BOOKS BY DAN KURZMAN

KISHI AND JAPAN

SUBVERSION OF THE INNOCENTS

SANTO DOMINGO: REVOLT OF THE DAMNED

GENESIS 1948: THE FIRST ARAB-ISRAELI WAR

THE RACE FOR ROME

THE BRAVEST BATTLE:
The 28 Days of the Warsaw Ghetto Uprising

MIRACLE OF NOVEMBER:
Madrid's Epic Stand, 1936

Dan Kurzman

BEN-GURION: PROPHET of FIRE

A TOUCHSTONE BOOK
Published by Simon & Schuster, Inc.
New York

For my dear wife, Florence,
whose gentle heart and innocent spirit
have made me the happiest author on earth

First Touchstone Edition, 1984
Published by Simon & Schuster, Inc.
Simon & Schuster Building
Rockefeller Center
1230 Avenue of the Americas
New York, New York 10020

TOUCHSTONE and colophon are registered trademarks of Simon & Schuster, Inc.

Designed by Karolina Harris

Manufactured in the United States of America

3 5 7 9 10 8 6 4 2
1 3 5 7 9 10 8 6 4 2 Pbk.

Library of Congress Cataloging in Publication Data

Kurzman, Dan.
Ben-Gurion, prophet of fire.
Bibliography: p.
Includes index.
1. Ben-Gurion, David, 1886-1973. 2. Prime ministers
—Israel—Biography. 3. Zionists—Palestine—
Biography. I. Title.
DS 125.3.B37K87 1983   956.94'05'0924 [B] 83-12010

ISBN 0-671-23094-8
ISBN 0-671-52821-1 Pbk.

CONTENTS

Book III: ISAIAH

Maps—pages 273, 331

Picture sections follow pages 198 and 310

ACKNOWLEDGMENTS

I wish to thank my wife, Florence, for her brilliant collaboration on this book. She edited with great skill, helped rewrite mangled passages, and knew exactly where a metaphor was needed. She also accompanied me to many interviews and helped evaluate much of the information obtained. Her partnership in this venture was indispensable.

I am also grateful to Yehiel Kirshbaum, my assistant in Israel, for his tireless efforts. He translated hundreds of pages from Hebrew and Yiddish with remarkable speed and precision, and he helped enormously with the research, digging into mountains of files. He served as an interpreter as well and interviewed a number of people.

Others whom I wish to thank include Michael Korda and Robert Bender of Simon and Schuster for their sensitive editing; my agent, Ruth Aley, for her counsel and encouragement; my brother Cal, who first suggested that I write this book, promising, as Dean of Learning Resources at the College of Marin, that I would sell at least one copy; Richard Deane Taylor for drawing the excellent maps in this book; and Sara Nicoll for typing the manuscript swiftly and expertly.

I am also indebted to the following for facilitating my research:

Baruch Arbel—director, Mehlman Library, Diaspora Research Institute, Tel Aviv University, Tel Aviv; Meir Avizohar —director, Ben-Gurion Research Institute and Archives, Sde

Boker, Israel; Malachi Beit-Arie—director, Jewish National University Library, Hebrew University, Jerusalem; Flory Chordeker—secretary, Sde Boker; Reuben Dassa—member of Israeli espionage team in Egypt; Joseph Delek—archivist, Vladimir Jabotinsky Institute, Tel Aviv; Yigal Donyets—assistant director, Sde Boker; Gila Fond—secretary, Sde Boker; Martin Gilbert—historian and specialist on Holocaust; Tivka Keidan—librarian, Mehlman Library; Yaakov Keinan—press officer, Ministry of Foreign Affairs, Tel Aviv; Sylvia Landress—director, Zionist Archives and Library, New York; Ralene Levy—information officer, Israel Consulate General, New York; R. R. Mellor—keeper, Public Record Office, London; Nehama Milo—archivist, Sde Boker; Issachar Miron—educational director, United Jewish Appeal; Hanna Moyal—secretary, Sde Boker; Malka Newman—librarian, Sde Boker; Gershon Rivlin—director, Ben-Gurion Research Institute and Archives (preceding Avizohar); Shlomo Simonssohn—director, Diaspora Research Institute; Esther Togman—assistant director, Zionist Archives and Library, New York; Irwin Weintraub—librarian, Sde Boker; Alexander Zvielli—director, *Jerusalem Post* Archives, Jerusalem.

Those who have contributed to this book with interviews granted over the last fifteen years include:

Zvi Ahroni—army intelligence officer; Moussa Alami—Palestine Arab leader; Yigal Allon—Palmach commander and Israeli foreign minister; Yosef Almogi—Ben-Gurion cabinet member; Arieh Altman—Revisionist Party leader; Meir Amit—army commander and chief of military intelligence; Chana Anavi (Yisraeli)—pioneer woman in Galilee; Ariel Ankorian—legal adviser to Histadrut; David Argov—brother of Nehemiah Argov, Ben-Gurion's military secretary; Samuel Ariel—Irgun official in Paris; Chaya Arkis—niece of Ben-Gurion; Reuben Aronovich—Hagana official and captain of the *Exodus;* Majid Aslan—Lebanese minister of defense; Shimon Avidan—army commander; Uri Avnery—Israeli magazine publisher and Knesset member; Ehud Avriel—a Ben-Gurion aide, troubleshooter, and diplomat; Abdul Rahman Azzam Pasha—secretary general of Arab League; Yochanan Bader—Revisionist leader and Knesset member; Harding F. Bancroft—U.S. State Department official; David Baniel—manager of Ben-Gurion's house in Sde Boker; Meir Bar-Eli—official in Mapai and Rafi Parties; Hasya Bar-Shira—friend of Ben-Gurion family; Yehuda Bauer—professor, Hebrew University (specialist on Holocaust); Bernard Beckhoeffer—U.S. State Department legal adviser; Lola Beer— Paula Ben-Gurion's dressmaker and close friend; Menachem Begin—Irgun commander, later prime minister; Ruth Beit-Halachmi—daughter of Rachel Beit-Halachmi; Yehuda Beit-Halachmi—brother-in-law of Rachel Beit-Halachmi; Yitzhak Ben-Aharon—leftist member of Ben-Gurion cabinet; Michael Ben-Ami—Irgun official; Lea Ben-Dor—*Jerusalem Post* editor; Shai Ben-Eliahu—official, *moshav* movement; Emanuel Ben-Eliezer —son-in-law of Ben-Gurion; Geula Ben-Eliezer—daughter of Ben-Gurion; Moshe Ben-Eliezer—grandson of Ben-Gurion; Orit Ben-Eliezer—granddaughter of Ben-Gurion; Yariv Ben-Eliezer—grandson of Ben-Gurion; Michael Ben-Gal—army commander; Amos Ben-Gurion—son of Prime Minister; Arye Ben-Gurion—nephew of Prime Minister; Benjamin Ben-Gurion —nephew of Prime Minister; David Ben-Gurion—founder and Prime Minister of Israel; Emanuel Ben-Gurion—nephew of Prime Minister; Henia Ben-Gurion—wife of Benjamin; Paula Ben-Gurion—the Prime Minister's wife; Eliahu Ben-Hur— army commander; Asher Ben-Nathan—director general, defense ministry; Mordechai Ben-Porat—Mapai Party official and government secret agent; Mordechai Ben-Tov—Mapam member of Ben-Gurion cabinet; Shimon Ben-Zemer—Histadrut leader; Leonard Bernstein—American orchestra conductor; Nahum Bernstein—American lawyer working for Hagana; H. C. Blackden—British colonel in Arab Legion; Zvi Brenner—Hagana leader and comrade of Ben-Gurion; Alexander Broida— Hagana officer (aide to Colonel Marcus); Nigel Bromage—British officer in Arab Legion; William Burdett—U.S. State Department official; Yosef Burg—Religious Bloc leader and member of Ben-Gurion cabinet; Dalia Carmel—secretary who played key role in Lavon Affair; Moshe Carmel—army commander and Mapam member of Ben-Gurion cabinet; Israel Carmi—army commander; Emanuel Celler—American congressman from New York; Amos Chorev—army commander; Clark Clifford— adviser to President Truman; Benjamin Cohen—adviser to U.S. State Department and delegate to U.N.; Mulah Cohen—army commander; Yehoshua Cohen—Stern Group commander and confidant of Ben-Gurion; Yeroham Cohen—Palmach officer; Pinchas Cruso—Second Aliya pioneer in Petah Tikvah with Ben-Gurion; Herbert J. Cummings—American diplomat in Israel; Sir Alan Cunningham—British High Commissioner in Palestine; Uri Dan—Israeli newsman and confidant of Ariel Sharon; Ezra Danin—Israeli specialist in Arab affairs; Aharon

Davidi—army officer; Carter Davidson—Associated Press correspondent in Jerusalem; Moshe Dayan—Israeli commander and chief of staff, later foreign minister; Ephraim Dekel—chief, Hagana intelligence; Jenny Denman—secretary to Ben-Gurion in London; Edouard Depreuse—French minister of the interior; Alexander Derczansky—French professor and Zionist; Raul Diez de Medina—Bolivian member of United Nations Palestine Commission; Mina Diskin—secretary to Ben-Gurion; Yaacov Dori—army chief of staff; Abba Eban—Israeli ambassador to U.S. and U.N., later foreign minister; Avraham Eisenberg —Plonsk resident; Yigal Elam—professor of Zionist history; Eliahu Elath—Israeli diplomat; Ezra Elnakam—Stern Group member; Judith Epstein—Hadassah leader; Miriam Eshkol— wife of Prime Minister Levi Eshkol; Dan Even—army commander; Ephraim Evron—aide to Ben-Gurion and to Lavon, later ambassador to U.S.; Walter Eytan—Jewish Agency official and Israeli diplomat; Munir Abu Fadil—Palestine Arab commander; Monroe Fein—American captain of the *Altalena;* Moshe Feldenkrais—scientist and Ben-Gurion's physical therapist; Meir Finkelstein—Plonsk resident; Arnold Forster— Anti-Defamation League leader; Shlomo Freidrich—French supporter of Hagana operations; Ze'ev Friedman—Ben-Gurion bodyguard; Berl Frimer—American Labor Zionist (Poalei Zion) leader; El'azar Galili—aide to Ben-Gurion; Israel Galili—Hagana commander and Mapam leader; Elkana Gali—political secretary to Ben-Gurion; Mordechai Gazit—army commander, later ambassador to France; Joseph Geva—army commander; Chaim Gevaryahu—rabbi, head of Ben-Gurion's Bible Circle; Emile al-Ghouri—deputy to mufti of Jerusalem; Tikva Gil— secretary to Ben-Gurion; Moshe Gilboa—aide to Ben-Gurion; John Bagot Glubb Pasha—British commander, Arab Legion; Stanley Goldfoot—Stern Group officer; Desmond Goldie—British officer in Arab Legion; Ralph Goldman—American Zionist leader; Nahum Goldmann—member of Jewish Agency Executive and president of World Zionist Organization; Ruth Goldschmidt—aide to Ben-Gurion; Israel Goldstein—president, Zionist Organization and Jewish National Fund; Shlomo Goren —chief rabbi of Israel; Yehuda Gothels—Israeli newsman and supporter of Lavon; Ernest Gross—State Department adviser; Yitzhak Gruenbaum—Israeli minister of the interior; David Hacohen—Mapai Party leader; Mordechai Halamish—editor, *Sefer Plonsk;* Gottfried Hammer—American Jewish Agency official; Raymond Hare—member of U.S. delegation to U.N.; Isser Harel—chief, Israeli security services; Yehoshafat Harkavi

—chief, army intelligence; Lee Harris—American adviser to Ben-Gurion; Gideon Hausner—Israeli prosecutor, Eichmann trial; Levi Yitzhak Hayerushalmi—Israeli newsman and Lavon supporter; Loy Henderson—U.S. State Department official; Aura Herzog—wife of Chaim Herzog; Chaim Herzog—chief, military intelligence; Ismail Hijazi—Palestine Arab official; Yaacov Hirsh—soldier and companion to Ben-Gurion in Sde Boker; Haj Amin el-Husseini—mufti of Jerusalem and Palestine Arab leader; Esther Izhar—daughter of Rachel Beit-Halachmi; Sheikh Mohammed Ali Jabary—mayor of Hebron; Charlotte Jacobson—president, Hadassah; Joseph Jacobson—member, Hagana High Command; Sir Barnett Janner—British member of Parliament; Julius Jarcho—director, American underground military procurement; Avraham Joffe—army commander; Joseph Johnson—adviser to U.S. State Department; Brigadier Sir Charles Jones—British commander in Jerusalem; George Lewis Jones—American diplomat in London; Dov Joseph—military governor, New City of Jerusalem, later minister of justice; Fawzi el-Kaoukji—commander, Arab Liberation Army; Shmuel Katz—Irgun leader and right-wing politician; Jack Katzman—American Labor Zionist (Poalei Zion) leader; Yona Kesse—Mapai Party leader; Zvi Kesse—left socialist youth leader; Yigal Kimche—aide to Weizmann; Sir Alec Kirkbride—British minister to Jordan; Ruth Kluger—Hagana agent abroad; Teddy Kollek—aide to Ben-Gurion, later mayor of Jerusalem; Lola Kramarsky—American Zionist leader; Yaacov Kvashner—boyhood friend of Ben-Gurion; Yitzhak Kvashner—Plonsk schoolmate of Ben-Gurion; Chaim Laskov—army commander and chief of staff; Naphtalie (Lau-) Lavie—aide to Dayan and Peres; Lucy Lavon—wife of Pinhas Lavon; Renana Leshem—daughter of Ben-Gurion; Shlomo Leshem—son-in-law of Ben-Gurion; Schneur Levenberg—British Zionist leader; Frank Lieberman—soldier in Jewish Legion, World War I; Malka Lif—secretary to Ben-Gurion; Eliezer Linski—Palmach soldier charged with accidental killing of Colonel Mickey Marcus; Joseph Linton—aide to Weizmann, later ambassador to Japan; Zivia Lubetkin—Jewish fighter in Warsaw Ghetto Uprising; Uri Lubrani—aide to Ben-Gurion; Sidney Luria—American Jewish Agency adviser; Ted Lurie—editor, *Jerusalem Post;* Robert MacAtee—American consul in Jerusalem; Mordechai Makleff—army commander, later chief of staff; Shmuel Makunis—Israeli Communist leader; Amos Manor—head of Shin Beth intelligence service; Mazal Giblie Mansour—Ben-Gurion's maid; Sir John Martin—British Colonial Office official; Will Masler—nephew of Paula Ben-Gurion; Robert McClintock—U.S. State Department official; General Sir Gordon McMillan—commander, British forces in Palestine; Golda Meir—Israeli foreign minister, then prime minister; Moshe Meisels—Israeli newsman and Lavon supporter; Yaacov Meridor—deputy commander of Irgun; Samuel Merlin—Irgun official; Hadassah Mor—Israeli writer; Said Mufti—aide to King Abdullah; Zakaraya Muhieddin—colleague of Egyptian President Nasser; Baruch Nadel—Israeli newsman; Uzi Narkis—army commander; Robert Nathan—American legal adviser to Jewish Agency; Yitzhak Navon—Ben-Gurion aide and confidant, later president of Israel; Arieh Nehamkin—general secretary, *moshav* movement; Shraga Netzer—Labor Party leader; Mordechai Newman—colleague of Ben-Gurion in Poalei Zion Party; Yorim Nimrod—Israeli writer; Moshe Nissim—Knesset member, son of Chief Rabbi Nissim; Francis Ofner—Israeli newsman; Yitzhak Olshan—Israeli judge; Meir Pael—military expert and Ben-Gurion critic; Amihai Paglin—Irgun chief of operations; Yehoshua Palmon—adviser on Arab affairs to Ben-Gurion; Dan Patir—Israeli newsman, later spokesman for Prime Minister Begin; Moshe Pearlman—Ben-Gurion confidant and army spokesman; Shimon Peres—director general, defense ministry, later defense minister and head of Labor Party; Mordechai Raanan—Irgun commander in Jerusalem; Yitzhak Rabin—army chief of staff, later prime minister; Yitzhak Rafael—Religious Bloc leader; Arie Rath—editor, *Jerusalem Post;* Ogden Reid—U.S. ambassador to Israel; Aaron Remez—Israeli Air Force commander; Kasim al-Rimawy—Palestine Arab leader; Lily Rivlin—Israeli writer; Enrique Rodriguez Fabregat—Uruguayan delegate to U.N.; Ahova Ron—bereaved mother and admirer of Ben-Gurion; Dorit Rosen—secretary to Ben-Gurion; Yehiel Meir Rosenberg—Plonsk resident; Zvi Rosenblatt—acquitted suspect in Arlosoroff murder; Fanny Rosenblum—friend of Paula Ben-Gurion; Shalom Rosenfeld—editor, *Maariv;* Moshe Rosetti—secretary of Knesset; John Ross—member, American delegation to U.N.; Mahmoud al-Rousan—Arab Legion officer; Esther Rubin—wife of artist Reuven Rubin and confidant of Paula Ben-Gurion; General Fuad Sadek—supreme commander, Egyptian forces in Palestine; Nahum Sarig—army commander; Eliahu Sasson—Israeli specialist in Arab affairs; Raquel Schanz (Ramati)—friend of Nehemiah Argov; Ze'ev Schiff—Israeli newsman and military expert; Al Schwimmer—American procurer of aircraft for Israel and founder of Israeli aircraft industry; Ada Sereni—chief Hagana agent in Italy; David Shaltiel—army commander;

Shlomo Shamir—army commander; Yaacov Shapira—Israeli cabinet member and well-known lawyer; Judah Shapiro—American Zionist leader; Moshe Shapiro—Israeli cabinet member; Ze'ev Sharef—secretary of Ben-Gurion's cabinet; Moshe Sharett—foreign minister, then prime minister of Israel; Yaakov Sharett—son of Moshe Sharett; Ariel Sharon—army commander, later defense minister in Begin government; General Shuquar Shawkat—commander in chief, Syrian army; Israel Sheib—ideological chief, Stern Group; Colonel Adib Shishekly—Syrian commander in Arab Liberation Army, later president of Syria; Shlomo Zalman Shragai—mayor of Jerusalem and chief of immigration; Paul Shulman—American commander of Israeli navy; Ruth Siegel—secretary to Ben-Gurion; Gabriel Sifroni—Israeli newsman; Moshe Sneh—Hagana commander; Rudolf Sonneborn—American industrialist and organizer of underground aid for Israel; Welles Stabler—American consul general in Amman; Avraham Sternberg—confidant of Lavon; Major General Sir Hugh Stockwell—British commander of northern Palestine; Josef Strumza—student comrade of Ben-Gurion in Turkey; Yosef Tabenkin—Palmach officer; Amnon Taub—Shlomo's son; Esther Taub—Shlomo's wife; Miriam Taub—niece of Ben-Gurion; Miriam Taub—secretary to Ben-Gurion in U.S.; Shlomo Taub—comrade of Ben-Gurion in Plonsk; Colonel Abdullah Tel—Jordanian commander, later military governor of Old City; Wasfi Tel—Arab Legion officer; Dan Tolkowski—commander, Israeli Air Force; Yaacov Tsur—Israeli diplomat; Shulamit Turel—daughter of Rachel Beit-Halachmi; Shlomo Tussia-Cohen—Jerusalem attorney; Lieutenant Colonel Robert W. Van de Velde—military attaché, U.S. mission in Israel; Ada Vereté—daughter of Shlomo Zemach; Yaacov Weinshal—Revisionist Party leader; Meyer Weisgal—colleague of Weizmann; General Karl Wolff—Heinrich Himmler's representative; Meir Yaari—Mapam Party leader; Yigael Yadin—army chief of staff; Yonai Yagol—Israeli newsman and author; Nathan Yanai—Israeli professor and writer on political affairs; Yaacov Yannai—commander, Israeli signal corps; Fanny Yassky—wife of Hadassah Hospital director Chaim Yassky; Yitzhak Yazernitzky (Shamir)—Stern Group leader, later foreign minister in Begin government; Nathan Yellin-Mor—Stern Group commander and Knesset member; Elchanan Yishai—comrade of Ben-Gurion; Chaim Yisraeli—aide to Ben-Gurion; Yehoshua Zetler—commander, Stern Group in Jerusalem; Seif ed din Zuabi—Israeli Arab leader; Dana Zvielli—neighbor of Ben-Gurion in Jerusalem.

The light of Israel shall be for a fire

ISAIAH 10:17

PREFACE

The life of David Ben-Gurion is more than the story of an extraordinary man. It is the story of a Biblical prophecy, an eternal dream. It is the story of Zionism and of the Jewish people in the last hundred years, of a nation's rebirth and its momentous consequences, which are reflected daily in the headlines. To fully understand these headlines and the passions behind them, the fears, the fantasies, and the frustrations, one must comprehend the character of the man who presided over the renaissance.

Ben-Gurion was, in a modern sense, Moses, Joshua, Isaiah, a messiah who felt he was destined to create an exemplary Jewish state, a "light unto the nations" that would help to redeem all mankind. He would allow nothing to distract him from this mission. He abandoned his beloved Rachel Nelkin (Beit-Halachmi), who would haunt him throughout his life; he blinded himself to the full meaning of the Holocaust until World War II was over; and he risked a new genocide in a war of liberation he seemed doomed to lose.

But he triumphed. He established a state, built a superb army to protect it, and brought his people home . . . only to die, in one of history's great ironies, a lonely, disillusioned man deserted by them—but with Rachel holding his hand.

I worked on this biography for three years, though I have included information gathered over the last fifteen years. The material, much of it new, has been culled in part from scores of

Ben-Gurion's unpublished private diaries and hundreds of private letters, including intimate correspondence between Ben-Gurion and the two women in his life—his wife, Paula, and Rachel. Other documents reflect Ben-Gurion's bitter feuds with Chaim Weizmann and Menachem Begin, and his strange affection for his most implacable enemy, Vladimir Jabotinsky.

This book is also based on interviews with Ben-Gurion himself shortly before he died in 1973 and with more than five hundred of his relatives, friends and associates from the time he was a boy in Plonsk, Poland. Additional sources include scores of oral histories, hundreds of books and thousands of documents. All sources are indicated in some fifteen hundred notes.

Exploring the heart and soul of Ben-Gurion was not an easy task, for he seldom revealed himself. His diaries and other writings fill a library, but while one might learn from them infinite details of everything from Zionist philosophy to Buddhism, one learns little about Ben-Gurion the man. It was only after enormous research that I began to grasp the essence of the man, his feelings and foibles, his virtues and vulnerabilities.

Gradually from the insulated recesses of the political creature emerged a lingering love from youth, a tormenting sense of guilt for his neglect of Paula, a troubling devotion to his father, who was both benefactor and burden to him. Yet, such sentiments are important mainly because their suppression was a measure of his phenomenal will. No human emotion could be permitted to drain the energy he needed to pursue his mission.

Ben-Gurion's successors, while less driven by a sense of destiny, cannot evade his shadow. They administer his democracy and command his army; they must appease his labor movement and obey his moral codes—or face outraged demonstrators at home and abroad. Though Ben-Gurion sometimes violated his own codes for pragmatic reasons, his vision of a quality Jewish state still stirs, and often disturbs, the Israeli conscience.

The story of Ben-Gurion is as vital today as it was when he was alive and at the peak of his power. For he remains the personification of the Zionist dream—and a reminder of the kind of nation Israel can be if it is true to its destiny.

Dan Kurzman
New York, N.Y.

PROLOGUE

My soul is among lions
PSALMS 57:4

TEL AVIV bakes in the sultry heat of a *hamsin,* a merciless desert wind that seems to suggest a desire by God to test the fortitude and endurance of His Chosen People even on this day of redemption—May 14, 1948. In the Tel Aviv Museum David Ben-Gurion, proud but apprehensive, slouches behind a battery of microphones at the center of a long cloth-covered table, waiting to preside over the rebirth of the Jewish state. Beside him sit members of his first government and, just below the dais, those of the first Knesset, or parliament. On the wall behind him a portrait of black-bearded Theodor Herzl, the founder of Zionism, hangs between two blue-and-white Zionist flags, benignly contemplating the sacred moment he had prophesied more than fifty years earlier. Ben-Gurion, his pink cheeks beaded with sweat, silently scans the semicircular rows of guests, about three hundred and fifty select people, who occupy brown wooden chairs or stand pressed together in the rear and in the aisles as if physically symbolizing the divine unity of Jewry on this historic day.

Palestine's two chief rabbis, sporting neatly combed beards and tall silk hats precariously balanced on uncut locks, rub shoulders with godless kibbutzniks wearing baggy pants and open-necked shirts. Reporters with notebooks in hand gaze around at the scene, wondering how they will ever capture the sublime texture of these moments on paper. Generals in khaki without insignia glance at watches, nervously counting the minutes until midnight, when disaster in the form of six Arab armies is expected to strike at the heart of the newly born Jewish state. Women in dark festive dresses fan themselves and stare into space, their eyes full of hope, full of fear; many have sons and daughters at the front.

The windows, draped with black cloth, are wide open, and the mirthful rhythms of celebration in the street filter in, blending with the restless chatter of the guests, the click and grind of cameras, and the whining complaints of those who arrive late and can't find a seat. Gradually the sounds from outside rise in jubilant cacophony as thousands of people clad in light-colored summer clothes gather under a hazy blue sky in front of the building on Rothschild Boulevard, waving flags, shouting, singing, humming in cadence with youngsters in shorts and sandals who have linked arms and hop around in circles to the quick beat of the hora. Automobiles honk with blasts of raucous revelry as they thread their way through the exultant throngs that surge toward the museum from every direction. Young boys and girls standing in army trucks en route to the front wave greetings, holding ancient rifles aloft.

Worried guards at the door frown at the mob. Wasn't this supposed to be a secret meeting? True, the press had announced that the ceremony would be broadcast at 4 P.M. today, but it wasn't supposed to reveal the site. For if the Arabs learned of it they might try to drop a bomb and eradicate all the Jewish leaders in one blow. The Jewish radio, however, had inadvertently mentioned the place, and so now, it seems, half of Tel Aviv has come to celebrate, certain that no bomb could be powerful enough to frustrate God's will.

After two thousand years of darkness and dispersion, *Eretz Yisrael*, the Land of Israel, would rise again from the ashes of history—but Ben-Gurion is beginning to wonder *when*. Like the generals, he too glances at his watch. It's now a few minutes to four, and still no Declaration of Independence! An official was to bring it from Keren Kayemet Hall, where a little earlier Ben-Gurion and his colleagues had met to put the final touches to it. But the official has not arrived. What is delaying him? After so many centuries, how much longer must the Jewish people wait?

It wasn't easy starting a state; the Jewish leaders had, in fact, decided to declare one only two days earlier. Scratching out a budget of four hundred and fifty dollars, they sent artist Otto Wallisch on a hurried search for the ceremonial props, and for hours he reconnoitered Tel Aviv in vain. Finally, he unearthed a portrait of Herzl in the dusty cellar of a Jewish institute and carefully wiped the soot off the great man's face. Elsewhere he stumbled on two Zionist flags, which were so dirty that he stopped off at a laundry to get them washed. It was harder still finding a parchment scroll that could be used for the Declaration, and when he did find one, he had to stay up all night testing its chemical makeup to be sure it would not disintegrate for at least another two thousand years.

Even the Declaration itself was a problem. Last-minute bickering over its contents left no time before the ceremony to inscribe it on the scroll. A secretary, Dorit Rosen, rushed out and bought a cardboard binder for the typed copy of the proclamation, which would later be transferred to the parchment. Meanwhile, Dorit invited the director of a local bank to the ceremony "in return" for permission to deposit the signed Declaration in his vault after hours. Let the bombs fall. Men might die but the Declaration would prove that the state existed.

Where was the Declaration? Ben-Gurion could not have known that Zeev Sharef, the official who was to carry it from Keren Kayemet Hall, was stranded there. Sharef had made sure that the Zionist leaders were safely whisked away in taxis but, ironically, not one vehicle remained to take him and Dorit to the ceremony. In desperation Sharef buttonholed a policeman and explained his predicament, and the policeman halted the first car that came along and asked the driver to give the pair a lift. "Sorry," the man replied, "but I'm rushing home to hear the Declaration of Independence on the radio." Sharef shouted a cataclysmic warning: "If you don't take us to the museum you may *never* hear the Declaration of Independence, because it's right here!"

Minutes later, at exactly 3:59 P.M., Sharef stepped out of the car, dashed into the packed hall, and handed Ben-Gurion the precious document. The Jewish state would not be delayed by a single minute after all. The "birth certificate" had arrived.

The comically amateurish ceremonial plans reflected the improvised nature of the Jewish state itself. It was in November 1947 that the United Nations voted to end the twenty-eight-year-old

British Mandate in Palestine and partition the territory into two states—one Jewish and one Arab. The Jews agreed, but the Palestinian Arabs, hoping to dominate the whole area, attacked them, and even at this moment battles were raging everywhere. Ben-Gurion, however, was far more alarmed about what would happen after midnight when the last British soldier sailed from Palestine, signaling the Arab armies poised on its borders to invade the infant state. His own commanders told him that they had only a fifty-fifty chance of succeeding.

Don't declare the state, the United States had pleaded; don't commit suicide; agree to a United Nations Trusteeship in Palestine. But Ben-Gurion would not listen. The United Nations had voted partition. Both Washington and Moscow, in a rare show of accord, supported a Jewish state. The world sympathized with the Holocaust survivors festering in European camps and clamoring to enter Palestine. The Arab states were still undeveloped and relatively weak. Such a propitious moment might never come again. Besides, the Jewish state was not simply a political issue but a moral one—for the Jews of the world. Its revival paralleled the Exodus from Egypt, the conquest of the land by Joshua, the Maccabean revolt. Would history, would his people, ever forgive Ben-Gurion if he now retreated before this new challenge? Through sheer will he had come this far, and he was not about to let this unique opportunity slip by; he pushed, he cajoled, he threatened, and his fearful colleagues finally fell into line.

Now, how should this decision be enshrined for posterity? Ben-Gurion and the others wrangled over the Declaration of Independence line by line until two hours before the independence ceremony. Everyone, it seemed, wanted to stamp his own indelible mark on this treasured document. Define the state's frontiers as drawn by the United Nations, demanded some. No, retorted Ben-Gurion; does the American Declaration of Independence mention borders? Of course not. Besides, "the Arabs are making war on us. If we beat them" the Jews will have additional land. "Why tie ourselves down?" No one had an answer; so Ben-Gurion won the argument.

Another acrimonious debate followed. How would they deal with God? The believers wanted a reference to "the God of Israel" or "the Almighty and Redeemer of Israel"; the nonbelievers wished to keep God out of it altogether. What about the "Rock of Israel"? Ben-Gurion suggested. "Rock" was another word for "God," he told the Orthodox; but not necessarily so, he assured the anticlerics. Everybody agreed on "Rock."

The state still had no name. Should it be called "Judea"? No.

That was the Biblical name of a small part of Palestine. "Zion"? Hardly. That was the name of a mountain and could be confusing. "Israel," advised Ben-Gurion. And again he prevailed.

Now he would embark on one of the greatest gambles in history. The survivors of the Holocaust would either join the millions already dead or be the vanguard of a powerful new nation.

At 4 P.M. Ben-Gurion rises, his five-foot, three-inch figure uncomfortably resplendent in a dark suit and, as a concession to history, a black silk tie set off with a silver pin, items that clash startlingly with his simple shirt-sleeve sartorial tastes. He looks dwarfish, especially in the shadow of Herzl's enormous image, but the odd proportions of his body, with a great round head atop a stubby torso, convey the impression of a giant in miniature.

His leathery lion's face, fringed with tufts of frothy white hair on either side of a shiny pate, is expressionless, reflecting his ambivalent feelings at this critical moment when the fear of destruction vies with the joy of deliverance. "I thought," Ben-Gurion said later, recalling this moment, "now we are responsible for our own destiny. . . . Coupled with [this thought] was the knowledge that . . . the [Arab] armies were massing on our borders ready to march across."

Penetrating feline eyes, humorless and unfathomable, bore into the shimmer of humanity from beneath bushy white-streaked brows—brown eyes that strangely seem to dissolve into blue in certain shades of light. A thick, pocked, slightly crooked nose overlooks a pair of dour pencil-line lips that curve down slightly at the ends in a perpetual scowl, and a powerful jaw juts forward, defiant, intimidating.

With a small, surprisingly delicate hand, Ben-Gurion picks up a walnut gavel and raps it on the table.

"*Eretz Yisrael* was the birthplace of the Jewish people. . . ."

Ben-Gurion, in his small monotone voice, begins reading the Declaration of Independence; and the people of Palestine, almost all of them tuned to the radio station broadcasting this historic event, listen with either rage or rapture. Only Jerusalem never hears it all, for the British-officered Jordanian Arab Legion, which had interrupted its bombardment of the Jewish sector of the city for afternoon tea, resumes it when cups run dry, drowning out the fateful words:

It is . . . the self-evident right of the Jewish people to be a nation, as all other nations, in its own Sovereign State. Accordingly, we . . . meet together in solemn assembly today . . . and by virtue of the natural and historic right of the Jewish people and of the Resolution of the General Assembly of the United Nations,

Hereby proclaim the establishment of the Jewish State in Palestine, to be called the State of Israel. . . .

Ben-Gurion then declares that British regulations limiting Jewish immigration are annulled, and the audience, rising, wildly applauds in acclamation. The first prime minister is handed a pen and signs the blank parchment on which the Declaration will be inscribed later, and his colleagues then scribble their names while Moshe Sharett straightens out the curling scroll. Suddenly, sounding like a blessing from heaven, the sad notes of "Hatikvah," the Jewish national anthem, drift down from a balcony where the Jewish Philharmonic Orchestra sits hidden from view. Ben-Gurion bangs his gavel on the table and declares the meeting over.

And then, as he steps down from the dais to be swallowed up by a mob of damp-eyed well-wishers, he breaks into a child's grin and exclaims to a British reporter, "You see, we did it!"

It was a long way from the Polish town of Plonsk, where Ben-Gurion had grown up as a boy full of heroic dreams. He had finally appeased a lifelong obsession and fulfilled the Biblical prophecy of Israel's rebirth. Ben-Gurion was himself a modern prophet. A flawed prophet to be sure; as with most giants of history, his follies were sometimes as monumental as his feats. But he perceived the need for a Jewish state when few others did, and he chipped away at centuries of inertia to meet this need. Like Moses, he led his people out of the deadly captivity of exile and shaped them into a nation. Like Joshua, he brought them into their land and smote those who would repel them. Like Isaiah, he taught that Israel must be an exemplary state that would redeem not only its own people but, in large measure, all mankind. Certainly Ben-Gurion was one of the greatest Jews since Biblical times.

Propelled by an unbendable will that he had cultivated since youth, Ben-Gurion harbored a mystical faith in Israel's destiny, which he viewed as inextricably linked to his own. He built a state brick by brick, according to a rigid system of priorities, concentrating completely on one brick at a time. He first organized a motley collection of starving pioneers into labor unions, then merged these unions into a monolithic labor-industrial movement, the Histadrut, which would serve as the infrastructure of a state. Then he united his labor party with others to form the socialist Mapai Party and trained it in the politics of redemption. When this party finally took over Palestine from its British masters and he became prime minister, he systematically siphoned the power of both the Histadrut and Mapai to the state, and used this power to build a mighty army and gather in Jews from the ends of the earth. In his extraordinary talent for focusing on only one goal at any given time lay both his greatest strength and his greatest weakness.

But if Ben-Gurion would not compromise on his goals, he would on his tactics, and he shifted policy and even ideology to fit events. Socialism? Simply a means to an end. He began in Palestine as a fiery young Marxist, moved toward moderate socialism, and finally forged a mixed economy with almost no hint of dogma. Before switching policies, however, Ben-Gurion would defend the prevailing one with such table-thumping vigor that even his supporters sometimes accused him of extremism. Yet, as Moshe Sharett, his foreign minister until 1956, said, "People call Ben-Gurion an extremist, but he is not. He is a radical who advocates all policies with extremism—even a moderate policy."

Ben-Gurion himself seemed to concede that his bitter challenges were essentially a tactic. "When I'm in a rage," he told an associate, "it's a sign I'm calm, and when I'm calm it's a sign I'm in a rage." Thus, the greater his show of rage, the more malleable he was likely to be.

But, once he had reached a decision, he would demand immediate action and bulldoze through every barrier. "If an opportunity arises we must seize it," he maintained. "If we are possessed by fear we will achieve nothing."

Ben-Gurion's pragmatism came naturally, yet he realized that he had to master the art of self-discipline in order to strengthen his will and better know when to compromise and when to change tactics, when to move and when not to. With so much at stake, he could not afford to act on impulse. He trained himself mercilessly. In 1940 he challenged both his son, Amos, and himself to stop smoking in order to test their wills. Amos agreed, but soon resumed smoking; his father never picked up a cigarette again.

Feeding Ben-Gurion's Zionist fervor, it appears, was a compulsion to compensate for a deeply ingrained inferiority complex. The potent blend of messianism and insecurity helped to shape his character and mold him into a paradoxical paragon of greatness. He was humble and boastful, forgiving and vengeful, shy and aggressive, alert and absentminded, generous and petty, considerate and cruel, sentimental and frigid. He treated many members of his own party contemptuously while using them as agents of his will, but he was gracious to most political foes, respecting them for daring to defy him. He bullied the Knesset like a dictator, but meticulously obeyed the rules of democracy. He helped build a socialist society, but relied on foreign capital to finance it. He strove desperately for peace, but would lead his nation through two wars. He learned the esoteric philosophies of the ancient Greeks and Buddha, but virtually ignored Islamic culture, though he dealt daily with the Arabs.

Most curiously of all, Ben-Gurion almost never attended synagogue, secretly ate ham for breakfast, and seldom wore a hat in Jerusalem as the rabbis urged (though he would often carry one in his hand as a concession to them), yet he mastered the Old Testament and sought to emulate the prophets. His feelings about God were as ambivalent as these contradictions. Thus, he once told a religious friend, as if summing up a lifetime of inquiry: "I've read much and thought much, and I've concluded that it is impossible to prove there is no God."

Earlier he had written: "We know what God is *not*—He is not a man, He has no ears, no eyes. . . . Nevertheless . . . I do believe that there must be a being, intangible, indefinable, even unimaginable, but something infinitely superior to all we know and are capable of conceiving."

However unorthodox his view of God, Ben-Gurion's character was anchored in the Bible. It was his principal source of inspiration. He used it as his guide in seeking Zionist goals and in setting moral standards, and he even dug in the Negev desert for precious minerals mentioned in it.

"Nothing can surpass the Bible at lighting up the manifold problems of our life," he said. "There can be no worthwhile political or military education about Israel without profound knowledge of the Bible."

According to Ràbbi Chaim Gevaryahu, head of the Bible-study group that met weekly in Ben-Gurion's home, the Prime Minister "unconsciously believed he was blessed with a spark from Joshua's soul. This helped give him the will to succeed, a sense of destiny."

The "spark" ignited Ben-Gurion's will in early childhood, when the youngster immersed himself in the Bible while other children romped in the garden, and the glow never dimmed through the years. The Bible gave him a historical frame of reference, validated his dreams, and justified his plea that his people uproot themselves and return to their ancestral home.

To Ben-Gurion, the new Israel was a "leap across Jewish history," an extension of the glorious Biblical era, with the two thousand intervening years in the Diaspora nothing but a historical aberration, a period of shame and humiliation to be ignored and even loathed. He seldom referred to Jewish life or accomplishment in exile or even the teachings of the Talmud that were formulated during those centuries, and he shunned the rich Yiddish culture that, in the greatest adversity, helped the Jews to survive as a people.

When a survivor of the Warsaw ghetto once appeared at a meeting and gave a moving account in Yiddish of the uprising there, Ben-Gurion rose after the talk and asked in cold anger how she could speak of so holy an event in the language of exile. And after the 1967 Six-Day War, he even wanted to pull down the ancient walls of the newly captured Old City of Jerusalem because they were a reminder of the medieval Turkish occupation of Palestine and thus interrupted the continuity of Jewish history.

"You know," he told a friend, "from the time of the Bible [until the state], we did not contribute anything to the world."

The key to Israel's rebirth and survival, Ben-Gurion believed almost fanatically, was the vision of "messianic redemption." God, he never forgot, told Moses that the Hebrews must become *am segulah,* a "unique" nation that would embrace the "higher virtues"—truth, justice, compassion. An exemplary Jewish state would synthesize the ethical teachings of the prophets, who would counsel man on *what* to do, and the discoveries of modern science, which would instruct him *how* to do it.

"It is only by the integration of the two that the blessings of both can flourish," Ben-Gurion said. "Our status in the world will not be determined by our material attainments or military prowess, but by the moral inspiration radiated by everything we do here, by the culture and society we create here; this alone will gain us friends among the nations."

Israel's integrated knowledge would be beamed to all peoples, for Jewish redemption was destined to be "intertwined with universal human redemption." Thus, the Jewish state would forgo the luxury of being "normal" and become "a light unto the nations," as prophesied by Isaiah (42:6), with a mission to bring salvation to mankind.

This sacred process would end with fulfillment of another prophecy by Isaiah (2:4): "Nation shall not lift up sword against nation, neither shall they learn war any more."

Ben-Gurion once told a colleague that he could lead a people in wartime because he "never shrank from giving orders that I knew would mean the death of hundreds of wonderful young men." Yet, the outlawing of war was to him the ultimate redemption. "There are movements," he declared, "which see war as an ideal . . . which claim that in war man becomes elevated . . . and the heroism of a people reveals itself. This approach is an abomination to us, it contradicts everything dear and holy in our movement and our people. . . . We shall make war only out of bitter, unavoidable necessity."

In practice, Ben-Gurion salted this promise with pragmatism, but it remained the guiding principle of his foreign policy.

Considering the moral tone of his rule, it is ironic that in the end Ben-Gurion toppled from his pedestal into bitter obscurity when the people who were to spread his messianic message perceived, rightly or wrongly, that his means were not always as lofty as his end. The unharnessed will that had created the state was thus to doom the man. Yet, Ben-Gurion never lost confidence that his people would ultimately help to redeem the world, and this faith was not a pretentious expectation; it was rooted in the paradox of his character, in the same contradictory blend of egotism and humility that shaped his personal life and career. He did not view the Jew as intrinsically superior to the gentile, but simply as more highly motivated to better himself and, therefore, uniquely qualified to aid others and set an example for them.

"In the majority of Jews," he wrote, "one finds something pushing from within to accomplish more, to do better, to follow a path of active virtue. . . . The Jews have little sense of a hell waiting under their feet. Their hell is more a personal dissatisfaction born of mediocrity."

Nor, he claimed, is Israel a "chosen people." God did not choose Israel; Israel chose God. All peoples had their own special qualities, and God, said Ben-Gurion, would not have selected one over another. What happened was that Israel chose God when all other nations rejected Him. And to support his view, Ben-Gurion quoted Joshua (24:22): "And Joshua said unto the people, Ye are witnesses against yourselves that ye have chosen you the Lord, to serve him."

Was Ben-Gurion as humble about himself as he was about his people? According to Teddy Kollek, a close aide who later became mayor of Jerusalem, Ben-Gurion "was a man of the greatest humility," who "would carry on a correspondence . . . with a simple citizen who had written him a letter."

And Ben-Gurion often seemed like a simple citizen himself. Once, when he was visiting the United States, an American reporter wrote: "There is a man in our town tonight who is to the little people [of Israel] what Abraham Lincoln was to the people of America in his day."

When Ben-Gurion read the story, he was furious. "When I think of a great man I think of Abraham Lincoln," he said. "Who am I? Just a little Jew." False modesty? Perhaps. But certainly Ben-Gurion considered Lincoln, with his human values, his decisiveness, and his rise from a log cabin, the kind of man he wanted to emulate. He also admired George Washington and carefully studied his military strategy in the Revolutionary War. But when someone suggested that he physically resembled Washington, he replied, "I would prefer to look like Lincoln." To Ben-Gurion, it was more important to be known as a humble liberator of the oppressed than as the great founder of a state.

Even when Ben-Gurion became prime minister, he lived with Spartan simplicity. He never lusted for money and seldom carried any in his pocket. Only once was he known to have rejoiced over the acquisition of "wealth"—when he was in New York in 1934 during the Depression. At a motion-picture theater that lured customers with Bingo prizes, he won two dollars and rushed to his office waving the money in glee.

Ben-Gurion's meager salary of about four hundred dollars a month, which he considered quite ample, went directly to Paula, his blunt, practical wife, and he never knew or cared how she spent it. He simply assumed that all his needs would be cared for. And they were, in fact, quite modest. He seldom found the time to be fitted out with new clothes, even when a pair of pants became too baggy or a jacket threadworn. He didn't have to be served gourmet food, either. "What difference does it make what I cook for him?" Paula once exclaimed. "He doesn't even notice what I put in front of him." Typically, at one dinner party he asked the guest next to him why she wasn't eating her steak—only to provoke the exclamation, "But this is fish!"

Nor would anyone who visited Ben-Gurion in his simple two-story, white stucco house in Tel Aviv doubt his humble tastes. This home, where he lived when he wasn't writing his memoirs in his even humbler dwelling in the Negev desert, was a model of utilitarianism. The only visible hint that an important person lived here was the presence of an armed guard standing watch in a tiny booth in the small fenced-in front garden. And sometimes even he wasn't around, for Paula would send him to the grocery store to buy vegetables for dinner. Once, when the guard protested that he had orders to "protect the Prime Minister," Paula retorted: "Never mind. You get the vegetables and *I'll* protect the Prime Minister."

The house, number 17 Keren Kayemet Boulevard (Ben-Gurion Boulevard today), was a little bungalow when Ben-Gurion bought it in 1927, one of a complex of homes constructed for workers in what was then an isolated section of Tel Aviv near the sea. For several years Ben-Gurion had to trudge through sand dunes to reach it, and to make do with kerosene lamps, since electricity still hadn't come to the neighborhood. The house was enlarged in 1946 and renovated in 1960, but it would never, by modern standards, be fit for a king—or even a prime minister.

Without air conditioning, Ben-Gurion and his family broiled in summer and, without central heating, froze in winter, when startled diplomats would sometimes find themselves consulting with the Prime Minister as he lay in bed under heavy quilts to protect himself from the cold. But whatever the weather, the atmosphere was always warm and cozy. Ben-Gurion entertained —when he had to—in a modestly furnished living room, while Paula poured wine and orange juice into glasses resting on lace doilies scattered on a long wooden coffee table. He would argue with his guests over the meaning of a Biblical passage or a point of foreign policy as they reclined on blue-upholstered chairs and a matching sofa and occasionally glanced at decorations on the wall, most notably a black-and-white drawing of King David by Marc Chagall and a landscape by Reuven Rubin.

Beckoning from an intimate alcove at one end of the room was a fireplace with a mantel that supported a small bronze head of Ben-Gurion and family photos. Here Ben-Gurion often listened to the news on an ancient radio, stubbornly refusing to accept the existence of television, which he barred from the land because, in his view, it blunted the mind and consumed precious time. The alcove was also a convenient place to corner and relentlessly grill a stubborn guest who might take issue with some point the Prime Minister had made. Prodded by Paula's nagging admonition, "Dinner is getting cold," guests would move into the small dining room, which was separated from the salon by a curtain, and squeeze into place around a mahogany table that could seat twelve in cramped splendor.

Except on the few evenings when the Ben-Gurions entertained, they dined in an old-fashioned white-tiled kitchen that would have horrified most American housewives. Ben-Gurion sat on a wobbly chair at a small wooden breakfast table, while Paula cooked over an old soot-blackened stove, served tea from a tarnished samovar, and weighed her husband's food on a little scale, so he could keep to the diet that she prescribed for him.

After dinner Ben-Gurion washed the dishes, and Paula, sometimes with the help of a part-time maid, cleaned up the kitchen. The couple then retired to their respective bedrooms. Paula's small room downstairs contained a narrow backless bed and other furnishings that reflected her simple tastes, with only a giant glass-enclosed, brightly robed Japanese doll relieving the drab decor. Ben-Gurion plodded upstairs to his bedroom, perhaps the most Spartan room of all, featuring a bed with three small, thin mattresses laid over a board that helped to ease his lumbago. Finally able to relax after a fifteen-hour work day, he read until about 3 A.M., hunched in bed or on a straw chair next to a table piled high with newspapers and books. No one knows how often he interrupted his thoughts in his last years to stare at the large color photo hanging on the wall over his bed—a scene of him strolling hand in hand with his young grandson that may have symbolized to him the passing of his mission to future generations.

The most distinctive feature of the house was an upstairs library of about twenty thousand books. They were stacked in four large adjoining rooms in wall-to-wall, floor-to-ceiling bookcases, a wealth of literature ranging from Spinoza to Lenin, from Thomas Aquinas to Churchill, with Bibles in a number of languages filling a separate shelf. This private collection, Israel's largest, was an index to Ben-Gurion's character and values. The Prime Minister was apparently never told that the government or wealthy supporters footed the bill for most of these books. (Sometimes he unwittingly boosted the price of a rare volume by requesting it from several stores, and they, after seeking it from one another, concluded that the book was in great demand.) He may simply have assumed that Paula or his aides were paying for the books out of his own earnings. No one, in any case, dared disturb him with the truth, nor is it likely that he would have wanted to hear it. A man who hoped to redeem mankind could not afford to know that he was himself less than morally impeccable.

Ben-Gurion spent most of his leisure time writing letters and memoirs in a little office that he had carved out of one of the library rooms. This glass-doored cubicle marvelously mirrored his spirit. From under the glass covering on his desk peered the images of his family, Albert Schweitzer, and his beloved deceased associates, Berl Katzenelson and Nehemiah Argov, all sharing his attention with inspirational, if somewhat yellowed, passages from the Bible. On the mantel of a marble fireplace stood a framed autographed sketch of Einstein, a statue of Buddha and small heads of Kennedy, Herzl, Plato and King David, some of his heroes of history. And all around him were small bookcases lined with volumes he most urgently needed. Here in this six-by-twelve-foot nook Ben-Gurion gathered all the symbols reminding him of the things that made life rich and worthwhile. It was his world in miniature, his past, present and future, integrated into timeless moments of meditative pleasure. It was an intensely personal world, the world of a humble man.

But in the impersonal political world, Ben-Gurion was less humble. From the time he was a child, he sought to compensate, and in fact overcompensated, for his early physical weakness, his shortness of stature, his family's relatively low social position in its Polish *shtetl*, and his limited formal education with a punishing effort to "prove" himself. His extraordinary political success did not satisfy him. He craved admiration while seeking to appear humble and even felt compelled at times to shower himself with praise. He would almost never admit to a mistake.

In his writings and statements, Ben-Gurion, usually referring to himself in the regal third person, made no secret of his view that he was predestined for greatness. More accurately than modestly, he described his decision to declare independence as an act of "boldness, courage and foresight." With straight-faced matter-of-factness, he quoted a companion of his youth as saying that he was "a man whose impulsive wisdom merged with profound morality," and that "God's spirit sometimes pervades him." And, characteristically, when someone told him that, like God, he had "not only . . . created the State of Israel, but . . .[had] modeled the new Israeli Jew in your own image," Ben-Gurion replied simply, "Well, that's not bad, is it?"

Ben-Gurion's ego problem, some associates think, was reflected even more in his reading than in his writing patterns. He was "a self-taught, learned man, but not the scholar he yearned to be, though he certainly had the mind to become one with formal training," says Yigael Yadin, a leading archaeologist, who was Ben-Gurion's army chief of staff in the War of Independence and later deputy prime minister in Menachem Begin's cabinet.

No one doubts that Ben-Gurion, who sometimes devoured a book a night, loved to read, that books relaxed him as a game of cricket might an Englishman; but some who knew him do not doubt either that he also felt a need to convince everyone, including himself, that he was indeed a scholar. Why, some people ask, did Ben-Gurion spend so much time wallowing in the philosophical, impractical themes of Plato and Buddha? Why did he choose to master Greek and Spanish rather than the more useful Arabic, which he learned only superficially? Politicians, others point out, read practical works, and Ben-Gurion had no wish to be stamped as simply a politician.

He deeply respected, even fawned on, scholars, and when they came to his Bible circle, he would actually drag in the chairs himself, arguing that it was his "duty to serve learned men." And since he wanted to be recognized as one himself, his reading had to show his scholarship. So, by this logic, he chose to be seen browsing through bookstores around the world, though he could have sent for the books he desired. Walter Eytan, an Oxford Greek scholar who served under Ben-Gurion, recalls that his boss never once discussed the language with him. Why? Ben-Gurion, says Eytan, apparently did not have a serious interest in it, though he wanted people to think he did.

Ben-Gurion, however, clearly loved languages, speaking Hebrew, Russian, Yiddish, French, German, Turkish, English, and a smattering of Italian, and reading Greek, Spanish, and some Arabic. One language he never learned was Polish, though he was born in Poland. Why waste time learning a "provincial" tongue when he intended to leave that country? Not practical! Yitzhak Navon, an aide who later became President of Israel, taught Ben-Gurion Spanish so that he could imbibe Spinoza and Cervantes in their original text. And the Prime Minister was so eager for lessons that sometimes he sneaked out of cabinet meetings so he wouldn't miss one. Cabinet members, of course, were impressed by such scholarly zeal—as Ben-Gurion must have noted.

He needed such small triumphs, for he was unable to overcome his complexes by poking fun at himself; he utterly lacked a sense of humor and almost never told a joke. But Ben-Gurion's ego would not allow him to recognize even so obvious a deficiency. No, it wasn't true, he assured his son-in-law Emanuel, who suggested that he was indeed humorless. Ben-Gurion then agreed to submit to a test. Emanuel would tell him a joke to see if his father-in-law understood the point.

"The day after the last election, when you were returned to the prime ministership," said Emanuel, "Begin's wife packed a bag, and Begin [Ben-Gurion's chief political opponent] asked her where she was going. 'To Ben-Gurion's,' she replied. 'You promised me that after the election I would be sleeping with the Prime Minister.' "

Ben-Gurion unsmilingly pondered the joke. "I don't believe Begin made such a promise," he said. "I don't like him, but he is a gentleman."

This response suggested not only Ben-Gurion's inability to perceive humor in life, which might have eased the tremendous burden of his mission, but also his intrinsic, almost naïve trust in people, even in his most implacable foe. When he felt that someone—especially a friend or colleague—betrayed this trust, he could become vicious and vengeful. But simple opposition drew little more than a biting remark or a withering glance. And though he might bitterly protest a majority decision by his colleagues, he would accept this decision as a matter of principle. He would, however, leap at any opportunity to reverse it.

Some foes called him a "dictator," and even some friends agreed that he sometimes acted like a typically intriguing Bolshevik leader; he had, after all, admired the Bolsheviks in the early days of the Russian Revolution. He was constantly seeking to unify labor, defense and other vital organs of the nation under his own unshakable control, constantly plotting against colleagues who dared to differ with him. Yet, how he actually dealt with these dissidents refuted the point. Instead of liquidating them he simply threatened to resign if they rejected his views. And since even some of his most unswerving antagonists recoiled at the thought, Ben-Gurion usually got his way.

Ben-Gurion cherished power, true, but he cherished democracy more. Thus, his power did not depend on military backing; in fact, he trained the army never to meddle in politics. He prevailed because of his persuasive arguments and the overwhelming strength of his personality. A speaker at a meeting who dared oppose Ben-Gurion might, on finding himself the object of the Prime Minister's mesmerizing stare, suddenly switch his position in midsentence, as if hypnotized.

While Ben-Gurion, as a dedicated democrat, had faith in people collectively, he was usually ill at ease with them as individuals. He was often alone but he was seldom lonely and, until his final years, felt the need more for books than for people. If he had many disciples, he had few friends, and except for acquaintances from his youth, even the people closest to him would not address him as "David." Since he regarded the designations "Mr. Prime Minister" or "Mr. Ben-Gurion" as unbecoming to a pioneer, they called him simply "Ben-Gurion"; in private they referred to him as the "Old Man." Even Paula addressed him by his last name, underlining her own sense of awe and the practical nature of their relationship. Ben-Gurion was not entirely pleased by this compromise. Why didn't people call him "David," he often asked, wishing to be loved and respected as a mortal, not worshiped and, ironically, virtually ostracized as a supermortal. Elchanan Yishai, a close aide, once replied, "I'm sorry, Ben-Gurion, but I just can't do it."

Ben-Gurion's relations were especially warm with members of his office staff—both in Jerusalem, where he sat as prime minister, and in Tel Aviv, where he served as defense minister. Members formed a kind of family group almost blindly dedicated to him, and Ben-Gurion tried in his own way to reciprocate. He would almost never fire anyone and would often saunter out of his office to exchange a few words with his secretaries. Actually, Ben-Gurion, his jacket draped over the back of his leather chair, did much of his own secretarial work. He never dictated, but, bent over his desk with pen tightly clutched in hand, he scribbled out his own letters in cramped, sometimes illegible, handwriting to be deciphered by a waiting typist. He also kept his own files, filled his own fountain pen, clipped articles from the newspapers himself. Nor did he seek aid in writing his speeches, which he often seasoned with passages from the thick Biblical concordance that lay on his desk.

Ben-Gurion also personally answered as many letters as he could, sometimes more than thirty an hour, including all those written by bereaved parents, and he usually recorded his own minutes at meetings. A caller might leave frustrated and bewildered after having performed a soliloquy while staring at Ben-Gurion's bald pate as the Prime Minister scrawled notes in a little black-covered diary that would preserve the man's unanswered proposals forever. Sometimes, if Ben-Gurion disliked the man or his ideas, his only answer would be silence or an irrelevant—and irreverent—question like, "Where did you get that funny hat?" Or he might abruptly change the subject with a comment on some Biblical passage or pointedly read a newspaper while the person expressed his view. If, however, he liked the view but not the speaker, he might later attribute it to someone else, perhaps himself. Occasionally, in his diary he described meetings that, according to one associate, never took place, apparently to influence future interpretations of history. At the same time he often concealed his real aims *from* history —and from his colleagues—so those aims could not be squelched before they were realized. Not surprisingly, perhaps, some colleagues panicked when Ben-Gurion summoned them.

"I would rack my brain guessing what made him invite me," said one. "On the day of the appointment, I couldn't think of anything else. Restlessly I waited my turn, and when the moment came to enter his room, I would frantically check whether I was buttoned up properly, if my tie was in place. Finally, I would clear my throat and 'cross the Rubicon.'"

Ben-Gurion never relaxed and sometimes kept his staff working late into the night. When one secretary asked him if he ever rested, he replied:

"What do you mean, rest? Do you mean sleep?"

"No," she retorted, "don't you ever just sit and rest?"

Ben-Gurion was startled. "You mean just stare at the wall?"

On another occasion he explained, in a sense, why he could never stare at the wall. Asked by a young student what day in his life had given him the most satisfaction, he replied: "Satisfaction? What's that? What does one need it for? If a man is satisfied, what does he do then? A man who is satisfied no longer strives, doesn't dream, doesn't create, doesn't demand. No, I've never had a single moment of satisfaction."

And woe to the aide who gave him information that wasn't specific enough. He had to know every detail about everything; otherwise, how could the Prime Minister make a practical decision? Even the Bible was not beyond microscopic scrutiny. Was it really David who slew Goliath? Ben-Gurion, who analyzed every line alluding to this question, was not at all sure.

Sometimes Ben-Gurion's fascination with detail could be embarrassing, even insulting, to his office help. "Why is your hair so kinky?" he asked one dismayed secretary, adding in a concerned tone, "And your eyes are so squinty." Nobody actually expected a compliment; after all, he didn't even compliment

members of his own family. Occasionally his alertness dissolved
into such extreme absentmindedness that he didn't even recognize the employee. At such moments, when he was concentrating especially hard on some problem, he seemed to lose almost
total contact with his surroundings. He didn't realize that he
was riding in a new car the government had supplied him until
he had been using it for days.

But Ben-Gurion's aides and office workers knew that careless
comments or temporary aloofness did not reflect his true ties
with them. He showed his real feelings in other ways. If any
staff member got married, had a baby, or was hospitalized, he
was likely to come to the wedding, *briss* (circumcision ceremony) or hospital to show his personal interest. When one secretary mentioned that her boyfriend was studying in the United
States, he arranged for her to work there so she could marry the
youth. Since Ben-Gurion wished to be liked as a person, he
would occasionally invite himself to a staff party—members
were usually too reverent to invite their god to a fun affair—
where he would sit and smile sadly amid the revelry.

Ben-Gurion found it still harder, of course, relating to people
he didn't know well. Many would gape speechlessly in awe of
him, while he dreaded the thought of chattering foolishly with
them. If they could not spout philosophy, Zionism, Biblical history or biology, there was likely to be a frozen silence until Ben-
Gurion and his embarrassed company parted. He is known to
have sat through entire social evenings without contributing a
word to the conversation. He even balked at shaking hands,
feeling that this custom was "un-Jewish," unnecessary and un-
sanitary. And while traveling by plane, he refused to let anybody but his wife sit next to him. How could he think with
someone beside him dying to banter with the Prime Minister?

If Ben-Gurion was criticized for his reticence, he would seek,
as always, to prove his critics wrong. Thus, when an aide told
him a visitor had complained that one couldn't "chat" with him,
Ben-Gurion indignantly asked to see the man again. The visitor
returned and had barely sat down when the Prime Minister
stared challengingly at him and exclaimed, "Well, chat!"

Yet, when Ben-Gurion did wish to speak, the words came
easily—even if he was standing on his head. United States Ambassador Ogden Reid once found him in that yoga position and,
on Ben-Gurion's invitation, balanced himself in the same pos-
ture. The two men then exchanged weighty world-shaking
views with their feet in the air. To Ben-Gurion, it was no mean
achievement to stand the American ambassador on his head.

The Prime Minister had not always found it hard communicating with people. Comrades from his youth were genuine companions, not like those of later years when his few deep relationships were essentially political or paternalistic. Until he was in his early thirties, he was romanticist as well as pragmatist, sentimentalist as well as hard-boiled politician. But, as his destiny drew closer, his human ties grew looser. No one must rob him of time and emotional energy that could be used to pursue his mission. True, until he died he loved his childhood sweetheart, Rachel Nelkin (Beit-Halachmi), who had come with him to Palestine in 1906. But when forced to choose between two obsessions, he left her and ran off to work in the wilderness, though he desperately tried to win her back, even after she had married someone else.

Ben-Gurion then married Paula on the rebound, finding her a convenient substitute for his mother, who had died when he was a child but lived in his dreams even when he was an old man. But there was almost no other emotional link between man and wife, though Ben-Gurion wrote Paula passionate love letters, apparently to ease his sense of guilt, when he left her alone and pregnant in New York and went to fight with the British in Palestine during World War I. Except at state functions, Ben-Gurion seldom even shared a social evening with his wife, and when she occasionally managed to drag him to a concert or an art exhibition, he felt he was wasting his time. Few people were surprised when, at one concert, he publicly referred to conductor Leonard Bernstein as "Rubinstein." Nor did many doubt the story that, at another concert, when Paula nudged him and complained that President Yitzhak Ben-Zvi was asleep, he grunted, "For that you wake me up?"

Yes, a most convenient marriage. Paula didn't demand, in return for her maternal attention, the adoration that might have drained him emotionally and possibly jeopardized his messianic plans. And he spent even less time with his three children than with his wife. On the other hand, Ben-Gurion did find time to enjoy the transient company of women who, unlike Paula, challenged him intellectually and could serve as sounding boards for his policies. And some could be doubly useful. According to his daughter Renana, he once expressed contempt for George Bernard Shaw on hearing that the British writer had lost his purity only when he was seduced at twenty-nine. Her father might be the founder of the state, but he was also a man.

Ben-Gurion could not always suppress his sentiment. He openly wept when people close to him died, and he did not conceal his grief in letters he wrote to the parents of fallen war heroes. Bereaved mothers held a special place in Ben-Gurion's heart, for he linked their love for their sons with his own mother's love for him. In fact, memories of his mother nurtured in him an infinite respect for all women, and he would tolerate blistering criticisms from females like Golda Meir that he would never have quietly accepted from men.

He could hardly imagine that Jewish women would stoop to crime or prostitution. When an associate, Meyer Weisgal, who resembled Ben-Gurion, once told him humorously that a girl had walked up to him on a London street and offered her services, overwhelmed by the idea of sleeping with the "Israeli prime minister," Ben-Gurion, clearly troubled, was interested in only one thing: "Was she Jewish?"

This question reflected not only his idealistic view of Jewish women, but apparently his fear that some Jews might not, after all, prove worthy of their nation's holy mission. Ben-Gurion could not permit himself to doubt that his people would meet the demands of destiny. He hadn't doubted since he was a boy in Plonsk, when Israel took root in his soul . . .

Book I

MOSES

CHAPTER ONE

The vision that I saw by the river

P LONSK in the late 1800s was an obscure outpost of the massive Russian empire, stretching somberly along the banks of the Plonka River, which wound like a blue eel through east-central Poland. It was an impoverished *shtetl*, or small town, of twelve thousand people, slightly more than half of them Jews, a town that steamed with quiet discontent and seemed to have little future. Few pillars of factory smoke spiraled into the usually sullen sky, and few echoes of a budding metropolis filled the air; the most familiar sound was the lazy whistle of a locomotive chugging between Warsaw and the Baltic coast with a trainload of goods. Yet Plonsk was more fortunate than many sister towns, for it was an island of tranquillity in the simmering Russian sea, still untouched by the typhoons that swept through the empire as rebels plotted revolution and mobs massacred Jews.

The Polish and Jewish communities had been living side by side since the end of the fifteenth century, when the village of Plonsk sprouted around a fortress built by a Polish prince. The local nobles encouraged Jews to settle there and develop the economy, and soon the village prospered. But jealous Polish merchants revolted and forced the nobles to shackle Jewish commerce. Anti-Semitism reached a peak in the seventeenth century, when Poles wantonly killed Jews, burned down their homes, and prevented them from opening their shops on market days.

Things had changed since then. Most Poles, now living on the outskirts of Plonsk, were either poor artisans or peasants who wearily pulled hand plows and extracted tons of rubbery corn and coarse grain from the reluctant earth. The Jews, who lived in the center of town, sold this produce in the market and dominated commerce in general. Others had varied skills. In his tiny shop or factory, or in a candle-lit nook of his dismal house, a bearded figure with side curls might weave fiber into rope, hammer tin into utensils, tan a cowhide that would be transformed into shoes and gloves, stitch by hand the traditional caftan that was worn by most Jews, or distill brandy or brew beer to be guzzled mainly by the tense, restless Poles, who were as unhappy under the Russians as the Jews were.

The *shtetl* of Plonsk was one of thousands scattered throughout the Pale of Settlement, the western zones of the empire where about five million Russian and Polish Jews were confined. Each *shtetl* was a semiautonomous area tied to the others with bonds of business and blood tightened by the frequent reappearance of itinerant rabbis, matchmakers *(shadchans)* and beggars. But if all had common problems and a common way of life, Plonsk had its own personality. It was more relaxed than most other *shtetlach;* since Jews outnumbered Poles here, they were safer from mob attacks and therefore slower to flee to the west or revolt against the Tsar. Having time to dream, they dreamed of eternal redemption. They were ripe for Zionism.

But their dream did not blind them to the misery of slum life, or to the physical dangers that might lie ahead. Most of the five million Russian Jews, including those in Poland, had long been doomed to an existence even more impoverished than that of the poorest gentile peasant. They were *Luftmenschen,* or "flying men," who gathered in marketplaces or in front of synagogues waiting for someone to come by and offer them even the lowliest job. Periodic pogroms added to Jewish suffering as the Tsars encouraged violence whenever they needed a scapegoat for Russia's crushing woes.

Jewish fortunes rose or plummeted according to the whims of the Tsar in power. Alexander III, who came to power in 1881, scrapped the reforms of his assassinated predecessor, Alexander II, and systematically stirred the rabble in many towns to assault the Jews. The random killing and wounding of countless innocents ended in 1884, and the sound of the mob—the thunderous pounding of leather on cobblestones, the jeers, the whistles, the cry, "Kill the Yids!"—subsided into an uneasy calm. Plonsk itself, with few revolutionaries and many Jews, had so far been

spared the terror, but the Jews had little doubt that their turn
would come. After all, Alexander III still sat on the throne and
the more his people despised him, the more he would need to
channel their hatred.

Still, most Plonsk Jews were consumed less by the fear of violence than by the fear of going hungry. Their *shtetl* festered in
indigence. Branching out from the huge market square in the
heart of town was a web of alleys paved with pink, red and blue
cobblestones that were often blackened with the slime of open,
overflowing sewers. Along the alleys were lines of rickety two-
story wooden houses that seemed almost to hold each other up.
Inside, wobbly, creaking staircases led to dark rooms with
smoky stoves, iron beds, and shelves laden with patched clothing—reeking dungeons totally cut off from sunlight by the
houses on the other side of the narrow street. The poorest Jews
lived here: the market women and their pale Talmud-studying
husbands, the seamstresses, the food peddlers who sold hot
beans to schoolboys.

One of the alleys led to a less congested section of town and
crossed a road called Goat's Lane. Just off this road, in a large
yard next to the home of a Catholic priest, stood two sturdy
timbered houses, back to back, with slanted red-tile roofs, each
crowned with two chimneys. These houses belonged to Avigdor
and Sheindel Green, who lived in the one facing Goat's Lane
together with their three children—Avraham, nine; Michael,
seven; and Rivka, five—and Sheindel's mother, who would
shortly die. The rear house was used as a *heder,* or religious
school, and would be inhabited by Avraham when he married.
Sheindel's father, David Yosef Friedman, a prosperous land-
owner, had given the two houses as a dowry to his only daughter's husband and distant cousin, Avigdor.

On October 16, 1886, while autumn leaves formed a golden
carpet in the yard, another baby was born to Sheindel, a dimin-
utive dark-haired woman in her late twenties with warm brown
eyes and a gentle manner. The child, named David after her
father, was Sheindel's sixth. (Two had died before he was born
and four others would die at birth or in childhood after he was
born, while one more child would survive.) David was born into
a happy harmonious household, full of the shouts of children,
the dreams of men, and the smells of delicacies. The house itself
was large and was fitted out simply but tastefully with wooden
furniture. Avigdor Green's family lived in the four rooms down-

stairs, while in the three upstairs dwelled a young couple and their two daughters, who cleaned the house, cooked, milked the cows, and worked in the garden, amid the apple, pear and plum trees.

The door was always open to visitors, and the table was always spread with delectable dishes. Among those welcomed were the *orkhim,* the poor, who knew they could always drop by for a plate of blintzes or gefilte fish. Nor did Sheindel's charity end in the kitchen. After finishing her regular chores, she would visit a sick friend or stitch wedding clothes for girls without dowries. Evenings were always lively, astir with people who plotted redemption while munching on Sheindel's cookies and sweets.

The host, Avigdor Green, was one of these people. Tall and lordly, with a carefully tended mustache and beard, Avigdor was one of the most elegantly dressed men in Plonsk. Certainly one of the most oddly dressed—for a Jew. Instead of wearing the traditional caftan and short-peaked cap, he decked himself in a frock coat, high starched collar, large bow tie, and often a high silk hat. He kept to a rigid schedule, was never late for appointments, and smoked exactly three cigarettes a day at fixed times, convinced that self-discipline together with a dignified appearance was the key to the respectability he coveted.

Although he was just an unlicensed legal counsel who represented clients in dealings with the government (a "fixer," some of his acquaintances joked) and barely earned enough to keep up his pretensions, he would show the "better people" in town who snubbed him that he was "somebody." And his son David would carry on the campaign after him, describing him as a "distinguished lawyer," though Avigdor never went to law school or even to a university.

The father's affectations did not always work. Though he had loyal friends, some were not as friendly as they seemed when they visited him or met him in the street. With a smirk, they called him "Avigdor *Rosh*," or "unclean head," viewing him as stubborn and arrogant, pompous in his peacock clothing. More serious, some critics, without offering proof, accused him of misusing funds he collected for the Zionist cause and denouncing government foes to the authorities.

Avigdor's bitterest foes were people who viewed him as an enemy of God. For his clothes and habits mirrored not only a deep inferiority complex—which his son would apparently inherit—but also a striving for a new life and state of mind free of traditional bonds. After centuries of conditioning, many Jews were timid and subservient and sought salvation not in action, not even in dreams, but simply in an unbounded faith in God. And the Hassidim, led by the rabbis and wealthy aristocrats who ruled the Jewish community of Plonsk, did not even want a Jewish state before the messiah came.

To the mystical Hassidim, God was ubiquitous. He was present in people, animals, plants; He controlled every act of man, even sin. This omnipresence made prayer not a mechanical duty but a means of directly communicating with God. One did not simply look up to heaven and beg for blessings; with wide-brimmed fur hat clamped on head and side curls swinging, one danced and sang oneself into a state of ecstasy. Since God was in every movement, in every sound, He would share the joy of the worshipers and listen to their prayers. It was therefore absurd to think that one could escape his fate—or to attempt to preempt God by seeking a Jewish state prematurely.

Avigdor Green had a different view. He considered himself a freethinker. Like other more sophisticated Jews, he was influenced by the Haskala, the movement of Enlightenment, which sought to merge Jewish tradition with modern secular thought, to reconcile Judaism to the new age. "Awake!" wrote one Haskala leader, Abram Ber Gottlober. "Israel and Judah arise! Shake off the dust, open wide thine eyes."

And thousands did, though their eyes reflected conflicting images. In Germany and other Western European countries, where this movement began in the early nineteenth century, the image was that of a world without Jews. Why suffer forever with the taint of a hated race when one could assimilate? In Eastern Europe, with its vast Jewish population and rich Yiddish culture, the eyes saw something else—a new and prouder Jew rooted in the glorious past while thrusting into a glorious future. The Haskala here revived Hebrew literature and rejoiced in Russian literature, finding in its themes of emancipation clues to the liberation of the Jewish people.

What path to freedom was best? The "enlightened" Jews split over this question. Stay where you are, said some, and help the gentiles oust the Tsarist regime; surely the victorious revolutionary leaders would grant Jews the rights and liberties they craved. Flee to the United States or to some other free Western nation, urged others. Set sail for *Eretz Yisrael*, demanded still others, and plunge into a wilderness that might one day blossom into an independent Jewish state.

Avigdor Green and most other Jews in Plonsk preferred the last course—*aliya,* a return to Zion, though it seemed at the time the least practical solution. A Jew without his own homeland was a Jew in chains. And so Zion, however impractical, was the *only* solution to Jewish oppression and insecurity.

Avigdor was, in a sense, born into this solution. His tall distinguished father, Zvi Aryeh Green, had mastered Hebrew and taught it at the famous Kuchary school run by a group of Haskala scholars. A brilliant scholar himself, Zvi Aryeh had amassed a large library and was especially familiar with Spinoza and Plato, philosophers who would later fascinate his grandson David. He also learned German and Polish and in his later years Russian, so that he could serve as an unlicensed counsel. A few prophetic Jewish philosophers like Moses Hess had already suggested that Jewish salvation lay in *aliya,* but in Zvi Aryeh's day neither he nor many of his contemporaries seriously thought of this as an immediate goal. However, he dreamed of an eventual return to Zion, and Avigdor, one of his four sons, inherited his dream as well as his job.

Since Avigdor dealt daily with the Russians and was friendly with them, he could hold political meetings in his home without fear of arrest. And this he did, especially after joining the new Love of Zion movement, the precursor of political Zionism, which spread throughout the Pale in 1884 in response to the powerful pleas of a Jewish philosopher, Leon Pinsker. A pamphlet by Pinsker entitled "Autoemancipation" appealed with devastating logic for a Jewish state (not necessarily in Palestine) as the ultimate answer to anti-Semitism.

People streamed into Avigdor's home, sat around on hard chairs or on the rugless floor, and spun out their fantasies of "going home." They argued how to teach Hebrew to the illiterate, recited Zionist proclamations and verse, and perused Hebrew pamphlets, while Avigdor busily collected three-ruble donations that would be sent to Love of Zion headquarters in Odessa. From the time he could barely toddle, David inhaled the exaltation of Zionist redemption, listening to rapturous voices as he lay in bed, glimpsing elated expressions from behind a half-opened door or—in the summer, when meetings took place under shady trees in the yard—from an upstairs window.

"In those days," he would recall, "I didn't understand much, but somehow it got into my blood . . . I sucked the dream of *Eretz Yisrael* with my mother's milk."

David's third year brought two memorable events. Amid great fuss and bustle, his mother gave birth to another baby, Feigele (Zippora), a homely, squirming "doll" that puzzled David at first, then intrigued him. The other children were too old to play with, but now he would have a younger sister, someone closer to his own age, whom he could coddle and love.

Then the other wonderful happening. He climbed on his grandfather's knees and began learning Hebrew from him. Zvi Aryeh would point with a gnarled forefinger and say, "That's a chair, that's a table," giving the meaning first in Yiddish, the everyday tongue spoken at home, and then in Hebrew, the language of the Bible, until the child learned the name of every article in his grandfather's house. Each lesson would end with a word game to test David's knowledge. Avigdor would then follow up. Sometimes on cold winter nights he would crawl into bed with David and carry on his instruction in Hebrew, as well as in Jewish history, Palestinian geography and other subjects, while both lay buried under thick quilts.

Even before David showed up for his first day in *heder* he could speak Hebrew as fluently as Yiddish. His teacher soon realized that he was the most gifted child in the class and was astounded when, after listening to a classmate read a page from the Bible, he repeated it word for word. One day, when David was five, his parents took him to the doctor, who was astonished at the size of his head. This was a sign, he said, that the boy, who was thin and sickly, had a brilliant mind. The parents exulted. "Duvcheh," Avigdor exclaimed, calling David by his nickname, would be a famous physician. No, retorted Sheindel, who, unlike her freethinking husband, was deeply religious. "Duvcheh" would be a great rabbi. And she never ceased repeating this prediction to the neighbors, or testing David's remarkable memory and encouraging him to improve it.

But Sheindel was more concerned about her son's frail body than about his brilliant mind. The doctor was adamant. The boy must spend the summer in the countryside, where he could rest and breathe good air. So every summer Sheindel would accompany her son to a country village, where they would stay with relatives. The boy was not sure whether his mother favored him over her other children because of his fraility or because of "that story with the doctor," but he loved her deeply for it. She was the center of his world.

When David was seven, Sheindel bore another child, but amid the joy, he experienced grief for the first time. His beloved grandfather, who had taught him Hebrew while bouncing him on his knee, was extremely ill at the time. Avigdor would later write: "On Thursday my wife gave birth and a neighbor went to Father and said, 'Mazal Tov.' He asked, 'She gave birth?' 'A son.' Then he said, 'I must die before the briss so the newborn can be named after me. . . .' " (Jewish tradition prohibits naming a child after a living person.) A week later, one day before the briss, he passed away, and the newborn was named after him— only to die also shortly afterward. David wept at both funerals, as he would at those of three more children. Perhaps he learned how little time one had to realize one's dreams.

Gradually, David grew stronger and was even able to climb trees. He would sit on a branch and scan the green countryside, happily chewing on lumps of sugar that he carried in a little bag. But withdrawn and rather contemptuous of games as a waste of time, he seldom romped with the other children, who, for their part, did not find him a suitable playmate. Nevertheless, he often joined the others in a rough and tumble fight with Polish youngsters, though always as "one of the rank and file, not what you would call a leader," he would later recall. "Somebody would perhaps throw a stone, or start an argument, and very often it was the Jews who started first. We used to get the upper hand."

The willingness of the Jews to fight earned them the gentiles' grudging respect, and this lesson would always remain with David.

But the boy shared with the other Jewish children more than the glory of street conquests. Apparently to prove that he was really one of them, he would occasionally help them steal apples, pears and cherries from his own yard. And sometimes on the Sabbath he and his classmates would gather in his garden to study while Sheindel passed around goodies. He seldom played any game but chess, which he learned from his father when he was only six. He would spend hours at a time matching wits with older children, learning to concentrate completely on his next move while blocking out all other thoughts.

But though David was introverted and serious-minded, he found a great deal of pleasure in daily life. He especially loved the pre-Sabbath and holiday rituals, the songs, the smells, the tastes, the gifts that all recalled Jerusalem, the tales of ancient Hebrew heroism he had heard so often when his father met with his friends. Yet his joy was tempered by a wistful sadness. How

could a boy be really happy so far from home, even while chewing on a Purim *hamintash* (prune tart) or spending his holiday
gelt (money)?

David did so well in his elementary classes that at the age of
eight he was chosen to attend a special school for gifted children, and there, in a musty little room with few chairs, he studied the Bible, the Torah, the Talmud and Hebrew grammar. He
was always attentive in class, except during the Talmudic lessons. The Talmud, a body of Jewish tradition assembled during
the dispersion, had little meaning for David. How valid were
laws intended for Jews in exile? Only the divinely inspired
Torah (the ancient five books of Jewish law) and the Old Testament would guide him in the future. So, while his teacher ex-
pounded on the wisdom of the Talmud, David sat reading
Zionist articles hidden between the pages of his textbook.

His classroom was part of the "new" *Beth Hamidrash,* or
house of study, one of several in Plonsk, each symbolizing a
sharply defined social class and embracing its own synagogue,
Talmudic school and social hall. When David left for synagogue
on the Sabbath or on a holiday, he would join most of the Jews
of Plonsk as they strode down the streets carrying Bibles and
wearing their best caftans—which differed only in the quality
of the fabric—en route to utterly distinct worlds.

His own family, together with most intellectuals, prosperous
merchants and professional men, filed into the modern "new"
Beth Hamidrash and prayed for deliverance to Zion; members
of the lower middle class attended the less fashionable "rear"
Beth Hamidrash and prayed for deliverance to the upper middle class; and the mass of poor peddlers, porters and artisans
crowded into the dilapidated "old" *Beth Hamidrash* and prayed
simply for deliverance. In addition, the Hassidim, including
most of the elite in their velvet caftans, had their own synagogue, called the *Shtiebel,* where they prayed for deliverance
from the Zionist challenge to their power. Many Jews also fre-
quented the Great Synagogue, an independent house of worship. The various classes seldom mixed; the elite contemptuously turned up their noses at the middle class, and the
middle class looked down theirs at the lower strata.

David's *Beth Hamidrash* was more than a school and a synagogue to him. Here David and his friends gushed verse from
the Bible, thrilled to sermons preached by Lovers of Zion and
enlightened itinerant rabbis, and hurled themselves into de-

bates often begun the night before in David's own home. As they grew older, they would thrash over the books they liked. Had anyone read *Ahavat Zion* ("The Love of Zion") by Avraham Mapu? Mapu, David assured the others, "breathed life into the pages of the Bible." And *Uncle Tom's Cabin* by Harriet Beecher Stowe movingly showed the horror of slavery and subjugation.

"These two books," Ben-Gurion would later recall, "more than anything else were responsible for my becoming a socialist."

But there was also *Resurrection* by Tolstoy, which helped him to "better understand" Russia's seething social problems. He was so impressed by this book that for a while he became a vegetarian as a mark of respect toward all living things.

David was delighted with a sudden new chance to plunge into Russian culture. His father enrolled him in a Russian government school, which he would attend in addition to *heder,* openly defying the Orthodox Jewish community. A Jewish boy sitting in a coeducational secular school, his head uncovered, under a picture of the Tsar and the crown-and-cross emblem? Disgraceful! Not, however, to the children of "enlightened" Jewish parents. At the age of seven, David, influenced by his *heder* studies, had experienced a year of extreme religious fervor. But this zeal gradually wore off and vanished completely in the temporal atmosphere of his new classroom. He finally stopped winding *tfillin* (phylacteries) around his left arm and forehead, a prayer ritual that most Jews followed, and he wouldn't give in even after his father, despite his own freethinking philosophy, slapped him for the first—and last—time.

When David was ten, his dream began to take concrete shape.

"There was a rumor," he would later reminisce, "that the messiah had come. He was said to be a tall handsome man with a black beard, a doctor. We heard his name too, Dr. Herzl."

Theodor Herzl, a reporter for an Austrian newspaper, had covered the treason trial of Alfred Dreyfus, a Jewish army officer, in Paris, and was so appalled by the anti-Semitism underlying the charge that he wrote a political booklet, *The Jewish State,* urging the Jews to set up a country of their own.

Although the idea was not new, the repercussions were explosive, for unlike earlier Zionists with their penny-ante fundraising campaigns and gradualist *aliya* schemes, Herzl would grandly negotiate with the great powers of the world to provide a Jewish home and finance it with millions of dollars from a Jewish international bank. His visionary plan swept the Jewish world with its dazzling detail and audacity. "The messiah had come!"

A year later, in 1897, Herzl imperiously summoned the First Zionist Congress in Basel, Switzerland, and, like a monarch dealing with his mesmerized subjects, masterminded the conversion of his idea into a political resolution: The aim of the new Zionist movement was "a publicly recognized and legally secured Jewish home in Palestine."

Like other Zionists, the Greens were ecstatic. Suddenly the vague longings of three generations had crystallized into a hard political pledge. The meetings in the Greens' house and in the *Beth Hamidrash* grew even longer, louder and livelier, and David founded a youngsters' Zionist Society, though he soon dissolved it when parents protested that their children were too young to indulge in political activity. Tragedy had in any case robbed him of his vigor and drive.

It struck when David was eleven, traumatizing him as no other event in his lifetime ever would. After Sheindel, at forty-one, had given birth to a stillborn child, Avigdor emerged from the bedroom, and one glance at his eyes told the boy that his mother had died. He was stunned, shattered. And tears did not ease the agony. He lost interest in everything, even in his precious Zionist dream. He would not eat, he could seldom sleep.

"I used to see her in my dreams, regularly for almost two years," he would say many years later. "Night after night, almost, I would dream about her, speak to her, and ask her why she did not come back."

Avigdor tried to fill the role of mother as well as father, feeding and caring for the children, but for David his rough kindness could not replace Sheindel's gentle voice, her tender caresses. Nor could David find consolation in close, soothing relationships with his brothers and sisters, with whom he shared little. Avraham was, at twenty, a fervent Hassid, though also a Zionist. Michael, eighteen, was not very bright or ambitious. Rivka, sixteen, was intelligent and warm, one of the few "liberated" young women in Plonsk, but she was occupied with her own teen-age affairs. And though David felt closest to his younger sister, Zippora, a girl of eight could hardly console a boy of eleven.

Despite his suffering, David managed to drag himself to class in both the religious and government schools, though it was a struggle to concentrate on his studies. Innately taciturn and introspective, he now grew morose, but also more self-reliant, assertive, demanding of life with its brutal uncertainties.

Several months after his mother's death, when he was twelve, David found someone who would help to fill the void in his soul. He met Rachel Nelkin, who, though only nine, was already regarded by many boys as "the prettiest girl in Plonsk." She was tall with striking dark eyes and black braided hair, and she had a shy, gentle disposition, a girl who seemed to possess many of Sheindel's qualities. In a sense, she was a phenomenon. She shockingly attended David's secular school, even though her stepfather was a Hassidic rabbi. One of the few Hassidim who had embraced Zionism, Simcha Isaac was, because of his prestige and standing in the community, a much more important spokesman for the movement than Avigdor Green. Nor did the two men resemble each other in demeanor or personality, Isaac being modest, unpretentious, subdued.

Like Avigdor Green, the rabbi welcomed many people in his home or in the back of his small grocery store, which buzzed almost every evening with talk about the joys of *aliya*. The numbers gradually grew, but not only because of reverence for the rabbi and sympathy with his cause. As Rachel approached her teens, they came also to see her, be near her, and be served cookies by her. As she flitted from one guest to another with a plate of sweets, their longing stares were seldom met; her dark eyes disappeared under lids fringed with long wispy lashes, and her pink cheeks flushed slightly.

David seldom attended the meetings in the rabbi's house, for he had his own Zionist sessions. Also, he was apparently reluctant to appear like just another of Rachel's young suitors, though he had little reason to be jealous. Rachel clearly preferred him, attracted, the more she knew him, by the fire she perceived in his soul. When they were older, they even dared once to stroll the streets together unescorted, to the hushed shock of the town. So scandalized were some parents that they forbade their daughters to associate with Rachel. On another occasion, a rival for her affection, Shlomo Lavi, flew into such a jealous rage that he drew a knife and chased David through the alleys until both boys collapsed from exhaustion. But even Lavi gradually reconciled himself to the tightening bond between David and Rachel.

The couple, however, would find no peace, for each was the child of a "heretic," in the eyes of Plonsk's Jewish fathers. Avigdor Green was a "low-brow" friend of the *goyim,* and Rabbi Isaac was a "traitor" to the rabbinate. Both had "forsaken" their people and their religion. And Hassidic leaders feared and hated Zionism still more after the First Zionist Congress, for even many rank-and-file Hassidim could no longer resist the attraction of a Jewish state.

In desperation the rabbis wrote pamphlets violently condemning Zionism and warned the people not to mix or "intermarry" with Zionists, while fathers beat and even disowned Zionist sons. David defiantly met with his two best friends, Shmuel Fuchs and Shlomo Zemach, to plot a bold act of revolt. Why not teach the mass of youth, the children of the poor, to speak Hebrew and persuade them to use it as their everyday tongue, filling them meanwhile with Zionist dreams? The three boys heatedly debated the plan. Could they so brazenly take on the Jewish establishment of Plonsk? If they failed, the whole Zionist cause might suffer. But despite the risks, the three agreed to start a new movement called the Ezra Society, after Ezra the prophet, who founded the Second Temple as they would help found the Third. And they prepared for the venture by making a pact: They would speak only Hebrew to each other and to their fathers.

For David, the decision was easy; his father would support him and even help to finance the society. But Shmuel and Shlomo agonized, for their fathers were Hassidim who ruthlessly attacked Zionism. Shmuel and Shlomo would have to fight and even humiliate them. And yet they did not hesitate. Shmuel, seventeen, was a brilliant organizer from a middle-class family and was loved by David as an elder brother. Shlomo, a handsome, dark-haired youth with classic features, was an aspiring writer and poet from the wealthiest and most aristocratic family in Plonsk, a family of great influence. He lived in one of eight large brick houses owned by the Zemachs, who, since the seventeenth century, had grown rich from a flourishing timber and wool trade.

Shlomo's father was a stern, arrogant man, so contemptuous of Plonsk's Jewish community that he sought husbands for his four daughters in other towns, where he could find richer, nobler young men. He especially despised the Zionists and snubbed the Greens when he passed them on the street. Once he slapped Shlomo's face on learning that his son had been to David's house. But this violent act did not stop Shlomo from visiting his friend. The two were, indeed, almost inseparable; each saw in the other qualities that were lacking in himself. David, who long resented the slurs cast on his father, envied Shlomo's social standing and was so proud to be seen with him that he even emulated his haughty air. Shlomo, on the other hand, wished he had David's talent for rousing people and winning their support. What did they see in someone who was so puny, with rough irregular features and thick wavy hair that rolled over a massive head?

But the two were extremely close and poured out their hearts to each other about more than Zionism and politics. David made no secret of his love for Rachel, and Shlomo did not hide his feelings for his own beloved—Shmuel's sister Rosa. Shlomo and Rosa had never met, for her father was a Hassid traditionalist and wouldn't let his daughter out of his sight. However, he couldn't keep her out of Shlomo's sight. Since they were neighbors, the two youngsters would sit by their windows and stare lovingly at each other.

Lovesickness, however, did not interfere with plans for a revolt. And one day in December 1900, David stood in the *Beth Hamidrash* before a group of about thirty comrades and announced the birth of the Ezra Society. The Zionist youth revolt had begun. But within minutes some twenty young Hassidim broke in and attacked the gathering. Somebody blew out the lamps and fists flew wildly. The attackers finally withdrew, and with the lamps rekindled, David brushed back his hair, straightened out his coat, and breathlessly affirmed that the meeting would resume.

The next day, David, Shmuel and Shlomo knocked on the doors of Plonsk's poorest Jewish homes and, without stressing their Zionist missionary aims, humbly asked to improve the children's knowledge of Hebrew. Some parents, obeying the orders of their Hassidic leaders, told the young Zionists to leave. But others were won over, and soon about one hundred and fifty children gathered daily for an hour and a half before the evening prayer in the *Beth Hamidrash* to learn Hebrew, study the Bible and read Zionist poems composed by David himself. Within months many of the youth of Plonsk were filling the air of this backward little *shtetl* with the harsh but exotic sounds of the ancient Hebrew tongue, and parents and friends, learning from them, soon joined in the phonetic symphony.

The Yiddish-speaking Hassidim, who viewed Hebrew as a language to be spoken only in prayer, were outraged, especially when many children dropped their Talmudic studies. They envisioned the whole traditional social and religious order crumbling into Zionist heresy. They even denounced leading Zionists to the Russian police, who vainly searched the Greens' house for "evidence" that Avigdor had illegally transferred money abroad. Rabbi Isaac paid dearly for his idealism. The fanatics first boycotted his shop, then dragged him from the synagogue while he was at prayer and beat him in the street.

But the three comrades had won an extraordinary victory, and the experience left a permanent imprint on David. He had visited dark stinking rooms where people with gaunt faces and vacant eyes lived and worked in squalor, people he would never have mixed with before. He had seen their depressed and lethargic children suddenly sparked to life by a dream. He had been physically attacked by religious fanatics, slandered by the greedy rich, shaken by the callousness of the poor toward those who were still poorer.

And so the idea of "messianic redemption," of creating a morally and intellectually superior nation that could ultimately redeem all humanity, began to give his Zionism a new visionary dimension. Zionism now had to be linked with a universal humanistic ideology. On a practical level, this was a matter not only of social justice but of smart politics. For did not ultimate power lie in the backing of the impoverished masses? Already influenced by the books he had read, David would link an ancient longing, Zionism, to a modern aspiration, socialism.

With remarkable daring, David alluded to this aspiration in public, even within earshot of the Russians, who constantly feared socialist revolutionary activity. When David's rabbi, who wanted to ease Russian concern about possible Jewish subversion, declared in the synagogue that the Jews were loyal subjects of the Tsar and none were revolutionaries, David jumped to the pulpit to respond. The Tsar's laws and methods, he cried, were pushing the Jews into the arms of the revolution. The audience gasped—and not without reason.

For Tsar Nicholas II, who had succeeded Alexander III in 1894, was determined to root out the revolutionaries. Many of the leaders, he was sure, were Jews, backed by international Zionists like Herzl who had the audacity to solicit his support for a Jewish state. Nicholas cracked down mercilessly, and in 1903 a pogrom in the Bessarabian town of Kishinev claimed the lives of eighty-five Jewish men, women and children, with hundreds more beaten and raped. A wave of horror rippled through Plonsk as elsewhere. The pogroms had begun again.

David called a meeting of all Plonsk Jews in the Great Synagogue, and hundreds, already aware of his reputation as a vigorous speaker, came to mourn the victims of Kishinev. With a trembling voice David entranced his listeners. Do not let the same thing happen in Plonsk; do not stand by passively and be massacred. Fight back! The audience was stunned. Nobody in Plonsk had ever suggested this before.

David, however, would not rely on fist-shaking alone. The real wound was not to the flesh of a man, but to the soul of a people, a wound that festered with the shame of passive martyrdom and could only heal in Zion. After his moving speech, David continued his campaign to exploit the slaughter, instructing Ezra members to ask the Jews of Plonsk to give their coins for the injured and the families of the dead. Even if one had no money to contribute, he would become aware of the tragedy, of the need to do something about it.

Although Avigdor was proud of his son and even endangered his family to help Ezra, he worried about David's future. The boy had left *heder* at thirteen, for he did not wish to labor over the Talmud, and he had been graduated from his government school. Where would he continue his education? In Plonsk there was no suitable *gymnasium* (high school) where he could train for a profession or trade. Could one make a living simply from a dream?

Avigdor remained close to his son after Sheindel's death; they even appeared together in amateur plays to the lively applause of less-than-discriminating audiences. Nevertheless, since his mother's death, David's relationship with his father had changed.

"When I was twelve years old," he would reminisce, "I was already busy with my friends, and I did not take what my father said seriously. . . . [He] did not generally interfere in my everyday affairs, and had he done so, I would not have accepted his guidance."

A barrier had come between them. Although Avigdor vowed after Sheindel's death never to remarry, he nevertheless took a second wife two years later. Tsivia Swistowski was a tall, elegant, intelligent widow with two grown children and was liked by most people who met her. But not by David, who, in fact, deeply resented "Aunt Tsivia," as he called her. How could his father share his life with another woman, especially after so short an interval? How could this woman dare try to replace his mother?

Avigdor, wishing to assure David's future and diffuse the emotional crisis at home, hoped to send his son to school abroad. In November 1901, he wrote a letter to Theodor Herzl himself asking for his help and advice.

> Leader of our people, spokesman of the nation, Dr. Herzl, who stands before kings [he reverently wrote]. God has blessed me with a superior son . . . His belly is filled with learning . . . and his soul yearns for study. I have decided to send him abroad, to study science, and several people have advised me to send him to Vienna . . . Thus, I am bringing this account before my lord so that he may command my son. . . .

David never knew until many years later that his father had written to Herzl, nor is there any indication that Herzl replied.

Herzl, in any event, was rather preoccupied at the time. Despite a Herculean effort, he had failed to persuade the Sultan of Turkey, who ruled virtually all the Middle East, to allow the Jews to build a national home in Palestine. Nor did European leaders support the idea. Herzl was downcast and disillusioned as he solemnly reported his failure to the Sixth Zionist Congress in Basel in 1902. Yet he saw one glimmer of hope—British leaders told him that Britain might agree to set up a self-governing Jewish territory in the highlands of Kenya, one of its African colonies, an area Herzl would mistakenly call "Uganda." Some of the other delegates, mainly those from Western Europe, shared Herzl's joy. A home at last! But the more traditional delegates from Eastern Europe were enraged. What kind of home was that? The Jews had only one home, the one God gave them— *Eretz Yisrael.*

News of the split soon reached Plonsk. David, Shmuel and Shlomo, while sunning themselves on the bank of the Plonka River, pored over the details in newly arrived Zionist journals. They were disturbed. The "messiah" wanted to set up a Jewish state in Africa! What was a Jewish state without a heart, without Jerusalem? The Zionist movement would soon reach a decision, and if "Uganda" won, it would be too late. The youths made a decision of their own: They would settle in Palestine and pave the way for other Jews in Plonsk and elsewhere. Political negotiations had failed. Now it was time to create a *fait accompli.* Only "practical" Zionism, the majesty of conquering the Palestinian wilderness with one's own hands, would lead to a state.

One of the three, the boys decided, would go first and then return to Plonsk with a report. They drew lots to decide who would leave first. Shlomo won, and David was almost relieved, for he was faced with a problem of the heart. A year later, when he was eighteen, he would write, clearly referring to his relationship with Rachel: "I was still a boy, about twelve years old and was already in love . . . My love was young like an early spring bird, but it grew in the course of time and burned like a flame—and last summer I learned that she loves me."

For the first time, David, who had secretly written love poems to Rachel that he never dared give her, had summoned the courage to confess his love for her, and she had confessed hers for him. But she would not leave without her family, and her stepfather, Rabbi Isaac, felt that he must still struggle to win over the Jews of Plonsk to Zionism. So let Shlomo leave first.

If David was at times overwhelmed by his love for Rachel, he was at other times tormented by uncertainty, by a vague sense of guilt that he was letting personal sentiments influence the course of his life. Occasionally he even tried to convince himself that he did not really love her. He could not go to Palestine without her—or stay in Plonsk with her. The only solution, he decided, was to go to Warsaw. Away from Rachel, his emotional confusion might unravel into some kind of rational understanding of himself and the road he must take. Besides, Warsaw was less than forty miles from Plonsk, and he could always return in two or three hours.

In Warsaw he would groom himself for the move to Palestine. The country would need trained technicians to design factories, plan irrigation systems, blueprint cities. And with his disciplined mind and flair for the grandiose scheme, he was sure he would make an excellent engineer. After high school in Warsaw he would go on to a technical college.

Avigdor approved his son's ambition. He wanted him to learn a trade or profession before immigrating to Palestine. At the same time he hoped to keep him within visiting distance for a while longer. But even with his father's permission, David kept postponing the date of his departure for Warsaw. First it was the summer of 1903, then autumn, then winter. He could not leave

Rachel. About a year later, on June 2, 1904, he would write to Shmuel Fuchs, who had left Plonsk:

> Yes, I loved—you know that—but you do not know how much . . . like the eruption of a flaming volcano, the fire of my love raged in my heart. All the poems I wrote were only its smoky shadow. . . . Suddenly, I began to cast doubt upon my love . . . did I really love? The question gave me no rest at night. . . . There were other moments when I was not able to believe that my soul could harbor such a foolish question . . . my love was still so strong. However, gradually I began to feel that I did not love her. . . . In my heart I continued to feel a strong sense of love, but not for her. (To this day, I do not know whether I ceased loving her, or whether I never loved her at all. . . .) It was the middle of the winter. Until then, I had been happy beyond bounds; afterwards, I was miserable . . . my heart pained me so, my sorrow disturbed me so that sometimes I sat in my bed all night and wept. . . . I could no longer live in Plonsk. That was one of the reasons why I traveled to Warsaw that summer—just as at the start of winter, love was my reason for staying in Plonsk.

David awoke the next morning embarrassed by his outpouring of emotion and continued his letter:

> "The morning is wiser than the evening," says the Russian proverb—and with justice. Recalling what I wrote last night, I laugh at myself. What an absurdly sentimental style—I even thought of starting the whole letter over again, but I am too lazy for that, and I do not have the time.

Shmuel Fuchs was the first to leave Plonsk for Palestine, despite the original plan to send Shlomo Zemach. Shlomo found that he could not defy his family so brutally, and he didn't have enough money for the trip anyway since his father would not give him one kopeck for such a journey. Fuchs decided to leave in spite of family pleas and managed to scrape up the necessary funds. So one day in May 1904, David and other Ezra youths went to the train station to see him off for London, where a ship would take him to Palestine. There was something almost holy in this moment; yet David had seldom felt as depressed as he did amid the cheers, the songs, the cries of "good luck." His comrades should be cheering him instead. He, David Green, should be sitting at the window radiantly waving farewell. Besides, he would write later, "I felt so lonely. As if I were left on a . . . deserted island."

David headed for Warsaw determined to strengthen his character for the ultimate ordeal. He would impose on himself an iron discipline, train himself to overcome his sentimentality and even his need for companionship. True to this vow, he refused to accept any money from his father, moving into a shabby room that he shared with other boys and surviving on bread alone, while he roamed the streets looking for a job.

At night David would sit in a corner and read by candlelight, refusing to visit friends and relatives living in Warsaw. Never again would he be a slave to his emotions. What did his soul matter when the soul of a nation was at stake? But he finally cracked under the tension of solitude and, putting down his book, dragged himself with a twinge of self-reproach to his relatives.

"This time," he would write, "my heart overcame my will."

Despite his loneliness and poverty, David found pleasure in the grandeur and sheer size of Warsaw. Unlike the alleys of Plonsk, the avenues here were broad and bordered by tall sturdy buildings and occasionally graced by splendid palaces and churches. And the shops were bulging with goods. Though he hardly had enough money for food, he borrowed some to buy a new short jacket and a straw hat to replace his long coat and peaked cap. What the rabbis in Plonsk would say if they could see him now!

David finally found a job as a teacher in a *heder,* and now he would have the money to pay for his studies. But the Russian high schools rejected him because their "Jewish quotas" were already full, and a technical college turned him down because he didn't have a high-school diploma, though he had passed the entrance examination with higher marks than the Christians who were admitted. David was outraged. Now he didn't even have a good excuse for delaying his trip to Palestine.

Then came more disastrous news. David received a letter from Shmuel Fuchs—he was in New York! While waiting in London for a ship to Palestine, Shmuel, who was supposed to be Plonsk's advance man in Palestine, had decided that life would be more fulfilling in the United States after all. David, however, did not abandon hope that Shmuel would eventually meet him in Palestine. With uncharacteristic delicacy, he tried to persuade him. In his letter of June 2, 1904, he wrote, gushing with almost feminine sentimentality:

> How great has become my longing for you. . . . Do you know, sometimes I am puzzled by it and look for explanations—but in vain. . . . Each time I sit down to write you, my heart overflows and I desire to write you everything—and I cannot! And when I read your letters, it seems to me I am being caressed, but, foolishness!

The biggest blow of all followed in July 1904: Theodor Herzl died. David was crushed. "It was as though the world was coming to an end," he would say later. Still hopeful that Shlomo would find his way to Palestine, David wrote to him two weeks after Herzl's death:

> There will not again arise such a marvelous man. . . . But today more than ever I have faith in and am certain of our victory. It is clear to me that there is a day—a day that is not far off—when we shall return to that wondrous land, the land of song and truth, the land of flowers and of the visionaries' visions.

Apparently to justify lingering in Warsaw and postponing his own "return to that wondrous land," David helped to found a Herzl Society, similar to his Ezra Society in Plonsk; but the struggle over "Uganda" had also split the Jews of Warsaw and so the organization soon disintegrated. Nothing seemed to succeed. David fell deeper into despair. And adding to his gloom was a masochistic tendency to dwell on the sadness of the past. He turned restlessly in bed and dreamed of his mother; he sat at the small table in his room and scribbled wistful letters to Shmuel.

> I am particularly influenced by [Bialik's] excellent love poems, arousing in my soul forgotten, sad memories. Beautiful are the roses blossoming in spring meadows, but how sad is the sight of white roses blooming on the mound of the grave under which is buried a boy who died in his infancy.

David remembered the baby brother who was born just before his grandfather died and who himself died shortly afterward. The other children who barely lived. The infant who never lived, dying in his dead mother's womb. . . . And Rachel. . . . Try as he might to tear her out of his mind, she kept returning, relentlessly, to haunt him.

> Even now at times, [he confided to Shmuel] love flashes within my heart like lightning; an ember will flare up—particularly when I am alone and I recall forgotten matters. . . . But a moment later, it has passed by. . . . Has my heart hardened, turned to stone? Who can read the riddles of the soul? . . .

David tried desperately to read the riddles. Should he continue his apparently hopeless effort to resume his education in Warsaw? Return to Plonsk, accepting failure and the renewal of his troubling relationship with Rachel? Leave for Palestine—and cut himself off completely from Rachel and his family, perhaps forever?

"I have a strong yearning for something," he wrote Shmuel, "but I don't know for what. . . ."

He must master his destiny, yet he still procrastinated, and the longer he did, the more tormenting was his sense of guilt. As his anxieties grew, his health began to deteriorate, apparently from psychosomatic causes, and he was bedridden for days at a time with high blood pressure, headaches, dizziness and heart pains.

No medicine helped him, but after he moved to a room in another apartment, his new landlord's daughter did. Genia, or Jenny, Ferenbuk was a sprightly, unpretentious Jewish girl, and she knew how to raise David's plummeting spirits. She was to be one of several women in his life who would do so at crucial moments of loneliness or despair. Jenny even managed at times to banish Rachel from his mind, though not for long.

"I feel in my heart," he would write of her to Fuchs, "a sentiment as powerful as an autumn storm, and I wish to cry in her bosom and pour out into her soul all my yearnings and longings unknown to myself. But this feeling does not persist and (sometimes) I laugh at such feelings."

When he would return to Plonsk, Jenny would visit him and, like Rachel before her, spark a scandal by strolling with him down the main street. Had David arranged this to arouse Rachel's jealousy, to hurt her in a clumsy attempt to build artificial barriers between them that might solve his dilemma? At any rate, Jenny would soon become but a pleasant memory, a tonic that he had gratefully sipped in a moment of despondency.

Another tonic turned out to be his old friend Shlomo Zemach. On November 20, 1904, he visited David and, excitedly pacing the floor of his room, revealed that he was leaving for Zion after all, despite his father's violent opposition. If necessary, he would "borrow" money for the trip from his father—without his father's knowledge, of course. David was delighted. Shlomo's decision would somehow make it easier for him to reach his own—when the time came.

Three weeks later, on December 12, Shlomo's father gave his son a bag of money to deposit in the bank. Shlomo saw his opportunity. In Warsaw he was greeted eagerly by David, who arranged for the "fugitive" to stay in a friend's house until he could obtain a forged passport (the government wouldn't grant passports easily).

Such caution proved justified. That evening, when David returned to his room, he found Shlomo's father sitting there. He wrote to Shmuel the next day:

"He spoke to me calmly, without any hint of emotion. . . . I assured him that Shlomo had already left. I don't know whether he believed me or not, but he did not come back again and has probably returned to Plonsk."

This account contradicted another that Ben-Gurion would give later. Shlomo's father, according to the new version, "got down on his knees," and begged him to reveal where his son was. "There was I," he would say, "an eighteen-year-old being begged by Shlomo's father, a rich and important man. I could not stand it any longer, so I asked him to swear an oath that he would not prevent Shlomo from going to Palestine. He swore the oath, and then I told him where his son was, and brought the two of them together . . . Shlomo's father made no attempt to stop him from going."

Shlomo later denied the accuracy of this version of the meeting and insisted that his father would never have acted so humbly. And, in view of David's earlier remarks to Shmuel Fuchs, it appears that David was unable to resist the temptation to feed his ego, to announce to the world that he had brought the most imperious member of Plonsk's elite to his knees.

On December 13, David once more gloomily bade farewell to a dear friend at the train station. Once more too, he tried to convince himself, as well as Shmuel in America, of the need to follow immediately. He wrote to Shmuel on December 18:

> Our situation is so terrible, so dreadful! Our era is the most dangerous period in all our history! . . . Unless we work with devotion, there, in Zion, we shall perish. Next summer I shall certainly go to *Eretz Yisrael*. Perhaps we, the three of us, shall soon meet there.

A few weeks later, on a trip to Plonsk, David was relaxing with his friends in the *Beth Hamidrash* when Shlomo Lavi rushed in, tears in his eyes, and cried, "Friends, a postcard from Shlomo (Zemach)!" As the boys surrounded him, he jumped on a bench and stammered out the precious message:

> I am in Rishon LeZion [a Jewish settlement in Palestine]. Now, as I write, there lie in front of me the first two *bishliks* [Turkish coins] I

earned with my own two hands. And my joy is great . . . Don't worry,
come, and you'll have work.

David and the others were overwhelmed. Their comrade was
actually working the soil of Zion with his own hands. A vague
image had suddenly crystallized into something real and tangi-
ble. Letters to David soon followed describing the hardships
but also the splendor of life in Palestine. The descriptions were
so vivid that David almost felt that he was there gazing won-
drously at the trees, the mountains, the sunlit sea; filtering the
cool earth through his fingers; savoring the dazzle of flowers
that bowed under a luminous sky; inhaling the perfumed fresh-
ness of the fields; tasting the golden fruit in the orchards; basking in the warm camaraderie of the settlements. Shlomo's
letters, however, intensified the cruelty of David's dilemma.
How long could he remain in the Diaspora?

Back in Warsaw, where he still worked as a teacher, David
found himself caught up in the revolutionary fever that was
gripping Poland and all of Russia. On January 27, 1905, he heard
that the Polish socialists planned to shut down commerce completely, and he rushed out to buy bread, only to find that he was
too late. The revolution began the next day. David watched
gangs of workers armed with rifles, wooden stakes and stones
run through the alleys firing and throwing their missiles, smashing into government stores, haranguing people to revolt. And he
saw the Cossacks, their capes rippling in the wind, sweep
through the crowds on their horses, whipping and shooting at
random and finally crushing the rebels.

David scurried to the safety of his room with mixed feelings.
He conceded that "the revolutionary movement has captured
my heart," and a part of him cried out that the struggle of any
oppressed human being was the struggle of mankind. The ultimate goal of his Zionism, after all, was to build an exemplary
Jewish state that would be a "light unto the nations" and lead
the way to the redemption of all humanity—including the
Poles.

But this cry was drowned out by another, his warning to
Shmuel: "We shall perish!" Whom could the Jews save if they
didn't first save themselves? After all, how thin could a man
spread his soul? *Eretz Yisrael* was a struggle to the death, and
David had to concentrate on it with all his energies and resources. So, though a socialist himself, a humanist who had

been outraged by the trials of Uncle Tom, he did not feel a part of this revolt in Warsaw.

"A vacuum was created in my heart," he wrote, "for I knew that the revolution would, perhaps, liberate Russia, but not the Jewish people."

David's reserve was all the more marked since many of the agonized faces he saw on the street were Jewish. In a sense, these Jews posed an even worse threat to Zionism than the Cossacks. For they belonged to the anti-Zionist League (Bund) of Jewish Workers of Lithuania, Poland and Russia, which had close ties with the Russian Social Democratic Party. The Bund urged cultural autonomy, especially Yiddish education, for Jews in Russian territories but opposed emigration as near-betrayal of the native land. The Jews, argued the Bund, should join the revolt against the Tsarist regime and help form a revolutionary socialist government that would grant them full political and civil rights. The Bund embraced most Jewish workers in Poland, though not in Zionist Plonsk. David admired the courage he saw in those Jewish faces on the streets of Warsaw, but to concede that the Jews should join in the fighting would be to concede that their philosophy might be right. This dilemma apparently nourished his melancholy.

And his spirits by no means rose when police, noting his long hair and Russian *rubashka* (a high-collared shirt), hauled him off to jail for looking like a revolutionary and threw him into a cell with common criminals.

"That was the first time I ever came into contact with the dregs of society," he would say. "I was shaken to the core at the language and the behavior. I never had the slightest notion that such people ever existed. . . . The thing that shook me most was that these criminals were Jews."

They were mainly Bundists and brothel keepers, arrested when the Bund attacked the brothels and tried to close them. To David, the Bundists, who "jeered" and "cursed" him and the other Zionist inmates, were the more dangerous criminals. A brothel keeper might wound a few souls, but the Bundists would doom a whole race.

Finally, after ten days in jail, David was released when his father came to Warsaw and convinced the police chief that the youth was harmless.

After vainly trying once more to wriggle into a technical school, David, in mid-1905, joined a new Workers of Zion (Poalei Zion)

Party, whose aim of building a socialist state in Palestine was based on the philosophy of Ber Borochov, a young Jewish Marxist. Borochov felt that since Jews were economically victimized in the Diaspora, Zionism was as inevitable for them as socialism was for the rest of mankind. David agreed completely, and never more so than in July, when the Seventh Zionist Congress declared that a Jewish homeland must be set up in Palestine and nowhere else. The "Uganda" proposal had failed. With new enthusiasm, David now helped to organize Jewish workers and instill Zionism in them. He worked side by side with other future leaders of Jewish Palestine, yet, perhaps because of his youth and his small-town origins, he was not then considered a major Zionist figure.

The battle between Zionists and Bundists for the sympathy of the masses in the Pale of Settlement now began in earnest. Both groups had long been caching arms, the Bund mainly to back the budding Russian revolution and the Poalei Zion to thwart the infectious spread of pogroms; now a fratricidal war between Jews threatened to erupt. David rushed home to Plonsk. His task was to convert Ezra into an arm of Poalei Zion and to woo local Jewish workers, who were being won over by a young Bundist organizer from another town. He invited the workers to his *Beth Hamidrash* and, with his usual rough eloquence, coaxed them to switch loyalties. Bund headquarters in Warsaw quickly ordered an agitator, Shmuel Segal, a sixteen-year-old oratorical prodigy, to meet David's challenge. When word spread that David Green would debate Segal, hundreds of people scrambled into the Great Synagogue to hear them, and shopkeepers even shut down for the day.

Each of the speakers was dramatically flanked by two bodyguards and carried a pistol in his belt, though both agreed to lay their weapons on a table to avoid any chance of a shootout desecrating this house of God. They climbed onto a bench, and David nervously surveyed the huge audience, knowing that his family and friends were there. He was proud to have this opportunity to convince the whole Jewish community that it should pack up and fulfill its long-delayed destiny. He was perhaps also ashamed, for he was talking and not acting, disobeying his own creed, delaying his own destiny.

After hours of debate, it was David who had made the deepest impact and won the most disciples. He spoke, said some, like the messiah himself, his high but carefully modulated voice rippling through the room like an echo from the Biblical past. His audience was spellbound—until someone in the rear suddenly shouted, "Police!" All socialist organizations were banned, and here was a debate between two of them!

Amid shouts and screams, people leaped from their seats and dived out of windows, piling upon each other in heaps of tangled flesh before scrambling to their feet and streaking away. David Green, breathless, his long hair disheveled, was among those vanishing into the shanty interior of the town.

David's membership in Poalei Zion helped to sharpen the image of his future role in Zion. If he could not serve as an engineer, he could serve as a labor leader. He would begin his education, he decided, by improving the conditions of some of the most exploited workers in Plonsk—the seamstresses. These young women, mainly in their teens, labored eighteen hours a day in dingy tailor shops. David set up a strike committee and personally visited the shops to explain workers' rights to the thin, pale seamstresses. He urged them to strike. The girls were dumbfounded. There had never been a strike in Plonsk before, but they agreed. And after a prolonged walkout, complete with pickets and "goon squads," the flabbergasted employers gave in. The girls would have to work only twelve hours for the same pay—a remarkable victory in those days.

David then forced the owner of the women's bathhouse to replace a well-off attendant with a needy widow, ordered the picketing of a tiny knitting shop, and even shut down a small rope factory belonging to Rachel's grandmother—with granddaughter's enthusiastic approval. He also unionized the house maids.

David was amazed by the power of organized labor. The authorities seemed helpless; when the police intervened to end violence during the tailor strike, a Polish judge actually sided with the strikers. David envisaged the potential of a mighty labor movement in Palestine, and he saw clearly for the first time the role he was destined to play there. He would start out in the fields and, rallying the other workers around the Poalei Zion banner, help to build a powerful political machine before the Turkish rulers awakened to Jewish aims.

If a labor movement could improve lives, it could not protect lives, certainly not at this time, when hundreds of Jews were dying in a rash of pogroms erupting throughout the Pale of Settlement. David called protest meetings and distributed leaflets condemning the attacks. But that was not enough—he needed an armed force. He urgently called a meeting of Ezra. Weapons must be bought, he cried, stolen if necessary, and stored for a possible uprising in case a pogrom struck Plonsk. Not everybody agreed. Such an effort might provoke the very pogrom it was meant to prevent.

The Jews must not be intimidated, David retorted; if they had to die, it was best to die fighting. Anyway, they needed arms "so as not to be dependent on others." They must act like the Israelites of the Bible, not like the Jews of the Diaspora. They would get the money for arms from the people, and the arms would be stored in his house. His father would agree; after all, Avigdor had allowed fugitives from Warsaw on the Tsar's blacklist to hide there. Later, David would explain:

> My father was not too happy about [storing the arms] but he did not stand in my way. . . . Had I asked his permission, he would have said "No," but since I never asked him he had a good excuse not to forbid me.

At the next meeting of Ezra, members showed up symbolically armed with knives, iron pipes, metal poles and other weapons. And David, trained to use a pistol by the Poalei Zion in Warsaw, proudly showed off his sharpshooting prowess while training them. He then sent them out to canvass Jewish homes.

"Do you think we ought to have a Jewish self-defense organization?" they would ask. "If you do, you must give us money for it." The potential contributors glanced at the pistol "on the table in front of their noses" and usually reached into their pockets.

In the shadows of night, David and his friends smuggled pistols and rifles into his house, carefully hiding them in the stove and in his sisters' room. They also stuffed the attic with forbidden Zionist literature, pamphlets on self-defense, and printing equipment. The Russian police, apparently hearing rumors of the operation, invaded the Greens' home one night, but made only a superficial search. Avigdor saw them off amid smiles and tinkling glasses of *Schnapps*. They wanted no Warsaw-style revolt in Plonsk.

David Green was an impressive figure as he strutted down the street, pistol in his belt, bodyguards at his side; and he enjoyed the power his new image implied. To accentuate this image, he occasionally resorted to adolescent bravado. Once he fired his pistol into the air inside the *Beth Hamidrash* and another time on the street when Rachel rode by in a carriage—hoping she would note that he was a man to reckon with. All the employers in Plonsk were terrified that his weapons would be turned against them, and even the police did not harass him. David was pleased with himself. He had gone far for a young man whose father had been vilified by the town's elite.

More important were the implications for his people. He had openly challenged the police and had triumphed, just as he had with his campaign to organize the town's workers. Even the most powerful oppressors would hesitate to confront a people ready to defend themselves with arms. Eventually, David believed, the Jews would all choose battle and martyrdom over the submission dictated by Diaspora culture.

Despite David's militancy on social and military problems, people so respected his wisdom that they came every day to ask him to mediate their disputes. Once, while in a nearby town settling an argument over who would be the new communal rabbi, he was arrested again as a suspicious character. His father rushed to the rescue once more—before police could carry out a threat to shoot the young man and thus cheat destiny just as it beckoned.

David would leave for Zion in late summer 1906, for not only did he know now what he must do there, but he was leaving with Rachel. Her stepfather had already left, and Rachel and her mother would follow on David's ship. They would be joined by Shlomo Zemach, who had come back from Palestine some months earlier and would now be returning. Shlomo had happily come to terms with his father, but now he had another heartache. He and David had tried to persuade Shmuel Fuchs's sister Rosa, whom Shlomo dearly loved, to join the group, but she wouldn't abandon her rigidly Hassidic family as her brother had done.

Shlomo had matured during the year and a half that he was away. He looked much tougher now, more muscular, with a complexion of soft leather deeply tanned by the relentless Middle Eastern sun. His haughtiness had melted into an air of self-confidence seasoned with a touch of humility. He sat in the Greens' home talking with David for hours about the sights and smells of Zion, but also about the disappointment and the disillusion. Despite the glowing descriptions in his letters, life in

Palestine was difficult, even brutal, he stressed, and the new-comers would have to change many of their preconceived ideas to meet local needs.

Shlomo glanced at David's revolutionary garb, his long hair, the pistol in his belt. He felt that David had moved too far to the left, too close to international socialism. Revolution? Yes. But a different brand, molded to circumstances. And few in the Dias-pora seemed to realize that Palestine wasn't inhabited by Jews alone, that Arabs lived there, too.

David was somewhat dejected, but he did not permit "reality" to dim his optimism; he was confident that he could fit his tactics to any new situation while always advancing toward his final goal.

A few days before his scheduled departure, David called a strike in a tailor shop where seamstresses were making a coat for Rachel to take on her journey. David adored Rachel, but this was a matter of principle, and he would not call off the strike so that the coat could be completed in time. Instead, he postponed their departure.

Finally an agreement was reached and the day came. David and all his friends and relatives met at his home for a farewell party, and never had the house been noisier. The guests laughed, cried, reminisced, sang, hugged, and took group pho-tographs in the garden, with David, wearing a *rubashka* and peaked cap, sitting cross-legged, proud and unsmiling, beside Rachel. Inside, Avigdor watched from a window, perhaps the saddest person at the party. His dear David was leaving to pick oranges in Palestine when he should be getting a formal educa-tion that would make him a great man. Avigdor had even offered to send him to study in Switzerland, but in vain. And he could not really argue with his son, for had he not preached a return to Zion even before the boy was born? And so Avigdor slouched at the window, his heart heavy with memories of the past and fears for the future—a future that would seem even bleaker the next year when he would run for the Duma (parliament) and suffer a humiliating defeat.

Forty-two years later, after David Ben-Gurion had proclaimed the rebirth of Israel, Rachel would recall those parting moments in a different light. She would write to the first Prime Minister:

I sat on that great and historic [Independence Day] next to the radio and listened with emotion and with my heart pounding to each word you spoke, and tears of joy filled my eyes. Is it true? Had the dreams we dreamed since childhood become reality forty-two years after our *aliya?* And a picture from the past appeared before me, the day when we left our town, Plonsk. The house is buzzing with relatives and friends who have come to take leave. And after we had taken leave of everyone and turned eastward and sung "Hatikva"—what excitement, what sacredness encompassed all of us. That was the first great day in our lives— the beginning. . . .

CHAPTER TWO

Time thou beginnest to put the sickle to the corn
DEUTERONOMY 16:9

IN the hazy glow of dawn, September 7, 1906, a seagull's screech welcomed the small cargo ship as it heaved through the waves past the reefs lying off shore and clangorously cast anchor. David Green, Shlomo Zemach and Rachel Nelkin and her mother stood by the railing and peered into the distance with joyful eyes that reflected little hint of their sleeplessness.

"Silently," David would write later, "I gazed at Jaffa, my heart beat wildly . . . I had arrived. . . ."

From the moment David and his companions had climbed into a horse-drawn carriage in Plonsk taking them to the train until they arrived in the port of Odessa, David was in a euphoric state. He was on his way to *Eretz Yisrael,* and sitting next to him was Rachel. All his emotional torment of the past two years had dissipated in final triumph. In Odessa he and Shlomo hastened to Love of Zion headquarters to see Menachem Ussishkin, leader of the movement, who in David's eyes had replaced Herzl as the Zionist god. The youths would ask him to finance a newspaper they planned to publish in Palestine in order to lure more immigrants there.

David felt a sense of awe as he and Shlomo faced Ussishkin, a heavy-set man with massive shoulders and hard blue eyes. But awe dissolved into hostility as David noticed the man was "looking at me as though I were crazy, and saying, 'Here's some idiot going to Palestine.' " Ussishkin made it clear that immigration to Palestine should be selective. *Aliya* wasn't for just *any-body*. David was shocked and disappointed. To help build a nation he might have to fight not only the Hassidim, the Turks, the Arabs and the whole gentile world, but also the Zionist fathers who had inspired him!

He was further disheartened when it seemed the whole trip might have to be canceled. The four travelers had no passports, and they couldn't find forged ones. Finally, at the port of Odessa, David met a rabbi with a wife and nine children—and a forged group passport. How would the rabbi like three more children and Rachel's mother thrown in? The rabbi agreed, and so, on August 28, David and his three companions, carrying bundles of clothing and food, tagged onto the rabbi and his family and trudged up a gangplank into an ancient 500-ton Russian cargo ship. This old tub was to be the ultimate link between David's past and future, the Diaspora and Zion.

As it pulled out and churned a path through the Black Sea, heading for the Dardanelles and the Mediterranean Sea, David's exalted mood withstood even the worst anti-Semitic indignities, the bitterest reminders of the life he was leaving behind. The entire crew, from the captain down, treated the Jews aboard contemptuously, abusing them, swearing at them, refusing to help the sick or clean the deck. And the deck was where David's group was quartered, together with peasants and their animals. The four slept side by side on blankets spread on the hard floor, with Rachel's mother pointedly bedding down between David and her daughter.

A little while out to sea, David learned that a young Jewish girl had been hidden aboard by a white-slaver who was taking her to Constantinople, with the apparent complicity of the captain. David and Shlomo boldly confronted the bearded white-uniformed skipper in his cabin, ignoring his order to leave.

"Under the Criminal Code," David coolly stated, "you are liable to life imprisonment and deportation to Siberia for conspiring to abduct a minor for purposes of prostitution."

The captain was startled—an arrogant little Jew laying down the law to a Russian sea captain! Nevertheless, the girl was not forced off the ship when it docked in Constantinople, and David once more savored the heady wine of triumph over authority.

David's spirits remained high not only because he anticipated a kind of magic fulfillment at journey's end, but because he was fascinated by many of the other passengers, especially the Arabs —the first he had ever met.

"They made an excellent impression," he would write. "They

were like overgrown children. They sang for us, asking us to join in."

One Arab even offered him candy in case he became seasick. David taught Hebrew words to some and in turn was invited to visit them. If these Arabs were typical, the Jews would have no trouble with them in Palestine.

David spent much of his time sitting on deck with Rachel, watching the sea and dreaming of tomorrow. But one day Shlomo, who had seen the realistic side of the dream, described the harsh life to Rachel, thinking it best to prepare her. He turned over her smooth delicate hands and told her that they would soon be rough and calloused. She would have to work in the fields like a peasant, with the sun beating down mercilessly and the mosquitoes tormenting her. There was malaria, bad food, little sanitation. Rachel wept. She had not fully realized what lay ahead, and perhaps she would be too fragile for the task.

David later tried to console her. She and her mother needn't worry. He would make sure they would lack nothing, even if he had to work as a teacher to earn enough money—a promise that sounded like a proposal of marriage.

But what of his dream, his plan for building a nation?

Could she doubt for a moment, he replied, that she had priority over any dream?

As the ship crashed through the leaping waves, David stared at the horizon, his carefully nurtured will a shambles.

Dozens of rowboats surrounded the ship and husky bronzed Arab porters, either bare-chested or in soiled white robes, attached ropes to the railing and climbed aboard like agile monkeys. Suddenly there was pandemonium as the Arabs, shouting and cursing in Arabic, Hebrew and Yiddish, raced about madly, grabbing bags and bundles and throwing them to comrades in the boats. David haggled with an Arab and agreed to pay the exorbitant sum of two rubles for each person and piece of baggage carried ashore.

David and the others climbed down a rope ladder into gleaming brown arms, and several oarsmen, singing the praises of Allah, began pulling their oars through the pounding waves. Despite his exhilaration, David was disturbed. Why in *Eretz Yisrael* should Arabs be doing work that Jews could be doing? But even this ideological problem faded from mind as the boat tumbled from wave to wave and finally splashed to a halt.

Thrust onto the quay of the Promised Land, David stood for a wobbly second in ecstatic contemplation. Home! . . . Then suddenly embittered cries:

"New victims!"

"Why did you come?"

Broken men with emaciated stubbled faces loitered on the waterfront like specters in a frightful fantasy. Hadn't the newcomers heard? The unemployment, the disease, the hunger? Thank God a boat had come to take them back to Russia! David apparently didn't take much note. He didn't want to.

The four newcomers were suddenly caught in a whirlpool of red-fezzed chaos as officials, porters and newcomers shouted at one another while pushing into the *Jumruk,* the Turkish customs house that smelled of seaweed, jetsam and rot. Before long, they were standing in the street devouring the sights.

"Waves of joy rose in me," David would recall. "The signs in Hebrew on the shops, the Hebrew spoken in the streets, the stores and the restaurants. Now one cannot doubt; now one must believe! . . . A Jewish boy rides a horse . . . ; a little girl of eight passes on a donkey pulling a heavy load; images of our renaissance."

But there were other, less cherished images, too: "Fat Arabs squatted next to their carts, and in between them was some miserable Jew's shop."

And while ragged idlers gathered around these carts and shops seeking handouts, customers barely better off eyed the dazzling displays and left with nuts, roots, seeds, cookies, candies, oranges, lemons, radishes, dates. Meanwhile Gramophones blared as men loafed in cafés, puffing on water pipes and jiggling dice. An Arab in a flowing *abaya* (robe) led a camel, hump heaving, nostrils sniffing, through a dung-strewn alley that twisted between rows of shanties with verandas that seemed about to collapse. There was a mosque with moldy green domes, a filthy bazaar scented with mint, dill and thyme.

David was not prepared for the despair and poverty of these Levantine scenes. "The air smelled of charity and *bakshish* (tips)," he would write his father.

Was this the home he had craved? Where were the pioneers and the workers, the dreamers and the builders, the Jews who would redeem their land and the world? David had been impressed by the educated, relatively prosperous Arabs on the ship, and he had been captivated by scenes of Arab life in the port towns he visited during brief stopovers. But similar scenes here, in the land that God had granted the Israelites, stung him like a desert wind.

He had given little thought to the Arabs in Palestine, although they now numbered about 700,000, compared to 55,000 Jews. They had been faceless shadows in the background, a problem of low priority to be dealt with only in the distant future. Certainly the Jews would not exploit them or drive them out; to do that would be to violate the very spirit of "messianic redemption." On the contrary, the Jews would help to raise Arab living standards—while progressively expanding into a majority as the Diaspora drained into Zion. The Arabs must accept the inevitable, and David felt they would when they realized what benefits awaited them.

While David and his friends stewed uncomfortably in the medieval "decadence," they were suddenly greeted by a group of ebullient, boisterous people. "Welcome home!" they cried, shaking hands and slapping backs. They were members of the two socialist groups that had sprung up here as they had in Europe during the past year—Poalei Zion, David's party, and Hapoel Hatzair (Working Youth), the non-Marxist party that Shlomo had joined when he was last in Palestine. David was delighted to see two familiar faces. There stood Shlomo Lavi, who had arrived some weeks earlier, and there, Rabbi Isaac, tearfully embracing his wife and his stepdaughter, Rachel. Meanwhile David and Shlomo each found himself surrounded by colleagues from his own party. This sudden separation was to symbolize the divergent paths they would shortly follow.

The two groups wound their way through the alleys to the Chaim Baruch Hotel, a run-down building known as the "flea house," which served as Poalei Zion headquarters; Hapoel Hatzair was based in the equally squalid Spector's Hotel, though it now joined with its competitor in welcoming the travelers. The party crossed a courtyard full of horse-drawn carriages and entered a lobby with dilapidated chairs in which unkempt men like those on the waterfront slouched with waxen lifelessness, prattling incoherently about their sufferings and shattered dreams.

When the newcomers had washed and changed clothes, they sat down with their comrades in the dingy dining room for a lunch of olives and fruit. One of the Poalei Zion chiefs, an angry-looking youth with curly black hair, a hooked nose, and piercing dark eyes, put down his cognac and introduced himself

as Israel Shochat. He seemed to be sizing up David: Would he
be a good leader? Was he tough enough? A Hapoel Hatzair man
was also scrutinizing him. David seemed to have substance;
perhaps he could be persuaded to switch parties. Later the man
took him aside. What did David think of "historical material-
ism"? He wasn't really a Marxist, was he? David was incensed.
Petty politics at this sublime moment?

Israel Shochat and his comrades invited the newcomers to
stay in Jaffa for a few days until they knew where they would
settle, but David was impatient. He had not come to Palestine
to stay in Jaffa—especially in such a dirty and depressing hotel.
He couldn't leave fast enough for Petah Tikvah, one of about
twenty Jewish settlements in Judea, the central part of Palestine, where he could start working. Rachel, Shlomo Zemach,
Shlomo Lavi and about ten other members of both parties would
go with him, while Rachel's parents would follow later in a
carriage.

Before leaving, David scribbled a postcard to his father:
"Hurray! This morning at nine o'clock I stepped on the soil of
Jaffa. This afternoon at four o'clock we leave for Petah Tikvah
from where I will write you in detail. I was not sick en route. I
feel healthy, courageous, and full of faith. Greetings from Zion.
David."

Dancing, singing and joking, the young people made their way
toward Petah Tikvah ten miles away, taking turns riding the
donkey that trotted alongside them. They sauntered over sandy
hills past wilting vineyards, fragrant orange groves and putrid
swamps alive with croaking frogs. Occasionally smoke curled
into the sky from the black tent of a Bedouin. David was the
envy of the others because Rachel was his girl, and when he
placed his arm around her shoulder, Shlomo Lavi, who still
quietly loved her, pulled it away. David would not dare do that
in Plonsk! Another would-be suitor in the group was Yehezkel
Beit-Halachmi, a modest, reserved youth from a town near
Plonsk, who had also long craved Rachel's affection.

If David sensed the envy, he didn't show it. While the others
frolicked in the desert, he seemed blissfully removed from reality, as if listening to the echoes of Joshua commanding his
troops, Jeremiah counseling the multitude, Bar-Kochba challenging the Romans. Suddenly a strange wail rose eerily in the
distance, like children crying. Don't worry, the veterans explained, smiling. Just little foxes "ruining the vineyards." The

wilderness thrilled David. And the answer to the riddle long tormenting him was already crystallizing.

At about 10 P.M. the hikers saw from afar what looked in the darkness like a great forest, but as they drew closer the moonlight revealed an orange grove. They had arrived.

"What a victory!" he would write. "In *Eretz Yisrael*, in a Hebrew village whose name means Gate of Hope."

Petah Tikvah was no "gate of hope" when its founders arrived there in 1878 with the First Aliya. They cast incredulous eyes on a swampy area so ridden with disease that the banks of the Yarkon River running through it were covered with the carcasses of cows and horses owned by Arabs living nearby. A doctor warned them that anyone who lived here or even breathed the air for long would surely die, but these pioneers were adamant. And, with the help of a handful of young people, they set about building Petah Tikvah—the first effort to lead the Jews back to the soil of Zion. They planted the roots of a state, and now David Green and his companions, pioneers of the Second Aliya, would help nurture the plant.

The group stayed up all night talking with friends from Plonsk who had settled here earlier, but David spoke little as he sat on the soft earth and drank in the scene.

> The howling of jackals in the vineyards; the braying of donkeys in the stables; the croaking of frogs in the ponds; the scent of blossoming acacia; the murmur of the distant sea; the darkening shadows of the groves; the enchantment of stars in the deep blue; the faraway skies, drowsily bright—everything intoxicated me. I was rapturously happy; yet, all was strange and bewildering, as though I were errant in a legendary kingdom. Could it be? Joy turned to exaltation. My soul was in tumult, one emotion drowned my very being: "Lo, I am in *Eretz Yisrael!*" and *Eretz Yisrael* was here, wherever I turned or trod. . . . All night long I sat and communed with my new heaven. . . .

The next morning, in the glare of a warm sun, David found that his "new heaven" was a rather barren place surrounded by orange and olive groves, with cypress trees bordering fields of corn and shading clusters of wooden huts and clay and plaster houses that sheltered about two hundred fifty families. David and Shlomo Zemach rented a room with furniture made of crates and boards, then set off to seek work, treading the sandy paths that led to each of the twelve farms there.

They knew that finding a job wouldn't be easy, for times had changed since the early pioneers started clearing the swamps twenty-eight years before; disease and hunger had ravaged not only the body but also the spirit. As in most of the Jewish villages, the survivors were no longer interested in building a homeland but wanted simply to make money. Instead of working the land themselves or at least hiring other Jews to do it, they employed cheap Arab workers who lived with the cows and donkeys. Why pay more to Jewish workers, who were seldom more than 10 percent of the work force in the Judean settlements, when most came from Europe and were unfit for toiling in the fields under a broiling sun? Nor did the Jews make good servants as the Arabs did.

The First Aliya pioneers, Ben-Gurion would write, "had become speculators and shopkeepers trafficking in the hopes of their people and selling their own youthful aspiration for base silver. . . . In their eyes we were a living indictment. . . . They could not bear the sight of us."

But David did not return the hatred, sadly viewing these people as fallen heroes. Ironically, they had been corrupted in large measure by the French Jew who had done more than anyone else to promote settlement in Palestine—Baron Edmond de Rothschild. The Baron had begun financing colonies in 1882 and had poured in money to drain swamps, plow land and construct houses. He was, however, a philanthropist, not a Zionist, and his donations were meant simply to help persecuted Jews who were fleeing from Eastern Europe to resettle in Palestine. He was not trying to build a nation or pursue an ideal. And with the money flowing in, the landowners dropped their shovels and abandoned their plows, moving into sprawling new Jerusalem homes and burying their dreams in soil worked by exploited and disillusioned men.

David and Shlomo now knocked on door after door, offering to do any kind of work. The farm managers shook their heads; try the next farm. Finally, after several days, David met Yitzhak Kvashner, an old classmate from Plonsk, who had arrived here a year earlier. They talked of old times. And since Kvashner was friendly with one of the farm managers, it seemed that half the *shtetl* of Plonsk would be working in the orange groves.

The next morning David, sore from sleeping on sacks of straw, awoke at six, washed himself in a pond, breakfasted on an orange, and with his comrades plunged into the clouds of dust that rose along the twisting paths as scores of Arab and Jewish workers, hoes and shovels balanced on their shoulders, headed for the fields and groves. In their assigned grove the Plonsk workers moved down the rows of orange trees, holding cans full of manure, which they spilled from tin cups into holes dug for saplings, working silently, swiftly, determined to prove themselves.

David was elated as he started his first job in Zion. The manure would nourish soil that was destined to support a nation, a nation that would eventually belong to him and his fellow workers. He felt especially driven with the Arabs working nearby. The Jews had to outwork the Arabs, not only to save their jobs but also to bolster their egos. A lively Eastern tune reached his ears as the Arabs, singing in unison, sped up the rhythm of their labor, deliberately, it seemed, to embarrass the inexperienced Jews. David groaned and his muscles ached. But the comrades from Plonsk would show they were men.

But not all were; two were women. One was Rachel and the other, Miriam Yoffe, who was also very pretty and a rival for David's affection. Miriam worked swiftly, but Rachel had to stop after a short while, for the wire handles of the can had cut into her hand and the pain intensified. The overseer walked over, looked at her bleeding wound, and said gruffly, "Your hands may be suitable for playing the piano, but not for working in an orange grove." And he fired her on the spot. Rachel gazed at her hands. Shlomo Zemach had warned her on the ship of the hard life here.

That night her comrades cruelly vented their fury. Why had she stopped working—because of a little cut in her hand? Hadn't Miriam Yoffe done *her* job? Rachel had soiled the reputation of the Plonsk workers! She wept but this time only Yehezkel Beit-Halachmi consoled her, while David kept aloof. His brief taste of life in Zion seemed to have confirmed what he had long feared: Marriage, or even a strong commitment, would inevitably quash his dream. Could one even consider raising children in this wilderness? Fulfillment of his love would have to wait. And Rachel's failure in the groves gave him an excuse to keep his distance from her. With the fate of his people at stake, not a single Jew could afford to show even the slightest weakness. Not even Rachel. And certainly not himself.

"*Yallah!* Faster! Faster!"

The sweat streamed down David's sunburned face as he dug in the hard earth under a torrid sun while the overseer pushed him and his comrades to the limit of their endurance. Look at the Arabs. See how fast they were working?

"Yallah!"

Day after day, David struggled to keep up the pace. His hands were "covered with blisters," and his limbs felt "detached from the body." Letters to his father, so euphoric at first, soon began to reflect a less rosy appraisal of daily life, though there was still evidence in them of an optimism, however guarded, that could only stem from supreme faith. Life here was "more difficult than in Russia," but his father shouldn't believe the letters of some Plonsk immigrants that depicted starvation and misery.

"No one has yet died of hunger," he wrote.

Wishing neither to worry his father nor to admit to weakness in himself, David grossly understated the "reality." Yet the drive for self-discipline led him, at times, to revel in his suffering. When malaria struck him two weeks after his arrival in Petah Tikvah, he said, "I was thrilled that I had the fever." Somehow, to have malaria in *Eretz Yisrael*—and most of the workers in the village had it—was a badge of honor.

Both Miriam and Rachel offered to nurse David back to health in their homes. He declined Rachel's invitation, apparently fearing that he would be drawn even closer to her, so it was Miriam who devotedly sat by his bed, applying cold compresses to his feverish forehead. When Rachel tried to visit him, Miriam stood at the door with arms folded and told her that David was asleep and couldn't be disturbed—especially, she implied, by someone who had given the people from Plonsk a bad name!

Thinking that David had fallen in love with Miriam, Rachel left in despair, to be consoled again by Yehezkel Beit-Halachmi.

When David recovered from that first attack he found himself out of a job. Most of the laborers were fortunate if they worked about two days a week, and they could be laid off at any time. So David became one of the horde of laborers who waited in front of the village synagogue until an employer came, felt their muscles, and selected one or two for a job. David was seldom chosen, however, especially after he tried—unsuccessfully—to foment a strike because he had been docked a quarter of his pay for being late to work one day.

The malaria attacks recurred every two weeks "with mathematical precision" and lasted for five or six days. The local doctor advised David to leave the country if he ever wanted to get well, but David was determined to stay in Zion until he died.

"Only two kinds of workers will remain," he wrote his father, "those with an overwhelming will and those who . . . have grown used to hard work."

But David could find little work, and the less he worked the weaker he became from hunger. On his "bad" days he could not even afford the soup and porridge in the tin-roofed workers' kitchen; and on "good" days all he could afford was one small flat *pita* bread.

> It was bearable during the day. I would talk to friends or try to think of other matters. But night was terrible. As soon as I shut my eyes, I would imagine pots full of meat, fried chicken, plates full of food. I feared I would lose my mind. In the morning, on waking up . . . exhausted, I would feel my head and clumps of hair would drop out and stick to my fingers.

Nevertheless, David's spirit never flagged. He wrote philosophically that "all three—work, malaria and hunger—were new to me, and interested me greatly. This was, after all, why I came to *Eretz Yisrael*."

Disturbing him more than the withering of his flesh was the withering of his friendships. Since he had decided to loosen his bond with Rachel, he seldom saw her. And even his ties with Shlomo Zemach were fraying since Shlomo, under pressure from his party, had moved out of the room they shared and was now a political rival.

But David would not confess his loneliness until some years later, fearing this would be an admission of weakness, and instead channeled his remaining energy into village politics. He took over the reins of the local Poalei Zion group and helped to persuade the workers to pool their wages so that, while all might be hungry, none would starve. When party headquarters in Odessa offered to send aid, most of the workers in David's group were ecstatic, but David voiced his objection with righteous fury at a meeting in the village school. They must live by the principle of self-help whatever the difficulties! If they accepted aid, they would be lost; Zion would be lost. He won the argument.

He lost another, however. When several women suggested setting up a laundry, David objected. Everybody must wash his own clothes. Most others disagreed; this was carrying ideology too far. So the workers set up a laundry anyway—and among the first in line when it opened was David Green, carrying a small

bundle of soiled shirts and underwear. After fighting tenaciously for his view, David surrendered to the majority, a principle even more important than ideology. But he had to keep
fighting for his views. And to strengthen his will for the long
pull ahead, he returned ten rubles his father had sent him. "I
have no need at all for the money," he wrote.

David now threw his growing political weight behind another
campaign that he considered vital to a national structure. He
would seek to merge the two parties, Poalei Zion and Hapoel
Hatzair, into a single labor party. Only a monolithic movement
backed eventually by the whole *Yishuv* (the Jewish community
of Palestine) would be strong enough to fight the landlords who
had sold out their ideals for money and to build an independent
socialist nation. Both groups, after all, were socialist, though
David's was Marxist and part of the world socialist movement,
while Hapoel Hatzair was neither, believing that Jewish socialism in Palestine should uniquely fit the special needs of Zionism. At first, Shlomo Zemach, like David, argued for a merger,
but he had since joined other members of Hapoel Hatzair in
firmly opposing such a union. And so David began his "unity"
campaign within his own party, trying to reconcile differences
among members from all over Palestine. He started building the
foundation of a structure that would one day be Israel.

In October 1906, Poalei Zion held its first conference. About
ninety members straggled into Jaffa from all parts of Zion, their
faces caked with dust, their only shirts soaked with sweat, to
officially found the Palestine branch of the party.

The situation was chaotic, for the numerous members from
Rostov, largely assimilated into Russian leftist society, had come
to Palestine more to "communize" than to "Zionize." They
knew little about Zionism and spoke only Russian. Wearing embroidered Russian blouses, they sang Russian songs and danced
Russian dances when not arguing violently for strikes, class warfare, and an integrated communist community embracing both
Jews and Arabs. And it appeared for a while that this thinking
might dominate the party. Israel Shochat would later say that
David "came and saved the situation."

He answered the Rostovians point by point. The party must
unite with non-Marxist groups. It must cast aside Yiddish and
speak only Hebrew. It must woo the whole *Yishuv* and not just
the workers. Without these basic conditions it would be impossible to build a Jewish state; and if there were to be no Jewish

state, why remain in Palestine? Moderate as well as radical members rebutted his views, but he carried his pragmatic arguments even into his room in the thin-walled Chaim Baruch Hotel, where he and his Rostovian foes shouted at each other all night long while other guests protested in sleepless rage. David found himself supporting arguments contrary to those he had backed in Plonsk. Marxism, he began to feel, could not be applied in this primitive land.

David was elected to the party's ruling central committee and to a special committee formed to draw up a party platform. Dominated by the Rostovians, who clung to the underground practices they had learned in Russia, the committee met clandestinely in a small caravansary tucked away behind thick walls in the Arab town of Ramle. Here members sat cross-legged on straw mats for three days, hammering out the aims of the party.

"During those three days," Shochat would write, "[David] revealed himself . . . as a dynamic force with an extraordinary ability to express himself, capable of bridging the gap between the two distant worlds—nationalism and socialism."

Was there to be a Jewish state or not? David demanded. The Rostovians stopped singing their Russian songs long enough to thunder "No!" And they pushed through a platform that read almost like the Communist Manifesto, with hardly a mention of Zionism. David was crestfallen. Zion, he vowed, would never be a communist state! And he moved still farther from Marxism.

Before long his fervent struggle began to bear fruit. At the second meeting of the Poalei Zion conference, he helped to ram through a resolution declaring that "the party aspires to political independence of the Jewish people in this country."

David's party thus stated flatly for the first time that its aim was a Jewish state, even though it still rejected what he felt were the two main requisites for one: union with non-Marxists, and Hebrew as the national language.

David stayed in Jaffa to add a few more bricks to the national edifice he was helping to build. As in Plonsk, he set up a string of about a dozen mini-unions in tailor, shoemaking and carpenter shops. Then, in March 1907, he thrust himself into an explosive labor dispute at the winery in Rishon LeZion, south of Jaffa, where the manager, a man named Gluskin, had fired "troublemaking" workers. A Rostovian-led work force went out on strike, standing at the winery gate with pistols and sticks to prevent anyone from entering.

Both labor and management gathered sympathizers for a showdown, and Israel and David rushed to the scene. While David supported the strikers, he opposed violence. At a tense meeting with Gluskin, Israel sat armed with a pistol, David with "arguments and proofs." The result was a compromise: The strikers would return to work and the dismissed employees, while denied reinstatement, would receive financial compensation. Shochat was again impressed. Thanks to David, he would say, "we got out of the business honorably."

But not everybody thought so. The extremists saw the deal as a sellout, and the moderates, including Hapoel Hatzair, viewed it as confirmation that the strike was unjustified and jeopardized the entire Zionist enterprise. Even Shochat, despite his admiration, began to edge away from David, apparently sensing that he was not a man who would play a secondary role to anyone.

The Poalei Zion's central committee crumbled under the tension of the strike, and David was blamed. He was angry and hurt. His foes didn't yet realize that one must be neither too provocative nor too pliant in an explosive situation if Zionism was to triumph in the end. One had to know how to tell principle from pragmatism. Regrettably, he might have to delay his grand plan after all—until his comrades came to their senses and listened to him. And he returned to Petah Tikvah, his ego in tatters, apparently deaf this time to the braying of donkeys and the croaking of frogs.

About three months later, in the summer of 1907, David returned to Jaffa, hobbling into a decrepit school that had been rented for the second Poalei Zion conference. From the outset he was the butt of attack. Why, his fellow members asked, had he split and almost destroyed the party? Speaker after speaker used him as a convenient scapegoat for their deep frustrations.

With icy calm, David stood up, eyes mocking, lips curled in contempt, and demanded that the party be less dogmatic and more practical. The World Zionist Organization should be urged to transfer its leadership to Palestine even if it was bourgeois. Then it would understand what was happening there. David's comrades scoffed. They would not "betray" the Jewish workers. There would be a Marxist Jewish state or none at all.

One man who listened with admiration, if not great sympathy, as David's voice rose over the tumult was a tall, slim youth with soulful eyes, a prominent nose and a shy demeanor. Yitzhak Shimshelevich, alias Yitzhak Ben-Zvi, had just arrived from Russia where, like David, he had led a secret self-defense group and had hidden arms in his house. But his family was less fortunate than David's; it was deported to Siberia. Yitzhak fled to Palestine and was welcomed by party members. Though he had a university degree and David lacked even a secondary-school certificate, the two young men had similar intellectual capacities, if contrasting personalities. Unlike David, Yitzhak was mild-mannered, malleable, even naïve, the kind of man who would listen to everyone, who would heal rather than split. He was elected co-chief of the new central committee, and David was ignominiously left out altogether—until Yitzhak brought him in on his own. Since David was too moderate for the Marxists and too abrasive as well, he would not be a good number-one man. But perhaps number three.

David exploded. Number three? Was he to take orders from people less able than he, with no imagination or vision, people who would never be able to build a nation? As the months rolled by, he met new defeats, new humiliations. Every one of his proposals was rejected. The party would publish its newspaper in Yiddish, not in Hebrew. It would not unite with Hapoel Hatzair. And it would not give immigration priority over socialist ventures.

Well then, *shalom* (goodbye). And David stalked off once again into the villages.

He went first to Ness-Ziona where, unable to find work, he nearly starved. When a friend took pity and invited him to dinner, pride proved stronger than hunger and he politely refused.

"Had he invited me in normal circumstances," he would later explain, "I'd have accepted the invitation. But under these circumstances . . . I said, 'No, I'm not hungry.' Actually, I thought I would go mad, I was so hungry."

In the end, David did go to his friend's home—but only after he had bought a meal on credit at a restaurant! He could thus "prove" to his friend that he was not hungry.

David drifted to Rishon LeZion, where he hoped to find work in the winery that had been the scene of his recent tainted triumph in the strike crisis. Large wagons bulging with cane baskets full of grapes ground to a dusty halt in the yard of the winepress, and workers carried the baskets to grindstones that gnashed out the grape seeds. Pumps rumbled without cease, and asbestos pipes trembled with purple rage. A job? The foreman scrutinized David. Someone was needed to tread grapes, but the person must have great endurance. David was undaunted. He might be skinny, he said, but he had the endurance of a camel. He got the job.

In the wine cellar, David undressed and stepped into a long sack with holes for the head, arms and legs. Then he was taken into a long narrow corridor with a dirty glass roof that led to the winepress. He was repelled by the mingling odors of alcohol, yeast, mold and fermented dough, but he climbed into a pitful of grapes and began treading with his bare feet. Despite his feebleness, he found the energy to move pistonlike, one foot after the other, on an endless march. What a fine way to bolster his will! He even wagered with another worker that he could outlast him and, incredibly, pounded the grapes almost nonstop for three days and nights, winning the contest in a state of near-delirium.

One day David met his old friend Shlomo Zemach at a festival in Rishon LeZion. Shlomo had long since left Petah Tikvah and gone north into the primitive, sparsely settled frontier region of Galilee, where fierce Arabs, not exploitive Jews, were the main threat. Shlomo, who had returned temporarily to Judea, described the tough, rugged but beautifully simple way of life in Galilee with great enthusiasm. There were no starving day laborers there, he said. Workers were employed annually and received good wages. The air was pure and so were men's hearts. There one found the real Zion.

David, though boiling with malarial fever at the time, listened raptly. Galilee! Perhaps that was what he was searching for. Besides, he was growing tired of the work he had been doing. He would write:

> The interminable hoeing and spading . . . did not satisfy me fully. It was too mechanical and monotonous. . . . I yearned for the wide fields, for the waving stalks of corn, for the fragrance of grass, the plowman's song.

Shlomo was returning to Galilee, and David decided to go with him. He went first to Petah Tikvah to bid Rachel goodbye and found her lying in bed with malaria while Yehezkel Beit-Halachmi ran in and out of the room with hot towels. She was hoping, it seems, to hear a tender word.

Had he come back to stay?

No, he was leaving for Galilee. There was so much to do.

And he hoisted his bundle to his shoulder and left.

Exhausted from a three-day hike to Galilee, David stood on a slope dotted with two vertical rows of red-roofed stone houses that reached to the hilltop, where the lush greenery of the model farm of Sejera sprouted like a fringe of hair. Amid eucalyptus trees and pepper plants, he scanned the wild beauty around him. To the east, veiled in a blue mist, were the mountains of Gilead and Bashan; to the west, the emerald heights of Nazareth; to the north, the majestic Mount Hermon wreathed in a snowy-white crown; and to the south, in proud solitude, Mount Tabor, the eternal guardian of the Valley of Jezreel. The smaller hills were rounded and verdant, and the fields at their feet were carpeted with multihued wild flowers, trees, grass and bushes.

"After Judea," David would write, "Sejera struck me almost as Petah Tikvah did after Plonsk and Warsaw."

It was only one of four small settlements in Galilee where even some of the hardiest pioneers hesitated to settle because of the rough primitive life and the constant danger of death from disease or an Arab knife in the night. All the work was done by the two hundred thirty-five Jews here on a cooperative basis, thanks to the vision of the Jewish Colonization Association, a Paris-based group that financed the project. On this farm worked not only young idealists from Eastern Europe, but a potpourri of people from many exotic lands—strapping medieval Jews from Kurdistan, thin wiry Jews from Yemen, even Russian proselytes, brawny peasants who had embraced Judaism after spiritual revelations and fled to Palestine. In the hillside village itself, small landowners and tenant farmers worked their own land and hired Jewish workers when needed.

Life had improved in Sejera since it was founded six years earlier, in 1901. Then the pioneers had lived in tents during the warm weather and in abandoned Arab huts with their animals during the winter. Disease had been rampant, but there was no doctor; the sick had to be carried by oxcart to a hospital in distant Tiberias. Sick or not, however, the settlers went on plowing, sowing, harvesting, fighting off bands of Bedouin robbers, building a community. Conditions had since improved, and now David and Shlomo resided in an old but "renovated" caravansary, while most other workers lived in relatively comfortable houses. A doctor came from Nazareth twice a week to treat the sick, and there was a nurse living in the settlement.

David and Shlomo were soon hauling the harvest from the threshing floor to the granary, and though they worked day and night in a race with the rainy season, David was consumed by

joy. He was no longer a "slave." The manager of the farm,
Eliahu Krause, and his overseers were workers themselves. On
some evenings all the men and the handful of women who
worked on the farm gathered in the social hall set up in a caravansary to eat, talk, sing and dance, while someone held an
empty oil can between his knees and drummed on it with lusty
abandon.

"Here," he would write, "I found the environment that I had
sought so long. No shopkeepers or speculators, no non-Jewish
hirelings or idlers living on the labor of others."

In striking contrast to his dry staccato utterances of later years,
he would wax lyrical:

> Beautiful are the days in our land, days flushed with light and full of
> luster, rich in vistas of sea and hill. . . . But infinitely more splendid are
> the nights; nights deep with secrets and wrapped in mystery. The drops
> of burning gold, twinkling in the soft blue dome of the sky, the dim-lit
> purity of the mountains, the lucid crystal of the transparent mountain air
> —all is steeped in yearning, in half-felt longings, in secret undertones.
> You are moved by urgings not of this world.

All of David's problems suddenly vanished, and he even
stopped brooding about his party's aloofness—until one day a
group of men, their Bedouin *abayas* billowing in the breeze,
their horses prancing with tassled saddles and colored bridles,
wound their way up the hill, followed by a horse-drawn cart
piled high with luggage. Who were these strutting intruders,
pistol handles gleaming in belted holsters, swords slapping
against dusty boots, whips cracking arrogantly? David came face
to face with their leader—Israel Shochat. If David was astonished, he soon understood why these romantically garbed men
from his party had come, and the truth, which he had long suspected, both elated and depressed him.

Shochat had brought a select group of party members to train
here as modern Zion's first soldiers. They belonged to Bar-
Giora, a secret underground watchmen's organization, named
after the last Jewish defender of Jerusalem in 70 A.D. Yitzhak
Ben-Zvi and Shochat had founded Bar-Giora at a clandestine
candlelight ceremony, and members took the oath "In blood
and fire Judea fell—in blood and fire Judea shall rise."

Such a force was necessary, David felt, but it should be controlled by the party, not by some power-loving leader—especially if he was not David Green. The hurt of being a party
pariah ran deep, and only the savage majesty of Sejera had eased
the pain. And now here were the men who had rejected him,

who had refused to believe in his destiny, taunting him with their presence. Why had Shochat not brought David into the group? Shochat would later explain, "We were afraid of another spiritual leader who was likely to arouse doubts and disputes on controversial matters."

When Manager Krause put Shochat in charge of the workers to mask the military aim of Bar-Giora, David, refusing to work under the "intruders," moved from the model farm to the village, where he found work with Abraham Rogachevsky, a saddler and tenant farmer. Away from the source of his anxiety, he once more began reveling in poetic fantasy. He had been thrilled by the experience of "conquering labor" on the hilltop farm, but hard physical activity was not David's forte. And now that he was working in the fields alone, his pride unchallenged by more productive comrades, he saw no reason to overstrain himself.

"Working is so easy, so agreeable," he wrote his father. "Taking the plow handle in my left hand and the goad in my right, I walk behind the plow and see dark sods turning over. The oxen advance slowly, like important persons; I have time to reflect and dream."

Then suddenly David's dreams dissolved in shock when a worker came from Petah Tikvah with devastating news: Rachel was engaged to marry Yehezkel Beit-Halachmi! David rushed to Petah Tikvah to prevent this catastrophe and found Rachel recovering from another attack of malaria, her delicate face still pale but never, it seemed, more beautiful.

Please wait, he begged. One day he would marry her. But nothing David could say would make Rachel reconsider. Hadn't he scorned her because she had failed at her job? He was married to his dream, and she was a woman, not a politician. Yehezkel loved her too, and he would never neglect her. Her mind was made up, she said.

Filled with fury and anguish, David departed. Rachel herself had finally resolved his dilemma.

David returned to Sejera and dreamed now more of the past than of the future as he lay on his cot in a corner of his boss's room and brooded. He had been shunned by his comrades and deserted by the only girl he had ever really loved. Not since his mother's death had he been so despondent. Never had the price of destiny seemed so unbearably high. He longed to be with his family but it was a world away, and even his talks at the dinner table with Rogachevsky and his wife about Zionism and the prospects of a state could not deflect his sad nostalgic thoughts. On the Sabbath he would walk to Tiberias just to eat fish that reminded him of the kind he had savored in Plonsk. And he would stare for hours at family photographs and actually converse with them, "but in vain. They are mute, mute!"

During one surge of melancholy, David wrote his father:

> Several times I have walked alone, my eyes on the stars and my heart with you. . . . Here is my land, a magic land, before me—so near, it touches my heart—and still my heart is crushed by longing for that foreign land, the land of the shadow of death . . . [I feel] like a liberated prisoner who has left all his friends and comrades behind him in jail.

As if in answer, his father urged him to come home, offering to pay expenses. David had been ordered to report for duty in the Russian army, and if he ignored the order Avigdor would be fined three hundred rubles. David knew he must go, but before leaving he would ask his father for forty rubles so he could pay his debts. Avigdor, after all, would still come out ahead.

As he prepared for the trip home, David tried to ignore the talk about Rachel's wedding, which workers from all over Zion had attended. What a celebration! And Rachel in her white linen wedding dress looked angelic. . . .

David could hardly wait to embrace his family.

David's homecoming, however, was not very cheerful. He could only have remembered with sadness the precious moments with Rachel, the sacred years with his mother, at whose grave he would mourn once more. Though he assured the military authorities that he had faulty vision in one eye, the Russian doctors declared him fit for duty, and he was sent to a training camp, where, with a sense of revulsion, he took an oath of allegiance to the Tsar. Shortly, however, David deserted the army. After all, once he had been conscripted, his father, under Russian law, could no longer be held responsible for his son's actions.

But before leaving Poland, David urged his father and other favored family members to follow him to Palestine and settle in Sejera. There were plenty of young men there for Zippora and for Rivka, who was still unmarried at twenty-nine. His brothers could come later—much later. Avraham would find the work too hard, and as for unambitious, untalented Michael, "if he was to be idle, it would be better if he were idle at home." Avraham's two young sons, however, would make good pioneers. Meanwhile those staying behind in Plonsk should send the others money. This advice hardly soothed the wounds David had already inflicted on his brothers. But his family, like all other Jews, he felt, had to play roles that best served the interest of the *Yishuv*.

With the authorities on his trail, David fled to Warsaw and hid out in the home of his old girlfriend, Jenny Ferenbuk. Then, about six months later, he continued on to Trieste, where he bribed his way onto a boat going to Palestine.

David landed in Jaffa in December 1908 and plodded up to Galilee again. He worked in the new colony of Kinneret for a while, then in the settlement of Melahemia. On one job there he toiled side by side with an Arab, trying again to prove that a Jew could outwork his Semitic cousin, and he succeeded; the Arab begged him to slow down so that he would not be fired for being put to shame. Even so, except in spurts, David was no match for many stronger, brawnier workers—Jews or Arabs. He was regarded more as a "philosopher" than as a farmer, since he was constantly preaching labor unity at meetings or in the field, undaunted by the yawns that greeted his pleas.

But his job had certain compensations—and one of them was a blue-eyed girl of seventeen named Chana Anavi, a teacher whose beauty was matched by her deep knowledge of Zionism and her pioneer fervor. David met Chana at her boss's home, where she lived and where he was invited to eat when he was out of work. Their friendship began with a furtive exchange of glances at the dinner table and was nourished by the lingering shock that David still felt in the wake of Rachel's marriage.

"It wasn't possible for a young girl not to like him," Chana recalls. "He wasn't a very good worker, but he was so intelligent, so intense and idealistic."

Chana already planned to marry another worker, David Rubin, but, confused by her feelings for David Green, she arranged to meet secretly with him outside the village to avoid gossip. Often they would sit amid the bundles of wheat and straw on the threshing floor, where she would teach him French in exchange for Talmudic lessons. They would also reveal their dreams and indulge in a "little romance." David Rubin would say many years later when Chana claimed she had simply "talked" with David Green, "It happens that I was hiding in the straw on the threshing floor. Do you think I didn't see what was going on?"

The two youths competed fiercely for Chana's affection. According to Chana, David Green even asked her to marry him, "but he knew he was too late"—and that was perhaps why he proposed. After about two months, possibly to clear her confusion, Chana returned to her native Bulgaria for a few years to teach Hebrew. David Rubin would eventually marry her and David Green would continue to yearn for Rachel.

In early 1909 David drifted back to the Sejera model farm after learning that Israel Shochat was no longer there. Shochat's Bar-Giora had left the settlement because of a conflict with the Circassian guards, members of a tough Arab tribe friendly to the Jews. Since they were hired in the early days, the Circassians, who lived in the nearby village of Kfar Kana, claimed that they had the sole "legal" right to protect Sejera. Krause thus sent the Bar-Giora away to avoid trouble.

The Jewish workers, however, resented having to depend on "foreigners" for their protection. And none pushed more avidly for Jewish self-defense than David, who now saw his chance to be the settlement champion. Krause sympathized with his view, but still feared that any attempt either to fire the Circassians or to reinforce them with Jewish guards would turn them into dangerous enemies. No talk about "Zionist idealism" could change his mind—until one night David and his comrades tried a ruse. They removed Krause's pedigreed horse from the farm, then ran to him with the story that his horse had been stolen.

Krause rushed out and whistled for the Circassian guard on duty. No reply. He looked everywhere. No guard. Finally the man was found fast asleep in his own village. Krause got the point; he put David and the other workers on guard. The furious Circassians fired into the settlement to frighten the Jews into changing their minds, but the new guards tenaciously clung to their posts behind rocks and cactus hedges, sometimes in the driving rain.

David and his comrades, who carried only pistols, demanded that Krause give them heavier arms, and soon a carriage rumbled in from Haifa bursting with ancient shotguns and hunting rifles. Suddenly, David would write, the big room of the main caravansary was "changed into an armory. Anyone entering in the evening was startled to see a score of young men seated on their beds, each cleaning, loading, testing or simply holding a beloved rifle."

David now commanded a force that guarded not only the farm but the entire village of Sejera.

On Passover in April 1909, after a number of Arab attacks had been foiled, Israel Shochat and his Bar-Giora guards returned to Sejera to take part in the *seder* and in a regional Poalei Zion conference the following day. For the *seder* everybody crowded into the main caravansary, where they found the walls adorned with eucalyptus and pepper branches, rifles, pistols, swords, daggers and farm implements, all wreathed in flowers. The celebrants, sitting at a long table, sipped wine and sang and were soon dancing wildly or clapping loudly to Arab and Hassidic tunes, spurring even David to forget his grievances.

Suddenly there was shouting outside and a young stranger burst in; the rejoicing faded into silence. The stranger, a photographer from Haifa, breathlessly reported that he and two others on their way over had been attacked and robbed by three Arabs; the photographer had fired his pistol and apparently wounded one of them.

Israel Shochat and his guards dashed out, leaped on their horses and galloped through the fields in pursuit of the bandits, while David and others followed on foot. But all anyone could find was a trail of blood. Later the Jews would learn that an Arab, after confessing his role in the theft, had died of a bullet wound in a Nazareth hospital. David and his comrades knew what such a killing meant—an Arab custom: blood revenge.

"A black cloud lowered upon us," David would write. "The shadow of death in ambush. No one spoke of it, but each of us sensed it in himself and read it in his neighbor's eyes; the sword of vengeance hung over us all—it must fall on the head of one among us. . . . Fate was still to choose its victim."

The morning after the incident, the Poalei Zion meeting opened, and would be described by Rachel Yanait, a party leader who had recently arrived in Palestine and had come to Sejera with Yitzhak Ben-Zvi, whom she would eventually marry:

> The room was crowded, the faces tense. All of us suddenly looked older. In one corner the rifles were stacked . . . The ever-threatening danger could be felt in [our] eyes. I looked from face to face and stopped at that of a young man. . . . There was something striking about him. At

first sight, he seemed tranquil, but his penetrating look revealed a stormy temperament.

The stormy-tempered young man was David Green, who presided over the meeting—until a guard rushed in with news that Arabs had attacked the herd and carried off several oxen and mules. David cut the meeting short and Ben-Zvi, Shochat and most others who had come to Sejera now left for another village, where they would transform Bar-Giora into a larger, more powerful military arm called Hashomer. But David, uninvited, stayed behind. Good riddance! Now he was in command once more. And though Krause asked the Turkish army for help against the Arabs, David went about organizing the colony's defense on his own—none too soon.

A shot rang out one night and a watchman, Israel Korngold, became fate's first victim. David, who was standing guard elsewhere, spotted two comrades chasing three Arabs and, with two companions, joined the chase, but they in turn were chased by the inhabitants of a nearby Arab village. One of David's companions fell dead while the settlement's alarm bell clanged ominously in the night, warning too late of the trap.

Covered with white sheets, the two dead men lay the whole night in the shed where the *seder* had been celebrated. Next day David helped to dig a grave and carry them to the cemetery. No one eulogized them, but in the silence David could hear the thunder of an army that would strike fear into the heart of any foe threatening Zion.

"That day opened my eyes," he would say. "I realized that sooner or later there would be a trial of strength between us and the Arabs. From that moment at Sejera I felt that conflict was inevitable. What happened that day in my village was child's play compared with the dangers that the future had in store for us. We had to be prepared to meet them."

If the killings stoked the fire in David, they quenched the low flame sputtering in the farm officials. The answer to the Arab marauders was not guns but negotiation, they argued. No more weapons; instead, a deal should be made to slaughter a sheep— in the traditional Arab peacemaking manner. This was better than risking the slaughter of more men. David was enraged. The Jews would never stand on their own as long as they had to depend on appeasement and other people's guns.

Then another disappointment. In August 1909 he called a strike to protest the dismissal of a comrade, and it failed. Put down by his employer, let down by his comrades, he reacted as he usually did when rejected. He packed his belongings in a small bundle and wandered off to find work in another village.

On the way a Bedouin shepherd stopped him and asked for a match, then tried to grab his bag and holstered pistol. Wrestled to the ground, the man stabbed his victim in the hand with a dagger and bolted with the bag. David rushed to the police and two officers accompanied him to the local *mukhtar*, the village leader, who was thought to be involved. The policemen accepted the *mukhtar's* hospitality, then showered blows on their host until he staggered out and returned with the shepherd and his loot. The thief was sentenced to two years in jail, but the Turkish authorities never got around to returning the bag to David. This only confirmed to him the cardinal Zionist doctrine that it was folly to rely on others for protection and justice.

In November 1909, David drifted to the settlement of Zikhron Yaacov, south of Haifa, where he lived in a cowshed that smelled of mice and manure. He tried once more to organize the laborers and persuaded them to set up their own bakery, which sold bread at half the price of the settlement bakery. Even so, most of the workers here, as in Sejera, were not interested in unions. David was depressed, but found temporary relief this time in the company of the farmer's daughter. And this was the one union, it seemed, that did interest his envious co-workers.

An unexpected twist of fate propelled David into a new phase of his thwarted crusade. In 1910, he plodded across steamy sands for two days to attend a Poalei Zion conference in Jaffa. When he arrived, he collapsed on his hotel bed for a twenty-hour sleep, the longest of his life. He awoke to find Ben-Zvi hovering over him with an offer to join the editorial board of a new Hebrew-language party newspaper, *Ahdut* ("Unity"), based in Jerusalem. A group of reform-minded Young Turks had grabbed control of the Ottoman Empire two years earlier, Yitzhak explained, and the time was ripe to organize the workers more openly, to raise money to buy more land for Jews, and to demand permanent residence permits for all immigrants. A party newspaper was needed to mobilize Jews for the struggle. David knew he wasn't Yitzhak's first choice, that others had already turned down the job. He thus found the offer insulting. The party, he was sure, still feared and envied him. No, he curtly replied, get someone else!

David left the conference angry and hurt. Why did they treat him so shabbily? In Plonsk, people had admired, even loved him. He thought of Rachel. . . . Swept up by nostalgia, David stopped at her home in Eyn Ganim, near Petah Tikvah, where she was now living with her husband and infant. He entered without warning and found her nursing her baby. Unable to restrain himself, he walked over and kissed her tenderly; neither seemed embarrassed. They talked of the past as if nothing had changed between them.

When David returned to Zikhron Yaacov, he could think only of Rachel. Ignoring her marriage to another man, he decided he must win her back. She had to come "immediately" to visit him, he wrote her, so she could see his beautiful village.

Ben-Zvi, meanwhile, kept urging David to reconsider his offer, shrewdly appealing to his ego. The paper needed someone with his practical farm experience, since it was intended mainly for farm workers. Besides, the job would greatly strengthen his influence in the party. David was suddenly roused, but he pretended not to be. Let them plead. After all, he replied with humility, he had never written for a newspaper before. However, since the party insisted . . .

And David, now twenty-four, packed his things and marched off to Jerusalem, his years of "practical" Zionism over.

CHAPTER THREE

I will teach thee in the way which thou shalt go

PSALMS 32:8

THE old one-story house squatted in the center of a court-yard amid shacks and shanties, its moss-trimmed stone walls a gleaming pink in the twilight. With bundle in hand, David entered a dark airless cellar room full of makeshift beds, mostly planks resting on empty oil cans and crates and covered with grimy blankets or threadbare coats. This was Floyd's Courtyard, a shelter for hungry art students who had come to Jerusalem to capture on canvas the city's sweep of purple hills, its maze of Biblical alleys twisting through history. It would also be David's new home, where, with his fellow editors Yitzhak Ben-Zvi, Rachel Yanait and Jacob Zerubavel, who had just come from Russia, he would write and edit the new party newspaper, *Ahdut.*

The darkness and dilapidation could not dampen David's exultation. He was in Jerusalem, the heart of his beloved land, and here he would live with the heroic past every day, every minute, drawing from it the inspiration to create a heroic future. On this first night the four editors sat on mats in the dull glow of a kerosene lamp and discussed their new journal. Its main objective, David argued, should be to pull the Jewish community together—the competing labor groups, the new and the old immigrants, the Ashkenazim (European Jews) and the Sephardim (Mediterranean and Middle Eastern Jews). He talked like a driven man. Now he would have the power to influence people, to pour new cement into the foundation of his state.

Living and working together day and night, the editorial board soon resembled a tightly knit family, and David was no longer lonesome. Ben-Zvi and Rachel Yanait were emotionally bound to each other, and David grew extremely close to them both, with rumor contending that at one point he and Yanait had more than a comradely relationship. At any rate, Yanait, a dark-haired girl with intelligent eyes that glared stubbornly through pince-nez glasses, was with David constantly, since she knew little Hebrew and needed him to translate her articles from Yiddish. Often they would work late into the night, then, sometimes with Ben-Zvi, stroll through the dimly lighted streets, reliving the tales of glory that had beckoned them to Jerusalem.

"Climbing onto the Wall," Yanait would write, "we would find ourselves imagining the last days of the Roman siege. We lived it over again, saddened and stunned by the memories. . . . There were times when we talked until dawn, often humming tunes."

Frequently David would go for midnight walks alone, composing an article in his mind. His landlady once commented to Yanait, "What an odd type he is—wanders about at night and sticks to his reading and writing all day long!"

His strolls into history not only gave David a chance to reflect but took his mind off his hunger, which he further eased by sleeping late in the morning. His meager earnings paid for just one meal a day, but at least now he didn't have to toil in the fields in his weakened state. When winter came, he wore an old black cape he had brought from Plonsk, using it also as a blanket at night. But whether hungry or cold, David worked with enormous energy—writing, editing, translating, and even helping to turn the big wheel that operated the press in the printing shop across the street from the *Ahdut* office.

His views were already stirring interest—and controversy—among his readers in Palestine and European Zionist circles, who knew him by a pen name that would become his legal name and eventually thunder around the world: David Ben-Gurion. He renamed himself after Yosef Ben-Gurion, a democratic leader of the Jewish revolt against the Romans in 66 A.D., who was killed by Jewish zealots for his political moderation. "Ben-Gurion" meant "son of a lion cub," a symbol that seemed to fit David's growling, aggressive personality.

But though his comrades now took him seriously, some still feared or disliked him. At one Poalei Zion conference in October 1910, all members except Ben-Zvi, Rachel Yanait and one or two others walked out when Ben-Gurion started speaking in

Hebrew, many because they didn't understand the language, others because they were "Yiddishists" in principle, still others because they scorned the speaker. He finished his talk anyway but, deeply wounded, refused to give any more speeches—until persuaded by his *Ahdut* colleagues to change his mind.

Ben-Gurion missed the day-to-day challenge of farm life, the challenge of survival. The agricultural workers were the real pioneers, the "practical idealists" who were willing to suffer, to endure great hardships, in the purest spirit and without complaint. Yet he found his new task even more fulfilling, for it had grandiose overtones. It also permitted him to live a more stable life—and to indulge more often in an old reverie. . . .

Rachel hadn't replied to his invitation to come to Zikhron Yaacov, but Ben-Gurion still longed to see her. How could he entice her to come to Jerusalem? Perhaps Shlomo Zemach, who was living here with his bride (he had given up on Rosa in Plonsk), could help him. Now earning a living as a writer, he looked far better off than Ben-Gurion, who struck Shlomo's wife as "poor and unclean." The two old friends played chess and reminisced about Plonsk, their comrades, Rachel. They agreed: All three of them would invite Rachel to Jerusalem with her baby daughter. On the invitation Ben-Gurion scribbled a personal plea:

"Rachel, though I didn't receive a reply to my previous invitation . . . one always pardons a friend, especially a lady friend. And now Rachel . . . come quickly. Dress your little girl and come!"

But Rachel did not come.

Once more drowning his disappointment in work, Ben-Gurion mapped a new pragmatic Zionist strategy. The Jewish settlers must strongly back the new young rulers of the Turkish Ottoman Empire. Together with the Jews in Turkey itself, the pioneers of Zion, working from the inside, could carve out of the empire an autonomous Jewish niche that would one day evolve into a state. To do this they must first bolster Poalei Zion's power by luring the Jewish workers in Turkey into the party, then groom these new Zionists for *aliya*. Finally, they must run candidates for the Turkish parliament, which the new Turkish government allowed minorities to do.

Ben-Gurion, Ben-Zvi and Israel Shochat all decided to prepare themselves to run for parliament. They would study law in Constantinople and then apply for Turkish citizenship, urging all other Palestinian Jews to become citizens, too. Meanwhile they would try to convert the Turkish Jews into Zionists.

Before leaving for Turkey, Ben-Gurion and Ben-Zvi would travel to Vienna to attend the Third Congress of the World Union of Poalei Zion. Ben-Gurion rejoiced at the chance to visit his family on the way—especially since he had to persuade his father to finance his studies. He must again be practical about this; the money would, after all, be an investment in the state. And this time Avigdor would not be so hard-pressed, for Rivka had been phenomenally lucky; she had married a rich Lodz merchant and would no longer be a financial burden on Avigdor. She even invited Ben-Gurion to stay at her sumptuous home, for he couldn't return to Plonsk, with Tsarist officials eager to arrest him for deserting the army. David was distressed, for Rachel, hoping to cure her malaria, had returned to Plonsk to stay with her grandmother. Before leaving for Poland, he wrote asking her to meet him in Lodz or Warsaw.

On June 13, 1911, Ben-Gurion stepped off the train in Warsaw into the arms of his waiting family—his father, brothers and sisters. Unlike his previous homecoming, this was a happy occasion, with joking, back-slapping, shoulder-patting, smiles all around. Rivka had married well; David would study to be a lawyer. They had something to celebrate this time. A carriage bounced them along the road to Lodz, where the horses snorted to a halt before Rivka's elegant home. Ben-Gurion could hardly imagine living in such a "palace" after his dank cellar in Jerusalem.

He soon learned from his sisters that Rachel had recently given birth to another daughter, but he still felt that he could win her. He wrote her a congratulatory note and was delighted when Rivka invited her to a reception for him. But Rachel sent her regrets; she was too busy with the children to come. David then wrote her another letter:

> . . . How much I would like to see you—I shouldn't have to tell you this. You certainly must sense it. I also believe that you want to see me. I'll be in Warsaw again during my four-week stay here, and perhaps you could come then to Warsaw. Write whether you wish to and are able to come, and I shall go to Warsaw any day you choose. . . .

Rachel replied with a polite "thank you" and a photograph of herself that Ben-Gurion would always cherish. But she still would not come.

Soon after his sister's reception for him in Lodz, David went to Warsaw to see his old girlfriend Jenny Ferenbuk. But no flirtation could alleviate his pain. In his despair he wrote Rachel again: Would she please meet him in Vienna, where he was to attend the world congress of his party? For the first time he declared that he wanted to marry her. He would take her and her two daughters to the United States and study there. He seemed ready to scuttle his whole plan—law school in Constantinople, a seat in the Turkish parliament, perhaps even leadership of his party—if only Rachel would leave her husband for him. His iron will had melted, and destiny might have to wait.

In July, Ben-Gurion traveled to Vienna for the Poalei Zion conference, and before it was over he and three others were named to the party's executive committee. Thus, one year after his farming days, he had risen to the international forefront of the party. Never again could he be ignored. Yet, ironically, at this moment of triumph he was consumed with anxiety. After the conference, other delegates went on to a meeting of the World Zionist Congress in Basel, but he remained in Vienna for weeks waiting for Rachel. Only when he learned that she had returned to Palestine did he too leave for home.

On October 28, 1911, shortly after his homecoming, Ben-Gurion set sail for Salonika, capital of the Ottoman province of Macedonia, where he would try to win over converts to Zionism before enrolling in the University of Constantinople. As the ship entered Salonika harbor and anchored in the jagged shadows of the mountains rimming the town, Ben-Gurion gazed with fascination at the sparkling white houses, the towering minarets, the dark cypress groves sloping up to an ancient Byzantine castle. He was surprised—and delighted—that in this Moslem land, the porters who grabbed his bags and the stevedores who unloaded the ship's cargo were Jews! Shortly, he rented a room in a Jewish home, where he was welcomed warmly if with utter bafflement.

The Salonikan Jews, whose ancestors had fled from Spain almost five hundred years ago, knew nothing about Zion, Ben-Gurion found, and showed little interest in learning about it. Nor could they easily learn from Ben-Gurion since they spoke only Turkish and Ladino, a derivative of Spanish. Ben-Gurion realized that he must learn Turkish quickly so he could communicate with them; besides, he needed the language to enter the law school. He hired a thin owl-eyed Jewish student, Josef

Strumza, who sat with him every day on a mat amid piles of books and papers and taught him Turkish until the pupil's mind reeled with fatigue. According to Strumza, Ben-Gurion made amazing progress and could read local newspapers after three months.

"My teacher," Ben-Gurion boasted in a letter to his father, "is astonished that in so little time I acquired a vocabulary of seven hundred words."

Even before Ben-Gurion could speak Turkish well enough to communicate intelligently, the young missionary tried to create a Poalei Zion cell in Salonika, lecturing in Hebrew on Jewish history and Zionism while Strumza stood beside him and interpreted. At first, Jews crowded into the classrooms where he spoke, puzzled by this strange man from Palestine, which might as well have been the moon. But soon the crowds tapered off, bored by the "secondhand" accounts cascading awkwardly from the lips of an interpreter. Even less attentive were the workers who belonged to socialist organizations. To them Zionism was nothing more than "bourgeois nationalist reaction." As usual, Ben-Gurion reacted bitterly to failure.

"In this animated port," Ben-Gurion wrote his father, "I live as in a desert. I don't speak to anyone. . . . I suffer much from loneliness."

After nearly a year of prodding and probing, Ben-Gurion finally had to give up. He now saw the difficulty of sowing Zionism beyond Eastern Europe, but he refused to be discouraged. With his newly acquired knowledge of Turkish, he would now enter law school in Constantinople and prime himself to run for parliament. Not even the Balkan War of 1912 could dim his optimism. When the Greeks stormed into Salonika shortly before he left for Constantinople, he was convinced that the Turks would soon drive them out. He trusted completely in the survival of the Ottoman Empire, in its hold on all its territories, including Palestine. His entire plan for creating a Jewish state was rooted in this premise. And he wasn't about to scrap it.

Ben-Gurion clambered ashore in Constantinople one hot day in August 1912, moved into a room with Ben-Zvi, who had arrived earlier, and plunged into chaos. He was out of funds, and money from his father had not arrived yet. And when he tried to register at the law school, he found himself mired in a swamp of Kafka-esque formality, especially since he still had no high-school certificate or passport. He would have to become a Turkish citi-

zen, it seemed. But this took time and money and, with the
sound of Greek cannons echoing ever louder in the distance,
the Turkish army might draft him in the bargain. Money finally
arrived from his father but with the war edging nearer, the university was shut down and turned into a hospital.

"You have certainly learned from the newspapers the stupe-
fying results of this war," he wrote his father. "The enemy is
only three hours from Constantinople. . . . Life is getting more
expensive; it is hard to find bread. It has become impossible to
devote oneself to intellectual life. The university is full of
wounded."

When the war finally ended in March 1913, Turkey had lost
some territory, but Ben-Gurion was still certain that the Ottoman Empire would endure, with Palestine safely under its imperial umbrella. He finally procured a forged high-school
certificate from Russia and permission from the university to
register as a foreigner even without a passport. He was elated.
The schools in Warsaw had spurned him; the university here
had blocked his enrollment with myriad obstacles. Yet now he
was a law student and would be a scholar, a man respected not
only for his political acumen but for his academic achievements.

Ben-Gurion studied diligently and, though ill during his examinations, mobilized his will so relentlessly that he passed
with the highest marks. Jubilantly he wrote his father:

> In international law I received 9½, in civil law 10 (the maximum).
> The three students who took the examination at the same time had 3, 6
> and 8. . . . [One] professor enthusiastically told me after questioning me:
> "I'll give you 10," and said to the following student: "I am happy to
> give this mark to a pupil like him." Hearing that I was a Jew from Russia,
> he told another student: "It is our misfortune that we have no such
> youth!"

In his letters home, Ben-Gurion ignored Ben-Zvi, except
when he boasted to Rachel that he had outshone him. In an
unusual gesture he sent regards to Rachel's husband, parents
and friends, apparently wanting Rachel to spread the news of
his brilliant performance.

Ben-Gurion had a greater problem nourishing his body than
his ego, but he did not let hunger sap his spirit. He even brought
Josef Strumza from Salonika and invited him to stay with Ben-
Zvi and himself in the room they had rented. Since no one had
the time or patience to clean up the room, conditions progressively deteriorated, but Ben-Gurion hardly noticed. When one
visitor complained to him that the teacups were unwashed, the

reply was cryptic: "Why wash them? Each one has his own cup."

One occasional visitor was Moshe Shertok, a fastidious fellow student who braved the aromas and disorder to argue with Ben-Gurion over Zionist politics—a dialogue that would continue, as in a stormy love affair, to a bitter climax fifty years later. Ben-Gurion did most of his arguing, however, at student meetings, serving as chairman of the Hebrew Ottoman Students in Constantinople, and he inspired such respect that people flocked to him with their scholastic and personal problems. But, though pleased by such attention, he deplored the cost in time and, in the dim light of an oil lamp, sat up all night hunched over his books to make up for these interruptions.

Such dedication took its toll. Ben-Gurion's health deteriorated dangerously under the pressure, and growing hunger and recurring malaria attacks weakened him further. When he complained to a doctor that he could neither sleep nor eat, he was told that he was suffering from "chronic starvation." With money from home still arriving late, he wrote his father that he had contracted scurvy, though he apparently had a less serious condition, an infection. Bitterly he wailed:

> My health is being destroyed more and more and, as always, at the most difficult moments I am without any money. Apparently we both made a terrible mistake: You assumed a responsibility you are unable to discharge, and I agreed to live under conditions that could destroy all my physical and moral strength. Forgive me, dear father, for causing you sorrow, but I am not writing out of joy.

Ben-Gurion believed that his father was damaging not simply his son's health but the whole Zionist cause. How could one prepare for a messianic role without funds? And if his father owed nothing to him personally, he owed much to the Jewish nation. Thus, Ben-Gurion never felt obliged to thank Avigdor for his money, and he demanded more when the sum was too skimpy. Thanking his father, Ben-Gurion apparently felt, would have implied gratitude for personal help, and the son would never admit that he needed such aid from anyone.

Meanwhile, Avigdor's burden grew: Son Michael was engaged to be married and would need financial help; daughter Zippora and her bridegroom were studying in Berlin and also required aid. To top it all, a deep recession had struck Poland, and even Rivka's rich husband could not bail Avigdor out. But to a man destined to save an entire race, the problems of a few individuals, even his own family, seemed insignificant.

On July 28, 1914, Ben-Gurion and Ben-Zvi, their faces gaunt and gray from fatigue, boarded a Russian ship that would take them to Palestine for a short vacation. Ben-Gurion could not imagine that his formal education was, in fact, over—even when two German warships sailed out of the horizon in pursuit. As bells on his ship rang and crewmen dashed around in near-panic, the captain shakily informed the passengers that a European war had broken out and the Russian ship was potential German booty!

The craft furiously chugged past Jaffa, since Turkey appeared ready to join the Germans in the battle against Russia, Britain and France, and glided into the port of Alexandria, in British-controlled Egypt, where Ben-Gurion and Ben-Zvi leaped aboard a Greek cargo ship heading for Jaffa.

"Our destiny is bound up with that of Turkey," Ben-Gurion told his colleagues sitting uneasily around the conference table in the editorial room of *Ahdut* amid bundles of newspapers that had arrived from abroad on one of the few foreign ships still allowed to anchor in Palestinian waters. He spoke calmly, as if unaware of the panic gripping the Jews of Palestine. Almost all contacts with Europe had been cut, no mail or money could enter, no citrus fruit or other produce could leave, banks shut their doors, prices skyrocketed.

If Turkey entered the war as Germany's ally, what would the Turks do to the Palestinian Jews from Russia, the vast majority of the Jewish community? Were they not Russian citizens? They could be deported, imprisoned, killed. After all the heartbreaking struggle, Palestine might be shorn of Jews. But to Ben-Gurion the solution was clear: Support Turkey.

"Only the Arabs will benefit from the weakening of Turkey, and who hates us as they do? . . . We need a strong Turkey—for only within a great Ottoman Empire embracing many nationalities and tribes, communities and sects can we too be important and have hopes of a future."

Most of his comrades reluctantly agreed. Did they have a choice? The Turks were not likely to harm Jews who backed Turkey and became Ottoman subjects. After all, they had never persecuted the Jews since they offered refuge to thousands who had escaped the Spanish Inquisition five hundred years earlier; and as long as the *bakshish* kept flowing they seldom interfered in internal Jewish affairs. On the other hand, if the Allies won

the war, Russia, the worst oppressor of the Jews, might grab
Palestine. What a cruel irony that would be for those who had
fled from Russian terror. Frightening images were conjured up.
The red-faced drunken policeman; mounted sword-swinging
Cossacks clattering through the streets; inflamed mobs crying
for Jewish blood. Yes, there was no other way: When Turkey
entered the war, the Jews must help it win.

But Ben-Gurion and Ben-Zvi knew they were fighting the
popular tide. For if Turkish officials had been relatively tolerant
toward the Jews, they had been vicious with other nationalities,
massacring thousands of Armenians and many Arabs too. The
best answer, many Jews felt, was to leave the country before it
was too late. Ben-Gurion was alarmed. If everybody left, his
dream would die. In his articles and lectures Ben-Gurion vigorously urged the community to apply for "Ottomanization,"
reminding it that Russian Jews had been persecuted ruthlessly
by the Tsarist government.

He and Ben-Zvi set up an "Ottomanization" committee in the
office of the chief rabbi, where they prepared the papers of Jews
switching nationality, though few found the nerve to exchange
their last tenuous connection with their miserable past for a
questionable future. The two Bens even tried to form a Jewish
militia, though, after they had begun to train about forty volunteers with official permission, the Turks issued a new order: No
armed Jews.

On October 31, 1914, Turkey entered the war. The Jewish
community trembled, not without reason, for Turkish officials
called for a *jihad*, a holy war, against the "infidels." They carried out searches and confiscated Jewish money, valuables, firearms and food; ransacked the Jewish emergency relief
committee; banished Jewish public figures to Tiberias; banned
Hebrew-language signs; and finally arrested and deported five
hundred Jews.

An even worse omen followed. A ship steamed into Jaffa port
and a short heavy-set man in khaki uniform and fur hat stepped
ashore. He had a swarthy brown-bearded Tartar face with burning black eyes and incongruously delicate features. Jamal
Pasha, one of Turkey's toughest military leaders, had come to
take over command of Palestine and make sure that hostile
forces did not subvert it.

Ben-Gurion and his colleagues had been plagued by indecision
since the expulsion of the five hundred Jews. Should they protest in print this shameful deed, which could presage the ban-

ishment of all Jews from their own land? This was the moral thing to do, but was such a move practical? The government would probably ban the newspaper and perhaps arrest them. Ben-Gurion weighed the alternatives and decided that a protest would be a practical gamble. Even if it didn't influence the Turks, it might influence the Jews. Many, in their fear, were now clamoring to leave Palestine without waiting to be deported or jailed. Thousands dragging suitcases with all their belongings had already jammed an American ship that had come with food and other supplies for the Jews. Those remaining had to be calmed and made to understand: In spite of hardship and danger, every one of them must stay, or there might never be a Jewish state.

"If it depended on me," Ben-Gurion exclaimed to his comrades, "I'd lock the gates of the land and wouldn't allow even one soul to leave. Five thousand Jews who might fall in *Eretz Yisrael* are more important to us, to our future, than ten thousand who might escape and save their lives in Egypt!"

Ahdut must publish a protest, he insisted, charging that the government had deported the victims not because they were aliens, as it claimed, but because they were Jews. This charge, however, should be diplomatically balanced with a plea to the Jews to back Turkey in the war. Ben-Gurion's colleagues agreed.

The protest appeared, and shortly afterward an *Ahdut* representative went to see Jamal Pasha, hoping to reach some understanding. But Jamal simply gave him a written statement that he wanted published in *Ahdut*. Ben-Gurion froze when he read it. While praising the Jews in Turkey, Jamal called the Jews in Palestine "enemies of Turkey" and warned that anyone found with a Zionist document would be executed. The *Ahdut* editors feverishly debated their response and decided on a trick. They published the statement as ordered but refrained from distributing this issue of the paper. Jamal learned of the ruse and ordered them to publish the protest again and distribute the paper this time. Left without choice, they obeyed and, as expected, public fear exploded into panic. The panic swelled as police began arresting any "foreign" Jews they could find in the streets and markets, releasing only those who vowed to become Ottoman subjects.

In their terror, people avoided Ben-Gurion and even crossed the street when they saw him coming. But they flocked to him when he sat in the chief rabbi's office, sweating over the many documents needed for "Ottomanization." The Turkish threat achieved what his personal appeals had not. From morning till night Jews queued in the large muddy square outside the office, ignoring a winter drizzle that soaked the long rumpled coats of the religious and the patched jackets of the workers.

Then one day a messenger wormed his way through the crowd and breathlessly reported to Ben-Gurion: "They've closed the printing shop and arrested the [paper's] administrator!"

Ben-Gurion rushed to the editorial office, and at a meeting of *Ahdut* employees suggested that someone sneak into the printing shop after dark to remove incriminating papers that might hang them all. Some employees dissented. Getting caught in the act would be even more dangerous, they argued.

One man turned against the Zionist idea itself. "The whole settlement policy in Palestine is sheer madness," he exclaimed. "We built on a volcano. . . . Do you know the Turks are capable of destroying us, of sweeping us out of this country with one stroke, as one sweeps a swarm of ants off a table?"

Ben-Gurion was aghast. If such thinking spread, Zionism might be doomed. Then came another shock. The *Ahdut* administrator told the police that Ben-Zvi had written the protest (though Zerubavel had).

"This is treason!" Ben-Gurion cried.

Now Ben-Zvi would probably be arrested; and in February 1915, he was—together with Ben-Gurion.

The Bens were charged not only with editing *Ahdut*, but with heading two "secret" political associations, Poalei Zion and Hashomer—though, ironically, Ben-Gurion had not even been asked to join Hashomer. They were thrown into jail, but bribed Arab guards proved lenient and all the Poalei Zion leaders came for a meeting, sitting on mats or on low straw footstools and sipping Turkish coffee served by a uniformed Arab boy. Both prisoners were stubborn. They preferred languishing in prison to leaving the country; they were even ready for hard labor.

"Jamal Pasha," said Ben-Zvi, "has issued an order not to accept me and Ben-Gurion as Ottoman subjects; he wants to deport us from the country as aliens."

Still hopeful, however, the pair wrote an appeal to Jamal: "We believe we have the right to be considered Ottoman citizens and ask Your Excellency for the favor of being treated—and, if necessary, punished—as Ottomans." There was no answer.

When the Bens were finally released on bail, Ben-Zvi and

Rachel Yanait went to see Jamal Pasha and then reported the results of the meeting to Ben-Gurion, who was waiting in Yanait's house. Jamal Pasha had torn up their letter; he wouldn't budge. Ben-Gurion did not reply. "[He] knew how to be silent, and his silence was very impressive," Yanait would later say of that moment. "We were all desperate."

The next day, the Poalei Zion leaders huddled in the Amdursky Hotel inside the Wall near Jaffa Gate, while policemen waited outside the door of their room. It was a sad farewell meeting, so tense that no one even sat down. Not only the Bens, but Israel Shochat and his wife, Manya, were to be deported. Ben-Gurion's worst fears were crystallizing; the top leaders of the party were being exiled.

The Bens, it was decided, would go to the United States and set up a volunteer pioneer force that would return to Palestine and fight for Turkey, which, after all, simply misunderstood Zionism. Then, after the war, this force would work in the fields and factories. Whether the Turks liked it or not, a Jewish army must fight *for* them—so that it would have the training to fight *against* them if necessary when the time came to set up a Jewish state. But, meanwhile, could the secondary leaders hold on in Palestine, or would they too be deported or perhaps abandoned by the people? Ben-Gurion was despondent. The base of the great Zionist structure he had been helping to build might disintegrate, and he would be powerless to act.

Yet, as the group talked of the future, it was buoyed by its makeshift plans. Perhaps, Ben-Gurion thought, their deportation would turn out to be a blessing. Perhaps it was time to rouse the Diaspora to the miracle of Zion.

"I can't forget that meeting, with all of us standing," Yanait would reminisce. "Shochat spoke with fervor, Ben-Gurion categorically, Ben-Zvi seriously and profoundly, and I too with enthusiasm. We didn't speak much, but felt each one of us had a mission to fulfill."

Ben-Gurion stared into the blue infinity of the sea as he stood by a window of the beach hotel in Jaffa where he and Ben-Zvi were imprisoned while awaiting a ship. The sea would separate him from his land; yet it would also be a highway for millions of Jews he would persuade to return with him. Now that his departure was inevitable, he was impatient to leave, to start on his

new "missionary" task. He was optimistic about the future—
until one day a new shock flashed visions of disaster. He met an
Arab student who was also being detained in the hotel, and they
became friends. In Turkish they spoke of many things—their
pasts, their dreams.

Why had Ben-Gurion been arrested, the Arab, Yahya Effendi,
wanted to know.

Because he was being deported on orders from Jamal Pasha.

The Arab responded in a sincere manner: "As a friend, I am
sorry, but as an Arab, I am glad."

Ben-Gurion was stunned. Suddenly he realized, as he hadn't
since his Sejera days, what might be ahead. "If a man like him
rejoiced at my expulsion," he would say, "what would Arabs
who didn't have his qualities do to the small numbers of Jews
in the country?"

He suddenly envisioned massacres, pogroms, holocaust.
Again he was haunted by fear; and his impatience to leave and
bring help grew with each passing day. Not even the visits of
friends like Rachel Yanait could cheer him or Ben-Zvi.

"Sitting silently in a room overlooking the sea," recalled Yanait, "they were sunk in their own thoughts. A candle flickered
on the table. I stood at the threshold in silence. Suddenly I felt
the pain of this forced parting. 'We'll be back, Rachel, we'll be
back soon. We'll return with many others—pioneers and volunteers. You'll see, Rachel,' [Ben-Zvi] whispered in my ear."

Finally, on March 21, 1915, police escorted Ben-Gurion, Ben-
Zvi and a procession of their friends through Jaffa's winding
alleys to a rowboat, still manned by raucous Arabs, that would
carry the two "martyrs" to an Italian ship bound for Alexandria,
from where they would sail to the United States. As the vessel
raised anchor, Ben-Gurion, standing on deck, narrowed his eyes
against the wind and gazed at the same scene that had mesmerized him nine years earlier when, with Rachel Nelkin beside
him, he had first set eyes on Zion.

He would be back. Destiny commanded it.

CHAPTER FOUR

He said, I will certainly return unto thee
GENESIS 18:10

S OME weeks later, in early May 1915, Ben-Gurion stood on the deck of another ship and stared at the silhouette of a tantalizing new world. He was thrilled by the sight of the Statue of Liberty and the skyscrapers "dozens of stories high," and he was so impatient to enter the United States that after being kept aboard for several hours he felt somewhat like Moses, who was permitted by God to glimpse the Promised Land but not to enter it.

"I always dreamed of America," he would write later of his thoughts during the voyage, "its vigorous ultramodern life, its capitalism in the most developed and most democratic country. We who want to build a new country in the desert, to raise our ruins, we must see how exiles, persecuted in England, constructed a state so rich, with unequaled power." He was a socialist, true, but he was ready to learn from the capitalists and adapt this knowledge to his dream.

En route to America Ben-Gurion had stopped in British-controlled Egypt and found that other exiled Jewish leaders wanted to fight *against* Turkey. In Cairo, Josef Trumpeldor was organizing a Jewish Mule Corps to help the British battle the Turks in Gallipoli, and in London, Vladimir Jabotinsky was trying to form a Jewish Legion to help the British battle the Turks in Palestine. How, Ben-Gurion asked, could the Jews support a country that was allied with anti-Semitic Russia, which could hardly wait to invade Palestine and turn it into another ghetto slaughterhouse? Besides, if the Jews backed Britain, the Turks might quash the *Yishuv* in revenge. Be practical! But nobody listened—except, of course, Ben-Zvi. Nor did the Bens' icy view of Britain melt when British police, noting their fezzes, detained them as "Turkish agents" in the port of Alexandria, releasing them only after the American consul rushed to their rescue.

Happily they were soon on a ship bound for America, and not even a stormy ocean could dampen their spirits, though it occasionally caused Ben-Gurion to lose his place in the English grammar book he was mentally photographing down to the last verb and participle. Then the white-tipped waves gradually calmed as the ship glided into New York harbor. When Ben-Gurion finally stepped ashore, he was so excited that he didn't even wait for Ben-Zvi to pass through customs. He jumped into a taxi and hurried to American Poalei Zion headquarters, ready to pursue his mission.

Within the fragmented, largely Yiddish-speaking Jewish community of New York, which resembled a giant transplanted *shtetl*, Poalei Zion floundered with the authority of a minnow in a pool of sharks. This East Side fringe party was nothing but a band of Communists, cried the more conservative political groups. But the two Bens, glamorous pioneers from *Eretz Yisrael*, turned the minnow into a respectable fish overnight. They were swept up in a flurry of receptions, parties and press conferences, and even the mayor appeared at one welcoming ceremony. Ben-Gurion detested the "American glitter," especially the exaggerated praise and empty rhetoric. He knew his American comrades did not really think he and Ben-Zvi were that heroic, but were using them mainly as exotic gimmicks to win new members. Even more irritating, the press always mentioned Ben-Zvi's name first, and sometimes referred to Ben-Gurion simply as a "dignitary from Palestine."

So dull and boring were the party functions that often he would sneak away with Ben-Zvi to his favorite haunt, the Shalom Café, a popular Broadway hangout for young Jews. Proudly wearing their fezzes, they would drink coffee and gaze at the girls who came and went, talking and dating easily, and Ben-Gurion recalled the sensation he had created in Plonsk when he merely walked down the street with Rachel. If only he had time to taste the delights of this strange new freedom.

But he didn't. When the big welcome was over, the campaign

for a pioneer army, the Hehalutz, began. A special party committee planned the campaign, but confusion reigned. Should
the Hehalutz fight in the war? And on which side? Help the
Turks! the Bens demanded. No, the British, cried others. Ben-
Gurion carefully measured party sentiment and led a tactical
retreat. Turkey? Britain? What did it matter? The important
thing was for the Hehalutz to build Zion *after* the war, which-
ever side won. And in the Jewish press, Ben-Gurion now wrote
only of the coming postwar struggle for a homeland.

Most party leaders supported this "neutral" approach and arranged for the Bens to lecture to party branches in major American and Canadian cities. Ben-Gurion now envisioned a great
crusade. He had only to tell young Jews about his dream, and
thousands would rush to enlist in the first Jewish army since the
fall of the Second Temple. Hashomer? A mere band of boys.
The Hehalutz would be a real army. And he, Ben-Gurion, would
be the commander, the new Joshua, who would lead his warriors into the Land—to fight, naturally, under the Turks.

But the "army" was elusive. In Buffalo, Ben-Gurion caught
diphtheria and was out for weeks. Detroit described him as a
mediocre speaker without warmth. Toronto reported that he
"isn't a public speaker." Montreal canceled his appearance. Ot-
tawa and Boston were "too busy" to book him. When the tour
ended, Ben-Gurion had signed up nineteen volunteers for Hehalutz, and Ben-Zvi, whose relaxed personality appealed to
more people, forty-four. Their Jewish audiences, mostly small
craftsmen, traders and sickly veterans of the sweatshops, had
little money for expenses and could hardly be imagined as bold,
aggressive soldiers or even as hardy pioneers. Ben-Gurion was
glum. One more failure. The American Jews would not listen to
him any more than his old comrades had listened during his
early pioneer years in Palestine. They were shallow and wanted
only to be entertained. They had no understanding of the past
—or the future—of their people.

Then another tour, and another trauma. Washington, D.C.,
was furious that they were getting him. Winnipeg complained
that he was a "very weak speaker and not a great agitator."
Pittsburgh preferred to give a Hannukah costume ball instead,
accepting him only under great pressure. St. Paul went "broke"
as a result of his lecture. Nor did Ben-Gurion enjoy the hospitality he did receive.

"The comrades," he wrote to a friend, "bother you all day

long in order, of course, not to leave you alone and lonely. . . . With great pleasure I would like to get rid of them and be by myself."

What is more, ill-fortune plagued Ben-Gurion all along the way. He lost his voice in one city, his money in another, and his underwear (when he sent it to the laundry) in still another. In Galveston, Texas, he was almost thrown out of a movie house for sitting in the black section. He found segregation "annoying, offensive and hurtful" and, referring to the Arabs in his own country, asked, "Couldn't the sons of free, cultured, progressive, and democratic America learn a little humanity from those savages?" About the only thing on the tour that didn't depress him were the comely girls of Texas.

Hurt and embittered by the apathy of his audiences, Ben-Gurion was ready to quit the tour and go home. Then, suddenly, people began challenging his views, and the atmosphere changed. He would ruthlessly strike at his foes—"bourgeois" Zionists and anti-Zionists—with stinging sarcasm, spouting facts that left them limp. He was back in the Great Synagogue of Plonsk devouring the Bund, and the people loved it. At one rally in Minneapolis, he verbally crushed an anti-Zionist foe and became an instant hero to American Zionists. Another victory at a Galveston rally spread his name further.

But there were new setbacks too. When Chicago asked for Ben-Zvi and got Ben-Gurion instead, it gave him a cool welcome. In Milwaukee he disappointed at least one admirer—an attractive young woman named Goldie Mabovich, who would one day govern Israel as Golda Meir. Because she missed Ben-Gurion's talk, she lost the privilege of hosting a luncheon for him the following day.

After an exhausting three-month tour, Ben-Gurion returned to New York in March 1916 with the feeling that, on balance, he had finally scored well. Because of his cutting confrontations, he was now much better known and respected than he had been at the start of his campaign. But both he and Ben-Zvi failed to achieve their goals: Only about a hundred persons had signed up for the Hehalutz. The trouble was, Ben-Gurion felt, people needed more than just lectures. They had to see as well as hear. Why not put out a Yiddish-language adventure book about the watchmen in *Eretz Yisrael?*

Party leaders agreed, but named Ben-Zvi editor. Ben-Gurion? Who could control this abrasive little "dictator"? Of course, he could contribute an article about his personal experiences. Ben-Gurion felt humiliated. They "stole" his idea, then chose someone else to carry it out! But in the end he triumphed, for the book, *Yizkor* ("Remembrance"), exploded into an international best seller among Jews. And since Ben-Zvi had temporarily moved to Washington, D.C., before it came out, Ben-Gurion found himself almost alone in the limelight, lionized as one of the heroic watchmen he had glamorously portrayed. He was suddenly besieged with speaking offers, and the publicity snowballed when anti-Zionists attacked him for building *Eretz Yisrael* "on the misfortune of the Arabs"—an attack that drew such an offensive reply from Ben-Gurion that the press refused to print it.

Ben-Gurion was then blessed with one of the biggest breaks of his early career. With Ben-Zvi away, he published an enlarged edition of *Yizkor* virtually by himself, and though Ben-Zvi had done most of the work on the original version, his name was deleted from this one. It was now Ben-Zvi who was furious, but Ben-Gurion could not let personal sentiment dilute his claim to destiny. No, he would never again be simply a "dignitary from Palestine," lurking in Ben-Zvi's shadow. Overnight the revised edition, far superior to the original, burgeoned into an even better seller. And the more famous Ben-Gurion became, the more resentful Ben-Zvi became, for he now found himself in Ben-Gurion's shadow, where he would forever remain.

Firmly on the road to destiny, Ben-Gurion, at thirty, felt that he could now afford to relax occasionally. But relaxation led to loneliness, and as he did so often when he was lonely, he pined for Rachel. While picnicking with his comrades one evening in Coney Island, he lay on the sand, melancholy amid the merriment, and wrote to her: "I stare into the sky and count the stars; or at the . . . crowds on the beach." But he could feel no joy, for "you are not here." Rachel, he pleaded once again, come—come with the two children. He would pay expenses.

But there was no answer. He wrote again. Still no answer. Brooding, he gave up. And with this wound, his soul was apparently sealed, marking an end to sentimental illusion. The process had been gradual. There had been his mother's death, his father's remarriage, his separation from his family, his estrangement from boyhood companions, his turmoil over Rachel, her marriage, and now this final rejection. Too many personal shocks for a messiah with a mission. And there was no one now he could bare his soul to—with the Germans occupying Plonsk, his father was cut off from the world.

Lonelier than ever, Ben-Gurion visited the home of his friend and party comrade Dr. Samuel Ellsberg. It was a cozy place, where he engaged in stimulating conversation with many writers and politicians. At one gathering in the summer of 1916, amid the chatter and the tinkle of teacups, the eminent socialist-Zionist leader Nachman Syrkin introduced Ben-Gurion to a young nurse who worked in Dr. Ellsberg's clinic. Her rather sad brown eyes behind pince-nez glasses seemed to contradict her cheerful smile, and her strong jawline and straight dark hair drawn tightly into a knot at the nape of her neck suggested a severity in curious contrast to her pleasant open manner. She had a rounded body and neatly curved thighs.

Ben-Gurion seems to have found Pauline Munweiss (originally Monbas) reasonably desirable, though they had little in common. He was an intellectual with his nose buried in books; she seldom read and knew little about the world. He was introverted and withdrawn; she was almost eccentrically outgoing, often asking embarrassing questions and uttering outrageous comments. He was a fanatical Zionist; she was sympathetic to Emma Goldman's anarchism. He dreamed of building a new nation; she didn't think beyond the little house she wanted in a "nice" neighborhood. Like Ben-Gurion, "Paula," as he called her, was on the rebound. She had been dating one of the American Poalei Zion leaders, Yitzhak Zelig Rabinovich, for about two years, but he had constantly evaded the question of marriage, and Paula, apparently with some apprehension, now considered herself free.

Physically Ben-Gurion was a big letdown after the handsome Rabinovich. Paula's friends ridiculed him and wondered what she saw in this joyless little man. Paula herself would later say of her meeting with Ben-Gurion, "You should have seen his appearance! Bleary-eyed and shabby. But as soon as he opened his mouth, I saw that this was a great man."

The fact was, however, that there weren't that many eligible bachelors around, nor was she *that* desirable. It was she who "dumped" Rabinovich, Paula assured Ben-Gurion—though Rabinovich would tell friends he was glad to be "dumped." Why concentrate on one man when there were so many others who wanted her? For example, Leon Trotsky, who was then residing in New York. She attended his lectures and in the midst of his fiery rhetoric, she boasted, he would passionately stare at her.

Paula also rattled off to Ben-Gurion a somewhat fantasized version of her life. She was six years younger than he, she claimed, though her sister Pesya would later say that she was actually four years older. Her father, she said, was a wealthy wheat merchant in Minsk, Russia, though he was only a poor grocery-store owner who had to ease his burden by sending four of his nine children, including Paula, to America in 1904. He sent her money for medical school until he died, she said, and then she had to quit. Which school? She never did say.

If Paula embellished some of the facts, however, Ben-Gurion did not question them. Her age and her family's social status didn't matter. After all, he portrayed his own father as a "distinguished lawyer" beloved by all the Zionists in Plonsk. He might "exaggerate" a little, but he was no hypocrite (except occasionally for the sake of the cause). Besides, Paula had many qualities he liked. She was one of the few people with whom he could feel at ease. She talked incessantly, but didn't necessarily expect him to answer or even to listen, and she always looked after his health and advised him what he should eat. After so many years of living alone, it was comforting to be cared for as he had been when he was a child.

And ironically, his obsession with Rachel made Paula all the more desirable. Now that he knew Rachel was lost to him, he no longer looked for the totally consuming love he felt for her. Never could he love like that again, so why not seek a less emotional relationship, one that would not impede his mission and might even help smooth the way to fulfillment? Why should he have to worry about feeding himself, paying his bills, meeting social obligations? All this took time, and there was so little time to waste. He had always feared the demands of love, but whatever his sentiment toward Paula, he apparently did not feel such fear.

Ben-Gurion was grateful that Paula asked to help him with his work. She not only eased his task, but tried to steep herself in Zionism despite her anarchist sympathies. She was especially useful when he started to research a new book, *Eretz Yisrael—The Land of Our Future,* in collaboration with Ben-Zvi, who had conquered his bitter feelings and returned to New York. This book, which would detail the history, geography and ethnography of the country, might be another best seller among the Jews and lure more young men into the Hehalutz. So Ben-Gurion began spending much of his time leafing through volumes in the New York Public Library with Paula constantly at his side, finding books and documents and copying extracts from them. They seemed to grow closer in the library than they did in the coffee houses and cinemas they went to—Dutch treat —when Paula could persuade him to take a few hours off.

On November 2, 1917, headlines heralded an event that would set Ben-Gurion's course—and ultimately that of Zion. Britain published a letter that Foreign Minister Arthur Balfour had sent to Lord Rothschild, head of the British branch of that illustrious Jewish family. Ben-Gurion read the words of the Balfour Declaration with startled joy.

"His Majesty's Government view with favour the establishment in Palestine of a national home for the Jewish People, and will use their best endeavours to facilitate the achievement of this objective."

Ben-Gurion had already dropped his plan for sending a Jewish force to Palestine to fight against the British, for the United States had become Britain's ally by declaring war on Germany on April 6, 1917. It hardly made sense for the Jews to join Turkey, the ally of America's enemy, when America would surely be on the winning side and, anyway, was too important a Zionist stronghold to turn into a foe. So Ben-Gurion went to American Zionist leader Louis Brandeis, who had just become a Supreme Court justice, with a *new* plan: Why not form a Jewish battalion in the American army? Brandeis relayed the idea to President Woodrow Wilson, who, though sympathetic, pointed out that the United States had declared war on Germany but not on Turkey. If the Jews wanted to fight only in Palestine, let them pull British lapels.

Ben-Gurion now found himself in a delicate position. In London, Vladimir Jabotinsky had been pulling British lapels since the war began, and Ben-Gurion had called him a fool. How could he now say Jabotinsky had been right all along? He couldn't. He would simply argue that, unlike in the past, it was now practical to back Britain.

Ben-Gurion was disturbed, however, by the explosion of euphoria and optimism that rocked the Jewish world when Balfour made his promise. Many Jews were acting as if the messiah had come and the Jewish state were about to blossom forth, though the struggle had only begun. In the party organ Ben-Gurion wrote:

England has not given us the Land. . . . [though it] has done much by recognizing our political existence and our rights to the country. The

Hebrew people . . . must, through its own labor and capital, build its national home and realize its full . . . emancipation.

To Ben-Gurion this statement was a personal pledge as well as a public plea. And with frenzy he thrust himself into a new campaign to enroll volunteers for the Hehalutz—this time to fight beside the British. As he stammered on from city to city, his voice almost giving out, only Paula, it seems, would sometimes intrude into his messianic mania. While he had not once said he loved her, he did feel close to her, probably as close as he could feel to any woman now that Rachel was beyond reach. If he left for Palestine without marrying her, certainly he would lose her forever. There was Rabinovich and apparently many others (though he didn't seem concerned about Trotsky). Had he not lost Rachel because of his procrastination? And while he was still very poor, he now had a certain stature and could afford to gamble on raising a family in *Eretz Yisrael*. He would ask Paula to marry him, but she would have to understand that nothing was more important than his mission.

Ben-Gurion went to Paula and was brutally frank. He wished to marry her, but only under certain conditions. She must let him return to Palestine with a Jewish battalion and, after the war, join him there permanently. Life would not be easy, he warned. The country was impoverished and there was no electricity or modern plumbing. Was she prepared to live a pioneer life? Paula shuddered at the thought, but if she wanted him she would have to accept his "ultimatum"—and she wanted him.

So they would be married. No formal wedding, he said. Not even a rabbi, though any marriage performed without one wasn't recognized under Jewish law. He was a socialist, she an anarchist—why be hypocrites? And so that no one would make a fuss, they would keep their intentions a secret until after the wedding. They were too mature for the usual romantic nonsense anyway. And besides, a conventional wedding wouldn't be practical. No time. Ben-Gurion looked at his schedule. Yes, he could squeeze in the ceremony during his lunch hour.

At 11 A.M., December 5, 1917, Ben-Gurion met Paula at the Municipal Building across from City Hall, and they walked together into the Marriage License Bureau, where he reached into his pocket for two dollars and applied for a marriage license. He was apparently so nervous that he forgot his mother's maiden name, for the license indicated it was "unknown." As the couple stood before the judge, with two hastily corralled witnesses looking on, his thoughts can only be surmised. Perhaps he was thinking of Rachel, who might now be standing beside him if his priorities had not been cast by destiny. Now he would finally extinguish the flame that had burned in his soul since childhood. Or would he?

When the ceremony was over, Ben-Gurion kissed his bride and then glanced at his watch. Good God, he would be late to the meeting of his party's executive! While Paula rushed off to her job at the clinic, Ben-Gurion raced to the meeting. As he burst into the conference room, his colleagues looked aghast. He was fifteen minutes late! It wasn't like Ben-Gurion. He was never tardy and regarded every second as valuable as a patch of land in *Eretz Yisrael*. Ben-Gurion sheepishly apologized, but he hoped they would understand. He had just gotten married. Silence. Then his colleagues congratulated him, though still unable to believe the news. Married? He was married to his mission.

That evening, Paula returned to the apartment she shared with two roommates, and her husband returned to the room he shared with Ben-Zvi. Ben-Gurion sat down at his desk and described the blissful event in his diary: "At 11:30 A.M. I was married."

Only three days after their wedding did the couple move into their own small apartment in Brooklyn. And when they did, Ben-Gurion didn't stay long. The following morning he was off on a speaking tour, and when he returned in a few days he spent one night at home and left on another trip. A night at home again and then still more travel. Each time he exhaustedly stumbled back into the flat and dropped his bag, he would rush to his desk and jot in his diary the size of the crowds that listened to him and how much money they donated. Imagine! Five thousand people had come to hear him in New England! Amid the clatter of pots and pans in the kitchen, Paula would gasp her admiration or—when Ben-Gurion tramped in angrily with bad news— her sympathy. Yes, it was disgraceful—the party wanting to use the money *he* collected for its own activities rather than for projects in *Eretz Yisrael*. Little wonder that he resigned from the central committee. But couldn't he forget his destiny for maybe a few hours?

Occasionally he did; when Paula coddled him, he felt like the child his mother had babied so lovingly. She treated his bloodshot eyes, washed and ironed his clothes and fed him nourishing food. Nor did Ben-Gurion resist when Paula "trained" him in personal hygiene. He now scrubbed his feet daily, changed his underwear often and brushed his teeth every morning. Grateful for Paula's care and attention, he replied with tokens of affection. Since she worked at night and therefore slept late in the morning, Ben-Gurion, before leaving for work, would sometimes wake her with kisses and caresses while her eyes implored him to stay "a little longer."

But Ben-Gurion seldom had time to stay longer. If he wasn't collecting money on tours, he was working feverishly on his new book with Ben-Zvi or exploring every path that could lead him back to Palestine as soon as possible, for British General Edmund Allenby had already captured the southern part of the land, including Jaffa. Finally, in February 1918, a cable from London opened a path. The British had agreed to form a Jewish Legion to fight in Palestine! At last a Jewish armed force, a force that could eventually be used to make the Balfour Declaration a reality. Ben-Gurion was jubilant. His efforts had finally borne fruit. Jabotinsky? What had *he* done?

The British set up offices in the United States to recruit alien Jews who could not be drafted in the American army, but Ben-Gurion, despite his joy, did not rush to sign up. For he had just heard another bit of earthshaking news: Paula was pregnant. Could he go away now, especially when he might die in battle, leaving his wife and child alone and almost penniless? He decided that he could. For did not destiny come first?

Ben-Gurion thus marched into the British recruiting office on April 26, enlisted, then returned home and cautiously broke the news to Paula. She absorbed his words in painful silence and burst into tears. He tried to calm her.

Hadn't he warned her before they were married?

But she was pregnant. She would be alone—maybe even a widow—when the baby was born. She might die in childbirth.

No need to worry. Nothing would happen. And he would leave her as much money as he could.

But Ben-Gurion felt a sense of guilt. Paula had chosen him over more attractive men and showered him with maternal attention. And he was repaying her with virtual abandonment when she was pregnant. But was this not the supreme test, the measure of his commitment to his mission? Whatever his regrets, he had not married Rachel when he had had the chance.

Now he must conquer himself again. Of course his wife and unborn child were important, but the Jewish state was transcendent. He *had* to go.

Meanwhile, would she please pack his things. They wanted him to speak in Chicago.

Ben-Gurion was relieved to learn that he would have enough money for Paula to live on when pregnancy forced her to quit her nursing job. The new book he and Ben-Zvi had written escalated into another international best seller among Jews, so now he could leave her eight hundred dollars plus whatever money trickled in from his articles and lectures. He would also send her twenty dollars a week from his soldier's pay. At the last minute he scribbled out his last will and testament, leaving all his assets to his unborn child and naming his wife and father as custodians of his meager inheritance. He also specified that if the baby was a girl, she be called Geula, meaning "liberation." She would be a living reminder of his role in conquering the Land.

On May 27, 1918, Ben-Gurion and Paula, dressed in their bargain-basement finery, went to a farewell ball for the departing Legionnaires. They stayed until 4 A.M., talking with friends, appearing to be joyous, though it isn't likely they were. If Paula saw only catastrophe ahead, Ben-Gurion obviously had mixed emotions, with the excitement of returning to Palestine tainted by the bane of guilt.

Paula begged him to change his mind until the moment of his departure two days later. Finally, in despair, she moved into her sister's apartment in Brooklyn, and he joined about three hundred other Legionnaires for a march down Fifth Avenue. Crowds cheered and bands played patriotic music all the way to the train that would take them to Pier 14 in Newark en route to a camp in Canada. At the pier, the recruits jumped off the train into a sea of sobbing well-wishers as loved ones embraced in touching scenes of farewell. It is not clear whether Paula was there. In his diary Ben-Gurion wrote only that when he had arrived in the United States he hadn't expected to return to Palestine "with a rifle in hand under the Hebrew flag."

"We sang all the way," Ben-Gurion would write Paula in Yiddish in his first letter to her from Port Edward camp in Windsor, Nova Scotia, describing his journey by boat and train.

In every city we passed through . . . we were welcomed enthusiastically. In Portland . . . the moment I emerged from the carriage and the people saw me, they lifted me up and cried "Hurray!" . . . [In] Bangor . . . the crowd, which had stood waiting all night, asked for me and looked for me.

Ben-Gurion clearly relished the role of hero and apparently wanted Paula to know that if she picked a rather unattractive fellow—compared to her former suitors—he was a person of some importance. He arrived in his camp with a joy he had perhaps not experienced since he first landed in Palestine. Greeting him and the others were smartly uniformed, flag-waving Legionnaires who had arrived some days earlier, among them, Ben-Zvi.

"Everyone came to shake hands with me," wrote Ben-Gurion. "The whole camp knew that I was coming, and they waited for me impatiently."

Acceptance by his comrades—idolization as he perceived it—kept Ben-Gurion's spirits soaring, and he marveled to Paula: "I feel drunk with my new life." In this "drunken" state no hardship or difficulty could daunt him. He described how he spent every minute of every day, dwelling on those minutes that reflected his comrades' esteem for him.

"My popularity here creates problems. . . . Virtually everything that happens in the camp is brought to me. One man asks my advice, another comes for information, a third simply wants to talk to someone. So I hardly have an hour a day to myself."

Ben-Gurion sometimes even boasted about his "humility." After he was elected to serve on the Legionnaires' committee, his sergeant "summoned me and said that the . . . major wanted to promote me to corporal. I declined. . . . The whole camp is talking about it."

He finally "gave in," however, and the sergeant told the major that "I was 'the best man in the Jewish Legion,'" explaining that "I had refused to be a corporal because as a private I had a greater moral influence in the Legion."

Ben-Gurion thus won his stripes—and his comrades' admiration too. He had objected to a promotion for *their* sake. But while he was certainly an important figure, not everybody considered him "the best man in the Jewish Legion." One comrade pointed out that "he was a very bad shot and couldn't even put his leggings on right." In other eyes he was too aloof and busy with committee meetings to earn the affection of the soldiers. He admitted to Paula that he was having problems with his instructors, though he felt they were to blame.

"I have been making good progress in my military training," he wrote her, "and if our instructors were better we could achieve a higher standard."

Whatever his efficiency or popularity rating, the more Ben-Gurion reveled in his growing importance, the more indebted he felt to Paula for suffering at home while he was getting "drunk" with his "new life." Paula did nothing to ease his feeling of guilt; in every letter she wrote, she flaunted her misery and fears, and voiced doubts of his love. Ben-Gurion sobered and, it seems, tried more desperately than ever to soothe and comfort her with endearing, if perhaps specious, phrases he had never dreamed of uttering at home.

He wrote on June 1, 1918, the day of his arrival:

> My darling, I miss only you. You are more precious to me than anything in the world. . . . Love me as much as I love you.

Two days later:

> I feel the love and longing in your heart, my darling. And I know and feel how unhappy you are. I promise you it won't be in vain. I will make you happy. I know you are suffering now, but I'm certain that I and my ideals will eventually compensate you.

In mangled but moving English, Paula responded to "Dear Ben-Gurion" with equal passion, diluted rather startlingly by an almost parental concern about his hygienic habits.

> I didn't realize before how hard it would be without you. . . . Since you have left I haven't slept one night yet, your image is always with me dear. My love for you is so sacred that this is not enough of a sacrifice yet. . . . I am not writing this letter with ink only, also with blood of my heart. Dear, one thing I will beg of you . . . keep yourself clean, clean your teeth, also wash your feet often.

As for her own well-being:

> I am not feeling very well. I got so thin that people don't recognize me, but this is not of great importance.

Also, her feet were

> swollen and [there is] nobody to help me, but what can I do. I suppose your ideal is greater then [sic] I and our future child.

Ben-Gurion replied:

It seems you don't know me very well! I doubt if there is a man in this world who could love a woman more than I love you, now that you have assumed the heaviest burden a woman can assume for the sake of the man she loves. . . . If I had remained with you, I wouldn't be worthy of the child you shall bear me. Our life together would be prosaic, petty and pointless. *This* is not the kind of life I wish for us; not a life so cheap, small and meaningless. . . . I am offering you the sacred human happiness that is bought with suffering and torment. It is with the greatest joy that I feel you were born for this kind of happiness. . . .

But Paula did not feel this at all, and continued to feed her husband's sense of guilt by alternately appearing brave and fearful, stoic and shattered.

"I am so worried about the future I don't know why I imagine I will die," she wrote. "I wouldn't care. But the child . . . it will be without a mother and father." And in another letter she assured her husband: "I will be all right. And if not, I don't care neither [sic] as life is miserable and lonesome."

Ben-Gurion replied: "Last night was the most miserable night I've spent here. I lay awake thinking about you and I couldn't even close my eyes."

Paula apparently felt that jealousy would further disturb his sleep.

One man [she wrote] fell in love with me. He always tries to come up and see me, but last night I told him how much I love you, . . . so he was so disappointed that I think he will not come up to see me anymore. . . . How are you, dear, are you lonesome for me?

Later she would cluck:

Liza Voran was . . . in my house. She was dressed up like a quin [sic]. So I asked her, where does she get so much money. . . . She told me that Wolkowisk an artist keeps her. . . . Then she says that I am a fool. . . . I told her, Liza I am sorry, but please do not come to my house anymore. . . . Darling papa, you ought to love me more than you do. . . .

Love her more?

I wish to fall at your feet and beg for forgiveness [Ben-Gurion wrote]. I want to embrace you and press you to me so tightly that you can feel my heart beating. I wish to cry in your arms and kiss you . . . to show you how much I long for you . . . I loved you even before we were married, though I never told you so. Now, my feeling is more than love. You are sacred to me, the suffering angel who hovers over me.

Paula:

> You are my all *[sic]* life . . . all the rest seems to be dead to me. I never thought I could love so sublimely . . . Dear let me know where I could let you know, when I will give birth if I will be alive.

In trying to compensate with gushing prose for the suffering and insecurity reflected in Paula's letters, Ben-Gurion may even have resorted, if perhaps unconsciously, to the ultimate deception. In one letter he wrote: "I have never felt for anyone else the tender love I feel for you. . . . I am a person who, having loved once, loves forever, with all the fire and strength of his being."

This was perhaps true, but was he thinking of Paula?

After more than a month of camp life in Canada, intoxication had gradually dissipated into boredom, anxiety and finally disillusion. For Ben-Gurion discovered that among the Legionnaires were some "born criminals." Not since he was jailed in Warsaw as a youth had he met such Jewish riffraff. Yet, were not the Legionnaires supposed to be an army of liberators? Were they not to form the core of a force that would revive the Jewish state and set the stage for universal redemption? They should be the cream of Jewish culture. Again he agonized over the reality that some Jews did not qualify as potential redeemers.

On July 10, Ben-Gurion's battalion finally packed its gear and left Windsor for Halifax, where, after a warm greeting by local Zionists sagging under tributes of cold kosher meats, it boarded one of the ships in a waiting convoy. Gliding through smooth waters infested with German submarines, the ship sailed toward England to the rhythm of an army band and, on one occasion, a flurry of cannon-shells aimed at a periscope that had been sighted.

The battalion arrived in Plymouth, England, on July 23, 1918, and Ben-Gurion shortly went on leave in London, where he began to feel that, for all the flags and heroic symbols, military life was shackling his independent nature. After speaking at two meetings arranged by his party, he refused to address a third "as I wanted an evening to myself. After two months of army life it's wonderful to be able to do as you please, with nobody giving orders or commands, and to know that you can go to bed and get up whenever you want, can eat anything you like when you feel like it." A far cry from his euphoric accounts of army life in his first letters from Windsor.

Soon army life would become almost unbearable.

Under a broiling Middle Eastern sun, the tents trembled in the familiar wind that swept through the bleak, glaring white reaches of Tel-el-Kebir, a stretch of sandy Egyptian desert east of Cairo. So close to home, yet Ben-Gurion was Moses again, trapped this time within sight of the real Promised Land. Could he still be Joshua? General Allenby had already captured Jerusalem and was now pushing north and east. "I'm afraid," Ben-Gurion wrote in his diary, "that our battalion will not take part in the conquest of the Land." "Anti-Zionist" generals like Allenby, he was sure, were deliberately keeping the Jewish Legion away, fearing that it might try to forcibly implement the Balfour Declaration.

But Ben-Gurion made the best of this forced encampment. From almost every tent wafted the ancient cadences of Hebrew, as he and Ben-Zvi, who were reunited here, taught their comrades the language of the land they wished to turn into an exemplary state. In any case, the men needed all the military training they could get—not for this war but for the one they might have to fight later.

Ben-Gurion's mood did not improve when he caught a severe case of dysentery. Hospitalized in Cairo, he now found plenty of time to ruminate on his personal problems. He was alarmed that Paula, who would give birth any day, had not written him a word, and a new surge of guilt overwhelmed him.

That same day a nurse handed him a cable and he shakily devoured the news: A girl! His Geula. He wrote Paula:

> My dearest treasure, I cannot tell you in words—in dead written words—what I have felt since receiving your telegram. . . . A few short words; but what a powerful message it was, and how happy it has made me. But this happiness is mixed with sadness. And my dearest wish at the moment is to leap over the oceans separating us and to be with you in the room where you are both lying, the two persons most precious to me, and to embrace you both. . . . But, dear Paula, this is the way it must be. Our suffering won't be in vain. Our first child comes into the world at a tragic and sacred moment, and from this experience a wonderful future will emerge and a bright light will shine over the life of this baby.

Impatiently, Ben-Gurion awaited a letter from Paula. When none came, he wrote again:

> Day after day I wait for word from you, as a thirsty man in the desert longs for a drop of water. As fate would have it, both of us were in the hospital at the same time (I with dysentery). . . . Dear Paula, are you angry with me for not being with you at a time like this? This is torture,

for me and even more for you, I know. But I also know that I have never
felt as close to you as I do now . . . Our souls are so intertwined that I
feel they love like one. . . . What does our baby look like? . . . Did you
have a hard time?

Dear and beloved papa [Paula finally replied], keep yourself clean, as
the disentary [*sic*] comes from uncleanliness. . . . In case you have a
slight cold stay in bed and call a doctor. Don't neglect yourself as we
need you. . . . You are asking me if I had a hard time. Of course dear,
especially after I was so lonesome without you. I was so miserable,
when I saw some other women have their husbands near them, and I
was all alone.

On his release from the hospital, Ben-Gurion felt as if he were
"being let out of jail." Now, at least, he could ease his anxiety
about his family by reverting to his even greater obsession, the
state. Not that he entirely ignored the subject while lying in bed
for about a month. Indeed, he had come to know a man who
would in the future help more than any other to guide him
toward his cherished goal. The man had written an article in a
Zionist periodical that uncannily might have flowed from Ben-
Gurion's own pen.

"When I read it," Ben-Gurion would recall, "I exclaimed—
heavens above! I'm willing to endorse on the dotted line every
word that's written there."

The writer opposed "class struggle" in undeveloped Palestine as unrealistic, arguing that the workers were not a separate
class, but "a part of the nation and . . . responsible for its fate."
Just the kind of pragmatic socialism that appealed to Ben-Gurion. And so, as he tottered out of the hospital, he had one aim in
mind—to join with Berl Katzenelson in a partnership that would
lead to a Jewish state.

When Ben-Gurion returned to Tel-el-Kebir and poked his massive head into the tent, he met the gaze of a soldier with gentle
eyes set deeply under brows as dark and shaggy as his thick
mop of hair and large mustache. Berl Katzenelson, who had
come here with the Palestinian battalion of the Jewish Legion,
had the demeanor—and reputation—of a humble man, unambitious, selfless, wise, a man who could inspire anyone but
threaten no one. Thirty-two years old, the same age as Ben-
Gurion, he was also about the same height. The perfect comrade!

Berl, as almost everyone called Katzenelson, had been a librarian and teacher in Russia before sailing in 1909 to Palestine, where he continued to teach, not in the classroom but in the fields and workers' meeting halls. He was too independent-minded to join either Poalei Zion or Hapoel Hatzair, but led a group of unaffiliated farm workers who, under his guidance, had reaped great political influence as well as a profitable desert harvest.

Squatting on the sandy floor of the tent, Ben-Gurion praised the ideas that Berl had floated in his article, and suggested transforming them into reality. Why shouldn't all the labor groups merge into one great workers' federation? Think of the power such an organization could wield, of the role it could play in building a state. Berl listened intently, but he was skeptical. Theory was one thing, practice another; the parties might not be ready. Some of his own workers would never join with those who had different views. But Ben-Gurion was more impetuous and less analytical. To hesitate, to worry about failure, was to fail in advance. The workers must understand that labor unity was an essential ingredient of the future state—then they would agree. Why not test their mood?

As soon as he and Berl could get passes, they would visit Palestine and dip their toes in its long-stagnant political water.

"At long last, I am going," Ben-Gurion wrote in his diary on November 4, 1918. Hours after receiving a pass he leaped onto a train headed for Palestine. He had no time to lose. The first Poalei Zion conference since prewar days had already opened in Jaffa, and he must get there in time to steer the party toward labor unity. It seemed strange—it was the goal that he had demanded at the first party conference in 1906. However, he had forged into international prominence since then, and now his colleagues would perhaps listen to the man whom Hashomer had once spurned.

Ben-Zvi was at his side, though no reader of Ben-Gurion's diaries would ever know it. As in past letters, he made no mention of Ben-Zvi, this time not because he envied his political stature and academic status, but apparently because he regarded him as a political underling. Ben-Zvi was less brilliant and more ambitious than Berl Katzenelson and never could qualify as Ben-Gurion's alter ego as Berl did. It was time for Ben-Gurion to ease his old comrade gently out of the political limelight.

After two days and several trains—Jaffa! The same Jaffa where Ben-Gurion first landed a dozen years earlier. The same bustling bazaars, exotic smells, lumbering camels. The same world doomed to disappear in the Zionist storm. As he had vowed three years and eight months earlier, when Jamal Pasha threw him out of the country, he was back "with a rifle on his shoulder." And Jamal? He was fleeing through the desert. Ironically Ben-Gurion might at this moment be wearing a Turkish uniform rather than a British one if Jamal had listened to him! Ben-Gurion was worried. Would he miss the Poalei Zion conference? Would vital decisions be made without him?

His exile suddenly dissolved into a mere blur in his life, as irrelevant and forgettable as the two thousand years of his people's exile. . . .

"General excitement," the minutes of the conference would note. "Comrades Ben-Zvi and Ben-Gurion enter. The chairman . . . greets them in the name of the conference as they are applauded by the participants."

Amid the bedlam, the two returning heroes proudly shook hands with their startled, delighted colleagues, who by coincidence had just elected them *in absentia* to the central committee. With the "generals" back, who could stop the army of Zion now?

The debate resumed. Had time really passed between conferences? The same arguments, the same attitudes, the same conflicts. Ben-Gurion wondered whether to bring up the issue of labor harmony now. True, he was a "hero," but his colleagues might oppose him anyway, and he wanted no defeat that could wreck his plan from the start. Berl had been right. Better to wait —and use the prestige of the Jewish Legion to set his plan whirring. If the Legion backed the idea, who would challenge it?

After ten days of plotting the future and exhuming the past, the two Bens bade *shalom* to their comrades and climbed aboard a train for the journey back to Egypt. Ben-Gurion left Palestine in a happy mood, for this time he knew he would be back soon.

"I never dreamed I would have such a marvelous return to *Eretz Yisrael,*" he would write Paula.

Even so, Ben-Gurion had not enjoyed peace of mind since hearing that Paula had given birth to a girl. Not a single word followed until letters mailed weeks earlier began to arrive. "Poor baby," Paula wrote of their daughter, "she came home without her father to welcome her." The child resembled him, and this made Paula cry uncontrollably. And she cried too because she hardly had any money. She didn't care about herself, but she couldn't let the baby starve. Milk cost three dollars a week and chicken soup too was expensive. Ben-Gurion must come home or bring his family to Palestine as soon as possible.

When mother and baby both fell ill in April 1919, Paula's pen quivered: "In case anything will happen to me come and take baby. I am all alone [and there is] nobody to give me a cup of water. . . . Be well and happy." In another letter she added: "If anything happens to me or Geula it will be your fault, as I am very weak and tired." She hoped that she would recover and Geula wouldn't be left alone. Meanwhile, she was teaching the baby to "drink from the bottle by herself" so she would learn to be independent in case her mother died. . . . "Probably we are not as dear as Palestine."

Still willingly accepting guilt, Ben-Gurion wrote Paula: "When I read what you are going through and how lonely and helpless you are, I felt that a sharp knife had been plunged into a hidden wound." As for their reunion, the time had "not come yet, but it is no longer distant." Either she and Geula would come to Palestine or he would continue on to New York when he had to visit Europe. "Dear Paula, I know what you must be enduring in your loneliness, and what a heavy burden you are bearing. But you are not entirely alone; you are together with the child—while I am all alone, far from the two people in the world who are closest and dearest to me."

Apparently noting that his degree of passion was proportionate to the fright she could arouse in him, Paula persisted: Geula was ill and if anything happened to her she would kill herself.

Despite his alarm and sleeplessness, Ben-Gurion would not let Paula's letters disrupt his mission. He strode into Katzenelson's tent, plopped down on the sand, and compared notes with Berl, who had also just returned from Palestine. His own people, Ben-Gurion was sure, would consider meshing with other labor groups. But what about Berl's? Katzenelson wasn't so sure. They agreed on their next step: Win the backing of the Jewish Legion. It reflected a cross section of Hebrew labor and would be a "laboratory for labor unity."

On November 26, 1918, the Legionnaires gathered in the camp library to hear Ben-Gurion and Katzenelson repeat their plea for unity. Did they want a state—a workers' state? Did they want to overcome cheap Arab labor? Then how could they refuse? The soldiers listened, argued—and agreed that they couldn't refuse. The two speakers were euphoric. Would their comrades in *Eretz Yisrael* deny the will of the glorious Jewish Legion?

Ben-Gurion received a coveted gift on his first wedding anniversary, December 5, 1918: assignment to Palestine. He and his fellow Legionnaires piled into trains and sped to Camp Sarafand, near Jaffa, where they set up bivouac in a driving rain. Ben-Gurion wasted no time. In the shadows of dawn he sneaked out of camp, feeling like a fugitive as he quietly sloshed through the mud past unsuspecting British guards. He then rushed around buttonholing political leaders. Follow the Legion, he pleaded. Unite!

Finally, on December 11, after a week of feverish campaigning, Ben-Gurion returned, exhausted and bedraggled, and was severely punished for going AWOL. He sheepishly wrote Paula: "I'm a private now, and not a corporal, because I went to Jaffa without a pass and was court-martialed."

On December 23, Ben-Gurion was transferred back to Egypt, but *Yishuv* leaders used their weight with British officials to get him frequent passes to Palestine to attend meetings. He was thus able to continue his crusade. However, each time his powerful friends requested a pass for him, the battalion major became more resentful, and he made sure that on his return Ben-Gurion would be assigned to midnight-guard or kitchen-police duty.

Still, Ben-Gurion gladly inhaled the stench of rotten eggs and spoiled fish for the sake of Zionism. On his leaves he not only pursued his campaign for labor unity but badgered his fellow Legionnaires to demobilize in Palestine and stay there. What pioneers they would make! But the British laid down an iron rule: Any discharged soldier who stayed in Palestine had to have a certificate from the Zionist Commission, which represented the W.Z.O. in Palestine, confirming that a job was waiting for him. The trouble was, there were few jobs waiting for anyone.

Ben-Gurion collared David Eder, the British chairman of the Zionist Commission, himself a Jew. Create jobs! Ben-Gurion demanded. Or issue false certificates!

Eder was contemptuous. What was Ben-Gurion doing anyway, steeped in Jewish politics while wearing a British uniform? Why didn't he first ask for a discharge of his own?

Ben-Gurion fumed. How could he live without his soldier's pay? How could he afford to bring over his family?

When more than fifty Legionnaires were court-martialed for refusing to leave Palestine, Eder scornfully shrugged off Ben-Gurion's call for a W.Z.O. protest. The fifty Legionnaires, Eder charged at a meeting of Jewish leaders, were bad soldiers anyway. Did Ben-Gurion want their misbehavior to spark anti-Semitism in the British army?

Lies! shouted Ben-Gurion, jumping to his feet. He threatened to sue Eder for slandering his brave soldiers.

The other Jewish leaders were shocked. Sue the W.Z.O. representative? Who was Ben-Gurion, after all? Just a small-time politician. In the end Ben-Gurion backed off, growling and snapping. The W.Z.O., he wrote, would be covered with "the shameful stain of the mass departure of the thousands of Legionnaires," whose vanishing influence meant a setback for labor unity, the state—and him. But if Ben-Gurion lost this round, he had at least served notice: He would fight the powerful bourgeois Zionist establishment until, at the head of his workers' army, he would wrench the Zionist movement from its grasp. And then he would take on the British—if they dared to renege on Lord Balfour's promise.

As he continued to shuttle between Egypt and Palestine, Ben-Gurion discovered that Rachel Beit-Halachmi had returned from Poland (she had been stranded in Russia during the war), and he stayed in her house, presumably with her husband and children. He avidly read letters that she had brought from his sister Zippora, the first word from his family since the war began. Zippora had married and was happy. So was Ben-Gurion as he lingered with Rachel; his own marriage apparently had not loosened his emotional bond with her.

But as usual, he did not let personal affairs interrupt his mission. After numerous meetings, debates and arguments, he finally managed to persuade his own party to merge with the other labor groups. No amount of talk, however, could move Hapoel Hatzair. Should a pedigreed dog mate with a mongrel? it asked. This was one of the most painful setbacks of Ben-Gurion's career. A few political chauvinists would sabotage his sacred campaign to set up a powerful Hebrew labor movement that could squeeze Arab workers out of the Jewish economy and spawn the Jewish state needed to save millions of Jews from further misery and possibly death.

But Ben-Gurion would not surrender. Out of the debris he

and Berl Katzenelson salvaged at least a partial victory. In late February 1919 their own two organizations met in a banner-strewn hall and, to the wild cheering of waiters and welders, farmers and fishermen, meshed into a single party called Ahdut HaAvodah (Union of Labor). Not untypically, Ben-Gurion crowed about *his* triumph, ignoring the important roles of Katzenelson and Ben-Zvi.

"Many people, including some in my own faction, were against the union," he wrote Paula, "and I had to persuade them. . . . I was the chairman, and . . . I had to maintain control. . . . I wish you had been there to see it."

And clearly, Ben-Gurion had been the hammer that finally nailed down the merger. Now he had the cornerstone of his Jewish state, and the chanting, clapping workers were excited. The state, they dramatically proclaimed, would rise again. Had not the British promised that it would?

Actually they had not. The Balfour Declaration called vaguely for a Jewish "national home," which did not necessarily mean an independent Jewish state. But why not interpret British promises as one wished? The Arabs did. After all, the British had also pledged to hand over former Turkish lands in the Middle East to *them.* And so the scene was set for a momentous clash of destinies. But the Arabs at this time were even more fragmented politically and ideologically than the Jews, and though a great Arab nationalist storm was gathering, many Arabs still did not feel buffeted by Zionist winds. Indeed the Palestinian Bedouin of northern Galilee were far more anxious about the European occupiers who would "temporarily" rule their lands.

Although the League of Nations formed after World War I would place Palestine under a British mandate and Lebanon and Syria under a French one, these Bedouin distrusted the French and feared that they would try to swallow up the northern Galilee bordering on Lebanon. So they went on a rampage against French troops in this zone, and two isolated Jewish settlements, Kfar Gileadi and Tel Hai, found themselves in the middle of the battlefield. The Bedouin mistakenly believed that a French officer was holding Tel Hai, though in fact the settlement leader was Josef Trumpeldor, who had led the Jewish Mule Corps that had fought with the British against Turkey. The Arabs thus stormed Tel Hai in February 1920, killing Trumpeldor and six other defenders, and forcing the Jews to evacuate both settlements.

No one was more impressed by the massacre than a twenty-

seven-year-old Arab leader in Jerusalem, Haj Amin el-Husseini,
a man of striking appearance with his reddish beard and shrewd
blue eyes. Haj Amin was a fierce Arab nationalist who had
vowed to "throw the Jews into the sea" before they grew strong
enough to take over Palestine. The British, he noted, hadn't
challenged the Arab sword, and now the way seemed clear. He
would keep up the momentum of murder in the very heart of
Zionism—Jerusalem. Passover would be a suitable time. It co-
incided with an Arab religious holiday, and a procession of worshipers could easily be turned into a bloodthirsty mob,
especially if they thought the Jews planned to seize the Moslem
Holy Places.

Early on the morning of Passover 1920, Ben-Gurion and Ben-
Zvi entered a stone house just outside the Arab Old City in
Jerusalem and were embraced by Rachel Yanait. She and Ben-
Zvi, newly married, lived here. The three old comrades sat
down and began "munching on matzos and sipping tea and
making ambitious plans," when suddenly they heard through
the windows the ominous rumble of people stampeding in the
street. Rachel's father, who had been out shopping, rushed in
"looking pale" and cried with "trembling lips," "People say
they're beating up Jews in the Old City!" The Arabs had attacked the Jewish quarter.

Yanait would later recount: "One cannot describe Ben-Gurion's reaction. How he jumped up . . . 'A pogrom in Jerusalem?
Beat up Jews in Jerusalem? Where are we?' "

Yanait, living in Jerusalem, was less surprised. Since Tel Hai
she had chilled to the Arab street cries: *"Itbah il Yahud!"*
("Massacre the Jews"); *"Yahud klabna!"* ("The Jews are our
dogs"); *"Al dola ma'ana!"* ("The government is with us"). One
day she confronted a member of the Zionist Commission and
demanded that the Jews form an underground army immediately from Hashomer veterans, former Legionnaires and other
young people. The man agreed and put Vladimir Jabotinsky,
founder of the Jewish Legion, in command. And thus was born
the Hagana, which almost thirty years later would burgeon into
the army of Israel.

But members of this new fighting force were too busy protecting the Jewish New City to adequately defend the Jewish quarter in the Arab Old City. Nor could they enter the Old City
anyway, since British troops had sealed off the area while doing
nothing to save the Jews trapped inside. The Bens were "pale,
furious, enraged."

They ran out the door and leaped down the stairs, determined to get into the Old City somehow and defend the beleaguered Jews single-handedly if necessary. Yanait quickly dressed in her mother's most elegant dress and a ribbon-decorated hat and, with pistol in purse, soon followed, entering the Old City disguised as an "English lady." She ran to the Jewish quarter prepared to shoot Arab rioters, and there, amid "feathers flying in the air, merchandise and property scattered" in the street, she glimpsed two figures—the Bens—carrying a wounded man on a stretcher. They were all too late; the killing had ended.

But the trauma had not. Back in the Ben-Zvis' house, the three sat sullenly over their half-eaten matzos and cold tea. "I've never seen Ben-Gurion so shocked," Yanait would recall. " 'A pogrom in Jerusalem!' he repeated." Was it possible?

But Ben-Gurion had little time to waste grieving. Especially after the British arrested twenty Hagana men, including Jabotinsky, and sentenced them to several years of forced labor for illegal possession of arms "with the evil intent of bringing about rapine, pillage, devastation of country, homicide, etc." As if the Jews had started the riots!

Neither the arrests nor the Jewish casualties—eight dead and more than two hundred wounded—would frighten the Jews, Ben-Gurion felt, and they might even serve the cause. Now, perhaps, the Jews would heed his call for unity to save both the national home promised by Balfour and those who lived in it.

And they did. Only a few days after the arrests that April, Jews streamed to the polls to choose an Elected Assembly, the first Jewish "parliament." Ben-Gurion had painstakingly organized the election in the face of bitter resistance from many groups, including rightist landowners who feared that he wanted to trick them out of their land, and the ultrareligious, who feared that even an unofficial parliament might lead to a Jewish state before the messiah came or, almost as shocking, encourage women to leave home and plunge into politics.

Would more than a handful of voters turn out? And would they vote for labor? Ben-Gurion anguished over these questions. But on election day, to his joy, 77 percent of the Jews jammed the polling stations to drop slips of paper into a ballot box and give the combined labor forces one-third of the vote, making it the largest faction in the assembly.

The British forbade the "parliament" to convene, but no matter. For the first time almost the whole *Yishuv* had thunderously acknowledged its ultimate aim: a Jewish state.

"Decide about your future," Paula wrote from New York. "You did your share for your ideals. Now consider your family, if not me, so your daughter."

But when Ben-Gurion promised to bring them to Palestine "as soon as possible," Paula was reluctant. Let him come to New York for a while. She was worried about fresh milk and eggs for the baby.

She needn't worry, replied Ben-Gurion. "You shall have so many eggs and so much milk for her that you'll be able to bathe her in milk. . . . Geula will have everything here that she has in Brooklyn and the Bronx, at least until she's ready to attend the Metropolitan Opera." He could not come to New York for he was still in the army and, anyway, his party needed him. "I am living in the expectation of your arrival," he wrote. "This is my personal messianic dream."

Paula was furious, but she agreed to come, and now demanded to leave immediately. "I cannot lead a life like I lead now," she lamented. And once more she cried that she would like to kill herself.

In desperation Ben-Gurion sought ways to bring his wife and child to Palestine while they were still alive. He tried, in vain, to send them with a Hadassah medical mission—no married nurses. Then, claiming that Paula was a "repatriated refugee" from Palestine, he sought financial and political help from Zionist colleagues in London and New York, and they, in turn, pressed the British War Office. The British finally relented, and in November 1919, after a six-week voyage by ship and train via London and Trieste, Paula and the baby landed in Jaffa. Ben-Gurion, who had been given a week's leave from the army—from which he would shortly be discharged—was overjoyed to see them, kissing and embracing his ecstatic wife and holding the child in his arms with all the love and gentleness he usually reserved for a favorite book.

Ben-Gurion would always be grateful to Paula for coming with their baby to this primitive land, sacrificing all the conveniences of American life just to be with him, even though Zionism meant little to her. But he would apparently never again write her letters of passion when separated from her; he no longer needed to. And, although he may still have longed to lavish his passion on Rachel, he was no longer able to. So, with his mind purged of guilt and his heart drained of hope, he could now concentrate on his mission.

CHAPTER FIVE

With the voice together shall they sing

ISAIAH 52:8

E VEN in the small dingy room he shared with his family, Ben-Gurion, in the spring of 1920, felt a peace of mind he had seldom enjoyed in past years. As he helped Paula wash the dishes in a tin basin, an activity he found relaxing, he could reflect happily on the way his mission was going. The *Yishuv* had taken great political strides toward a state, with labor leading the march. A British High Commissioner instead of the present military governor would soon be presiding in Jerusalem, presumably to carry out the Balfour Declaration. And Paula and the baby were now at his side. But though he was grateful to Paula for her sacrifices, he wished she wouldn't *kvetch* (complain) so much. So there was no electricity. So the plumbing was bad. Didn't he warn her about pioneer life?

Meanwhile, Ben-Gurion plunged into this life with renewed energy. Since Hapoel Hatzair had turned its back on Ahdut HaAvodah, he would gather the workers of both parties in a nonpolitical labor federation. Such an organization might not be able to govern *Eretz Yisrael,* but it could build factories and settlements in the wilderness, furnishing the money as well as the muscle. It would be a labor enterprise with tentacles curling around every pillar of the economy. A state would evolve not from the fine talk of the diplomat but from the sweat and ingenuity of the worker.

Before Ben-Gurion could bring this proletarian monster to life, however, his party decided to send him to London, where he would take charge of the Poalei Zion World Federation—now a faction of the Ahdut HaAvodah Party—and press the British politicians to swiftly fulfill Balfour's promise of a national home (the time was not yet ripe to use the more explosive word "state"). The Zionist leaders based in London had the ear of the Conservative government, and now Ben-Gurion would woo the Labour Party, though it already championed Zionism and shared the social ideals of Ahdut HaAvodah.

Ben-Gurion was chagrined that he would have to let others create his labor monolith, but he was also content. With all the modern conveniences in London, perhaps Paula would *kvetch* less. He could not leave her behind. After having left her "in such difficult circumstances during the war," he wrote his father, "I have no right to abandon her here even for half a year" —certainly not when she was pregnant again. Paula was euphoric. London! At last a tile bathtub and a flush toilet.

For Ben-Gurion, London's bathroom fixtures held no more joy than its Victorian buildings, its broad traffic-crammed streets or even its magnificent museums.

"In London," he wrote Rachel Yanait after arriving in June 1920, "you always live in a cold and monotonous fog."

And somehow poverty was more humiliating here than in *Eretz Yisrael,* where almost everyone was poor. He stayed with his family in a cheap hotel, ate the cheapest food in Lyon's restaurant, and got off the bus a station before his stop in order to save a few pennies. And though he haunted the bookshops, he could buy only a fraction of the books he wanted. In the small, smoky East End Poalei Zion office, crowded with gossiping demobilized Jewish Legionnaires, he sat silently in a corner grinding out letters, reports, articles, press releases, unnoticed and known mainly by his Yiddish nickname *der grosse Schweiger*—"the big silent one." "Ben-Gurion" was not an illustrious name amid the cosmopolitan Zionists of London. He was just a provincial, rather shabby trade-union leader from *Eretz Yisrael* who sometimes met with his British Labourite brethren but who could not be imagined sipping sherry in Lloyd George's drawing room.

Ben-Gurion was thus happy to surge back into the limelight at the first conference of the World Zionist Organization since 1913, held in Albert Hall about a month after he arrived. Even

in the limelight, however, he remained in the shade, for many
of the world's giant Zionists were sitting in the crowded hall.
Among them was a tall slim man with a craggy, Lenin-like face
dominated by a black mustache and goatee and bushy-browed
dark eyes that alternately mirrored deep melancholy and twinkling humor—Chaim Weizmann, who would be elected president of the W.Z.O. at this meeting. Though Ben-Gurion
respected Weizmann, he felt that the man did not understand
the problems in Palestine or how to achieve a Jewish state. But
it was pride, not politics, that often made him refuse to be seen
in Weizmann's company. Why stress his own shortness by
standing next to his towering foe? It was difficult enough standing in Weizmann's intellectual and political shadow.

Born near Pinsk, Russia, in 1874, Weizmann had first helped
to shape the Zionist movement while the youthful Ben-Gurion
was still dreaming of redemption as he lay on the banks of the
Plonka River. The elder man helped to turn the tide against
Herzl's "Uganda" proposal, then went to Britain and used his
charm, elegance and wit to win his way into the confidence of
its leading statesmen. They found him comfortably compatible,
for he was a person of breeding who had studied in Germany
and Switzerland and was a world-renowned chemist. Good food
and fine wine always graced his table, while he entertained in
lavish style largely with the money he earned from his scientific
patents. Nothing impressed his British friends more than his
discovery of a formula during World War I for the manufacture
of synthetic acetone, which was needed to make ammunition. It
was said that the Balfour Declaration was his reward.

While Weizmann had never latched onto any political party
or ideology, he backed the pioneering struggle of the socialist
parties, as long as it didn't hinder his diplomatic moves. The
neat white suit he incongruously wore when he waded through
the mud or sand of the primitive settlements perhaps reflected
his ultimate faith in diplomacy. After all, didn't he wrest the
promise of a national home from the British? Eventually he
would persuade them to meet their pledge, though he wasn't
sure whether such a home would ever really evolve into a state.
His central tactic was to accept "the virtues of the [British] Empire and [assume] that one of the tasks of the Jewish nation
would be to protect Britain's Imperial interests on the Suez
Canal." Move slowly, he warned, and don't ruffle the British,
who were really good honest chaps.

Weizmann's grandiose style and gradualist philosophy vexed
the impetuous, earthy Ben-Gurion. One couldn't buy a state

with good food and wine or with "decadent" Yiddish humor. Only manual labor, the "religion of toil," could create the conditions for a state. Hungry workers were infinitely more important to the cause than well-fed luxury-loving diplomats, even well-intentioned ones. And the rate of immigration should be unlimited, whatever Britain said. Who cared about "absorptive capacity"? Let the Jews live for a while on *pita* and olives, as he had done; at least they would be free in their own land. What was necessary now was money—rivers of capital for settlements, industries, roads.

Weizmann and other Zionist leaders, their dress impeccable, their manner genteel, stepped to the rostrum in Albert Hall and eloquently lamented the lack of funds to spark immigration and develop *Eretz Yisrael*. They must proceed with patience. His voice calm, his manner stately in the British tradition, Weizmann loosed a muffled barrage. The *Yishuv*, he charged, was excitable and impulsive, entirely unreasonable; the political parties were thinking only of themselves. Ben-Gurion silently boiled.

When his turn finally came, he stood up, his inexpensive, ill-fitting suit a symbol of contempt, and heaped scorn upon Weizmann and his fellows. Proceed with patience—and snuff out the zeal of the pioneers? Absurd! If the workers of *Eretz Yisrael* could make enormous sacrifices, couldn't the W.Z.O. at least give them the means to succeed? On the other hand, why should private Jewish farmers who hired *Arab* workers get Zionist aid?

"Because you are useless!"

This cry shook Ben-Gurion. His magnificent pioneers—useless? Unless the "slanderer" retracted his words, Ben-Gurion snarled, "we'll throw him out of the hall!" And the man apologized.

But Weizmann, vain and imperious, would apologize for nothing. He again attacked the Palestine delegates with blistering sarcasm. And after a great burst of applause, the Diaspora delegates, though moved by Ben-Gurion's passionate appeal to Zionist nationalism, voted against his "unrealistic" views. A lot of *chutzpah* for a provincial farmer! Even little Geula, sitting in her mother's lap, could not help him with her cries, "Papa, papa!"

"Who is that child?" the presiding officer demanded.

And he ordered her out of the hall in a ludicrous parody of the bitter, often irrational conflict that would escalate during the next three decades into a monumental struggle for power between two immovable pillars of Zionism.

In August 1920, Ben-Gurion decided that he had to attend the Poalei Zion World Federation conference in Vienna to keep it from splitting apart. As he had done once before—when he joined the Jewish Legion during World War I—he was leaving Paula behind shortly before she was to give birth. But this time, he assured her, he would return before the event. Extremists in Poalei Zion were eager to join the Communist Third International and cut links with the "bourgeois" W.Z.O. He had to stop them; a split in Poalei Zion might doom Ahdut HaAvodah and ruin his whole plan for creating a state. Surely Paula could understand.

Whether she did or not, Ben-Gurion rushed off to Vienna, where he found himself mired in the mud of intraparty strife. Despite his fervent plea that Zionism, not socialism, must be the party's central goal, the majority demanded amid pandemonium that the Poalei Zion join the Comintern immediately. Ben-Gurion and his comrades rose and angrily stalked out. The feared split had materialized. But Ben-Gurion now wondered if it was not for the best. After all, the moderates in Poalei Zion would no longer have to compromise with the extremists. Almost everyone now left in that party, as well as in the umbrella Ahdut HaAvodah, was a real Zionist.

Ben-Gurion felt drained from the ordeal, and his old sense of guilt about leaving Paula pricked his conscience again. Nor did nagging thoughts of his family in Poland boost his spirits. He had written to his father after three years of war-imposed silence and bragged about his recent successes and new life. What a book he had written! An English critic had called it "the most complete and authoritative work on *Eretz Yisrael* in print today in any European language." Having lavished praise on himself, Ben-Gurion focused on Paula. She had shown such love and courage when he went off to war leaving her pregnant and alone. And as for Geula, even his "most objective friends" agreed that "there did not exist a child more beautiful or healthy looking."

Avigdor wrote back: Would his son please help him come to Palestine? The postwar anti-Semitic Polish government now heading an independent Poland refused to let him represent clients before the courts, leaving him almost without income. But Ben-Gurion, already distracted from his mission by his immediate family, cautiously replied: "This question depends largely on my future. I definitely do not yet know how I will manage."

Apparently troubled that he had written such a cold reply, Ben-Gurion tried to soothe his father's feelings in a letter inviting him to Vienna. He offered to pay all his father's expenses, and even to send him a permanent monthly allowance. But his invitation was limited. He did not invite "the aunt," his father's second wife, whom he still resented.

Before Avigdor could reply, a telegram arrived from Paula: Come home quickly! He rushed back to London just in time to take Paula to the hospital, where she gave birth to a boy on September 28, 1920. Ben-Gurion was joyous on seeing the child and, as his own parents had when he was a child, he marveled at the size of his son's head. "I can't say anything yet about his intelligence," he wrote his father, "but his skull is larger than average and holds promise."

Avigdor had asked that a boy be named after Ben-Gurion's grandfather, but the new parent refused. He preferred to name his son after the prophet Amos, who had championed the poor and the oppressed, promised the Israelites that they would return to their land, and assured all other peoples that God loved them too. Rather callously, Ben-Gurion wrote his father: "Excuse me for not acceding to your request . . . but your suggestion conflicted with my own idea."

Certainly he had loved his grandfather, but whose memory, after all, more aptly symbolized the spirit of the Jewish state—his grandfather's or that of the prophet Amos?

With Paula recovering from a difficult childbirth, Ben-Gurion had to play nursemaid to his two children, a role he humbly accepted. Visitors were astonished to find him holding Geula in his arms or rushing to the cradle with a bottle for Amos. "I can't leave the house," he wrote Avigdor, "and I have learned what raising children means." According to one visitor, Ben-Gurion "was very modest at that time." It was a period of "weakness," perhaps intended to compensate for his untimely departure for Vienna, a temporary domestication that would seldom be duplicated in the future.

Meanwhile, Avigdor wrote that he was unhappy that his son would not help him come to Palestine, and Ben-Gurion replied: "I am extremely sorry that you think I am to blame," but he was terribly busy. Since he was now back in London, however, his father would be welcome and "[Paula] especially insists that you come here with the aunt." The family had moved into a three-room apartment, the son said, and a room was being reserved for the couple. But then, suddenly, Ben-Gurion and Paula had a change of heart and switched to a small two-room apartment. Would he kindly come alone, Ben-Gurion now wrote Avigdor. There was no room for two guests, nor could he afford to keep more than one. Avigdor did not come.

In March 1921, Ben-Gurion would have to leave London, for his budget had almost run out and he hardly had enough money to pay office expenses. The British Zionists did not contribute very generously to the cause anyway. Ben-Gurion even had to solicit alms from James Rothschild of the philanthropic family, though, as a good socialist, he had always opposed asking the rich in the Diaspora to save the poor in Palestine. His own savings were dwindling fast, partly because he had spent two thousand dollars on books, and he barely had money left to buy milk for the children. He was also in poor health, having almost died from blood poisoning. These problems merged into an even bleaker portrait of London than he had drawn when he first arrived.

"It is so cold, empty, freezing and boring here," he wrote the Ben-Zvis in January 1921. "And there is nothing to nourish the soul."

So one day in March 1921, the Ben-Gurions crossed the English Channel, crowded into a dirty French railway cabin that smelled of garlic and echoed with the cackle of chickens carried by unwashed peasants, and arrived in Vienna in tattered misery. Ben-Gurion went to work in his party office there, but Paula, after a short impoverished stay in a tiny cold-water hotel room, gratefully accepted an invitation from Avigdor to visit Plonsk with the children until her husband could join them. Even life with Avigdor, her chief rival for Ben-Gurion's affection, would be more bearable than life in a Vienna "slum."

White-haired, white-bearded and still distinguished in dress and demeanor, Avigdor greeted Paula, Geula and Amos with great warmth, feeling that he knew them intimately from the descriptive letters of his son. But he would soon realize that he knew very little about Paula. Hardly had she entered the guest room when she gasped in horror: How could the children live in a room so damp and cold? She looked at the water in the pitcher. It was "muddy"! She had barely unpacked when both children fell ill. Thunder rumbled. Turn the oven on full force! Find some pure water! Where was the maid?

Relations between Paula and her in-laws steadily declined,

reaching a critical stage when Ben-Gurion finally arrived in July 1921, after almost four months in Vienna. So many years had passed, and now father and son were at last reunited—only to be ripped from each other's embrace by the force of the storm. Ben-Gurion, the reputed mediator, listened quietly to the near-hysterical complaints of father and wife, and the house was soon heated and the water less murky. But the bickering continued.

Not only was Ben-Gurion disturbed by the family friction, but he was depressed by bittersweet memories of the past, and he could hardly wait to return to *Eretz Yisrael*. He devoured the news from home. To his surprise, the first British High Commissioner in Palestine had turned out to be a Jew—Sir Herbert Samuel. And the first thing he did was to lift curbs on Jewish immigration. A Jewish state, it seemed, was now inevitable.

Then, in December 1921, more good news. Ben-Gurion's teen-age vision of a great state-building labor army crystallized when most Jewish workers joined hands in a General Federation of Hebrew Workers in *Eretz Yisrael*, known as the Histadrut. Ironically, Ben-Gurion, who had largely laid its foundation, had been out of Palestine when it was founded. And now he still was—at a time when decisions that could shape the fate of Palestine were being made.

One decision had been made shortly before Ben-Gurion reached Plonsk. He tore open a telegram and digested the news with rising fury. On May Day Communist and moderate members of Poalei Zion had come to blows in Jaffa in a violent manifestation of the struggle that had split the party at the August 1920 Vienna conference. Rumors then spread that Jews had attacked Arabs, and Arab gangs went wild, beating and stabbing to death fifty Jews and wounding many others. The High Commissioner reacted strongly but, to the bewilderment of the *Yishuv, against* the Jews; Jewish immigration must be halted, he ordered—just what the attackers wanted!

Sir Herbert, it seemed, wanted to "prove" he was a fair man, despite his Jewish background. Although the previously reigning British military government had found Haj Amin el-Husseini guilty of inciting the 1920 Arab massacre in Jerusalem and forced him to flee the country, the High Commissioner curried favor with the Arabs by pardoning him. Suddenly Haj Amin reappeared, carried on the shoulders of a worshipful Arab crowd. And Sir Herbert named Haj Amin the new mufti, or Moslem religious leader, of Jerusalem.

Ben-Gurion was now more impatient than ever. He had to return home, he cabled his comrades, before the mufti and his

mobs could further sabotage the Balfour Declaration. Paula and
Avigdor could barely hide their joy at the prospect of parting,
but to their mutual astonishment Ben-Gurion insisted that Paula
and the children stay in Plonsk. He would send for them, and
Avigdor and "the aunt" could follow later. Nothing could
change Ben-Gurion's mind. If he was to help save the state at
this critical point he could not be burdened with daily personal
problems. His father and his wife must somehow learn to live
with each other. Ben-Gurion borrowed some money for Paula,
boarded a train, waved goodbye to his loved ones and, with the
controlled compassion of a cockfight promoter, left them to fight
it out.

In late 1921, fifteen years after brawny, boisterous Arabs had
first thrust him onto the pier of the Promised Land, Ben-Gurion
stepped ashore once more, determined to finally redeem the
promise. From Plonsk he had returned to Vienna, where he
engaged in Zionist work for several months while waiting for a
ship that would take him from Trieste to Palestine. But now he
was back, and he had the tool he needed for redemption: the
Histadrut. Here was the labor army that he felt had really been
born in Plonsk when he had called the seamstresses and bath
attendants out on strike, the army that would create a new economy, a new culture, a new Jew, a new state.

The problem was that the Histadrut was like a mother to almost all the workers' groups, with all of them yelling "mama"
and pulling her apron strings at once. So Ben-Gurion decided
that his party, Ahdut HaAvodah, must control the strings. But
there was also strife within the party, even though most extremists had split off at the Vienna conference. The Histadrut should
be an end in itself, some members cried, a collection of socialist
trade unions seeking fatter paychecks and greater medical benefits while preaching class struggle. It must not be corrupted
into a political tool.

Nonsense! replied Ben-Gurion. Histadrut was not an end but
a *means* to an end—a Jewish state. Socialism was important,
yes, but precisely as a political tool; it would build the state.
The party, he demanded, must become a "labor army" under
military discipline, a force that would gradually turn the whole
Yishuv into one giant Soviet-style commune, or kibbutz, the
pioneer collective settlement that had taken root in the countryside. Without the Soviet terror, of course.

Ben-Gurion's comrades both on the left and on the right

shouted him down, and so he resigned from the party's central committee and tramped away. But as he had done at Sejera many years before, he kept one ear cocked waiting for the call. When it didn't come, he returned to his party anyway. All right, no commune!

The important thing to Ben-Gurion was that he had the Histadrut. With his peerless pragmatism, hypnotic intensity and sheer drive, he convinced his colleagues that, whatever their differences, they needed him. And they chose him to be one of the three secretaries of the labor federation. He soon dominated it alone.

At this time only about eight thousand workers, an eighth of the *Yishuv*, belonged to the Histadrut. But membership spurted as the Third Aliya, which began after World War I, gradually flooded Palestine. Encouraged by the Balfour Declaration, about thirty-five thousand Jews flowed in, especially from Russia, where troops and peasant mobs attacked Jews in the worst pogroms to date amid the anarchy of the Russian Revolution. Ben-Gurion was blindly optimistic. The Histadrut would lead a workers' society as a pioneer "work-creating" force with its own industries, companies, cooperatives, mines, banks and a socialized medical system that would shortly serve nearly 80 percent of the Jews. It would bring to life isolated stretches of wasteland where no private profit-seeking firm would think of venturing. Nor would the Histadrut simply exercise the power of the pioneer. It controlled an armed force, or at least the embryo of one —the Hagana, which was born during the 1920 Jerusalem riots.

In February 1922 Ben-Gurion decided that since the Histadrut was to be the hub of his state, it would move its headquarters from Tel Aviv to Jerusalem, the traditional capital of Zion. The actual transfer symbolized the poverty and amateurism plaguing the infant labor federation at this time, with Ben-Gurion himself helping to push the sluggish truck loaded with furniture and files up the hilly road. And his inauspicious arrival did not signal greater prosperity. Moving into a small room with a colleague, Ben-Gurion found his living standards plummeting to the depths of a decade earlier when he first arrived in Jerusalem. Once more he slept on boards resting on two oil cans—half the time; since there was only one bed, he and his companion took turns sleeping on the floor.

So small was Ben-Gurion's salary that he had to borrow from the Histadrut treasury or from friends, and his debts kept mounting. Yet, he deliberately lowered his pay, feeling that all members of the federation should get the same, and he refused even to accept bonuses as others did. Nor was he careless with his expense account, recording even his most trivial expenditures.

One problem was that Ben-Gurion compulsively spent much of what he did earn—or borrow—on books. He sent another large chunk of his income to Plonsk each month to cover the living costs of Paula, his children and his father. How grateful he was that he had not brought his family to Palestine with him. This was a period of sacrifice, and nothing could stand in the way of the Histadrut taking root. How could he concentrate on his work, on his books, the key to an exemplary state, amid the whimpers of his offspring and the wails of his wife?

When Ben-Gurion was lonely, he often sought Rachel's company. Rachel and her husband had lost everything in Jaffa during the 1921 riots there, and Ben-Gurion now visited her in their new home in Givatayim, outside Tel Aviv, though he still resented her husband, who was sometimes present. He spoke to her about politics, but also about his children. Rachel was moved, he happily noted, when he told her that Geula had eyes like hers.

Still, Paula was on Ben-Gurion's mind and he tried to ease her pain—and his own recurring sense of guilt—by taking her side in her dispute with his father.

> In vain did I seek a way to bring you closer to each other [Ben-Gurion wrote Avigdor]. You were unable to penetrate into her soul and feel her strangeness in these unusual surroundings . . . You did not imagine that Paula's demands were . . . required, just like air for breathing.

Ben-Gurion was hard on Paula too. Didn't she realize there was a gap in education and manners "between the city world and the little Polish town?" Nevertheless, he clearly implied that Avigdor was more at fault.

Paula aggravated the friction with Avigdor when she packed her things and hustled off with the children to live in the country with Ben-Gurion's relatives, as her husband had done in the summer when he himself was a child. She fled because Amos had been ill and needed clean air, she wrote her husband.

Please return to Plonsk for Father's sake, Ben-Gurion pleaded.

Reluctantly Paula complied, but she soon went back to the village and asked Ben-Gurion to rush money for rent and a servant.

No, he responded, she must go back again to Plonsk, and as a concession, he asked his father "to clean her room well and hire a maid for her."

Once more Paula bundled her children back, but she would not relent. "Amos looks . . . half his size," she reported. She herself had "fainting spells and pain in my heart. . . . Life is unbearable."

It grew even harder. Ben-Gurion's brother Avraham, who with his wife, Tauba, and their three children had taken refuge in Russia during the war years, now returned with his family and moved in with Avigdor. Thus, thirteen people, including six children, stumbled over one another, and echoes of family strife resounded throughout Plonsk. Finally sheer chaos broke out when Michael's wife, unable to stand the tumult, fled into the night. "They all say she became a prostitute," Paula chirped.

She then charged that Avraham and Tauba "took" a suit Ben-Gurion had left behind, and implied that they stole her gold pin. And yet Avigdor had the *chutzpah* to ask Ben-Gurion for money so their daughter Sheindel could complete her schooling!

"I beg you, papa," Paula wrote, "don't send any money to Avraham. . . . He has gold and silver and more than we have. . . . If you have any respect for me and the children don't send them anything."

Nor should he help anyone except his father to come to Palestine. "I will not have them in my house one day." Yet Paula felt kindly toward "the aunt," who despite earlier disputes now treated her well. Why not send her "one pound and I will buy her something?" After all, "the aunt" was not a threat; Ben-Gurion despised her.

He did not send for his wife and children until the spring of 1922, more than a year after they had arrived in Plonsk. He grew tired of his bachelor life, the loneliness, the daily meals of pickled herring and bread in the workers' kitchen. When he heard they were finally coming, he sent Paula's sewing machine to the repair shop; bought chairs, a stove, and a broom and pail; hired a carpenter to build shelves for his books and a cleaning woman to scrub away layers of grime that had accumulated in the small two-room apartment he now rented; and, just before heading for the train station, had his shoes shined.

In his diary on the day of his family's homecoming, he noted: "I went down to Lydda to meet [Paula] . . . They came! . . . Geula is wonderful. Amos has an unhealthy complexion. . . . [Paula] is thin and worn out." He carefully listed the expenses of picking them up, then went on to describe in detail other apparently more important events of the day.

Paula was shocked when she entered his apartment. She looked in every corner, opened every cupboard and closet. Where was the furniture? Except for a few pieces of junk, the place was almost empty. Not even a sink; she would have to wash the dishes in a pan on the floor! No hot water, no gas, no electricity. In the morning she handed Ben-Gurion a shopping list. He shouldn't come back without soap, kerosene, meat, milk and vegetables. Later she sent him out to buy two beds, a table, and other household items. She scrutinized him. Look at his clothing! She would have to sew a whole new wardrobe for him. And when did he last have a haircut? *Oy gevalt!*

When Ben-Gurion finished his errands, he slunk out and went back to running his labor colossus—and let no one tell him how!

No one dared to, as he lectured day and night at workers' meetings, dressed perhaps in a white cotton jacket and sport shirt, standing with dramatic assertiveness, one hand on a table and the other in his pocket. Or as he negotiated labor disputes, called for strikes, argued with British bureaucrats, or bounced around the country from factory to kibbutz to housing project. Ben-Gurion demanded that all labor unions bow to the Histadrut and that all Histadrut co-leaders bow to him.

Many agreed, relieved to surrender the responsibility. For with almost no money dribbling through its veins, the Histadrut was withering. At conference after European conference, Ben-Gurion squeezed the moneybags of the W.Z.O., but not a dollar, shilling, mark or franc dropped out, though many W.Z.O. leaders wallowed in wealth. Contribute to socialism? A droll thought! Ben-Gurion himself was so poor that he would often buy only a one-way ticket to these meetings and then demand that his comrades in Palestine wire him the return fare if they wanted to see him again. His rage swelled. Should he have to beg the capitalists to keep his workers alive?

Maybe the Communists would be more generous. If the Russians let him set up branches of the Histadrut Workers' Bank and a joint commercial company in Moscow, he could rake in money since he was sure many rich Jews lived there even under the Communist system. He fiercely fought the local Jewish Communists, for they demanded a Jewish-Arab labor federation and a ban on immigration. They wanted to sabotage Zionism, and once they even revolted against the Histadrut, seizing its

Tel Aviv office before his men threw them out in a bloody battle. The Russian Communists, however, were another story. He remembered the horrors of Tsarist Russia; who could have imagined then that the workers would one day run the country? Besides, three million Jews still lived there, and what better way was there to get them out than to build a bridge to Moscow.

The Soviet government, it seemed, read Ben-Gurion's thoughts, for it invited the Histadrut to show Palestinian fruit, grain, farm machinery and other rural products at Moscow's International Agricultural Exhibition in the summer of 1923. Ben-Gurion would personally lead the Histadrut delegation.

"Moscow is animated, lively, active," Ben-Gurion scribbled in his diary when he arrived in the Soviet capital on August 31, 1923. "Without the newspapers and the posters on the walls, one would think he was in a peaceful prewar country."

Ben-Gurion thrashed in conflict as he savored the bristling revolutionary atmosphere.

> This revolution has become much closer, much more precious to me [he wrote]. Sometimes it seems to me that it would be worthwhile to remain here, that one should dedicate himself to it totally. . . . For I feel in it the throbbing pulse of a profound fundamental revolution, struggling in its severe and terrible birth pangs toward a new world and a new life. . . . If this revolution succeeds . . . it will gather you in its wings wherever you are, whether you like it or not.

Here could be the beginning of universal emancipation, which, in essence, was the ultimate aim of Zionism—"messianic redemption." Was Russia not serving Zion's great mission?

But on the other hand, it called the Zionists "imperialistic" and "counterrevolutionary." Somehow the Bolsheviks must be convinced that the new state Ben-Gurion wanted to create would help, not hinder, the professed Communist aim of liberating mankind. Surely Lenin would understand. Lenin, he wrote,

> is a great man. He possesses the essential quality of looking life in the face. . . . His eye looks afar at the forces dominating the future. Nevertheless he follows a single path, one that leads to his goal, while taking various detours according to circumstances.

A man, Ben-Gurion apparently felt, with a character like his own.

Anyway, if the Bolsheviks were overthrown, the Tsarists would reap their revenge on the three million Russian Jews, many of whom backed the government or actually held the reins. But while it was important to teach the Kremlin the truth about Zionism, it was even more important to teach the Russian Jews this truth. They must pour into Palestine with the irresistible momentum of an avalanche. And he would loosen the first stone at the Moscow exposition.

The exposition hall was impressive, with many countries flaunting their prize crops and machines amid festive floral arrangements spelling out Leninist slogans in praise of the peasants. Atop this and other buildings, huge red flags fluttered side by side with those of the invited countries, while on the plaza outside the hall folk songs burst harmoniously from the throats of Soviet youth. In the Histadrut stall, Ben-Gurion busily built pyramids of oranges, lemons, jams, cereals, wine, honey and oil.

Would many Soviet Jews come? He knew they were split over Zionism. The few but powerful Jewish Communists despised the concept, and the government's Jewish Section, or *Yevsektzia*, had even tried to bar the Histadrut from the fair. To his shock, Ben-Gurion read in an article apparently inspired by the Jewish Section that the Histadrut's wares were actually grown and processed by exploited Arabs and that he himself "belonged to this group that had seized the Histadrut in its dirty paws to make it its private property."

Such savage taunts, however, seemed only to loosen the stones Ben-Gurion hoped to set rolling, as Zionist Jews began visiting the exhibition in growing numbers despite fear that their mere presence could mean arrest. Ben-Gurion spent hours talking with them, and was especially taken by a Zionist scout leader, El'azar Galili, who had served in the Tsar's army. Would Ben-Gurion like to meet some of his scouts?

Shortly the pair entered a small dismal apartment, and Ben-Gurion was startled to find a group of youths who stood up, saluted, and greeted him in Hebrew. As he spoke of *Eretz Yisrael*, his poetic descriptions were suddenly punctuated by the clap of boots outside. The G.P.U. (secret police)! Galili ordered two comrades to guide Ben-Gurion to safety, and the visitor calmly donned his Russian cap, bade *shalom* to his hosts, and urged them to "come home."

As he left, someone exclaimed: "What a man!"

Word spread of Ben-Gurion's "escape" and his pleas for *aliya,*

and soon Jewish youths were stumbling across forbidden borders en route to Palestine. But the avalanche never quite began,
for many others were afraid. Some even asked Ben-Gurion to
remove the blue-and-white Zionist flag flying from the roof of
the exposition pavilion after the Jewish Section threatened to
shut down the Histadrut exhibit if the banner remained in
place. But he refused. It was important, he wrote his colleagues,
that in Moscow, where everything "smelling of *Eretz Yisrael*
and Jewish nationalism was forbidden and banned," Jews
should see "the national flag fluttering openly." And non-Jewish Russian officials let it flutter. Ben-Gurion thus won a symbolic victory, and he was gratified as the news spread.
Especially when an old Jew hobbled in and said, "My son, I
heard there was an exhibition on *Eretz Yisrael* and I have come
to see the fruits of the Holy Land." Could he please have a few
grains of wheat to show his synagogue?

As Ben-Gurion sailed back to Palestine across the Aegean, he
sat on deck watching the sea and reflecting on his conflicting
passions, on the bitter paradoxes he had found:

> We discovered Russia, [he wrote] a Russia that calls for class struggle
> to give power to the international proletariat and that deprives its work-
> ers of all the rights of man and citizen. . . . One does not know what
> remains from the past and what forbodes the future.

And now Lenin was no longer simply the determined far-
sighted realist.

> There is a man with a will of iron who worried little about human life
> and the blood of innocent victims of the revolution. An incurable sick-
> ness has struck this giant of thought, this great captain, and the ship
> struggles in the storm to reach the distant bank of a magic land that no
> man has yet contemplated. And in the uncontrollable sea amid the ruins
> of the cruelest struggle in human history float the remains of Russian
> Judaism.

But on arriving in Palestine, Ben-Gurion still thought Russian
Judaism could be saved, though his optimism dimmed as his
disillusion with the Russian Revolution grew. When Lenin died
in 1924, paving the way for Stalin, Ben-Gurion felt for a time
that the new dictator would revive the revolution. But his hopes
slowly withered and he began to view Bolshevism as inherently
brutal, hopelessly impractical, and incapable of accepting so-

cialist Zionism as a natural ally. The Russian leaders, it now seemed, would never let his people go. Stalin finally took the form of a monster. He betrayed not only Lenin but Ben-Gurion and his dream of mankind's redemption.

Ben-Gurion spoke now of a "working nation" rather than a "working class" and branded the local Communists as "scum" and "traitors." He threw most of them out of the Histadrut and virtually blackballed them from jobs.

The Zionist far-leftists—especially those under the influence of Israel Shochat—did not accept Ben-Gurion's growing anti-Communism quietly. Ben-Gurion had felt a quiet delight when Hagana, the military arm of his Histadrut, had swallowed up Hashomer, Shochat's old guerrilla band. This seemed a fitting end to his festering conflict with Shochat, who had banned him from Hashomer years earlier. But for Shochat it was not the end. In 1927 he decided it was time for Hashomer to splinter off from Hagana and become a separate force as before. His men robbed smugglers of a fortune in gold, which he used for buying weapons and training fighters. Shochat even asked the Soviet ambassador in Berlin to give his men pilot training in the U.S.S.R., and then visited the country to ask the Russians if they would support a Communist-Zionist state.

Ben-Gurion was unyielding; he must break up Hashomer once and for all. In the ensuing struggle, he allegedly accused it of murdering one of its foes and Shochat's wife, Manya, wrote in reply that his methods might "destroy us, but also you." Ben-Gurion interpreted this to mean that Shochat wanted to kill him too, and his suspicions grew when Hashomer leaders tried to "lure" him into one of their settlements. He told Manya that this "threat arouses in me only pity for those who threaten me." Shochat bitterly retorted that Ben-Gurion simply wanted to avenge his rejection by Hashomer many years before; but he eventually surrendered to a Histadrut ultimatum and gave up his weapons. His more extreme comrades fled to Russia, where they tried to practice pure communism—until Stalin, ironically, wiped them out.

Ben-Gurion's book on Hashomer was finally closed.

If Ben-Gurion attacked the leftists after returning from Russia, he fought the rightists with equal fervor. For in early 1924 the Fourth Aliya began, and this time it was largely a middle-class flood pouring in from Rumania and Poland. With anti-Semitism rampant in these countries and Jewish property in danger, thousands of Jews fled to Palestine. Since few came for idealistic reasons, they shunned pioneer life in the wilderness and settled instead in the cities, where, as in Europe, they opened up shops and built factories that turned out every kind of consumer item from diamond rings to doilies.

Tel Aviv, which had once been a quiet Jewish suburb of Arab Jaffa, burgeoned into a lively, horn-honking, café-happy town, and prosperity kissed the land. Women in high fashion strolled the potholed streets; bow-tied waiters served vintage wine in fine restaurants; real-estate speculators sold new stucco seaside homes, which the owners furnished with expensive imports. What the labor idealists couldn't do in decades, the capitalists chortled, *they* had achieved in months. And many Zionists around the world agreed.

Ben-Gurion seethed. Had he struggled to build a nation of fat "profiteers" who dreamed simply of earning quick money? Look what was happening to the workers as prices soared and salaries plunged. Meanwhile *aliya* filled the Histadrut offices with jobless newcomers willing to work for a crust of bread. Ben-Gurion was ready to call for a strike that would shut down the whole economy if necessary.

If the bourgeoisie succeeded in their plans, what would happen to his "exemplary state"? Zion would be one big commercial ghetto—hardly an inspiration for the world. But they would fail, because they were spoiled and self-seeking. A country founded on hard physical labor and a consuming drive to save its people had to be compassionate to survive and grow. And the lust for profits, Ben-Gurion felt, was not compatible with compassion.

By 1926 the profits petered out and the economy nearly collapsed, with many firms, including the Histadrut construction company, Solel Boneh, going bankrupt, shops shutting their doors, and thousands of workers losing their jobs. Ben-Gurion's remarkable ignorance of finance did not help, but he did occasionally bail out the penniless Histadrut executive committee, using his own money to send urgent cables and buy stamps. The fine wine and high style vanished, and people went hungry, their suffering compounded by a typhoid epidemic. Many rushed to the docks as others had done in the early days to leap aboard any vessel they could find. And Ben-Gurion reacted as he had then. Scanning the alarmed expressions at a meeting of his party's central committee, he calmly assured his colleagues:

"Let's not blame the people who are leaving. . . . They have no strength. They are weak. . . . Shall we surrender? We shall not! Those who have the strength shall remain!"

And he was prepared to ruthlessly test their strength. Better days ahead? the workers would ask him, seeking assurance in his eyes. They saw, however, not a pledge but a prophecy. Thus, when at one huge meeting in Jerusalem his audience waited for him to talk about splitting up jobs and other emergency measures, he bluntly declared, "I can promise you neither a day of work nor a piece of bread." Instead he promised them a magnificent state.

"At that moment," says one Jerusalemite, "we forgot our suffering, our depression, and to a large extent our despair. . . . He instilled hope and confidence. . . . What other leader would have come to a meeting of workers, of destitute, barefoot, hungry people, and not speak about bread but about vision?"

Sometimes Ben-Gurion would go out of his way to make sure that an impoverished worker was offered relief, especially if the person was too proud to ask for it. But he was against granting such aid as a matter of principle, arguing like an arch conservative that it would only make parasites out of pioneers. Better to let the jobless go hungry than to give them charity. "They can break our office windows," he cried, "but we shall not destroy the people."

Were they not to be a model of moral fortitude for the world? But as he gazed at silent, scrawny children and saw the misery in their parents' eyes, he began to change his mind.

"Should help be given to the hungry?" he agonized in his diary. And he relented to some degree, though with tormented misgivings.

But whatever compassion Ben-Gurion may have felt for the unemployed, he would seldom show it openly. Once when a jobless worker stormed into his office demanding help, Ben-Gurion looked up at him and quietly said, "You're complaining? You're not satisfied? How can one be dissatisfied in our Land?"

When the man had bitterly departed, Rachel Yanait, who was present, admonished Ben-Gurion: "Do you think he feels like you do—that he is placing the foundation stones of the Jewish state? He is hungry."

Ben-Gurion was silent. Every Jew must learn to conquer hunger. Hungry Jews could survive; Jews without a state could not. As for those who fled, they were mainly bourgeois anyway. Had he not predicted they would choke on their greed?

"The middle class came—and failed," he wrote. "It had to

fail, for it wanted to gain its livelihood in Palestine as it had in the Diaspora. It didn't understand that Palestine was not Poland."

In Ben-Gurion's view, some of the Jewish landowners had no more noble a motive. Like those he had worked for when he first set foot in Palestine, they still hired cheap Arab labor, though they treated such labor less callously now. As head of the Histadrut, Ben-Gurion was now the chief champion of *Avoda Ivrit*, "Hebrew Labor," the policy of excluding Arabs from jobs in the Jewish economy. He still felt, or rationalized with lingering Marxist logic, that if the Jews stopped exploiting Arab workers, barriers between the two peoples would ultimately crumble and they would live in peace. Surely the Jews were not morally superior to the Arabs, nor were they better workers; they had in fact learned a lot about farming from the Arabs. Also, the Arabs, like the Jews, worked the land with their own hands, meeting his moral criterion for the right to own this land. Nevertheless, Ben-Gurion argued, the Jews had a greater right to it because the Jewish *need* was greater; world Jewry was threatened with extinction, and the Palestinian Arabs were not.

Ben-Gurion wanted the Jews and Arabs to run their own separate economies down to the municipal level, thus permitting the Jews to cultivate an autonomous self-sufficient society that would eventually blossom into an independent state. The Arabs too would nurture their own society, but it would be absorbed into that state—and the Jews would help them as they would any struggling people in the spirit of "messianic redemption." Was he not being fair to the Arabs? He based his whole moral case for Zionism on his concept of "fairness," since to doubt it could be to doubt Zionism itself. And Zionism—ultimately meaning a Jewish state—was a *principle* that *no* argument could shake.

"According to my moral judgment," he wrote in 1924, trying to justify his stand, "we have no right whatsoever to deprive a single Arab child even if through such deprivation we shall realize our aims."

Ben-Gurion sounded all the more righteous after Jabotinsky and other extreme nationalists blasted him as a dogmatic socialist and cosmopolitan Jew for proposing an agreement of cooperation with the Arabs. The Arabs, these extremists felt, should be forcibly removed from *Eretz Yisrael* if necessary. No, Ben-

Gurion argued, just kept off *Jewish-owned* land. And even years
later he fought an unsuccessful battle to keep the word "Hebrew" in the Histadrut's official name, The General Federation
of *Hebrew* Workers in *Eretz Yisrael.*

But Ben-Gurion was perfectly willing to let the Arabs work
on *Arab* land in *Eretz Yisrael.* And he held that most Arabs,
wishing to benefit from Jewish prosperity, would accept such
an arrangement if it were not for the power-hungry *effendis*
(notables) like the mufti, who, he charged, stirred up the miserable, ignorant Arab peasants, the fellaheen. Ben-Gurion apparently ignored the fact that Palestinian Arab nationalism had
been simmering since the middle 1800s, as had Jewish nationalism. And he was encouraged to do so by the past willingness
of some Arab chiefs to compromise with the Jews. Evidently
such Arabs failed to gauge the rising nationalist temperature of
their Palestinian kinsmen. And perhaps *because* Ben-Gurion
was a prophet, he too failed to gauge it, for could a man who
focused so intensely on a distant vision always see the reality
around him? Especially when this reality threatened Hebrew
Labor?

Attacked by the left, threatened by the right, challenged by the
Arabs, harassed by the British, Ben-Gurion, in the middle 1920s,
almost never had free time, even for his family; he confessed
that he was "unable to fulfill my duties toward my wife and
children." Still, sometimes when he was traveling he would be
seized by nostalgia for them, especially after receiving letters
from Paula intended as usual to frighten him into rushing home.
He had apparently become immune to her tales of calamity, for
he seldom replied now and expressed little alarm when he did.
But, typically he would jot in his diary:

"I shall soon again embrace Amos and Geula and their mother
will be happy. My dear—how many times have I abandoned
you and how many times shall I still?"

With her husband seldom at home, Paula was both mother
and father to her children, somehow eking out a life for the
family on Ben-Gurion's small salary. She had returned from
Plonsk with a new sense of marital realism, convinced that Ben-
Gurion was less a husband than a messiah, and that a messiah
needed a protector and servant more than a wife. She learned
these roles well, no longer demanding a maid as she had done
in Plonsk, and resigning herself to a pioneer's life.

When Histadrut headquarters was shifted back to Tel Aviv,

Paula, with Ben-Gurion away, supervised the moving job alone. This exhausting task presaged the harsh, bitter life that would follow. Impoverished and lonely, Paula was apparently even more miserable than she had been in Plonsk.

"I cannot go out without shoes, without clothes," she wrote Ben-Gurion when he was visiting Europe in March 1926. Things grew worse. She developed "heart trouble" but didn't have the money to buy milk and bananas as the doctor ordered, and once she "had a fit." Paula was livid when the postman knocked on the door one day and hauled in huge cartons of books; her husband had plenty of money for books, but did he have enough for a feather quilt or the dozens of other things she had asked him to buy abroad? Meanwhile, he was driving the family deeper and deeper into debt and couldn't even pay his taxes. "You only think about yourself," she charged. "For what does it matter to you? You have a faithful servant at home. The day will come when I'll kill myself. . . . And what do you care? You play the gentleman. It's nice to be a good actor."

However hyperbolical her letters, life was indeed arduous for Paula. Every morning, in the courtyard of the house, she would chop wood to build a fire so she could heat water. Then, after scrubbing the soiled clothes in a basin, she would join the crowd of housewives fishing for bargains from grocery carts that creaked down the sandy street. Once the iceman accused her in public of stealing some ice, while other peddlers deplored her habit of squeezing every tomato and examining every potato. "It's for Ben-Gurion!" she would exclaim, feeling that was explanation enough. When a baker tried to sell her burnt bagels, she admonished him, referring to her husband's political enemy, "Give them to Jabotinsky!"

Paula spent much time mending clothes and for a number of years Amos wore items that his sister had outgrown. His mother also gave him enough bus fare to take him only halfway to school, and he had to walk the rest of the way and all the way back. Yet Paula refused to send the children to a Histadrut school, enrolling them in an expensive "bourgeois" school instead. And she made them take piano lessons, though she could not pay installments on the piano. When she showed the bills to Ben-Gurion, he wrote the dealer that he would pay him as soon as he had the money, but that "you have the full right to come at any time and take back the piano."

Finally the children were sent home from school because there wasn't enough money for tuition. Paula managed to dig up the funds and humbly paid it, but was less humble when the teacher dared to give her children poor marks. She stormed into class and demanded that they be given a new examination. After school, they had little time to play, for Paula put them to bed at six every evening, until they were about twelve, so she could devote herself completely to feeding and caring for Ben-Gurion.

Thus, the children saw little of their father, who came and went like a ghost. He almost never knew when they were ill and sometimes did not even recognize them. Once Ben-Gurion boarded a bus, sat next to a neighbor's son, and proceeded to scold him for some mischievous act—without realizing that the boy was not Amos! Paula was so embarrassed by his inattention to the family that she sometimes dragged him to the roof at dinnertime and, with the command, "Louder! Louder!," forced him to shout at the top of his high-pitched voice for the children to come home so that the neighbors would think he cared about them.

But, for all his neglect, he did care about them—especially about his third child, born in 1925. Though sick in bed when a neighbor burst in with the news that Paula had given birth to a girl, he rushed to the hospital and, in an expression of his own euphoria, named the baby Renana, meaning "exultation." Nevertheless, he was subdued and not nearly as boastful as he had been after Geula and Amos were born.

He had taught himself to appear reserved when he was really exhilarated, and he apparently sensed the special relationship that would flower between him and Renana. Surely he would lavish his affection on her as he would not on his other two children. Every day he recorded in his diary her weight before and after nursing, and one day he proudly reported, "Today we weaned her." Later he would rejoice over Renana's first tooth.

Never was Ben-Gurion closer to Renana than on the day she fell dangerously ill, several months after birth. He ran out into the night like a madman, banging on the doors of three doctors. "I was not sure I would find her still alive," he would write that night.

When the doctors came and couldn't decide what was wrong, Ben-Gurion almost went to pieces, and his diary began to look like a medical record. "At noon her condition deteriorated again. She was seized by a terrible fit. She was all blue and cold. Her eyes were glasslike. Her teeth were clenched and her mouth tightly closed. Foam streamed from her lips."

Finally a doctor told Ben-Gurion and Paula the grim news: "There is no hope, she will die."

Paula shouted, "No, she won't die!"

But tests showed that the doctor was probably right. Renana had meningitis. Thunderstruck, Ben-Gurion sat silently by Renana's crib, applying compresses, feeding her, holding her hand, praying to a God he was not sure was in the business of helping people. He even missed a day or two at the office, an extraordinary concession to personal interest. And Renana somehow recovered.

But Ben-Gurion did not give up his habit of sitting by her bed and comforting her. He would tell her stories, bathe her, seat her on the potty. Later he would play word games with her and, when he was away, write more often to her than to the other children.

"I received your drawings," he wrote her once at the bottom of a letter to Paula. "Very nice. I was pleased with them. Send me more and more. Learn to write and write me a letter. I miss you, my lovely, and I love you so much. Kisses, Father."

He added almost as an afterthought, it seemed: "And also to Geula and Amos." Thus, even in these early years resentment began to simmer within the family.

Paula was hurt by the amount of attention Ben-Gurion paid to Renana when he could find almost no time for *her*. Since Geula was also perturbed, they found in their common feeling of rejection a link that was to draw them closer over the years. Once when Paula broke an ashtray in Ben-Gurion's library, Geula took the blame and the brunt of her father's anger—though she won his praise after Paula told her husband the truth.

Amos was less sensitive to Ben-Gurion's apparent favoritism and lack of attention. His father seldom gave him a present, but "I respected him and looked up to him," Amos would later say. "That was enough for me." On one occasion Amos, a mischievous child who would sometimes strike his sisters, had a rare opportunity to test his sentiment toward his father in a personal encounter with him. After he had misbehaved, Paula, at her wits' end, sent him to be spanked by a paternal hand. Ben-Gurion, lying on a sofa, greeted him with a mild, almost apologetic expression. "Amos," he said, sitting up, "when I am old, the one thing I'll regret is that I didn't pay enough attention to you in your early life. But I have a mission to perform and I cannot divide my attention. So please, Amos, try to reduce the burden that I shall feel when I am old."

Deeply moved and upset that he had caused his father distress, Amos replied, "Don't worry, Father, I'll find my way. You go ahead with your mission."

Every time Father tried to, it seemed, some member of his family—either at home or back in Plonsk—would suddenly demand his attention. With borrowed money, Ben-Gurion financed the studies of Avraham's daughter, Sheindel, despite Paula's objections, and brought Zippora's son Benjamin to Palestine. After Benjamin came Zippora and her elder son Arye. Zippora's husband, a physician whom Ben-Gurion had known and liked, had been mysteriously shot to death in Odessa, where the family had been living. Ben-Gurion had written to Avigdor when Zippora informed him of the tragedy:

"My dear father, I have bad news for you. . . . Our [Zippora has become] a widow with two children. . . . I have no words to console you. . . . But I promise you I shall do all I can to bring [Zippora] here at once. I shall share my bread with her and adopt her children . . . and shall be a father to them."

And Zippora warmly wrote Paula: "Let us be friends forever, for I have dreamed all my life of being with David's wife."

But shortly after she arrived, she moved out of Ben-Gurion's house and went to live in Haifa, for Paula showed little desire to share even a slice of bread with her. Zippora's sin was that she was especially close to Ben-Gurion and was a dangerous rival for his affection. In a brief note to Paula, Zippora bitterly wrote: "You have apparently lost all your feeling for the family."

Though Ben-Gurion was willing to bring to Palestine a young pioneer like Benjamin and a trained nurse like Zippora, he felt that his burden was already too heavy for a messiah and refused to help other family members come, at least for the time being. Avraham had to wait because his old job—selling lottery tickets —would not make him a very useful pioneer. As for Michael, would the country *ever* need him? Nor would Ben-Gurion help Rivka leave Plonsk, though her husband had died after losing all his money.

He felt "her terrible situation with all my heart," Ben-Gurion wrote his father, referring to her "heart-rending letter," but she probably couldn't find work and "she needs at least three to four thousand pounds" to be able to live on the interest. Thus, Ben-Gurion, oddly for a socialist, suggested that unless she could live like a "parasitic capitalist," she shouldn't come to Palestine!

Avigdor had written in January 1920, when he was sixty-three, that he himself hoped to celebrate his sixty-fifth birthday in Palestine "together with all the children." But when he now reminded his son once again of his wish, Ben-Gurion threw up his hands in despair. He would have to find his father a job while others were out of work. About the only person for whom he had ever found a job was a desperate man who barged into his office and threatened to shoot himself on the spot. But his own father . . . ?

"Any public body here . . . will gladly provide employment for anyone I propose," Ben-Gurion wrote Avigdor. "That is precisely the obstacle . . . in using my influence on behalf of those who are close to me."

In one stroke Ben-Gurion bragged of his power and expressed his fear that nepotism might soil his moral image. He then told his father how he could come without dishonoring his son: "I want you to [be] recognized not as Ben-Gurion's father, but as yourself, and [to be] offered a job not because of me. . . . I also hope you'll be able to find work suited to your talents and knowledge."

Avigdor would thus have to "prove" himself, to earn his way in competition with younger men. As for "the aunt," she should stay behind in Poland until Avigdor came and could personally afford to bring her to Palestine. Meanwhile, since his father would have to sell his house to finance his *aliya*—unfortunately dispossessing Avraham and Michael—"the aunt" would have to live with relatives.

One day in July 1925, with Zippora's younger son, five-year-old Emanuel, at his side, Avigdor arrived in Haifa harbor and watched as a rowboat pulled closer with grimacing Arabs at the oars. In the center of the boat sat a man waving and smiling sternly, a man with gray in his hair, who had grown much older and heavier in the last few frenetic years. Ben-Gurion climbed aboard Avigdor's ship and embraced his father. Well, there was always room here for another Jew, even one who might give him problems and slow up his mission.

Refusing to accept Paula's begrudging hospitality, Avigdor moved into Zippora's house in Haifa. His son found him a job as an accountant with Solel Boneh, the Histadrut construction firm, painfully conceding that it was impractical to make his own father hostage to a moral notion. "The aunt" soon followed, only to die a few years later in 1930, and Rivka, Avraham, Michael and their families would arrive in the next few years—in the order prescribed by Ben-Gurion.

But Ben-Gurion seldom spent time with any of his relatives, for Paula managed to keep them away from him. She stood defiantly at the door with a slightly malicious stare and a thrust of her chin, and growled that he couldn't be disturbed, treating all of them—even Avigdor—no differently from anyone else who didn't have urgent business. Occasionally one would slip by Paula, and Ben-Gurion would warmly welcome the "intruder." Why, he would ask, didn't the person visit him more often, though he could hardly have been unaware of his wife's watch-dog role. Paula, in fact, served him well. The unessential visitor would unleash his anger on Paula rather than on Ben-Gurion for being turned back at the door, and Ben-Gurion would not have to waste precious time. Besides, since he couldn't give Paula herself much of his time, why not allow her the pleasure of depriving others of it, too?

And Paula pursued this pleasure without prejudice, dealing with her own kin no less severely. Her younger sister, Pesya, arrived from Russia in 1924 and stayed with the Ben-Gurions. But not for long. Paula ordered the young woman around like a servant until she fled to a kibbutz. Now Paula would have her husband to herself again.

Meanwhile, Ben-Gurion flung himself anew into the steaming caldron of Histadrut politics, and to raise spirits—and funds—he dashed from city to city, country to country. In the evening he would sit down and record his experiences in his diary, sometimes daring to deviate from the mundane facts of his mission to comment on less weighty matters: stuffing himself with Gallic delicacies aboard a French liner, flying in a "whistling, creaking" plane for the first time, discovering Freud in the British Museum library, a revelation that inspired him to interpret his dreams.

Occasionally there was a spark of sentiment, sometimes romantic, at other times melancholic or even morbid. Thus, nostalgia colored his description of a trip in summer 1928 to Istanbul, formerly the Constantinople of his student days. He strolled the twisting lanes of the university and visited the room where he had lived in filthy Bohemian splendor with Yitzhak Ben-Zvi and Josef Strumza, vainly asking neighbors where he might find diaries, letters and books he had left behind. And aboard one ship he sat on deck and briefly opened his soul to his diary:

> Evening twilight. The sight of the sea, the boat is sailing, the waves are caressing. Silence. . . . The sky is studded with bright agitated twinkling sparks. Depression in my heart. Everything will pass, vanish. Eternal cold, destruction, annihilation, nothingness without end. What is the meaning of all our wretched fleeting existence?. . . Who will reply, who will tell? The grave—the only reply. The only purpose.

But the next morning he would be thinking again of life, not death, the life of his people, which he must secure before he could rest in his grave.

In the late 1920s, Ben-Gurion grew ever more sullen as he sat at his desk, head in hands, pondering his plan to secure the life of his people. In a few years he had moved dramatically toward this goal, and the Histadrut, though still flirting with bankruptcy, now virtually controlled the Jewish economy, thanks more to Ben-Gurion's ability as an organizer than to his skill as an economist.

But while Ben-Gurion built the core of what he hoped would be an exemplary state, his egalitarian principles, ironically, encouraged Histadrut leaders to behave in less than an exemplary manner. Unable to live on their low salaries, they raided their treasury for bonuses, advance wages and loans, which were often written off—benefits that were denied common workers. Though Ben-Gurion himself was a beneficiary, he agreed, under pressure from many Histadrut members, to investigate the charges, but laundered the investigating committee's report. Lost in the suds were the most serious accusations along with the names of "guilty" persons, including his own.

Ben-Gurion felt no qualms. He had not spent one *grush* of Histadrut's money for his personal needs—only for the "cause." Certainly he borrowed funds for books, but how else could he learn the fine points of building a state? Certainly he borrowed money to construct his large house in Tel Aviv, but how else could he find space for his books and all the people a prophet needed to see? When Avigdor had sent him money to study in Turkey, did he have to pay his father back—or even thank him? Of course not. By aiding him, his father had simply been serving the cause, as the Histadrut was doing now. But it would be disastrous to reveal everything and endanger the embryo of his state, not to mention himself. People might not understand his higher motive. Ben-Gurion, however, began to see the question of egalitarianism in a new light. Could a man with his mission really earn just a little more than the most humble worker and perform adequately?

The Histadrut had its problems with the Diaspora as well. In August 1925, speaker after speaker at a Zionist Congress in Vienna condemned the labor organization for its "waste" and "greed," ignoring the waste and greed of the middle-class "profiteers." Dressed in an open-necked work shirt to emphasize his contempt for his starched-collar foes, Ben-Gurion jumped to the rostrum and hissed:

Let me inform you gentlemen that Zionism has no content if you do not constantly bear in mind the building of a Jewish state. And such a state is only possible on the basis of a maximum number of workers. And if you cannot understand that, woe to your Zionism!

But it was also woe to the Histadrut, for the Congress cut it off without a *grush*—until a chastened Ben-Gurion agreed to let a member of the Zionist Executive sit on the Histadrut board to keep tabs on the leaders. Better humiliation than bankruptcy.

Ben-Gurion would now try again to achieve what he had been seeking almost since the day he first got off the boat in Palestine —a united labor political party that would lead the way toward national and universal redemption. And he was optimistic. "My forecasts are coming true," he rejoiced in his diary. "Histadrut is forcing all the parties that hate each other to work together for the good of Palestine."

Ahdut HaAvodah, which was already a union between Poalei Zion and the independent farm workers, must finally hitch up with Hapoel Hatzair. And who would be the perfect *shadchan?* Berl Katzenelson, of course. As his party's chief theoretician, Berl ideally complemented Ben-Gurion, the chief practitioner. With his disciplined mind, he knew more than he understood, while Ben-Gurion, with his uncanny intuition, understood more than he knew. In speeches as well as in print, Katzenelson was more inspiring—despite a disturbing platform habit of sipping a glass of water after almost every sentence. And among those he inspired most was Ben-Gurion, who would listen only to *his* advice, finding him a model of logic, a moderating influence, and a man he loved deeply as a human being.

Katzenelson was loved by many people, mainly for the quality Ben-Gurion seemed to lack. The "conscience" of his party, he cared for the individual more than Ben-Gurion did, identifying with his problems, advising, consoling, encouraging, constantly seeking out new potential leaders. Nor did he want personal power or a place in the limelight, preferring to work inconspicuously behind the scenes. He thus posed no threat to the normally distrustful Ben-Gurion, who could afford to listen to him—and to love him, too. As a common friend observed, "One of Ben-Gurion's signs of greatness was that he recognized Berl's spiritual supremacy." And Katzenelson, though apparently less charmed personally with Ben-Gurion, viewed him as a "gift of history," a gift he would handle with deftness and care. When

Ben-Gurion would rush to him with some pet plan, Berl, if he didn't like it, would simply ask a few probing questions, and "each time the tone of Ben-Gurion's reply would drop lower and lower until . . . the whole plan evaporated as if it had never existed."

Now, as he described his plan for labor matrimony, Ben-Gurion did not lower his tone once, for Katzenelson liked it. And immediately, with his slim torso bent resolutely over his typewriter, Berl hammered out a series of articles passionately proposing marriage. To dwell on differences between Ahdut HaAvodah and Hapoel Hatzair, he argued, was to "split hairs." The Hapoel Hatzair leaders, Josef Sprinzak and Chaim Arlosoroff, read the pieces stone-faced. They would never yield their power to Ben-Gurion and kowtow to a man so impetuous, impatient and aggressive. But their followers disagreed. Both parties held a referendum in 1926 and voted for fusion.

But it was only at a Histadrut conference in October 1927 that the leaders of the two parties met to iron out their differences. Day after day Ben-Gurion, his eyes fiery slits, his hair feathery chaos, hunched over the conference table, arguing, demanding. Elation vied with exhaustion as history rumbled through his mind. Twenty years earlier he had urged these same parties to meet and merge, and almost nobody had listened. A naïve dreamer, they called him. And now, to spice his thoughts with poignancy, Shlomo Zemach, who had vehemently opposed union then, was sitting at the table as a Hapoel Hatzair negotiator. But their relationship was strained. Ben-Gurion had become perhaps the leading political figure in the *Yishuv*—and who was Shlomo Zemach? An unsung writer who dabbled in politics. Shlomo Zemach, whose name had once awed all of Plonsk!

After seventeen days of almost nonstop quarreling, Ben-Gurion felt he had had enough. Things had not really changed in twenty years. He claimed he had a pounding headache and irately stomped out of the conference room.

At dawn the next day there was a different kind of pounding. The door of Ben-Gurion's house, it seemed, would fly off its hinges. Paula woke up with a start. What was all the noise outside? Who would dare disturb Ben-Gurion at this hour? Slipping into her robe, she shuffled angrily to the door and listened.

"Let us in! Let us in!" a great crowd roared. "We must see Ben-Gurion!"

Paula opened the door slightly and suddenly found herself

swimming in a sea of swirling flesh. My God, had these madmen come to lynch her husband? In a moment Josef Sprinzak was standing by Ben-Gurion's bed.

The wedding was on!

Barely awake, Ben-Gurion looked startled. Then he scrambled from bed and, arm in arm with his new partner, stumbled out onto the balcony in his nightshirt to be greeted by the hysterical cries of their followers, who burst into a hora in the middle of the street, waking the whole neighborhood. Ben-Gurion waved, smiling wanly.

It was a premature celebration, for it took another two years to complete the marriage contract. At a final meeting in January 1930 in Tel Aviv, wedding bells tolled throughout the land. The Eretz Yisrael Workers' Party, to be known as Mapai, would embrace about 80 percent of the Jewish workers. Again Ben-Gurion was the hero of the hour as thunderous applause greeted him when, with his hands in his trouser pockets, he tramped to the rostrum in high boots to make the last speech.

Moshe Gurari, one of his lieutenants, describes the moment: "Pale and moved, he stood there moving his lips, making an effort to speak. His voice couldn't be heard. He was unable to overcome the stormy emotions that flooded him when he saw the fulfillment of his dream of unity. . . ." But then his voice rose over the din: "We know our sin . . . This sin we shall not be forgiven, even if we are thoroughly righteous men, the sin of weakness. We are weak. Woe to the weak!" But Mapai would not be weak. It would "show the way to a state and seize political power."

When the conference ended, reports Gurari, "heavy rain fell in Tel Aviv. But it didn't stop [Ben-Gurion's] followers from strolling with him along Allenby [Road] to his home. . . . Ben-Gurion, as he marched along, scanned the surrounding scene as if he wanted to escape. When he reached his house he was surprised to find another crowd . . . awaiting him in the garden."

Everyone began dancing and singing "God Will Build Galilee," and Ben-Gurion, no longer able to control his emotions, lustily added his voice to the cacophony of joy.

But not for long. For despite the miracle, he sensed, the cheers were premature. He could feel the first ominous gusts of a gale that would sweep through the edifice he was so painstakingly building.

CHAPTER SIX

I will make a covenant of peace with them

EZEKIEL 37:26

A T 11 A.M., August 23, 1929, Haj Amin el-Husseini, the mufti of Jerusalem, greeted his guest with an Oriental majesty vividly embellished by his pointed red beard and white flat-topped turban. The British police chief, "nervous and worried," wasted no words: Why had a huge screaming crowd armed with knives and daggers gathered in the Old City?

Only to protect themselves in case the Jews attacked, His Eminence calmly replied.

And the Jews *would* attack, Haj Amin had been predicting for months. They flocked to the Wailing Wall for prayer, he charged, because they yearned to seize the Mosque of Omar nearby; they wanted to destroy it and rebuild the Temple that two thousand years earlier had rested on the same spot. Mohammed's magic horse was tied to the Wall when the prophet, according to legend, rose to heaven from the site of the mosque; so what right did the Jews have to claim the Wall as their own? The Arab press echoed these arguments and called for *jihad*, while Jabotinsky's rightist Revisionist Party ignored Ben-Gurion's plea for calm and demonstrated feverishly at the Wall, crying, "The Wall is ours!" Now, in response, as Ben-Gurion had feared, thousands of Arabs from all over the region had swarmed into Jerusalem on this Moslem religious day to pray in the mosque—armed with deadly weapons.

Haj Amin's studied reply did not seem to ease the anxieties of the police chief as he stared into the mufti's cool blue eyes. The Arab leader had every reason to be cool—and confident. For never were his people more insecure, and insecurity bred violence. They were worried about the mosque, about Jewish restrictions on Arab labor, about the waves of Jewish immigration that might soon flood the land. It was time to strike, too, because the tattered economy had sent Jewish morale plunging, and violence could further stem the flow of Jewish investment money into the country. And since the British forces resented the Jews, they would most likely stand by and do nothing. Who, after all, could enjoy a cup of tea with Ben-Gurion and his crowd when they were constantly, scowlingly, demanding a national home? Yes, the Arabs must attack soon, before the whole Jewish population drained into the Hagana, before the newly united labor party could infect the Jewish mainstream with its militancy—and before the newborn Jewish Agency grew into a powerful international organ.

The Agency was the latest threat, though almost as much to the Zionists, it seemed, as to the Arabs. In July 1929 Ben-Gurion had raced off to a Zionist Congress in Zurich and, with throbbing uncertainty, stammered his approval of the Agency, which would hover over Zionism as a kind of shadow government for Jewish Palestine. Trouble was, it would embrace non-Zionists as well as Zionists in order to attract funds from the world's more affluent Jews, and this could mean pressure on the Zionists to lower their voices.

Pragmatism had triumphed, however, and Ben-Gurion reeled out of the hall in exhaustion onto a train bound for Nice, where he would relax for a day or two. This town, with its clean streets and cheerful façades, so delighted him that he wrote in his diary: "Why can't Tel Aviv be like Nice?" The next morning this question took on added meaning. After a restful night in a seaside hotel, Ben-Gurion went to buy the morning newspaper and, amid dripping bathers and gay holidayers, stared with horror at the headlines: Arabs had surged like a raging sea through Jerusalem's Old City, stabbing Jews to death.

The mufti had struck a far more brutal blow than he had in 1920 and 1921. And over the next few days, the murder spree would spread like a Biblical plague from Jerusalem to Hebron, Haifa, Safed and dozens of Jewish settlements. More than a hundred and thirty Jews and about a hundred Arabs would hug in death the ground they had so uncompromisingly claimed in life, many of the Arabs felled by British soldiers who were finally ordered to end the fighting.

Shortly Ben-Gurion boarded a ship bound for Palestine, and

he sat on deck penning angry thoughts in his diary. Certainly the riots would deepen Jewish despair, interrupt work, and temporarily block the flow of immigrants and capital into Palestine. But they might also set the Jewish soul afire. For this was not simply a pogrom, but an assault on the Jewish nation. The national consciousness would swell and perhaps spark massive immigration and swifter moves toward statehood. Ben-Gurion rallied other Jews on the vessel, and they cabled the Zionist office in London:

> The events in the Land require a response from the *Yishuv* and from the Jewish people. Our response must be an immediate mobilization of men and capital. There must be thousands more pioneers. The bloodshed requires neither aid nor mercy but more forces and more work.

Ben-Gurion believed, as he had after the earlier riots, that the mufti and other "bloodthirsty agitators," encouraged by the British, had simply whipped up gangs of Arabs to a frenzy, that most Arabs were passive and fairly immune to nationalistic fever. But the mufti's work, he felt, had fueled Jewish nationalism, ironically helping the Zionist cause. And reflecting this optimism, Ben-Gurion began to act the moment he jumped ashore into his family's welcoming arms. He dashed off to a conference with his colleagues and demanded that they press the British to punish the rioters. Then he cabled pioneer groups abroad to round up at least ten thousand people for immediate *aliya*, pushed for a harder-hitting Hagana and finally, clutching a briefcase packed with plans for exploiting the massacres, pleaded with colleagues to help him form a Jewish police force of new pioneers to protect every Jewish town and settlement. But he pleaded in vain.

Violence to meet violence? they cried. Insanity!

Then the British delivered an even more devastating blow. Two commissions of inquiry took tea with select Arabs and Jews and decided that the promised national home should remain a Jewish dream rather than an Arab nightmare. And in October 1930, Colonial Secretary Lord Passfield framed this sentiment in a White Paper: Henceforth only a limited number of Jews could set foot on Palestinian land, and only a limited amount of this land could be sold to Jews. Ben-Gurion was aghast, and some Zionists, in their shock, were even ready to give up on a state. Manya Shochat urged Ben-Gurion to make a deal with the Arabs and forget about a Jewish majority, and her husband, Israel, agreed.

Ben-Gurion could hardly believe what he heard. The Arabs now outnumbered the Jews 800,000 to 150,000. Were the Jews forever to be a persecuted minority in their own land? Had his whole life been a waste? Some of his own comrades, the cream of the pioneers, would abandon the Jewish state itself! Like a maddened lion, he clawed at Manya with insults.

Ben-Gurion then replied to the British Labour Party's "betrayal" with a "White Paper" of his own, sending pamphlets to all groups affiliated with Histadrut and the Jewish labor movement throughout the world. Rebel! he cried. Rebel against the British even if this means the third destruction of the Temple! The Jews were threatened with extinction! He even took his message to the street. Late one night he stood on a corner surrounded by sweepers with long brooms, waiters from nearby cafés, street vendors and an assortment of other people, and cried to them:

"No White Papers or papers of any other color will decide our fate. We will determine our own destiny. We must resist!"

"But we are only a handful," someone replied. "How can we resist the British army?"

Ben-Gurion answered furiously: "Numbers are not important! Only the will is, the will of the people!"

And the sweepers returned to the street, the waiters to their tables, the vendors to their stalls, still doubtful, though somehow enthralled by this man's faith in their invincibility. But his comrades were less enthralled. How could a man reputed for his rationality, they asked, suddenly become so irrational? Were the Jews to fight the whole British Empire? Would mass suicide bring a state any closer? Ben-Gurion cooled down. He didn't want to rebel against the British now, he explained, only later, if all seemed lost. But he had frightened many Zionists. Would he eventually lead the Jews to some apocalypse?

The fearful were mainly those who didn't understand that Ben-Gurion's verbal extremism was often only tactical artillery meant to terrify the enemy. When one avenue of advance was blocked, as it was now, he would simply ram down another. Few of his colleagues really comprehended the subtleties of his political guerrilla strategy—when to feint, when to retreat, when to thrust ahead, with the mind never deviating from the central goal. His new Mapai Party would have to conquer the whole Zionist movement and then, with himself at the helm, no Zionist would dare challenge destiny.

Thus, on September 27, 1930, in Berlin, Ben-Gurion rose and hammered his gavel to open the founding conference of the World Congress of Labor *Eretz Yisrael*. This would be the workers' answer to the W.Z.O., which for so long had feared and fought labor power in Palestine. Since stealing the reins from the bourgeois W.Z.O. seemed impossible, Ben-Gurion's new organization would have to devour it. But his Mapai colleagues did not think it could. Wasn't it strictly Ben-Gurion's personal toy? Who would accept him as the leader of world Zionism— this scruffy little man who hated diplomacy? Besides, they had not forgotten his "irresponsible" call for a revolt against the British. No, they would not give up their seats in the Zionist Executive and join his maverick group. Ben-Gurion grumpily accepted the decision. Somehow he would scratch his way to the Zionist summit and topple Chaim Weizmann from his perch.

Weizmann was already in trouble. He had been the defender of Britain, the intimate friend of its leaders. Trust the British, he had repeatedly urged Zionist skeptics; they would not let the Jews down. And then came the Passfield White Paper, virtually canceling the Balfour Declaration! Weizmann fought to stay in the W.Z.O. presidential chair, begging his British friends to annul the White Paper. Did they want to see an extremist replace him and stir up more trouble for them in the Middle East? They did not. So finally, in February 1931, Prime Minister Ramsay MacDonald wrote Weizmann a letter partly rescinding the Passfield White Paper; there would be fewer restrictions on immigration, settlement and land purchases.

But would this letter be enough to save Weizmann? The Seventeenth Zionist Congress, convening in Basel in July 1931, would decide. Worker unity in Palestine had cleared the way for a great victory by labor, which had won 29 percent of the delegates and for the first time emerged as the largest single group in the Congress. Ben-Gurion was as delighted as he was surprised. Labor might, after all, soon dominate the W.Z.O. Could he then more easily thrust to power inside this organization than outside it? This possibility intrigued him as he considered the opposition.

First there was Weizmann. Ben-Gurion had long thought he should retire from the presidency, noting once in his diary that the man was "ridiculous and wretched." Still, he saw merit in the view of other Mapai leaders who argued that Weizmann was "the best of the bourgeoisie." The man, after all, supported the "conquest of labor," even if he synthesized the party's "practical" Zionism with his own "political" brand. The real danger to labor, they stressed, was Vladimir Jabotinsky, whose right-wing Revisionist Party had gained a highly respectable 21 percent of the delegates and could be the wave of the future. So now Ben-Gurion played with a new tactic: Let Weizmann hold on to the presidency until labor could crush Jabotinsky and surge to the top in the next Congress two years later.

Jabotinsky, in any case, had to be stopped, in Ben-Gurion's view. He was fanatical, unrealistic, antisocialist. Besides, he had occasionally been more visionary than Ben-Gurion, backing, for example, the formation of a British-led Jewish Legion in World War I, while Ben-Gurion still plumped for Turkey. He was, moreover, a noted poet, playwright, philosopher and linguist, a powerful speaker and a magnetic personality despite his mild professorial appearance, with high forehead, tight thin lips, stubby nose, and eyes that probed through round black-rimmed glasses. He was, to Ben-Gurion, a man to be feared—and envied.

At the same time, he viewed Jabotinsky's Zionism as one-dimensional and fascistic, and the ideological struggle raging in Europe between social democracy and fascism deepened his distrust. Jabotinsky demanded a state immediately at any cost, one that embraced not only all of Palestine but Transjordan as well, since Transjordan had been a part of Palestine until 1922, when the British turned it into a separate country under the rule of the Hashimite dynasty. Ben-Gurion wanted not simply a state but an exemplary one that would ultimately lead to universal redemption, and he was willing to wait for the pioneers to carefully cement every brick in place.

These diverse aims and tactics perhaps stemmed from their contrasting backgrounds. Ben-Gurion was born into Zionism and Jewish tradition. His vision was rooted in the Bible and geared to eternity. Jabotinsky, born in cosmopolitan Odessa and reared in a non-Jewish environment, seethed with an impatience triggered by sudden revelation. He wanted instant results; he would worry afterward about the quality of life and the purity of ethos. If the state to Ben-Gurion was mainly a Biblical injunction, it was to Jabotinsky primarily an assertion of national honor.

Ben-Gurion, somewhat paradoxically, admired Jabotinsky with the disturbing ardor of a warrior finding something of himself in the soul of the enemy. For Jabotinsky too was single-minded, decisive, utterly unshakable in his convictions. Ben-Gurion, however, had only scorn for his foe's tactical thinking. Jabotinsky had been a powerful member of the Zionist Executive in the early 1920s but, hoping to force a showdown with the British, he resigned so he could organize a hard-line party. This party seemed doomed to remain a black-sheep minority in the Zionist movement, while Jabotinsky himself had been banned from Palestine as a troublemaker and was living in London. No, not pragmatic at all. Yet now, to Ben-Gurion's surprise and chagrin, Jabotinsky stood as the central threat to his quest for world Zionist domination.

Hardly had the Seventeenth Zionist Congress opened in Basel in 1931 when it almost disintegrated into bedlam. Ben-Gurion, dressed in a dark suit and sport shirt, ripped into the Revisionists with scowling frenzy, charging they were "chauvinistic" and filled with hatred toward the workers and the Arabs. Jabotinsky icily demanded a tougher policy toward the British. And Weizmann asked for a softer policy, even saying that a Jewish majority in Palestine, the main requisite for a state, was not really necessary. Ben-Gurion's comrades began to waver. After Weizmann's "treasonable" remarks, could they still back him as the "best of the bourgeoisie"?

Weizmann realized how fragile his chances were and desperately turned once more to his British friends. Again he asked: Did they want to deal with a fanatic like Jabotinsky, or even Ben-Gurion? If they didn't, they should help him win Ben-Gurion's support before it was too late. Only Ben-Gurion could save him. They agreed, and Weizmann rushed to see his old foe with a letter from Ramsay MacDonald indicating that the Prime Minister might be willing to set up an Arab-Jewish legislative assembly in Palestine on a basis of parity, equal representation, even though the Arabs still greatly outnumbered the Jews. Fly to London immediately, Weizmann urged. See the Prime Minister and return with a deal. The trip could yield an important victory for Zionism—and, presumably, for Weizmann. How could Ben-Gurion oppose a man who handed him such a political plum?

Ben-Gurion was eager indeed to exploit this opportunity, for a legislative assembly would enable him to proclaim a Jewish state when enough immigrants poured in to give the Jews a majority. With another Zionist leader, Lewis Namier, he flew off to England for a talk with Ramsay MacDonald at his country home in Chequers. This would be his first meeting with a chief of government, a job always left to Weizmann, and the prospect excited him.

When the two guests had breakfasted with the Prime Minister and his family amid awkward attempts at conviviality, the men moved to the host's elegant office, sank into soft leather chairs, and got down to business. Ben-Gurion was startled by the Prime Minister's remarks. Here was the man who had approved the anti-Zionist Passfield White Paper—before being forced to rescind most of it—sounding almost like a Zionist himself. He supported the "parity" idea, he said, and he would try to dismiss British officials in Palestine who were unfriendly to the Jews.

But it was clear that without Weizmann the Prime Minister's enchantment with Zionism might quickly wither. MacDonald was so worried about Weizmann's future that he even wanted son Malcolm, his aide, to rush off to Basel to plead the old Zionist's case. Chilling at the thought of British intervention, Ben-Gurion politely dissented. Then he and Namier raced back to Basel—in a train. The fate of Palestine might hang in the balance, but the two men, having missed their plane, refused to spend fifty pounds to hire a private aircraft. English eyebrows rose in astonishment, but the visitors were unembarrassed. How could a couple of poor workers afford a private plane?

Their frugality may have helped doom Weizmann. (The trip was a failure in any case, since Britain would never follow up on the Arab-Jewish legislature.) For by the time the travelers got back to Basel, the delegates had nudged Weizmann off his presidential pedestal and installed in his place Nahum Sokolow, a handsome, eloquent, passionless figure—though in reality Weizmann would still rule from behind the scenes. Ben-Gurion, no longer "anti-Weizmann," was disappointed. Would Ramsay MacDonald, with his favorite Zionist toppled, now find the anti-Zionists in his government less repugnant? Anyway, it seemed to Ben-Gurion that his rival had been "voted out in an unfair manner." But he was buoyed when Jabotinsky's hard-line proposals bounced off a stone wall. And he was even happier when Jabotinsky climbed onto a chair, thundered, "This is not a Zionist Congress!" and stomped out of the hall. With luck perhaps he wouldn't return.

Especially welcome too was the decision of the Congress to form a Zionist Executive with delegates from all parties—except the Revisionists. Would he himself join the Executive? Ben-Gurion shook his head. Too busy with the Histadrut, which he still viewed as Zionism's spearhead in the drive to a state.

But he was delighted that two of the five members of the Executive were from his party. Things hadn't turned out too badly. He could now discard his new plaything, the World Congress of Labor *Eretz Yisrael,* and focus on conquering the World Zionist Organization. He would finally harness the whole Zionist movement to his destiny—if only his comrades would find the courage and vision to help him.

Ben-Gurion's next step was to turn Mapai into a political juggernaut. It must pulverize the Revisionists and all other foes while grooming itself to govern an exemplary Jewish state. As Histadrut chief, Ben-Gurion doled out the best jobs to Mapai loyalists, declared war on all landowners who tried to profit from Arab sweat, and fought Histadrut's ultraleftists, who pulled the labor strings in some villages.

Revisionist labor unions, backed by brawny members of Betar (Jabotinsky's uniformed youth group), were a more serious menace, especially when Revisionist scabs boldly crossed the picket lines of striking Histadrut workers. Ben-Gurion shook with rage. There was only one way to deal with them—strong-arm squads. Thus he took a sudden interest in the Histadrut sports organization, Hapoel. He had finally found a good use for muscle power. "Sport," he had told a meeting of Hapoel, "is not an end in itself. It is only a means." A means now of physically crushing the Revisionist forces.

Who would lead the goon squads? Israel Shochat. It seemed fitting—the founder of Hashomer doing Ben-Gurion's dirty work.

More powerful than ever at home, Ben-Gurion now felt confident enough to prod his reluctant comrades toward the summit of the Zionist movement. In July 1932, at a meeting of the Mapai Council, he made his move. Standing before them with icy calm, his gray hair loosely combed back in reluctant waves, his jaw thrust forward with snarling arrogance, he sprang to the attack. The bourgeoisie wanted to exploit *Eretz Yisrael* for its own personal gain, and the Revisionists were its "black wing." And while the workers in Zion were building a state, the world Zionist movement, led by the middle class, was impotent, waiting for Britain to magnanimously offer it the territory as a Hannukah gift. This scandal must end!

Everyone agreed, but only Ben-Gurion claimed he knew *how* to end it. Labor must capture the world Zionist movement, he proclaimed. Mapai could no longer call itself a *class* party; it

must be a *national* party. The ruling party. Ben-Gurion's colleagues were stunned. Impossible! *Meshuga!* ("Crazy!") But at
a party conference in October 1932, they agreed to reach for the
reins of the next World Zionist Congress.

Not since World War I days, when he tramped from one American city to another croaking appeals for a Palestinian armed
force, had Ben-Gurion worked so hard. Not since he led the
Jewish battalion from New York to Canada had he been so
showered with adoration. The ghettos of Eastern Europe rose
up to welcome him as he blazed through a campaign in April
1933 to persuade Zionists in the Diaspora to vote for labor delegates to the Eighteenth Zionist Congress the following July.
But he had no illusions. Jabotinsky had left giant footprints in
some cities; the people had greeted him tumultuously too. And
he had given them a better show. His speeches had rung with
jingoistic slogans. His Betar youth had marched in perfect step
to inspiring Zionist tunes. His banners had screamed for an
instant state.

Ben-Gurion, however, was not discouraged. His voice was not
as compelling as Jabotinsky's, but his language was as colorful.
Slamming his fist on the table, he raged against Revisionist "de-
generacy," "chauvinism saturated with racial hatred," "incite-
ment" against the workers. He even called Jabotinsky "Vladimir
Hitler," harping on his "fascist" tendencies. In this way he cast
a frightening shadow upon Revisionist militancy, especially
since Hitler had just come to power.

The Revisionists struck back—not only with epithets like
"British agent" and "traitor," but with eggs and "stink bombs."
One young woman flung a heavy package at Ben-Gurion, barely
missing him. And, ironically, Communists often joined the Revisionists in the heckling and violence. But his foes could seldom get near him, for husky workers from his own party formed
a human wall around him, letting fly with fists and clubs at
anyone who threatened him.

Meanwhile, as Jew fought Jew, the real Hitler watched from
afar, perhaps amused by what must have seemed to him the
ultimate futility of Zionist politics. If Ben-Gurion spoke often of
"Vladimir Hitler," he spoke seldom of Adolf, though even then
Nazism was hovering over European Jewry like a thundercloud.
Apparently there was no time to worry about a storm that might
never break. Ben-Gurion had to devote every word of every
speech to the election; it was crucial to the cause. And even the

direst emergencies could not sidetrack this cause, for was it not hitched to eternity? He thus hardly reacted when European Jews complained about the anti-Semitism plaguing them. After all, a Jewish state would save them all eventually. The British, anyway, would let only a trickle of refugees into Palestine now, and if these Jews went to other "safe" countries they might be lost to Zionism forever. So why waste precious time worrying about ephemeral hardships, especially when a show of too much concern might trigger a premature exodus?

Ben-Gurion was even wary when the Jewish Agency sent its political secretary, Chaim Arlosoroff, to Berlin to negotiate the transfer of German Jews to Palestine. If the Germans agreed, the Agency felt, Britain would certainly fling open the door of Palestine to these refugees. But to the Revisionists, this was "trafficking with the enemy." Ben-Gurion was displeased for more practical reasons. Why give priority to saving the German Jews? On July 9, 1933, he wrote to his party:

> If the situation in Germany offers us new groups of volunteers, fine, but I view Zionism in its totality: The Jews of [Eastern Europe], and especially the youth, are as important as the German youth. They must be saved no less rapidly than the young Jews of Germany.

Arlosoroff should be in Eastern Europe campaigning for an electoral victory as he himself was. Could anything have higher priority? Why didn't Arlosoroff view Zionism "in its totality"?

Meanwhile, Ben-Gurion felt he was making headway as he trudged from town to town in Poland, Lithuania, Estonia, Latvia. In one letter to Paula he wrote, typically boasting of his popularity: "People walked for four or five hours to [hear me], sometimes in the pouring rain." At another meeting a "human sea" overflowed the hall, and the street was "black with people."

But as the election neared, Ben-Gurion noted with concern that Jabotinsky also continued to draw big crowds. And the atmosphere of violence all around him nourished this concern. What if—God forbid!—the Revisionists won a majority and the whole Zionist movement fell into their hands? They would pack Palestine with *their* followers, sabotage the pioneering movement and demolish the Histadrut, while building a fascistic bourgeois society with the same corrupt moral standards found in other countries. They would foul his dream and perhaps wreck his career—and fail anyway to win a state. For the British would certainly crush any attempt to set one up by force as the Revisionists threatened to do. Zionism had reached a supreme crisis; destiny itself seemed in danger.

And never more than on June 17, 1933, when Ben-Gurion's train steamed into Vilna to another rousing welcome.

> We went to the hotel [Ben-Gurion would later write Paula]. Our comrades told me that a telegram had arrived for me, but that they had left it home. . . . They asked . . . if I had heard the news from Tel Aviv. What news? I asked. Riots, attacks? What's happened? . . . Then someone said: . . . Something has happened to Arlosoroff. Arlosoroff? What do you mean? Then they found the "misplaced" cable and gave it to me: Arlosoroff had been murdered in Tel Aviv.

Turning pale, Ben-Gurion called out, "What!" Then "my whole world went black, and I fainted."

On the previous evening, June 16, Chaim Arlosoroff and his wife, Sima, had dined on the veranda of Tel Aviv's seaside Kaete Dan Hotel, a kind of headquarters for the elite despite its rather dingy inelegance, and then went for a stroll on the beach. The night was oppressively warm and few people were around, for it was Friday and most Jews were at home savoring the Sabbath meal with their families in the shadowy light of prayer candles. Arlosoroff had returned from his mission to Germany three days earlier and seemed pleased, for the Nazis had agreed in principle to allow Jews to emigrate in exchange for their property.

But he also had reason for concern. The day before, the newspaper of the extremist Revisionist wing, the *Biryonim*, had viciously attacked the "criminal Arlosoroff" as "Mapai's Red diplomat crawling on all fours before Hitler." "The Jewish people," the journal threatened, "will not forget your visit to Nazi Germany, and it will know how to react appropriately to this crime." And Arlosoroff knew that even some of his own colleagues, including Ben-Gurion, were upset by his trip. Yet what choice had he had? One of the few Jews who foresaw the Holocaust, he had felt that even if he could save one Jewish life, the trip would be worth it.

Chaim Arlosoroff was an unusual man. A master politician, administrator and orator, he was also a sensitive intellectual, as one could surmise from his ascetic face dominated by a prominent nose, sensuous lips, and thoughtful eyes hidden behind thick glasses. He had gone far in his thirty-four years. Born in the Ukraine in 1899, he received a doctorate in Berlin at twenty-three, then, on arriving in Palestine shortly afterward, began a meteoric rise to Zionist stardom. Even some of his most brilliant colleagues stamped him as their finest ideologist and a man likely to lead the world Zionist movement one day. Ben-Gurion, understandably, was not among these forecasters, harboring this ambition himself and possibly envying his rival's academic success.

As Arlosoroff and his slim brunette wife tramped along the beach in the moonlight, two men approached, and one of them shone a flashlight in Arlosoroff's face.

"What time is it?" the man asked.

When Arlosoroff reached for his pocket watch, the other man suddenly pulled out a pistol and fired at him point-blank. The strangers fled, and shortly Sima stopped a car, which sped the victim to the hospital. But it was too late. Arlosoroff died, and Palestine was soon to explode into a caldron of hate, anger and fear.

Who killed Arlosoroff? Before he died, the doomed man himself told a visiting colleague, Eliezer Kaplan, that the murderers were not Jews. And Sima Arlosoroff told Jewish officers working for the British police that the killer and his companion were Arabs. Earlier, she had assured the two men who drove her and her wounded husband to the hospital that she was "one hundred percent sure that the attackers were Arabs."

No one at this point seemed to doubt that Arabs had murdered Arlosoroff.

Ben-Gurion didn't. When he learned that Jabotinsky had received two cables from his followers in Palestine, he noted in his diary on June 18, 1933: "The first said that the Communists had killed Arlosoroff, the other that it was the work of an Arab. This seems to be the right hypothesis."

But as he wrote to Paula a few days later, on June 26, suddenly a "terrible suspicion entered my mind. . . . The murderer couldn't have been an Arab. Arlosoroff lived in Jerusalem. Why didn't they kill him in Jerusalem? How did the murderers know when he would be in Tel Aviv? How was an Arab able to escape from such a place at ten o'clock at night? And why Arlosoroff? . . . The terrible suspicion wouldn't leave me. . . ."

Ben-Gurion's colleagues in Tel Aviv, far better informed, of course, were thinking along the same lines. And so were the

British police, who were now closely collaborating with them. Hadn't the *Biryonim,* who were fascistic and had even praised Mussolini, warned that the Jewish people "will know how to react appropriately" to Arlosoroff's "crime"? And wasn't it logical that the Revisionists, proven addicts of violence, had committed the murder? Whether the approach of the elections reinforced this logic can only be surmised.

The machinery of justice thus creaked into gear. A Jewish employee in the immigration department informed the Hagana that a man named Avraham Stavsky, who belonged to *Biryonim* and resembled one of the assailants, was planning to leave Palestine urgently. The Hagana men immediately fetched a copy of Stavsky's photograph from the department files and showed it to Sima Arlosoroff. Was this not the man with the flashlight? Yes, it was, she agreed. And when she was later shown police photographs of ten different people, she understandably had no trouble picking Stavsky as the guilty one. Then, apparently to be consistent, she switched her original story. She was now 100 percent sure that the attackers were Jews. And her original testimony mysteriously disappeared from police files.

Stavsky was arrested along with the *Biryonim* leader, Abba Achimeir, who was charged with instigating the crime, since he had written an inflammatory article a few months earlier that appeared to justify political murder under some circumstances. Hagana and British police now looked for the triggerman and used a woman of dubious moral reputation to help them. Rivka Feigin had been thrown out of a Revisionist cell, and she accused the cell leader, Zvi Rosenblatt, of the murder. Rosenblatt was arrested, and with the leading suspects in hand the prosecution doggedly tried to prove its case.

Meanwhile, an Arab held in prison on an unrelated murder charge called for the warden and made a sensational confession: He and another Arab were the two men who had accosted Arlosoroff on the beach, and his friend had fired the fatal shot "accidentally." They had only wanted to "have some fun" with the victim's wife. The British—and the Arab leaders—were aghast. Such a confession was in the interests of neither. Didn't he know he could be hanged for the crime? the prisoner was asked. He suddenly withdrew his story and it was not investigated. Two years later, however, the Arab would again insist that he and his friend were the culprits, but official ears remained plugged.

Whatever the truth, perhaps the most damaging evidence against those who tried to convict the three Revisionist suspects

came many years later from Yehuda Arazi, a Hagana man and
police inspector who conducted the original investigation for
the British and, after World War II, headed the secret Hagana
network that brought illegal immigrants and arms into Palestine.
His impeccable Mapai-Hagana credentials make it difficult to
ignore his published allegations that the British, prodded and
helped by those two Jewish organizations, deliberately sought
to place the blame on the Revisionists. In a report to the British
intelligence chief on August 28, 1933, he had written: "It is my
impression that all the witnesses, beginning with Mrs. Arlosoroff, have wanted to incriminate the suspects at any cost."

After writing this, Arazi was abruptly removed from the case.
At the showcase trial that followed, Rosenblatt and Achimeir
were acquitted, and Stavsky was found guilty and sentenced to
hang, though he was finally freed for lack of sufficient evidence.

While Palestine simmered in the heat of this violent controversy, Ben-Gurion, under heavy police guard, continued to ha-
rangue crowds in Eastern Europe, charging everywhere that the
Revisionists had created the atmosphere conducive to the murder—though he would write in his diary: "One cannot yet state
that a Revisionist was the murderer."

In a letter to party leaders on July 9, he wrote typically that
"this is the moment when I find myself steeped in bitterness
before . . . the profanation that surrounds us. Still drenched with
Arlosoroff's blood, impure forces raise their heads and try to
make us serve them. . . . The coming Congress will be decisive.
It will be our last chance."

In the violent climate of the campaign it is not surprising that
he suspected the Revisionists. But he publicly implied their
guilt before the facts fully emerged, and he did not bother to
check them when they did trickle out. The details were not
important; only the principle was, the principle of winning the
election so that, ironically, he might create an exemplary state.
The killing of one man, however terrible, was not the point.
And he admitted he was "less interested in whether Stavsky is
the murderer or not than in Jabotinsky." Ben-Gurion apparently
believed, as one Mapai leader openly proclaimed, that the suspicion itself showed that Revisionist philosophy incited such
crimes. In other words, the Revisionists were guilty of complicity in the murder even if they didn't actually commit it.

By hammering the suspicion into the Jewish consciousness,
Mapai was certain to win votes. And it was evident when East-

ern European crowds began greeting Jabotinsky with taunts and stones that Ben-Gurion's strategy was working. The Mapai chief relentlessly attacked the Revisionists; he even threatened to quit his party when he learned that his comrades had met with the "enemy" for "peace" talks and wanted to postpone the elections until the inflamed atmosphere cooled down. Let up on his foes when they were on the run? Not before he destroyed them!

In mid-July, as returns from around the world poured in, Ben-Gurion sat in his Warsaw hotel room reading them with joy. He scribbled a note in his diary: "Cable from America that we got 50 percent! Is it true?"

It was. Labor had won 44 percent of the total world vote, a gain of 15 percent, and the Revisionists only 16 percent, a loss of 5. With the help of a few small sympathetic parties, labor would enjoy a majority and for the first time grace the throne of Zionism. Ben-Gurion had won his gamble.

As Ben-Gurion stepped to the rostrum to greet the Eighteenth World Zionist Congress meeting in Prague on August 25, 1933, he listened silently, almost incredulously, to the ceaseless applause, his stubby figure carelessly wrapped in a rumpled gray suit and open-collared white shirt. Had he finally stumbled to the summit? From the day twenty-seven years earlier when he hiked to Jaffa for the first Poalei Zion conference clad in a sweaty Russian shirt and rope sandals, many of his comrades doubted him, attacked him, even scorned him. And now he was being acclaimed by the whole Zionist world. Destiny, with all its devious tricks, had been true to him.

But Ben-Gurion still brooded. The Revisionists, after all, had 16 percent of the seats, and he wanted to shrink that figure to zero. Why let the predator wriggle off the hook to attack another day? Throw the Revisionists out of the organization—and force all other bourgeois members to toe the labor line or get out, too.

"There will be no negotiation; no concession will be made to those who don't agree with us," he cried. "Those who accept the majority program will make themselves part of it; the others, too bad for them! If they threaten to quit the Congress, let them go. If they protest, we won't be afraid. What is a majority for?"

But Ben-Gurion *was* afraid. Would Jabotinsky do at the Congress what Hitler and Mussolini did in their countries—destroy the parliament? "There is serious danger," he wrote almost paranoically to a colleague, "that the Duce [Jabotinsky] will try to break . . . up [the Congress] forcibly. Before I left Warsaw I heard he wanted to mobilize five thousand Betar members who would be concentrated in Prague."

Hardly had the Congress begun when Ben-Gurion and his comrades rammed through a resolution condemning "tendencies that are contrary to Jewish ethics and constitute a danger to the rebuilding of *Eretz Yisrael*," and calling for a committee to "take all steps that can . . . eradicate from the Zionist movement any elements . . . responsible for such tendencies."

When the Revisionists tried to protest, labor delegates walked out—but rushed back in time to ban them from the Congress leadership, censor their declarations, and scrap their proposals. The Zionist movement was now irrevocably split. And Ben-Gurion was content, hoping that Revisionist power would now simply wither away. His own would grow, though—by his account—only after being thrust upon him. His comrades insisted that he join the Zionist Executive.

> To my surprise and fear [he later wrote to his two elder children], I seemed to be the only man in the Zionist movement whom all the parties trusted. Even the Revisionist leaders wanted to meet me. This alarmed me. To bear so heavy a responsibility in the Zionist movement is beyond the power of any man—in any event, beyond my power. [Besides,] my deepest links and aspirations, my spiritual and human contacts, my private and public life, my real world as a man, a Jew, a worker, a man of our times are all bound up with the Histadrut.

Ben-Gurion may have felt that he could wield more power at this time as a "general" commanding an army of loyal workers —and playing the role of "gray eminence"—than as a political leader commanding only the language of politics and diplomacy. But he also seemed to be playing "hard-to-get" again. Finally, his colleagues agreed to let him keep his Histadrut post while he simultaneously served as chairman of the Zionist Executive.

He was now the world's most powerful Zionist.

Soon aware that politics and diplomacy were a full-time job, Ben-Gurion gradually gave up his old duties and plowed into his new ones with the same brash dynamism that had fueled the spectacular growth of the Histadrut. He ran a bristling, no-nonsense Zionist Executive, forbidding frivolous conversation and ripping newspapers from the tremulous hands of those who dared let their attention stray. Later, in 1940, when he would give up smoking, he demanded that his colleagues stop smoking in the room. Yet he was less tense than before, for now he could more openly serve the national cause before the needs and ideals of the workers. He refused to "take a position" on anything not directly related to the winning of a state.

Living much of the year in London, where the Zionist Executive was based (it would eventually move to Jerusalem), Ben-Gurion drew on a liberal expense account but still earned only his Histadrut salary, a little more than the thirty pounds a top worker was paid each month. Despite Paula's pleas, he refused to accept an additional salary of seventy pounds for his political duties. Paula, however, found ways of augmenting the family income. With Ben-Gurion abroad so often, she moved into one section of their house with the children and rented the remaining part to tourists, apparently without telling her husband. She also worked as a nurse in a first-aid station on the beach.

Meanwhile, Ben-Gurion envisaged days of catastrophe for his people—unless they could escape to *Eretz Yisrael*. On one trip home, at a meeting of the Histadrut Council, he prophesied:

> Hitler's rule places the entire Jewish people in jeopardy.... [His] regime cannot long continue without war, a war of vengeance against France, Poland, Czechoslovakia and other countries where a German population is to be found, or against Soviet Russia with its vast expanses. ... What will be our strength and weight in [Palestine] on the awful judgment day, when the great catastrophe bursts upon the world? Who knows—perhaps only four or five years ... stand between us and that terrible day. During this period we must double our numbers, for the size of the Jewish community then may determine our fate in that decisive hour.

With a new sense of urgency, Ben-Gurion fought to bring in every Jew. Since Britain granted Palestinian visas only to those who were assured jobs in the shops, factories and settlements, he demanded that every possible slot be occupied, from barber to botanist. But this was not enough. The British had to open the floodgates of Palestine and let waves of Jews flow in. Should he threaten force as he had in the past, or use diplomacy? He decided, after dealing daily with British leaders, on diplomacy.

Actually, Ben-Gurion's own ambivalent attitude toward the British began to crystallize into the kind of affection and respect that Weizmann had always felt. A Jewish state could, after all, learn much from this civilized nation, with its rich culture, democratic politics and system of justice, which, enriched with traditional Jewish values, would help groom the state for its redeemer's role. These were rational, humane people whom he could persuade. At the same time, he understood what most Zionists did not—that only common interests, not friendships, existed between countries. In any case, he bantered in London with newsmen who could sway British opinion, negotiated with British diplomats, buttonholed members of Parliament at the cocktail parties he hated. Give us more visas, he pleaded. Give us a national home. A state? It still wasn't time to ask for one. First, fill up the country with Jews. Create power. *Then* demand a state.

The problem was that the Revisionists were still demanding a state *now*. However humiliated at the Eighteenth Congress, they refused to wither away; in fact, they were making a comeback, for after Stavsky's acquittal in the Arlosoroff murder case, popular sentiment began turning against Mapai. And now the Revisionists were threatening Ben-Gurion's power again, and were continuing to break strikes called by the Histadrut. Ben-Gurion was exasperated. His strong-arm squads had been showing restraint, but now, he decided, they would "wage war to the end." And the streets echoed with curses and the clatter of men running, the thud of stones hitting.

The echoes suddenly terrified Ben-Gurion; did they not sound like those out of Germany? At a moment when Jews most needed to embrace, they were flinging missiles at each other. "I soon realized," he would later write to his children, "that we faced total destruction if we continued the internecine strife."

Perhaps he had erred in sparking these battles. What worried him most was the pessimism of his comrades. Was the whole cause, they asked, to be ground underfoot by rightist forces? His colleagues were "defeatists," Ben-Gurion cried, hiding his own great concern. "They do not believe in our strength. They have despaired."

In the midst of this despair, in September 1934, a letter from the Revisionists shook Mapai headquarters. Would Mapai agree to direct talks with the Revisionists on how to end the "violent actions of Jews against Jews and against Jewish property?" Did the Mapai want a *"modus vivendi"*? No, replied most Mapai leaders. But Ben-Gurion, who more than anyone else had wanted to "punish" the Revisionists, was now ready to listen to them.

When he had thought he could destroy them, it seemed foolish to compromise. But now that they were surging back, splitting the labor movement and rioting in the streets while Hitler tightened his noose around the Jewish neck, why carry on the vendetta and weaken his influence with the British, who held the key to a state but wished nothing more than to divide and conquer? The right tack now, it seemed, was to neutralize and absorb the Revisionist movement. And so he persuaded his comrades to talk with the enemy.

Delegates of the two parties met in London in early October 1934, and the gray clouds overhead seemed to characterize the atmosphere as they heatedly flung invective at each other. With the talks on the verge of collapse, a common friend of Ben-Gurion and Jabotinsky quietly called on both men. Would they agree to meet? Jabotinsky, who had little to lose, jumped at the chance; Ben-Gurion weighed the offer carefully. His colleagues, he knew, would violently object, but he finally decided to present them with a *fait accompli*. He would test his power.

That night he wrote in his diary about his meeting with Jabotinsky in their friend's hotel room:

"I said *shalom* to him without stretching out my hand. He got up, extended his hand, and asked: 'Don't you want to give me your hand?' I was surprised and extended my hand."

Ben-Gurion had been sure that Jabotinsky detested him. But, in fact, the Revisionist leader reciprocated Ben-Gurion's own secret admiration for him. Their handshake symbolized the strange warmth of the encounter as the two men, after cautiously feeling each other out, exchanged opinions over coffee like old friends. Jabotinsky even flattered Ben-Gurion; he expected him to answer his questions "in the Ben-Gurion manner —without fear."

Both men were surprised to learn that their views were not as contradictory as they had imagined—until they considered joint action. Two million European Jews, Jabotinsky proposed, should petition their own governments and that of Britain to let them enter Palestine, and they should demonstrate around the world.

"You don't understand or appreciate the value of the demonstration and the slogan," he said.

Ben-Gurion would comment in his diary: "I sensed that here we had come to the fundamental conflict." Petitions? Demonstrations? No, only pioneer action, underground action, could win a state.

But conflict did not taint the sudden sanctity of their relationship. They reached no decisions but agreed to talk again the

next day. As they walked together to the subway station, Jabotinsky asked Ben-Gurion in an almost hurt tone, "Why didn't
you extend your hand?"

"I didn't want to put you to a test," Ben-Gurion dryly replied.

And so did human feeling triumph over political fetish. The
two men met almost daily for a month, if not in their friend's
hotel room then in either one of theirs, and even dined together
in restaurants—though Ben-Gurion constantly glanced over his
shoulder to see if anyone recognized them. He could imagine
the repercussions in his party, which had opposed even low-
level talks. "Miraculously nobody saw us go or return," he
noted with relief in his diary.

The two men continued to bicker and bargain until finally, on
October 26, after a harrowing all-night session, they wearily
scratched their names on an accord and with stunned joy staggered out into the foggy London dawn. The agreement forbade
all "acts of terror or violence in any shape or form," as well as
"libel, slander, insult to individuals or groups."

The pair were to hammer out more accords, but Ben-Gurion
was so delighted with the first one that he rushed to his hotel
room and mused in his diary: "I don't know whether all the
comrades in Palestine will welcome this agreement. As for me,
this question is so important and meaningful that it is still hard
to believe that it can be implemented." And he added in English: "It is too good to be true."

The following day, still intoxicated with his triumph, Ben-
Gurion sat down and wrote to "Dear Jabotinsky":

> I hope you will forgive me if I address you as a colleague and friend,
> without the ceremonial "mister" . . . I am not sentimental, and it seems
> to me that you are not either. But I did not tell you what was in my
> heart. . . . However, nothing that might happen from now on will change
> the fact that both of us met and in the course of many hours forgot all
> that had occurred in the past, and that a great concern for the [Zionist]
> movement and the success of its work moved us, in mutual trust and
> respect, to a joint effort. This fact will not be rooted out of my heart. As
> you know, whatever may happen in Zionism in the future, my hand will
> always be extended to you in times of friendship and stress in spite of
> all party opposition.

Jabotinsky immediately replied: "My dear friend Ben-Gurion: I am moved to the depths of my being to hear, after so many
years—and what years!—words like 'colleague and friend' coming from your lips. . . . I grasp your hand in true friendship."

On October 27, the day after the signing, Ben-Gurion shakily wrote his colleagues about it, then penned in his diary: "Won't they stone me for the sin and treachery of meeting with Jabotinsky?"

The first stone was flung the following day. Berl Katzenelson read about the pact in the Palestine press and, in astonishment, telephoned Ben-Gurion to warn him: "The comrades take a negative view of the agreement."

Then a cable from the "comrades": "Return home at once!"

Ben-Gurion angrily ignored the order, and sat for three days writing a detailed report that read like the brief of a defense attorney desperately pleading his case before a biased jury:

> I am sorry that our party does not yet fully appreciate the . . . responsibility thrust upon it . . . , bearing now, more than anyone else, the burden of the entire Zionist movement, and that in its hands lies the fate of the Jewish people in one of the gravest and most fateful moments of our generation.

More cables from Zion, most of them blasts of fury. Ben-Gurion wired Moshe Shertok, who had replaced Chaim Arlosoroff as head of the Jewish Agency's political department: "What is the meaning of the panic and excitement?"

The meaning was that while Ben-Gurion would take almost any road that might shorten the distance to a state, his comrades couldn't be led down a path pitted with so many bitter memories. Katzenelson then cabled:

> Movement has been wounded and danger is very great. . . . Continuation of negotiations pushes people to anarchy and destructiveness. . . . No reconciliation with fascist Zionism. . . . Do not commit yourself until your arrival. Hasten your return. Every moment precious.

This harsh message from the one man he fully trusted and even loved shattered Ben-Gurion. Did Katzenelson distrust him, too? Ben-Gurion signed a labor truce with Jabotinsky that would presumably bring peace between the Histadrut and the Revisionist trade-union movement, then gave up before he could conclude other accords.

"Negotiations called off," he cabled. And he left for home.

Though Ben-Gurion was now the most powerful man in the *Yishuv,* he was still not powerful enough to impose his will on his colleagues. He had taught them to hate Jabotinsky, and now, ironically, they would not stop hating him even though this feeling was no longer practical. Nor would Ben-Gurion dare tell them that Jabotinsky, fascist or not, was really a great man. How could he let them think that, in a rare moment of exultation, his armor had melted and he had waxed sentimental?

Meanwhile, Jabotinsky was having trouble with some of *his* followers, who couldn't bear the thought of dealing with men who had tried to hang three of their members in the Arlosoroff case. But he could openly defend Ben-Gurion because his domination over his own party was far greater than Ben-Gurion's over Mapai. At the Sixth Revisionist World Conference meeting in Cracow, Poland, in January 1935, a young supporter, Menachem Begin, replied to his leader's appeal for approval of the pact, "You may have forgotten that Ben-Gurion once called you 'Vladimir Hitler,' but we have a better memory."

The conference, however, overwhelmingly endorsed the agreement.

Ben-Gurion's turn came at a Histadrut meeting in March 1935. Most speakers ripped into the accord, but Ben-Gurion would not retreat. Let the members of the Histadrut decide! he demanded. Hold a referendum! And in a highly charged atmosphere, amid fistfights, stone-throwing and name-calling, workers crowded to the polls that same month to resolve this momentous question. By a vote of 16,000 to 11,000 they rejected Ben-Gurion's rapprochement with the Revisionists.

"You have sinned against the Histadrut!" Ben-Gurion cried, bitterly aware that his vast prestige had suddenly eroded.

When Ben-Gurion explained to Jabotinsky that "the opposition was largely psychological," his old foe consoled him: "On receiving the news . . . , some inner weakness whispered to me: 'Thank God!' And perhaps Ben-Gurion feels the same at this moment."

Jabotinsky then pulled his party out of the W.Z.O. and would shortly found a separate Revisionist Zionist world movement. But this did not keep Ben-Gurion from babbling to him with an affection he seldom lavished even on his own family:

> Perhaps we will have to appear again in opposing camps. . . . And if we are destined to fight, remember that among your "enemies" there is a man who admires you and shares your suffering. The hand you felt I wanted to stretch out to you at our first meeting will be there even in the storm of battle. . . . I would not want you to "change." I want to carry with me your image as I remember it from London.

But their hands seldom clasped again, while the battle continued to rage. Some years later, in 1938, Ben-Gurion would even

scrap an agreement that the Hagana had reached with Jabotinsky's military arm, Irgun Zvai Leumi. No, he would never cooperate with the Irgun—not until it accepted the authority of
the W.Z.O. Was he, as some critics felt, simply spiting Hagana
comrades who had quashed his own earlier deal with Jabotinsky? The Revisionist chief reacted like a spurned lover, charging that Ben-Gurion quivered before the British. But the strange
and moving friendship between the two leaders did not entirely
fade, and Ben-Gurion sometimes visited Jabotinsky in London.

He would not, however, welcome him at home. Still exiled
by the British, Jabotinsky asked in his will shortly before he
died in 1940 that his remains not be brought to *Eretz Yisrael*
"except at the command of the Hebrew government of a free"
Jewish nation. But Ben-Gurion, while he led Israel, would refuse to issue such a command, arguing that the country "needs
living Jews, not the bones of the dead." He had enough political
tsouris without helping to enshrine the god of the Revisionists,
who were still the "enemy." And when his successor as prime
minister, Levi Eshkol, did allow the transfer of Jabotinsky's
bones, Ben-Gurion would not attend memorial ceremonies. Jabotinsky had been a dear friend, true, but he never understood
that Israel must be an exemplary state—generous, tolerant,
compassionate.

While Jabotinsky skidded into relative obscurity, Ben-Gurion,
despite his humiliation, began rapidly scaling the political
heights after his comrades refused to accept his resignation. At
the 1935 World Zionist Congress in Lucerne, Switzerland,
where half the seats were filled by his party, his colleagues
beseeched him to head the Jewish Agency Executive in addition to the Zionist Executive, and become, in effect, the "prime
minister" of a shadow Jewish government. Once again he
balked; he wanted nothing more than to be a "soldier in the
ranks." But after colleagues had pleaded with him for hours,
Ben-Gurion, crumbling into a state of "collapse, helplessness
and hysteria," finally accepted the power he always knew he
was meant to wield.

Some colleagues even wanted him to be president of the
W.Z.O., but this was one job he really didn't want, for it was
more diplomatic than political, and promised more publicity
than power. Who, then, was most suited for this role, which
Nahum Sokolow had played without a hint of distinction since
replacing Chaim Weizmann in 1931? Chaim Weizmann, of
course. Though Ben-Gurion still had little rapport with Weiz-

mann, he perceived a "holy flame" in the man and thought he could still be useful; after all, the Diaspora Jews and the British leaders adored him. And surely he had been "purified by the pain" of his 1931 defeat.

So, in Lucerne, Ben-Gurion pushed his comrades to make Weizmann president again. Naturally he would not be a real leader this time, but a kind of Zionist ambassador who would take orders from the Zionist Executive, that is, Ben-Gurion. And Weizmann, under pressure from his ambitious wife, Vera, agreed to come back. But Ben-Gurion had better understand: Chaim Weizmann had no intention of taking orders from a crude labor leader who never wore a suit that fit!

On returning home, Ben-Gurion described his great triumph over and over again to his children and friends, and among his most interested listeners was Rachel, whom he visited when he could, sometimes when their spouses were present, though Paula was as jealous of Rachel as Ben-Gurion was of Rachel's husband. Paula, it seems, went more to keep watch than to be entertained, and she was doubtless irked by the contrast between his ebullient mood at Rachel's house and his normally taciturn disposition at home.

Rachel was still an attractive woman with large expressive eyes and silken dark hair drawn with stunning simplicity into a bun, a gentle woman who radiated warmth—especially in Ben-Gurion's presence. Did she, as some acquaintances thought, harbor fantasies that someday she would have him? Paula apparently suspected so. Nor did Paula doubt that Ben-Gurion still fantasized about Rachel—though she could not know that he had told his first love in an unguarded moment that "if I had married you, I would not leave home as often as I do now."

Paula was by no means happy about the links that Ben-Gurion and Rachel had cultivated between the two families, almost, it seemed, as an extension of their own youthful bond. The Ben-Gurion children spent many of their vacations with Rachel's family, while Ben-Gurion regarded her three daughters virtually as his own. Rachel's obvious pleasure in Ben-Gurion's emotional ties with her family only darkened Paula's scowls. Didn't that "vamp" know who married him?

Ben-Gurion was apparently oblivious to this subtle rivalry; he was too busy building a state. With the Zionist movement now in his hands, it was time to leave Histadrut behind and focus on Mapai, so that it would effectively lead the W.Z.O. and one day the Jewish state. Never mind what he said in the past; this party must not threaten the nonsocialist groups but join with them in meeting the common challenge. It must no longer bring in only idealistic pioneers, but "simple Jews, not all of whom studied Marx." Mapai must convert itself from a class party into a *national* party, powerful enough to make the British open the door to Palestine—and the Arabs, the door to peace. . . .

Was peace with the Arabs possible? In early 1933, Ben-Gurion decided to find out. He went in secret to Moshe Shertok's Jerusalem home one night, and the two men waited anxiously for a knock on the door. Ben-Gurion braced himself for what he felt would be a memorable meeting. For the first time he would have a long serious talk about peace with a leading Arab. Up to now he had been too busy saving Jews to think much about wooing Arabs. But now, as a political figure, he must think of how to live in peace with them.

The knock came, the door opened, and Ben-Gurion stared curiously into the good-humored eyes of a chubby man with a toothy smile that stretched broadly under a white brush mustache. He was Musa Alami, attorney-general in the British administration and a relative of the mufti. The three men sat down over tea and Ben-Gurion and Alami instantly liked each other, though the Arab's smile soon dissolved into a frown of frankness. It would be better to let the land remain poor and desolate for another hundred years, said Alami, than to let more Jews enter Palestine.

Ben-Gurion was startled. "The prevailing assumption in the Zionist movement then," he would later relate, "was that [the Jews] were bringing a blessing to the Arabs of the country and that they therefore had no reason to oppose us. . . . That assumption was shattered."

He might have corrected it many years earlier, but his tardy enlightenment did not leave him angry or resentful. "I felt that, as a patriotic Arab," he would say, "[Alami] had every right to this view."

Ben-Gurion then made an ingenious proposal: The Jewish state would join a regional federation, something like the British Commonwealth, in which the Arabs would be the overwhelming majority. So what if the Jews enjoyed a majority in a tiny part of the federation. Their state would be no more than a star in a galaxy. No matter what happened in Palestine, the Arabs would remain a powerful force in the world, while the Jews, without a state, would remain weak and vulnerable.

Alami was impressed with this logic, and many talks followed, interrupted by visits to several *kibbutzim* and finally culminating in an accord that delighted Ben-Gurion. In principle, the Jews could immigrate without limit and settle even in Transjordan; take part in a British-led government on a parity basis with the Arabs; ultimately set up a state linked to an Arab Federation; maintain a system of Hebrew Labor within the Jewish economy, while working with the Arabs to build industry; help local Arabs to raise their living standards and the Arab states to achieve unity.

Alami now reported on their talks to the mufti, who would have to back any agreement.

"This came as a bombshell to the mufti," Ben-Gurion would later write. "He had not imagined that there were Jews who sincerely wished an understanding and an agreement with the Arabs . . . He, Musa Alami, had assured the mufti that I was speaking honestly and sincerely and that he could rely on me. The mufti heard the plan with great interest."

The bombshell ricocheted back on Ben-Gurion. He too was stunned. Haj Amin interested? Incredible! But true, Alami assured him. Now, he said, Ben-Gurion had to win over two highly influential Syrian leaders who were living in Geneva. Ben-Gurion rushed to Geneva, but both men disdainfully rejected the accord.

This negotiating experience had driven home a salient point: Thousands of Jewish youths might have to die to realize Ben-Gurion's dream of a Jewish state. No longer able to shunt this apocalyptic thought from his mind, Ben-Gurion now leaped at every opportunity to talk peace with Arab notables. He met with George Antonius, the "theoretician" of Palestine nationalism, and others, including the head of the Palestine Istiklal ("Independence") party, two officials close to Saudi Arabia's King Ibn Saud, and more Syrian nationalists. But preliminary interest always fizzled as these leaders glanced over their shoulder at unseen assassins. The fact was that Ben-Gurion would not and could not make the one compromise they wanted: He refused to settle for less than a Jewish majority in Palestine.

And in April 1936 the Arabs punctuated their demands with gunfire, which would finally lay to rest Ben-Gurion's vision of peace on Zionist terms.

1

1. *Farewell gathering at Ben-Gurion's house
in Plonsk, Poland, 1906, for Ben-Gurion (front
row, center), Rachel Nelkin Beit-Halachmi (to
Ben-Gurion's left), and Shlomo Zemach (to
Rachel's left), before they departed for
Palestine. Among those bidding goodbye were
Ben-Gurion's sister Rivka (to his right), his
father, Avigdor (at right window), and his
stepmother, Tsivia (at left window). Ben-
Gurion would always resent his stepmother
for replacing his mother, Sheindel. Sheindel's
death, when he was eleven, scarred him for
life. [Israel Government Press Office]*
2. *Shlomo Zemach, a close boyhood friend of
Ben-Gurion, came from the richest family in
Plonsk and was the first Jew from there to
emigrate to Palestine. [Ada Vereté]*

2

3

3. *Rachel Beit-Halachmi with two of her children. Ben-Gurion secretly loved
Rachel from childhood to his death. He abandoned her to work in the Palestine
wilderness, but he sought to win her back even after she married someone else and
had children. He once offered to run off with her to America. [Ruth Beit-Halachmi]*
4. *Farm and winery workers in Rishon LeZion, Palestine, 1907. Ben-Gurion (front
row, center) nearly starved before getting this job. He treaded grapes here, one time
for three days nonstop. [Zionist Archives and Library, N.Y.]*

4

5. *Staff of Ahdut,* *the first Hebrew language newspaper in Palestine. Members, photographed in 1910, included Ben-Gurion (front row, second from right), Yitzhak Ben-Zvi (front row, second from left), Jacob Zerubavel (center), and Rachel Yanait Ben-Zvi (second row). Ben-Gurion's fiery articles catapulted him into international prominence. [Yad Ben-Zvi]*

6. *Ben-Gurion (center) with Israel Shochat (left) and Yitzhak Ben-Zvi as students in Constantinople. They studied law there in 1913–14 and prepared to run for the Turkish parliament in order to fight for an autonomous Jewish state within the Ottoman Empire. Shochat headed the Hashomer, Palestine's first Jewish armed force. He excluded Ben-Gurion from his elite fighting group for seeking too much power. [Israel Consulate General Library, N.Y.]*

7. *Ben-Gurion and his bride, Paula, shortly after they married in New York in 1918 ... during his lunch hour. He had fled to the United States when the Turks expelled him and other leading Zionists from Palestine after World War I broke out. [Israel Consulate General Library, N.Y.]*

6

7

8

9

10

8. Ben-Gurion wearing the uniform of the British-led Jewish Legion, which he helped to organize in the United States for dispatch to the Palestine front in World War I. [Israel Government Press Office]

9. Zionist leader Chaim Weizmann (seated, right) and former British Foreign Minister Lord Balfour (far left). In 1917 Weizmann persuaded the British leader to issue the Balfour Declaration, which promised to establish a Jewish national home in Palestine after World War I. [Israel Consulate General Library, N.Y.]

10. Ben-Gurion harangues workers as chief of the Histadrut in the early 1920s. He nurtured the Histadrut, Jewish Palestine's giant labor federation, as the nucleus of a future state. [Zionist Archives and Library, N.Y.]

11. Family portrait taken about 1926. From left to right: son Amos, Avigdor, daughter Geula, Paula, daughter Renana, and David. In his obsession with a state Ben-Gurion had little time for his family, though he felt a special bond with Renana from her infancy. [Ben-Gurion House]

12

12. *Ben-Gurion's younger sister, Zippora, and her two sons in the mid-1920s. Because David favored her, she and her children were the first members of his family that he brought to Palestine. [Ben-Gurion House]*

13. *Family portrait, late 1930s. From left to right: Paula and Geula (standing); Ben-Gurion, Renana, Avigdor, and elder brother Avraham. Paula was deeply antagonistic toward Avigdor and Avraham and once accused Avraham of stealing a gold pin from her. [Ben-Gurion House]*

13

14. *Ben-Gurion, Paula, and Renana return to Palestine from abroad in the 1930s. He traveled overseas constantly but seldom with Paula, who in her despair often tried to lure him home with claims of family illness. [Zionist Archives and Library, N.Y.]*

15. *Vladimir Jabotinsky (front row, right), leader of the right-wing Revisionist Party, poses with his paramilitary commanders, including Menachem Begin (front row, extreme left). Ben-Gurion and Jabotinsky slandered each other during the Zionist Congress elections of 1933, then, two years later, secretly met and became close friends. They were, however, driven apart again by political and ideological pressures. [Vladimir Jabotinsky Archives]*

16. *Haj Amin el-Husseini, the mufti of Jerusalem, who called for the massacre of Jews in 1920, 1921, and 1929, and led a full-scale Arab revolt against the Jews and British from 1936 to 1939, turning Palestine into a bloody battleground. Ironically, he thus encouraged the Jews, under Ben-Gurion, to build an armed force of their own that would one day crush the Arabs. [Author's photo]*

17. *Berl Katzenelson was Ben-Gurion's closest friend and adviser.* [Israel Government Press Office]
18. *Moshe Shertok (later Sharett), Chaim Weizmann, Berl Katzenelson, and Ben-Gurion in 1935. Ben-Gurion surged to the top of the world Zionist movement in the early 1930s.* [Israel Labor Party Archives]

17

19. *Geula, Renana, and Amos Ben-Gurion. The family was so poor that Amos often wore Geula's hand-me-downs.* [Ben-Gurion House]

18

19

Book II

JOSHUA

CHAPTER SEVEN

Who casteth firebrands, arrows, and death?
PROVERBS 26:18

THE first Arab bullets tore through the night of April 15, 1936, ripping into two Jews on the Tulkarm-Nablus road and setting off a chain reaction of violence in the dark twisting alleys of several towns. Four days later, Arab bands thundering over the cobblestones of Jaffa wantonly knifed and shot sixteen Jews to death. Were these attacks simply a spate of common Arab street crimes? Though many Jewish leaders thought they were, Ben-Gurion was doubtful. Even if the murders had been spontaneous up to now, the mufti and his men would surely exploit them to spark others. The crimes had made the Palestine Arabs look odious to the world anyway, so why not seize this opportunity to detonate a full-scale rebellion?

Ben-Gurion's suspicion proved well-founded. The *effendis* called a general strike on April 22 and formed a Supreme Arab Committee, which vowed to close down shops, factories and ports until the British stopped Jewish immigration, banned land sales to Jews, and formed an Arab-majority government. The aim of the strike was to fuel new violence, and it did. Palestine exploded into a battleground with Arabs, daggers raised, guns drawn, attacking Jews and Britons alike and even uprooting trees the Jews had planted on barren land. Had the great bloodbath begun?

Ben-Gurion was not too worried at first. Though he now realized that Arab anti-Zionism was a true nationalist phenomenon and not simply a phobia of the *effendis*, the Arab masses, he felt, surely opposed the revolt even if they sympathized with the aim.

"This is no national uprising," he wrote. "The Arab people is not involved, not even the bulk of it; it lacks the will, the capacity and the strength to revolt. At the same time, they are not just highwaymen and thugs."

But as violence spread, he grew alarmed, and he was soon convinced that the Jews were in mortal danger, not only from the Arabs but from the British and even themselves. In desperation High Commissioner Sir Arthur Wauchope wanted to give the Arabs almost everything they demanded. He would cut down Jewish immigration and land purchases and set up a legislative council with an Arab majority. As if that were not trouble enough, Mapai began to disintegrate, with workers led by leftist leader Yitzhak Tabenkin screaming for more independence and party posts—while Palestine burned.

In the dazzling glow, Ben-Gurion stood by helplessly as the flames threatened to devour the harvest of three decades of heartbreaking toil. All he could do now was to pull out of the embers what could be saved. It was time for the Jews to show their military strength, however limited. He ordered Hagana fighters to open their hidden caches and remove the new greased rifles they had stolen from the British or smuggled in from abroad. But they must remember that their job was to defend, not to kill indiscriminately. They must be guided by one word: *havlaga*, "self-restraint." No Jew was to let the smell of blood go to his head. The Jew was to be the purest fighter in the world, for he was defending a people destined to purify the human spirit.

"Terrorism benefits the Arabs," he wrote. "It may lay waste the *Yishuv* and shake Zionism. But to follow in the Arabs' footsteps and ape their deeds is to be blind to the gulf between us."

Besides, there was now a practical side to *havlaga*. The Jews had to win the sympathy of Britain no matter how some mandate officials felt. The British, it seemed, bore gifts for everyone. With one hand they were giving the Arabs concessions, but with the other they were giving the Jews at least some arms and military training, and this aid must not be jeopardized. The British represented a last-ditch security barrier against Arab mobs threatening to massacre the Jews, and any Jewish attacks might weaken this barrier. The *Yishuv* couldn't take the risk.

The Hagana was now emerging as a far stronger guerrilla army than ever before. It was a national force, no longer tied exclusively to labor, and led by an excellent commander, Eliahu Golomb, who was close to Ben-Gurion. Golomb's command now embraced men who wore not only the working clothes of the Histadrut, but the baggy suits of the new middle class. All Jewish fighters obeyed its orders except the Revisionist military arm, the Irgun Zvai Leumi. But even Jabotinsky endorsed *havlaga*, though he could not restrain some Irgunists from hurling bombs into Arab marketplaces.

Actually, the *Yishuv* did not have to rely entirely on the Hagana for its strength to resist. The Arabs were inadvertently helping it not only by pushing the British into Jewish arms, but by spurring the Jewish economy with their strike. For the jobs they vacated could be filled by Jews climbing off the ships anchored in the murky waters of the Mediterranean. Had not the British tied immigration quotas to available jobs? Soon, with the Jaffa docks shut down, the Jews were carrying timber on their backs to build new docks in Tel Aviv, and Jewish rather than Arab stevedores were hauling freight.

The Arab leaders grew desperate. They stepped up their attacks, promising not to let up until the British shut off the flow of Jews streaming in, at least temporarily, and the British began to quake. Reluctant to stir the wrath of the whole Moslem world —especially while Hitler and Mussolini threatened war—mandate officials avoided cracking down on the *effendis* even though Britons as well as Jews were their victims.

Ben-Gurion rushed to London, where, with Weizmann, he stormed into the offices of almost all British leaders from the Colonial Secretary down. Don't give in! he pleaded. Don't be blackmailed!

Meanwhile, both Parliament and the press lauded the "brave" and "humane" Jews. The British public had long been confused, seeing justice in the claims of both Arab and Jew, but the wanton murder had begun to erode sympathy for the Arabs. The problem was Weizmann. Fearing that the whole *Yishuv* might perish, he suggested that the Jewish Agency *volunteer* to halt immigration temporarily "in order to help the government," and actually assured Iraqi Prime Minister Nuri Said, who was in London, that it would. Ben-Gurion was horrified. How could Weizmann even think of compromising *aliya*, the most sacred principle of Zionism? When Weizmann refused to retract his promise to Nuri Said, Ben-Gurion reported to his comrades back home, "I was unable to foresee the disaster that now awaits us because of this man."

Ben-Gurion threatened to resign but, as he apparently expected, his colleagues "persuaded" him to stay on the job. Meanwhile, his policy of *havlaga* helped to persuade the British to let the creaking tubs bulging with Jews discharge their human cargo as usual. The British also handed out arms and police uniforms to thousands of Hagana members, who stood guard in the settlements. And London even funneled more troops into Palestine.

Finally, in October 1936, the Arabs held their fire, hid their weapons, and unbolted the doors of their shops and factories. *Havlaga* had proved more devastating than bullets in imposing peace. But Ben-Gurion was by no means sure that peace would last. On Amos' sixteenth birthday he took his son to lunch in Haifa and, instead of ordering a cake with sixteen candles, gave him a pistol with six bullets. What else should a father give a boy at a time of such tension and uncertainty?

Before the fighting ended, the British sent over a new Palestine Royal Commission under Professor Earl Peel to examine the causes of the Arab revolt and seek ways of healing the festering Palestinian wound. And while Ben-Gurion feared that this commission, like all the others, would simply slam the door on Jewish immigrants, he saw it as an opportunity to woo the British. After all, *havlaga* had already won many British friends.

The British, Ben-Gurion was sure, would never agree to set up a Jewish state now, so why ask for one? Better to demand simply swifter immigration; the land would then soon swarm with Jews, and a state would automatically spring forth in a few years anyway. Nor should the British be encouraged to leave Palestine while the Nazis and Arabs threatened his people. No, it was not the time to reveal his real aim.

On January 7, 1937, Ben-Gurion thus told members of the Royal Commission:

> For the solution of the Jewish problem . . . it is not necessary that Palestine should constitute a separate state and we should be only too glad if, when the Jewish national home is fully established, Palestine shall be a member of a greater unit. . . . the British Commonwealth. [For one thing,] there are Holy Places in Palestine that are holy to the whole

civilized world, and it is not in our interest that we should be made responsible for them.

Then the Jews didn't want a state?

A Jewish state would be less than a national home to the Jewish people. Why? . . . [The inhabitants could] decide without giving any reasons who shall or shall not come into that state.

"You mean," asked an incredulous Commission member, "there might come a moment when, if there was a Jewish national state, they might say, 'We have enough people here, we do not want any more of you?' "

Yes, without giving any reason for it, but they cannot do it when there is a national home for the Jewish people. . . . If Palestine were an empty country we could say [we wanted] a Jewish state. . . . But there are other inhabitants in Palestine . . . and as we do not want to be at the mercy of others, they have a right not to be at the mercy of the Jews. . . . A state may imply a wish to dominate others.

Those who knew Ben-Gurion could barely suppress their laughter—and awe. A state was unnecessary? The Jews would be reluctant to rule over an Arab minority? Jews might keep Jews out of *Eretz Yisrael?* What nonsense! Yet Ben-Gurion spoke with the same burning intensity as he had done when pushing for a state.

Only a day after Ben-Gurion explained why there shouldn't be a Jewish state, one Commission member suddenly asked his colleagues, "If there were no other way to peace, might it not be a final and peaceful settlement—to terminate the mandate by agreement and split Palestine into two halves, the plan being an independent Jewish state . . . and the rest of Palestine, plus Transjordan, being an independent Arab state?"

Ben-Gurion was stunned. Partition! The Commission was talking about a Jewish state! And from this moment on, so was he. On February 4, 1937, about four weeks after he had testified *against* a state, he was again arguing *for* one—before members of his party's central committee.

"At first," he told them at a meeting in his Tel Aviv home, "this plan might seem utterly fantastic. And indeed it might have seemed fantastic a year ago, and could appear absurd in another year. But at this particular moment it is *not* fantastic."

And on returning to London, Ben-Gurion wrote Paula: "My nerves are tense and almost ready to snap, and I can't sleep at night. Lying before us may be an unprecedented battle"—the battle to win a reasonably large slice of Palestine. . . . "We are facing a complete revolution in our life in Palestine, and perhaps in Jewish history."

On July 2 an aide rushed into Ben-Gurion's London office waving the first of four long cables from Moshe Shertok in Jerusalem —the report of the Royal Commission. Ben-Gurion grabbed it and devoured its contents with the excitement that Moses might have felt when he first read the Ten Commandments. The Jewish state would embrace about one-fourth of the country, including the Galilee, the Jezreel Valley, and the coastal plain, with about 260,000 Jews and 225,000 Arabs. The Arab state would comprise the rest of Palestine plus Transjordan. The British would keep enclaves under permanent mandate, including Jerusalem and several other major towns.

"When I . . . weigh . . . the advantages and disadvantages of the Commission's proposal compared to my own [partition] plan," Ben-Gurion wrote Amos with low-key satisfaction, "I find that, generally speaking, it is better." And in his diary, he declared simply on July 2: "The Jewish state will rise in our time."

But in addressing the Mapai central committee, he could no longer suppress his exuberance. He was, he cried, "moved to the depths of my heart and the chasm of my soul by the great and wonderful redeeming vision of a Jewish state, whose hour has pealed." The Peel report was the "beginning of the redemption, a greater redemption than in the days of Ezra and Nehemiah." The miracle was happening, the dream coming true.

Most of his comrades, however, were not ready to settle for a partial miracle, for half a dream. How could he abandon claims to most of the Promised Land? Such a small state could not survive. Ben-Gurion found himself in curious company. His closest associate and friend, Berl Katzenelson, opposed partition, while his fierce foe and rival, Chaim Weizmann, backed it.

When Amos wrote him that he had mixed feelings, Ben-Gurion tried his best to convince him with a lesson on pragmatism.

> Sentimental considerations have no place in politics, [he wrote back]. The only thing we must decide . . . is: What is desirable and good for us, what path will lead to the goal, what policy will strengthen us and what policy will weaken us. . . . Naturally, I would prefer not to partition the country. . . . But . . . would we get more if there were no partition?

Besides,

> the more Jewish strength increases in the country, the more the Arabs will realize . . . that it would be in their interest to work together, to accept our aid, and to permit us to settle in all parts of the country, of their own free will. . . . I act on the assumption that a partial Jewish state will not be the end, but the beginning. . . . It will be a powerful lever in our historic effort to redeem the country in its entirety . . . whether by agreement and mutual understanding with our Arab neighbors or *in another way.* . . . The rest [of the land] will come eventually. It must come.

But Ben-Gurion didn't want Britain to know at this time that "it must come," or even that he and some other Jewish leaders backed partition. After all, he had assured the British that the Jews didn't want any state at all. Would they not find him "opportunistic" if he suddenly changed his mind? At the same time, the Jews could better bargain for a larger state if Britain thought they opposed any partition at all.

In late July, Ben-Gurion climbed to the visitors' gallery of Westminster Palace and anxiously watched as his British parliamentary friends plunged into turbulent debate. Certainly they would demand a larger Jewish state than the Commission recommended. The Honorable Winston Churchill, portly and impetuous, rose and spoke with cutting elegance. Partition? Utterly unacceptable! How could the British so flagrantly "betray" their Jewish friends? Former Prime Minister Lloyd George stood up, a model of white-mustached imperialistic dignity. He would never agree to partition either. And so Parliament voted against it. Ben-Gurion was shocked: His tactic had backfired. He and his comrades had attacked partition so persuasively that their British friends thought they were doing the Zionists a favor!

Like most setbacks, however, this one only hardened Ben-Gurion's will. His main problem now was to persuade his own people to back the idea of partition, and he would have his chance at the Twentieth Zionist Congress meeting in Zurich in August 1937. But there too he met defeat. Still, Ben-Gurion, hoarse, sweaty, weak from fatigue, managed to scrape out a compromise: The proposed partition was unsatisfactory, a patched-together resolution declared, but the Zionist Executive could sit down with the British and negotiate for a more viable state. Then, however, the Jewish Agency Council met and came up with a new scheme: The British should call an Arab-Jewish conference to consider how to improve the mandate! Gloom.

After two thousand homeless years, the Jews trembled before the millennium.

Only the League of Nations now supported partition—conditionally. Britain, meanwhile, sent another more "reasonably minded" commission to Palestine under Sir Charles Woodhead, and it returned with a plan that the government knew nobody would accept: The "Jewish state" would be a kind of Hebrew Vatican, a spiritual center squeezed into ten thousand square kilometers!

Ben-Gurion's spirits plummeted and he turned to his closest friend, Katzenelson, for consolation—though, ironically, Berl's opposition to the partition plan had helped to feed Ben-Gurion's despondency.

"He was on the verge of a complete breakdown several times," Katzenelson would write a friend. "He even despaired of himself. And I had to dress his wounds."

Ben-Gurion sought relief as well in thoughts of his family, which normally found it hard competing for his attention. And Paula revealed her own loneliness in a spate of frantic prose, apparently igniting her husband's old sense of guilt. His response, which both served his ego and soothed his agony, lacked the passion of earlier years, but nevertheless glowed with rare flashes of sentiment.

> Life is very difficult, Paula. . . . I have never complained, and I am not complaining now. . . . [But] I stand alone, and I bear a heavy burden. . . . Yet I bear it with love, and with all my being. As I try to strengthen the party, encourage the comrades, increase their confidence, I sometimes find myself consumed by bitter feelings, which I keep hidden. . . . I find myself overwhelmed by a terrible loneliness, as if I were living in the desert, buried in its utter emptiness. So every indication of love and friendship on your part is precious to me.

As he bent over his desk in London one day in September 1938, Ben-Gurion read the headlines in the morning newspaper: "Peace in our time!" What kind of peace? The British and French had betrayed Czechoslovakia at their meeting with Hitler in Munich.

"Hitler's prestige will rise even higher in Germany and the world," he wrote Paula. "America will retreat into its shell and will recoil in disgust from European affairs. The Central European countries will rush to make peace with the Nazis, and a new and terrible threat will confront the Jews of Europe."

Palestine? "They handed Czechoslovakia over. Why shouldn't they do the same with us?"

Frantically, Ben-Gurion met with Malcolm MacDonald, now Colonial Secretary, at Weizmann's sumptuous home. MacDonald had always seemed friendly to the Zionists, more so than his father, former Prime Minister Ramsay MacDonald. Would he allow such a crime?

Over dinner the secretary chillingly analyzed Munich: "This time the Germans have a case. . . . Hitler is an intelligent and practical man who wishes to free the Rhine area and to annex Austria and Sudetenland, and nothing more. . . . The arrangement with Hitler ensures peace in the world."

In shock Weizmann asked, "Have you read *Mein Kampf?*"

But the secretary moved on to the Palestine problem. If a world war exploded, the Arab and Moslem world could rise up and threaten the British Empire. Thus, Britain must slow down Jewish immigration to make sure the Jews stayed a minority in Palestine, at least for a while.

Ben-Gurion furiously argued for more immigration to Palestine—not less—and for a Jewish army, but MacDonald would not budge. At midnight the secretary rose and departed, and Ben-Gurion remained in his chair, alone with his terrible thoughts. He had glimpsed the future as filtered through British fear. It was clear that Britain would sell out the Jews as it had sold out the Czechs at Munich. London planned to let the Arabs rule all Palestine. No Jewish immigration, no Jewish state.

Ben-Gurion returned to his hotel room and wrote Paula: "I can foresee global cataclysms that will turn the earth almost upside down."

For days he roamed the streets of London, weighing and reweighing the chances of the *Yishuv*'s survival. Then he cooped himself up in his room and, continuing to meditate bitterly, once again sought solace in thoughts of his neglected family.

"When I returned to the hotel last night," he lamented to his wife about a week after his talk with MacDonald, "I felt a terrible loneliness; everything seems empty and hollow. I am used to being alone and lonely. But this time I feel lost."

But gradually Ben-Gurion's depression lifted, and a few days later he assured Paula: "I believe in the days of the messiah. The wicked shall not be triumphant forever."

On the same day, he wrote his children: "If only the *Yishuv* . . . stands firm, . . . without fear, I am absolutely certain we can thwart this plot."

And then Ben-Gurion told his children how to do it: "Youth

of all ages, those who are young in spirit, will raise high the torch of revolt and fight."

In December 1936, Ben-Gurion had secretely met in his Tel Aviv home with some of his closest comrades, including the Hagana leaders, to thrash out plans for survival. Ben-Gurion grimly predicted the future. Britain might in the end betray the Jews, especially if a new world war threatened its own existence. Then, not only the local Arabs but also the Arab states would try to liquidate the *Yishuv*. Hagana, therefore, must form regular army units, manufacture its own arms and train the pioneers to use them.

Actually, Ben-Gurion stressed, an ill wind was not necessarily bad. Had not the *Yishuv* grown stronger from past crises? Would there have been a Balfour Declaration without World War I, a strong Jewish economy without Arab boycotts, a united Hagana without Arab attacks? If, God forbid, another world war broke out, a Jewish state would surely bud.

The atmosphere was electric; few of Ben-Gurion's comrades had thought that far ahead. And the voltage soared as Ben-Gurion plunged into a campaign to create a powerful Jewish army that could fight the Arabs—and perhaps even the British. Nor was his threat of revolt merely tactical bombast this time, for the only alternative might be to renounce a state.

Ben-Gurion sent agents abroad to buy more arms, which they would smuggle into Palestine in iron pipes and barrels of cement. He sought advice from B. H. Liddell Hart, the British military historian and analyst, who told him over dinner in London how to mobilize thirty thousand Jewish soldiers. And then he selected another Briton to command these men—Captain Orde Wingate, who had been sent to Palestine in 1937 to help quell the Arab revolt.

Wingate was a Biblical scholar of ascetic appearance, with deep-set penetrating blue eyes and beautiful hands that attested to his artistic nature. He excelled in painting watercolors—and waging war. But when he first stepped off a troopship in Haifa one day in 1937 he could not have imagined that he would shortly be waging it at the head of a Jewish force. It took him less than three months, however, to become a mystical Zionist as militant as any Jew and far more aggressive than most Jews in asserting Zionist rights.

"When I was at school," he later explained to a friend, "I was looked down upon, and made to feel that I was a failure and not

wanted in the world. When I came to Palestine I found a whole
people who had been treated like that through scores of generations, and yet at the end of it they were undefeated, were a
great power in the world, building their country anew. I felt I
belonged to such people." And he wrote to his uncle, Sir Regin-
ald Wingate: "I have seen Jewish youth in the *kibbutzim,* and I
assure you that the Jews will produce soldiers better than ours."

He did his best to prove he was right. There must be less
havlaga! he told Ben-Gurion and the Hagana commanders. The
Jews must do more than passively defend themselves; they
must strike back. Spare innocent lives, yes, but *havlaga* must
not guide Jewish military strategy. The Jews, like the ancient
Israelites, must attack, attack, attack! And he would teach them
how. He would create a new Jewish soldier in the mold of the
old one—aggressive, self-confident, unconquerable. His listeners were entranced. A *goy* with the soul of a Maccabee!

Wingate persuaded his British superiors to let him organize
the best Hagana fighters into special "night squads," and soon
Jewish guerrillas, among them future leaders like Moshe Dayan
and Yigal Allon, were storming Arab bases, their pistols stutter-
ing, their knives flashing. But they remained true to the spirit of
havlaga, discerning to the degree possible between the innocent and the guilty. The embryo of a superb Jewish army thus
took form, shaped by a British officer. But the British command
recalled Wingate, whom they found far too friendly to people
who might have to be abandoned. And so one dreary day he
stood before his men and told them in halting Hebrew:

"I am sent away from you and the country I love. . . . They
want to hurt me and you. I promise you that I will come back,
and if I cannot do it the regular way, I shall return as a refugee."

But even as a "refugee," Wingate (who would die commanding
British troops in Burma in World War II) or any other Zionist
would have found it hard to return. For Britain, as Malcolm
MacDonald had hinted to Ben-Gurion, would soon close the
door of Palestine and the Jews could do nothing about it. Ben-
Gurion, true, was building up a Jewish force, but he was not yet
ready for a military clash with the British. Instead he clung to
havlaga, not only as a moral doctrine but as a political tool, a
temporary way to sway the British. He even obliquely cooperated with the British in a common struggle against the Irgun Zvai
Leumi. When British troops captured and executed one member, Shlomo Ben-Yosef, in June 1938, Ben-Gurion was furious

on finding that someone had hoisted a black flag on the Histadrut building. Why should the Histadrut grieve over the death of a Revisionist who had violated *havlaga?* And he spurned an accord between Hagana and the Irgun partly because he didn't want to jeopardize relations with the British.

Nor would Ben-Gurion agree to bring in Jews illegally aboard Hagana ships for fear of a British backlash. When a Hagana leader informed him in January 1938 that a Greek fishing boat, the *Poseidon,* was about to land and disgorge sixty-seven Polish Jews, he sputtered in rage:

"When the boat arrives I shall go down to the shore, take off my shoes, wade into the water and help the boys disembark the newcomers and bring them to shore on my own back. But then I shall go directly to a meeting to have you all disciplined for your utter irresponsibility."

Ben-Gurion not only hesitated to force the door, he also shrank from appealing to world opinion. What would happen if the Zionists harped on the misery of the Jews penned up in Germany and threatened in the rest of Europe? With British bayonets gleaming along the beaches of Palestine, other countries might agree to accept the refugees. Yet the Jews could have only one destination—*Eretz Yisrael.* So in June 1938, shortly before Allied representatives met in Evian, France, to seek ways of rescuing Jews, Ben-Gurion frankly voiced his concern to colleagues in the Jewish Agency Executive.

He did "not know if the conference will open the gates of other countries. . . . But I am afraid [it] might cause tremendous harm to *Eretz Yisrael* and Zionism. . . . Our main task is to reduce the harm, the danger and the disaster . . . and the more we emphasize the terrible distress of the Jewish masses in Germany, Poland and Rumania, the more damage we shall cause."

So be silent, Ben-Gurion cautioned his comrades, unable to imagine the unimaginable. And in the silence, broken only by the wails of the doomed, Evian failed.

A few months later, in November 1938, Hitler hinted at the unimaginable. After a Jewish youth shot a German diplomat in Paris, the Führer unleashed his stormtroopers one night and by dawn forty thousand German Jews had been dragged out of bed and thrown into jail, scores had been killed and wounded, and thousands of Jewish stores, homes and synagogues lay in ashen ruins grotesquely overlaid by a glitter of broken glass.

With the plight of the German Jews now more desperate than ever, another emergency conference was called in London to try to save them from other "Crystal Nights." And again the

Jewish Agency Executive met to debate Zionist strategy. It hadn't changed, even though the vise was tightening. In fact, to emphasize that he had not panicked, Ben-Gurion began speaking about Arab-Jewish relations—until Weizmann reminded him why the group had gathered. His colleagues then agreed that, as Moshe Shertok said, the Agency should not "participate in any activity dealing with emigration to other countries." One member, Nahum Goldmann, even warned that if the German Jews were given refuge outside Palestine, other anti-Semitic nations in Europe might insist that their Jews leave, too. Was Zion to lose the whole European Diaspora? Ben-Gurion listened without dissenting; he seldom spoke at meetings when others voiced his own opinion—especially if this opinion could be morally controversial.

After all, Jews had suffered much in the past, but they had survived. Had not the tears of the persecuted watered the Zionist plant? After the Kishinev pogrom, many Russian Jews had scrambled into boats bound for Palestine, finally realizing that only in Zion would they and their children be safe forever. What could Hitler do to the Jews now? Beat them, jail them, maybe kill some? Like their brothers before them, they would survive this pogrom too. Hitler would learn how futile it was to kill a Jew. And the Jew, in his misery, would learn that he must come home. . . . So the conference in London, like that in Evian, failed.

But there would be one more—to decide whether the Jew could in fact come home.

On the morning of February 7, 1939, Ben-Gurion, stuffed into a morning coat and striped trousers, sat restlessly on a chair still warm from the equally restless flesh of an Arab who, with his colleagues, had refused to talk face to face with the Jews. The Jews, led by Ben-Gurion and Weizmann, now sat at the negotiating table in St. James's Palace listening to the same welcoming speech that Prime Minister Chamberlain had just given the Arabs. "Concentrate on the realities of the present situation," he admonished the Jews.

With his tight stiff collar perhaps aggravating his distress, Ben-Gurion glowered at him even more severely than did Queen Victoria, imperiously staring down from the wall above. Yet he was impressed. Remarkable, the British—full of pomp and dignity even at an execution. Ben-Gurion offered three options: a Middle East federation, partition or a temporary settlement allowing large-scale immigration. But Malcolm MacDonald merely repeated what he had told Ben-Gurion and Weizmann privately: No unbridled immigration. The Jews must remain a minority within an Arab state.

Ben-Gurion tore off his velvet gloves, and for the first time challenged the British to their faces: "Jews cannot be prevented from immigrating into the country except by force of British bayonets, British police and the British navy. And, of course, Palestine cannot be converted into an Arab state over Jewish opposition without the constant help of British bayonets!"

The British were shocked. How very un-Jewish! Was the British Empire to tremble with fear?

Not with fear, Ben-Gurion was sure, but with a sense of injustice. The British might "betray" the Jews if it were expedient, but they were incapable of charging at them with bayonets. Nor would public opinion in Britain stand for such barbarism. He knew the British.

Finally, a miracle! The delegates from Egypt, Iraq and Saudi Arabia agreed to sit and talk in the same room with the Jews. While logs in the fireplace blazed away, the main Arab spokesman, Egyptian Prime Minister Ali Maher, said:

> If Palestine were empty, we, the Arab states, would invite the Jews to come to Palestine and establish a Jewish state in it. For we understand the Jewish ideal. It is a beautiful and just ideal. It is necessary that the Jews also have a state, and it would be good for the Arabs too. But the country is not empty. . . . Arabs have lived there for centuries. . . . Go slowly. Halt immigration for a while, peace will be established, you will win Arab friends. . . . With their goodwill you can continue your activities later. Perhaps you will even become a majority. But do not hurry. Let there first be peace, and if for that purpose you have to slow down —is peace not worth it?

While stirred by this conciliatory plea, Ben-Gurion replied by asking who broke the peace and who could restore it. Not the Jews. And Jewish immigration was hardly a valid reason for Arab violence. Jewish claims to Palestine were a reality too, and it would be unrealistic to halt immigration. Could a mother in labor stop giving birth? he asked. "It is possible to kill the child or to kill the mother; but it is impossible to expect her to cease giving birth."

Then Weizmann declared in so many words that the mother could do just that—at least for a while! "For the first time in twenty years I heard from a Moslem words of friendship and appreciation," he said. "In this spirit we shall be able to talk.

... If we are told, 'We'll reach an agreement, slow down a bit,' we can find common ground."

Ben-Gurion and his colleagues were stunned. Moshe Shertok would say, "I thought my hair was turning white. I sensed that a chasm was opening up at our feet." But Malcolm MacDonald smiled with the euphoria of a man who had just won the sweepstakes. "This meeting has not been in vain after all," he glowed. "It seems that there is common ground on a slowdown of immigration for a time."

Livid, Ben-Gurion cut in: "I am sorry to disrupt the rejoicing, but I still do not see any 'common ground.' ... There can be no talk of a slowdown; that is a unilateral assumption."

MacDonald's smile vanished. "We shall continue the discussion tomorrow," he said.

"When we resume our discussion," Ben-Gurion persisted, "will it be possible to consider a speedup of immigration?"

"No!"

"Why not?"

"Because on the basis of a speedup there will be no agreement."

"I am afraid that on the basis of a slowdown there will also be no agreement."

And there was none.

Ben-Gurion was crushed at first, traumatized by the vast implications of this final failure, and one colleague even described him as "quite hysterical." In a rage he stammered in his diary:

"M.M. [Malcolm MacDonald] revealed himself in all his hypocrisy, crookedness and mendacity." He had tried to "distort, tempt, incite, frighten, deceive" as he stooped to the "intrigues of a cheap shyster ... worthy of serving only a bunch of gangsters and racketeers."

When Ben-Gurion fell ill from the strain, a bouquet of flowers arrived accompanied by a note: "With the best wishes of the Colonial Secretary for a speedy recovery." Even worse than he thought—a hypocrite with *chutzpah!* Ben-Gurion finally calmed and, as the five-week conference drew to a close without him, he scrawled his feelings to Paula:

> I have never experienced anything like these last three weeks ..., the unequal struggle, like that between David versus Goliath, which was fought here in St. James's Palace between the representatives of a poor, homeless, hopeless people and His Majesty's Government, ruler of the mightiest empire on earth.

And Ben-Gurion left no doubt about who really played David's role. Having put up such a good fight, he almost exulted in adversity. True, the British had "betrayed" the Jews, declaring in a White Paper shortly after the London conference that:

1. Only 75,000 Jews could immigrate to Palestine in the next five years and none after that unless the Arabs agreed.
2. The British could forbid the purchase of Palestinian land by Jews.
3. Within ten years an independent Palestinian state dominated by the Arabs would be set up—though the Jews could veto such a state, presumably in favor of continued British rule.

But so "evil, stupid and shortsighted" was this annulment of the Balfour Declaration that Ben-Gurion actually felt relieved. For he was "absolutely certain that this policy cannot be carried out for long," especially since the Arabs also spurned the British paper. And the British would certainly not use bayonets to force the policy down Jewish throats. It was now time to be tough.

For the first time in the history of Zionism and in the history of the Jewish people after the Roman conquest [Ben-Gurion wrote] we faced serious combat with a mighty power and did not rely only on pleading, requests for mercy or appeals for justice. For the first time we used a new argument: our own strength in Palestine. . . . They could hardly believe their ears.

Aboard the ship en route home, Ben-Gurion dwelled on the details of a plan for Jewish resistance when he wasn't glancing at a sociology book or playing a game of chess. On arriving, he immediately met with his colleagues to map out action. He stared at them with the arrogant, impatient eyes of a professor lecturing his pupils and spelled out his plan:

Refuse to cooperate with any scheme for "Arab independence"; build military industries; reorganize Hagana under a central command, and mobilize every adult between eighteen and thirty-five; inject the entire fighting force with the Wingate spirit. Ben-Gurion, as head of the Jewish Agency, was automatically the nominal commander of Hagana, which was an arm of the whole world Zionist movement. Now he would take over direct command and become a kind of "defense minister."

His first order: Activate *Aliya Gimel* ("Immigration G"). Bring in Jews "illegally" and settle them, forcing the British to use bayonets until conscience and publicity gave them pause. This was a complete reversal of his earlier stand, but had not circumstances changed? And besides, Berl Katzenelson had soundly

scolded him for his "excessive" caution in banning such land-
ings. Ben-Gurion would later say, explaining his plan:

> We would organize armed immigration, and members of the Hagana
> would stand on the beaches with weapons in their hands to welcome
> the immigrants. . . . [And] if there was no alternative, the settlers would
> defend their home against the government [also] with weapons in their
> hands. . . . We would show decent men in Britain that what their govern-
> ment was doing was not right; we would show practical men that what
> their government was doing was not practical.

Ben-Gurion's colleagues now thought he was going too far.
Were the immigrants trained soldiers? Sheer suicide! The Jews
of Europe would never submit their families to such a risk, nor
would the boat-owners rent craft that might end up at the bottom of the sea.

But Ben-Gurion would not listen. Was it not worth risking a
few lives to turn the White Paper into ashes and thus clear the
way for all Jews?

The dispute came to a head when the *Colorado*, carrying 380
illegal immigrants, steamed toward shore. Bring them into Tel
Aviv! Ben-Gurion demanded. The Hagana would meet them
with guns drawn. But his colleagues voted him down. He ignored this setback, and when the British seized the vessel and
brought it to Haifa, he bellowed another challenge: Take over
Haifa by force! But once more his colleagues shrank back—No!
He growled defiance, but finally accepted the majority decision.
The Jews would *not* use force to help fellow Jews land.

At the critical moment fear and uncertainty had triumphed
again.

In August 1939, Ben-Gurion traveled to Geneva for the Twenty-
first Zionist Congress and assured hundreds of despairing delegates that the Jews would snip the White Paper into shreds. Too
late, too late! many cried. Hitler was about to pounce. And while
they talked with trembling voices of a dream betrayed, the
Führer signed a nonaggression pact with Russia, freeing him for
an assault on Poland and Western Europe. Chaim Weizmann
plodded to the rostrum and said:

"There are some things that cannot fail to happen. . . . The
remnant shall work on, fight on, live on until the dawn of better
days. Towards that dawn I greet you. May we meet again in
peace."

When he finished, Weizmann embraced Ben-Gurion and

other colleagues "as though he would never let them go," while hundreds of others, most of them doomed, applauded wildly.

"Everybody sobbed, not Ben-Gurion," says one delegate. "Ben-Gurion was already working on illegal immigration, and where the young people would go, and how they would manage. He had no time for [talk about] when we would meet again."

A few days later, on September 1, Ben-Gurion was on a ship heading home. As he sullenly searched the sea, perhaps for his precious boats packed with escaping brethren, momentous news ricocheted around the deck: Germany had invaded Poland. Just as he had learned aboard a vessel taking him home from Constantinople that World War I had broken out, he now learned aboard another taking him home from Geneva that World War II had exploded.

. . . Too late, too late.

CHAPTER EIGHT

Or darkness, that thou canst not see
JOB 22:11

"THE die is cast. Today his Majesty's Government declared war against Hitler's Germany. At this hour of emergency, the *Yishuv* must embark on a three-fold struggle: for the defense of the Homeland, for the welfare of the Jewish people, for the victory of the British Empire. . . ."

Drugged with hope, driven by fear, Ben-Gurion pored over the press release he had helped to draft. As soon as his ship docked on September 3, 1939, he darted to his office in Jerusalem to meet with Hagana leaders and members of the Jewish Agency. This statement reflected their talks. The outbreak of war had changed everything. Before, Ben-Gurion wanted to fight against the British; now he had to fight beside them.

But not every Jew was eager to fight beside men who would snuff out the Zionist dream. Some Mapai leaders even cried that the war was "imperialistic," parroting the Moscow line despite Stalin's honeymoon with Hitler in the wake of a German-Soviet pact. And Ben-Gurion himself was troubled by the dilemma of supporting a government hostile to Jewish immigration. But he solved it a few days after his return with some tortuous Solomonist logic, telling his Hagana commanders:

"We must help the British in their war against Hitler as if there were no White Paper; we must resist the White Paper as if there were no war."

Hardly had Ben-Gurion issued a call to arms when 130,000 men and women besieged recruiting centers. With Britain fighting for its survival, how could it now ban a Jewish army? But it did. For as Ben-Gurion himself explained to Mapai leaders:

"The British understand very well the true reason for our enthusiasm about volunteering for military service; they are not so naïve as to imagine that our only motive is the altruistic desire to help them in their war."

The British understood very well indeed. No, they would not create a Frankenstein army that might push the Arabs into Hitler's arms and then crush the British Mandate in Palestine after the war.

On February 28, 1940, the British struck yet another blow—new Land Regulations. Jews could settle only in a narrow "Pale" embracing 5 percent of Palestine, mostly urbanized, west of the Jordan. Ben-Gurion exploded. He called an urgent meeting of his colleagues and cried that "war on the White Paper now takes precedence over everything else!"—apparently even over the war against Hitler. The Jews had to strike at Britain in any way they could.

"We should break off relations with the hostile administration in Palestine," Ben-Gurion cried, "and not let Jews be mobilized as 'hewers of wood and drawers of water.' "

Was Ben-Gurion serious? his comrades asked. Such a policy would hurt the British struggle against Hitler.

Perhaps. But when the government realized this, it would change its policies. And besides, said Ben-Gurion, reflecting his ambivalent view of the British, they were in no immediate danger. Let it be clear that he was a "patriot of the British Empire, a great Anglophile, and may our lot always fall with the British Empire." But he was a Jew first, and "the problem of the Jewish people comes before anything else."

Ben-Gurion's colleagues were unmoved; they wanted no confrontation. Their leader then reacted as usual with a sulky tantrum—he resigned. Predictably, his comrades called him back. Very well, he could lead a protest campaign against the British —but only in Palestine. Ben-Gurion wasted no time: Strike! Demonstrate! Jews clashed with police. Ambulances sped away with dead and wounded. Enough! cried Ben-Gurion's comrades. And peace settled over the land. Ben-Gurion was enraged. They still didn't understand the logic in his "madness."

On May 1, 1940, Ben-Gurion returned to England to continue a more peaceful campaign for a British-backed army in Palestine. He was hopeful now, for Winston Churchill, a friend of Zion, had become prime minister and his government might be more reasonable than the others. But he found that it wasn't. Frustrated, Ben-Gurion released his fury in Zionist headquarters, a three-story, yellow brick building on Great Russell Street, where he ruled imperiously from a small office overlooking the red-tiled roofs of Bloomsbury. He goaded his aides and secretaries into frantic activity.

"He had a very arrogant manner," one secretary recalls. "He would scream at meetings and mumble bitterly to himself. If his typist left out a word in a report, he would smash his fist on the table and shout at the poor girl."

But not every assistant was terrorized. Doris May, who had long been Weizmann's secretary but also served Ben-Gurion, felt a deep affection for him, as he did for her. Doris was a plain-looking but highly intelligent woman in her early forties, a Catholic who zealously embraced Zionism. But it was not only ideology that sparked their friendship; loneliness—and language—also did. Doris was a Greek scholar, and Ben-Gurion leaped at the chance to learn a tongue that would permit him to savor Plato and other Greek philosophers in the original, feeling that reading translations was "like kissing a woman through a veil." If they weren't bent over a Greek grammar book in Doris' modest home or browsing together in the bookshops along Charing Cross Road, they were speaking Greek in the dim light of an air-raid shelter during the many alerts.

Soon Doris was punctuating her explanations with "darling," though apparently without romantic intent, for she was in love with another Zionist official, Arthur Lourie. Ben-Gurion clearly cherished the intellectual exchange, the swap of views on British and Greek culture, on Judaism and Christianity—the kind of relationship he could never have with Paula. Doris was the ideal companion. She taught him, challenged him, amused him. A *shiksa* (gentile girl) with the gently domineering nature of a Jewish mother, even better, a *scholarly* Jewish mother.

When Paula later visited London she immediately suspected an affair and struck violently at Doris' supposed vulnerabilities. Doris was, after all, a *shiksa*, she constantly reminded her husband. And to make the point, she loudly asked her "rival" once how she could "believe in all that Catholic rubbish." Nor did Paula ignore a hearing problem the woman had. While Ben-

Gurion was talking on the phone with Doris one day, Paula cried: "Speak louder! She's deaf!"

But so was Ben-Gurion—to Paula's jealous tantrums.

When the Nazis began bombing London in September 1940, Ben-Gurion didn't always rush to a shelter and practice his Greek between explosions. He also found other ways to while away the time—often to the dismay of the air-raid wardens. Once his colleagues, unable to find him after a raid, concluded the worst, until he casually sauntered into his office explaining that he had sat out the attack in a cinema, apparently the only spectator not to run for cover when the sirens sounded. He hated crowds and preferred to remain alone so he could think. What picture was playing? Who knew? He could think better with his eyes closed.

Another time he was visiting a Scottish church when the thunder broke. But no one moved as the minister calmly read from the Book of Exodus while lightning flashed through the windows. This was one crowd he loved. "I shall not forget this experience," he wrote a friend. "This little scene symbolizes for me the whole situation of England."

Years later he would recall how he had walked the rubble-strewn streets and seen the taxi drivers and the workers who were not afraid, even as the bombs fell, for to them country and freedom were dearer than life. They would be a model for his own people when the time came for them to fight for *their* life. And his own model would be Winston Churchill. Not since Lenin had a leader so moved him. Ben-Gurion would later say:

> Not only was he the greatest leader Britain ever produced, but he was . . . among the greatest statesmen of all time. . . . He lifted an entire nation out of the depths of humiliation and defeat . . . He was able to do so by his unique combination of qualities—magnetic leadership, powerful eloquence, contagious courage, supreme self-confidence, a deep sense of history and an unshakable faith in the destiny of his people. . . . History would have been quite different if there had been no Churchill.

Was Ben-Gurion identifying with Churchill as he had once done with Lenin? He would surely feel his imprint, even justifying the British leader's failure to annul the White Paper and intervene more effectively for the creation of a Jewish army and ultimately a state. "He was a Zionist sympathizer, but he was first of all an Englishman. He was busy conducting the war and the struggle for victory."

Ben-Gurion was, paradoxically, less understanding of Chaim Weizmann's effort to press Churchill for a Jewish army. For if he viewed Churchill as a model, he still saw Weizmann as a rival. Ben-Gurion, as chairman of the Jewish Agency, was the real leader of Zionism, Weizmann, though undaunted by the movement's recurrent lack of confidence in him, still considered himself its living spirit, and with reason. In the Diaspora, especially in the United States and Britain, it was Weizmann, not Ben-Gurion, who was revered. Weizmann was the great father figure of Zionism, the diplomat, the professor, the scientist, who orated in rich, inspirational language. He was the genius of the movement. Ben-Gurion, on the other hand, was viewed as a tough little trade-unionist who spoke common sense, but dryly and inelegantly, a smart fellow, if obviously self-educated. And he was resentfully aware of Weizmann's image—and his own.

In September 1940 Weizmann finally plucked a promise from Britain to form a Jewish military force. "It is almost as great a day as the Balfour Declaration," he exclaimed.

Ben-Gurion, however, was less euphoric. Why didn't Weizmann get a guarantee that the force would fight *only* in Palestine? The conditions were unacceptable.

Weizmann was indignant. He was lucky to have made the deal he did! And the Jewish force would have only symbolic value anyway. It would surely be wrong to use it as a conquering army after the war. Wrong? Not to Ben-Gurion. He demanded that Weizmann take him along to all future talks on a Jewish army, but Weizmann angrily spurned this "ultimatum," and his colleagues backed him. Ben-Gurion retreated home and scratched in his diary: "A bitter disappointment." And, as he had done so often when his views were rejected, he fled the scene of his defeat, heading this time for the United States.

Ben-Gurion would urge American Jews to press Washington on two fronts: It must step up war aid to Britain, and it must push Britain to form a Jewish army that would fight in Palestine. He would forge iron links not with unreliable statesmen or fearful Jewish leaders but with the great Jewish masses. Weizmann was betting on Britain, but it would certainly be America, in Ben-Gurion's view, that would replace the ghettos of Eastern Europe as the center of Diaspora life after the war. And the Jews of America must make sure that Washington would never let *Eretz Yisrael* be turned into a new ghetto.

America was another world to Ben-Gurion. In Britain, sirens
screamed and bombs exploded, but people joked in the shelters.
Here there was peace, business as usual and, among the Jews,
fear. Not of the Nazis, but of their fellow Americans! They
feared charges of dual loyalty. They feared outbursts of anti-
Semitism. And to prove their "patriotism" some of them
sounded as isolationist as the militants of the antiwar America
First movement. Yet, wasn't Britain fighting for its life, for the
life of the whole free world? Wasn't the fate of the Jews tied to
that of Britain?

Nevertheless, Ben-Gurion scurried from meeting to meeting
trumpeting his views, arguing, demanding. Utterly exhausted,
he relaxed only on weekends when there were few people
around to badger. He would stroll the twisting lanes of Central
Park or the twig-strewn paths winding through lush suburban
forests to remind himself of the woods, lakes and flowers that
would one day replace the windswept desert still blanketing
parts of his *Eretz Yisrael*.

But whether on a stroll or on the run, he was seldom alone,
for he had a new companion, Miriam Taub, a bright, vivacious
employee of the Zionist Organization of America, who chauffeured him and did his secretarial work. Like Doris May in
London, Miriam eased his loneliness and his occasionally in-
suppressible need for affection. He never thought of taking her
to the theater, a film or a concert, but he often dined with her in
a particular Rumanian restaurant where he savored his favorite
calf's liver while exchanging views on Zionism, philosophy or
American-Jewish psychology.

Ben-Gurion was stymied by this psychology. Yes, he met
some Jews who would listen to him, especially members of
Hadassah, the Zionist women's organization, who once kept
him talking all night. But most American Jews were adamant.
They would not put President Franklin D. Roosevelt "on the
spot." Ben-Gurion finally gave up and, after ten months abroad,
returned to Palestine in January 1941.

On arriving home, Ben-Gurion found himself in a wonderland
even more removed from reality than the United States. While
millions of Jews in Europe writhed under the Nazi whip in
ghettos and concentration camps that would soon empty into

gas chambers, their brothers in Palestine haggled over how to build socialism and when to hold party elections.

Yitzhak Tabenkin now headed a leftist group called "Faction B," which had won over the socialist youth and threatened to turn even the Hagana into a political tool. Ben-Gurion was appalled. This wasn't the time to pursue politics, he cried. Debate on all political questions must stop until the war ended! What should they discuss? Defense of Palestine, a Jewish army, immigration, construction, a state. He did not mention the captive millions who might not live to inhabit the state.

Meanwhile, the Germans crept closer to Palestine. The Balkans fell, then Crete. A pro-Nazi regime took over in Iraq, backed by the mufti, and the French Vichy regime clamped a grip on Syria. More ominous yet, General Rommel's tanks were slithering eastward across the North African desert toward neighboring Egypt, and the British were getting ready to pull out of Palestine. But, with a grotesque persistence, the Jews went on squabbling. Ben-Gurion met with the Hagana commanders to seek a way to save the *Yishuv* despite itself.

If the British withdrew, all Jewish soldiers serving in the British army would desert wholesale with their arms and remain behind. Most of the other Jews would join them on Mount Carmel in Haifa, where the *Yishuv* would fortify itself against a Nazi assault and fight to the death as Jewish zealots did at Masada in 70 A.D.

And the survivors, what would happen to them? a colleague asked. They would work for the Germans until they were liberated, Ben-Gurion replied. The Nazis would need workers and technicians.

As Rommel inched closer, party leaders finally agreed in June 1941 to stop bickering and build barricades. And Ben-Gurion decided to go abroad once more to win backing for a postwar state even if Zion should fall. On June 22, 1941, the day Hitler invaded Russia, Ben-Gurion flew off to London en route to the United States. He was in such a hurry that he neglected to leave his family "even a penny" to live on in the frightening days ahead. He might never see his loved ones again but his mind was on the state.

Lord Moyne, the new British Colonial Secretary, greeted Ben-Gurion warmly, then made a chilling offer. "We shall drive the Germans out of East Prussia, settle the Jews, and establish a Jewish state there."

Incredulous, Ben-Gurion replied: "You can drive the Germans out of East Prussia with machine guns—but even with machine guns you will not be able to bring masses of Jews to East Prussia. The land of the Jews is Palestine."

Ben-Gurion then tramped out and decided to play his wildest card. With a ticket to the United States in his pocket, he sent a farewell note to Weizmann: "I am departing not very encouraged—but not despairing. We shall overcome the difficulties."

And they would, he felt, if only Weizmann, whose genteel diplomacy had miserably failed, would now let him move toward the millennium in his own way.

On November 24, 1941, Ben-Gurion plunged once more into the seething chaos of New York. A taxi rushed him to his hotel and, though dazed as usual by the crass rhythms of this frantic city, he immediately set telephones ringing around the country. Top Zionists and non-Zionists alike picked up the receiver and heard his impelling voice: Come to a meeting that could set the future course of Judaism!

Until now, Ben-Gurion would never ask the great powers for too much or demand that the Diaspora push them too hard. Why frighten Zion's benefactors? But now he had to frighten them. He would take an extreme stand—like the one the Revisionists had been taking all along—and tell the world that the Jews must have an independent state in all of historic Palestine, including Transjordan. Unlike the Revisionists, however, he would settle in the end for an ample chunk of Palestine and membership in the British Commonwealth or a Middle East federation. But meanwhile, let the world think he was an extremist who would not compromise.

Carefully weighing every word, Ben-Gurion revealed his demands to the gathering of Jewish leaders, who, after coming out of shock, asked to see a detailed proposal. While drafting it on Sunday, December 7, Ben-Gurion turned on the radio and listened in dismay to a news bulletin: Japan had attacked Pearl Harbor! America was in the war! Hitler's fate, it seemed, was sealed. Yet Ben-Gurion's first reaction was not joy, for his state was in jeopardy. The United States would surely tighten its ties with Britain now and do nothing to antagonize that country. And the American Jews would be more afraid than ever to press their government on so "marginal" a question as Palestine. What would Pearl Harbor do to his dream?

Ben-Gurion soon recovered from the news, however, and buried himself in his new campaign. He rejected support from no one—except his old enemies, the Revisionists, though they were the most fervent supporters of his plan! Jabotinsky had died in 1940, and his more militant followers had snatched the reins of the Revisionist remnant—the Irgun Zvai Leumi. Now the Irgun chief in New York, Peter Bergson [Kook], who had been campaigning for an American Jewish volunteer army, offered to join forces with the American Zionist Organization. Ben-Gurion shrugged contemptuously. No deal. Not unless Bergson's group agreed to take orders from *his*. He would work with non-Zionists he trusted, but not with Zionists he distrusted.

Ben-Gurion's scenario now called for a cosmic American Zionist conference unmatched in importance since Herzl's founding convention of the Zionist movement in Basel almost forty years earlier. If that initial meeting vaguely defined the aims of Zionism as it was being launched, this one would, for the first time, sharply define the final goal. As Ben-Gurion rushed plans for the grand opening in May 1942, he learned with chagrin that Chaim Weizmann had decided to come. Was he to be upstaged again? He tried to discourage Weizmann, but the elderly Zionist leader sailed from London even though he was still mourning the death of his son, a Royal Air Force pilot who had plunged to his death.

Weizmann had not changed. He still ignored Ben-Gurion's views and saw important people on his own. Ben-Gurion again protested, and again colleagues backed Weizmann. How could anyone humiliate their hero, especially at this time of grief? But Ben-Gurion persisted.

"He put a terrific strain on everyone," charged a Weizmann aide. "He was tempestuous, convulsive and threatening. He berated people and was intolerant of any point of view that seemed at variance with his own. He acted as if he alone were conscious of the war and the danger to Palestine."

Ben-Gurion, however, felt he had good reason to "berate" Weizmann, and would later tell his colleagues that Weizmann "instigated others to oppose me, and I was obliged to push through [what] I considered no more than a compromise." Ben-Gurion would now demand a Jewish "commonwealth" in all of present Palestine, though *not* in Transjordan as he had planned earlier.

Weizmann had himself appealed for a state in all of Palestine in an article he wrote for the January 1942 issue of the American periodical *Foreign Affairs*. But Ben-Gurion didn't believe for a moment that he really meant to campaign for such a state. And in fact Weizmann regarded his magazine appeal as a political slogan, a negotiating position that might gradually bear some fruit, with immigrants allowed to trickle into Palestine over a number of years. Ben-Gurion, on the other hand, viewed his own plan as a tool to pry as much territory as possible out of the British when the war ended. And he would never retreat, even for a day, on immigration. At least two million Jewish survivors, he insisted, would crowd into *Eretz Yisrael* immediately after the war—with the help of American and British troops. The Allies, after all, would be under intense pressure to resettle the homeless millions.

Actually, by the time of the conference in May 1942 about a million Jews were already dead, though even Ben-Gurion, whose ear was close to the best sources of information, could not imagine the scope of the slaughter. There were rumors of gas chambers in Chelmno, Belzec and Auschwitz, but who could believe them? Not Ben-Gurion. Since he had geared his mind from youth to focus completely on one goal at a time, it was easy for him to ignore news that might compel him to juggle his delicately calculated priorities.

The conference coming up would be a Zionist milestone. Was he to blur its importance because of such unconfirmed reports? To focus on the present rather than on the future, on immediate rescue rather than eternal redemption—especially when the Allies could do little to save the Jews anyway? Before the war he had not made too much of Jewish suffering under Hitler for fear that other countries would take the victims in before the British opened the door to Palestine. Would it be sensible now to make too much of the "rumors" when his high contacts in Washington and London were already engaged in a campaign for a Jewish army that could eventually force open the door? Wasn't his primary duty to Zionism?

On May 9, 1942, over six hundred delegates streamed into the Biltmore Hotel on the corner of Madison Avenue and 43rd Street after squirming their way through swarms of uniformed servicemen and others out to inhale the excitement of wartime New York. As they took their seats in the great banquet hall, they hardly seemed aware of the historic role they were about to play. Their minds were really on the war; they were worried about their sons who had gone off to battle. But they were, at the same time, buoyed by the certainty of victory and the pros-

pect of an idyllic postwar world—and this is where Zion fit in.
It might take years, perhaps decades, or even forever, to create
a Jewish state, but this was the time to declare one's dreams.

Ben-Gurion spoke slowly, lovingly of *Eretz Yisrael*, its history, its land, its people. He rhapsodized on the great green
expanses where he had once trod on sand. He recalled the
prophets of the past and dwelled on plans for the future. He
touched on the Persians and the Byzantines, on Jewish sailors
and Jewish fishermen. And he cherished this mystical moment
when he and his listeners would proclaim to the world that
Palestine would become a Jewish state.

Then Weizmann spoke and others followed, and on the third
day the delegates approved the Biltmore program almost unanimously: The White Paper must be scrapped, and the Jewish
Agency would deal with immigration and settle the land; a Jewish army must be formed; and Palestine must "be established as
a Jewish commonwealth." The hall shook with applause and
Ben-Gurion stared into a galaxy of beaming faces. How many
realized what they had done? How many could imagine that
their voice would echo through the generations? A state. A refuge for the survivors.

Yet, Ben-Gurion and his colleagues barely mentioned these
survivors. A resolution referred only to "a message of hope and
encouragement" and prayers "that their hour of liberation may
not be far distant," while Weizmann estimated in his speech
that 25 percent of central European Jewry would be "physically
destroyed." Twenty-five percent! . . . Even so, that would still
leave millions to populate *Eretz Yisrael*—enough to give the
Jews a majority.

Ben-Gurion basked in his victory, one of the most important
since he launched his mission in the fetid alleys of Plonsk. But
two days after the conference, joy faded into sorrow, and memories of those youthful days flooded his mind. A cable arrived:
Avigdor was dead. Ben-Gurion had spent little time with his
father in recent years, partly because Avigdor and Paula tried to
avoid each other. Yet, how often Avigdor had turned up at meetings where his son spoke, sitting in the front row, leaning on his
cane, his white-bearded face aglow and his eyes seeming to ask:
Was that really his son David standing on the podium, David
the sickly boy who had given him so many problems? He had
even written Herzl asking what to do about him. And now his
son was as great a man as Herzl himself. Ben-Gurion wrote

Paula and his children: "I inherited from him my love for the Jewish people, *Eretz Yisrael,* the Hebrew language. He was a rare father, full of love."

It seemed fitting that Avigdor had lived to hear his son's voice echo from the Biltmore around the world: "Give us a Jewish state!"

Before the echo faded away, Ben-Gurion held the Biltmore banner aloft and charged at the next "enemy" who, he felt, threatened the drive to destiny—Chaim Weizmann. Weizmann had dared to meet alone with Undersecretary of State Sumner Welles even though he had promised to take Ben-Gurion along! Weizmann, he was sure, actually wanted to sabotage the Biltmore conference, to keep him from pressing Washington to carry it out. This was "treachery"! Weizmann had outlived his usefulness to Zion—and to him.

On June 11, Ben-Gurion wrote him: "I do not see that I am . . . any longer associated with you. . . . Since you came here you have acted entirely on your own, consulting and cooperating . . . with people of your personal choice as one does in his private affairs."

In an angry reply, Weizmann called the note a "rather amazing document" and denied the charge that he had failed to consult with his colleagues, accusing Ben-Gurion of refusing to come to his meetings. He then wrote one of his colleagues in London:

> Ben-Gurion has been extremely difficult, grumbling and grousing, most secretive. . . . He announced to me, among many complaints, that in London he came to the meetings merely out of courtesy, as he did not think them important enough. . . . I was aghast when I heard that. . . . I think the man suffers from some mental aberrations.

Meanwhile, Ben-Gurion asked Rabbi Stephen S. Wise, the American Zionist leader, to arrange a meeting with Weizmann and the other Zionist chiefs, and before a tense gathering of nine people in the rabbi's home, he hurled his challenge. He once more criticized Weizmann for "acting alone," then suggested that he resign.

There was a moment of awkward silence, and then Weizmann, his wrinkled, bearded face surly, cried that the charges were "painfully reminiscent of purges" and amounted to an "act of political assassination."

Ben-Gurion soon realized that he had blundered—just as he had in London. He had attacked before a forum heavily

weighted in Weizmann's favor. The struggle was still one between a revered statesman and a smart little labor leader. His
accusations were baseless, the group decided. And as the meeting ended, Ben-Gurion sat in curdled silence absorbing the outraged blasts of his colleagues. How dare he profane their god?

But Ben-Gurion wasn't defeated yet. The Zionist Executive
was based in Palestine, and there *he* was god, or at least he soon
would be. He wound up his work in the United States and, just
before leaving, told a select group of his comrades exactly what
they and the other delegates had done at the Biltmore conference. They had voted not for an illusive dream, but for the
transfer of two million Jews to Palestine immediately after the
war. They had voted not to plead with Britain for a state, but to
demand one of her.

Weizmann could barely contain himself. Pure fantasy, he
would later rage. The Biltmore declaration was "just a resolution, like the hundred and one resolutions usually passed at
great meetings." Ben-Gurion "had absolutely nothing to show
by way of achievement, and so he stuck on the Biltmore resolution, more or less conveying the idea that it is the triumph of his
policy, as against my moderate formulation of the same aims,
and he injected into it all his own extreme views." Why hadn't
Ben-Gurion told colleagues of his intentions before? Instead he
"blurted it out in a few hysterical sentences" just before leaving.
All these "mock heroics were disquieting, most harmful and
demoralizing."

Ben-Gurion was disdainful. What was harmful or demoralizing about fighting for a state? And now the world—and the
Zionists themselves—could not ignore the Biltmore commitment.

Nor he the threat to it.

After fourteen months abroad Ben-Gurion returned to Palestine
on October 2, 1942, courtesy of the British, who, despite severe
wartime flight restrictions, flew him back so he could no longer
attack Weizmann and weaken his standing in the United States.
He found that the mood of his country had changed drastically
since he had departed. General Montgomery had smashed Rommel's tanks at El Alamein and fear of another Masada, with the
Jews bunched atop Mount Carmel, had dissipated. And the British, while still ignoring the sobs and cries emanating from rickety refugee vessels that they had chased back to sea, informally
recognized the Hagana and trained its best fighters to prowl

Nazi-backed strongholds in the Middle East, where they gathered information and gutted installations.

At the same time, with more and more Allied troops pouring in and two thousand war-supply factories spouting pollution into the autumn sky, Palestine had emerged from depression and was zooming toward prosperity. There was excitement and even a certain gaiety in the air as Tommies tarried in the cafés with their Jewish girlfriends and people packed the shops casually dispensing their pounds.

Most of them didn't know, and didn't want to know, the ghastly truth that local newspapers had barely hinted at in the back pages during the past months to avoid causing undue alarm. But Ben-Gurion and his colleagues had heard more than mere rumor. Jewish leaders based in Switzerland had told them in August 1942 about the extermination of Jews deported from the Warsaw and Lvov ghettos and elsewhere, and even about the construction of factories to utilize Jewish bones and fat. And they warned, "We must keep in mind that the fate of the great majority of the Jewish community in Europe conquered by Hitler is sealed."

Yitzhak Gruenbaum, who served under Ben-Gurion as a member of the Jewish Agency Executive, would later say that "we knew about the massacres in August [1942] but didn't reveal the information in public because Rommel was then threatening Palestine and the *Yishuv* had to devote all its attention to making a last stand. . . . We had to instill in the people's hearts the recognition that it was necessary to fight and not to be like sheep led to the slaughter. How could we then talk about what was taking place in Poland?"

But even after Rommel was repelled at El Alamein, the Zionist leaders remained silent; perhaps the report was exaggerated after all. Moshe Shertok, for one, saw no reason to spread the news. Why press the Allied governments to take action when they were *already* fighting the Germans? On a trip to London, he even refused to attend a rally to protest the massacres, especially since a non-Zionist Bund leader, Artur Ziegelbojm (who would later commit suicide to protest Allied inaction), was sponsoring it. And when Gruenbaum finally asked for a hundred pounds to cable the Swiss report to Jewish organizations abroad, Eliezer Kaplan, the Jewish Agency treasurer, was indignant. Fifty pounds would be enough!

Ben-Gurion, who was in America at the time but kept abreast of all developments back home, apparently approved this policy of caution. In any case, on returning he showed no public sign of even knowing. At a press conference he held in Jerusalem less than a week after his arrival, he spoke of the Biltmore conference, a Jewish army and other subjects, but not a word about the mass slaughter. A few days later he addressed the Zionist Executive and made just one passing reference to the "disaster that has happened to Polish Jewry." His job was to preach Biltmore to the *Yishuv*, spur Britain to forge a Jewish army, and propel Weizmann into political oblivion—essential steps toward a state. And he would not let any passing clouds obscure his path.

The sun seemed especially bright on October 11, when the Zionist Executive unanimously approved the Biltmore program, making it the official program of the world Zionist movement. Biltmore would now channel Jewish energy into a state—even as Hitler was channeling gas into his death chambers. Ben-Gurion had won a great victory over Weizmann, finally swapping the image of an artless provincial politician for that of an illustrious national leader.

It was time to dispose of Weizmann once and for all and preempt the international arena as well. And so, prodded by Ben-Gurion, the Zionist Executive invited Weizmann to Palestine "for consultations and clarification of current problems," but the elderly scientist was not about to make Ben-Gurion's mistake and meet the "enemy" on his home turf. He wasn't well enough to come, he wrote back, but he would make a few comments:

> I have watched Mr. Ben-Gurion carefully during his stay here. His conduct and deportment were painfully reminiscent of the petty dictator, a type one meets so often in public life now. They are all shaped on a definite pattern: They are humorless, thin-lipped, morally stunted, fanatical, and stubborn, apparently frustrated in some ambition, and nothing is more dangerous than a small man nursing his grievances introspectively.

In his bitterness Weizmann plotted to split the Zionist Executive and isolate Ben-Gurion, who had tried to do the same to him. He thought of Moshe Shertok, who headed the political department of the Zionist Executive. Was he not a "moderate" like himself? Shertok too felt it was unrealistic to bring millions of Jews to Palestine in a single stroke, that one had to move slowly and surely. Weizmann and his American colleagues invited Shertok to the United States in a brazenly transparent move that even the old scientist doubted would work.

When Ben-Gurion learned of the invitation, he summoned Shertok. Certainly Moshe would not betray him. Short and dark with wavy black hair and a Chaplinesque mustache, Shertok was witty, sophisticated, the picture of diplomatic dignity. And his quick mind, which could dispense polished logic in eight different languages, had long marked him as a future top leader of the Zionist movement. His feelings toward Ben-Gurion were ambivalent. He viewed him with awe, yet, as a highly cultured Russian Jew who loved art and had exquisite table manners, he showed a certain contempt for Ben-Gurion's "provincialism," artistic illiteracy, and disdain for the most rudimentary etiquette. Imagine, meeting diplomats tieless and sometimes in shabby attire!

Ben-Gurion was equally torn in his feelings toward Shertok. He had recognized his potential when they were students in Constantinople, but he felt that this potential could only flower if controlled by someone with greater vision—for example, Ben-Gurion. Shertok, like his mentor, Weizmann, was too eager, in Ben-Gurion's view, to please the *goyim* and too timid to defy them. Nor could Ben-Gurion, with his pangs of inferiority, ignore Shertok's delicate sneers. Yes, Shertok knew more languages than he did and could speak more eloquently. Yes, he had studied at the London School of Economics. But look at his failings!

"He isn't a man of vision," he wrote Paula. "His thinking is not profound; he sometimes does not understand complex problems. He doesn't always see far enough, and he is unable to make decisions that require considerable intellectual and moral courage." Of course, he had some good qualities too. "He knows his job, he is talented in many ways, he is devoted and loyal. And I think Moshe himself knows that he needs to be directed, and largely accepts this."

And surely he would accept direction now. Did Shertok plan to go to New York?

New York? Oh, no. Just to London. Had some business there.

Shertok stalked out and, on arriving in London, found a message from the Mapai leadership—minus Ben-Gurion: Continue on to the United States! Shertok did, and was greeted in New York by Weizmann, who begged him for permission to open a branch of the Zionist Executive in Washington. Shertok thought it over. Ben-Gurion would explode—Weizmann invading *his* domain! But he agreed.

The explosion was not long in coming. "B.G. saw in my acceptance of Weizmann's request," Shertok would write in his

diary, "an act of treason and desertion to his sworn enemy. . . .
He ceased to call me Moshe and began calling me Shertok; he
informed me that all relations of mutual trust were gone, subjected me to a murderous interrogation . . . and literally mal-
treated me."

But early the next morning Ben-Gurion phoned him. "From
his hoarse voice," Shertok would inscribe in his diary, "I understood that he had had a sleepless night. . . . The main thing is he
called me 'Moshe' again."

Ben-Gurion needed Shertok if he was ever to bring Weizmann down, even though he thought of him as a pale, more
malleable version of the old professor. This was, after all, the
first time Shertok had openly defied him. But relations between
the two men would never be the same.

While Ben-Gurion and the other politicians intrigued in the
name of saving their people, they appeared to take little note of
events in Germany that were daily demolishing this cause. At
least the press they controlled did not reflect undue concern.
Thus, on November 15, 1942, *Haaretz* wishfully editorialized:

"The reader should be reminded that all the information from
the occupied areas comes from doubtful and unreliable sources
and should be treated with caution and suspicion."

And on the following day, November 16, *Davar*, the Mapai
daily, edited by Berl Katzenelson and strongly influenced by
Ben-Gurion, published an article on the cultural life in the Warsaw ghetto—90 percent of whose inhabitants had already been
liquidated!

Ironically, that same day a group of sixty-nine British and
Palestinian Jews who had been exchanged for German prisoners of war arrived in Palestine from occupied Europe, living
testimony to the horror. After being interviewed by members of
the Jewish Agency, one of the survivors would write:

> They did not believe me! They said I exaggerated. They asked me
> questions and subjected me to an interrogation as if I were a criminal
> inventing a story in order to cause somebody harm, in order to deceive
> people deliberately and for ulterior motives. . . . They tried hard to
> weaken my certainty, so I should doubt the veracity of my information.

Eliahu Dobkin, one of the Jewish Agency interviewers,
would tell his colleagues afterward that Hitler was operating
"something like a [murder] apparatus," something that "was

going in the direction" of total extermination. And on November 23, 1942, the press finally reported on the atrocities that the survivors had witnessed, corroborating what newspapers elsewhere had reported much earlier, though still refusing to acknowledge a Nazi plan for killing all the Jews in Europe.

The Palestine Jews were distressed, no longer able to doubt that their kin were being systematically murdered. But apparently still noting their leaders' calm, which gave them an excuse to be tranquil too, they showed "no outward signs of shock," according to the Hebrew newspaper *Hatzofe*. The writer had believed that the shopkeepers would shut their doors, that the people would spontaneously gather in the streets, rip their clothes, sit on the sidewalks, and bitterly lament the destruction of European Jewry. But they didn't. Life went on as usual and the cafés still catered to gay throngs.

"How does one explain this criminal indifference?" the *Hatzofe* writer asked. Dobkin would later reply: "If the *Yishuv* had gone out into the streets in protest and demonstrated every day, would that have helped? It wouldn't have."

Yet Dobkin, after questioning the survivors, became so emotional that some colleagues warned him not to "speak loudly" about what he learned and unnecessarily "panic" the people. And Ben-Gurion? He "accepted [my] appreciation," Dobkin would say. "He saw very clearly [in late 1942] the danger of extermination. He knew—though not the full extent; not about the six million."

Ehud Avriel, who helped to form a Rescue Committee, would say that his mentor, Ben-Gurion, knew as early as summer 1942. But Ben-Gurion would never admit that he knew what he did when he did, claiming after the war that news of the Holocaust "reached us late, and then [the people] wouldn't believe us for a long time." In 1942, however, the Nazis were in an *early* stage of their extermination program, and there is no evidence that Ben-Gurion seriously tried to inform his people about the catastrophe at any time during the war.

Still, he was sufficiently shaken after the survivors told their story to implore other countries to take in any Jews they could free from Hitler's grasp. Addressing the Allies, he thus urged in a speech:

> There are German nationals in the United States, in England, in Russia and other countries. Demand that they be exchanged for the Jews of Poland and Lithuania and other countries under Nazi rule. Allow those who are able to, to escape. Do not close your gates to them. First and foremost, rescue the Jewish children. Bring them into neutral countries. Bring them to your own countries.

This plea contrasted sharply with his view before the war, when he and other Zionist leaders had discouraged such non-Zionist rescue efforts. On another rare occasion, he blasted the Allies for their passive attitude toward the slaughter:

> What have you allowed to be perpetrated against a defenseless people, while you stood aside and let it bleed to death, without offering help or succor, without calling on the fiends to stop, in the language of retribution, which alone they would understand? Why do you profane our pain and wrath with empty expressions of sympathy that ring like a mockery in the ears of millions of the damned in the charnel house of Nazi Europe? . . . Would you have kept silent if every day thousands of your infants and children had had their skulls cracked against stone pavements and walls?

But Ben-Gurion made this dramatic appeal in connection with his struggle for a Jewish army, using it as a form of psychological pressure on the Allies:

> If it is not in your power to put a stop to the slaughter, why do you not let us avenge the blood of millions of our brethren and allow us to take up arms against the Nazis as a nation, as Jews in a Jewish army, under a Jewish flag?

Ben-Gurion's reference to "millions of our brethren" in the first years of the war was as unusual as his public charges. His recognition of the "truth" did not normally extend to accepting stories about the murder of *millions,* the millions he was still hoping to bring to Palestine. Thus, Ben-Gurion told another gathering about two weeks after hearing the testimony of the witnesses to the horror:

"We do not know exactly what is happening in the Nazi field of slaughter; how many Jews have already been slaughtered, murdered, buried alive. . . . But we know what Hitler is scheming against our people and what he wrote in his book *Mein Kampf.*"

Unable to suppress his own nationalist optimism, Ben-Gurion addressed the doomed: "We shall bring you all to us, to our land." And in still another talk, delivered after the world press had reported that more than half the Jews in Europe were already dead, he spoke of "the days of big massacres—tens and hundreds of thousands, we do not even know their numbers."

Did Ben-Gurion, a compulsive researcher on subjects he wanted to know about, try very hard to know about this one?

Later in the war, when he did speculate on the worst, he did so mainly in the light of what the destruction of European Jewry would mean to the Zionist cause. According to S. B. Beit-Zvi, an

Israeli scholar and expert on Zionism in World War II, "the Holocaust as the destruction of Jews was for the Zionists a tragic problem of good friends. The Holocaust as a factor liable to affect Zionism was for them a matter of life and death."

Typically, Ben-Gurion said:

> If there is, God forbid, no remnant except the Jews of America and the Soviet Union, perhaps there will be no Jewish immigration after the war, and our future in the Land will be like the future of Yemen's Jews and the Assyrians of Iraq, and that of the Jews of Germany after Hitler.

He would also say that "the dead millions had borne the torch of rebirth and possessed the power to realize it."

At the same time, he perceived how catastrophe could actually keep the Zionist lamp burning:

> It is possible to convert the great disaster of our people in exile into a powerful lever of redemption. A catastrophe of millions is also capable of redeeming millions. And Zionism's message . . . is to cast the great Jewish catastrophe in mighty molds of redemption.

It appears, then, that Ben-Gurion did not focus on trying to stop the catastrophe as it was happening, but on making the most of what might emerge when it had run its course. As head of the Jewish Agency, the shadow Jewish government, he made no real attempt to lead a crusade—for example, to press the Pope to cry out, or the Allies to bomb the gas chambers or the railroads leading to them. Nor did he vigorously push the large influential American Jewish community to conquer its fears and complexes and relentlessly demand that its government take action.

Ben-Gurion's small Rescue Committee, which operated mainly out of Istanbul in neutral Turkey, gathered information on the Holocaust and helped the handful of escaping Jews get to Palestine. But he took little personal interest in this committee and did not create a "brain trust" that would rescue and propagandize in a broader, more systematic way, that would dedicate itself to awakening the world and exerting maximum pressure on its leaders to do something, anything, however "impractical," to stop, or at least slow down, the horror. Meanwhile, his party newspaper *Davar*, as well as other Hebrew papers, continued to underplay the Holocaust, even after there could be no doubt that the killings were massive.

Avriel says in defending Ben-Gurion, "With his realism he knew that we could at best give comfort to a few people, but to

save many we were not strong and powerful enough. . . . Only
ending the war could save large numbers of victims."

But this was also the realism of Roosevelt and other Allied
leaders in failing to make a supreme effort to cheat the gas
chambers.

Lova (Arie) Eliav, who returned from Italy on leave from the
British army in late 1943, a year after the survivors' revelations,
would later reminisce:

> I came back to a satisfied *Yishuv* enjoying a prosperity it had never
> before experienced. . . . I felt a certain shock. . . . [It] was terrible. . . .
> My friends and relatives . . . had virtually no conception [of the Holo-
> caust] or didn't want to think about it. . . . They were content and calm.
> . . . As for Ben-Gurion, he interrogated me for hours. . . . Wasn't I exag-
> gerating? Weren't the Jews themselves exaggerating? . . . Ben-Gurion
> didn't react with an "oy" or "oh" . . . or any other expression of woe. He
> just noted down everything I told him.

Though the British railed against Ben-Gurion as a fanatic in
his struggle against the White Paper and for a state, they too
found him cautious when dealing with the Holocaust. In 1944 a
Jew named Joel Brand arrived in Istanbul from Hungary with a
proposal from the Nazis: They would liberate a large number of
Jews in return for a fleet of trucks and quantities of coffee, tea,
cocoa and soap. But on the way to Palestine to meet Zionist
leaders, who presumably would obtain the ransom from the Allies, Brand was arrested by the British and prevented from
going back.

At a meeting with High Commissioner Harold MacMichael
on June 15, Ben-Gurion, apparently, was not overly concerned
about this decision.

"It is quite likely that the whole business was a trick,"
MacMichael, in a report, would quote him as saying. Of course,
"if there was anything which could humanly be done in such a
way as not to be of any advantage to the enemy or prejudice the
war effort, he pleaded that it should be done."

Grateful for Ben-Gurion's "moderate" stand, one British official who discussed the Nazi plan with him and Shertok wrote
his superiors:

"Ben-Gurion, who is in many ways more extreme than Mr.
Shertok, sees the problem more clearly. . . . [He] spoke with obvious sincerity, dignity and appreciation of the dangers." And
this official added, "It is to be observed that we ourselves from
the first have considered this scheme to be a fantastic piece of
blackmail with political warfare motives. . . . It appears to be
sympathized with by Mr. Ben-Gurion."

In June 1944 the Jewish Agency Executive debated whether

to ask the Allies to bomb Auschwitz. The question was: Would the bombs kill more Jews than they saved? Ben-Gurion was adamant:

"The true situation in Poland is unknown to us," he said, though by now multiple reports had indicated that Hitler planned to kill every Jew in his hands. "And it appears to me that we shall be unable to propose anything on this subject."

When others agreed, he concluded: "The view of the Executive is that bombing places where there are Jews should not be proposed to the Allies."

A few months later, Weizmann did request the bombing of Auschwitz, but a British Foreign Office official wrote back that the Royal Air Force could not agree "in view of the very great technical difficulties involved." Nor could the Allies disrupt strategic plans for a nonmilitary purpose. Ben-Gurion, however, bore no grudge, and would even write that "in Churchill's view the salvation of England had priority over everything else, and I am not certain whether the bombing of Auschwitz would have saved Jews."

If Ben-Gurion did not give the Jews who were doomed priority attention, he did give such attention to those few who were saved—the future *aliya*. In December 1944, shortly after the Russians had liberated Bulgaria, he rushed there to see his future pioneers and soldiers. When he stepped off the Orient Express in Sofia, local newspapers heralded his coming, and the nation's top leaders welcomed him—the first "foreign statesman" to visit liberated Bulgaria. Ben-Gurion was overjoyed as he stood before thousands of cheering Jewish survivors who had jammed into the city's largest cinema to hear him speak. He spoke to them of life in *Eretz Yisrael*, of the future they would share, and shouts echoed through the hall, "*Aliya*, no more slavery!"

But then Ben-Gurion glimpsed other Jews, the ones who had returned to homes that were no longer there and had been piled together in a cold prisonlike building. Hungry, barefoot, shivering on the stone floor, they were silent as Ben-Gurion walked by trying to encourage them with "a word, a smile, a gesture." He was appalled. These were the more fortunate Jews of Europe?

"The first thing I will do when I return," he said to an aide, "is to send you five thousand pairs of shoes for the children." Then he added with a "whimsical twinkle in his eyes": "Or perhaps, should we not try to bring the feet to the shoes?"

The great bulk of European Jews, however, no longer needed shoes. They were dead—and lost to Zion. Could some of them have been saved? No one will ever know. But after the war Ben-Gurion would say that he thought so. The Allies "might have rescued perhaps not all of our doomed brethren, but surely hundreds of thousands of them." But could he claim to have forcefully urged them to?

Speaking of Pope Pius XII, Ben-Gurion told a reporter that "to the best of my knowledge [he] made no attempt to stop the annihilation of the Jewish people, nor did he ever publicly denounce it." This was true. But while the Pope's voice would have resonated like thunder against Ben-Gurion's squeak, the fact remains that Ben-Gurion barely squeaked, though he was himself a Jew, indeed the leader of the largest and most powerful Jewish organization in the world.

Actually, the psychological rationale of the two men, it appears, was not dissimilar. Both placed the long-range interest of the institution before the salvation of individuals, however agonizing the choice. The Pope feared mainly that if he publicly denounced the Nazi crimes, Hitler would carry out a blackmail threat to invade the Vatican and kidnap him. And Ben-Gurion feared mainly that if he pressed the Allies too hard he would lose many of the chips he needed to first win a Jewish army and, after the war, the ultimate prize, a Jewish state.

A leader of Ben-Gurion's Rescue Committee, Anshel Reiss, would say many years after the war: "Ben-Gurion did not have too much understanding in [rescue] matters. Either he did not believe in it or he was occupied with Palestine affairs. . . . He didn't live with [the Holocaust]."

And another associate, Arie Tartakower, would say: "I don't remember a conversation when we spoke in particular about . . . the Holocaust. . . . His thoughts, initiative, and will were devoted only to questions involving *Eretz Yisrael* and the state. There were people in our movement active in Holocaust matters and rescuing Jews, but I didn't see Ben-Gurion among them. As far as I know, Ben-Gurion didn't take an interest in these matters."

Surely, Ben-Gurion was as horrified as anyone else about the destruction of his people, perhaps even more so than many, for he had brought the victims to the brink of Zionist salvation. Why then was he so reluctant to believe? Perhaps because he couldn't permit sentiment, and the unbearable sense of guilt it would breed, to influence his priorities and steer him off his messianic course. Anyway, the fate of a few million Jews today was not as important as the fate of countless millions in the future. On the other hand, when reality finally forced him to believe, the Holocaust was in its last stages or past. And to dwell on the past, whether on the horror or the heroism, was to waste precious emotional energy needed to save the future millions. One had to be ruthlessly practical to reach an "impractical" goal —even when dealing with genocide. And this rationale would not permit even the smallest admission of error. Yet Nahum Goldmann, who had also tried hard not to believe, would dare to admit after the war in reference to Jewish rescue efforts:

"What matters in a situation of this sort [the Holocaust] is a people's moral stance, its readiness to fight back instead of help-lessly allowing itself to be massacred. We did not stand the test."

If Ben-Gurion "didn't take an interest in [Holocaust] matters," his interest in political matters did not wane, especially where Chaim Weizmann was concerned. Weizmann must resign, Ben-Gurion continued to demand. And he condemned his foe so scathingly at one meeting in July 1943 that Berl Katzenelson, who himself had little noted the Holocaust in his *Davar*, shouted at him:

"All of Zion is standing on the edge of the abyss. There are problems now much more important than Weizmann: The loss of European Jewry. That is much more of an anti-Zionist factor than anything else. I am shocked by Ben-Gurion's talk, not be-cause I differ very much from him. . . . Ben-Gurion's preoccu-pation with Weizmann now is, in my view, what in literature is called escapism—flight from reality. I say this to Ben-Gurion: 'You are occupying yourself with something that is not impor-tant at this time!' "

Ben-Gurion, however, would not relent. If he couldn't do any-thing about the Holocaust, he could do something about Weiz-mann. When his colleagues refused to ask Weizmann to resign, Ben-Gurion cried that *he* would then resign. So they compro-mised, inviting Weizmann to Palestine once more, ostensibly to chair a world Zionist conference. But Weizmann again refused, determined not to "fight a madman on his own ground." And even if Ben-Gurion came to London, Weizmann would "not sit at the same table with [him]." In a rage Ben-Gurion decided not to sit at any table at all. He bellowed at a Jewish Agency Exec-utive meeting that he would no longer accept Weizmann's "treacherous policy." He would now carry out his threat to resign.

Ben-Gurion's colleagues were, even more than in the past, stunned by this announcement. Moshe Shertok would write: "It was like a child being asked what would be worse, the death of his mother or of his father."

Finally, in February 1944 a *Yishuv* delegation went to Weizmann and mediated a compromise. Weizmann promised to consult with Jerusalem, and Ben-Gurion agreed not to resign after all.

Soon there was more *tsouris*. The conflict within Mapai between the moderates and Tabenkin's leftist Faction B erupted into a crisis. Tabenkin had violently opposed partition in 1937, and he was now convinced that the Biltmore program was nothing but a smoke screen for a new partition plan. It was stupid to demand a state right after the war, he cried. Settle all the land in Palestine first, and then a state would come automatically—embracing the entire country.

At a Mapai conference in March 1944, Tabenkin walked out of the meeting with some of the finest pioneers and activists, including many members of the leftist kibbutz-dominated Palmach, the spearhead elite of Hagana. After all the struggle to unify labor, it had now split again.

And then, an even worse disaster . . .

At about midnight, August 15, 1944, Ben-Gurion, on vacation in a rest home in the hills of Haifa, received a surprise visit from his Mapai colleague David Hacohen.

"Ben-Gurion," said Hacohen, "I have something to tell you. I've just been told—Berl is dead."

Ben-Gurion's iron discipline suddenly dissolved; his face turned pasty and his eyes stared with the glaze of shock. Falling on his bed, he covered his head with a sheet and beat it against the mattress. "Berl, Berl," he moaned, "how can I live without you?"

He quickly dressed and with Hacohen rushed off to Jerusalem, where Berl Katzenelson's body lay in the home of a friend. He pushed through a crowd to Katzenelson's room and, glancing at the corpse, fainted. When he revived, he remained with his beloved comrade for two hours, sobbing, "Berl, you can't do this to me. . . . Berl, you can't."

Katzenelson had been for him—and for the nation—a spiritual crutch, an intellectual compass, an emotional tranquilizer.

Whenever Ben-Gurion had chosen the expedient route or surrendered to impulse, there was Berl, almost maternal in his gentleness, to calm him with logic or to scold him like a schoolboy. Now Berl was gone and he was alone, as he had been when his mother died and when Rachel married another.

"How dear you were to me, Berl," he would write in a letter to comrades, as if speaking directly to the deceased.

> Dearer than brother and friend! Since I first met you in khaki in our bivouac in the Egyptian desert, and together we dreamed a dream of perfect unity among the workers of Israel that they might fulfill their tremendous destiny: to build the Homeland and establish in it a Jewish state, to make a living socialism and exalt man upon earth . . . since that day I have loved you with love everlasting. Unto yours my soul was bound.

How could he pursue destiny with only part of his soul?

Ben-Gurion's colleagues felt almost as desperate as he, for who could rein him in now that Berl was gone? Who would give his policies poignancy and perspective? And one of Ben-Gurion's first actions following Katzenelson's death did not ease their anxiety.

It came after the British showed signs of agreeing to some of the Jewish demands. Winston Churchill felt he could defy his Arabist commanders after Rommel's defeat at El Alamein, for with the Nazis no longer a threat in the Middle East there was less need to curry Arab favor. So he agreed in August 1944 to the most unrelenting Zionist demand—a Jewish military force —and this time, like a bulldog protecting a bone, he snapped contemptuously at anyone who tried to change his mind.

To Ben-Gurion's joy, the British soon formed a five-thousand-man Jewish Brigade and sent it to fight in Italy, where, Ben-Gurion hoped, it would gain the experience it could use after the war to create a state by force if necessary.

At the same time, Churchill set up a ministerial committee to carve out a partition plan and the war cabinet approved it. More joy. Ben-Gurion would gladly water down the Biltmore program if the British were really serious. But the Revisionist Irgun Zvai Leumi would not. It wanted all of Palestine or nothing, and an extremist wing led by Avraham Stern broke off and demanded all of it *now*, while World War II was still raging.

When the war had broken out and Jabotinsky was still alive, the Irgun, ironically, had stopped hurling its bombs and gre-

nades and volunteered to help the British in the Middle East
with even greater enthusiasm than the Hagana registered. But
soon after Jabotinsky's death, another Revisionist leader
emerged—Menachem Begin. He had come to the Middle East
with a Polish brigade formed in Russia, where he had been
jailed for his Zionist militancy until the Nazis invaded that
country. To Begin, who deserted the Polish force in Transjordan, fighting the White Paper was more important than helping
the British fight the Nazis—especially since Palestine was now
safe from Rommel and an Allied victory seemed certain.

But even Begin was too soft for the Stern Group. Attacking
British military installations, as Begin had ordered, wasn't
enough. One had to assassinate British soldiers and officials.
Then, the Sternists believed, Britain would understand—and
leave. And whose murder would make the most impact? A man
the Jews hated anyway: Colonial Secretary Lord Moyne, who
had just agreed, if reluctantly, to Churchill's plan for partition.
One day in November 1944, two Sternists shot him to death
while he was visiting Cairo.

When Ben-Gurion learned of the murder, he exploded. Just
when the British had agreed to form a Jewish army and were
even talking of a Jewish state, the Jews struck down a British
leader! One bullet could reverse the trend toward Zionism—
and would. Churchill hinted as much in a bitter address to the
House of Commons, declaring that "many persons like myself
will have to reconsider the position that we have maintained so
firmly for such a long time."

Furthermore, that bullet symbolized the danger to the Jewish
unity that Ben-Gurion had always thought must bind together a
state. Should a small group of fanatics be allowed to steer Jewish policy? Assassination was, in any case, morally abominable
and unworthy of a model people. But though Ben-Gurion continued to rage over Lord Moyne's murder, it was, he decided, at
least timely.

He issued an ultimatum: Either the dissidents would halt all
terrorism and take orders from him or he would crush them. The
Sternists grew fearful and agreed to Ben-Gurion's conditions.
Begin, however, did not. He would place the Irgun under Hagana command only if Ben-Gurion formed a "committee of national liberation" or a "Jewish provisional government" and
launched a war on the British.

Contemptuously, Ben-Gurion stood before the Jewish Agency Executive on November 7, 1944, and pushed through a drastic order that would strike not at the "guilty" though compliant

Stern Group, but at the "innocent" though defiant Irgun. In the long run, the larger, more influential Irgun posed a greater threat to his dream, regardless of who committed the ugliest crimes.

"The Jewish community is called upon to spew forth all the members of this harmful, destructive gang, to deny them any shelter or haven, not give in to their threats, and to extend to the [British] authorities all the necessary assistance to prevent acts of terror and to wipe out [this] organization, for this is a matter of life and death."

Thus began the "Hunting Season." For four months Hagana patrols picked up Irgunists, took them to an outlying house or cave in the hills and interrogated them, then turned them over to the British. But though the public would not cooperate, Ben-Gurion was immovable. Any means, he felt, could justifiably be used to wipe out "maniacs" and "criminals" who would block the path to destiny—even if they were Jewish. But though terrorism ceased for the remainder of the war, the leading "maniacs" and "criminals," including Begin, were never captured and would return later to plague Ben-Gurion.

The war years were a tremendous challenge for Ben-Gurion, but also an enormous strain. There had been Weizmann, Tabenkin and Begin, British intransigence, German infamy, Berl's death. His activities had never played greater havoc with his family life. He was abroad more often than not, and when in Palestine he was home even less often than usual. But not always because of his punishing schedule. As so often in the past when he was under great stress, he needed an outlet for his feelings, a sounding board for his thoughts. In New York he had Miriam Taub, in London, Doris May. In Palestine Rachel Ben-Zvi met Ben-Gurion in a resort with a "young new immigrant," for whom she bought clothes since "she was practically barefooted."

Paula was convinced her husband was unfaithful, and she desperately poured out her woes to the Ben-Zvis one day, even though she had always resented them for knowing Ben-Gurion before she did. Her husband, she sobbed, regarded her as little more than a maid. She might even commit suicide.

Nonsense! said Rachel Ben-Zvi. Why didn't she take a greater interest in her husband's political life so they would have more in common?

Paula would try. Her husband had run the Histadrut for years but she had never learned much about it, so now she sat down for hours with Histadrut officials asking questions. One of these officials, Israel Meriminski, was soon escorting her to concerts and other social events when Ben-Gurion was abroad, and he finally asked a question of his own:

Would she marry him?

But she was already married.

So let her get a divorce.

Paula's starved ego bulged, but she declined. How could Ben-Gurion survive without her? Besides, one marriage was enough. One suitor, however, was not. She found more, including a Histadrut lawyer named Israel Bar-Shira. Meanwhile, she crammed into her mind everything she could absorb about the Histadrut and Palestine politics and, when her husband was in town, showed off her knowledge at the dinner table. Whether Ben-Gurion was impressed, no one can say. Nor is it clear whether he knew—or cared—about her "affairs." But relations between them improved, if only because Paula learned to live with her suspicions.

Ben-Gurion spent even less time with his children, though when he was in Jerusalem he shared an apartment with Renana, a student at Hebrew University. With lively blue eyes and an infectious smile, Renana had grown into a comely young woman, but Ben-Gurion apparently noted only her brilliant mind. Stingy with compliments, he once said to her, "You're not very pretty. How do you get all those boyfriends?"

But Renana didn't need compliments to love her father. Yes, he had always been too busy with his mission to devote much time to his family, but she remembered the precious moments he did spend with her, how he would sit reading in her room while she did her homework so he could answer questions, how sometimes he would read aloud to her from Plato and other learned works. Instinctively, she understood his priorities.

Sometimes Ben-Gurion would also visit Geula, who was attractive too, though far more subdued and far less intellectually inclined than her sister. She had married in 1937 while studying in a teacher's college, and life had not been easy since her wedding. Ben-Gurion had refused to wield his influence to get his new son-in-law a job, offering only to feed the couple at home until the youth could find employment on his own. The righteous father even returned a check that his Jewish Agency sent the newlyweds.

Now Geula lived alone with her small son, Yariv, while her husband served in the British army. Ben-Gurion had been so excited when he learned in London of Yariv's birth that he dashed into the street crying, "I'm a grandfather! I'm a grandfather!" He constantly admonished Geula to have three more children and pressed her to take full advantage of her husband's furloughs.

Ben-Gurion hardly ever saw Amos, who had also joined the British forces. The Royal Air Force had rejected him because of his father's anti-British utterances, but the infantry accepted him. Whenever he came home on leave, Ben-Gurion would marvel at him, as if he were confronted by his own younger self. Amos in his uniform was the picture of his father in Jewish Legion days—the same piercing eyes, thick wavy hair, and powerful jaw.

"Amos, stay a private," Ben-Gurion urged, recalling his own reluctance—for a while—to accept a promotion in the Legion. "Don't command people. Live with the troops."

But when Ben-Gurion saw Amos again, in early 1945, the young man was wearing a Jewish Brigade officer's uniform. He had just been discharged from a military hospital in Liverpool, where he had lain ill for several months. Meeting in London, they lunched in a kosher restaurant and, over pickled herring, Amos summoned the courage to reveal a shocking bit of news:

"Father, I'm going to do something that might hurt you politically."

"What are you going to do?"

"Marry a *shiksa*."

Ben-Gurion put down his fork and stared at his son. Who was this *shiksa?*

A nurse at his hospital.

Father pondered the news. "Amos," he finally said, "never mind what happens to me. If you think you're doing the right thing, go ahead and do it."

With gratitude and relief, Amos brought his attractive, dark-haired Mary to London, and Ben-Gurion, looking her over as he might a new car, "fell in love" with her. The rabbis would gasp, but let them; they didn't recognize his own marriage, since a rabbi had not performed it. Anyway, their attitude was not important. Hadn't many Biblical figures married *shiksas?* The rabbis ignored the Bible and lived by Diaspora law, while he did the reverse.

Now to tell Paula, who, he knew, would be disturbed. Amos, he wrote her, wouldn't change his mind. He had even found an

American Reform rabbi who would perform the ceremony without first requiring a formal conversion. So they might as well accept the decision.

Besides, he couldn't let a personal matter divert him from his task in life. He would save his fighting for a state. The war would soon be over—but not for him.

CHAPTER NINE

Shall a nation be born at once?

ISAIAH 66:8

A<small>MID</small> a blazing flutter of banners and flags the people of London swirled through the streets, singing, cheering, shouting in rapturous response to Prime Minister Churchill's announcement in Parliament on this historic day, May 8, 1945. Germany had surrendered! Peace at last! Ben-Gurion struggled through the bubbling maelstrom of humanity, his melancholy demeanor in jarring contrast to the public mood. He scrambled into the solitude of his flat and, while the echoes of ecstasy wafted through the window, slumped over his desk and wrote in his diary: "V-E Day—sad, very sad."

Sad that so many of his people were dead, that so few would come to Zion. Sad that the world, savoring peace in anticipation of Japan's collapse as well, would surely try to forget the Jewish problem that threatened more tension, more bloodshed, more moral and strategic dilemmas. It would soon be time for the world to relax—but for the Jews to fight the final battle. With the victors preparing to reapportion the earth among the nations, the Jews must win their share before it was too late. Too late to save the remnants, to secure the dream.

"Rejoice not, O Israel," he would write, quoting the Bible as the sounds of celebration filtered in, "for joy is for the other peoples."

Ben-Gurion had flown to London in March to appeal once more to the British. The White Paper must be swept away to permit a million Jews to crowd into Palestine immediately—a grudging concession to reality; he no longer demanded two million, for the liberation of Buchenwald and other death camps dispelled all doubt that far fewer than he had thought remained alive. Anyway, even a million immigrants would give the Jews a majority in Palestine. He still did not know, and could not conceive, that only about a million non-Russian European Jews in all had survived.

Britain's response came on June 9, after Weizmann had sent Churchill a list of Jewish demands: Sorry, wrote Churchill, but no requests would be considered until the Allies sat down at the peace table. Ben-Gurion sank deeper into gloom. Churchill? The greatest Briton, the most pro-Zionist of all?

Nor could Ben-Gurion count on American support. Roosevelt had met with Saudi Arabia's King Ibn Saud after the Yalta Conference and then had written him promising not to "undertake . . . any action likely to be hostile to the Arab people." The President did not even invite the Jews to the founding conference of the United Nations in San Francisco. To Ben-Gurion he was "two-faced," claiming that he supported Zionism while quietly stifling it. Nevertheless, the American Jews wielded great power in their country, politically and financially, and he would tap this power and use it in the last battle for a state, indeed for sheer survival.

He hurried off to the United States on a new mission. His last one had yielded a platform; this one must yield a pledge.

Ben-Gurion lay "stretched out on a big bed, pasha-like," when Meyer Weisgal entered his room in Hotel Fourteen, at 14 East 60th Street, a kind of Hagana headquarters in New York. Weisgal was Weizmann's chief aide and was well-connected with leading Jews throughout the United States. Ben-Gurion had urgently summoned him on this day in late June to ask him for a list of wealthy Jews "who will follow me blindly, who will do what I want without asking questions."

The British, Ben-Gurion predicted, would be leaving Palestine soon, and the Arab armies would then try to destroy the *Yishuv*. The Hagana had enough men and arms to hold off local Palestinian gangs, but not regular Arab armies. And though most of his soldiers would come from the refugee camps in Europe, the required weapons—and the dollars to buy them—were available only in the United States. He must meet a group of wealthy American Jews who would "mobilize money, arms, machinery, science, professionals, et cetera."

Weisgal was riveted. No other Jewish leader had painted the

future danger with such bleak strokes. He sent Ben-Gurion to see Henry Montor, director of the United Jewish Appeal, who knew every Jew worth knowing. In no time Ben-Gurion left Montor's office with a list of eighteen millionaires and was lunching with one of them, Rudolf Sonneborn, an industrialist whom he had met many years before.

On July 1, 1945, a steaming Sunday in Manhattan, Sonneborn's doorbell rang seventeen times as the other millionaires filed into his luxurious duplex penthouse, bewildered by the telephone calls and wires summoning them to an urgent meeting. Sonneborn, tall and lanky, towered over his pudgy friend from Palestine as he introduced him to the gathering. Sweaty in his shirt sleeves, Ben-Gurion leaned against a grand piano and described the danger he foresaw.

"On that memorable day," Sonneborn would write in a confidential memorandum, "we were asked to form ourselves into an ... American arm of ... Hagana. We were given no clue as to what we might be called upon to accomplish, when the call might come, or who would call us."

But all agreed to answer the call.

July 1945 brought other good news too. Ben-Gurion and many colleagues, sailing from New York to London for the first postwar international Zionist conference, suddenly heard a loudspeaker blare that the British Labour Party had crushed Churchill's Conservatives in the first postwar election. Waves of euphoria rippled around the decks, for had not the Labour Party condemned the White Paper from the start? Only a few months earlier it had gone even further than the Zionists had—demanding that the Jews receive not only all of Palestine, but Transjordan as well, with the Arabs in both lands to be shipped to neighboring countries! This was a new Britain.

But Ben-Gurion did not celebrate with his comrades. He knew the Labour politicians. They were frantically pro-Zionist while in opposition, but when in power? He was not at all sure. And as professed anti-imperialists they were even more likely than the Conservatives to dissolve the British Empire *before* the Jews had the means to defend themselves against the Arabs. It was more urgent than ever, he sensed, to set up a Jewish state. And now aware of the full horror of the Holocaust, he was ready to demand immediate entry for only the hundred thousand survivors who crowded the displaced persons' camps.

At the conference, which started on August 1, Ben-Gurion

cried, "Either we stand on the threshold of a state . . . or we stand on the threshold of a grave." If the Labour Party, he warned, didn't scrap the White Paper, "we in Palestine . . . shall fight" England!

Chaim Weizmann winced. Fight England? Ben-Gurion was *meshuga*. Then he himself roared, "Palestine as a Jewish state should be one of the fruits of victory, and with God's help it shall be!"

Before a startled Ben-Gurion could rejoice, Weizmann was Weizmann again. . . . Of course it might take five years to achieve this goal. The important thing now was to get a hundred thousand immigration certificates. . . .

This was too much for Ben-Gurion. He rushed to the rostrum, slammed down his fist, and stormed, "This man is speaking in his own name. Nobody empowered him to propose anything totally opposed to the decision of the Zionist Executive in *Eretz Yisrael!*"

The session ended in an uproar and with a militant resolution backing the Biltmore program.

Ben-Gurion kept up the momentum and, after the conference, led a Zionist delegation to the Colonial Office, barging into the domain of the new Colonial Secretary, Glenvil Hall. The secretary, Ben-Gurion growled, must issue a hundred thousand immigration certificates immediately and declare Palestine a Jewish state! Hall shook with anger at the roughneck intrusion and later told Parliament that this behavior "was different from anything . . . I had ever experienced!" Then the Arabs warned of a "new crusaders' war" if Jewish demands were met, further hardening British intransigence. Even a plea by President Truman for the hundred thousand certificates did not help. The White Paper, virtually banning Jewish immigration, would stand. Although Ben-Gurion had foreseen this, he felt that the British Labour Party had betrayed him.

Ben-Gurion would now launch a revolt—a "restrained" one. The Jews must strike hard enough to chip at British policy without provoking a dangerous backlash. Blow up a few installations, engineer some jailbreaks, fire over British heads. Weizmann mockingly called such controlled guerrilla action "hot ice," which would, he thought, melt into pure terrorism. But to Ben-Gurion it was time for "hot ice," and who could challenge him? In his dual role he would carry both a briefcaseful of papers and a bagful of bombs. He had never been stronger, and Weizmann never weaker. The Holocaust had shown what happened to people who didn't fight back. The *Yishuv* was with him. And it didn't even know about the American pledge.

"The time has come!" said the anonymous voice on the phone. Rudolf Sonneborn slammed down the receiver and swung into action. He formed his group of millionaires into the secret Sonneborn Institute, which cooperated with Hagana agents in setting up dummy companies to buy tons of government surplus arms and ships from any source it could find, including the Mafia. American-Jewish war veterans left souvenir firearms at "gun drops." Gambling casinos gave a percentage of each pot to the cause. Even Hitler's victims helped, contributing their gold teeth, which the American army had found in the death camps and sold cheaply.

The arms collected would be used against the British if they didn't scuttle the White Paper, or against the Arabs if they tried to scuttle the state. The ships, packed with immigrants, would run the blockade of Palestine. Meanwhile, the Jews would fight the British with the wile and weapons they had. On October 1 Ben-Gurion, without informing his comrades in London, rushed off a letter to Moshe Sneh, the Hagana chief in Palestine, ordering what amounted to an armed uprising: Begin *Aliya Gimel!* Land refugees in Zion at the point of a gun. Set up a central command in Paris to direct and finance this operation. Sabotage and retaliate—without killing people indiscriminately. And make a deal with the Irgun Zvai Leumi and the Stern Group for unified action under the Hagana command—yes, with the same terrorists he had tried to wipe out a year earlier! Had not circumstances changed? And might not British Labour policy change too as headlines blared British atrocities—and humiliation?

Ben-Gurion then left for Paris, where he personally helped to organize *Aliya Gimel* with Hagana officials before moving on to Germany to see the human wreckage that would be loaded aboard his armed ships—just to make sure they wouldn't arrive half empty.

On October 19, 1945, a train pulled into Frankfurt, and a few hours later Ben-Gurion was at the gates of the displaced persons' camp at Zeilsheim. As Ben-Gurion sat in a car, a Jewish D.P. peered in.

"Ben-Gurion! Ben-Gurion!" he shrieked.

The others gathered around and joined in the shouting, and

soon the crowd was so large that Ben-Gurion's guide, Rabbi Judah Nadich of the Hagana, feared a riot.

"He was the embodiment of all their hopes and aspirations," Nadich would report. "The black night was over, and the first rays of a new dawn were bursting over the skies of their miserable camp."

Nadich led Ben-Gurion through the multitude to an auditorium, and the whole camp followed. As Ben-Gurion stood on the platform, the people cheered, sang, and finally wept.

"At last he began to speak, his voice choked up, his eyes filled. He had to stop as he broke down for a moment. In the sudden quiet one could hear the muffled sobbing from all sides of the auditorium."

Zion was waiting for them, Ben-Gurion said, and would bring balm to their wounds. Patience. They would leave soon. More cheers and sobs. Yes, they listened; they trusted and loved. And Ben-Gurion returned their love. They would be good pioneers and soldiers.

That afternoon Ben-Gurion went to military headquarters and met with Supreme Allied Commander General Dwight D. Eisenhower, who greeted him warmly. It was not in his power to help the refugees settle in Palestine, the General said, but he would do his best to help them while they were in Germany. Ben-Gurion saw a unique opportunity to turn the D.P.s into fighters right there and catapult them directly into the armed struggle in Palestine. The General wanted to help the refugees? Then why not clear Germans out of a zone in southern Germany and concentrate all Jews in a kind of miniature autonomous "Jewish state"? But even without such a "state," the camps should be self-ruling and the people given agricultural and vocational courses and physical training. Also, a military plane should shuttle to Palestine every week to bring back books, teachers and mail.

Shortly afterward Ben-Gurion received word that the "chiefs of the military government" had rejected his proposal for a "Jewish state," though approving his other requests. He was not surprised by the turndown and did not blame Eisenhower, who, he was convinced, had Jewish interests at heart. Nor was it the General's fault that Washington, under British pressure, canceled the air shuttle service.

Anyway, the refugees, he was sure, would soon be home regardless of Allied policy. After being welcomed in every camp like a god, Ben-Gurion was convinced that what the D.P.s might lack in training they made up for in spirit. A spirit born in death camps like Dachau and Belsen that for the first time brought home to him the full truth.

"I saw the gas chambers," he would later tell his comrades. They "were made as if there were showers in them. The Nazis would peep in from the outside and watch the Jews writhing in pangs of agony. I saw the crematoriums in which hundreds of thousands and millions . . . were burned."

However cataclysmic the cost, the Holocaust had turned the survivors into fanatical Zionists. They all longed for *Eretz Yisrael.*

"This is the last will of the millions . . . who went to their death . . . only because we were a nation without a homeland and state."

The Hagana, the Irgun and the Stern Group, now linked in an unholy alliance called the Hebrew Resistance Movement, launched a series of daring operations. On October 10, 1945, they burst into the Atlith detention camp, and two hundred illegal immigrants burst out. On November 1 they sabotaged the railroad in Palestine and blew up British coast-guard vessels. Ben-Gurion was delighted; the British were shocked. And this shock was reflected in a speech that Foreign Secretary Ernest Bevin planned to make in Parliament.

Ben-Gurion knew even before reading an advance copy of it that there would be bad news, for he knew Bevin. The secretary was, in his eyes, the most treacherous and insensitive of the Labour Party leaders, though Prime Minister Clement Attlee ran a close second. As a trade-union leader, Bevin had been fiercely pro-Zionist, and it was largely he who forced Prime Minister Ramsay MacDonald to scrap his plan for keeping Jews out of Palestine in 1930. Now, with equal ferocity, he was himself keeping Jews out of Palestine.

Sarcastically dismissing "the view that the Jews should be driven out of Europe," Bevin proposed setting up a joint Anglo-American Commission of Inquiry to investigate where the refugees should lay down their pitiful bundles once and for all. But Britain would feel bound by the recommendations *only* if the Commission agreed to them unanimously, an unlikely prospect.

So in March 1946 a group of distinguished Americans and Britons went to Palestine and investigated, then issued a report calling for a United Nations trusteeship, an end to the White Paper and Land Regulations, and the immediate entry of a hundred thousand refugees. And they agreed on these measures *unanimously,* meeting Bevin's condition. But the Foreign Secretary wriggled out of his promise. For the sake of racial harmony, he explained, he had to turn down the Commission's proposals. This was more important than keeping a promise.

Ben-Gurion went wild. Resume the battle! he ordered. And strategic bridges, roads and railroads exploded into rubble all along Palestine's borders, while Ben-Gurion hurried to Paris en route home to step up *Aliya Gimel.* He apparently miscalculated, for British fury soared to the boiling point.

The caldron finally boiled over as "Black Saturday" dawned—June 29, 1946. Tanks and armored cars slithered through *kibbutzim* and city streets hushed by a general curfew, people screamed into phones that were dead, and anyone trying to leave the country was greeted by cocked guns at the border. The British had launched a drive to intimidate the *Yishuv* and destroy the Hagana. All over Palestine, troops broke into homes, ripped open floors and walls looking for arms, and dragged out Jews by the hair, locking them in cages, then dumping them into detention camps, where some were beaten, tortured, even killed.

Weizmann, who was in the country, was one of the few Jewish leaders who remained free. He was a reasonable man, the British felt, just the man to cooperate with them. But Weizmann was angry and disillusioned. He had placed his faith totally in Britain despite the warnings of many colleagues. Now the British had let him down, and then dared humiliate him by asking him to collaborate against his comrades. Weizmann replied by throwing them out of his home in Rehovot. But he demanded, as W.Z.O. president, that the Hagana "cease all armed action." Hagana chief Moshe Sneh, who had escaped the British net, testily resigned and smuggled himself out of the country to join Ben-Gurion in Paris.

At 6:30 A.M., shortly after the British struck, the telephone rang in Ben-Gurion's room at the Royal Monceau Hotel. Still bleary from sleep, he answered and heard the excited voice of Ruth Kluger, one of his chief conspirators in Europe. Frenziedly she blurted out the news that practically the whole Jewish leadership in Palestine was behind barbed wire. Ben-Gurion grimly replied, "I expected this. I must go back immediately."

"What could you do in jail?" Ruth asked.

"All right," Ben-Gurion replied, "but this may be it. Now we may have to throw them out and declare a state."

But he still seemed a bit uncertain. Was he now to risk the very existence of the *Yishuv* with so drastic a move? The British might even join the Arabs in fighting the Jews. Within minutes members of the Hagana team had gathered in Ben-Gurion's room and silently awaited runners bringing information from their secret radio station. Finally, near midnight, Ben-Gurion went for a ride with one of them, Ehud Avriel.

"Although he was sitting next to me," Avriel would report, "Ben-Gurion was worlds away. I could feel his mind at work like a calculating machine dissecting details, conjuring up alternatives and gradually constructing a coherent scheme. His face was expressionless. His sad eyes looked into an infinite distance."

When Ben-Gurion had alighted from the car, he said, as if finally having conquered all doubts, "I'll tell you what we must do. We must establish a Jewish state."

Avriel followed Ben-Gurion into the hotel and told a comrade, "I believe I have witnessed the thought process that led to the decision on the proclamation of independence."

Ben-Gurion immediately plowed into a personal campaign to win international support for a state. One national leader even offered to let him set up a Jewish government-in-exile in his land. Ho Chi Minh, the wispy-bearded Vietnamese Communist chief who was soon to return home to lead the battle against French rule, also lived in the Royal Monceau Hotel, and the two men often met for long talks about their respective struggles. In broken French Ben-Gurion politely rejected the offer, but he was happy to know that the possible future head of a distant Asian nation backed the Zionist dream, a nation the Jews might one day redeem with the light of the prophets.

Ben-Gurion returned to the United States to carry on his campaign, pushing the Sonneborn Institute to swiftly collect more funds for the purchase of more arms and ships to transport "illegal" immigrants. But for all his vigor and determination, Ben-Gurion was apparently still frightened that he might be gambling too boldly. When a Mapai official, Chaim Gvati, arrived from Palestine and visited Ben-Gurion at Hotel Fourteen, he found a deeply dejected figure. As they talked, Ben-Gurion suddenly pressed his hands to his head and cried, "Berl! Where is Berl?"

Berl Katzenelson had always told him when he was going too far. Now he had to decide alone. . . . Carry the message to Zion, he instructed Gvati: The British must go! And to prod them, he approved the most daring act of defiance yet: The united Hebrew Resistance Movement would blow up the King David Hotel in Jerusalem, seat of the British bureaucracy. But then he changed his mind. Whatever the British provocation, the Jews could not ignore *havlaga;* the cost would be too high—morally and politically.

Irgun leader Menachem Begin, whose identity was unknown to the British, didn't agree. Hagana had committed itself to the operation, together with the Irgun, and Begin, pale, gaunt, trigger-tempered, was adamant. His own men would carry out the attack with or without the Hagana's approval, he bluntly told Israel Galili, who had taken over as Hagana chief when Moshe Sneh fled. Fearing that the Irgun would ignore *havlaga* if it acted alone, Galili shrugged his approval. And in the ensuing explosion almost a hundred people were killed after the British refused to heed a telephone warning to evacuate the hotel.

Ben-Gurion was enraged when he learned of the disaster and bitterly denounced the Irgun for its action, apparently unaware of Begin's deal with Galili. The Irgun had done exactly what he feared it might do. Scores of innocent people had died in a massive violation of *havlaga*, warning or no warning. And, in his view, whatever propaganda advantages Black Saturday might have netted the Jews, this terrible atrocity would cancel them out. In fact, the British Parliament ominously placed more blame on him than on the Irgun and might even be in a mood to let the mandate forces snuff out Zionism altogether.

Meanwhile, the explosion was reverberating politically. The Hebrew Resistance Movement was dead, and Jews were turning away from Ben-Gurion and toward Weizmann. Had not Weizmann warned that "hot ice" would bring catastrophe? Even *Haaretz* condemned Ben-Gurion and demanded his resignation. A Jewish bomb had achieved what British raids had not: It had split the *Yishuv* and threatened the very existence of the Zionist movement. Ben-Gurion knew it was time for a change in tactics. To mend the split Ben-Gurion would stitch a delicate seam. He would needle the British enough to appease the militants in his party, but not enough to frighten the moderates who were abandoning him.

At a meeting of the Zionist Executive in Paris on August 2, 1946, Ben-Gurion started melting the "hot ice." No more armed struggle until the next Zionist Congress, the majority ruled. And

Ben-Gurion agreed. Still, he had to consider the reaction of his militant friends—especially Abba Hillel Silver, a bullheaded hard-liner who had succeeded the cautious Stephen Wise as the undisputed leader of American Zionism. Ben-Gurion feared his power but needed his support at the Congress, which would map the final lap to statehood. So when the Zionist Executive voted to approve partition, Ben-Gurion sheepishly abstained.

Partition, yes. But the record must not show that the father of Biltmore had helped to kill his child.

In edging toward "moderation" Ben-Gurion had a familiar problem—Weizmann. How could an activist like himself compete with Weizmann for the moderate vote? But he finally figured out how to get rid of the man without humiliating him—make him "honorary" president of the W.Z.O. Ben-Gurion spread this word behind the scenes of the first postwar World Zionist Congress before it opened in Basel in December 1946. This was the perfect job for Weizmann; he would have the honor but not the power. The old scientist, however, fought back ferociously and seemed to be gaining ground, until Ben-Gurion resorted to a sure-fire trick: He walked out and threatened to go home. His comrades, of course, begged him to return, and when he did, most delegates were so glad to see him that they agreed to any terms he wanted. Very well, Weizmann would be "honorary" president.

No, he wouldn't! Weizmann raged. And when one delegate cried, "Demagogue!" he stormed back: "I—a demogogue! . . . The person who flung that word in my face ought to know that in every house and stable in Nahalal, in every little workshop in Tel Aviv or Haifa, there is a drop of my blood!"

The audience stood up and applauded, and Weizmann, taking heart, decided to test his power. Zionist leaders, he demanded, must take part in a new London conference with the British. Ben-Gurion rose and roared defiance. And in a dramatic showdown vote, the delegates backed Ben-Gurion. Weizmann slouched away, a bitter, defeated man. Who would replace him? Nobody. Why hurt this great human symbol more than necessary?

Weizmann later plotted a last-gasp rebellion, beseeching his followers to resign from the Zionist Executive and turn out the "unclean ones." But no one listened. And so Ben-Gurion now stood alone at the Zionist pinnacle. He could act like a moderate without appearing to mimic Weizmann, and like a militant without fearing a revolt by moderates.

Demonstrating his new freedom, Ben-Gurion went to London a few weeks after his victory for the conference that Weizmann had demanded—at the cost of his job. He could now afford politically to sit down and bargain with Bevin. Black Saturday had backfired on the Foreign Secretary, Ben-Gurion and not Weizmann had sprung to the top, and the terrorists, to the horror of British mothers, were on a rampage. Thus, pressed at home and abroad, Bevin had been forced to release his Jewish prisoners. Was he finally ready to let the Jews set up a state?

Bevin proposed a four-year British trusteeship, followed by independence for Arabs and Jews if they could agree on terms. Ben-Gurion spurned the proposal, sensing that Bevin was playing his last desperate card. Even Attlee had begun to question whether Palestine was worth it all. Bevin wanted the troops to stay, but could he pay the price? Ben-Gurion felt that he must find out and asked to see him alone.

"I would like to know what your needs and your fears are in Palestine," Ben-Gurion said with measured coolness as he sat facing Bevin.

The Foreign Secretary resembled a huge frog as he sprawled bulbously behind his desk, glaring at his visitor through round heavy-rimmed glasses. His jowly face with thick stubborn lips mirrored a will perhaps as unbendable as that of his adversary. And like his adversary's, it had catapulted him to the top of his country's trade-union movement. But it was an uneducated will hitched to impulse and immediate gratification rather than to an eternal dream. He was a politician; Ben-Gurion was, too, but he was also a prophet.

"Is it possible," Ben-Gurion went on, "to find a solution that will satisfy both you and us?"

He didn't *need* Palestine, Bevin huffed. If both sides were incapable of compromise, the British would leave the country.

"Neither we, you, nor—I believe—the Arabs, can apparently wait much longer," said Ben-Gurion.

"We can't force a Jewish state on the Arabs," Bevin grunted. "We have no authority for that from the United Nations. No one helps us. The Americans bring pressure to bear on us."

Bevin then made a momentous pronouncement: He would let the United Nations determine Palestine's future. And the meeting ended.

On February 18, 1947, the Foreign Minister rose ponderously to the rostrum in the House of Commons and repeated this private promise. Was Bevin, Ben-Gurion wondered, simply playing a game, figuring that the United Nations would quickly toss the ball back to Britain and then let the Foreign Secretary do as he wished in Palestine? If so, Ben-Gurion was sure, Bevin would be disappointed, for the Jews would never agree.

The time was past for "hot ice." It was time for cold steel.

"This meeting must be strictly confidential," Ben-Gurion rumbled, staring into the slightly oriental eyes of Chaim Laskov, a Jewish Brigade veteran, shortly after returning to Palestine from the London conference. "Do you know what keeping a secret means?"

He did, replied Laskov, wondering why this talk in Ben-Gurion's home was clandestine. Ben-Gurion explained that whatever the United Nations decided, the British would soon march out and the Arabs, in. The *Yishuv*'s life was at stake, and a real Jewish army must spring forth urgently.

"What must we do to build a force?" Ben-Gurion asked. "What do we need to hold out?"

This question tormented Ben-Gurion, who now devoted almost all his time to defense matters, educating himself overnight in a field that he had known little about. The time for "night squads" was over, he realized, and he needed Laskov because, as a veteran of the Jewish Brigade, he had been trained in the British army. The homegrown Hagana commanders, though brave and able guerrilla fighters, could not stand up to regular armies. Besides, the best guerrilla fighters belonged to the Palmach, which was dominated by the Mapam Party, formed by most of the leftists who had bolted Mapai in 1944. Ben-Gurion feared that after the war Mapam might try to seize power. Why should he build up a possibly dangerous private army? Already the Palmach founder and commander, bald, white-bearded Yitzhak Sadeh, was threatening to become a legend. And one legend was enough for the country.

Shortly before this meeting with Laskov, on June 18, 1947, Ben-Gurion had called his commanders together and gravely told them that the main mission of Hagana had changed and so, therefore, must the character of Hagana. It would have to fight not British forces bound by conscience, but regular Arab armies bent on carnage. Thus, it must urgently build its own regular army. The Hagana-trained commanders were shocked. They could envisage guerrilla warfare with the British and local Arabs, but a clash with the Arab states?

Soon after that meeting Ben-Gurion tried to set up a secret

department in Hagana headquarters to blueprint a conventional army, though the opposing commanders made such a commotion that he could proceed only gradually. His army would be a unique blend of foreign and domestic brands, a large regular force, yet one that would strike with the speed and mobility of a Wingate patrol. And he would not tolerate the Palmach or any other private "political" army. Above all, his army must embody the messianic ideal. It must be morally impeccable, with officers who would fill the role of mother to their unit family with the same love that had glowed in his own mother's heart.

But first Ben-Gurion would have to make his officers—and his people—realize that the *Yishuv* tottered at the edge of the precipice. In speech after speech, he shouted his message: "We shall stand face to face, not with political opponents, but with disciples—perhaps even teachers—of Hitler, who know of one way alone to solve the Jewish problem: total annihilation."

"Alarmist!" came the echo. And so Ben-Gurion would have to save his people despite themselves.

He now asked Laskov again: "What do we need?"

Twelve infantry brigade groups, one to three armored brigades, as many aircraft as possible, one hundred twenty thousand rifles. . . .

The top commanders, Ben-Gurion said, must be trained to operate regular army units.

No time, replied Laskov. First train the corporals and sergeants, because their men would be in the front line.

Ben-Gurion agreed, and Laskov immediately began designing the army that had to save the *Yishuv*.

Meanwhile, Ben-Gurion issued orders to his agents in Europe to rush arms shipments that had been trickling in since late 1945. These were weapons that the Jewish Brigade stole from British depots and smuggled into Palestine hidden inside tractors or in crates of onions that tearful inspectors rushed through customs. And in the United States, the Sonneborn Institute worked full-blast buying up surplus World War II weapons.

At the same time, Ben-Gurion ordered a speedup of illegal immigration. More ships, more people! He needed men quickly for his new army. From the end of World War II to the birth of the Jewish state three years later, more than sixty vessels carrying almost a hundred thousand refugees would sail the stormy waters of the Mediterranean, though only a handful would slip by the British watchdog fleet to land clandestinely. But, never mind. Scenes of British soldiers and sailors dragging people ashore in Haifa, often after deadly battles, and whisking them off weeping and screaming to detention camps in Cyprus, if not back to Europe, made sensational front-page drama around the world. The refugees were useful whether as fighters or martyrs.

But useful or not, Ben-Gurion was determined to "save" every one of them—including the "endangered" Jewish women in Sweden! He had visited that country and was shocked to see how Jewish female refugees were behaving. "When they recovered [from their ordeal in the Nazi camps]," he told a comrade, "they could not control their sexual impulses. . . . Cold Swedish men, drunkards—a disaster!" These young women might be lost to Zion forever! So, shortly, the threatened females kissed their "cold, drunken" boyfriends goodbye and were flown to Palestine.

In June 1947, a United Nations Special Committee on Palestine (UNSCOP) flew to the Holy Land to sort out once more the tangled claims of Arab and Jew. Ben-Gurion greeted members with a question:

"Who is willing and capable of guaranteeing that what happened to us in Europe will not recur? Can the conscience of humanity . . . absolve itself of all responsibility for that Holocaust? There is only one security guarantee: a homeland and a state."

The Committee searched its collective soul and saw sense in this argument. And the British helped in their own way. While members looked on in horror, British troops wielding gun and club stopped the refugee ship *Exodus* from disgorging its pathetic load, which was finally sent back to the graveyards of Europe. On September 3, 1947, UNSCOP issued a historic majority report: The Palestine mandate should dissolve into two sovereign states—one Arab and one Jewish—with Jerusalem internationalized. Now it was up to the United Nations General Assembly to consider this recommendation. Bevin, it seemed, had lost his gamble.

Ben-Gurion kept his people at the U.N. working day and night trying to convince American and other delegates that the Jewish state must now rise again. In his desperation he even recruited Chaim Weizmann to help in the campaign, despite his fear that this old foe might try to settle for less than a state. Weizmann,

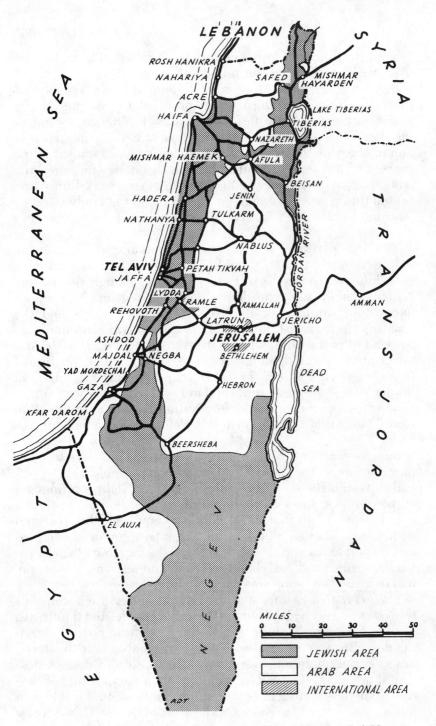

THE UNITED NATIONS PARTITION PLAN

though in ill health, left London for Washington to make sure that President Truman continued to back partition.

Ben-Gurion had been especially alarmed when Truman approved a U.S. State Department proposal to give the Negev region to the Arabs. To Ben-Gurion this desert area, including the port of Eilat on the Gulf of Aqaba, was the potential economic heart of the Jewish state, since it would constitute 60 percent of its area. Without it, he felt, the state would be little more than an oversized ghetto. And Weizmann so skillfully presented this view to Truman that the President not only stood by partition but decided that the Jews should get the Negev after all.

The final partition plan was now acceptable to Ben-Gurion: Palestine, with 1,200,000 Arabs and 568,000 Jews, would be split into two states linked economically, though the United Nations would rule Jerusalem under a trusteeship. The Jewish flag would ripple over the Negev, eastern Galilee and the coastal strip from just north of Haifa to the Gaza Strip border— 55 percent of the land, with a citizenry 58 percent Jewish. And the Arab flag would flutter over the west bank of the Jordan River, western Galilee, the Gaza Strip and an Egyptian-Sinai border zone—45 percent of the land with a population 99 percent Arab. A five-member United Nation Palestine Commission would join Britain in administering Palestine to prepare for partition.

But two-thirds of the General Assembly would have to bless partition under the plan. The United States would vote "yes," and so would Russia and its satellites, since Stalin's prime aim at the time was to root Britain out of the Middle East so Russia could move in. It was not at all clear, however, that partition would win, though Ben-Gurion's agents vigorously wheeled and dealed to line up delegate votes, even bugging official British limousines and Arab hotel rooms to find out what the enemy was doing. The enemy was dangling huge bribes.

Yet, even a victory for partition would not assure a state—or the *Yishuv*'s survival. War would surely explode, and the British wouldn't even be around to save the Jews from possible annihilation. But Ben-Gurion was ready to gamble that the Jews, however outnumbered, would win. He wouldn't sidetrack destiny at this point. Instead he would explain the meaning of destiny to the one Arab leader who might understand, for this man too had a dream. He sent Golda Myerson, a Jewish Agency leader, and another colleague to visit the man with a plea for mutual fulfillment.

The two Jewish emissaries stole into Amman and there, in the royal palace, found that King Abdullah was understanding indeed. Over a magnificent meal of mutton and rice, he told them jokes and then, over Turkish coffee, what they had come to hear. With merry eyes, he said that if the Jews let him gobble up the projected Palestine Arab state, he would keep any Arab army from crossing Transjordanian sands to attack the Jews. His guests agreed, and Ben-Gurion was delighted when he heard the news. He wanted Abdullah to absorb the West Bank before the mufti could. Nor did he wish the Jewish state to take over this Arab-populated region and risk losing its Jewish character if the Arabs were given the full rights of an Israeli citizen, or its democratic character if they weren't.

On the chilly starlit night of November 29, 1947, Ben-Gurion, contrary to habit, went to bed early, though few of his compatriots would get any sleep at all in these historic hours. He and Paula were trying to relax in the Kaliya Hotel on the northern shore of the Dead Sea, even though they knew that at any moment they would learn whether the U.N. General Assembly had voted to sanction a Jewish state.

Hardly had Ben-Gurion fallen asleep when the door swung open and a man burst in, ignoring Paula's shrill protests. He was a comrade from the Jewish Agency, and he had just come from Jerusalem. *"Mazel tov!"* he cried. "We won!"

The partitionists had gained the necessary two-thirds majority. Ben-Gurion stared up at him with joy. A state! He slowly rose and, slipping on his robe, shuffled to a table, picked up his blue Parker pen and began writing a declaration. When he ran out of paper he asked for more and scribbled the last words on a sheet of brown toilet tissue:

> ... The Jewish people, which has never given way to despair, even at the darkest moments of its history, and which has never once lost its faith in itself and in the conscience of humanity, will not fall short at this great hour of the opportunity and the historic responsibility that have been given to it. The restored Judea will take an honorable place in the United Nations as a force for peace, prosperity and progress in the Holy Land, the Near East and the world at large.

Suddenly there was a commotion outside and some young people crashed in singing songs and dancing a wild hora around Ben-Gurion. How great to be alive at this moment! He had given them a state! They asked him to join in, but he simply smiled and stood, awkward and silent, watching their euphoric faces. Could they know as he did what tomorrow would bring?

"Crowds danced in the streets," he would say later. "But I could not dance. I knew that we faced war and that we would lose the best of our youth."

Two hundred Bren guns, fifteen hundred rifles, four hundred submachine guns. . . . Back in his office the day after the United Nations vote, Ben-Gurion brooded over his small arsenal. So much trouble and risk for so little. He had been counting on arms from Russia and its satellites, but they had attached strings to their aid, demanding to know the political views of the Hagana. In reply, he angrily ordered his agents to stop all payments to these countries. The price of pride, however, was high. How could the *Yishuv* face the tanks, artillery and planes of the Arab states with a few rifles?

Ben-Gurion would have to depend on his own agents abroad, especially Yehuda Arazi, his chief arms procurer in Europe. Arazi planned to buy a ship, fill it up with arms, and sail it home on the day the British left. But he too was having trouble getting enough arms and needed help. So Ben-Gurion called in Ehud Avriel, handed him a shopping list, and said, "Those are the items we need."

But since Avriel and other agents needed at least twenty-five million dollars, Ben-Gurion sent his treasurer, Eliezer Kaplan, to raise the money in the United States. Kaplan returned with only five million.

The American Jews, Ben-Gurion felt, didn't understand what was at stake. He would go to them personally and make them understand. But his colleagues protested; he must stay home to direct the coming war.

"What you are able to do here, I cannot do," said Golda Myerson. "But I can do what you would do in America. So *I* shall go."

Golda was always ready to perform the hardest tasks. Stout and striking with black hair knotted in the back and eyes that perpetually reflected an inner sadness, she had migrated with her parents from Kiev, Russia, to Milwaukee as a young girl before moving to Palestine in the 1920s. She learned English well enough to work as a teacher, and she knew how to deal with American Jewry.

Ben-Gurion brushed Golda's offer aside, but his colleagues voted him down, and so without luggage or even a change of clothing, and with only ten dollars in her purse, Golda rushed to the airport to catch the next plane to the United States.

The urgency of the Avriel and Myerson missions struck with greater impact each day. On December 2, 1947, Ben-Gurion peered through the window of the Jewish Agency building in Jerusalem and watched helplessly as howling Arab mobs broke into Jewish shops and set them ablaze—while British policemen passively looked on. The Arabs, with British help, would try to make it clear to the world that partition would not work.

In the Jewish quarter of the Old City they even tried to break into the Warsaw Synagogue, which the British finally saved by flashing their bayonets. But Arab snipers on the rooftops had forced shops and schools to close and turned the quarter into a silent maze of death. Then, on January 14, 1948, a thousand Arab villagers stormed the Etzion Bloc of settlements perched atop the rolling Hebron hills, surging up the rocky gray slopes wave upon wave. The Jews managed to push them back, but when a Hagana force of thirty-five tried to reach Etzion with arms and food, it was ambushed and, after a dramatic battle from rock to rock, wiped out.

As usual when Ben-Gurion was shaken by heavy blows, a calm surface masked his inner turmoil. Was this an omen? As if in answer, his officers rushed to him with more devastating news: Foreign Arab "volunteers" had marched into Palestine from Lebanon and Syria, urged on by the blood-curdling war cries of their commander, Fawzi el-Kaoukji, an Arab adventurer well known for his terrorist role in the 1936–39 Arab revolt. And the British let him stay after he promised that he wouldn't attack the Jews until every British soldier had sailed off, presumably in mid-May 1948.

Even when Kaoukji broke his word and pounced on one set-tlement, the British did not move against him; only the Jews did, finally driving back his troops with a few old rifles and homemade bombs that were more deafening than deadly. But Kaoukji simply stumbled off to his headquarters village cursing Jewish "luck" and plotted a new assault. Meanwhile, the mufti, distrusting him as an agent of the "treacherous" Arab states that hoped to snatch Arab Palestine for themselves, stepped up his own campaign of violence to show his people that he was still boss. In Jerusalem his men blew up the English-language *Palestine Post,* a block of houses, and even part of the Jewish

Agency building, from where Ben-Gurion and his colleagues miraculously escaped unscathed.

Each day the thought of another Holocaust haunted Ben-Gurion more, and even the British, he now felt, wouldn't try to stop it. His agents were still his main hope. Arazi? Little progress. Avriel? Not a word from him; what the devil was he doing? Ben-Gurion sent cable after cable to him. No reply. Finally, he would learn with enormous relief that Avriel was doing quite a bit. Over oysters and wine in a Paris hotel, he had persuaded an agent of a giant Czechoslovakian arms firm to take him to his boss in Prague. On arriving, Avriel pulled Ben-Gurion's shopping list out of his pocket and handed it to the "boss," who glanced at it and smiled. Yes, he had everything on the list.

And the Jews had the money to buy it all, too, for Golda Myerson had charmed American Jewry into stuffing her kitty with some fifty million dollars—double her goal! Then more good news. Agents were smuggling tons of war equipment out of the United States and Mexico, partly with the help of the Sonneborn Institute. And as British soldiers began trickling out of Palestine, several of them agreed to turn over tanks and guns they managed to hijack from their camp, if not for the money then for the sake of Hagana girlfriends. Meanwhile, Hagana agents sank a huge shipload of arms destined for the Arabs before it could leave an Italian port.

But there was bad news too. The American ambassador to the United Nations, without consulting President Truman, announced to the Security Council on March 19 that the partition plan could "not now be implemented by peaceful means" and that his government therefore "believes that a temporary trusteeship for Palestine should be established."

Then, even worse news. The Arabs, unable to smash into the settlements, began ambushing convoys along the main roads, cutting communications everywhere, slicing up Jewish Palestine into isolated pockets and sealing off Jerusalem, which was swiftly running out of ammunition, food and water. But Ben-Gurion ordered the Jews to defend every colony, every town, whatever the odds. Each one abandoned could mean that much smaller a state. What was more important—ephemeral human life or land that would eternally protect and nourish the survivors and their descendants?

Even Ben-Gurion's most sacred military tenet—*havlaga*—began to crumble in the face of the growing threat. He still forbade attacks on peaceful Arab villages but, with a shrug of regret, conceded now that "it is impossible in time of war to keep from hurting innocent people." Perhaps he had been "too optimistic and didn't appreciate sufficiently the Arab character," he wrote in his diary. Some villages would have to "be taught a lesson."

It was time for Plan D.

Plan D called on the Jews to strike back remorselessly and consume all areas granted to them under the partition plan—and any Arab sectors within them—especially the enemy-infested highlands overlooking the Tel Aviv–Jerusalem road, a deadly gauntlet of fire and lead. With the first arms from Czechoslovakia about to arrive, the Jews must attack without delay in order to defend the little territory they still controlled. For the first time they would seize and hold Arab villages, though the inhabitants would be allowed to remain in their little stone houses if they didn't revolt against Jewish military control.

But even at this magic moment of commitment, Ben-Gurion was his practical self. "We'll grow vegetables there," he said. "Afterward, when there is peace, we'll give them back the land with the vegetables."

Peace—survival—was more important than land, at least in the short term. The Jews could wait for destiny to run its course.

At a meeting of Hagana chiefs on April 1, Ben-Gurion ordered them to rustle up two thousand rifles so they could storm the village of Kastel overlooking the road to Jerusalem. With the fortress there in Jewish hands, the road would be open. The full impact of his lifelong obsession with the Bible struck with blistering force when it appeared that Jerusalem would fall to the Arabs and perhaps be lost forever to the Jewish state. Whatever happened to any other Jewish areas, the Holy City must be saved. It was the soul of the Jewish people, the fount of the light to be cast unto the nations. He had agreed that it be internationalized as a *temporary* concession. But an Arab flag over Jerusalem? Not for one minute!

And the next day fifteen hundred men with rifles, drawn from settlements and battle lines around the country, were ready to launch Operation Nahshon, named after the first Israelite to leap into the Red Sea during the exodus from Egypt.

"At 0330 we shall [move up toward] Kastel. You all have your instructions. Remember, this objective is a must."

The commander of the Palmach unit calmly briefed his men on the morning of April 3, 1948. Kastel! After all these centuries, still a monstrous sentinel blocking the way to Jerusalem, dominating the region for miles. But now the Jews, armed with brand-new Czech rifles miraculously flown in the night before, seized Kastel in a quick thrust at dawn, and the dust of death hovering over the road to Jerusalem suddenly vanished in the sunlight. Shortly afterward the Arabs stormed the height and recaptured it, but the Jews took it back again. And within hours, Jerusalemites deliriously welcomed three supply-crammed convoys, leaping on running boards, crawling over every vehicle, screaming and weeping and throwing kisses.

Ben-Gurion rejoiced, too; the Jews had conquered Kastel, and the British had not joined the Arabs. The sands of war were shifting. In fact, more swiftly than he imagined—thanks largely to his Jewish foes. When the Jerusalem commanders of the Irgun and the Stern Group learned about the Hagana's plan for Operation Nahshon, they felt left out. Why not, they asked, attack some Arab target of their own? And they settled on the village of Deir Yassin, a picturesque complex of flat-topped, sun-baked stone huts mounted in tiers to the crest of a hill outside Jerusalem.

After warning the inhabitants by loudspeaker to flee (few could hear it), they smashed into the village—only to find themselves bogged down by Arab fire from almost every house. Maddened by the unexpected resistance, the attackers dynamited each dwelling systematically, burying scores of Arabs in the debris. They also shot many other Arabs at random. When the smoking village finally fell silent, more than two hundred bodies lay, piled up in heaps, though most inhabitants had escaped.

When Ben-Gurion learned of the massacre, he was "filled with shock and disgust"—not only because the terrorists had grossly violated the sacred rules of *havlaga*, but because King Abdullah might now hesitate to make a deal with the Jews. He immediately whipped off a wire to Abdullah expressing his deep regret and disavowing the bloody event. But the King replied caustically that the Jewish Agency was indeed responsible for Jewish actions.

Panic spread in Arab Palestine, and within weeks fighting in Tiberias, Haifa, Safed, Jaffa and other places would end with hundreds of thousands of Arabs dragging themselves beside their heavily laden donkeys toward the safety of the bordering Arab states. In Haifa not even the pleas of Jewish leaders and neighbors could stem the flow.

Ben-Gurion was startled. He had not planned this massive exodus and apparently never imagined that it could happen. In fact, when one of his officers suggested that his men kill the inhabitants of another Arab village, Tul Kerem, in order to frighten others into fleeing, Ben-Gurion was so furious that he expelled the officer from his post. Still, pragmatism went hand in hand with humanism. Why were the Arabs fleeing? Less because of Deir Yassin, he seemed sure, than because of orders from the mufti and other Arab leaders, who presumably promised to lead them back with the conquering Arab armies. This would be the official Zionist view, though there is no evidence to show that the Arab leaders actually issued such orders.

Anyway, the Arabs, Ben-Gurion felt, could have stayed but chose to flee. And almost overnight the Jews had become the predominant people in all of Palestine. He would govern a *real* Jewish state, and there would be few Arabs left to sabotage it.

"It is not our duty to be concerned with the return of the refugees," he would now say. Let the surrounding Arab states absorb them. And he ordered that Jews be settled in the abandoned villages immediately. The devil in Deir Yassin had played into the hands of Providence.

Arab fighters desperately sought to avenge Deir Yassin and raise the sagging morale of their people. They bombed to a halt a convoy of buses and trucks winding up to Hadassah Hospital atop Mount Scopus in Jerusalem and set fire to some of the vehicles, burning alive seventy-six doctors, professors, nurses, students and hospital employees before British forces careened to the scene and stopped the massacre. When Ben-Gurion learned of this tragedy in Tel Aviv, he was close to tears. He had known the victims, and one of them, a physics student, was the fiancé of Renana, a fellow student in Jerusalem and now a Hagana defender who carried bombs instead of books.

Despite such incidents, Ben-Gurion was now more optimistic than he had been for months, for the Jews had won most of their battles and would be stronger in the future, with arms starting to flow in. He was also relieved to learn that the U.S. State Department, after being quietly upbraided by Truman, was no longer pushing for a U.N. trusteeship but calling simply for a truce. When the British departed, the Jewish Agency and the Arab Higher Committee, under this proposal, would peacefully rule their own communities without either declaring a state. But Ben-Gurion rejected this "compromise" too, provoking State Department threats to "expose" the "pressures" that American Jews were exerting on the United States government.

How desperate were the Americans? Would they try to sabotage a Jewish state? A week before the British were to leave Palestine, Ben-Gurion cabled Moshe Shertok in New York: Go to Washington and find out. Neither man knew that Nahum Goldmann, while resenting American intimidation, had, in his fear of a new Holocaust, advised American officials to oppose a state. Within hours, on May 8, Shertok was sitting in the office of Secretary of State George C. Marshall.

There must be an immediate truce, Marshall exclaimed. The Jews must postpone a state for the sake of world peace.

But the Jews, Shertok revealed, had an understanding with Abdullah, and the Arab states would probably not attack.

Marshall, however, was skeptical and made it clear that if the Jews declared a state and the Arab world did attack, the United States would not come to their aid.

Shertok was crestfallen. The Jews, he was persuaded, could not afford to defy the United States. He gloomily departed and was about to board a plane at La Guardia Airport for Tel Aviv when he heard himself being paged and went to a telephone. It was Chaim Weizmann: "Tell B.G., tell everyone: It's now or never! Fear not, nor be dismayed!"

Still in doubt, Shertok flew off to Tel Aviv and hurried to Ben-Gurion's home with Marshall's proposal.

"What do you think of the idea?" Ben-Gurion asked.

"I think he is right."

Ben-Gurion was relentless. "Moshe," he said, "listen to me as a friend. If you don't want to ruin your life, don't say that in your report."

Ben-Gurion faced the challenge of Shertok's message only hours after Golda Myerson had rushed to him with news of even greater import. She had met King Abdullah secretly in Amman on May 11—their second meeting—after slipping through the lines disguised as a veiled Arab woman.

The King, under heavy pressure from his Arab colleagues, had dourly asked the Jews to cancel plans for a Jewish state— the plans that he had approved at their first meeting—if they wanted to avoid war. They must agree to autonomy for one year, and then Transjordan would absorb all of Palestine. A joint parliament and perhaps a joint cabinet would be set up and Jews would fill half the seats in each.

"We can give you the answer here and now," Golda had replied. "If Your Majesty has turned his back on our original understanding and wants war instead, there will be war."

So Marshall was right—the Arab states *would* invade. But they would do so, Ben-Gurion was convinced, even if the Jews did not proclaim a state. At least with a state it would be easier to buy arms, hire foreign officers to train the army, and win international support. Besides, he could not be less militant than Chaim Weizmann—it was, as Weizmann said, now or never.

On May 12, three days before the British were to depart, Ben-Gurion strode into a Jewish Agency conference room in Tel Aviv, his face haggard and grim. He solemnly greeted fellow members of the National Council of Thirteen, a body that had replaced the Jewish Agency Executive as the supreme Jewish ruling body and would become the provisional government when the mandate ended. Would they listen to him? Would they show the courage and foresight of Abraham, Moses, the prophets? Could he expect them to, when he himself was filled with fear? The cries from the Etzion Bloc were terrifying. Abdullah's soldiers had joined local Arabs and were about to attack these settlements, and others were also in peril. Perhaps sixty thousand Palestine Jews, almost one out of ten, would die.

On paper, Ben-Gurion felt, the Jews seemed to be holding their own. They occupied almost solidly the coastal strip of Palestine from Tel Aviv north to Haifa, eastern and western Galilee and the Beisan Valley. They controlled much of the Negev network of roads that linked twenty-seven dispersed settlements, and they were standing fast in Jewish Jerusalem despite renewed Arab attempts to strangle this hungry besieged city.

Yet, something of a miracle was still needed. Arabs entrenched in the hills less than ten miles from the coast could sweep down and slice the Jewish state in two. Arab Ramle and Lydda were deadly arrows aimed at Tel Aviv, only twenty minutes away. Arab guerrillas dotted the heights twisting from Jerusalem to Hebron to Beersheba, and once more blocked the Tel Aviv–Jerusalem road. And while Arab arsenals bulged, the Jews were still looking out to sea for their precious ships to come in.

At the same time, the Jewish command was almost as splin-

tered as the Arab leadership, with the Mapam-dominated Palmach determined to remain a semiautonomous force. To
disband it, Ben-Gurion would have to dismiss Israel Galili, the
chief of national command, who served as a liaison between the
Jewish Agency and the general staff. No easy matter, since he
was an extremely influential Mapam leader. Ben-Gurion had
already tried to get rid of him, but had had to back down when
some of his best officers threatened to mutiny.

Now, at this historic meeting on the morning of May 12, Ben-
Gurion could not afford to antagonize anyone. He called the
National Council of Thirteen to order and posed the most important question they would ever have to answer: Should they
accept the American truce plan? If the majority replied "no," he
would proclaim a state. If "yes" . . . He shuddered to think of
that happening. Gazing at the faces around the table, he found
them even more anxious than his own. At least a third of his
own party was leaning against a state. He tried to remain calm,
to appear confident.

But the mood grew more morose by the minute as speaker
after speaker analyzed the danger. Moshe Shertok reported on
Marshall's warning—without revealing his own reaction. Golda
Myerson described her bleak talk with King Abdullah. Then
Ben-Gurion called in Israel Galili and Yigael Yadin. An arche-
ologist like his father, Yadin was the Hagana chief of operations
and acting chief of staff in the absence of Yaacov Dori, who was
in the United States seeking arms and would later be too ill to
serve in his post. In Ben-Gurion's eyes, Yadin, though only
twenty-eight, was a brilliant strategist and organizer. He had an
independent mind, yet, unlike Galili, could be trusted to follow
orders. Surely these two military leaders would stiffen the
Council's back. He posed the crucial question: From a military
point of view, would it be wise to call a truce?

Galili, short, pudgy, white-haired, equivocated—a truce
would be helpful militarily, but it had to be weighed against
political considerations.

Yadin's thin poetic face, projecting birdlike from a long neck,
paled when his turn came. He could not reply, he said, since
the responsibility was too great. But after a heavy silence, he
went on: The fact was, a concerted invasion would give the Arab
armies a "distinct edge." A truce would help, for at least the
army could obtain more arms.

And what were the chances for victory now?

Perhaps fifty-fifty.

Only a fifty-fifty chance to survive? A chill wind of desperation swept through the room. Set up a "government" instead of a state, one Council member cried. Accept the truce, demanded another. Ben-Gurion tried to tame the tempest. They must understand.

"Do we envisage any realistic possibility of resisting invasion?" he said. "My reply is: . . . given our moral values, and on condition that our manpower is wisely used and equipment is increased, then we have every prospect of success. . . . The outcome depends on our wiping out most of the Arab Legion."

Wipe out the Arab Legion, King Abdullah's powerful British-led army? The Council members were appalled by Ben-Gurion's impudence, enthralled by his pluck.

"And now we shall vote on whether to accept the truce proposal," Ben-Gurion declared calmly.

Would they hear the whispered pleas of the murdered millions? Would they seize this moment of destiny? The air was electric, as if God Himself were cocking an ear. Those in favor of a truce? . . . Those opposed? . . . Ben-Gurion announced the results as casually as he might the date of their next meeting. Six of the ten Council members present had voted to reject the truce. He glanced with the faintest smile at Moshe Shertok, who had cast the deciding vote.

Two days later Ben-Gurion proclaimed the rebirth of Israel.

CHAPTER TEN

Thus the Jews smote all their enemies
ESTHER 9:5

"**A**RE you sure?" Yaacov Yannai shouted into the telephone.

"Yes, that's what it says," replied the operator of his secret radio station, who had just jotted down a message from the United States.

Yannai, who commanded the Hagana signal corps, could hardly believe it. The clock had barely tolled midnight, May 15, 1948, and the British Mandate had just ended. Yet Washington had already recognized the State of Israel! He sped to Ben-Gurion's home, knocked on the door and stared into Paula's grim, suspicious face.

"Ben-Gurion is exhausted," she snapped. "I will not let anybody wake him up!"

But Yannai slid past Paula and bounded up the stairs to Ben-Gurion's room. Shaking the Prime Minister awake, he blurted the news.

"I don't believe it!" Ben-Gurion cried.

"But the operator took down every word."

"Take me to the station. I want to check it myself."

Ben-Gurion leaped out of bed, slipped into his robe, and ran down the stairs and out the door, with Paula at his heels crying, "Come back! Come back!" even as she scrambled into the back seat of Yannai's car. In minutes the vehicle skidded to a halt in front of a small wooden hut on the beach, and Yannai rushed in and made contact with New York.

"It's definite," he told Ben-Gurion. "Truman has recognized us."

The Prime Minister embraced Yannai and agreed to speak by radio to the United States. The officer drove the couple home and picked them up again about two hours later for the broadcast. As the three waited outside the hut for the operator to contact New York again, they suddenly heard an ominous hum. Egyptian planes! In a moment bombs were screaming down on a nearby power station. The invasion had begun! Then it was Paula who screamed. "You are killing Ben-Gurion! Let's get out of here before he's killed!"

But at that moment the radio operator called out that New York was on the line. Yannai was in turmoil. Should he whisk Ben-Gurion to safety or push him into the hut? He watched the planes circle for another try. Didn't Israel desperately need American support? He dragged Ben-Gurion into the station while Paula continued to yell, "You are killing him! You are killing him!"

Yannai slammed the door shut behind Ben-Gurion to keep Paula out and, at 5:20 A.M. (10:20 the previous night in New York), the Prime Minister sat before a microphone and began speaking from hastily scribbled notes, ignoring the shouts and wails of his wife as she pounded on the door. Then more bombs, and the walls of the hut trembled and the lights winked on the control panel. Ben-Gurion paused, then calmly injected an incidental remark: "The explosions you can hear are Arab planes bombing Tel Aviv."

After thus scooping the whole press corps, he returned to his message while the walls continued to tremble—from the cries of Paula, who was still demanding that her husband come home and get some sleep before he was killed.

Soon he did go home—after he had driven to the airport with some soldiers to see what damage the bombs had done there. He sat down at his desk and drowsily scrawled in his diary: "Outside stood people in pajamas. I looked at them and saw that there was no fear in their eyes. I knew then we would win."

"I'm sorry, but we have nothing. We have a front in Jerusalem, a front in Galilee, a front in the Negev. There are not enough arms anywhere."

Ben-Gurion paused, and suddenly one of his visitors broke into tears. The group had come on May 19 from Kibbutz Degania in the Galilee, where Syrian troops were threatening to wipe out the settlement. In desperation the emissaries were appealing to Ben-Gurion for cannons, planes and reinforcements before it was too late; even now their wives and children might be dead. But what could he do? The Arab Legion had cut the road to Mount Scopus in Jerusalem. The Egyptians had captured key fortresses in the Negev and bombed Tel Aviv's central bus station. And the arms that Ehud Avriel had bought were still, eternally, "on the way." Hold on! Ben-Gurion ordered. Every settlement must fight until overrun by enemy forces, emulating Kfar Etzion—where dozens of defenders had fought to the death.

When the visitors had left, crestfallen, Yigael Yadin protested that there *were* arms; four 65-millimeter guns of 1870 vintage had just arrived from Europe.

But Jerusalem needed them, Ben-Gurion replied.

It could be fatal to base war strategy on the needs of Jerusalem, warned Yadin. He knew Jerusalem, and it could hold. But Degania probably couldn't. For God's sake, send two of the guns to Degania! After a lengthy argument, Yadin smashed his fist on the table, breaking the glass covering it and severely cutting his hand. Ben-Gurion was impressed. Yadin stood up to him as few of his colleagues would. Apparently as a concession to his grit, Ben-Gurion let the guns go to Degania for twenty-four hours.

Shortly, these sightless cannons were in action and, though missing their targets by far, made so much noise that the Syrians fled in terror. Ben-Gurion was relieved, but he was still apprehensive. Was the survival of Israel to depend on sheer luck and a few gimmicky guns?

Within days the luck and the gimmickry began to run out. An Egyptian armored column crawled to within twenty-five miles of Tel Aviv; other Egyptian forces blasted into Beersheba, the largest town in the Negev; Arab Legionnaires and Iraqis were thrusting toward the sea; the Jewish quarter in the Arab Old City of Jerusalem was overrrun; the isolated Jewish New City was under murderous bombardment; and settlements everywhere were fighting, bleeding, begging for help. But there was none to give.

Ben-Gurion paced the floor, his jaw taut and tyrannical, his eyes remote mirrors of anguish. Occasionally he would sit down and demand the latest battle reports or growl orders to intimidated subordinates, then stand up again and study the huge maps on the wall, tracing the fronts with his finger. What did his staff officers know? Some of them doubted the Jews could hold out another three days. Three days! His people would hold out for as long as they had to. Even if the enemy reached Tel Aviv, the battalions of civilians being formed there would fight with sticks, stones, bare fists.

Yet even at this desperate moment, on the brink of total destruction, Ben-Gurion clung to his ultimate goal. Israel would not only survive but would prepare for its universal mission. Thus, he overruled Yadin when a young scholar requested that his army call-up be delayed until he could finish writing a book on the prophet Jeremiah. The draft board, Yadin argued, could not play favorites, especially at this critical time in the war.

"The war is very important indeed," Ben-Gurion replied. "But how many Jeremiahs are there? The book must be finished. That's part of our war effort. The war is not only shooting." And the scholar was given two months to complete his book—provided that Israel would last that long.

It would. On May 23 an aide burst into Ben-Gurion's office with the news that the infant state now had more than sticks and stones—the Messerschmitts had arrived! The Prime Minister stared at the man as if he were a messenger of God. Assemble them quickly, he ordered, and send them to the fronts! Then more good news: A ship was nearing Tel Aviv loaded with almost fifty cannons and five thousand rifles.

"That will mean the turning point!" Ben-Gurion joyfully jotted in his diary. Now he could save Jerusalem.

Jerusalem again! Yadin and most of the other commanders argued, as they had many times before, that the best way to save Jerusalem would be to save the rest of the country first. But, reluctantly, they agreed to attack Latrun. Latrun was a clump of rocky hills overlooking the Tel Aviv–Jerusalem road, a pinkish-brown mass dominated by a police fortress that reached into the sky like a gnarled claw. Hit this stronghold head-on, Ben-Gurion ordered, then push down the branch road to Ramallah skirting these hills and strike at the Old City from the rear, trapping the occupying Arab Legion forces within its walls. The key to victory was speed.

But his men were not ready yet, Yadin protested. Anyway, a head-on attack would leave the hills freckled with bodies. Outflank the fortress, that was the way.

"There is no time for that," Ben-Gurion replied. "We'll have to improvise. And I'm not interested in the obstacles. It's your job to overcome them."

"A direct attack will be sheer suicide," Yadin insisted. "I implore you to postpone the attack for just one week."

"Not for one day."

But Ben-Gurion finally relented. All right, one day. Twenty-four hours.

At dawn, May 25, the Israelis, mainly untrained refugees just off the boat, stumbled through a wheat field toward the forbidding heights until greeted by a stream of shells and bullets that sent the survivors staggering toward the rear. Officers shouted for them to halt, but everyone, it seemed, spoke a different language and would not listen to reason anyway as they frantically fled their Tower of Babel.

"You must look at the general picture," Ben-Gurion argued when Yadin told him the attack had failed, with about one hundred forty dead. "We forced the enemy to divert forces to Latrun that would certainly have attacked the New City."

"But if a diversion had been our aim," Yadin replied with exasperation, "it would have been much easier and cheaper to attack elsewhere. The immediate objective of the attack was to open the roads to Jerusalem and Ramallah, and we failed miserably."

Ben-Gurion waved away this logic and insisted that his forces attack again. And they did—under Colonel David "Mickey" Marcus, a jovial, pot-bellied American Jew, who had just arrived from the United States to help organize the budding Israeli army. He would be Israel's first *aluf*, or general, since Judah Maccabeus held the rank two thousand years earlier. But the new attack failed too, after a unit had reached the fortress but took too much time trying to blow the door open—not realizing it was unlocked!

Marcus now had a new idea. He gathered an army of civilian men and women and put them to work with chisels, wooden mallets and shovels in a massive effort to carve out of the limestone hills a "Burma road" that would bypass Latrun. After five days, Ben-Gurion exulted as the first trucks, hidden from enemy missiles, slowly ground their way over a precarious stony path.

But Ben-Gurion and Marcus feared that the Arab Legion was getting set to attack the new road, and they ordered another assault on Latrun. This time the Israelis attacked the wrong hill in the dark and were mowed down again. And now it was too late for another go. The United Nations called for a truce.

Ben-Gurion was shocked as he sat in bed reading the radio message. Mickey Marcus was dead! A guard at central-front headquarters had mistaken him for an Arab in the dark and allegedly shot him during the truce. An accident? Ben-Gurion was skeptical. A strange coincidence—just when he had named Marcus commander of the Jerusalem front, infuriating the Palmach commanders, who wanted no "outsider" telling them how to fight. He summoned Yaacov Shapira, a lawyer who would soon become attorney general, and said, "Yaacov, I want all the facts in the Marcus case. I want you to make a thorough investigation and then report to me."

Shapira immediately investigated—without going to the scene—and prepared a report that raised more questions than it answered. Several shots were heard, though the guard fired only once, and a doctor testified that the fatal bullet appeared to have been fired from a Sten gun, not from the guard's Czech rifle. But, Shapira concluded, "Commander Marcus was killed by a shot fired upon him by Private Eliezer Linski" in the line of duty. (Linski, whose identity was supposed to be secret, would later tell the author that he was not at all sure his bullet had been the fatal one.)

Ben-Gurion would publicly agree with Shapira, but years later he would assure the author that "the Palmach deliberately killed" Marcus. "It couldn't have been an accident," he said, rising from his desk and tensely pacing the floor. "It isn't logical. It was the Palmach."

Although Ben-Gurion conceded that he had no proof to support this conclusion, as in the Arlosoroff case fifteen years earlier, proof was not essential. It was more important to eradicate a perceived threat to his dream of a messianic state. In 1933 the Revisionists were the most immediate threat. In 1948 the Palmach was. It blocked the creation of a unified army, the key to his state, and might, as an instrument of the Mapam Party, even try to devour him after the war. Suspicion was enough to fuel his moral outrage, to help justify his campaign to weed out wayward military groups. As he had in the past glued together the labor unions and the labor parties, he would now fuse all fighting units into a single national army under one command—by whatever means.

On June 11, 1948, almost a month after the Arab invasion, a truce settled over the body-littered land like a massive shroud. The Arabs had spurned a cease-fire at first when it looked as if their armies might grind the new Jewish state into dust. But as they started to choke on the dust, they changed their minds and approved a truce plan proposed by the United Nations mediator, Count Folke Bernadotte. Ben-Gurion distrusted the lanky, stern-faced Bernadotte, a member of the Swedish royal family and president of the Swedish Red Cross, considering him a pro-British foe of partition. But Ben-Gurion too backed the plan, hoping to give his exhausted, depleted forces a chance to recover and reorganize.

With the battlefields silent, Ben-Gurion met at general headquarters with his commanders, who, haggard and mud-stained, swapped horror stories of impossible struggle. The troops, they agreed, had fought to the breaking point and were near collapse. But Ben-Gurion looked at the broader picture. No reason for pessimism. The Israelis, after all, had held out against the regular Arab armies in almost every settlement within the territory that the United Nations had allocated to Israel. The big problem for him was not the suffering of the individual, but the individualism that caused the suffering.

"Because of lack of discipline," he said, "we have lost positions; because of lack of discipline we have not fully exploited possibilities and have not made gains that were within our reach. If we had one army rather than a number of armies, and if we had operated according to one strategic plan, we should have more to show for our efforts."

Ben-Gurion's obsession with "one army" even overshadowed his hunger for arms, as the tragic odyssey of the LST *Altalena* would demonstrate. The ship sailed from a French port crammed with almost a thousand Jews and a huge cargo of weapons secretly delivered by a French army convoy—a token of France's sympathy for Israel in the midst of its own battle against Arab nationalists in North Africa. The problem was that the vessel, and the Jews aboard, belonged not to the Israeli government but to the Irgun Zvai Leumi. On the morning of June 12, Irgun chief Menachem Begin announced dramatically to Israel Galili and other Israeli officials:

"The *Altalena* is carrying men and iron to Israel that can win the war for us. She's carrying enough arms to equip ten battalions. She will arrive in five days."

It seemed only fair, Begin said, that the Irgun keep 20 percent for its own fighters in Jerusalem.

Galili telephoned Ben-Gurion, who was enraged. Had not Begin already agreed to integrate his units into the army and turn over all their arms to it? And Ben-Gurion wasn't impressed by Begin's argument that since Jerusalem was, under the partition plan, to be outside the Jewish state, his men there could operate independently of the army and equip themselves with their own weapons.

Ben-Gurion was convinced that Begin planned to use the arms to seize the government by force—a charge that the Irgun leader denied, though some of his extremist followers were, in fact, plotting a coup, apparently without his knowledge. Amihai Paglin, who was then Begin's chief of operations and would eventually head an antiterrorist unit in the Begin government, admitted to the author that, during the *Altalena* incident, he and another Irgun leader, Bezalel Stolnitzky, conspired to overthrow the government. And they were prepared, Paglin said, to "wipe out" Ben-Gurion and his cabinet if necessary. But before they could round up an Irgun "commando force" for the operation, Paglin was arrested and the plot fell through.

In any case, Ben-Gurion ordered his commanders to let the *Altalena* come. All the weapons, however, would go to the army. Galili then told Begin that the ship could land.

"What about the arms for Jerusalem?" Begin asked.

"We'll work that out," Galili replied. "I think twenty percent can go to Jerusalem."

Begin was delighted. Apparently he hadn't listened very carefully; Galili had not specified *who* in Jerusalem would be getting the 20 percent. At any rate, the two men clashed when Begin insisted on storing the arms in an Irgun warehouse. The government didn't agree? Too bad. His men would unload the arms themselves and keep them all!

In fury, Galili sent an urgent note to Ben-Gurion: The Irgun was challenging the authority of the state and the Prime Minister should take "swift and clear action" to meet this "internal threat" to Israel. Ben-Gurion agreed. Yes, action—and he had a perfect excuse for the world. The Irgun was trying to smuggle in soldiers and arms in violation of the cease-fire! Never mind that his own agents were doing the same thing. Here was a chance to destroy an "internal threat," procure a shipload of arms, and win the sympathy of the world all at once.

On the afternoon of June 20, Ben-Gurion called a secret meeting of the cabinet and persuaded it to make a grave decision. The army would seize the weapons by force if necessary.

The *Altalena* anchored that night at Kfar Vitkin on Israel's northern coast, and the men and women aboard, tense and excited, immediately began unloading their precious cargo into motor launches and rowboats, which rode the waves to shore.

The work went on at a dizzying pace through the night and the next day in a festive atmosphere, as Irgun sympathizers from all over the country swarmed over the beach, as if at a picnic, to take part in this glorious episode in Irgun history.

Suddenly, a Hagana officer drove up and handed an ultimatum to Begin: Either he turned over the arms to the army or they would be confiscated. He had ten minutes to make up his mind. Begin didn't need ten minutes. His answer was "No." Let the officer's commander come to *him!*

Hardly had Galili reported to Ben-Gurion on Begin's defiance when the Prime Minister fired back a note: "This time we cannot compromise. If they don't accept orders we must shoot. . . . If force is available, it must be used without hesitation." He added: "Immediately!"

Within an hour a hail of bullets sprayed the beach. As Irgunists toppled to earth, several men grabbed Begin, who was imploring everyone to stay and fight, and dragged him kicking and cursing to a motor launch that sped to the *Altalena.* With most of the Irgunists and arms aboard—those people still ashore surrendered—the ship raced southward toward Tel Aviv and possible civil war.

The *Altalena* zigzagged along the coast to avoid fire from pursuing corvettes and, on reaching Tel Aviv, came to an abrupt halt atop the remains of an old refugee ship the British had sunk before World War II. One of the Irgun passengers suddenly realized that it was he who had sent the ill-fated vessel, loaded with Jews, to Palestine. When he gazed ashore he was seized by another terrible recollection as well. There, about a hundred yards away, was the spot where Chaim Arlosoroff was killed in 1933. The doubly-stricken passenger was Avraham Stavsky, whom Ben-Gurion's followers had accused of the murder. Now, once more, Stavsky and his comrades, many of them gathered on the beach to welcome the ship, would face their Jewish enemies in a traumatic confrontation.

A few hours later, on the morning of June 22, Ben-Gurion sat with his cabinet, his eyes inflamed from sleeplessness, his hair in even wilder disarray than usual. Solemnly he exclaimed, "What is happening endangers our war effort and, even more important, it endangers the very existence of the state, because the state cannot exist until we have one army and control of that army. This is an attempt to kill the state."

After the meeting, Ben-Gurion telephoned Yigal Allon at Palmach headquarters in the Ritz Hotel, which stretched along the beach within sight of the *Altalena*. The Prime Minister would use the Palmach to execute the Irgun before he executed the Palmach. Allon, who had succeeded Yitzhak Sadeh as Palmach commander, was to take command of the Tel Aviv area, a tough assignment, for he might have to kill Jews. Perhaps many, for the ubiquitous Irgunists were marching on the city from all directions, while there were few army troops around. Allon should start firing only if the foe fired first—or tried to unload the arms.

While Ben-Gurion addressed his cabinet, Begin addressed the local population through a loudspeaker rigged on the ship: "People of Tel Aviv, we of the Irgun have brought you arms to fight the enemy, but the government is denying them to you. . . ." Then, directing his appeal to the army, he shouted, "Use your heads. Help us unload these arms, which are for the common defense. If there are differences among us, let us reason later. . . ."

On the veranda of the Kaete Dan Hotel, due west of the ship, a group of United Nations observers listened in astonishment over breakfast. At press headquarters in a nearby building, correspondents scribbled notes as Begin spoke. At Palmach headquarters in the Ritz Hotel, Yitzhak Rabin, deputy Palmach commander, handed out grenades to his men.

Meanwhile, army troops cleared the beach front of civilians as a motor launch carrying arms chugged from the *Altalena* to shore, delivered its contents to waiting sympathizers, and returned for more. But as the launch approached shore once again, a machine gun sputtered a murderous welcome, and within seconds the antagonists on shore and aboard ship raked each other with gunfire. At the same time, Irgunists—many of them deserters from the army, which they had recently joined—began storming the beach from the city, and all along the waterfront and on nearby streets Jews shot at Jews, sometimes mistakenly at friends, since all wore the same uniform.

Soon the larger Irgun forces, it seemed, had won control of Tel Aviv.

Ben-Gurion remained icily calm in the face of this threat to his rule and his state. In fact, when one official rushed into his office with news of the battle, the Prime Minister was calculating with a colleague how to fit out the army with more pants, undershorts and shoes.

"What shall we do?" the official cried desperately.

Ben-Gurion thought for a moment and replied: "There's no other way. We must shell her."

Shortly the *Altalena* was hit by an artillery shell and burst into flames. The survivors aboard jumped into the sea to be picked up by Irgunist boys in small boats, leaving the dead—including Avraham Stavsky—to go down with the ship. Begin, who had wanted to be the last man off, was hurled overboard by his men, picked up in the water, and safely carried ashore. Pondering his losses—almost a hundred casualties—he broke into tears as he defiantly cried over the secret Irgun radio that evening, "Irgun soldiers will not be a party to fratricidal warfare, but neither will they accept the discipline of Ben-Gurion's army any longer."

Ben-Gurion contemptuously replied: "Blessed be the gun that set the ship on fire—that gun will have its place in Israel's war museum."

The Palmach then arrested all the Irgunists it could find, but Begin slipped through the dragnet. The arms were to rot at the bottom of the sea. Too bad, Ben-Gurion felt—they might have fired the decisive volleys in the struggle to save the state. But what was a state without authority—plagued, and perhaps seized, by parochial men like Begin with no sense of *havlaga*, social justice or universal mission, and lacking even the majesty of their late spiritual mentor, Jabotinsky? Men who would challenge his destiny and cheapen his dream.

On June 29, one week after the *Altalena* went down, Yadin dropped a sheaf of papers on Ben-Gurion's desk—a plan for reorganizing the army. The Prime Minister glanced at the lists of proposed commanders. What was this? Yigal Allon, central-front commander? Other Palmach officers in most of the other choice posts? Not while *he* was prime minister! He had dealt with the right; now he would deal with the left—but not in the way the High Command wished. In his view, the Palmach, under Mapam influence, had already disposed of Mickey Marcus. When would it emulate the Irgun and revolt against *him*? He summoned the High Command and firmly announced: Shlomo Shamir, a British-trained veteran, *not* Yigal Allon, would command the central front. And other British-trained officers would get their share of top posts.

"We believe that Yigal Allon is the best man for the job,"

Yadin protested. And he would resign if Allon was not appointed central-front commander.

If Yadin did that, Ben-Gurion raged, he would be court-martialed! Yadin and his colleagues stood up, announced their resignations, and marched out. Ben-Gurion then met with his cabinet and said, "What this business really amounts to is an attempt at revolt by the army. A war is being waged on me. . . . I demand that a committee of three ministers be appointed to examine the matter and draw conclusions."

Ben-Gurion thus decided to stake his political career, and possibly the security of Israel, on the outcome of this secret investigation. And the outcome seemed clear from the moment a cabinet committee began its inquiry on July 3, 1948, only five days before the U.N. truce was to end. He found himself reeling under a rain of blows from his commanders. He had unnecessarily sent hundreds to their death at Latrun. . . . Not a soldier, not a cannon could be moved without an order from him. . . . He second-guessed his top officers. . . . He was a dictator.

The committee was impressed by these charges. A war cabinet would be set up to formulate war strategy, it decided. And two directors general would be appointed as aides to the Prime Minister. One of them, presumably Galili, would also continue as liaison officer with the High Command. Galili had triumphed after all—for the moment. Silently rising, the Prime Minister stomped out of the room, strode to his office, and scribbled out his resignation.

The truce was about to end, and the country would find itself without a prime minister or a defense minister. It was a good time to fall ill.

"B.G., what in heaven does your letter mean?"

A doctor standing by Ben-Gurion's bed put a finger to his lips and whispered to the visitor, Moshe Shertok: "Please, Mr. Ben-Gurion is ill."

"No, I'm all right," the Prime Minister groaned, opening his eyes slightly. "But no business, Moshe. I just want to rest."

Shertok stared at the patient with restrained sympathy, not sure whether he was really that ill.

"Are you prime minister or not?" he asked.

"No," Ben-Gurion moaned, and the doctor whisked Shertok from the room.

The cabinet was stunned by Shertok's account of the "talk." One member took Galili aside and said, "We are facing the first big crisis of our new state, and it could have severe repercussions. We must pay the price to solve it."

"I am the price and you may pay it," replied Galili.

Everybody was relieved—Galili was willing to sacrifice himself. Shortly a note from Ben-Gurion arrived. He would withdraw his resignation, but the proposals of the committee would have to be shelved. More relief. Yadin then went to see Ben-Gurion, who agreed to compromise. There would be no central-front commander, but Yigal Allon would lead the offensive in that area, playing the same role without the title.

Ben-Gurion suddenly made a remarkable recovery. In no time at all he was out of bed, dressed, and drumming out orders to his grateful court. He was not yet able to place the Palmach under the command of British-trained officers, but he had proved that he was indispensable, at least while the war was in progress. Nobody wanted him to fall ill again.

The Prime Minister never seemed fitter than he was when the fighting resumed on July 9, 1948, for he had a freshly rested army with new rifles, mortars, machine guns and even bombers that enterprising agents had purchased or stolen abroad. Were these the same fighters who had cried to him in desperation when the Arab invasion began less than two months earlier, pleading for help, predicting catastrophe? Now they were placid, proud, undemanding.

They had conquered the Ramle-Lydda wedge and many parts of Galilee. They had blocked an Egyptian drive in the Negev and had broken through to isolated southern settlements. They had broadened the corridor to Jerusalem, knocking out every strong point except the high fortress at Latrun. And they would certainly have seized the fortress if a tank operator had not misunderstood his commander, who spoke a different language, and retreated instead of advanced—though the defenders had already fled! They had bombed Damascus, Cairo and the Egyptian bases at El Arish and Rafah. They had even shelled the Lebanese port of Tyre from naval vessels few Israelis even knew they had. And they had done all this in ten days.

Yet Ben-Gurion could not exult. For the longer the war dragged on the more dead there were to be counted. And since he, almost alone, had pushed his people into war, unprepared as they were, he felt a deepening sense of guilt as the casualties mounted, a feeling that victories could not assuage. At times the strain buckled the wall containing his emotions, particularly when he wrote to bereaved parents.

"Every Jew in the world is happy about the victories and the conquests and the independence," he typically wrote one father, "[but] there has been no joy in my house, for I see before me always these precious sons."

Ben-Gurion was especially saddened when he learned that Yitzhak and Rachel Ben-Zvi had lost their son, and Shlomo Lavi, his two. The ravaging of his beloved soldiers was so agonizing that he couldn't bear during this period to see anybody experience the slightest pleasure. Once, in August 1948, after he fled from a reception given in his office for visiting Zionist leaders, a colleague, Moshe Gurari, found him working at his desk and criticized him for leaving his guests. Gurari recounts:

> [Ben-Gurion] sat frozen, gazing straight ahead, not batting an eyelash, [then] suddenly shook his head, contracted his eyebrows, and began talking in a whisper, as though to himself:
> "I thought . . . we would sit quietly and discuss the tasks before us . . . and, instead, what we have is a shindig and a feast—a *hassene*," he added in Yiddish. "You know, sometimes I attend soldiers' funerals, or take part in meetings of bereaved parents, and I always wonder: No one has yet insulted me, no one has tried, in his grief, to throw a stone at me. No one has shouted at me and called through his pain: 'You wanted a Jewish state and we are paying the price for it; we have lost our sons!' "
> Ben-Gurion took a small book from his desk, opened it with a shaking hand and read in a choking voice: "To David Ben-Gurion—at your orders he fought, and at your orders he fell; may your name be blessed."
> "Did you hear?" he asked. "Did you ever hear such a dedication from a parent of a soldier who fell? This is stupendous, incredible!"
> He hid his face in his shaking hands. He appeared to be holding back tears.

Ben-Gurion's colleague urged: "Let us return to the guests now." And the Prime Minister rose obediently and went back to the hall.

If Ben-Gurion was troubled despite his victories, Count Bernadotte, the United Nations Mediator, was troubled *because* of them. He had wanted to shrink the Jewish state, and during the first truce, had pressed the Israelis to accept the idea. He had called for an alliance between Transjordan and Israel, with King Abdullah absorbing all or part of the Negev, the Israelis, all or part of western Galilee. Abdullah would rule all of Jerusalem, with the Jews enjoying municipal autonomy. Haifa would be a free port, Lydda a free airport.

Ben-Gurion had rejected this plan with contempt.

Bernadotte's offer of a new plan now, in the wake of Israeli gains, did not change Ben-Gurion's mind, even though the Mediator finally agreed to internationalize Jerusalem—as the United Nations had proposed in the first place. If Bernadotte wasn't a British agent, Ben-Gurion felt, he was certainly doing the job of one.

"If the world listens to Bernadotte and pressures our weakling government into making compromises," said Israel Sheib, "we will have lost our state. We can't let this happen."

Sheib, a wizened little man with a small dark beard, was the ideological leader of the Stern Group. He had just arrived at the Tel Aviv apartment of Nathan Friedman-Yellin, the Sternist commander, for a fateful meeting that would shake the world. Also present was a colleague, Yitzhak Yazernitzky, who, more than thirty years later as Yitzhak Shamir, would become foreign minister of Israel in the government of Prime Minister Begin.

The three men had plotted the assassination of Lord Moyne and Sir Harold MacMichael, who had been British High Commissioner for Palestine. Moyne had been killed and Mac-Michael had escaped with a wound. Now it was Bernadotte's turn. Over wine and fruit the three decided to kill the Mediator and have a phantom organization called the "Fatherland Front" publicly claim responsibility for the crime.

The decision was immediately relayed to the Sternist commander in Jerusalem, Yehoshua Zetler, who, with Stanley Goldfoot, his intelligence officer, and Yehoshua Cohen, his deputy, would carry out the plot. Goldfoot, lanky and elegant, had immigrated from South Africa, where he had passionately backed apartheid. With the same passion he now learned every detail he could about Bernadotte's habits and schedule, and as an accredited journalist he had access to vital information.

Yehoshua Cohen, a wiry good-natured Sabra, was reputed for his courage and ingenuity. He did not hate, or need to hate, his enemies in order to "execute" them in cold blood and in good conscience. His devotion to Zionism was undiluted and unsophisticated, with roots deep in the earth he had plowed as a farmer's son. He had been taught early that it was necessary to destroy the insects that threatened the crop.

On the afternoon of September 17, 1948, Bernadotte was scheduled to visit the Jewish sector of Jerusalem, but he was behind schedule. As tensions rose in the Sternist camp, Goldfoot sped in a jeep to the government press office, hoping to learn something, and there he heard an amplifier feeding information to the press officer. Bernadotte would enter the New City at five o'clock and pass over the road that ran near the Sternist camp. Goldfoot rushed back to the camp, and just before four o'clock four men in khaki drove their jeep to a point some five hundred yards away.

About two minutes after five, they sighted a convoy of three cars approaching, the third one with a United Nations flag flying from one front fender and a white one from the other. The jeep swung around into the middle of the road, forcing the convoy to a halt. As one of the men in the jeep approached the last vehicle, the passengers in the rear seat reached for their passes. Yehoshua Cohen calmly stuck the barrel of his weapon through the open window and fired a burst.

Count Bernadotte sank back in his seat, riddled with bullets, though as a hemophiliac he might have died from a scratch.

Ben-Gurion was studying the new Bernadotte plan when, at about 5:45 P.M., an aide rushed in with the news. He felt horror, anger, revulsion. Did the man deserve to die just because he was unfriendly to Israel? This crime would repel the whole world at a time when Israel was fighting for its life. But even if the country survived this catastrophe physically, could it survive spiritually? It was to be a "light unto the nations," and here his people had murdered a representative of the nations.

But, as after Lord Moyne's slaying, he at least had an excuse now to take drastic action. He would push through an antiterrorist law and eradicate, with blood and steel if necessary, the last remnants of all terrorist groups not already integrated into the army. And those in Jerusalem would no longer be immune. He would arrest every member of the Stern Group, which he was sure had committed the crime. Coming on the heels of the *Altalena* sweep, this purge would finally cleanse Israel of the dissidents on the right, leaving only the Palmach on the left.

The Irgunists bowed to Ben-Gurion's ultimatum and dissolved their organization. And while Sternists soon packed the jails, most of their leaders eluded arrest. Friedman-Yellin had been captured, but he was freed after winning a seat in the first Israeli Knesset in early 1949. In fact, the jail door soon swung open for all the Sternists as world outrage over Bernadotte's assassination mellowed. If the world could so quickly forget, why shouldn't he, Ben-Gurion? The crime itself was less important than world reaction to it. Besides, many of the dissidents, especially the Sternists, were really heroic and pure-hearted patriots, however revolting their methods. And the fact was that, as much as Ben-Gurion deplored the murder, Bernadotte's "abominable" plan had died with him.

It was time for Chaim Weizmann to come home. Though ill, he had longed to leave for Palestine before the state was declared, but Ben-Gurion and his Jewish Agency urged him to stay in the United States so he could deal with any last-minute problems, since he was the only Zionist leader President Truman would see. Weizmann wasn't doing much, his colleagues felt, but who really needed him in Palestine? Certainly not Ben-Gurion. And as Truman had pledged him to secrecy, Weizmann couldn't even let his colleagues in Tel Aviv know that it was *he* who had persuaded the President to recognize the Jewish state as soon as it was formed.

On May 14, Weizmann had rejoiced when an aide rushed into his room in the Waldorf-Astoria Hotel in New York gasping the news that the state had been born. But as the day wore on, his joy melted into dismay. Was he not Herzl's successor? Had he not fathered the Balfour Declaration and paved the way to this great moment? Yet not a word from Tel Aviv. Finally, the next day, after some prodding from American Zionist leaders, a cable arrived:

> On the occasion of the establishment of the Jewish State, we send our greetings to you who have done more than any other living man towards its creation. Your stand and help have strengthened all of us. We look forward to the day when we shall see you at the head of the state established in peace.

The message was signed by Ben-Gurion and three other colleagues.

That day Weizmann was elected president and the blue-and-white Israeli flag fluttered from the Waldorf-Astoria. A few months later, in August 1948, Weizmann left for home. And in what luxury! His plane was an oil-leaky DC-4 that had been flying supplies to the front lines, but for this trip from New York it had been converted into Israel's first "airliner." A sofa and armchairs had been nailed to the carpeted floor. Curtains had been hung. Hotel waiters, dressed in hastily tailored uniforms decorated with winged Stars of David and flying-camel symbols, had been recruited as stewards. When the plane landed and the President emerged, flashbulbs popped, hands reached out, flowers were thrust into his wife's arms, a band blared a welcome, a guard of honor stood at attention, and customs officials, drafted for the occasion, respectfully declined to open baggage or check passports.

But once settled in his large comfortable house in Rehovot, he would wonder in restless anguish why no one ever consulted him any more. Ben-Gurion would not even let him sign the Declaration of Independence. Weizmann, he explained, was not a member of the People's Council and was not in Palestine at the time of the signing; he was thus ineligible to sign. And he never did.

Later, Ben-Gurion would argue that he had forgotten to leave a place for Weizmann's signature. But perhaps more important was what he may have remembered—Weizmann's unseemly "affair" with the British, his insults, his lone-wolf tactics and illusions of political supremacy. Or was the Prime Minister simply reluctant to share his messianic glory with Weizmann and remind future generations that he had a rival? No one can be sure.

So Weizmann was left only with the trappings of power and glory. And even the luxury "airliner" was repainted, shorn of furniture, and rushed back into the reality of battle.

The show was over.

But the battle was just beginning. Before the first truce, the Israelis had barely held their own, and at a huge price. After the truce, they had swept to stirring victories. A second truce had gone into effect; but, like the first, it would eventually collapse. When it did, Ben-Gurion decided, the Israelis must seize almost all of Arab-held Palestine. Where would they strike first? Ben-Gurion stood for hours by his wall map, and his roving finger always came to rest on Jerusalem. The Israelis, he told the High Command, must attack the whole West Bank from the Judean hills in the north to the heights south of the Holy City. This military decision clashed with his political goal, which was to let Abdullah absorb this area, but he apparently felt that he could eventually trade territory for peace. And on September 26, nine days after Bernadotte was killed, he presented the plan to his cabinet, expecting a quick "amen." It didn't come. Take over the West Bank, the "Arab state"? What would the United Nations say—especially after Bernadotte's murder? It might even send troops to stop Israel. And Ben-Gurion lost by a single vote.

He was dismayed. His own cabinet? His own party? They were still cowards. He went home and with a tremulous hand raged in his diary:

"The plan has been dropped. Fortunately for us, most of the offensives we've launched this year were not put to the vote of that lot!"

Yadin now called for a drive against the Egyptians, arguing that "Egypt . . . is our principal enemy" since it "controls the Negev." And Ben-Gurion began to feel that this might be true. But before making up his mind, he decided to visit the front, as he often did anyway to raise morale. Once when bombs started to fall near a dugout he was in, he agreed to leave only after his guard was wounded. Another time, on a trip to the Negev, he found himself caught in the middle of a mine field and calmly threaded his way to safety while his commanders trembled along beside him.

And once he even ran the gauntlet between Tel Aviv and Jerusalem so he could celebrate Passover with his besieged brethren, barely escaping with his life as bullets peppered his convoy going there and coming back. At one point, his aides had to pull him back when he tried to jump from his armored car to care for a man wounded in the vehicle behind him. So worried were his commanders about Ben-Gurion's safety that on one occasion, while he was reviewing his troops, they almost panicked when Paula breathlessly interceded, crying: "Move him from here, quick!"

Ben-Gurion was in danger?

Yes, it was windy here and he had a cold!

Most fretful of all about Ben-Gurion's daring was his new military secretary, Nehemiah Argov, a young officer who worshiped his master and felt personally responsible for his safety and health. On one visit to the front, Argov went pale when Ben-Gurion drank some sour milk with his coffee. He alerted a doctor and observed his idol's every move and expression until finally "I saw to my joy . . . that our fear was unfounded."

Now Ben-Gurion was touring again, and Argov's anxiety was rekindled as he assessed the dangers—a bullet, a bomb, a bellyache. At Negev headquarters, the Prime Minister listened to Yadin describe his battle plan. Once the Egyptians were crushed, he said, those entrenched in the Hebron hills would flee, clearing the way for an all-out assault on the West Bank. Ben-Gurion's eyes gleamed. He would have the Negev and the West Bank too!

On the way back to Tel Aviv he told Argov that "now the issue is completely clear.... We must open the way to the Negev settlements." He hoped his commanders understood the need!

"We have just made the gravest decision since the proclamation of the state," he wrote in his diary.

Too grave, Ben-Gurion decided, to permit any more chauvinistic factionalism in the army. The Palmach's time had come. He would finally purge its separate command and see that it took orders directly from general headquarters. To ease his task, he first agreed to let Yigal Allon lead the attack when the fighting resumed. Then, with little time left for argument, he simply informed the High Command of his decision: No Palmach command. Either accept this order, he warned, or risk destruction of the state. Mapam yelped and threatened to form an underground inside the army. Ben-Gurion cried back that Mapam was "a danger to the integrity of the state." The army was on the verge of disintegration. But finally the Palmach command, though seething with bitterness, dissolved itself. Allon was no longer Palmach commander, but simply commander of the southern front.

Ben-Gurion was jubilant. The armed forces of Israel were unified at last—under him. He had finally wiped out all traces of the humiliation still lingering more than forty years after he was frozen out of Hashomer. Could the Hashomer leaders have imagined that one day he would command a national Jewish army unchallenged by lesser men like themselves?

Now he would put *his* army to the test.

Ben-Gurion sat down with his commanders and predicted what would happen in the next campaign. He told them how the British and Americans would react, how long it would take the United Nations to cry "Cease fire," how far the Israelis must thrust ahead each day to reach their goals in the eight to ten days he estimated they would have. And the commanders, though having revolted against him, trusted his calculations. Maybe he *was* a military amateur and a political tyrant, but was he not also a prophet?

Now all the Israelis needed was a pretext to attack, and they soon had one. The Egyptians violated the truce agreement by refusing to let Israeli trucks drive through the lines to supply the besieged settlements. So, on October 15, Ben-Gurion gave the signal. His army rumbled across the dusty red earth of the Negev to detonate Operation Ten Plagues, a reference to the horrors that God had inflicted on the ancient Egyptians—and to those the Prime Minister hoped to inflict on their descendants. His spirited troops smashed open the road to the Negev and, in a surprise attack, even seized Beersheba. On October 22, after stalling the United Nations for a few days, Ben-Gurion had to give the cease-fire order to his commanders. He had largely won the race against time. The Egyptians still held part of the Negev —but, he felt confident, not for long.

As Ben-Gurion sat at his desk studying reports of his army's great victories, he was determined to maintain the impetus. The Arabs were on the run, and he had to keep them running. But not for the moment in the Negev. If he defied the United Nations now, Truman himself might give up on Israel, and the new state could not risk losing American support. But perhaps if he attacked elsewhere, Truman would look the other way. Jerusalem? No, it was the same old cabinet. The Galilee? Perhaps. Moshe Carmel, commander of the northern front, vigorously urged that "we should use this opportunity to liberate" the whole region.

Only six days after the cease-fire in the Negev, Carmel, given the go-ahead, ordered his brigade to attack Fawzi el-Kaoukji's renovated Arab Liberation Army, which the Israelis had battered before the British left. In sixty hours Carmel's troops captured all of Galilee. His men then blasted into Lebanon, where they were molested less by Kaoukji's troops than by relentless Levantine salesmen armed with fountain pens, nylons and souvenir trinkets from the markets of Beirut and Tyre. When the brigade had halted at the Litani River, Carmel sent his commander, Mordechai Makleff, to Tiberias to see Ben-Gurion, who was resting at the Galei Kinneret Hotel there.

"Let us push all the way to Beirut," Makleff urged. "Just give us twelve hours more to get there."

"No," Ben-Gurion replied, "I've got enough trouble with the United Nations over the Negev."

Makleff then desperately appealed to Ben-Gurion's political instincts: "If we take Beirut we can establish a Mapai government there!"

Ben-Gurion smiled. "Cheer up," he said. "After all, we've captured the whole Galilee."

With the truce that followed came another United Nations resolution: Both sides must return to the boundaries they shared
before the last Israeli offensive.

Not an inch back! exclaimed Ben-Gurion.

Ralph Bunche, the thoughtful black American who had replaced Bernadotte as the United Nations Mediator, suggested a
compromise. Mobile Israeli troops would evacuate the Negev,
but those in the settlements could stay. Israel would thus still
control most of the Negev.

Ben-Gurion agreed.

Now, with the United Nations pacified, it was time for a new
Israeli thrust, one that would finally win the whole Negev. But
since this operation would put the Israelis on King Abdullah's
border, Ben-Gurion feared that the Arab Legion might try to
block the way. Better to make peace with the King, who now
had what he wanted. On December 1 Abdullah had fused
Transjordan with the West Bank, which was to have been the
heart of the new Palestinian Arab state, to form the Kingdom of
Jordan—as the Israelis had suggested before the war. Moshe
Dayan, the new commander of Jewish Jerusalem, approached
his Arab counterpart in the Old City and shortly was sipping
Turkish coffee with Abdullah in his palace.

As a result of this meeting, the King did not protest when the
Israelis hit the Egyptians in mid-December. After all, King Farouk of Egypt had backed the mufti and condemned Abdullah's
seizure of Arab Palestine. And so, by the end of the month,
Allon's troops had not only swallowed up almost the entire
Negev, but were grinding over the trackless Egyptian Sinai
Peninsula toward El Arish on the Mediterranean coast, threatening to encircle the Gaza Strip and the remnants of the Egyptian army.

Ben-Gurion was aghast. Allon had no orders to advance that
far! America would never stand for an invasion of Egyptian-held
territory. And the British might even attack. Hardly had the
Prime Minister ordered Allon to halt when, on December 31,
1948, the American envoy to Israel, James G. McDonald, delivered to him an ominous cable from Washington sent in the name
of the President. The message paraphrased a cable from Britain
confirming Ben-Gurion's worst fears. Unless the Israelis withdrew from Egyptian soil, British forces would, under a 1936
defense treaty with Egypt, throw themselves into the battle.
Also, Washington would reexamine its relations with the Jewish
state and might even refuse to back Israeli admission to the
United Nations.

The British threat did not surprise Ben-Gurion. Britain was

Israel's "invisible enemy"; it wished to strangle Israel. But the United States? Would it really intervene against his country—perhaps even militarily? This possibility alarmed him. He told his American guest that he had ordered all Israeli troops out of the Sinai immediately.

But shortly afterward, on January 2, 1949, Allon flew by Piper Cub to Tel Aviv and pleaded with Ben-Gurion for a campaign south of Rafah that would cut off Egyptian forces in Gaza from those in El Arish. After all, the area was barely across the border. Ben-Gurion looked away, agonizing in indecision. What if Britain attacked? He stared at the sandy-haired, blue-eyed commander, unable to suppress his admiration for him. Allon was aggressive, imaginative, confident—and uncomfortably persuasive. A magnificent product of the kibbutz, however politically innocent.

Ben-Gurion agreed.

By the next evening, January 3, Allon had done exactly what he had said he would do, and the Egyptian army on the coast was cut off. But what should Israel do now? Keep the Egyptians hemmed in and under constant fire at the risk of British intervention? Or withdraw—the Egyptian condition for immediate armistice talks? Late into the night Ben-Gurion sat at his desk pondering the question.

The next morning an aide hurried into Allon's stone headquarters hut in Beersheba and handed the commander a radio message from Yadin: "All our forces should be evacuated from beyond the border. . . . Complete evacuation by Monday January 10. Carry out without reservation. . . . Start evacuation immediately."

"Shocked by this order," Allon flew to Tel Aviv again to beg Ben-Gurion to rescind it. But the Prime Minister was adamant. He laid a hand on Allon's shoulder and, like a father admonishing his child, said, "Commanders must obey orders even if they don't like them."

Allon knew then that Ben-Gurion would not change his mind. He abruptly left and, when he arrived at his headquarters, radioed his commanders: "There is no room for any appeal or delay in carrying out the order, however harsh it may be."

Soon, on the lovely island of Rhodes, armistice talks with Egypt began in the Hotel des Roses within view of majestic Greek

ruins and white-washed huts that graced green hillsides alive
with peasants riding their donkeys. Allon, in his bitterness, sent
his deputy, Yitzhak Rabin, to represent him. Meanwhile, Allon
made a new plea to Ben-Gurion. Before the war ended, let him
take over the West Bank. After all, the Prime Minister himself
had wanted to do this earlier in the war. And the British
wouldn't intervene; his men had intercepted a British message
to Abdullah saying that he should not expect their help unless
the Israelis attacked Jordan proper.

But Ben-Gurion now rejected the idea. Circumstances had
changed, and just as peace with Egypt was more important than
Sinai territory, peace with Jordan was more important than West
Bank territory. Indeed, the closer he came to peace, the less
ambitious he became. He wanted armistice agreements with the
bordering Arab states, and he would have them. So he wouldn't
win everything in one war, he conceded. Nor would he in his
lifetime.

"I do not know any generation in Jewish history," he would
write, "that completed its task." And he quoted from the Book
of Joshua, Chapter 13: "Now Joshua was old and stricken in
years; and the Lord said unto him, 'Thou art old and stricken in
years, and there remaineth yet very much land to be possessed.' "

Joshua, in fact, didn't even capture Jerusalem. Yet, his battles,
though "conducted in a natural way," were won with the help
of a "superior power." So were his own, Ben-Gurion mused.
But as Joshua understood, one had to be patient with God; He
could not be expected to mass-produce miracles.

Biblical philosophy, however, could not console Yigal Allon,
though after a truce accord with Egypt was signed on February
24, 1949, a dip in Biblical waters would. The southern wedge of
the Negev leading to Eilat on the Gulf of Aqaba still lay out of
Israeli reach.

Couldn't he at least grab this enticing triangle? Allon pleaded.

Send a patrol, Ben-Gurion agreed. See if the Israeli troops
could seize it without a battle that would threaten the truce
accords and perhaps spark a British assault.

A patrol thus plodded southward over the sun-baked sands—
until it sighted a group of Arab Legionnaires in the distant glare.

Not an inch more! Tel Aviv ordered.

And Allon's men complied—in a sense. They *didn't* move an
inch more; they moved, after bypassing the Legion unit, all the
way to the sea! Tearing off their clothes as they ran, they dived
into the welcoming glassy bay where Solomon's ships had once

sailed laden with gold from Ophir. Ben-Gurion exulted, but in silence. The Palmach had disobeyed orders again—and won the whole Negev!

The war was over and Israel had triumphed. Now could it survive the crushing burdens of peace?

20. *Chaim Weizmann addresses the historic conference at the Biltmore Hotel in New York City in 1942. Ben-Gurion (at Weizmann's right) organized the meeting to demand publicly that the British establish a Jewish state in Palestine after World War II. He concentrated so completely on seeking such an Allied commitment that he blinded himself to the full truth of the Holocaust. [United Jewish Appeal]*

21. *British troops board a Jewish refugee ship in 1947 before it can land illegally in Palestine to discharge its human cargo. Ben-Gurion organized a massive illegal immigration movement after World War II, ordering ships to land in defiance of British bayonets. [Zionist Archives and Library, N.Y.]*

22

22. *Ben-Gurion reads Israel's Declaration of Independence, May 14, 1948, in Tel Aviv under a picture of Theodor Herzl, founder of modern Zionism and Ben-Gurion's childhood hero. Meanwhile British Mandate forces were leaving Palestine, and six Arab countries prepared to invade the infant Jewish state. [Israel Government Press Office]*

23. *Ben-Gurion signs the Declaration of Independence as Moshe Sharett assists. Sharett regarded Ben-Gurion with awe but when Sharett's dovish tendencies brought the two men into conflict and he was forced to resign as foreign minister in 1956, he turned vehemently against Ben-Gurion. [Israel Consulate General Library, N.Y.]*

23

24. In the 1948 War of Independence, Ben-Gurion demanded that every Jewish settlement hold out against Arab assault. He armed civilians with rifles smuggled out of America and Europe or stolen from British Mandate forces. [Zionist Archives and Library, N.Y.]

24

25. Yigal Allon, hero of the 1948 War of Independence. His skimpily armed but high-spirited troops routed the invading Arab armies. [Israel Government Press Office]

25

26. Ben-Gurion visiting his troops with Chief of Staff Yigael Yadin during the 1948 war. Yadin would turn down an offer by the Prime Minister in 1963 to succeed him in that office. [Israel Government Press Office]

26

27

27. *The LST Altalena, crammed with weapons from France intended for Begin's Irgun Zvai Leumi, burns in Tel Aviv harbor after Ben-Gurion ordered the Israeli army to fire on it during the 1948 war. The incident symbolized the fierce conflict between Ben-Gurion and Begin, who Ben-Gurion feared would try to overthrow his government by force.* [Vladimir Jabotinsky Archives]

28. *Ben-Gurion guides President Chaim Weizmann, who had become nearly blind, toward the rostrum at a ceremony marking the opening of the Weizmann Institute in Rehovot, Israel, in 1949. The two men had bitterly competed for leadership of the Zionist movement before the state was founded. As President, Weizmann deeply resented Ben-Gurion for ignoring him and not inviting him to sign the Declaration of Independence.* [Israel Consulate General Library, N.Y.]

28

29. *Ben-Gurion presents a menorah to President Harry Truman in 1951, while Israeli Ambassador Abba Eban looks on. Despite bitter State Department opposition, Truman supported the creation of a Jewish state and recognized it as soon as it was born.* [Israel Government Press Office]

29

30

30. *Ben-Gurion is welcomed in Boston during his first U.S. tour as Prime Minister in 1951. The trip produced large-scale American aid to finance the Ingathering of the Exiles, probably the most ambitious planned immigration in history. [Israel Consulate General Library, N.Y.]*

31. *Ben-Gurion visits immigrant Sephardic children from the Arab world in the early 1950s. The Sephardim received his love but not, they felt, a fair share of the national* *wealth or power. [Israel Consulate General Library, N.Y.]*

32. *Ben-Gurion feeds a lamb in Kibbutz Sde Boker while Paula looks on. He temporarily resigned from the premiership in 1954 in order to live in the desert as some of the prophets did. Although he hoped to recapture the spirit of his early days in Palestine, Ben-Gurion found that he was too old to do hard pioneer labor. [Israel Government Press Office]*

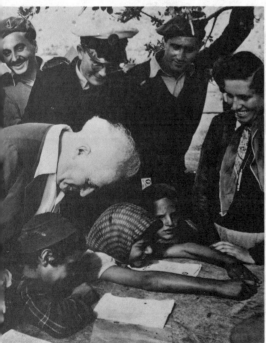

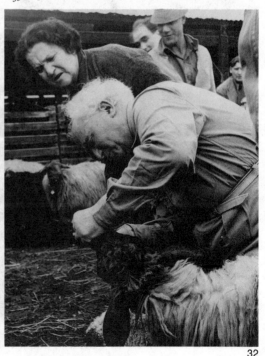

31

32

33. *Paula Ben-Gurion at work in Sde Boker's communal kitchen. She was reluctant to cook for anybody but her husband, and when she lived in the city she sometimes even tested butter at a laboratory to make sure it was the best quality. [Israel Government Press Office]*

34. *Ben-Gurion and U.N. Secretary-General Dag Hammarskjold being shown a vegetable garden in Sde Boker by a settler. Ben-Gurion courted the Swedish diplomat as part of his campaign to win the friendship of the world. [Israel Consulate General Library, N.Y.]*

35. *Ben-Gurion confers in the early 1950s with Ariel Sharon (left), whom he considered a great warrior but too undisciplined and ruthless to qualify as chief of staff. [IDF Archives]*

36. *Israeli tanks grind through Egyptian-controlled Gaza in 1956 during the Sinai Campaign. Israel attacked toward Suez, seeking to end Arab terrorist raids and to force Egypt to open the blockaded Straits of Tiran, the gateway to Africa and Asia. Between the 1948 and 1956 wars, Ben-Gurion, with the help of Moshe Dayan and Ariel Sharon, had built one of the finest armies, man for man, in the world. [Israel Consulate General Library, N.Y.]*

37. *President Eisenhower greets Ben-Gurion in 1960. Ike refused to heed Ben-Gurion's pleas for weapons. [Israel Government Press Office]*

38

38. *Ben-Gurion meets with President Kennedy in 1961. Kennedy asked his visitor how he could repay the American Jews for helping to put him in the White House. [Israel Consulate General Library, N.Y.]*

39. *Ben-Gurion with French President Charles de Gaulle, whom he considered the greatest leader in modern history. De Gaulle admired Ben-Gurion too, but when he granted Algeria independence and started to woo the Arab world, French-Israeli ties began to loosen. [Israel Government Press Office]*

39

40. Ben-Gurion meets West German Chancellor Konrad Adenauer in New York in 1960 in a dramatic reconciliation of their two peoples. Begin and other Israelis violently opposed any Israeli-German ties. [Israel Consulate General Library, N.Y.]

40

41. Ben-Gurion in native dress on a visit to Burma in 1961 as the guest of Prime Minister U Nu (left). The Israeli leader meditated in a Buddhist monastery for eight days to understand the spiritual experience. [Israel Consulate General Library, N.Y.]

41

42. Ben-Gurion greets visitors from Ghana. One of his principal foreign policy aims was to "cast a light unto" the African nations and win them as permanent allies. [Israel Consulate General Library, N.Y.]

42

43. *Ben-Gurion chats with Golda Meir. An early ally, Golda turned against him when she suspected he wanted to replace the veteran Zionist leaders with young "technocrats" like Moshe Dayan and Shimon Peres. [Israel Government Press Office]*

44. *Levi Eshkol, Golda Meir, Ben-Gurion, Yitzhak Ben-Zvi, and Rachel Yanait Ben-Zvi waiting at the airport to greet a visiting dignitary. Ben-Gurion chose Eshkol as his successor, but later called him "unfit to be prime minister" for daring to back policies Ben-Gurion opposed. [Israel Government Press Office]*

43

44

45. *Defense Minister Pinhas Lavon (left) talks with Chief of Staff Moshe Dayan in the early 1950s. Lavon and Ben-Gurion clashed savagely some years later when Ben-Gurion refused to clear Lavon in an intelligence scandal, detonating the Lavon Affair, which would prove to be Israel's Watergate and Ben-Gurion's Waterloo. Dayan, Ben-Gurion's favorite protegé, tried to pin the blame for the episode on Lavon. [Israel Government Press Office]*

45

46   47

46. *Ben-Gurion shakes hands with Shimon Peres, who, under the Prime Minister's
tutelage, set the stage for the 1956 Suez War and initiated Israel's nuclear and
aircraft industries. In 1977 he took over the reins of the Labor Party.
[Israel Government Press Office]*

47. *Ben-Gurion with Yitzhak Navon, his political secretary, who felt Ben-Gurion
was the "greatest Jew in two thousand years." Navon would become president of
Israel in 1978. [Israel Government Press Office]*

48. *Ben-Gurion lunches with Menachem Begin and Air Force Chief Ezer Weizman.
Ben-Gurion rarely met with Begin, considering him a threat to democracy and
peace. [Israel Government Press Office]*

48

49

49. *Ben-Gurion and Nehemia Argov, his military secretary. Argov was Paula's counterpart away from home, worshiping Ben-Gurion and guarding him closely. He committed suicide in 1957, feeling he had in some way failed Ben-Gurion. [Israel Government Press Office]*

52. *Ben-Gurion gives a Bible lesson to an army commander. Though unreligious—he even ate ham for breakfast—Ben-Gurion lived by the Bible, which he considered more a historical than a spiritual document. [Joseph Geva]*

50. *Ben-Gurion and Dr. Moshe Feldenkrais, his look-alike physical therapist. Feldenkrais "magically" eliminated Ben-Gurion's back pain in the mid-1950s and turned him into an enthusiast of physical exercise.* [Moshe Feldenkrais]

50

51

51. *Ben-Gurion practices yoga. On one occasion he discussed world-shaking events with U.S. Ambassador Ogden Reid while both men stood on their heads.* [Jewish Observer *and* Middle East Review]

53

53. Ben-Gurion attends the wedding of his niece, Miriam Taub (on his right). Also present were Paula (on his left), his sister Zippora (with white collar), his brother Michael, father of the bride (behind Zippora), and Michael's wife (at her husband's right). Michael, who operated a refreshment kiosk in Tel Aviv, was never close to his illustrious brother. Except on such special occasions, the Prime Minister seldom saw any relatives outside his immediate family, and sometimes Paula wouldn't even have his relatives in the house. [Miriam Taub]

54. Family portrait, 1949. Left to right: Emanuel Ben-Eliezer, Geula's husband, holding their daughter, Orit; Mary Ben-Gurion, Amos' wife; Yariv, Geula's eldest son; Geula; Amos, holding his son Alon; Galia, Amos' daughter; Ben-Gurion, holding Moshe, Geula's younger son; Renana; and Paula. To Amos' surprise, his father agreed that he could marry Mary, a British shiksa (gentile girl). She turned out to be a more observant Jew than most of the family. [Israel Government Press Office]

54

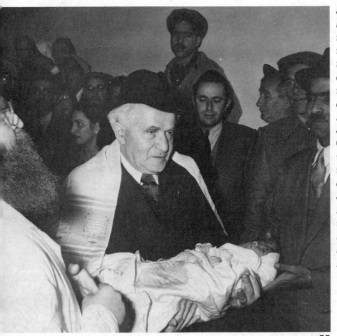

55. *Ben-Gurion officiating at a briss (circumcision ceremony). He regularly attended weddings, bar-mitzvas, and brisses celebrated by the families of his employees. He once secretly gave money to his maid so she could buy an apartment. [Israel Government Press Office]*

56. *Ben-Gurion and Ruth Goldschmidt, a British journalist with whom he had a romantic interlude in the late 1940s and early 1950s. [Ruth Goldschmidt]*

57. *Ben-Gurion and Rachel Beit-Halachmi, shortly before they died in 1973. She held his hand as he lay dying; a few months later she herself passed away. [Ruth Beit-Halachmi]*

55

56

57

58. *Ben-Gurion's house in Tel Aviv. Here he lived in spartan simplicity and greeted world leaders who, in winter, were sometimes startled to find him bundled in blankets for lack of central heating. [Ben-Gurion House]*

59. *The library in Ben-Gurion's Tel Aviv home. Crammed with twenty thousand books, it is the largest private collection in Israel if not in the Middle East. [Ben-Gurion House]*

58

60. *Ben-Gurion's austere bedroom in his Tel Aviv home. [Ben-Gurion House]*

61. *Graves of David and Paula Ben-Gurion in the Negev desert. Ben-Gurion wanted to be buried in what he hoped would become a populated, industrial area that would eventually serve the needs of the whole Afro-Asian world. [Ben-Gurion House]*

59

60

61

Book III

ISAIAH

CHAPTER ELEVEN

Then the remnant of his brethren shall return
MICAH 5:3

BEN-GURION watched in wonder as his dream dissolved into reality. The door of the plane opened, and out shuffled a bearded old man followed by a woman with a baby strapped to her back. After them came an endless line of young people. The men wore rumpled white robes, embroidered caps and side curls, and the women, colorful flowing dresses and magnificent hand-carved silver necklaces. They were dark-skinned with fine features and brown eyes that gleamed with the light of redemption. Operation Magic Carpet had begun, carrying them home on "eagles' wings," as the Bible had promised.

Some had squatted in the aisle because the seats were too soft for them; others, to the horror of the crew, had lit portable stoves in midair to cook their rations. Across desert and mountain they had trudged from the primitive interior of Yemen to British-ruled Aden on the Red Sea. Bandits had robbed and shot at them, starvation and thirst had made every step agony, and Arab nationalists had pounced on them, knives raised, in the Aden camps. But after this final terrible test, God had opened the door to Jerusalem for the survivors. And now, with centuries of misery and degradation behind them, they were home.

As they knelt and kissed the earth, Ben-Gurion remembered. Had he not wanted to do this when he was heaved ashore for the first time more than forty years earlier? But then the Holy

Land had been a steaming, disease-ridden Turkish colony. Now it was a Jewish state with modern towns, factories, settlements. Now all Jews, for eternity, could come freely and live in dignity and build an enlightened nation. They had started streaming in, mainly from D.P. camps, the moment the last Briton had leaped aboard a departing troopship, and many had been hustled directly to the front. Now, with the War of Independence over, the stream had become a flood, and they poured in by the thousands and tens of thousands.

"Never before," Ben-Gurion would write, "was the sea to us a way for the redeemed. And now *aliya* is as an ocean current, and what the sea does not bring, . . . aircraft bear aloft." What a difference, he noted, from the Ingathering twenty-five hundred years earlier when exiles returned riding horses, mules, camels and asses. From many lands they now came—hunched carpet weavers from Iran, swaggering street urchins from Morocco, powerful porters from the Kurdish mountains, pale shopkeepers from Brooklyn. The modern Ingathering of the Exiles. But many might still be in exile if Ben-Gurion had not defied logic. Devastated by war, virtually bankrupt, still imperiled by the Arabs and distrusted even by many American officials, Israel had nevertheless decided to bring in almost at once every Jew who wished to come. Early in 1949 the economic experts in the cabinet, Eliezer Kaplan, Pinhas Sapir and Levi Eshkol, had tried to argue "sense" into him. Immigration must be gradual, they said —according to the country's ability to absorb newcomers.

Ben-Gurion was furious. That was the old British formula— before the White Paper cut off immigration almost completely.

There was simply no money, the economists argued. It cost twenty-five hundred dollars to transport a Jew to Israel, keep him in a reception camp, build him a home, find him work, and assimilate him into the life of the state. To settle a million people in five years, as Ben-Gurion wanted to do, would cost two billion, five hundred million dollars. Where would Israel get that kind of money—even with aid from abroad? He must be practical.

What was more practical, cried Ben-Gurion, than assuring the security of his people? The state needed as many soldiers as possible to face the countless millions of Arabs surrounding it; the Diaspora needed to come home before new Holocausts struck. The Ingathering was the very meaning of his life, the very essence of the state. And it was the state, not the government, that gave all Jews the right to come at any time. Had he been practical when he defied the Turks, and then the British?

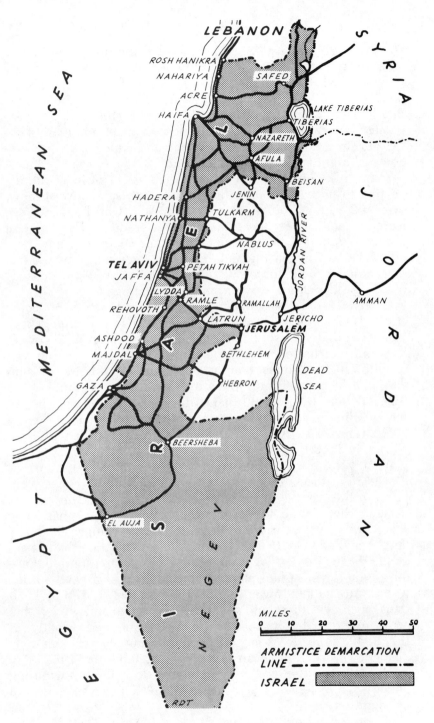

THE FINAL ARMISTICE PARTITION

Had he been practical when he gambled the life of the *Yishuv* on a war nobody thought he could win? As a politician, yes, he was practical. But as a messiah? Only in defense of the principle. Go to the Jews in the Diaspora and ask them for the money, Ben-Gurion admonished the skeptics. If they didn't give enough, every family in Israel would take in an immigrant family. But they would come! And in one of the most extraordinary epics of migration in history, they did.

Some, like the Yemenites, came mainly out of idealism, expecting to find a golden millennium in Jerusalem. Most, however, were less Utopian. Many in the Arab world and Eastern Europe came to escape tyranny, their freedom bought with Diaspora dollars. Others came to break the chains of ghetto poverty. As Ben-Gurion watched, his joy was tempered by the fact that so many came not to satisfy an ideal, but to "avoid catastrophe." Could a nation survive simply as a refuge?

Even more disappointing, many of his people would not come at all. How could any self-respecting Jew refuse *aliya*? Ben-Gurion verbally blasted American Jews for choosing the comforts and corruption of Diaspora life. And, some people say, despite official denials, that he detonated a *real* blast in Baghdad; that his agents there blew up a synagogue—empty at the time—so that Jews would blame the Arabs and, in fear, flee to Israel. (Pinhas Lavon, who was defense minister in the early 1950s, referred to this plot in a recorded conversation with Ben-Gurion in 1960.)

Whatever the truth, immigrants from about seventy countries flowed in at the rate of about a thousand people a week—but not into the paradise many expected. The ground they kissed became the ground they slept on in windy tents that some shared with two or three families in makeshift camps. The lucky ones crowded into the dark stone huts that Arabs had abandoned during the 1948 war. Arabs who wanted to return to these huts, which were often painted blue to keep away evil spirits, would thus be kept away too. The newcomers cooked their rations on smoky stoves and spent the day looking for work as the economy crumbled and a black market flourished. Finally, in July 1949, an army of ragged, raging unemployed immigrants marched on the Knesset in Tel Aviv and, shouting "Bread and work," stormed the gate in a pitched battle with club-wielding police—while legislators inside searched for ways to step up immigration!

The sounds of mutiny struck Ben-Gurion with shattering impact as he was suddenly flung back into a barely forgotten night-

mare. "Bread and work!" An echo from the hungry 1920s when
Communists had screamed those words. Who said the rebirth of
a nation would be easy? Didn't the newcomers realize that they
were home and would never be mistreated again? Bread and
work . . . in time, in time. If his foolish government would just
listen to him.

Like the Israelites in the Bible, everyone in modern Israel
wanted to run things. The Mapam wanted its own "private
army"—the Palmach. The religious and leftist groups wanted
their own schools. The Histadrut wanted its own employment
and health agencies. Enough! cried Ben-Gurion. This was now
a state! There would be one army, one educational and health
system, one government. Only the survival of the *state* really
mattered. When a powerful state was already built, then he
would think about ideology.

Now he would think about democracy, the umbrella for all
ideologies and the prime requisite for an exemplary state. In
January 1949 he thus gave his people a free election, complete
with posters deifying or insulting candidates, sound trucks that
made eardrums rattle, torchlight parades that turned Israel into
a circus. The trouble was, under Israel's electoral system of
proportional representation—a carry-over from Zionist Congress days—a splintered, unstable government was almost inevitable. And since the smaller parties were not apt to vote
themselves out of existence in favor of a two-party system, chaos
would continue to reign. Thus, Ben-Gurion's Mapai, which
founded the state, gained only about 36 percent of the vote, with
Mapam winning about 15 percent and Menachem Begin's new
Herut Party, 11 percent. In all, members of eight separate parties would pummel each other in the Knesset, which was less a
debating chamber than a platform for party propaganda. Some
deputies, especially Begin, attacked Ben-Gurion ruthlessly, but
the Prime Minister usually outfoxed them. He countercharged
even more ruthlessly, often without grounds, and forced his foes
to change the subject.

How, Ben-Gurion wondered, could he run a coalition composed of tiny, quarreling special-interest groups, of men from
every political, social and religious stratum—pale, hollow-
cheeked men who wore *yarmulkes,* bronzed men in open-
necked shirts, pink-skinned men in business suits. Skeptically
he struck a deal with several groups, including the Religious
Bloc with its 12 percent of the vote. He wanted a free hand in

political and foreign policy? Fine, said the rabbis. But *they* wanted a free hand in religious matters. No buses on the Sabbath, no civil marriage or divorce. No nonkosher food in the army. Though Ben-Gurion rode on the Sabbath, had a civil-marriage certificate, and ate ham for breakfast, he agreed. The nonobservant would be inconvenienced, but this was a small sacrifice to make for national unity. He even proposed a ten- or twenty-year accord between Mapai and the Religious Bloc, arguing that together they would make Israel a light unto the nations and thus guarantee its survival.

But the "inconvenience" soon became intolerable as immigrants from North Africa and the Middle East continued to flow into Israel, some right out of the thirteenth century, and almost gave the Sephardim a majority. With many of them educated mainly, if not only, on the Bible, the Religious Bloc confidently viewed them as potential supporters. But Ben-Gurion and the Histadrut were resolved to turn them into modern-minded Mapai enthusiasts.

The Prime Minister desperately searched for alternative partners. He appealed to the leftist Mapam; they wanted more socialism. He appealed to the rightist General Zionists; they wanted more capitalism. More religion, he decided, was better than more socialism or capitalism. At least he wouldn't be shackled politically. So he resorted to an old trick. In October 1950 he phoned President Weizmann: He was resigning! Within hours, as Ben-Gurion expected, the rabbis protested, fearing that another prime minister might be even worse. They compromised with Ben-Gurion on several issues, but by February 1951 he again clashed with them. This time Ben-Gurion carried out his threat. A new election would be held the following August and maybe he would come back strong enough to do without his religious friends.

Meanwhile, Ben-Gurion struggled to save the economy from complete collapse and give his people "bread and work." But he needed billions of dollars, and while only the United States had the wealth to help, American Zionist contributions and American government aid together fell far short. Ben-Gurion was angry with the American Zionists. They collected little money for Israel, but wanted to influence Israeli policy. Before the state they had an important say, but now that Israel was a sovereign nation, he proclaimed, they would have none unless they moved there. True, they had helped to create Israel, but should they be thanked for trying to buy their way out of their *real* duty—*aliya?* They didn't even deserve to be called Zionists, he cried. At least non-Zionists, the great majority of American Jews at that time, were honest with themselves. They might not have contributed to Israel's birth, but most, he was sure, still felt a sentimental attachment to the country—and they had the money. It seemed only practical (if treacherous to some American Zionists) to lavish most of his attention on the least faithful. And in August 1950, Ben-Gurion invited Jacob Blaustein, president of the powerful non-Zionist American Jewish Committee, to Israel.

Would his group help Israel raise a billion-dollar loan? Ben-Gurion asked.

Yes, replied Blaustein, if Israel stopped trying to pressure American Jews into *aliya.*

Ben-Gurion agreed. And with Paula, he flew off to New York on May 9, 1951, to help his capitalist non-Zionist friend collect the funds needed to save the socialist Jewish state.

It was a nostalgic moment. Thirty-three years earlier, during an hour's break in his schedule, Ben-Gurion had rushed with Paula to the Municipal Building across from City Hall, paid his two dollars, and walked out with a wife and a guilty conscience for being late to an important Zionist meeting. Now they were back at the scene, after threading past a million frenzied New Yorkers who had cheered them through a storm of ticker tape along the flag-draped streets of Manhattan. Flanked by Paula and Mayor Vincent Impelliteri, Ben-Gurion stood outside City Hall and, facing a packed plaza, screeched into a microphone: "I am a happy captive of your city."

Actually, the city was *his* captive. He had captured the people crowding the streets and would capture others that night at a rally where he would open a "Bonds for Israel" drive that would sweep the American Jewish community. Other cities too would find themselves captive. In Washington, D.C., he presented a bronze menorah to President Truman, thanking him for his role in Israel's rebirth and admiring him for his decisiveness in dismissing General Douglas MacArthur and asserting civilian control over the military, a tradition he himself had begun at home. He didn't seem to mind at all that MacArthur's return to the United States had edged his own trip out of the top headlines.

As crowds greeted Ben-Gurion in cities across the country, memories seized him of the cities where once many groups had only reluctantly booked him as a speaker. Now, in Tulsa, Oklahoma, his train pulled in during a midnight rainstorm, yet almost the entire Jewish community of several hundred was waiting for him under dripping umbrellas.

Paula was almost constantly at Ben-Gurion's side, shooing away hordes of women, who she suspected were plotting to drag him off to bed and breakfast. Occasionally, however, she stole off to see old friends or go shopping for a few hours. One day she went to Garfinckle's, a chic department store in Washington, D.C., but quickly rejected every garment she tried on, informing the sales manager that her Israeli dressmaker made much better clothes. When she couldn't find a hat, she simply lifted one she fancied from the head of a friend, who never had the nerve to ask for it back.

Meanwhile, in Princeton, New Jersey, Ben-Gurion fidgeted uncomfortably in his dark statesman's suit as he sat beside Albert Einstein, who sported slacks, sweater, open-necked shirt and shoes without socks. The two sages, among the greatest Jews of modern times, pondered the enigma of God in wispy, white-haired communion. Was there a supreme being "infinitely superior to all that we know and are capable of conceiving?" They agreed there was. They also believed there was an absolute truth. There had to be, reasoned Einstein, for without it there could be no relative truth.

By the time he was ready to leave for Israel after crisscrossing the United States for two weeks, Ben-Gurion's sixteen major addresses had yielded about fifty-five million dollars in bonds for Israel—a promising start for his campaign to save the state he had wrought.

Though his people greeted him with ringing cheers back home, they did not translate their affection into votes in the election of August 1951. Mapai scored about the same as it had in 1949 and remained a minority party, while the Religious Bloc once again held the balance of power. So Ben-Gurion had to go on haggling with the rabbis over the Jewish debt to God.

Meanwhile, Ben-Gurion was trying to assess the German debt to the Jews. In the wake of the Holocaust, the German Federal Republic, it seemed to him, should be Israel's chief benefactor. And he had to strike while at least some Germans were tormented with a sense of guilt.

Thus, in March 1951, he submitted a claim to the four occupying powers—the United States, Britain, France and Russia—for one and a half billion dollars covering the Jewish property looted and burned by the Nazis. But the powers balked. Deal with the Germans directly, they replied. And Ben-Gurion announced that he would—setting off an emotional explosion that threatened to rip Israel apart.

Accept blood money from the fiendish murderers? cried Mapam and Herut.

Not blood money, Ben-Gurion retorted. "There was no atonement for genocide." But, he reasoned, the sins of the fathers should not be visited on the sons, "for that is racial theory." He would demand only compensation for lost Jewish property. And he quoted the Bible to "prove" that this was proper. The Nazi victims, in dying, had themselves called out for a strong and prosperous Jewish state that would protect its people from another Holocaust. And this was one way to meet their demand. Israelis must be practical.

But some were not. When violinist Jascha Heifetz came to Israel intending to play the works of the German composer Richard Strauss, one young Israeli struck the musician's hand with an iron bar. Ben-Gurion respected the protester's view despite his own feeling that music should be judged only on its own merits, but now he advised Heifetz to play Strauss as planned and agreed to attend the performance himself—"even though I don't understand music."

Ben-Gurion tackled reparations no less defiantly. In December 1951 he called in Nahum Goldmann, chairman of the Jewish Agency, which still represented world Jewry, and blurted out an order: See Chancellor Konrad Adenauer and ask for a billion dollars! (East Germany, he calculated, owed the remaining half-billion but would surely not pay it.) Goldmann flew to West Germany and presented the aging, stone-faced German leader with the bill, expecting to be shown quickly to the door. But instead Goldmann walked out leisurely with a promise of more than eight hundred million dollars.

Ben-Gurion was delighted and called a meeting of the Knesset to approve negotiations on the basis of this promise. By the time the session opened in Jerusalem on January 7, 1952, Israel was in violent ferment. Unperturbed, Ben-Gurion stood up and stressed again the need for German reparations. "Let not the murderers of our people be also their inheritors."

An emotional storm suddenly swept the Knesset, and one member shouted that his small son had asked him: "What price will we get for Grandpa and Grandma?"

A few blocks away Menachem Begin stood on a balcony in Zion
Square haranguing a crowd about the evils of Ben-Gurion's proposal. Relations between the two men had not improved since
the 1948 war, though politics, not "terror," was now the issue.
Ben-Gurion treated Begin's Herut Party like a pariah, charging
that it was as dangerous to the state as the Communist Party.
Though Herut was legal, he cried, it was beyond the pale. He
refused to let his government grant pensions to the widows of
Irgunists or Sternists killed in the 1948 war though it granted
them to Hagana widows. And in the Knesset he wouldn't even
call Begin by name, contemptuously referring to him as "the
member sitting next to Mr. Bader." Begin had to be totally dis-
credited and kept out of the government at all cost. If he ever
came to power—God forbid—he would, in Ben-Gurion's view,
destroy the Histadrut, antagonize the world, and betray the destiny of Israel as mankind's redeemer. He would foul Ben-Gurion's dream.

But to Begin, Ben-Gurion, with his "soft," "expedient" tactics, was fouling *his* dream—a Greater Israel, proud, militant,
middle-class. And now he held up a slip of paper and cried with
inflammatory zeal:

> I have not come to inflame you, but this note has just been handed to
> me. It says that the police have grenades that contain gas made in Ger-
> many, the same gas used to kill your fathers and mothers. We are pre-
> pared to suffer anything—torture chambers, concentration camps and
> subterranean prisons—so that any decision to deal with Germany will
> not come to pass. . . . This will be a war of life or death.

The crowd dispersed, and several thousand youths raced toward the Knesset, many lugging sacks of stones. Policemen on
nearby roofs dropped tear gas bombs and fired over the heads
of the attackers, who threw stones at them, burned automobiles,
and halted ambulances loaded with wounded policemen. Amos
Ben-Gurion, now a police chief, rushed into the Knesset to see
his father.

"Can we fire at them if we need to?" he asked breathlessly.

"Even if they destroy the Knesset, don't fire at them!" the
father roared.

Suddenly stones crashed through the windows, hitting one
member while the others scrambled for safety. Tear gas puffed
through the broken panes as handkerchiefs were pulled from
pockets amid coughs and cries of fear. But Ben-Gurion did not
reach for his as he listened to the shouts of the mob, the wail of
police and ambulance sirens, the explosion of gas grenades, and

the crackle of flames from a burning car. Let his eyes tear, his throat burn. Was the Temple toppling again, demolished by his own people?

Begin then stormed in and strode to the platform as stones continued to whiz through the shattered panes. He glared at his audience cowering in the corners. Reparations from Germany? Shameful! And he read off a list of rabbis, scholars and poets who had signed a petition rejecting such a deal. Ben-Gurion rose and, pointing to the windows, cried, "They are not identified with your hooligans in the street!"

Begin shot back, "You are the hooligan!"

The chairman of the session demanded that Begin apologize, but he refused. "If I am not permitted to speak, no one will speak!"

And no one did. The Knesset was recessed.

The day after the riot Ben-Gurion's voice thundered over the radio:

> Yesterday the hand of evil was raised against the sovereignty of the Knesset and the first steps were taken toward the destruction of democracy in Israel. A wild mob composed of Irgunists and Communists stormed the Knesset. . . . I consider it my duty to tell the nation of the gravity of the criminal and treacherous plot. . . . I do not underestimate the declaration of Menachem Begin that he is preparing for a war of life or death. . . . I know that it is not difficult to carry out acts of murder against members of the government. . . . Nor am I ignorant as to who is the principal target of Mr. Begin's plans. . . . But do not panic or be afraid.

A few days later the Knesset convened to vote on the reparations question, and hardly a member was missing. One Begin follower who had just suffered a heart attack was carried in on a stretcher. Ben-Gurion calmly kept count, his face expressionless even when the results were announced—a victory for him by sixty-one to fifty. A great triumph! he exulted. Pragmatism, not emotionalism, would guide Israeli policy. His people were learning. Now the state would benefit from about eight hundred million dollars' worth of machinery, raw materials and rolling stock. And who cared if it came from the devil—or his sons?

To protect his huge human investment, Ben-Gurion needed security even more than money. But despite Israel's overwhelming victory in the 1948 war, the country was not secure. The Prime Minister had signed armistice agreements with the bordering Arab states but no peace accords. (This no-war, no-peace situation would not change until the Camp David accords between Israel and Egypt nearly thirty years later.)

Thus, while Ben-Gurion had correctly prophesied the state, he had not foreseen the terrible intransigence of the Arabs after fulfillment, having always said they would fight to prevent Jewish statehood but would accept a *fait accompli*. Here Israel *was* a *fait accompli*, and they still denied its existence. His fears grew that there would emerge a charismatic Arab leader who would train and unite the Arab armies and lead them into a new war of vengeance.

To meet this possible danger, Ben-Gurion felt, he must build a powerful, modern, apolitical army. An army with superior spiritual values that could stand up against a superior force, that could wield the rake as well as the rifle and teach table etiquette to the primitive, science to the educated, Hebrew to the newly settled. An army with a high command constantly replaced so there would be no military caste. But first he had to deal one final time with the sectarian Palmach. During the 1948 war he had abolished the separate Palmach command; it was now time to abolish the Palmach itself, especially since its patron, the Mapam Party, backed Stalin on every issue except Zionism, which the Soviet dictator fiercely opposed.

All Palmach units, Ben-Gurion ordered in 1949, must be dissolved and absorbed in the army. In a rage, Yigal Allon flew off to Paris to study; when he returned after several months, he learned that Moshe Dayan had replaced him as southern commander. Ben-Gurion was apologetic. He deeply esteemed Allon. Had he not been the "MacArthur" of the 1948 war? What a great chief of staff he would make—if only he belonged to the Mapai Party. Allon angrily resigned from the army, together with most of the Palmach commanders, depriving Israel of some of its finest officers.

The results were catastrophic. Concluding in 1950 that only reprisal raids could stop the Arabs from terrorizing across the armistice borders, Ben-Gurion hurled his troops time and again against enemy villages, only to suffer heavy losses. In one raid on a Jordanian hilltop village, the Israelis couldn't even find their way in the dark. Adding to the chaos, Yadin, in a quarrel over the military budget, resigned as chief of staff in 1952, even turning down an offer by Ben-Gurion to make him defense minister.

If the Prime Minister, in his alarm, could not sleep at night, neither could his people in the frontier settlements. Would Israel be able to survive a massive attack? This terrifying question sparked a new decision by Ben-Gurion. He had originally wanted a small elite professional army, but after the 1948 war he had let Yadin coax him into forming a "people's" army with a huge civilian reserve that the Prime Minister feared would be unwieldy. Now he felt that within this army he needed an elite force to deal with "peacetime" violence and set an example for other units. This new army must be commanded by a young man who would inspire the youth to fight and build at the same time. And so he turned to Moshe Dayan.

Even before World War II, Ben-Gurion had sensed that Dayan, a veteran of the Wingate night squads, had the makings of a great commander. He didn't look the part, with his baggy trousers, unshined shoes, and socks falling around his ankles; nor did he understand, or have the patience for, administration or teamwork planning. He was a lone wolf, or—as he viewed himself—a "wily fox." He was also adolescent in many ways. But there was no commander, in Ben-Gurion's view, who was more aggressive, imaginative or courageous, no leader so admired by his men. His officers cried not "Forward!" but "Follow me!" And he worked out of a cubbyhole office without air conditioning. He was a true Maccabee—and politically reliable too.

Short, cherub-cheeked, with a cynical lopsided smile, Dayan exuded a *macho* charisma, which a black patch over one eye enhanced. He had lost the eye while on a mission for the British during World War II, but this misfortune had not dampened his ardor for battle. It was, however, more than simple reckless bravery that drew Ben-Gurion to Dayan; he detected something of himself in him. Dayan was the ultimate pioneer. His Russian-born parents were among the founders of Degania, the first kibbutz in the Holy Land, and then of Nahalal, the first *moshav*, or semicollective settlement.

Dayan commanded almost without advisers, and held authority and convention in contempt. He thus avidly dug for ancient columns and jugs to decorate his home—using military men and equipment—though such archeological scavenging was illegal. And he lured countless young women, including the wife of one trusting comrade, into transient affairs, making little effort to keep them secret. He seemed to savor his reputation as a dashing romantic, much as Ben-Gurion enjoyed his as a book-greedy scholar. When one husband wrote a letter to Ben-Gurion accusing Dayan of seducing his wife, the Prime Minister philosophically replied, citing King David and Lord Nelson: "You must get used to the idea that, in the case of great men, the public and private lives will run parallel, but will never meet."

Should a personal moral infraction, however distressingly un-Jewish, outweigh a man's value to the cause—especially when he himself was sometimes guilty of such infractions?

Dayan needed political seasoning, Ben-Gurion felt, but the main thing was that his young protégé had an original mind and a vigorous spirit. Like his mentor, Dayan focused on the central goal, though he himself conceded that he lacked Ben-Gurion's vision. Even more important, Dayan was, like the Prime Minister, coldly pragmatic. Both would analyze all available information, draw practical conclusions and, spurning consensus, simply bull ahead with their ideas, popular or not. Dayan's pragmatism, however, seemed almost flighty, sometimes even to Ben-Gurion. He would make a quick decision, then contradict it the next day and decide on something else the day after—according to circumstances.

And often his pragmatism was far less humane than the Prime Minister's. While Ben-Gurion brooded over war casualties, Dayan regarded casualties dispassionately, apparently feeling that it was a sign of strength to overcome one's sensitivity to tragedy. Thus, it was no surprise that Dayan shed few tears when his men occasionally overreacted and inadvertently killed innocent people in his reprisal raids. Yet he thought of himself as an Arabist. Unlike Ben-Gurion, he was enchanted by the culture of the Arabs and stimulated by their company. His Arabism, however, had a paternalistic ring. Give the Arabs their rights, he pleaded, but make them understand who was boss.

Ben-Gurion named Dayan chief of operations and planned to make him chief of staff when he was ready. But Dayan wielded virtually as much power as his superior, Mordechai Makleff, who had succeeded Yadin as chief of staff. He cracked down hard on the army, ordering his officers not to halt an attack unless more than 50 percent of their own men lay dead or wounded on the battlefield—otherwise they would be dismissed.

Dayan clashed with Ben-Gurion and Makleff when they formed the elite force. The whole army should be elite at once, he cried. But when Unit 101, commanded by a young Israeli "Patton" named Ariel "Arik" Sharon, struck at the enemy with all the daring aplomb of Wingate's raiders, Dayan was sold. And in late 1953, as chief of staff, he would merge this aggressive but slovenly unit with his polished but battle-shy parachute battalion to set off a chain reaction of inspired fighting that would soon turn the Israeli army, man for man, into perhaps the best combat force in the world—a force that, as Ben-Gurion had hoped, could build as expertly as it destroyed, and help to blend young men and women of varied background into a homogeneous Israeli society.

To supply this army, Ben-Gurion decided to build an arms industry dwarfing that of any other small nation. This task he turned over to another young man, Shimon Peres, an ambitious technocrat with shrewd eyes, a high sloping forehead and a strong cleft chin. Attracting Ben-Gurion's attention with his creative drive and arrogant dynamism, Peres, at the age of twenty-three, had served in 1947 as an aide to the Prime Minister in Hagana headquarters. After the 1948 war he launched a search for weapons as head of the defense ministry's purchasing mission in New York.

When Peres suggested that Israel build its own aircraft industry, the experts at home were dismayed. It would be a "white elephant"! they cried. Ben-Gurion, however, was intrigued. If he could build a state, why not an aircraft industry? Do it! he told Peres.

After boning up on American technology, Peres came home in 1952 to become deputy director general of the defense ministry, and three months later he moved into the top post. He now approached Ben-Gurion with an even more daring idea. How about a nuclear industry? Israel needed energy and irrigation—and, apparently, atomic bombs. Ben-Gurion this time was incredulous. But he thought it over. If the plan worked, he perhaps felt, Israel would have the ultimate security guarantee. And had he not always viewed science as a key to human progress?

In 1954, a nuclear reactor began to sprout in the Negev desert. Nothing but a textile plant turning out nice suits, explained the government.

Though Dayan and Peres manipulated vital strings of power, their influence could not equal that of the young man who controlled access to Ben-Gurion. Nehemiah Argov, Ben-Gurion's military secretary, had little army experience and was no intellectual giant, but as the link between the Prime Minister and his aides and commanders, he would decide with a motion of

his dark handsome head who would pass into the throne room
and who would not. And very few would. He was Ben-Gurion's
"Paula" at the office, and was just as jealous of anyone who
unduly attracted his master's attention. Even the normally in-
trepid Dayan is said to have feared this moody watchdog. "He
was afraid," said one observer, "because Nehemiah whispered
things in Ben-Gurion's ear. And Ben-Gurion usually believed
what Nehemiah whispered."

Anyone who dared voice a word of criticism about the Old
Man or tried to get too close to him could find himself virtually
blackballed. Argov's extraordinary devotion to Ben-Gurion bordered on slavish piety. Like his Biblical namesake, he was the
king's cupbearer and the guardian of the royal apartment. When
Yitzhak Navon came to work as Ben-Gurion's political secretary,
Argov spelled out instructions:

"When the Old Man asks for something, leave everything immediately and do what he wants. He doesn't like to wait . . .
When he asks you a question and you don't know the answer,
don't be evasive. Say: 'I don't know' and run to find out. Don't
bring half answers, otherwise you'll have to run again. We do
everything. We remove coffee cups, sweep away the dust. Don't
let anything be beneath your dignity! And don't try to lie to him.
. . . If he catches you lying, you're finished! If you have made a
mistake, confess. If you've sinned, tell him. He doesn't like
fools, but he hates liars. And there's something else—and this
is the most important thing: Love him! Without love it's impossible to work with him."

Argov proved his love for Ben-Gurion in his every waking
moment. He became his alter ego, sensing what his master
wanted from his expression and even emulating his manner-
isms, voice and walk. He drove the Prime Minister home at
night and sometimes removed his shoes and socks. Once he
rushed out in the middle of the night awakening friends in a
frantic search for a book Ben-Gurion impulsively wanted. Another time, when his boss ran out of ink, Argov jumped up and
roared to the office help: "Children, where is the ink?" When
he had found a bottleful, he raced into the Prime Minister's
office and solemnly filled his inkwell, then his pen, which he
carefully tested. Satisfied, he handed the pen to Ben-Gurion as
if it were a sword of honor and returned to his desk with the
pride of a soldier who had just won a major battle for his idol-
ized commander.

At other times Argov would play the commander, or at least
the Jewish mother:

"B.G., put on your coat!"

"I don't want to. I'm not cold."

"B.G., you'll put on the coat."

Ben-Gurion put it on.

If the Prime Minister was grateful for Argov's extraordinary loyalty and love and responded with paternal affection, he was also, apparently, somewhat disturbed. Love, fine, but blind worship? Ben-Gurion didn't even worship God! Yet he felt trapped. How could he throw aside a slave so emotionally dependent on him—especially when he had also become dependent on the slave? Could he possibly get through the day without Nehemiah solving every minor problem?

Still, Ben-Gurion would defy Argov on matters that counted to him. Nehemiah once criticized Renana for riding on the Sabbath, arguing that her behavior might, in rabbinical eyes, reflect on the Prime Minister.

"Renana has a right to do what she wants," interrupted the irate father. And besides, didn't he himself ride every Friday night from Tel Aviv to Jerusalem—behind drawn curtains?

Another aide who became a trusted confidant was Chaim Yisraeli, who, like Argov, began his career at the summit during the 1948 war. He was put in charge of Ben-Gurion's defense ministry archives and soon amassed an awesome knowledge of ministry secrets possessed by no other person. With his phenomenal memory, he became an indispensable human encyclopedia for Ben-Gurion, who eventually entrusted him even with his most intimate personal secrets. He decided whose letter or message Ben-Gurion should read and he paid (or didn't pay) the Prime Minister's bills. Yet Yisraeli's genius was reflected less in the vast power he thus wielded than in his utter invisibility. The public, which was at least vaguely aware of Argov's role, hardly knew that Yisraeli existed. Shy and taciturn, he yearned for none of his master's reflected glory, feeling simply that it was his destiny to serve the "messiah." And he would serve him even after the Old Man's death—as the jealous custodian of his property and papers.

Two other young men were also especially valued by Ben-Gurion. Yitzhak Navon, charming and brilliant, an aide who had taught Ben-Gurion Spanish, served, in a sense, as the "house Sephardi." The other was Teddy Kollek, director general of the Prime Minister's Office, who dealt only with such secondary matters as radio, press and civil service. Kollek, though able and warm, was viewed by Argov and Navon as loquacious, brash, strictly a public-relations man. Not someone who should see state secrets or take the Prime Minister's time.

With his young protégés and others guarding the nation and

reporting to him, Ben-Gurion thought the future of the state was in excellent hands—a view shared by few of his old colleagues, who felt threatened by these ambitious men. With vehemence, the "old guard" deplored their cold technocratic philosophy, which preached that science and technology rather than ideology should pave the path to Eden, that the state, rather than the political parties or Histadrut, should lead the way. Ben-Gurion's "youngsters" were, charged the veterans, men without a soul, men who asked not "What shall we be?" but "What shall we do?" This was the question the old Zionists had to ask too as they pondered the threat.

Ben-Gurion felt that Israel needed at least one major foreign ally. Where else would sophisticated arms, money, spare parts, know-how and diplomatic backing come from? Even an atomic bomb, once built, could be used only in a desperate last stand. His hopes of winning Asian support had fallen through; the two giants, China and India, refused even to recognize Israel. As he had foreseen early in World War II, the United States had emerged as a superpower and could help Israel the most. But there were also France and Britain, though he was still wary of Bevin's motives in the Middle East. The three powers had already offered Israel a bullet-proof vest of sorts when they jointly proclaimed in 1950 that they would keep an arms balance in the region and would oppose the use of force there. Also, the United Nations had in 1949 voted the Jewish state into its family—still further protection. But these moves did not ease Ben-Gurion's fears. He craved closer ties with the Western powers, either individually or through the North Atlantic Treaty Organization.

But the demands of destiny forced him in the first years of independence to hew a neutral path in the Cold War. Refugees were, after all, cascading in from Communist Eastern Europe, and he couldn't jeopardize the Ingathering, his most important goal. A swing too far to the West could also be politically disastrous, for the left wing of the Mapai Party might swing all the way East—into the arms of the pro-Soviet Mapam Party. Nor had he abandoned hope of luring the left back into the united labor party that had split during World War II, or at least into a ruling labor coalition. In 1951, however, history swung Ben-Gurion pell-mell into the Western camp. With Korea in flames, Israel could not reject Truman's request that it back the United Nations forces against the Communists. As a consequence, labor split more deeply than ever, with Mapam supporting Stalin and the North Korean government.

Fearful that Mapam might even stage a coup, Ben-Gurion ordered his secret service director, Isser Harel, to closely watch Mapam and Communist leaders. Harel shadowed them, bugged their offices and tapped their telephones. The only top official who could walk into Ben-Gurion's office at will, right past Nehemiah Argov, Harel breathlessly reported to the Prime Minister in early 1952: Not only had Mapam obtained secret military and political information but, unknown to its chiefs, Communists had infiltrated the party and were trying to take it over. Ben-Gurion appreciated the information—and the informant. Harel had a special hold on him. He was short, shiny-domed, steely-eyed and iron-willed. He got things done. A clone of himself in some ways.

If the Mapam leaders were startled to learn of the Communist intrigue, they were shocked when, that same year, Communists abroad openly betrayed them. With Stalin now convinced that Israel would not join his satellite empire, Czechoslovakia dutifully placed fourteen people on trial, including eleven Jews, for supposedly plotting under Zionist command to overthrow the government. One of the Jews was a member of Mapam.

Ben-Gurion saw his chance. What member of Mapai, however leftist, would move to Mapam now? Mounting the Knesset tribune, he cried, with a mocking glance at his helpless Mapam foes: "Why are you so two-faced? . . . How can you recognize the anti-Zionist aspects of this so-called trial, yet deny its blatant anti-Semitic features?"

Ideologically shaken to its foundations, Mapam crumbled, with one group led by former Hagana chief Moshe Sneh defecting to the Communist Party. Since the left wing of Mapai now had nowhere else to go, Ben-Gurion felt free to commit an ideological heresy: He summoned members of the right-wing General Zionist Party and, to their shock, suggested a deal. He would dilute his socialism in exchange for their support in the Knesset, especially for an alliance with the West. Smiles and handshakes. What a pleasure to be able to tell the rabbis: Keep God out of the government!

But Ben-Gurion's socialist colleagues were less enthralled. They shuddered when their former Marxist comrade declared that "this state cannot become either capitalist or socialist— both private enterprise and national control are essential for the fulfillment of Zionism."

Ben-Gurion then proceeded to whittle down the power of the Histadrut, dismantle the separate Histadrut public-school system, and offer all kinds of economic sweets to Israeli businessmen and foreign investors. Was this pragmatism—or was it treason? The socialist traditionalists were in turmoil, and some even threatened to wreck the coalition. For all the shabby furor, however, Ben-Gurion conquered his own party.

But not the Western powers. They had their own priorities, and Israel's security was not one of them. The Arabs could give them oil and strategic advantages. What could Israel give them —except trouble?

Take Jerusalem. When the United Nations voted in December 1949 to internationalize the Holy City as recommended under the original partition plan, Ben-Gurion typically balked. By attacking Israel, he argued, the Arabs had nullified that plan. Tel Aviv was only a temporary Jewish capital; Jerusalem was the eternal one. And to make this point, after the United Nations vote he ordered his stunned colleagues to "pack up. We're all moving to Jerusalem tomorrow." He then forced the Knesset to agree and, before the world could react, men, furniture and files were haphazardly piled into new makeshift quarters. The government, Ben-Gurion announced, was open for business—in Jerusalem! And the world could do nothing. Yes, the Western powers concluded, Israel would make a difficult ally.

An ally nevertheless—if Ben-Gurion had his way. Still, his distrust of Britain lingered, as the British would learn. Sir Brian Robertson, commander of the British forces in the Middle East, stopped by in February 1951 and casually dropped a momentous hint: Britain might, after all, want a base in Israel. The Prime Minister was excited, but hesitant. Only if Britain agreed to an alliance with Israel, he replied. He would even be willing to "associate" Israel with the British Commonwealth. But nothing came of either man's proposal.

Ben-Gurion was more trusting of the United States. He suggested to Secretary of State Marshall the same year that Israel would welcome American bases in Israel. But all he received was a promise to "cooperate" in case of war. When Eisenhower came to power, Ben-Gurion decided to try again with *his* secretary of state, John Foster Dulles. And he saw the opportunity when Dulles stopped off in Israel in May 1953.

Hoping to soften him up, Paula arranged an elaborate welcome. Although she usually served guests herself, sometimes with the help of her husband's secretaries, this time she would need real waiters. Well, not *truly* real ones—the state couldn't afford them. She called in the guards and ordered them to rip off their insignias. Fine! They were waiters. Then she prepared the twenty-seven-kilo fish someone sent her from Iceland and dumped it into a tin bathtub of cold water in the garage.

Dulles came, and everything went smoothly, even after Paula admonished him to have more chicken soup or "I'll have to throw it out." Finally coffee and cookies were served, and Paula could relax.

"Are these cookies homemade?" the secretary asked appreciatively.

Paula paled. "Yes, of course. . . . But I don't know in whose home."

He had to ask about the one thing she hadn't prepared herself!

Nor was Ben-Gurion any happier than Paula when Dulles departed. The secretary had shown no interest in an alliance. And the Prime Minister would be eating fish for a week.

By 1953, five years after independence was proclaimed, Ben-Gurion was growing weary. For almost a half century he had struggled to create the state he now led, starving his body, stifling his emotions, neglecting his family, demolishing his enemies, abandoning his friends. Now, at sixty-seven, the strain of these decades of turmoil and trial was etched on his face. He was still robust, but the wrinkles were much deeper, and the flesh sagged like stretched leather. How much longer should he remain at the helm?

He stole away on a number of hurried holidays in this period. In November 1950 he vanished from the country, only to turn up as in the past—to great headline fanfare—rummaging through the stacks in his favorite bookstore in Oxford, England. In Athens he toured the Acropolis, basking in the glory of ancient Greece but showing only contempt for modern Greeks who couldn't understand him when he spoke their classical language. On the French Riviera he nearly killed himself learning how to drive, skidding to a nerve-tingling halt after an aide grabbed the steering wheel. But he had greater success at the roulette wheel; with an incredible application of logic, he developed what seemed like a foolproof system for winning. If one had to waste time, why not be proficient at it?

At home, Ben-Gurion relaxed mainly after midnight, when he would submerge himself in a book. But sometimes he also put aside his work to visit with Rachel and her children, usually at her home—meetings that still left him exhilarated. And he occasionally enjoyed relationships with other women, who, as one aide said, "were all cultured and proud." He would meet them in his office when all his aides and secretaries had gone, or else at the home of an understanding colleague.

Ruth Goldschmidt, tall and slim with reddish-brown hair, was a brilliant young British reporter for a Zionist news agency. She worked with Ben-Gurion in London before World War II, though he first took note of her only in 1941, during the "blitz." She went to do some typing for him while he lay in bed ill, and found him asleep. "I picked up a book from his night table," she says, "and then he awoke and said, smiling; 'So you're reading Aristophanes.'"

Aristophanes was thus midwife to a budding relationship that blossomed in 1947, when Ben-Gurion "insisted" that Ruth come to Israel. To Ruth, only in her twenties, Ben-Gurion was apparently the ultimate father figure or, as she puts it, "grand-father" figure. To Ben-Gurion, Ruth, it seems, was a mirror of his own youth, a reminder of past vigor and vitality, as well as a reflection of the dreams and doubts of the younger generation that he sought avidly to understand. She was also the new sounding board for his political ideas and philosophical views, though there was apparently a stronger romantic link between them than there had been in Ben-Gurion's previous short-term relationships. During the 1948 war, the most brutally demand-ing period in his life, Ruth served him well as a tranquilizing influence, usually in the home of an aide, Zeev Sharef, where she lived.

Ruth also developed a close friendship with Renana, who understood her father's need for affection and intellectual chal-lenge. Paula usually sensed her husband's "affairs" and was, of course, less understanding, once rabidly scolding Renana for having dared to bring home "your father's mistress." The Prime Minister was always delicate when the time came to end a rela-tionship. As Ruth was leaving Israel in 1951, he told her that "personal happiness is more important than Zionism," encour-aging her to find such happiness in the United States—though he himself had sacrificed it for Zionism and chided other Jews who would not live in Israel.

Shortly Ben-Gurion found himself involved with another woman, Yael Uzai, a secretary and later an official in the defense ministry. Perhaps there were others as well. In any case, it was not always easy dealing with or breaking off these relationships, and in the end the emotional strain possibly outweighed the therapeutic benefits. Was this one reason for Ben-Gurion's fa-tigue and low spirits by 1953? If so, it was ironic in light of his lifelong attempts to avoid such strain in order not to jeopardize his mission. Underscoring the problem, Nehemiah Argov in-scribed in his diary in June 1954, after Ben-Gurion had tempo-rarily resigned from his post to live in the Negev:

X phoned. She asked to see me, came to my room. She began to explain her feelings toward the Old Man. She is willing to follow him and wash his feet, in any place he wishes. She had not seen him for a long time and his image does not leave her. She wants to see him, asks my advice—should she go? She had never loved her husband and children. Her feelings toward the greatest man in our generation are . . . unrestrained. She wants to be near him, even for a few moments. . . .

However diversionary such ties may have been, Ben-Gurion scored many political feats in the first five years of independence. He more than doubled the Israeli population through immigration, built an army that could defend it, and assured the flow of funds from abroad needed to absorb it. Naturally, there were disappointments too—especially his failure to hitch Israel to a Western armory. Even more distressing was his need to do so. The Arab states still rejected peace.

Ben-Gurion's hopes had risen in 1952, when a coup plotted by Colonel Gamal Abdel Nasser overthrew Egypt's King Farouk, but the new Egyptian government, ostensibly led by placid, pipe-smoking General Mohammed Naguib, ignored the Prime Minister's outstretched hand. This snub helped to assure that Israel would spawn a great spirited army bred in danger. But the danger was costly and, he feared, might presage a new Holocaust.

Ben-Gurion had other worries too. The smaller parties, still unwilling to sign their own death warrants, blocked all attempts to set up a stable two- or three-party system that would permit him to build an exemplary state more swiftly. His cabinet was now simply a vessel of vested interests, the Knesset a platform for party propaganda, every government agency a nest of nepotism. How disgraceful that, with food rationed and prices controlled, some officials dined on imported steak and dressed in designer suits, often purchased in a flourishing black market. How shameful that the rich doctored their tax forms and the poor refused to exert their muscles, if they could find jobs at all. While most American Jews sent their money rather than themselves to Israel, many Jews from other lands who had kissed the earth when they arrived were now disillusioned, demoralized and dismayed. They languished hungrily in their tents and huts, staring at empty bowls that they had thought would overflow with milk and honey. Thousands of European immigrants were already packing their meager belongings and cramming into ships that would whisk them from this nightmare.

And the pioneers and soldiers he had already molded? He couldn't even count on them—the true idealists and Maccabees

—to beam Israel's light unto the nations. How could he, when they had switched off the light on their own people? They hadn't welcomed newcomers into their homes. They hadn't offered them jobs. And even many *kibbutzim,* the fountainhead of Zionist purity, had refused to admit them as members or hired workers. Not only were the kibbutzniks ideologically opposed to hiring help, but why, they asked, share with outsiders the fruit of their terrible labor—their factories, fisheries, gardens and groves? They confined their idealism to their small communal world, failing to grasp the real meaning of Zionism.

"I am ashamed of [their] attitude," Ben-Gurion rasped, like Moses decrying the Golden Calf.

And with the newcomers blaming mainly the government for their lot, it was little wonder that socialism and Mapai were losing popularity.

So frustrated were some of Ben-Gurion's aides that in 1952 they reportedly urged him to launch a *coup d'état* and declare himself dictator. Dictator! Ben-Gurion could barely choke out his contempt for the idea. And after the report leaked, he became so sensitive to the charge that he even lashed out at a colleague who told him jokingly about a "proposal" that American Jewish leaders had made to him. Ben-Gurion, they said, should abolish the republic and crown himself King David II!

Whatever the answer to Israel's chaos, few Israelis blamed Ben-Gurion for it. He was adored as a paternal symbol of authority, as a messiah, and if things weren't going too well, the people around him were at fault. Even the Orthodox liked and respected him. True, he wouldn't follow God's rules, but was there not something of God in his Zionist mysticism, which had, after all, yielded a state? And his friendship with the leader of religious Zionism, Rabbi Yehuda Maimon, born in the politics of the early 1920s, blossomed as never before—especially when they visited each other's library and argued over the nuances of some obscure Biblical passage. The rightist General Zionists also got along with him, though abhorring the welfare state. For was he not flexible, even jolting the system with large infusions of capitalism? In fact, only the Communists and Begin's Herut Party really wanted him out of office.

But perhaps the greatest tribute of all came from one of the most unlikely people—Chaim Weizmann. Weizmann was driving in the country one day, marveling at the homes and factories that sprang up almost daily. "Between you and me," he whispered to his secretary, Yigal Kimche, as if revealing a terrible secret, "this wouldn't have happened without Ben-Gurion."

Yet Weizmann remained bitter and lonely amid the cheerless luxury of his home, wasting away in body and spirit as he waited in vain for the government to consult with him or even show him its protocols. Ben-Gurion treated him with touching fondness at the inauguration of the Weizmann Institute for Scientific Research in November 1949, leading him to the platform by the arm and extolling his virtues. He was "the only head of state in our generation . . . in many generations, whom the state did not make but who made the state."

But Ben-Gurion visited him only about once a month, and then more to pay his respects to the President than to ask the opinions of the man. In Ben-Gurion's mind, apparently, Weizmann threatened him even as a figurehead. He wrote in his diary after the President had returned from America: "Weizmann is liable to inconvenience the government."

And time and again Weizmann, for his part, had sat at his desk to shakily scribble a letter to Ben-Gurion hinting that he might resign. "I am . . . standing before an unpleasant choice," he once wrote, "of either continuing to work in a manner . . . which is neither dignified nor useful, or to cut myself adrift and create an unpleasant situation. . . . This dilemma has been haunting me all these months, and I don't see what useful purpose it will serve by continuing this state of affairs."

But Kimche would read such a letter, praise it, and persuade him to keep it as a memento of a desperate but passing moment. The wound continued to fester, however, even as Weizmann revealed his grudging admiration for his victorious rival.

Ben-Gurion would soon have the opportunity to return the compliment—posthumously. Weizmann died in November 1952 at the age of seventy-eight, and Ben-Gurion paid him effusive homage at his funeral. Yes, Weizmann was a great man. But for the next president, why not an even greater man? A man respected and viewed with awe around the world, a universal man, a scientific humanist who would symbolize to mankind the promise of its redemption—Albert Einstein.

A week after Weizmann's death Ben-Gurion telephoned Abba Eban, his ambassador to the United Nations in New York, and ordered him to contact Einstein and offer him the presidency of Israel. Eban was astonished by the "audacity of this idea," but wrote to the scientist in Princeton, New Jersey, making the offer. Einstein shortly replied that he was deeply moved but had to decline the invitation because he had "neither the natural ability nor the experience necessary to deal with human beings and to carry out official functions."

Ben-Gurion then thought of Yitzhak Ben-Zvi, who was now a member of the Knesset. He had not seen him or his wife Rachel often in the years of mourning since they lost their son in the 1948 war, and even before then his ties with them had disintegrated over the decades into a few threads of nostalgia. Perhaps remembering the years when Ben-Zvi had overshadowed him, Ben-Gurion treated his old friend callously as his own power ballooned. He would interrupt him at meetings, slight him, ignore him. Yet, how precious was the memory of their pioneer days together. He could still recall those cool Jerusalem nights when the three would, in shabby splendor, lounge over a Turkish coffee in a noisy little café, arguing over the contents of the next issue of *Ahdut*. And now, forty years later, Ben-Gurion was the first prime minister of a Jewish state—and Ben-Zvi the second president.

Stop here!

The jeep ground to a halt in the burning Negev sands before a scattered jumble of old Byzantine ruins about fifty miles south of Beersheba. Ben-Gurion, on his way back from a trip to Eilat, climbed out. He stood and savored the thought that less than two thousand years ago a Nabataean civilization had flourished in this barren wasteland, that the earth had been green, nourished by water from vaulted cisterns now jaggedly poking from their burial ground. Suddenly several young men approached, like phantoms out of a mirage. Who were they? Veterans from the 1948 war, they said. They had fought here and now they had returned to build a kibbutz in the desert.

Shortly Ben-Gurion found himself in Kibbutz Sde Boker (Shepherd's Field), staring at a cluster of wooden houses built around a single tree, which bowed with naked humility before these determined pioneers.

How was life here?

Hard. When the wind came up, the sand blinded them, burned their throats, singed their souls. Arabs stole their sheep and once killed the shepherd. It was lonely, especially at night when one lay counting the stars, alone in the universe.

Was he back in Petah Tikvah? In Sejera? Was this the beginning again? . . .

Paula was stunned. The desert? They were going to live in the desert? The Prime Minister and his wife living like Bedouin?

Ben-Gurion understood Paula's chagrin and tried to calm her. He would resign and they would go into the desert, at least for a couple of years, for he was spiritually exhausted, a victim of routine, and only in the wilderness could he renew his vigor and refresh his vision. After all, was he a prophet or simply a politician? Did not Abraham pitch his tent in the Negev? Did not God pass the Ten Commandments to Moses in the Sinai? Did not Elijah and Jeremiah leave their unruly people to seek in solitude communion with God?

Perhaps too by pitching his tent in the desert he would recharge the pioneering spirit of the youth, who entrenched themselves in the crowded big towns and shunned the open spaces. He would be a Jewish Pied Piper, leading them into the Negev, which would one day be the industrial heart of Israel, the pathway to Africa and Asia. And even if his people didn't follow him, they would learn the lesson that no leader was indispensable. As for the thousands of Bedouin who roamed the desert, why not convert them to Judaism and let them stay?

But Israel's renewal offered little consolation to Paula. How could she leave everything—Geula and her three children; Amos and his two; Amos' *goyisha* wife, who had turned into such a good Jew that she even lit the candles on Shabbat; Renana the professor, who still lived with them in Tel Aviv; friends who kept her informed about every scandal and love affair.

Ben-Gurion had seldom seen Paula so distraught—perhaps not since he told her during World War I that he was joining the Jewish Legion.

She didn't have to go. Let her stay in Tel Aviv, and he would come home every weekend to be with her.

Was he *meshuga?* How could he survive in the desert without her? Someone had to wash his shirts and protect him against the snakes and people who might drop in.

Being the Prime Minister's wife had not spoiled Paula, and she still served her husband with the protectiveness of a German shepherd, the tenacity of an English bulldog. All other functions in life were *kutch-mutch,* an expression that she coined to indicate trivia or odds-and-ends. She had come to terms with the loneliness and injured feelings that had driven her to threaten suicide some years earlier. Not every solution worked. She had tried to understand politics so she would have something to talk about, but Ben-Gurion would remain as silent as a giraffe. She was only able to learn about secret political goings-on by ambushing callers as they stepped out of Ben-Gurion's study and making them think she knew more than she did.

Nor did her husband ever notice a new hairdo. Did he like it? Like what? When Golda Meir (who had changed her name from Myerson) came to the house, it was a different story. He could talk all night with *her*! How could he enjoy being with a woman who had such "fat legs"? Still, Paula enjoyed being the Prime Minister's wife, if only because the excitement and attention helped to compensate for the barrenness of her emotional life. Everybody looked up to her and crowded around crying, "Paula! Paula!" The grocer always gave her a discount. And she met presidents, kings, even movie stars.

At first the social limelight confounded Paula, and she asked rich friends how to entertain and what things to buy, from clothes to cutlery. But she virtually ignored their advice and wouldn't even hire full-time help. Her part-time maid, Mazal, was a hard-working Yemenite girl, and she constantly shuttled from one home to another, since Ben-Gurion spent part of the week in Jerusalem as prime minister and the other part in Tel Aviv as defense minister. One maid for two houses—a real steal. And it literally was. Paula had lured Mazal away from her best friend, Esther Rubin, the wife of famed painter Reuven Rubin. Mazal was treated almost like a member of the family. Paula showered her with gifts she herself had received and didn't like, and Ben-Gurion, without informing his wife, slipped the young girl a large sum of money to help her family buy an apartment. But good as Mazal's work was, Paula would follow up with broom and dust cloth. And she did all the cooking. She wouldn't take a chance that the Prime Minister would get diarrhea!

Yes, Paula had been a good wife. Every morning she got up at five and, in bathrobe and slippers, shuffled into the kitchen to prepare breakfast, cutting the grapefruit in sections so that Ben-Gurion would need only to pop the pieces in his mouth, mixing together some white cheese and plum jelly, dissolving saccharin in the coffee, placing the morning newspapers on the table to the right of his plate so he could easily reach for them. As soon as Ben-Gurion waddled in and sat down, one dish followed another without a second's delay. Then, while he read over coffee, she would vanish upstairs to brush his suit, pull out a clean shirt, insert stays in the collars. She had laid out his socks and underwear the evening before so he could put them on as soon as he got up and wouldn't catch cold.

While he was at work she would often call his office to speak with Nehemiah Argov, her office counterpart. Did Ben-Gurion have his warm milk? At what time? And his pills? Were the windows closed? Only when Argov assured her that everything had been done could she relax. But not for long. It was time to make lunch. When Ben-Gurion was late she would call Argov again. What was so important that her husband couldn't come home in time to eat and rest? And she made sure he ate only the best, even sending chunks of butter to a laboratory for analysis. If the Ben-Gurions were staying in an Israeli hotel, Paula would insist on cooking for him in the kitchen. And if he was going abroad, she would call up the president of El Al Israel Airlines and make sure her husband would be served grapefruit and salad aboard. But no bread (too fattening) or eggs (too much cholesterol). She herself would prepare the borscht and send it to the plane. Once she instructed a startled airline stewardess: "Ben-Gurion likes pickled herring, but don't give him more than one piece even if he asks for it."

Paula also presided over his nap. She would scream out the window for the neighbors' children to be quiet, and if they weren't she would grab a broom and chase them down the street. And when the barber came, she observed every snip of the scissors, overruling her husband (who apparently saw the theatrical value of his disheveled locks) when he ordered the barber, "Enough."

No, *not* enough. Still another centimeter.

Paula was also a good hostess at parties, preparing all the food herself, even calling diplomatic wives into the kitchen to teach them how to cook. Nor was she extravagant when she entertained, especially if the guest could not be of great service to Ben-Gurion or herself. When Helena Rubinstein, the cosmetic tycoon, visited her she got cookies instead of the elaborate chocolate cake a friend had baked for the occasion.

"I'll keep the cake," Paula told the friend. "Cookies are good enough for her."

Nor did she appreciate Rubinstein's gift of cosmetics. "Does she think I want to look like her?"

But Paula's manner was often so disarmingly folksy that guests didn't mind her bluntness. Still, one British political leader almost swallowed his soup spoon when she remarked to him: "Your wife is older than you, isn't she?". . .

Paula was at least relieved that she and her husband wouldn't be leaving right away. First, Ben-Gurion told her, he had to make sure that the country was secure. He would go on leave for three months, visiting all the army camps and drawing up a defense plan for the future. If he found the country was not in peril, he would then resign. But no one was to know about his plan until he returned, or the pressure on him to stay would be unbearable.

"Er geht! Schweig!" ("He's going! Don't say a word!")

Who was going where? asked Fanny Rosenblum, Paula's friend and neighbor in Jerusalem.

Ben-Gurion was going into the desert. He must be stopped. Wasn't Fanny a friend of Shalom Rosenfeld, the Jerusalem bureau chief of *Maariv?*

"Invite him to meet me at your house," Paula urged. "I'll tell him everything, and he will tell the world."

The world presumably would not let her husband resign. So Paula met with Rosenfeld, sputtered the news, and prayed, it seemed, to some unknown god as he rushed out with the scoop, his teacup still full.

Actually, Ben-Gurion had already revealed his plans to top members of his party, and they were begging him not to resign. Seated in a circle in his Jerusalem home one day in October 1953, they bombarded him with arguments, while Paula served tea, her face aglow with hope after each one.

Finally it was the turn of Moshe Sharett (who had changed his name from Shertok). Foreign minister since the birth of the state, he was also acting prime minister while Ben-Gurion was on leave—to the dissatisfaction of both men. Ben-Gurion had always distrusted Sharett's dovish approach to the Arab problem and world diplomacy. But Sharett nevertheless played a valuable role. He presented a moderate Israeli face to the world, and at the same time helped Ben-Gurion see more clearly how the world perceived Israel—though the Prime Minister sternly admonished him: "What is important is not what the *goyim* say, but what the Jews do!"

To Ben-Gurion their relationship was a political convenience, seasoned perhaps with a dab of affection and a touch of contempt. But to Sharett, it was a bond of submission, a tie of torment. With all the other old comrades of the Second Aliya gone, he would be Ben-Gurion's logical successor. Yet, he knew, he would still not be free. Ben-Gurion might be planting trees in the desert, but his shadow would stretch to Jerusalem. Hardliners like Dayan, Peres and Deputy Defense Minister Pinhas Lavon would all remain loyal to Ben-Gurion, and Sharett would be a historical joke, a cinder in the afterglow of the Old Man's greatness. Better that Ben-Gurion stay in office.

Sharett now bluntly criticized Ben-Gurion for "abandoning the state and the party to incalculable shocks." How could he be so "irresponsible"? Other ministers were also hard on the Prime Minister, and they all threatened to resign. But when Ben-Gurion remained adamant, they backed down. Sharett was thus fated to become Israel's second prime minister—until fate took an unexpected hop. After one meeting with Ben-Gurion, Yitzhak Navon handed Sharett a note: "B.G. is thinking of Eshkol as prime minister."

The final humiliation! Sharett hurried to his office and wrote a note to Ben-Gurion: In case the Prime Minister resigned, he, Sharett, would not accept the post. In this way, he would not be embarrassed if Ben-Gurion did not offer him the job. Would the torment never stop?

On October 14, 1953, Sharett sat at his desk and read the reports with alarm. Another Arab atrocity! Infiltrators from Jordan had crept into an Israeli village and hurled a hand grenade into a house, killing a woman and two children. Lavon, Dayan, Peres and the other hawks were screaming for a terrible reprisal and Ben-Gurion backed them, but as usual, Sharett protested, especially since the Jordanian leaders themselves mumbled their shock. As usual too his protests went unheeded—even though he was acting prime minister.

Thus, on the breezy starlit night of October 14, a hundred parachutists and Unit 101 fighters under the command of Ariel Sharon swept into the Jordanian village of Kibya, about two miles east of the Israeli border. The fifteen hundred inhabitants appeared to have fled when the Israelis stormed in, leaving the radio in the village café eerily blaring an Arab tune. Sharon had told his soldiers that "we don't return unless we carry out our mission." The future of Unit 101 might depend on what happened, and Sharon was not a man to accept failure. He barked an order and his men swiftly ran from house to house planting dynamite in each one; after about three hours the night exploded. The attackers then stalked off congratulating one another. A job well done. And Dayan sent Sharon a message: "There's nobody like you."

Within hours many other people thought so too. For Sharon's soldiers had killed more than seventy civilians, including many women and children. They had been hiding in the dynamited houses, which his men had only superficially searched before setting the charges. The United Nations Security Council condemned Israel. The United States sent angry messages. Churchill protested to Ben-Gurion, as did members of his own government.

Ben-Gurion hurried to Jerusalem to grab the scepter from Sharett, while back in the "palace" Sharett paced the floor in outrage after learning of the killings. Finally he sat down to note in his diary: "Had I feared such a slaughter I would have made a tremendous fuss."

Now, as Ben-Gurion rushed in, he made one—too late. Ben-Gurion, Sharett insisted, must issue a statement expressing regret that the army did such a thing.

No, Ben-Gurion would blame the Israeli border settlers, who, he would say, had lost patience with the Arabs' ceaseless acts of murder and had understandably retaliated on their own.

But no one would believe such an obvious lie, Sharett protested. Ben-Gurion ignored him. He had to protect the army, for the army protected the state. He would guard its good name whatever its shame. He recalled Victor Hugo's *Les Misérables*, in which a nun lied to the police that she had not seen a fugitive they were chasing. Could her lie, rooted in noble purpose, be condemned? Could his own? So he lied to the world. And having done so, he seemed to find it easier deceiving himself about the horror of the deed itself. After the Deir Yassin massacre, committed by "dissident" forces, Ben-Gurion had reacted violently, even apologizing to the King of Jordan. Jewish terrorists had flagrantly violated the treasured Zionist code of *havlaga*. But now, after Kibya, he was more understanding. For did not the interests of the army—and thus of the state itself—have priority even over *havlaga?*

Ben-Gurion called in Sharon, whom he viewed with mixed feelings. This handsome, solidly built warrior had the military genius of Orde Wingate but was also, he felt, tainted by ruthless, undisciplined tendencies and impatience with *havlaga*, which, to the degree practical in a besieged state, still underpinned Israel's military philosophy. Sharon, Ben-Gurion felt, would never qualify as chief of staff.

What happened in Kibya? the Prime Minister asked.

He hadn't meant to kill all those people, Sharon replied.

Ben-Gurion, according to Sharon, accepted this explanation. The important thing now, the Prime Minister stressed, was not what the world said, but what the Arabs would conclude. Nine years later, however, perhaps for the sake of Israel's messianic mission and his own conscience, Ben-Gurion was less pragmatic. He growled to Sharon that the attack was "shameful." In any case, Ben-Gurion had less appetite for reprisal raids after

Kibya. But the incident seemed to harden his conviction that Sharett was too "soft" to be prime minister.

On November 2, 1953, in Jerusalem, members of the Mapai political committee listened silently, as if to a funeral oration, while Yitzhak Navon mournfully read Ben-Gurion's letter of resignation to President Ben-Zvi. Then tumult. . . . "No! No!" Ben-Gurion climbed to the rostrum, proud but determined. Yes, he was leaving. And he hoped Levi Eshkol, his finance minister, would replace him as prime minister, with Pinhas Lavon moving up to be defense minister. Ben-Gurion ignored Moshe Sharett, the elder statesman of the pioneers, as if he didn't exist. Sharett was devastated.

Eshkol, however, would not agree to be prime minister. And in the next few days Sharett's friends worked on Ben-Gurion ceaselessly. If the Prime Minister really planned to quit, he must place his "crown" upon Sharett's head. Finally Ben-Gurion agreed.

Sharett's gratitude oozed with bitterness. Ben-Gurion had made it clear to the world that he didn't want him. "Was there really no alternative but to make the transition so ugly?" Sharett groaned to a colleague. "Was it necessary to be so cruel?" In his diary he likened his relations with Ben-Gurion "to a precious crystal vessel that had been cracked. The vessel still stands, is still fit for use, but the crack, it too remains and is irreparable."

The Mapai central committee unanimously approved Sharett as the new prime minister, and Ben-Gurion "came up to me [Sharett] with firm steps, looking excited but restraining his emotions with a smile, shook my hand strongly, and said: 'I'm strengthening your hand, Moshe.' After a moment he added in Arabic: '*Maalesh* (It doesn't matter).'"

What mattered was that Sharett's hand be guided. And Ben-Gurion knew that Lavon and Dayan would not hesitate to do it.

Ben-Gurion had achieved much of what he had set out to do when he boarded an old Russian freighter bound for Palestine almost fifty years earlier. Despite all the obstacles and setbacks, he had carved a Jewish state out of the desert exactly as he had planned, finally rescuing his people—those who had survived the Holocaust. Israel still must help to redeem the world, of course, but that task would be left to others, when peace in the region prevailed. Yes, he came from a family scorned by the elite of Plonsk, and he did not even have a high-school diploma. Yes, his comrades had cruelly spurned him in the early pioneer years. But he had triumphed; he had served destiny. Shochat, Jabotinsky, Weizmann and others, however militant or scholarly, all in the end had to bow before him. He could afford now to be humble.

> I have endeavored [he would tell the nation in a farewell broadcast] to fulfill my mission as far as it lay in my power, with devotion and in all humility. But I do not claim to have been free from fault and error. With complete sincerity I can repeat literally the words of the psalmist in the first verse of Chapter 131: "Lord, my heart is not haughty, nor mine eyes lofty; neither do I exercise myself in great matters, or in things too high for me."

A few days later, on Sunday, December 13, 1953, the Ben-Gurions rose early to do last-minute packing, then welcomed close friends and relatives who had come to bid goodbye. Paula was finally resigned to exile, though finding little consolation in her husband's Biblical ode to her courage, repeated to all who would listen: "I remember thee, the kindness of thy youth, the love of thine espousals, when thou wentest after me in the wilderness, in a land that was not sown."

What else could she do? He had even offered to scrub the floors.

When several trucks had been loaded with books, furniture and other household goods, the couple stepped out into the front garden, shook hands with their bodyguards and, amid applause from a cheering crowd that had gathered, started climbing into their car, which would be followed by a caravan of press and other vehicles. Suddenly Ben-Gurion paused and with a wave of his finger sternly admonished some people he noticed with tears in their eyes:

"Do not weep! Follow me!"

CHAPTER TWELVE

He shall return to the days of his youth
JOB 33:25

MANURE held special meaning for Ben-Gurion. His first job in the Holy Land had been spilling this natural fertilizer in the orchards of Petah Tikvah. And it had been Rachel's failure at this job that led to a fraying of their ties and her marriage to another man, one of the greatest traumas of his life. Now, almost fifty years later, his once starved body rotundly snug in khaki shorts and shirt, he was spilling manure again, this time on the crusty earth of Sde Boker.

"I feel," he wrote Sharett, "approximately as I felt on my first day in the Land." Yes, a fitting second start.

Not everything, of course, reminded him of the first one. Now the geography was even more challenging. The kibbutz lay in a desert flatland girdled on three sides by low stony hills and bordered in the south by a higher range leading to the Biblical Wilderness of Zin. And the social conditions had drastically changed. The dreaded cry *"Yallah!"* no longer pierced the air, warning workers to speed up if they wanted to keep their jobs. Absentee landlords and their exploitive system had long since vanished, thanks in large measure to Ben-Gurion's own struggle as labor leader, and now the land he worked belonged to the pioneers, the people.

Still, the past was all around him. There was the same wasteland, the same bright dusty days and warm shadowy nights echoing with the howl of the jackal and the fox. There was even a living reminder. Working side by side with Ben-Gurion was the grandson of Abraham Rogachevsky, whose fields he had plowed in Sejera.

But the sense of changelessness only magnified the change in Ben-Gurion. The youth he sought to recapture eluded him. With his sensitivity blunted by decades of emotional discipline, the primitive raw material of a state no longer seemed to stir the same poetic imaginings in his soul. His feelings were more practical now, and nature, though still breathtaking, had become more functional. The stars suggested Einstein's theory, a tree or a flower indicated soil fertility. Indeed, science would one day transform the whole desert into a garden. And even if he still could express himself poetically, who was there now to share his joy? Paula? How long had it been since he really communicated with her? Besides, she hated the desert.

Ben-Gurion scanned the thirty acres of peach trees, vineyards, vegetables and pasture. A shepherd was tending several hundred sheep, while two cows and a dozen Arabian and Yugoslav horses grazed nearby. The whole area was surprisingly green, for water trapped by low dams of earth rushed through a channel leading from the hills into the fields during the occasional heavy rainstorms—the same system used by the Nabataeans two thousand years earlier. All was tranquil, though the settlers were reminded of the turbulent outside world by the more than thirty young armed soldier-pioneers based here, the ugly entanglements of barbed wire, and the high-powered electric lights that obscenely illuminated the whole kibbutz at night. Ben-Gurion, after all, was no longer an itinerant laborer who had to show his muscles to get a day's work. He was the founder of Israel and had to be protected.

It was because he was so important that the kibbutz committee had blackballed him from membership in the kibbutz, though they had given him "residence" rights and would eventually accept him as a member. Not only did his fellows consider him too old, but how could they work in peace with the nation's father living among them? Sde Boker would be another Jerusalem, with national and even international figures popping in and out. They had wanted to get away from the world, and now the world would come to them. But this skepticism only fed Ben-Gurion's determination to prove himself worthy of membership. He would work as hard as the youngest of them. He dug into his pail to scoop out more manure.

Having started work at six o'clock, he was panting by lunchtime. If once he raced against the Arabs in the fields of Petah

Tikvah, now, he realized, he was racing against time. Yes, at sixty-eight he was perhaps a little old for a pioneer—but, damn it, look at the long trail of manure behind him! He puffed his way to the small communal dining room and sat down on a bench next to Paula, who had squeezed her bulk into what would be her desert uniform—a frayed sweater and his old pants. The food was bad, she warned, but she would be working in the kitchen and would prepare the old vitamin-crammed dishes for him. In fact, she would, without his knowledge, cook *only* for him—to the ire of her fellow kitchen workers. At any rate, Ben-Gurion enjoyed the food, if he realized at all what he was eating. And though the room was crowded, his comrades, he gratefully noted, tried not to take special note of him.

But they couldn't entirely ignore his status, so they had built for him and Paula a special one-story, four-room, Swedish pre-fabricated house. Painted green with a red-tile roof and a screened porch, the house was cozy, centered around a den that would eventually bulge with about five thousand books. There were small statues of Socrates, Buddha and Moses on a shelf and, in the bathroom, rationed quantities of hot water—heated by a primitive device for capturing solar power, a symbol, he felt, of what was to come. Paula even had a kerosene-operated refrigerator, a gift from the kibbutz. And there was a pantry full of fruit, wine and canned food, offerings from well-wishers around the world. Ben-Gurion would return here after lunch, take a nap, and spend the rest of the afternoon and part of the evening—when visitors weren't dropping in—writing his memoirs. Before going to sleep he read as usual.

Though he and Paula still slept in separate bedrooms and he spent much of his time alone in his study, they were together much more often than they had been in the hectic political days. But if this greater proximity did little to improve communication, it did give Ben-Gurion a greater appreciation of his wife's energetic and devoted nature. She had no maid here to help her wash, iron and dust, and she still refused his offer to scrub the floors himself. Nor did Paula challenge callers at the door any less fiercely than she had done before; she was still the loyal watchdog. Yes, she had dreaded coming here, and even greeted visitors sometimes with the salutation: "Welcome to h-e-l-l!" But her unhappiness did not mellow her spirit.

Helping Paula to bear the loneliness of desert life were Ye-hoshua and Nechama Cohen, who lived in a neighboring house and came over often for a cup of tea and a chat after putting their small son to bed. Even Ben-Gurion could sometimes be drawn away from his books to join in, almost grateful that there were people in the kibbutz not afraid to be with a "great" man, a fear that had begun to give him a sense of isolation. But he also took a special liking to Yehoshua, who personified to him the ideal pioneer type—a Zionist in the old Second Aliya mold. In fact he was the same Yehoshua Cohen who had assassinated Count Bernadotte a few years earlier.

Ben-Gurion knew that Cohen had belonged to the Stern Group, and later would learn of his role in the murder. But though he still deplored the act as a blot on Zion's good name, he would overlook the past, because to a prophet only the future really counted. And some Sternists, after all, were true idealists, however misled—Yehoshua certainly. He would even become Ben-Gurion's personal bodyguard and confidant, and perform, in a sense, the function that had once fallen to Nehemiah Argov, escorting him on long hikes, fixing things in his house, catering to his needs. At the same time, Cohen's wife affectionately took the place of all the women Paula had captivated over the phone with gossipy tidbits and exotic complaints. Now her main complaint was about her husband's job: Would the founder of Israel be dumping manure all his life?

He wouldn't. For carrying manure and plowing, which he also did occasionally, were too wearing for Ben-Gurion, and for the guards as well. There were too few of them to keep an eye on him in the fields and no one wanted the responsibility anyway. So he was put to work in the settlement's small meteorological station. No, he wanted a harder job. He had one as soon as a guard was found who had the courage to work in the sheep shed with the first prime minister of Israel. The sheep had been brought into the kibbutz to harvest the grass and provide wool and meat for sale. Now Ben-Gurion would feed them. The hardest part of this task was rolling a sluggish wheelbarrow loaded with orange peels into the shed, and though he often fell down, Ben-Gurion refused to let his protector, a youth named Yaacov Hirsh, help him up. He would unload the wheelbarrow into troughs and then bottlefeed the newborn lambs. Ben-Gurion was delighted when these lambs would chase him.

"Look! They like me!" he would exclaim. It was nice to be liked, and not simply worshiped—even by animals. Yaacov didn't have the heart to tell him that the lambs merely wanted more milk.

Was Ben-Gurion just grateful to the lambs for their "affection," or did he return the sentiment? Clearly he was humane toward animals. Seeing that the larger sheep tended to push the younger ones aside in the rush for food, he exhibited his sense of justice by feeding the younger first.

A healthy tan replaced the pink in Ben-Gurion's face and he felt stronger than ever, but so eager was he to emulate the fever-ishly working David of his pioneering youth that he damaged his back carrying a lamb, an injury that would keep him in pain for the next several years. However, he still wouldn't waste a minute, and if anyone, even Prime Minister Sharett, visited him during working hours, he would make him wait. Sorry, he would explain, but the animals depended on him.

No one had the courage to say that the politicians and officials did, too. But they did, shuttling to Sde Boker in droves to tap his wisdom on every issue.

"He still kept his hand very near, if not actually on the helm of the ship of state," Golda Meir would write.

And while Ben-Gurion despaired over the little time that was left for reading and writing, he was glad, it seemed, that the world had not forgotten him.

"I received the impression," Sharett would say, "that he enjoyed the publicity he got in the world press and was pleased that guests came to visit him, especially those from abroad."

Besides, the visits helped him to keep pace with events, though not all the news was soothing. Few young people, he learned, were heeding his call to follow him. What kind of state had he created? Simply a huge ghetto, dark and devoid of soul? But this disappointment did not alone feed his insomnia. Visitors like Dayan, Peres and Lavon were convinced that Egypt was plotting to attack Israel eventually. And if the British pulled out of their Suez Canal Zone base, as Egypt was demanding, could Israel halt a thrusting Egyptian army before it smashed into Tel Aviv? Ben-Gurion scrutinized the map and ruefully noted the barren lands between the Jerusalem highway and the Negev, between the Gaza Strip border and the Hebron hills. A miracle had stopped the Egyptians in the 1948 war, but would Israel have to depend on another miracle? Israel *must* conquer the desert, or the Egyptians might conquer Israel first.

The Israelis, Ben-Gurion decided, would have to build fortified colonies to block Egypt's path and serve as maintenance centers for tanks and other equipment. The Negev had to be turned into an obstacle course. At the same time, settling the Negev would fulfill his dream of a small industrial empire in the south. New immigrants must be brought straight from the ship and plopped down in the desert, taught and led by idealistic pioneers who had already succeeded in their task. Youths who had not stopped dreaming.

Ben-Gurion asked his aide Elchanan Yishai, who had followed him to Sde Boker, to urge Mapai leaders and ministers to put up the money and clear the way. But he shouldn't explain the military purpose of the plan. For how many politicians had the courage and vision to understand that the countdown to war had already begun? They could not see "a meter beyond their nose. They have to be shown the way."

Yishai rushed off on his mission and was soon sitting with Minister of Finance Levi Eshkol, who listened with astonishment.

"The Old Man is *meshuga,*" he said. "We have land and water right in the center of the country, which we haven't settled yet. Why *shlep* us to the desert?"

Then he pondered the question a few moments, and a smile illuminated his face. "But how often has he been wrong? And who am I to challenge his vision? Very well, I agree."

But though Ben-Gurion dragged himself from town to town beseeching the youth, he was unable to persuade them to abandon their cars and comforts for the rigors of the desert. Moshe Dayan then came to his rescue, eager to help, for as chief of staff, he too saw the need for fortified Negev settlements. Since his parents had helped to found the first *moshav,* Nahalal, he knew the people there well. They would listen to Ben-Gurion. And they did. About twenty-five hundred of them, sitting on the grass or atop haystacks, silently weighed his appeal, recalling the days when this lush settlement with its comfortable cottages, pruned hedges and flower gardens had been a vast wasteland. Standing on a tractor-trailer, bent over slightly from his lumbago, Ben-Gurion gazed down upon his audience with the wistful intensity of a man pleading for his life. And as he ended his talk, there was thunder in the sunshine. They had listened.

And so was born the Movement Without a Name. About two hundred youngsters from Nahalal and other settlements moved, some with their families, into the bleak reaches of the Negev to take part in an amazing social experiment that would test the adaptability of people to a complete change in environment, vocation and way of life. They were joined by hundreds of incredulous newcomers from Morocco and Cochin, India, who tumbled out of buses that had come directly from the port and would race back for more.

When would the buses be back to take them the rest of the way?

This *was* the rest of the way. They were home!

The people looked around in disbelief. This barren wilderness? The caves and shacks they had left behind had at least given them shelter.

But soon the veterans were teaching them how to build a house, as well as to speak Hebrew, plant trees, grow vegetables, even to eat without dipping dexterous fingers into the stew. Ben-Gurion was sure these newcomers would be good farmers. But it pained him to depend on illiterate, ideologically innocent people to do the job that most educated political activists had spurned. Except for a handful of true idealists, the youth had failed him, as the ancient Israelites had failed Moses. Yet, like Moses, he would save his people regardless—with the help, ironically, of the new settlements they would not stoop to build.

Ben-Gurion would, first of all, have to save the Israeli government. One by one Israel's leaders traipsed into Ben-Gurion's desert lair, each with a horror story to tell about some colleague. And most of the tales revolved around Pinhas Lavon. Ben-Gurion listened in sorrow, and in some embarrassment, for he had chosen Lavon defense minister against the judgment of many military and political leaders, including Sharett himself.

His reasons had seemed sound. Since Lavon was a hawk, Ben-Gurion had felt, he would clip Sharett's dovish wings when necessary. Also, at forty-nine, Lavon stood in age between the two feuding generations and perhaps could serve as a kind of bridge even if he was not especially liked by either. Besides, excluding himself, was there a politician in his party more brilliant, more charismatic than Lavon? Thin, a bit stooped, with a hangdog look accentuating the dry irony in his heavy-lidded eyes, Lavon was a man nobody could ignore, a man who either captivated people with his charm, wit and oratorical power or outraged them with his sarcasm, rudeness and arrogance. A man, Ben-Gurion had judged, tough and smart enough to be a leader and possibly prime minister—until Moshe Dayan was seasoned enough to take over.

Ben-Gurion had not always been so drawn to Lavon. Until the 1948 war, Lavon, a kibbutz leader and hero of the Mapai left wing, had been more dovish than Sharett, and had even opposed proclaiming the state. But after the 1948 war, as minister of agriculture, he began showing hawkish tendencies that eventually earned him the post of deputy defense minister. Political opportunism, his critics charged, arguing that he wanted to win over the dubious general staff. Not true, his supporters replied. After Israel's birth he was simply obsessed with visions of an Arab holocaust and thus felt that he must be militant. Ben-Gurion didn't ask questions about motivation. It wasn't often one found a superintellectual bird of prey like Lavon.

Sharett had never been happy with Ben-Gurion's choice. He had accepted Dayan as his chief of staff only after vigorously protesting to Ben-Gurion that the man would "politicize" the army and turn it into a nest of intrigue. But Lavon's appointment as defense minister had frightened him even more. Not only was Lavon a military novice but, it seemed to Sharett, he openly sneered at higher authority. Lavon, Sharett now hysterically charged in his diary, "has proved that there are demonic elements both in his character and in his intelligence." He devised horrifying "atrocities." Sharett did not specify what they were, but Teddy Kollek and Abba Eban told the author that Lavon proposed, for example, the poisoning of wells in some hostile Arab villages.

Nonsense! reply Lavon's supporters. No wells were poisoned and Lavon never wanted to poison any. Dayan, they claim, would initiate extreme military action, then tell Sharett it was Lavon's idea. Whatever the truth, Dayan—and Peres—clearly deplored the defense minister's effort to control personally the purchase of every ministry item from cannons to can openers. Not at all like Ben-Gurion, who had given them a free hand.

Finally, when Lavon refused to buy a certain French tank favored by Dayan, the chief of staff resigned. Lavon retreated and wooed Dayan back, but he continued to "undercut" him by dealing directly with other senior officers. This was too much for Dayan. And so did Lavon stumble into a trap that, if not laid by his enemies, was not pulled out of his way either. A trap that would, in the end, ensnare Ben-Gurion as well. . . .

Colonel Gamal Abdel Nasser was, in a sense, the bait. To the Israeli hawks, he was deliberately plotting war, hoping to wipe out Israel and become the heroic leader of the Arab and Moslem worlds. He refused to let Israeli goods pass through the Suez Canal, and he blockaded Israel's southern sea outlet through the Gulf of Aqaba and the Tiran Straits in violation of international law. Worse, charged the Israelis, he was sending Palestinian killers across the border from the Egyptian-held Gaza Strip to shoot and stab innocent civilians.

Actually Nasser was not *at that time* sending the killers across the border; in fact, he was trying to stop them before they pro-

voked an all-out Israeli attack that would embarrass him and
perhaps propel him out of power. And he had largely succeeded. The Gaza frontier under Nasser and Sharett was relatively calm, the main attacks into Israel coming from Jordan.

"We have been keeping track of acts of infiltration and
blocked them," wrote the Egyptian governor of the Gaza Strip
in his 1953 secret annual report. "Close to fifty persons have
been arrested and these incidents have just about come to an
end."

In another report, the chief Egyptian intelligence officer,
Mustapha Hafez, wrote in 1953: "The principal reason for the
presence of forces along the cease-fire lines is to prevent acts of
infiltration; attacks carried out from these borders will only result in increased tension."

Persuaded that Nasser wanted to ease the tension, Sharett
urged negotiations, and each man sent agents to Paris to meet
secretly and iron out their problems. One Egyptian agent even
asked Nahum Goldmann to arrange a meeting between Nasser
and Sharett. And shortly, Nasser invited an Israeli, Yeroham
Cohen, to visit him and renew a friendship born in the Negev
during truce talks in the 1948 war. He wasn't discouraged either
when Israeli officials banned such a visit by a private citizen.
He used the Indian ambassador to Cairo, K. M. Panikar, and a
British member of Parliament, Maurice Orbach, to feel out Sharett about a meeting. Nasser once sent Orbach to the Prime
Minister with a note that greeted him as "My brother Sharett."
But Sharett was too weak to defy the hawks, who distrusted
Nasser's hints of peaceful intent.

Besides, the hawks, especially Dayan and Peres, had the sympathy of Ben-Gurion, who was no longer the man who did all
the thinking himself. In any case, he felt that the Arabs would
not agree to an "acceptable" peace—if they ever would—until
they were further convinced that a perpetual state of war was
unprofitable and even counterproductive.

"Why," he asked a visitor, "should the Arabs make peace? If
I was an Arab leader, I would never make terms with Israel. . . .
Sure, God promised [the country] to us, but what does that mat-
ter to them? Our God is not theirs."

Hard reprisals, Ben-Gurion argued, also had vital educational
value. The Jews from Arab countries had been brought up to
accept abuse, mistreatment, torture. "We must straighten their
backs," Ben-Gurion said. They must see that the guilty would
not go unpunished. Retaliation was the expression of the proud
new Jew—the Jew he had started to mold in Sejera.

But if the new Jew was proud, he was also wary and frustrated, and he feared a full-scale Egyptian invasion. Lavon even suggested a preemptive assault on the Gaza Strip and the Golan Heights. Then came the most frightening news of all—the British, tired and overburdened, agreed to Nasser's demand that they get out of the Suez Canal Zone.

So this was why Nasser was holding back on massive forays or even all-out war, reasoned the hawks. He was waiting for the British to leave! Then he would get his hands on their airfields, arms dumps, military installations. And the United States, hoping to lure Nasser into a defense pact, was pressing Britain to agree and might even sit back and do nothing if the Egyptians stormed through the desert.

Could the Israelis stop them? This question helped spark Ben-Gurion's drive to set up fortress settlements in the Negev . . . and now it would trigger a plot that would ultimately shake Israel to its roots. The plotters had one aim: To persuade the British—whom the Jews, ironically, had pushed out of Palestine —to stay in the Suez Canal Zone.

Colonel Benjamin Gibli, the tall, slender chief of military intelligence, sat down with sharply creased elegance to explore the options with some of his men. Since Lavon virtually ignored both his superior, Sharett, and his subordinate, Dayan, Gibli wielded a unique influence for a person in his job. Lavon met directly with him and, knowing little about military matters, picked his brain and listened to his advice. Gibli, for his part, felt that he understood the kind of decisions Lavon wanted, and he had just the instrument to carry them out—an espionage ring in Egypt.

In 1951 an Israeli officer had slipped into that country and recruited a group of young Egyptian Jews to help their comrades get to Israel and to spy and sabotage when necessary. And now it was necessary. Why not blow up American and British property in Egypt? Washington and London would think Nasser couldn't control the extremist Moslem Brotherhood or the Communists. And if he cracked down on them, all the better. They would retaliate and there would be no end to violence in Egypt. Would Britain leave the strategic Suez Canal to a nation in flames? Would America let it? Presumably not.

Gibli apparently decided to act on his own without inflicting the burden of final decision on his superiors. He sent a subordinate, Lieutenant Colonel Mordechai Ben-Zur, to Paris in spring 1954 to unveil his plan to the spy who would pilot the operation, Avri Elad. A former Palmach officer who had been dismissed from the army for "behavior unfitting an officer" (he was suspected of stealing), Elad arrived in Egypt in late June 1954, checked into a hotel, and turned on the radio. Shortly he heard the Voice of Israel announce a recipe for English cake— the signal to begin the operation.

On July 2 two Jews casually walked into Alexandria's general post office and each slipped a package into a mail box. They sauntered out, just before the building echoed with two rather feeble explosions. On July 14 several young men in Cairo and Alexandria strode into the United States Information Service libraries in the two cities and left their eyeglass cases on bookshelves. Again smoke and flames. On July 22 saboteurs bought tickets to two theaters in each of those cities, ripped open seats and inserted more deadly eyeglass cases. But one man in Alexandria never completed his mission. His case exploded prematurely in his pocket and he was dragged off by the police, screaming in agony. Other arrests soon followed, though Elad managed to fly off to Europe.

Gibli was horrified when he read a message from Elad about the disaster. He didn't dare mention the arrests to Lavon until the defense minister learned of them from the press four days later. When Lavon queried him about the report, Gibli confirmed in a note that there had been a police crackdown but said nothing about the plot itself. Several months earlier, Gibli had outlined it to Lavon, but there appears to be no valid evidence showing that Lavon agreed to it or gave the go-ahead.

Dayan too was aware of the sabotage plan and had rejected it outright. But was it a coincidence that he left on a tour of the United States on July 12, after the operation had begun (a tour that the Pentagon supposedly sponsored, though it could not recall doing so)? When Dayan was in Washington, Gibli informed him in a letter dated July 19 that the order to start the operation in Egypt had been given. But why did Gibli so apprise Dayan when the first bombs had exploded in Egypt on July 2—ten days *before* the chief of staff left Israel? Was the letter meant to "prove" that Dayan could not have known about the operation until he was harmlessly abroad? Whatever the answer, Dayan did not react like a man seized with shock or anger. He apparently made no frantic call to Lavon or Sharett to protest or demand more information; he simply burned the letter as required by security regulations.

Did Dayan's silence mean that he condoned the operation

even though he had formally rejected it? This is not clear, but one thing is: He desperately wanted to get rid of Lavon, who, in his view, was a threat to army morale and to the nation, not to mention himself. And a harebrained plot that was bound to fail could give Sharett a perfect excuse to fire Lavon, and Ben-Gurion a compelling reason to emerge from the desert and replace both men. The minister of defense, Dayan felt, surely not the chief of staff, should be held ultimately responsible for any military blunder. (Dayan's view of ministerial responsibility would apparently change many years later, after the 1973 Yom Kippur War, when *he* was defense minister; then he laid the blame for the Israeli blunders that could have cost Israel its life on the chief of staff.)

When Dayan returned from abroad in August 1954, he rushed to Sde Boker and, though he had not yet investigated the fiasco, assured Ben-Gurion that Lavon had given the order. Ben-Gurion, who would claim this was the first he heard of the so-called "security mishap," jotted in his diary: "He informed me about a strange order by P.L. [Pinhas Lavon] during his absence for an operation in Egypt that failed. How could it help but fail—criminal irresponsibility!"

Again Ben-Gurion believed what he wanted to believe. He was not interested in evidence; he had a deeper, more practical interest. Even if Lavon denied giving the order, would it not be the word of a civilian against that of a soldier? Could he, Ben-Gurion, let the good name of his beloved army, his incorruptible army, be soiled to protect a man who had disappointed him anyway, a man who was trying to whittle down the power of his young protégés, the future hope of the state? What an egregious error he had made choosing Lavon as defense minister!

But if Dayan had rather easily convinced Ben-Gurion that Lavon had given the order, he had a problem with Gibli. The intelligence chief himself had not yet blamed Lavon for the disaster. Dayan soon straightened him out: Gibli must accuse Lavon explicitly or Gibli himself could be the goat. Choose! Gibli chose. At a general staff meeting on November 1, 1954, he detonated the explosion that would be known as the Lavon Affair. With immaculate cool, he hurled for the first time his momentous charge: Lavon gave the order!

Now, how to prove it? Dayan scanned the report of Gibli's deputy, Mordechai Ben-Zur. Not a word about Lavon's "order." Obviously the report was "incomplete." Dayan fired it back to

Gibli for the appropriate correction, and Ben-Zur agreed he had "inadvertently" omitted this point. Gibli would claim that Lavon had orally authorized terrorist action at a meeting between them on July 16, four days after Dayan had left Israel and one day before Gibli himself gave the signal for the abortive third attack that took place on July 22. This meant that all trace of Israeli involvement in the first two attacks taking place before July 16 would have to be erased.

Propelled by a Watergatelike desperation, the conspirators went to work. Ben-Zur handed Gibli's secretary, Dalia Carmel, a copy of the letter that Gibli had sent to Dayan in Washington announcing that the ill-fated operation had begun. Would she please type in the words: "as Lavon has instructed." (Dayan would later tell investigators that he could not remember whether those crucial words were in the original letter.) Dalia was soon working overtime; she sat at Ben-Zur's kitchen table typing and altering document after document, including some to show that Gibli had kept Lavon abreast of the situation in Egypt.

When the Egyptian government put the captured agents on trial and one of them committed suicide, a storm of emotion swept Israel, feeding Gibli's fear that the people, who considered the spy charges absurd, would learn the truth. He took another desperate step, calling in Avri Elad, the spy leader, who had returned to Israel. Did Elad care about the army? Of course! Then he must doctor his records, deleting any mention of the first two bombing attacks, and answer any questions asked by investigators accordingly. When Dayan later asked Elad, for the record, if he was involved in the first two bombing attacks, the spy replied no. That was apparently all Dayan wanted to hear.

Lavon fought back ferociously. Confronting Gibli, he warned that he could prove they had not met privately on July 16, but Gibli unblushingly refused to yield. Lavon then burst into Sharett's office and demanded an investigation. Sharett, who hadn't even known that the Cairo spy ring existed before the bombings, wearily assented, and in January 1955 a two-man committee listened to perjured testimony, waded through forged reports, weathered hysterical accusations—including a nightmare account by Peres of what it was like working for a madman —and staggered out completely baffled, heads spinning. Sorry, the committee told Sharett, but it couldn't determine *who* gave the order.

Then came the verdict in Cairo: Two of the accused spies were sentenced to death and six to prison, while two were acquitted. Near-panic in the government. The public still didn't know the truth, nor did the Knesset or even the non-Mapai cabinet ministers, but many people would surely ask questions now.

Meanwhile, Lavon, enraged that the committee had not cleared him, rushed to Sharett again and scathingly attacked the inquiry. He would demand a Knesset investigation. Sharett froze. "That would be a bombshell shaking the party . . . to the core," he would confide to his diary.

Sharett secretly summoned his Mapai colleagues. What should he do—fire Lavon? Let Ben-Gurion decide, they replied. And a delegation scrambled into the desert.

"He must go!" exclaimed Ben-Gurion.

And shortly afterward, when Lavon demanded that he be allowed to reorganize the defense ministry and dismiss his enemies, Sharett refused, conveniently forcing Lavon to resign. The scandal was thus buried—for a while.

Was Ben-Gurion aware of all the intrigue? Did he know of Dayan's role in it and perhaps even encourage him? One cannot be sure, but it is doubtful whether he would have *discouraged* him. Not with the honor of the army at stake.

Delegations now streamed into Sde Boker. Ben-Gurion, they pleaded, save the army, save the country—and, of course, the party. Elections would be held in the summer, only a few months away, and the party was in a shambles. He must come back and take Lavon's place as defense minister. Ben-Gurion hesitated, for he loved the life of a pioneer, and he had to write his memoirs, to let the young know how their nation was built. Besides, the world, he perhaps calculated from press notices, esteemed a prophet in the desert more than a politician in a smoke-filled room. Did the Bible immortalize politicians?

But gradually his "no" seemed less firm. Ben-Gurion didn't like to admit it, but it was getting harder every day to engage in physical labor. His lumbago was painful, and so was Paula's arthritis, but how could they beg off work without looking like slackers? Far more important, the army and the state were in trouble. After a long talk with Labor Minister Golda Meir—whom Sharett had sent to Sde Boker in a final effort to lure him back—Ben-Gurion noted in his diary with thunderous humility: "Lavon is definitely going, and there is no one else. They asked

me to return. I was overwhelmed. I decided that I must accept
the demand and go back to the defense ministry. Defense and
the army have first priority."

Ben-Gurion and Paula would return to Sde Boker often; it was
now their home. As a farewell gift, the Old Man bought the
kibbutz two camels to help herd the sheep. He would miss the
lambs; surely they would miss him.

When Golda Meir returned from Sde Boker with the news that
Ben-Gurion would be defense minister, "a wave of happiness
swept over" Sharett. But then Sharett began to wonder: Could
he work with Ben-Gurion, especially as his boss?

Rushing off to Sde Boker to thank the Old Man personally,
Sharett had hardly buried his cold feet in the hot sand when his
suspicions grew. Ben-Gurion stressed that Sharett would indeed be the boss. But, of course, he must pursue the right priorities. Though peace was important, security was even more
important. Thus, retaliation was permissible even if it "made
peace more distant."

The following day Ben-Gurion wrote Sharett that if he
learned in the coming weeks "that the foreign ministry [which
Sharett personally ran] interferes in defense matters . . . and the
Prime Minister approves the intervention, as prime minister
you will have to take over the defense portfolio from me or
appoint someone to replace me."

"Great God! What a person!" Sharett exclaimed in his diary.
Ben-Gurion hadn't even come to work yet and he was already
threatening to resign! He scribbled a note to Ben-Gurion: "It is
difficult for me to express my sorrow and disappointment that
you chose . . . to speak already about returning the portfolio.
Yes, it makes one despair of any possibility of joint comradely
work."

The massive public turnout to welcome Ben-Gurion back on
February 21, 1955, did not ease Sharett's anxiety. Huge crowds
frenziedly hailed the founder of the state as he edged into the
Knesset and took his place while colleagues surrounded him
and reached for his hand. Sharett, dressed as usual in a neatly
pressed suit and a tie, greeted the distinguished member, barely
hiding his ire at his undistinguished attire. Ben-Gurion was still
wearing open-necked khaki, with sheep dung clinging to his
shoes and only a brown jacket as a concession to parliamentary
dignity. Who could miss the point that the prophet had returned
from the desert to stiffen the spine of Moshe Sharett?

The stiffening process soon began. Four days after the welcome, just before Sharett was to preside at a cabinet meeting, Ben-Gurion resolutely strode into his office. Sharett's old awe returned. Ben-Gurion "stood in front of my desk . . . just as I used to . . . stand in front of his desk. But there was no time to think about the quirks of destiny." Dayan appeared beside Ben-Gurion with rolled maps in hand, and Sharett immediately realized what was expected of him. The day after Ben-Gurion's return, a gang of infiltrators had ambushed a bicyclist and killed him. This crime could not go unpunished—especially since identity papers that the killers had abandoned indicated they were working for Egyptian intelligence.

Dayan unrolled his maps and laid them on Sharett's desk. Two companies of soldiers, he explained, would storm an Egyptian army camp at the entrance to the city of Gaza. Sharett's mind churned with doubt as Dayan sketched the battle plan on his desk with a forefinger, but he approved, since a "lack of reaction to [the Arab crime] will not be reasonable." In any event, Ben-Gurion proved that he wanted to act properly and with complete loyalty by bringing the matter to him. "I didn't doubt that he would." It was a great feeling for a prime minister to know about an action before it took place.

With the matter settled, Ben-Gurion and Sharett went to the cabinet meeting. After agreeing to take orders from the Prime Minister and deal only with security matters, Ben-Gurion redefined security. Security, he said, "doesn't mean only concern for the army. It necessitates dispersion of the population and settling the Negev. [It means] a pioneering movement, moral recovery, a different electoral system. Therefore [I] would deal with all these things as 'a citizen.' "

Sharett caught his breath. "I saw ahead of me," he would write, "a course planted with mines, for me and for him."

The first mine exploded that night—literally.

Ariel Sharon, who had commanded the deadly operation in Kibya as a kind of farewell party for Ben-Gurion about a year earlier, would now welcome him back with another daring raid. At about 8:30 P.M., February 28, he led his commando unit through a shimmering field of grain and halted it in an orange grove outside the Egyptian military camp on the northern outskirts of Gaza. Then he gave the order and suddenly the sky

exploded, astir with missiles and aglow with flames that consumed trucks, tents, buildings. Dynamite added to the din as
the water-pumping station crumbled into a scorched ruin and
stone huts vanished. Meanwhile a truck crammed with thirty-
five Egyptian soldiers racing to the rescue struck a wire
stretched across the road, pulling Molotov cocktails against the
sides of the vehicle and turning it into an inferno. When the
carnage ended, the casualty list attested to the bitter fighting:
thirty-eight Arabs dead and thirty-one wounded, eight Israelis
dead and nine wounded.

On learning of the casualties, Sharett was "shaken." Would
the Egyptians "really exercise self-restraint after the burning
insult we inflicted on their army? . . . How many victims in the
settlements would their reaction cost?" And what would the
raid do for the prospect of peace? Apparently referring to his
contacts with Nasser, he told the cabinet, "It must render more
distant the chance of peace, where lately some progress was
registered, precisely in regard to Egypt."

Furthermore, the United States would not be likely now to
give Israel the security guarantees it wanted. He was "tortured
by the thought whether what happened . . . is not my greatest
failure as prime minister."

Yes, Ben-Gurion had returned. And without hesitation he
publicly excused the high casualties, which Sharon explained
to him with cold military logic. Was it Israel's fault if Egyptian
reinforcements tried to meddle in the battle? Besides, Ben-Gurion wrote Sharett, almost all the enemy casualties were soldiers,
not civilians. He was proud of his heroic fighters. Nor should
Sharett worry about world opinion. "Our isolation," said Ben-
Gurion, "is not a result of the incident; it existed earlier, when
we were as pure as doves."

But unlike Dayan, Ben-Gurion did not want to push the Arabs
into more violence or possibly war; he wanted simply to pressure them into peace—if this could be done without war.

As Sharett had guessed, Nasser vowed to avenge the "burning
insult." He felt especially humiliated since he had visited Gaza
shortly before the attack and assured his troops that there was
no danger of war. Now he would back the terrorist *fedayeen*
groups he had been trying to rein in. And soon the Gaza frontier
region echoed almost nightly with the roar of rage and revenge,
most devastatingly on March 24, 1955, when terrorists turned a
wedding feast in the immigrant village of Patish into a bloodbath with hand grenades and machine guns.

Ben-Gurion had taught Nasser a lesson, but not the kind he

had intended. Now, prodded by Dayan, he would try again. After all, "who is he anyway—that Nasser-Shmasser?"

Pain once again "gnawed at [Sharett's] soul" after a late-night meeting with Ben-Gurion in the Defense Minister's library. Ben-Gurion had summoned the Prime Minister on March 25, 1955, to feel him out on a sensational reprisal attack. Israel, Ben-Gurion said, should swallow up the whole Gaza Strip and clean out the *fedayeen* once and for all. He apparently felt that his troops could withdraw before full-scale war with Egypt erupted.

The whole Gaza Strip? Sharett was incredulous. Dayan, he felt sure, was behind this plan. He was "corrupting" Ben-Gurion more and more. Recently there had been the Bedouin murder case. After the Bedouin had killed a young Israeli and his fiancée, the girl's brother and three comrades allegedly slew five innocent Bedouin in revenge. They were arrested, but Dayan urged Ben-Gurion not to prosecute them since they were all paratroopers. (Sharon, who himself was accused of condoning the plot, would later say that Dayan knew about it in advance.) Though Sharett reminded Ben-Gurion that "in the days of *havlaga* . . . we curbed the instincts of vengeance," Ben-Gurion would not listen, for Dayan, in Sharett's eyes, had convinced him that the "higher" morality was to protect the good name of the army—even if this meant covering up crimes committed by individual soldiers. In any case, the suspects were freed without a trial.

Still fuming from this "betrayal" of Zionist ideals, Sharett, as he listened to Ben-Gurion's new proposal on Gaza, decided he would "take no more" from him. He would no longer deny, apologize, explain to an outraged world. "I was filled with anger and refused to lift a finger. How long will I be B.G.'s nanny, cleaning up after him?"

And the next day, Sharett warned his cabinet that the capture of Gaza would spike world sympathy for Israel and perhaps spark British retaliation. And his colleagues agreed, voting against the plan, eleven to five.

Dazed but still dogged, Ben-Gurion made another demand: Junk the armistice accords! Israel didn't need United Nations mediation. It must rely for its security only on its own strength.

Sharett hollered back: It was no insult to the national honor to accept foreign mediation. Israel needed the world. The cabinet thought so, too, and turned down Ben-Gurion again.

Sharett also spurned a plan by Ben-Gurion to thrust into

Lebanon and help the Maronite Christians there form their own state if Syria and Iraq united in moves against Israel. Nor would Sharett agree to finance a Christian separatist movement, arguing that the Maronites were too divided for such a venture.

Ben-Gurion was now livid. How could he protect Israel with the Prime Minister cajoling the cabinet to gang up on him! He would be patient, though. Elections were due in July 1955, and then he, Ben-Gurion, would be prime minister again, and Sharett would be simply his foreign minister, as in pre-Sde Boker days. Meanwhile, he would keep Sharett in line with a personal war of nerves.

In Sharett's state of mind, even Ben-Gurion's aloofness toward the Prime Minister's family was devastating. Once Sharett proudly showed Ben-Gurion an article from an American newspaper about his son, Yaacov. But Ben-Gurion's reaction, the father wrote, "bore witness to his character . . . Not a warm word . . . not a smile . . . , really nothing, as if I had lent him a pencil and he returned it to me."

Nor did the elections, won as expected by Mapai, settle the conflict. The party, including Sharett, agreed that if Ben-Gurion wanted to be prime minister, the job was his. But Ben-Gurion haggled with his colleagues over policy like a vendor in a Levantine *souk* (bazaar), changing his mind almost daily. Sharett grew frantic, until finally Ben-Gurion publicly announced what, it seems, he had privately decided long before—that he would accept the top post. But only, he said, if Sharett agreed to be foreign minister. Sharett, after coaxing from his party colleagues, agreed, saying that he had "no choice but to surrender." He was crushed yet somehow relieved that he would keep his old post, even under Ben-Gurion, who, despite his many faults, was, after all, a great man. But let Ben-Gurion understand: Moshe Sharett would fight any decisions that violated his conscience!

Some time later, on August 30, Sharett (who was still prime minister, since Ben-Gurion had not yet formed his government) showed that he meant business. After Dayan, in response to a terrorist raid, had already ordered troops to assault an Egyptian fortress in the Gaza town of Khan Yunis, Sharett dared call them back. Dayan wrathfully handed his resignation to Ben-Gurion, who, in protest against Sharett's move, didn't show up at his office the next day. At noon Sharett summoned his ministers and sadly noted his master's vacant chair. Dayan, he said, should, of course, attack.

The thunderous collapse of the town fortress upon the heads of more than thirty defenders had an ominous echo. Nasser sent his troops into the Gaza Strip, then, on September 27, at the opening of a military exhibition in Cairo, crowed that he had closed an arms deal with Czechoslovakia—Czech weapons for Egyptian cotton and rice.

Ben-Gurion was shocked when intelligence gave him the list: two hundred Mig-15 fighters, fifty Ilyushkin bombers, three hundred tanks, and a great variety of guns, naval vessels and other military equipment. Enough to destroy Israel in two days! "If they really receive the Migs," Ben-Gurion exclaimed to colleagues, "then we should bomb them!"

Though Ben-Gurion fell ill, he was so alarmed by Nasser's arms deal that, while in bed, he hammered together a government and prepared for possible war. He cabled Moshe Dayan, who was vacationing in France, to return home immediately and report on secret arms purchase talks Israel was conducting with the French. More than a year earlier, after failing to get weapons from the United States or Britain, Ben-Gurion, from his desert throne, had sent Shimon Peres to Paris. During the next months Peres clinked *apéritifs* with top French officials, who found that France and Israel had much in common—especially an obsessive fear of Nasser. The Egyptian leader was, after all, helping the enemies of each—the Palestinians against Israel, the Algerian rebels against France. At the same time, some French leaders, especially the socialists, remembered the Holocaust and sympathized with Zionist aspirations. France would sell arms to Israel.

After being told of future deliveries, Ben-Gurion instructed Dayan to draw up contingency war plans immediately. Israel must be ready to invade the Gaza Strip, thrust into the northern Sinai and, more urgently, grab the islands and land around the Straits of Tiran so that ships flying the Mogen David (Star of David) could again plow through the Gulf of Aqaba and the Red Sea.

Contingency plans? Dayan was disappointed. It was time, he felt, for preventive war. Reprisal raids, however massive, had not kept the Arabs from burning, shooting and stabbing, and such incidents had multiplied since the Gaza attack. Israel could not afford to let Egypt digest the Soviet arms. But to Ben-Gurion, war was still a last resort, an option valid only when the life of the nation was at stake.

"I gathered," Dayan would lament, "that he tended to favor a political rather than a military solution."

Even so, on November 2 Ben-Gurion agreed to use limited force to pry open the Straits of Tiran—only to have his cabinet, under Sharett's influence, reject the plan. But then, suddenly, a political solution to the crisis seemed possible.

Robert B. Anderson, a Texas oilman who had held high posts in the Eisenhower Administration, arrived in Israel in January 1956 on a supersecret mission. Eisenhower had sent him to the Middle East to mediate peace between Israel and Egypt, hoping to replace Nasser's Russian connection with an American one. Anderson had just met with Nasser in Cairo and was now eagerly greeted by Ben-Gurion in his Jerusalem home.

"Nasser said he could assure you," Anderson reported, "that he did not want any more acts of hostility," but he demanded, in exchange for peace, that Israel grant the Arab refugees a "free choice" either to return home or to receive compensation, and give up a slice of the Negev so that Egypt could share a common border with Jordan.

Unacceptable! said Ben-Gurion. But they could discuss all conditions. If Nasser would meet with him, he would be surprised how far Israel was ready to go. . . . "Peace might be attained in ten days. . . . I see no other way. . . ."

Nasser, however, refused to meet with Ben-Gurion, perhaps recalling that Jordan's King Abdullah had been assassinated for talking peace with the Israelis. Even these indirect contacts, Nasser said, had to be kept secret, and he himself would dare tell only one or two close associates, apparently fearing blackmail. On Anderson's last trip to Cairo, the Egyptian leader, while promising not to attack Israel, stated flatly, "I cannot stake myself and my government on this game!"

Disheartened, Ben-Gurion made one final appeal for the "only way to prevent war": America must give Israel arms. When Anderson replied equivocally that Washington would, of course, "consider" this request—as it had been doing for months—Ben-Gurion glumly warned, "We will have to devote the last drop of our energy to prepare our people to meet Nasser with all his Migs."

Perhaps Dayan was right, the Prime Minister now thought. Preventive war might be the only way to end the *fedayeen* killings and crush Nasser's new military machine before his Czech planes and tanks could lay waste the land. At a secret Mapai meeting in January, he argued that Israel might have to attack, but Sharett violently disagreed. A war, he warned, could mean "the destruction of the Third Temple." And with the doves out-numbering hawks in the new cabinet birdhouse, most of the ministers backed him, as they would whenever a demand was made for armed action.

Sharett, ironically, was now more influential as foreign min-ister than he had been as prime minister. And Ben-Gurion felt exactly as Sharett had when he had been top man. Didn't a prime minister have the right to lead his own government? He would have to get rid of Sharett in order to pave the way for possible war.

It was not an easy decision. In almost any other country, the chief of government has the right to dump a subordinate who is sabotaging his policies. Not so in Israel—at least in its early years. A politician might feel compelled to resign, but only to return the next day after an apologetic plea by his comrades. Or he might be transferred to another important post. After all, to fire anybody or even air government disputes or scandals in public would hurt the feelings of old comrades, damage the reputation of party and government, sow doubts about official policy, and thus endanger the state.

Consequently, Sharett hid his despair from the public, which viewed him as a man who happily bowed to the demands of the group. And Ben-Gurion hid his feelings toward Sharett from all but his most intimate collaborators—though his hostility slipped through when he stopped calling Sharett by his first name. He had urged Sharett to stay on as his foreign minister partly because he was popular and could help heal party schisms. Now he could not fire him without risking new splits and provoking a barrage of embarrassing questions from the public. He must prod him to resign of "his own accord."

An opportunity arose in May 1956, at a Mapai meeting in Ben-Gurion's Jerusalem home. Party leaders tossed about the names of those who should be urged to run for Mapai secretary general. Suddenly Sharett said in jest, "Well, maybe I should become the secretary general."

While others laughed, Ben-Gurion stared at Sharett and said, "Marvelous! A wonderful idea! It will save Mapai."

Sharett smiled uncomfortably and claimed that he had only been joking. He wouldn't dream of leaving the cabinet.

Desperately, pathetically, he clung to the "last threads some-how connecting" him with Ben-Gurion. But for Ben-Gurion, the time had come to unceremoniously cut them.

On June 6, two Mapai officials knocked on Sharett's door and delivered an ultimatum from Ben-Gurion: Either Sharett resigned by 5 P.M. or the Prime Minister would return to Sde Boker. Sharett had guessed before they said a word why the two men had come. He had shortly before written in his diary, even while clinging to the threads:

> The curse of my relations with this man has been compressed into my conscience, hard and dark, choking all my joy of life, fettering my drive, robbing me of all initiative . . . And now he wants my blood.

Sharett cried to the visitors, "I know why you have come. To slaughter me! I agree!"

The visitors glanced at each other and hastened to see Ben-Gurion. When they told him the news, he stared at them with sorrow in his eyes and clasped his hands to his head. Deeply moved, the guests left, and one of them phoned Navon.

"Yitzhak, go to the Old Man. He's alone. . . ."

Navon was puzzled. "Don't bother me," he said, "he's now being interviewed by American TV."

Sharett sweated through his last cabinet meeting on June 18 and, in his farewell speech, said, "I cannot force myself upon Ben-Gurion, and I've decided that my resignation is the lesser evil." Some members protested, but not too much, for the alternative was Ben-Gurion's resignation. And "this sword of Damocles . . . hovered . . . over the cabinet table."

Sharett gathered his papers and shook hands with Ben-Gurion, then walked out, as "the cabinet sat silent. None of my colleagues raised his head to look at me. Nobody got up to shake my hand. As if their feelings had been paralyzed, as if their limbs were unable to move, as if . . . the freedom of expression, as well as the freedom of action, as dictated by conscience, had been taken from them. . . . They sat with vague expressions in heavy silence."

Ben-Gurion was working in a Haifa hotel room on July 26, when an aide burst in with the news. Nasser, celebrating the anniversary of his revolution, had stood before a great crowd in Alexandria and made a momentous announcement. The Suez Canal was Egyptian property and its international operators must turn it over to Egypt and leave.

Ben-Gurion's reaction was ambivalent. He envisioned disaster, for Nasser would wield great power as the keeper of the canal. But he also envisioned opportunity, for the Western nations might now try to get rid of the new pharaoh. If they did not, Israel might have to act alone, and with Sharett out of the way, maybe the cabinet would now be less "cowardly." Earlier, in May, Peres had gone arms hunting again in Paris and was asked by Defense Minister Maurice Bourges-Maunoury, "How much time do you think it would take your army to cross the Sinai Peninsula and reach Suez?"

Rushing back to Israel, Peres informed Ben-Gurion that France would help to build up the Israeli army on a massive scale. Ben-Gurion was delighted, and in June Peres and Dayan were back in France. The pair met in an old château near Paris with France's highest military leaders, and eager eyes read the Israeli shopping list. *Mais oui!*

Within weeks Ben-Gurion stood elatedly on a Haifa pier watching thirty tanks and numerous crates being lowered to the dock from a French ship in the black secrecy of night. Then he plodded up the creaking gangplank to the applause of French sailors and Israeli soldiers, shook hands with the officers, and returned to his hotel. "It was as if the days of Hagana had returned," he jubilantly noted in his diary.

Two days later, Nasser claimed the Suez Canal, contemptuously waving his Russian weapons in the face of Israel and the West. But Ben-Gurion was not ready to wave *his* new weapons back; he was still wary of all-out war. The following day he went to Nahalal to attend the funeral of Dayan's mother, and hardly had the rabbi's prayerful laments died away when Dayan urged an immediate attack. Patience, Ben-Gurion urged. And his prudence was not misplaced.

French and British leaders met, kissed each other on both cheeks, and vowed not to turn either one in facing Nasser's challenge. But after Dulles warned against an attack and two international conferences on the future of the canal collapsed, Britain backed off and France turned to Israel. Diplomats shuttled between Paris and Jerusalem drawing up a French-Israeli pact. And in late September, Bourges-Maunoury posed the crucial query to Peres: Would Israel agree to a joint attack on Egypt —with British help if possible? There were more talks, and a coordinated plan emerged. But Ben-Gurion was cool to it, for the British would take part in the operation only if Israel agreed to appear as the "aggressor." The scheme was simple: Israeli forces would crash through the Sinai almost to Suez, and *then*

Britain and France would unleash their troops. After warning Israel to stay out of the canal zone and Egypt to evacuate its troops from there, the two powers would fly men into the area to keep the waterway open and presumably spark Nasser's overthrow.

Why, Ben-Gurion wanted to know, should Israel be cast as the villain in the world's eyes while the British and French appeared as angels of peace? Besides, if Israel attacked first without the help of the other two powers, Nasser's Migs might swoop down on Israeli cities before these powers could act. True, victory could mean that Israeli ships would sail through the Straits of Tiran, permitting Eilat to burgeon into a great port and injecting the whole Negev with new life. But defeat could mean the end of the state. Was the prospect of some gains worth the terrible risk—when even victory, under the British plan, could stain Israel's honor? He decided it wasn't.

Nevertheless, Ben-Gurion accepted an invitation by French Premier Guy Mollet to personally attend a final conference in the Paris suburb of Sèvres, after Dayan and Peres convinced him that a compromise might still be possible. But even while secretly driving to the airport in a curtained car, his telltale feathery locks tucked under a wide-brimmed hat, he almost turned back. For, compromise or not, the thought still haunted him: How could he gamble the very existence of the Jewish state, his precious creation, in a possibly needless war?

In a magnificent villa surrounded by hedges and rosebeds that cast a spell of peace, Ben-Gurion met with his French and British conspirators to talk war—war against Nasser, though at times they seemed at war with each other. Ben-Gurion and British Foreign Secretary Selwyn Lloyd glared disdainfully at each other and made mutually extreme demands. Lloyd "may well have been a friendly man, pleasant, charming, amiable," Dayan would later write. "If so, he showed near-genius in concealing these virtues. . . . His whole demeanor expressed distaste—for the place, the company and the topic." As pure and lofty as each leader judged his own motives, the atmosphere of conspiracy and suspicion suggested a meeting of robbers quarreling over the best way to heist a bank. And Lloyd was like some Mafia godfather who resented having to deal with a man he suspected couldn't hold up a grocery store.

Israel had to appear in the eyes of the world as the "aggressor," Lloyd demanded, or else Britain would. And surely she could not agree. Dayan didn't dare glance at Ben-Gurion, fearful that the Old Man "would jump out of his skin." He suggested a compromise: Israel would attack first, but only with a paratroop battalion that would be dropped about thirty miles from the Suez Canal. The attack would appear as simply a large-scale raid, not all-out war, and thus Nasser wouldn't bomb Israeli cities before the French and British joined in the fighting. But the assault would be close enough to the Suez Canal to give Israel's conspirators an excuse for stepping in to "keep the canal open." Meanwhile, an Israeli armored column would smash through the southern Sinai to link up with the paratroopers, and then, when the French and British had stormed the Suez zone, the whole Israeli army would push through the Sinai.

Lloyd was doubtful. He feared that the paratrooper force would be too small, that the world might not think that even its presence near the Suez was threatening enough to justify an Anglo-French invasion. Israel, he demanded, must commit a "real act of war."

Ben-Gurion bristled. Real enough to provoke an air attack on Israeli cities? The British should remember the horrors of London during the blitz!

A French general then suggested that Israel's air force could bomb the Israeli town of Beersheba when the fighting began and the world would, of course, blame the Egyptians. British and French planes could then rush to Israel's help immediately.

Shocked by the idea, Ben-Gurion cried: "But . . . how can we deceive the world? . . . To lie to the whole world to make the matter easier and more convenient for Britain? Never!"

Bombing his own people was going too far—even to achieve what he considered a moral end.

Finally, everyone—except Ben-Gurion, who remained non-committal—agreed on a final version of Dayan's "Israeli pretext" plan. After the first day of fighting, Britain and France would give ultimatums to both Egypt and Israel: The two sides must cease fire and withdraw ten miles from the Suez Canal while Anglo-French troops moved in and temporarily occupied Port Said, Ismailia and Suez in order to guarantee that the canal remained open. If these terms weren't met within twelve hours, the British and French would seize the Suez Canal Zone by force. Israel would "give in," but Egypt almost certainly would not—and thus the pretext for an Anglo-French attack.

What did Ben-Gurion think? Not even Dayan or Peres knew. To avoid committing himself, he had allowed Dayan to present the plan, but only in his own name. The Prime Minister was in turmoil. On the eve of the final meeting, October 23, 1956, he sat alone in his room listening to the radio. Another Arab terrorist raid in Israel. How many Jews had died? How many would die in a full-scale war—a war in which Israel would have to gain its objectives in a week or so, before Washington and the United Nations could clamp a cease-fire on his troops. Was such a feat even possible?

"None of us envied him the long evening that lay before him," Peres would write. And Dayan would comment, "He was still grappling with the basic question. Should we or should we not go ahead?"

Ben-Gurion felt lonely. "The whole gang is in town," he noted in his diary. But members of the "gang" weren't enjoying themselves. Even the most exotic Parisian stripteasers, Dayan would say, could not arouse them. Not with history about to bare a momentous decision.

Shortly before noon the next day, October 24, Dayan and Peres found Ben-Gurion relaxing in the shade of a fine old tree in the garden of the villa. It was a sunny autumn day, a day that soothed the soul and augured peace. But war was on his mind, and apparently had been throughout a sleepless night. Would Dayan please sketch the battle plan? Since Dayan had no map, Peres took out a packet of cigarettes and handed it to Dayan. The general drew on the back of the wrapper an outline of the Sinai Peninsula and marked it with three arrows, indicating the projected paths of Israeli advance. Ben-Gurion studied the diagram, then asked dozens of questions. At two o'clock the three men rose, breathed in the fragrance of the flowers, and started toward the villa. Did this mean the Old Man agreed?

"Moshe's plan is good," he finally said. "It saves lives."

Then Ben-Gurion suddenly switched to another subject—Procopius. On the flight to Paris he had read a book by this Byzantine historian referring to a Jewish kingdom that existed in the fifth century on the island of Tiran at the eastern edge of the straits. "I wonder," Ben-Gurion mused, "how a Jewish realm could have subsisted [there] without water. Why, the Jews almost destroyed Moses over the problem of drinking water."

He would soon have a chance to find out.

CHAPTER THIRTEEN

Conspired all of them together
NEHEMIAH 4:8

ONE night in October 1956 Fanny Rosenblum answered the door and found Paula standing outside in robe, nightgown and slippers. She had rushed across the street from the Prime Minister's residence in Jerusalem and had to see Fanny immediately. Not since she was about to be exiled to the desert had she seemed so disturbed.

"We're leaving for Tel Aviv!" she exclaimed as she entered. "You must stay in our place for a few days."

"Why?"

"On Sunday we start, and on Tuesday *they* will come. You must stay in our shelter."

Fanny now knew. War was about to explode. Few others knew, however, and even the leftist Mapam ministers would not be told until shortly before the cabinet met to vote on whether to carry out the attack, scheduled for the following day. (Only these leftists voted no.) Ben-Gurion was so anxious that he fell ill and had to stay in bed as soon as he and Paula arrived in their Tel Aviv home. He would stay in the ground floor room that Renana had vacated a few months earlier when she married a young army officer. A concrete wall had just been built outside the window to shield him from shrapnel, but the ominous shadow it cast only heightened his fear. His fever edged up, but the doctors couldn't understand it. Could anyone understand the stress of a man who was risking the life of his country?

After the cabinet meeting, generals, cabinet members and Knesset leaders, ignoring Paula's protests, crowded into his room and sat at his bedside, calming and congratulating him for negotiating the plot. To the amazement of the others, Menachem Begin took Ben-Gurion's hand and held it "as if they were lovers." Shortly, two cables arrived from President Eisenhower. He feared that Israeli mobilization indicated Israel was about to attack *Jordan.*

Could American intelligence be that bad? Ben-Gurion wondered. Obviously the secret was not seeping out—a hopeful sign that the attack would succeed. But how would Eisenhower react when he learned he had been duped? Ben-Gurion had wanted to reveal the plot to him, but his allies would not agree. Now, bent under the moral burden of concealing it from so trusting—and powerful—a friend, he ordered an aide to write a reply but to avoid committing Israel not to attack. The reply would read: "My government will be failing in its essential duty if it were not to take all necessary measures to assure that the declared Arab aim of eliminating Israel by force should not succeed."

Was it his fault if Eisenhower expected Israel to attack Jordan —and not Egypt?

Had they jumped yet? Ben-Gurion demanded to know as Moshe Dayan entered his room in the afternoon of October 29. They had. At 4:59 P.M. about four hundred paratroopers under Ariel Sharon's command had floated into the Mitla Pass some thirty miles from the Suez Canal. The world wondered what the attack signified. Was it just a large-scale reprisal raid or all-out war? Even Israeli envoys were not quite sure. At the U.S. State Department, Ambassador Abba Eban was assuring an assistant secretary of state that Israel's military buildup was only defensive when someone burst in with news of the attack. There was an embarrassed pause.

"I'm certain, Mr. Ambassador," said the assistant secretary, "that you will wish to get back to your embassy to find out exactly what is happening in your country."

In New Delhi, Moshe Sharett, on a goodwill tour of Asia, was en route to an audience with Prime Minister Jawaharlal Nehru to assure him also of Israel's peaceful intentions, when he happened to see the headlines at a street newsstand. He was incredulous. He had reluctantly undertaken the tour at the government's request and, once more, Ben-Gurion was making a fool of him. What if he hadn't seen the headlines? Now he would have to explain to Nehru that this catastrophe was really an action of self-preservation.

The next day, October 30, the Israelis proved that they were quite able to preserve themselves. They had opened up several gateways to the Sinai the previous night and now the main Israeli forces began smashing through the desert toward Suez— still without help from the British and French, who were not to start bombing Egyptian air bases until dawn on October 31, after issuing ultimatums to both sides.

The ultimatums were announced, and that night Dayan was back at Ben-Gurion's bedside. The Prime Minister was in an agitated mood. While Israel, as planned, had accepted the demand, Egypt, as expected, had not. The British and French were thus to bomb Egyptian air bases the next morning—but, claiming that they weren't ready, they postponed the attack for twelve hours. And so the Israeli forces would still be fighting alone until late the next day, October 31. Ben-Gurion was enraged. His allies had betrayed Israel! Meanwhile, Sharon's paratroopers in Mitla were trapped. Bring them out immediately, the Prime Minister commanded. But Dayan assured him that the forces in Mitla and elsewhere could fight and win even without outside help.

In fact, the Mitla fighters on the following day wouldn't even wait for their own army to link up with them. Misleading the general staff about his intentions, Sharon led an assault against the Egyptians entrenched nearby and his men seized the area in a costly—and unnecessary—battle.

Shocked by the unexpected Israeli attack on Egypt, President Eisenhower rushed a message to Ben-Gurion asking Israel to "return to the border, since it has completed its task, namely elimination of the *fedayeen* bases." He would then, he promised, "issue a declaration of profound admiration and firm friendship toward her."

Ben-Gurion rejected this demand, and a second one from Eisenhower as well. The Security Council hastily met, and the United States and the Soviet Union for once locked arms instead of horns. Cease fire! But France and Britain vetoed the call.

The full conspiracy then flowered as British planes finally bombed Egyptian airfields at 5 P.M., October 31. Ben-Gurion's temperature dipped, and the heat on Israel diminished too. Britain and France—angels of peace? To the world they suddenly seemed more like the Godfather to Israel's mere grocery-store robber. Israel, it appeared, would be the big winner in this war. The Israelis had captured the Gaza Strip and almost the whole Sinai Peninsula; they would soon storm Sharm el-Sheikh, opening the Straits of Tiran; and now the Anglo-French forces were finally in action. Ben-Gurion's illness vanished.

"At first," he wrote euphorically, "the matter looked like a daydream; then like a legend; finally, like a series of miracles."

Still, sadness and anger soured his joy. Israeli casualties were light but too high for him, and largely because of Sharon's "unnecessary" attack, they would reach 174 dead by war's end compared to about 1,000 enemy dead. Nor did he mourn only for Israeli Jews. In the Israeli Arab village of Kfar Kasim near the Jordan frontier, residents were toiling in the fields when a curfew was imposed on all Arabs in the area. Unaware of the curfew, the villagers were walking home when Israeli soldiers shot down 43 of them. Ben-Gurion court-martialed the responsible soldiers and vowed that "nothing like this will ever happen again in Israel."

The British were his most immediate worry. Not only had they held up the air attack, but now, he learned, they would need several days to pull together their forces for a landing in the canal zone. On the one hand, Israel no longer required military support, and on the other, it was under mounting pressure at the United Nations to cease fire. Yet the British were quietly pushing Israel to continue fighting. Political disaster in the midst of military triumph!

On November 5, a few hours after the Israelis bulled into Sharm el-Sheikh, the disastrous situation swiftly worsened. An aide hurried to Ben-Gurion with a letter from Soviet leader Nikolai Bulganin, and the Prime Minister read in disbelief:

> The government of Israel is criminally and irresponsibly playing with the fate of the world, with the fate of its own people. It is sowing hatred of the State of Israel amongst the Eastern peoples . . . and places in question the very existence of Israel as a state. . . . The Soviet government is at this moment taking steps to put an end to the war and to restrain the aggressors. The government of Israel should consider before it is too late. We hope that [it] will fully understand and appreciate our warning.

A naked threat of force! Bulganin also sent notes to Britain and France, but couched in far less scornful terms.

Meanwhile, on November 5, Anglo-French airborne troops scrambled for a toehold in the Port Said area, only to stop shooting after twenty-four hours as the two governments caved in under world pressure, their intricately conceived plan a fiasco. But while British and French leaders agonized in humiliation, Ben-Gurion beamed as he stepped to the Knesset rostrum on November 7 to address a packed hall thundering with applause. Defying his doctor, he had traveled to Jerusalem so that he could now bask in Israel's glory. The eyes of the world were fixed on him—though Paula's focused only on the back of his head. Waiting for him with a hot drink in hand, she stood peeping through a thick curtain behind the rostrum.

"The revelation of Sinai has been renewed in our time by our army's thrust of heroism," Ben-Gurion rhapsodized. "This was the greatest and most glorious military operation in the annals of our people, and one of the most remarkable operations in world history."

The armistice agreement with Egypt was dead and the armistice lines invalid, he cried. And no "foreign" troops would be allowed to enter Israeli-occupied territory, though Israel was ready for face-to-face peace talks with the Arabs. Later he would crow: "Yotvat [the island of Tiran] will once more become a part of the Third Kingdom of Israel!" Ben-Gurion remembered the book he had read by Procopius, noting that the Jews had conquered this island in the fifth century. The rest of the world, however, viewed the situation through a different prism.

The United Nations General Assembly voted ninety-five to one (Israel) for a stiffly worded resolution ordering the Jewish state to leave the Sinai at once.

U.N. Secretary General Dag Hammarskjöld grumbled to newsmen that Israel was endangering world peace and its own future "existence."

President Eisenhower sent a thinly disguised threat to Ben-Gurion: Israeli actions, he hoped, would not "impair the friendly collaboration between our two countries."

A State Department official warned Israeli diplomats that their country might lose American aid, be expelled from the United Nations or have sanctions slapped on it, and even be attacked by Russia.

In the wake of Bulganin's note, this last threat did not seem far-fetched. Moscow, having crushed the Hungarian revolution, was now reportedly pouring arms and "volunteers" into Syria and planning to "flatten" Israel within twenty-four hours. Meanwhile Washington, though promising to retaliate if the Soviets hit Britain and France, ominously offered no such assurance to the Jewish state. As Ben-Gurion had predicted,

Eisenhower felt that his allies had betrayed him and he was venting his rage mainly on Israel—though, ironically, Israel alone had wanted to be frank with the President. With Britain and France involved, Suez had become a focal point of big-power struggle, and Israel, now viewed almost universally as dragging the world to the abyss, was becoming more and more dispensable to almost everybody. A small-time bandit, it turned out, was a more inviting target of abuse than a Mafia godfather.

Had Israel's great victory, Ben-Gurion wondered, been the prelude to another Holocaust? He noted in his diary:

> [Ambassador] Eban phoned me, filled with fear. His cables also sow fear and terror. . . . It was a nightmarish day. From Rome, Paris and Washington there is a succession of reports on [Soviet designs against Israel].

The world froze. Was it about to disintegrate in a nuclear conflagration? If so, Ben-Gurion knew, Israel would be the first country to go. He now admitted, as he had seldom done in the past, that he had gravely erred. "I made a few mistakes in that speech, saying that the armistice agreement was dead and buried, that Egypt would not be allowed to return to Sinai. I went too far. . . . But you see, the victory was too quick. I was too drunk with victory."

Now, the morning after, November 8, Ben-Gurion and his people nursed an almost paralyzing hangover. Dayan found the Prime Minister in his office "very pale, and as angry as a wounded lion." Around him, sleepless aides frantically telephoned instructions to Israeli diplomats at home and abroad while shuffling through reports or sipping cold coffee. Ministers nervously sat outside Ben-Gurion's office and one of them, Pinhas Sapir, who headed commerce and industry, kept shouting, "Withdraw! Withdraw! Withdraw!," smashing his fist on a table in violent rhythm with the demand. Another minister who paced the floor puffing furiously on a chain of cigarettes cried, "We must tell B.G.: '*Aroys!* Out of the Sinai!'"

But who would do it? Who could face down the devastating stare?

As mankind seemingly hurtled toward Armageddon, Dayan was little impressed. Defy Russia! Defy the world! he urged Ben-Gurion. The Kremlin was bluffing. And Ben-Gurion thought it was, too. But who could be sure? Even if Russia didn't attack, could Israel afford to so blatantly challenge America, its ultimate defender? Ben-Gurion decided he must talk with President Eisenhower.

He called Ambassador Eban at the United Nations. Arrange a meeting with Eisenhower immediately, he ordered, if necessary in secret. Eban, aloofly urbane, eloquently articulate, his small bespectacled eyes cool and shrewd, was not a man to lose his composure easily. But he nearly did now. Didn't Ben-Gurion understand? Did he think that the President, in his punitive mood, would give him the prestige victory of a private meeting? Ike had even asked one American Jewish leader whether "Ben-Gurion's reputation for balance and rationality was really well-founded."

Withdraw from the Sinai, Eban advised Ben-Gurion, and the Prime Minister finally agreed—on the condition that an international force police the area and that "satisfactory arrangements" be made with the United Nations. With luck, a debate on what constituted satisfactory arrangements could stretch on forever. Would such a withdrawal accord appease the Soviets? Ben-Gurion asked. If not, Israel would have no choice but to withdraw unconditionally. He had written two speeches, one proposing the compromise, the other announcing surrender. Which speech should he make?

Eban was overwhelmed. "I was now to be faced," he would write, "by one of the most extraordinary situations in which an ambassador has ever found himself. Ben-Gurion did no more or less than transfer the crucial decision to me!"

The ambassador feverishly buttonholed top American officials, and they agreed to the conditional option. Now that Washington was backing the Israeli plan, Eban calculated, Moscow wouldn't dare attack Israel and risk a big-power clash. Within two hours he called back to Israel: Ben-Gurion should give the speech proposing compromise.

The Prime Minister was relieved. He went on the air after midnight, his voice not euphoric this time, but "weary and restrained," and even hinting agony. The Israeli army in the Sinai would come home.

"But there is no power in the world," he told his people, "that can reverse [its] great victory. . . . Israel after the Sinai Campaign will never again be the Israel that existed prior to this great operation."

Painfully, almost sheepishly, he would later tell his army commanders, "You advanced to Sinai, and I withdrew from there."

Yet he could not risk the immediate demise of the state in order to pursue its perceived long-term interests as some extremists would have done. It simply wasn't practical. And he did, after all, pull out of the ashes a remnant of victory—time. Israel would withdraw from the Sinai and Gaza in installments, about fifteen miles a week, quickly enough to avoid a political showdown with the United Nations and the United States, but slowly enough to gain perhaps a permanent foothold in the two coveted regions.

Eisenhower, however, snapped the lash. The threat of World War III had receded, but the injury to his pride still festered. Aggression could not be rewarded, he insisted. When he threatened to punish Israel if it didn't clear out of all the occupied areas at once, Ben-Gurion growled to his aide Yaacov Herzog, "Write and tell him to bomb us with guided missiles. . . . Let them carry out their sanctions!" But he settled for a mere charge that Washington was discriminating against Israel.

As American threats continued, the struggle degenerated into what seemed like a personal vendetta between the two leaders, a confrontation especially traumatic to Ben-Gurion because of Ike's sympathetic attitude toward the Jews when the pair had met in Germany after World War II.

"This president hardly does any work," Ben-Gurion remarked contemptuously to his army commanders. "He spends his time playing bridge or golf, and in the morning he reads a short page his secretaries bring him on what is happening in the world."

But when Washington began cutting off its aid, Ben-Gurion began cutting down his demands. And French Foreign Minister Pineau, sensing that the time was ripe for a compromise, concocted one. Golda Meir would make a speech in the General Assembly—approved by the United States, France and other nations—promising that Israel would evacuate the occupied areas on three "assumptions": Israeli ships would be allowed to sail through the Straits of Tiran; United Nations troops would march into Sharm el-Sheikh and the Gaza Strip; and United Nations, not Egyptian, administrators would make Gaza run. If Egypt tried to overrule these "assumptions" by force, Israel would have the right to strike back.

Ben-Gurion was back in bed gulping down Paula's pills, but none was as bitter as this proposal. Israel could "assume" it would continue to exist? Still, it was better to gain a bad peace than to lose a good partner. France might cut off arms to Israel if it turned down Pineau's plan. Rejecting Dayan's advice to stand firm and ignoring Begin's warning against "betrayal," he called his top commanders to his bedside and told them, "Tomorrow there won't be dancing in the streets." But the straits would be open, and ships from all over the world would come.

Israel would thus prosper and "there will be rejoicing." As for Gaza, Nasser would soon fall, he predicted, and there would be peace in that region. One had to trust America.

Hardly had Golda Meir delivered her address to the General Assembly that evening of March 1, 1957, when American Ambassador Henry Cabot Lodge stepped to the rostrum and declared that the straits must remain open—*but* that the future of the Gaza Strip would have to be worked out "within the context of the armistice agreements."

"Perhaps," Golda would write, "not everyone at the United Nations that day understood what Cabot Lodge was saying, but *we* understood all too well. The U.S. State Department had won its battle against us, and the Egyptian military government, with its garrison, was going to return to Gaza."

Despite reassurances from Eisenhower that Israel's hopes would "not be in vain," Ben-Gurion despaired. All those months of planning, agonizing, fighting, dying, winning, arguing—and now losing. Perhaps Dayan was right. Perhaps he should have held out to the end. But could Israel risk complete isolation and possibly final destruction? No, he would not gamble with destiny. His soldiers would withdraw.

If it hurt Ben-Gurion to lose what he had gained in war, peace served as a soothing salve. Israel's borders no longer erupted with violence, and its ships no longer were barred from the Gulf of Aqaba. The army had brilliantly made its point. Thus, Ben-Gurion, like his compatriots, soon realized that Israel had actually achieved its basic war aims. It was time to focus again on building an exemplary state with bridges spanning to all corners of the world.

But could he drive himself forever? Ben-Gurion was tired and still suffered pain in his back that sometimes incapacitated him. If he had any doubts about his ability to function, however, Dr. Moshe Feldenkrais, his physical therapist, who was also a leading scientist, helped to dispel them by early 1957. Ben-Gurion was skeptical when, shortly before the Sinai Campaign, a friend introduced him to the stout, fuzzy-haired doctor, who closely resembled the Prime Minister. Why waste precious time exercising—except to sow the earth or thrust the sword? But magic hands soon eased his pain, and suddenly exercise had a practical value. Now he would secretly disappear from his office— sometimes in the middle of a conference—to spend an hour a day with Feldenkrais, usually on his back twirling one leg in

the air. Shortly, both legs were in the air. People strolling along
the beach in Herzylia at the break of dawn were sometimes
startled to see an urn-shaped silhouette etched against the orange sky. A closer look would reveal a chubby man standing on
his unmistakable white-thatched head. Ben-Gurion was irri-
tated. Couldn't a man draw blood to his brain without people
gaping at him?

What did he expect? Paula snapped. "Let him open a circus.
So at least he will make more money." And he would never sit
still any more. Walk, walk, walk! In Sde Boker he hiked six
kilometers in the morning and six in the evening. At home in
Tel Aviv, he paced the corridors for hours, counting every stride
with his fingers and forcing everyone to remain silent so he
wouldn't lose count! Feldenkrais, Paula felt, was wasting her
husband's time. What did "Hocus-Pocus" want—some cheap
publicity? Anyway, she feared that he was drawing too close to
Ben-Gurion. He had almost become a confidant—some people
even thought a kind of Rasputin. Perhaps, but for his services,
he received little more than "cheap publicity." When Ben-Gurion once learned that Feldenkrais had not been paid, he promised to tell his aide, Chaim Yisraeli, to "take care of it." But the
therapist remained unpaid, and nobody ever brought up the
question again.

Paid or not, however, Feldenkrais worked on Ben-Gurion
until the Old Man's back pain vanished. And soon, for the first
time in years, the Prime Minister could sleep a full night and
climb into a car without help. In the Knesset he no longer
gripped the arms of his chair to jerk his body up, trying to suppress a grimace of agony. Thrilled that he was fit again to pursue
his mission at full speed, he showed off his new mobility by
running up to the speaker's desk faster than any other Knesset
member.

Unfortunately, Ben-Gurion wasn't in motion on the cold gloomy
day of October 29, 1957. He sat behind the long table in the
center of the chamber-jotting notes on a piece of paper as he
listened to a colleague pontificate on some point of foreign policy. Meanwhile, in the circular spectators' gallery overhead, students, soldiers, tourists and curious passersby watched the
Knesset in action. Suddenly a young man in the top row rose
and hurled a small egg-shaped object that barely missed Ben-
Gurion's head and dropped about a yard behind him. The Prime
Minister jumped up and knelt behind his chair, and for a mo-

ment there was stunned silence, broken only by a cry from the gallery: "What *chutzpah!* Throwing a stone here!"

The "stone" then exploded. Screams, gasps, moans. Moshe Shapiro, minister for religious affairs, slumped in his chair, blood oozing from his head and stomach. Golda Meir clutched one of her legs. And Ben-Gurion, ignoring wounds in his arm and foot, cried, "Sit down! Stay in your seats!"

Meanwhile, doctors present rushed to help the wounded, and police hustled away the "stone-thrower," a young Jew with a history of mental illness, who claimed the Jewish Agency owed him money. The siren of an ambulance soon echoed through the acrid-smelling, shrapnel-pocked hall, and Ben-Gurion was helped outside. But, waving off an ambulance, he stoically hobbled to an automobile, which rushed him to Hadassah Hospital.

Not serious, the doctors reported after removing the shrapnel, but he would have to remain in the hospital for a while. Ben-Gurion was grateful that he was alive and that his colleagues would also recover. But he was alarmed. This was not an Arab terrorist attack. A Jew had tried to kill him. How could a Jew do this? Even a *meshuggener.* The day after the shooting, he propped himself up in bed and wrote a letter to the parents of the would-be assassin:

"I know that you regret, as do all the people of Israel, the abominable and senseless crime that your son committed yesterday. You are not to blame. You are living in Israel, where justice reigns, and I wish you and your sons good luck. May you succeed in educating the rest of your children to do good deeds and to love Israel."

Paula couldn't be kept from his side even when she herself contracted the flu. She simply moved into a room in the hospital one floor above that of Ben-Gurion, without telling him about her illness, and continued to visit him every morning and evening, carrying shopping bags full of food and reading material and wearing her usual street apparel, even a hat. Let him think she was coming from home. Why worry him when he was so weak? Some who knew her well were puzzled. Had she changed that much since those days when she would write Ben-Gurion desperate letters wailing about her every ailment, real or otherwise? Or did she hope to impress him with her extraordinary thoughtfulness when he would eventually learn of her "plot"?

A far more serious plot was hatched one day when Ben-Gurion's friends learned what happened to Nehemiah. He had driven to Tel Aviv on business, and while heading back to Jerusalem he struck a bicyclist, knocking him unconscious. He drove the man to the hospital, then went home. The next day, when Argov did not turn up for work or call in, a security officer went to his apartment, peered through a shutter and saw him with his head resting on his desk and a pistol beside him.

Why had Nehemiah Argov killed himself? When Ben-Gurion had returned from Sde Boker and asked Argov to work for him again, Nehemiah joyously told a colleague: "I would like to die now. I have reached the peak of happiness. What further purpose is there in life?"

But his euphoria waned after a love affair with a younger woman went sour, and it vanished when he learned that Ben-Gurion had barely escaped death while he was not around to protect him. Finally, adding to his sense of guilt, he thought the bicyclist would die (though he would, in fact, live). In a farewell letter addressed to "My dear friends," he pleaded for the victim's forgiveness and left all his money to the man's family. He could "not bear living in the circumstances which have occurred" and was "not worthy to be mourned."

But his friends did mourn him—all but Ben-Gurion, who did not know he was dead. On the advice of the Prime Minister's doctors, news of the tragedy was kept from him. Thus, the "plot." The Voice of Israel received instructions not to broadcast news of the suicide, and the newspapers were asked to print a few copies with no mention of it. A messenger picked up these specially printed copies and delivered them to Ben-Gurion. But the day after the funeral a group of aides visited him and Dayan bluntly said, "We have bad news for you. Nehemiah is dead."

Ben-Gurion turned pale and cried, "What?!" Dayan then related the tragic story and handed him a farewell letter from Argov personally addressed to the Prime Minister, who, with trembling fingers, tore open the envelope and silently read it . . .

No, this was not the deed of a strong man, but he was no longer strong. And Ben-Gurion needed strong men around him. On the other hand, the "stiff-necked" Jewish people needed Ben-Gurion, who ranked in his opinion with Moses and King David as one of the three greatest men of all time . . .

When Ben-Gurion finished reading, he put down the letter and stared straight ahead, his face taut, furrowed with pain, the

color of curdled milk. Then he turned toward the wall and
sobbed. A feeling of guilt deepened his sorrow, and later he
would broodingly badger colleagues for clues to Argov's motive
for ending his life.

Hardly had Ben-Gurion checked out of the hospital when he
limped into the Knesset and said in a broken voice: "I doubt if
two men ever worked so closely together before. . . . And if I
had some share in the achievements [of this decade] it was the
result of [our] partnership. . . . Permit me to stand here alone,
silent, for a brief moment, in respect for his memory."

And all members of the Knesset stood and remained silent
too, honoring the memory of the Prime Minister's military secretary. But some, especially those out of favor, were resentful.
Did one have to fill Ben-Gurion's inkwell to earn such reverence?

It was now time to woo the world that still chillingly recalled
peering into the abyss after the Sinai campaign. Israel, as always, needed foreign allies and, in any case, had to clear the
path that would one day lead to universal redemption. And in
the next few years Ben-Gurion wooed passionately. His campaign was perhaps symbolized by Dag Hammarskjöld's visit to
Israel shortly after peace had settled over the Middle East. Ben-
Gurion was resolved to win the sympathy of this man who had
so angrily condemned the Sinai attack, for he did, after all, represent the world that Israel was destined to help redeem.

Paula, however, seemed more interested in redeeming the
man. At an official dinner she stared at her distinguished guest
as he sipped his soup and asked, "Hammarskjöld, why don't
you get married?"

The Secretary General, spoon in shaky hand, smiled and replied that he had no time.

"Ben-Gurion also had no time, yet he found me!"

"But why should I get married?" asked Hammarskjöld in astonishment.

"Personally I don't care whether you do or not. But married
people have trouble at home with the children and problems of
money and making a living. You would have so much trouble of
your own, you wouldn't have time to give us any!"

Later, in Sde Boker, there was another dinner. Paula sat Hammarskjöld down in the communal dining hall, placed a bowl of
tomatoes, onions and radishes before him and commanded:
"Eat! Don't talk!" After the "feast," however, Paula remem-

bered the cause and made a nearly supreme sacrifice. She let the Secretary General have the bathroom in the family cabin all to himself while she and the Prime Minister washed and brushed their teeth in the kitchen sink.

The next morning Hammarskjöld dragged himself along on a six-kilometer hike with Ben-Gurion and Yehoshua Cohen, whom the Prime Minister jocularly introduced as a "former terrorist." One can only speculate how the Swedish visitor would have reacted if he had known that he was matching strides with the assassin of Count Bernadotte, a countryman who had represented the very organization that Hammarskjöld now headed! But the Ben-Gurions had not done too badly. The Secretary General left Israel alive—if a bit humbled—and more sympathetic to Israel than he had been before. He clung to "rich impressions," he said. Also to bachelorhood.

Though satisfied with the Hammarskjöld visit, Ben-Gurion wanted to give the people of the world, at least the Third World, more than impressions. With the borders now calm, he would begin casting a light unto the nations. He was driven, however, not only by Israel's destiny but by the need to keep Nasser from fulfilling his. The Egyptian president dreamed of reigning over the whole Islamic-African world, with the support of the Communist bloc, and if he succeeded, Israel would be left with almost no backing in the United Nations.

Nasser had already helped to block an opening to the People's Republic of China. This was a heavy blow to Ben-Gurion, who, defying American pressure, had recognized Peking without being recognized in return. He had delved into Chinese history and culture and even studied Buddhist thought. China, he was convinced, would inevitably evolve into the greatest power on earth, and its support would be invaluable. The Chinese leaders were militant Communists, yes, but the best way to moderate them, Ben-Gurion felt, was to talk and trade with them, not force them into snarling isolation. David Hacohen, the Israeli envoy to Burma, had actually met in Rangoon with Chinese Premier Chou En-lai, who hinted at diplomatic and economic ties. But Chou, at a conference of Third World nations in Bandung, Indonesia, in 1955, was lured into Nasser's camp.

Now Nasser was courting the Africans, who had started to break away from the colonial powers, and Israel had to move swiftly. In spring 1957, Ben-Gurion called in Ehud Avriel, and the air was almost as electric as it had been during the 1948 war when he sent Avriel off to Europe to seek arms. Avriel reminded him of that meeting a decade earlier and Ben-Gurion replied:

"You are right. I must once more ask you to accept a mission as crucial, perhaps, as in 1948."

He turned to the huge map of the Middle East on the wall behind him, pointing to a tiny white spot—Israel—an island in an enemy sea of bold color.

"Nasser," said the Prime Minister, "has formed an alliance of Arab countries against us. He is working hard to gather all the Moslem states together in a union against us. We must prevent the development of a third encirclement—of the countries in Asia and those to emerge soon in Africa." Unlike the Asians, African leaders "are Christians, they know history, the Bible and the Jewish fate. . . . It does not matter that we are a small country; on the contrary, they will understand that we can have no desire to dominate them. . . . We shall help them and they will help us by opening for us new horizons, by breaking the siege."

Avriel left on his new assignment—Israel's ambassador to Ghana and Liberia.

Ben-Gurion thus embarked on an adventure almost as spiritually rewarding as the Ingathering and the pioneering of the Negev. In the next few years, as new states sprouted, hundreds of Israeli experts fanned out all over Black Africa and thousands of Africans streamed into Israel. A kibbutz farmer would bury his naked feet in frugal African soil and teach a peasant how to plant cotton or corn. A public-health specialist, stripped to the waist, would sweatingly supervise the building of a bamboo clinic in the dark lushness of the jungle. An engineer would squat outside an adobe hut helping a young apprentice to blueprint plans for a new road to market.

In Israel itself, eager black fingers scribbled notes in the university classroom, while heads covered with embroidered African caps absorbed some of the prophets' teachings together with algebraic equations. Black politicians, educators and poets also came, to be greeted by a prophet thankful for the chance to prove that his Biblical forebear, Isaiah, was right.

But Joshua was right, too. Israel must be secure so it could carry out its mission. And its Afro-Asian friends could be a bridge not only to destiny, but to Dulles. Ben-Gurion still hoped to forge an alliance with the United States, but President Eisenhower, heeding Dulles' advice, continued to balk while nursing his

Sinai grudge. Nevertheless, the Prime Minister saw an opening in 1957, when Syria began firing across the Israeli border with Soviet weapons. The Kremlin was, in fact, stuffing Syria with arms and seemed ready that summer to devour it.

Playing upon America's dread of the Red peril, Ben-Gurion wrote Dulles: "The establishment of Syria as a base for international Communism is one of the most dangerous events that has befallen the free world in our time. . . . Everything depends on a firm and purposeful position taken by the United States." And of course, Israel would be glad to help in any way it could.

Thanks for the advice, replied Washington, but it didn't need any. The United States clearly favored a Middle East defense alliance against Soviet aggression but, because of Arab pressure, Israel would be frozen out of it. So Ben-Gurion decided to form an "alliance" of his own. He glanced at his great map, and his eyes roved to the periphery of the Arab world—Iran, Turkey, Ethiopia. They were not Arab countries, and all feared Communism and its Egyptian ally. Ben-Gurion called in his agents and in late 1957 and early 1958 they secretly flew off to see whether the leaders of the three countries would cooperate with Israel in warding off the twin dangers. All three were willing to listen. Ben-Gurion followed up with a letter to Shah Pahlavi of Iran. The Jews, he wrote, would always remember King Cyrus, who centuries earlier had protected the Jews. The Shah warmly replied: He "cherished the memory of Cyrus' policy and planned to continue this ancient tradition."

Ben-Gurion was delighted. He would soon have allies! And if the United States approved, how could it refuse to give Israel arms and security guarantees? But in the summer of 1958, while the Prime Minister was forging his Middle Eastern and African links, tanks operated by local disciples of Nasser blew the pro-West governments in Iraq and Lebanon out of power and were threatening to blast apart the Jordanian regime as well. American Marines stormed the beaches of Beirut, and task forces rushed to the Persian Gulf and Turkey. Overnight, Israel's frightened new friends moved closer to the Jewish state. The Turks were "taking [defensive] action similar to ours," Ben-Gurion happily recorded in his diary, "and are eager to coordinate their political moves with ours. We are entering historic times, and the opportunity for such action is unique."

This was the time to test Eisenhower's mood again. Surely Ike would now invite him to the White House for talks on mutual defense. On July 24, 1958, he wrote the President a note. Israel and its three allies "will be able to stand up steadfastly against Soviet expansion through Nasser." All they needed was political, moral and—of course—financial support. The next day, Ike replied that Ben-Gurion could be "confident" of his "interest in the integrity and independence of Israel."

Not even a hint of an invitation!

"Why doesn't the President invite me," Ben-Gurion fumed in his diary, "when he invites prime ministers from countries big and small?"

Finally, word from Dulles. If Israel wanted to form an alliance of its own, fine.

Ben-Gurion wasted no time. On July 28, dressed in khaki to make people think he intended to visit Israeli army bases, he was driven by a circuitous route to the airport, where he secretly boarded a plane with several aides. He was excited. His last clandestine trip—to Paris—had ended with the momentous decision to attack Egypt. What prize would he bring home now from Turkey? Little could he have imagined when he sailed from Turkish shores as a student that he would one day return as the prime minister of a Jewish state. Still, the need for secrecy somewhat tempered his elation. It seemed rather shameful that even friendly nations in the region feared to reveal their close ties with Israel, like a man afraid to be seen with the woman he is courting. A virtuous woman yet!

The next morning, in Ankara, Turkish Premier Adnan Menderes entered the luxurious guesthouse where Ben-Gurion was staying, and the two men, nibbling on Turkish snacks, discussed the Russian and Nasserite threats to the region. They agreed to consult often on these dangers, exchange ambassadors and extend trade. Little more was said, and nothing was written, but the implications of the meeting were clear: If either nation was in real danger, the other would come to its aid. Here in a sense was the tie with the Turks that Ben-Gurion had so avidly sought before World War I.

A few months later, in early 1959, Ben-Gurion sent Chaim Herzog, his chief of military intelligence, to Teheran, where the officer haggled with the Shah and gleefully strode out with a signed—and secret—agreement for "military cooperation." When Herzog returned with the accord, the Prime Minister kissed him on the cheek, a gesture that even Paula seldom rated. And while on a trip to Burma in 1961, according to an aide, Ben-Gurion stopped off in Teheran for a clandestine meeting with the Shah to personally reinforce the pact. The Arabs were now outflanked to the north and the east.

That left Ethiopia in the south. One of the African nations
benefiting from Israel's technical-aid program, it also agreed to
jointly resist Nasserism. Israel would, in fact, help save Em-
peror Haile Selassie's throne—not from Nasser, however, but
from some of the monarch's own officers, who, in 1960, seized
the royal palace in Addis Ababa while the black-bearded em-
peror was out of the country. Selassie used the Israeli embassy
radio in Liberia, where he was visiting, to find out what was
happening back home and to rally his forces, and soon his slight
beribboned form was firmly planted on the throne again—a
most grateful ally.

In the steamy summer of 1958, Israel needed every ally it could
find. Although it had won the Sinai Campaign, Egypt, ironically,
was now more powerful than before. Russia was pouring in new
arms, and Syria, having merged with Egypt in February 1958 to
form the United Arab Republic, was providing new blood. Also,
Lebanon and Iraq had fallen under Nasserite influence, and
Jordan was tottering. As the danger grew, Ben-Gurion met with
his lieutenants to decide whether Israel should invade the west
bank of the Jordan if Hussein toppled. The Prime Minister
longed to revive all of Biblical Israel, if only to secure the state.
But, he wondered, would he be securing the state—or sabotaging it? This dilemma had been tormenting Ben-Gurion ever
since the 1948 war (and would continue to perplex Israel down
to the present day). Pragmatism finally triumphed. He wrote in
his diary on August 19, 1958: "Our burning problem is lack of
Jews, not lack of territory." On October 7 he added: "The addition of one million Arabs to Israel is liable to bring about the
end of the state."

Since the Arabs had a higher birth rate than the Jews, and the
Jews were, it seemed, hopelessly divided, "the Arabs would
eventually rule the country." Of course, the Jews could force
them to flee, but this they would never do. Jewish destiny, after
all, was to enlighten the nations, not brutalize them.

Ben-Gurion thus cabled Ambassador Eban that if Jordan fell
to the Nasserites, Israel would take only limited action to
achieve small border revisions. The real question was how to
keep Hussein on the throne, and to help do this Ben-Gurion
agreed to let British planes fly over Israel with troops and supplies for Jordan—until, frightened by Russian threats, he ordered Britain to halt its flights. Both Britain and the United
States were furious. Ben-Gurion, Eisenhower charged, had
"surrendered" to the Soviet Union. Now Ben-Gurion was fu-

rious. Would Ike come to Israel's aid if Russia attacked it? Would he give arms to Israel so it could at least fight back? Was Jordan's survival more important than Israel's? Washington's reply was clear—even Israel's peripheral alliance was not enough to pry open America's arsenal. "Eisenhower's honor has declined," the Prime Minister groused to colleagues.

Ben-Gurion now wistfully looked to France for more arms, but General Charles de Gaulle became president in May 1958 and soon started to loosen French ties with Israel. No more quiet deals between friends. And the ties might grow even looser if, as Ben-Gurion predicted, the Algerian rebels won their struggle for independence, for De Gaulle would surely try to improve relations with the Arabs. After a rebuff from Britain as well, Ben-Gurion, in his desperation, invited the Soviet ambassador to Sde Boker, gave him a locally woven rug, and even asked *him* for weapons. The ambassador's frozen stare flashed the expected *"Nyet."* Finally, the Prime Minister began dickering with West Germany, though he knew such talks would set off a political earthquake at home. He remembered the one that shook Israel when he closed a deal for German reparations a few years earlier.

Shimon Peres charmed German Defense Minister Josef Strauss with the same skill that had untied the strings of the French purse—though *Schnapps* and a sense of guilt replaced champagne and war camaraderie as the catalysts of understanding. Would Israel like to buy two World War II submarines? Israel would, Peres replied, and Chief of Staff Dayan prepared to join him in the talks. But the news leaked, and the earth shook. The protesting leftists in Ben-Gurion's cabinet slammed their fists on the table, and the thumps sent tremors throughout Israel. The head of the Israeli army going hat in hand to Germany to plead for submarines once commanded by Hitler? Begin's voice added to the rumble, and Ben-Gurion was forced to cancel Dayan's trip. In the end, Israel did buy two submarines—from Britain.

Soon afterwards, Israel quaked with even greater intensity. This time Ben-Gurion apparently tried another ploy. Speaking in a low, almost inaudible voice at a cabinet meeting on December 14, just loud enough for the stenographer to record his words, Ben-Gurion proposed that Israel sell its own small arms to several countries, and he listed them with slurring speed. Everybody agreed that Israel needed the money and thus approved the proposal—until they learned to their dismay that one of the countries was West Germany!

We will never accept such a deal, cried the leftists.

But they already did! replied Ben-Gurion, showing them the minutes of the meeting.

A trick!

A triumph! Ben-Gurion retorted. The Germans acknowledged that the Jews can produce something superior to theirs.

This tremor too gradually abated. And shortly, German soldiers were firing Jewish machine guns.

By early 1960, Ben-Gurion feared that if he didn't get more sophisticated weapons soon, Arab soldiers would be firing Russian missiles. Egypt seemed poised for another strike, and the Syrian border was aflame. Free-world leaders, the Prime Minister felt, would understand Israel's perilous position if he personally gazed into their doubting eyes and explained. They would listen to him because they would realize that Israel was important for the world; because their conscience told them to.

First he must see Ike. Searching his files, he pulled out a letter from Brandeis University announcing that he was being awarded an honorary degree. Just the thing. White House aides were notified that Ben-Gurion would visit the country to accept the degree. Awkwardly they suggested that if the Prime Minister had the time, let him stop by the White House. Ben-Gurion had the time. And in early March 1960, after dining or taking tea with such luminaries as Vice-President Nixon, Nelson Rockefeller and his old friend Dag Hammarskjold, Ben-Gurion was ushered into the Oval Office. There was the man he had greeted fifteen years earlier in Germany. Then he had urged a heedful general to help ravaged people find a new life; now he must urge a harried president to help them preserve this life. Ben-Gurion droned on about the Arab lust for revenge, the Israeli longing for peace, the Arab deal with Russia, the Israeli debt to the dead. Israel was in danger. It needed arms; it needed missiles.

The President was vague, even cool, though he promised never to let the Arabs annihilate Israel. Later, Ben-Gurion asked Secretary of State Christian Herter whether Israel could expect to receive the arms it needed from the United States.

"This is a fair assumption," replied Herter. But it wasn't a correct one.

On the morning of March 14, Ben-Gurion stepped out of his suite on the thirty-seventh floor of the Waldorf-Astoria Hotel in New York and climbed down two flights of stairs to another suite that was roped off to keep scores of journalists and photographers at bay. As Ben-Gurion entered, a tall man with a crinkly smile on his frozen face rushed to greet him and vigorously shook his hand. It was a handshake that would again send Ben-Gurion reeling back fifteen years, that would conjure up memories of man's basest moment, yet stir hope for his ultimate redemption. A historic handshake that would both sicken and soothe the Jewish soul.

Ben-Gurion had been secretly planning to meet Chancellor Adenauer for some time, and since both were to be in the United States on unofficial visits simultaneously, the meeting would finally take place. Powerful forces drove these two old men into each other's arms. Adenauer had six million murdered Jews on his mind, and Ben-Gurion had two million menaced ones on his. German reparations were running out, and now the Prime Minister would seek long-term economic and military aid, regardless of the anti-German sentiment at home. And he expected to get it, deeply respecting Adenauer for the moral courage reflected in his public vow to do all he could to make amends for the Holocaust.

Adenauer, he would write, "will be remembered in German and European history as one of the great statesmen of our time."

Shimon Peres and Defense Minister Strauss had already reached a secret preliminary accord that would deluge Israel, free of charge, with such military ware as aircraft, submarines, helicopters and air-to-air missiles. But how much money should Ben-Gurion ask in economic aid, for industry, shipping, agriculture? A two-hundred-fifty-million-dollar loan over ten years, his experts suggested. But the night before the meeting with Adenauer, Yitzhak Navon protested, "Not enough! Ask for a billion."

"Nonsense! He would refuse."

"Ben-Gurion, if you don't ask for a billion," Navon persisted, "you will be making a grievous mistake."

As Ben-Gurion left his suite for the meeting, he turned to Navon and said, "All right, for your sake, I'll ask for five hundred million."

Partly appeased, Navon told the interpreter: "If Ben-Gurion hesitates, you say 'five hundred million.' "

Ben-Gurion laughed, but he was deadly serious as he sat down with Adenauer. "Hitler almost murdered the State of Israel," he said. "One cannot talk of compensation, for there is no compensation for the loss of human life. It is possible to help in reducing the damage. And it is here we want your help." He then asked for five hundred million dollars over a period of ten years.

"We will help you for moral reasons and for reasons of political logic," replied Adenauer vaguely. "We will not desert you."

"I understand that you agree in principle to my proposals."

"That is correct."

And Israel would also get free arms from Germany?

That was correct, too.

Ben-Gurion felt vindicated for his pragmatism. Many people, he told Adenauer, had criticized him for meeting with the Chancellor and distinguishing between the new Germany and the old. "But this view is not in the spirit of Judaism—my conscience is clear. I feel that I have done my duty as a Jew and as a human being."

After the talk, both men walked out with tears in their eyes. Ben-Gurion exultantly reported to Navon, "I asked for five hundred million dollars and he agreed!"

"Why didn't you ask for a billion?" replied Navon.

En route home, Ben-Gurion stopped off in London to see Prime Minister Macmillan, and he proved to be Eisenhower's match —stiffly correct and just as "even-handed." He was unwilling to supply arms to Israel.

Britain, however, wasn't a total loss. As usual when he was there, Ben-Gurion lodged in a small Oxford hotel and lingered in his favorite bookstore, ordering forty books on the philosophies of the Far East, India and Greece, which would ease his disappointment. But even the wisest philosophy could not erase the irony of his trip. For all the prestige and goodwill he had gained in the United States and Britain, the only country that concretely offered to help Israel survive was the one that had tried to systematically murder the whole Jewish nation only fifteen years earlier. But he was ready to visit every country in the world until he got the arms, money and diplomatic support he so urgently needed.

Indeed, hardly had he flown home to a rousing if rainy welcome when he planned new journeys. He even asked the Soviet ambassador, who was at the airport to greet him, if he couldn't arrange a meeting with Russian leader Nikita Khrushchev. Meanwhile, he must see De Gaulle. His fears about France seemed to be justified. After offering to negotiate with the Algerian rebels, France was already cooling toward Israel, though, Ben-Gurion convinced himself, the French foreign ministry and not the General was at fault. Great men like De Gaulle, Churchill and himself could, in any case, be excused for pursuing national goals that might conflict with their personal sentiments or even their moral codes.

To Ben-Gurion, De Gaulle was an even greater man than Churchill. For while Churchill had rallied his people from near-defeat to glorious victory in World War II, they were eager to follow him. De Gaulle had, on the contrary, confronted *his* people, dragging and shaming them into resistance. Nor would the French leader compromise with his people after the war, accepting the reins of government only when they concluded that he alone could save them. Was not De Gaulle the soul of France —as Ben-Gurion was the soul of Israel?

Yet Ben-Gurion had hesitated to meet with De Gaulle until now, even though Yaacov Tsur, the Israeli ambassador in Paris, had long urged such a meeting. He felt a strange awe before the General, it seems, the kind that many people felt before *him.* Perhaps each man perceived the messianic qualities in the other. But if a messiah knew how to deal with mere mortals, how did one messiah deal with another? Especially when the other was as proud, aloof—and tall—as De Gaulle, whom Ben-Gurion would be facing eye to tie. The Prime Minister apparently recoiled before the prospect of emerging as the lesser god. The aides of both leaders worried, too, because both were obstinate, if not immovable. What if the meeting disintegrated in argument and injured ego?

But now, in the summer of 1960, Ben-Gurion would see De Gaulle regardless, for Israel's ultimate security was at stake. France had earlier agreed to secretly help Israel build a nuclear reactor, but now it halted this aid. This installation, De Gaulle was to write later, "would convert uranium into plutonium from which, one bright day, atomic bombs could emerge." Aid would continue only if Israel agreed to international inspection.

Ben-Gurion was crestfallen. Inspection? He didn't want the world to know that Israel even *had* a nuclear reactor!

At noon, June 14, 1960, Ben-Gurion, his wife and his entourage ambled up the steps of the Élysée Palace in Paris between two motionless rows of Republican Guards who, resplendent in three-cornered hats and shiny black boots, presented their glistening sabers. President and Madame De Gaulle greeted their guests with Gallic warmth, the General stooping slightly in a gallant attempt, it seemed, to diminish his figure in deference to the short, tubby Prime Minister. Soon all were seated at a flower-decorated banquet table in a huge reception room illuminated by the glow of tinkling chandeliers. Paula, matronly chic in her six-year-old black suit, imbibed the elegance of the moment. She looked to her left—President De Gaulle. To her right—a gentleman whom she did not know. She addressed him: "Tell me, please, who are you and what is your occupation?"

Slightly taken aback, he replied, "I am Maurice Couve de Murville, the Foreign Minister of France."

"Oh!"

Then, through an interpreter sitting behind them, De Gaulle began speaking to Paula in French.

"I know that you speak English," she interrupted. "You simply don't want to because you're angry with the British for what they did to you in the war. Well, you're right!"

Israelis sitting nearby who heard the remark froze as they watched for the General's reaction to this allusion to his differences with the British in World War II. They breathed again only when De Gaulle smiled in amusement.

Later during the lunch, Paula's voice reverberated around the hall: "Ben-Gurion, you've already had one portion of ice cream. That's enough!" Caught in mid-swallow, Ben-Gurion was presumably relieved when De Gaulle finally raised his glass for a toast:

"You symbolize in your person, Monsieur Ben-Gurion, the amazing rebirth, the pride and prosperity of Israel; to me, you are one of the greatest statesmen of this century."

Ben-Gurion was overwhelmed. De Gaulle thought that? He would go him one better. Rising, he replied, "It is *you* who are the greatest statesman of our time." Then he humbly added: "It was the Jewish people, not I, who created the State of Israel."

Over coffee in the beautiful tree-shaded garden, De Gaulle spoke to Ben-Gurion about Israel: "Monsieur le Président, tell me what your real ambitions are for the frontiers of Israel. I promise to keep it secret."

"If you had asked me that fifteen years ago," Ben-Gurion said, apparently sincere, "I would have answered: 'I want the State of Israel to include the hills of Jordan and all the land up to the

Litani River in Lebanon.' But since you're asking me today, I'll tell you quite frankly that I am more concerned with immigration and peace problems. I can content myself with the present frontiers if we can attain peace and bring in more Jews. . . . We want to double the number."

De Gaulle smiled and called two of his ministers to his table. "What do you think," he said with a doubtful twinkle in his eyes. "Prime Minister Ben-Gurion is not satisfied with two million Jews. He wants people more than he wants territory."

(In his memoirs, De Gaulle claims that Ben-Gurion "revealed to me his intention of extending" Israel's frontiers "at the earliest opportunity" and that he urged the Prime Minister "not to do so." But Israeli officials deny that Ben-Gurion told De Gaulle he had such an intention.)

The President then asked if Israel was "really in serious danger."

It was, Ben-Gurion replied. But President Eisenhower had promised not to let the Arabs annihilate Israel.

"Neither will France!" the Frenchman declared.

He would continue shipping arms to Israel, he promised. . . . But the atomic reactor was a more complex matter. He would negotiate the issue in the coming weeks.

The Israeli leader was delighted with the success of his trip; each man had appreciated the genius of the other.

Ben-Gurion was less delighted with the aftermath of his visit. Shimon Peres flew to Paris and reached a nuclear accord with the French, calling for the supply of any materials on order, but no new aid. And when the news leaked in December 1960, the world press suddenly exploded in huge headlines: "Israel building a reactor!" "An atomic bomb within five years!" No!, Ben-Gurion bellowed, Israel was *not* making atomic bombs. But eyebrows arched skeptically in Washington, and in January 1961, American Ambassador Ogden Reid went to see Ben-Gurion in Sde Boker. What would Israel do with the plutonium it produced? Could outside scientists inspect the reactor? Did Israel plan to make the bomb?

"You must talk to us as equals, or not talk to us at all!" the Prime Minister growled. And he curtly replied to Reid's questions: Plutonium always went back to the uranium seller; no snoopers, though friendly scientists could eventually come; only one reactor was planned, and it would not turn out bombs. . . . What did the United States want from Israel anyway?

Reid told him—immediate inspection by American scientists. Ben-Gurion reluctantly agreed to let two scientists visit the secret site. If he refused, American pressure, he feared, might shatter Israel's whole nuclear program. And surely, with John F. Kennedy about to move into the White House, now was the time to court the United States with new vigor.

Ben-Gurion was, indeed, so eager to redeem Kennedy's campaign promises to Israel that he demanded to see the new president almost before the man could settle into his rocking chair. Israeli diplomats were incredulous. Not a single foreign leader had met with Kennedy yet. He hadn't even formulated his policies; anyway, he wanted to keep the Arabs off his aching back for a while. But when Ben-Gurion insisted, the diplomats conveyed the "demand"—only to receive a terse reply that the President would see Ben-Gurion only in June, six months later.

"I can't wait," Ben-Gurion howled. "I must see him *now!*"

Canadian Prime Minister John Diefenbaker "cooperated," inviting Ben-Gurion on a state visit to his country. Muttering under their breath, White House aides agreed to squeeze him in right afterward—in late May. (He couldn't wait until June!) And then only for an *unofficial* talk in New York, where Kennedy would be stopping on the way to Europe for a summit meeting with Khrushchev.

"It is hoped," presidential aides wrote in a memorandum, "that this arrangement will produce a minimum of publicity with respect to the President's talk with Ben-Gurion."

Ben-Gurion sized up with uncertainty the slim, youthful man with a shock of sandy hair. The Prime Minister had met Senator Kennedy years before and had not been very impressed. He seemed too young and inexperienced to hold a top political position. Now Kennedy was president of the most powerful nation on earth.

But if Ben-Gurion harbored doubts about Kennedy's presidential stature, he was pleased by the tenor of the meeting. American scientists, Kennedy said, were satisfied that Israel's reactor was designed for peaceful purposes. He pressed Ben-Gurion, however, to take back a token number of Arab refugees. The Prime Minister's advisers had warned him that Kennedy would propose this. Agree to do it, they said. The Arabs would surely reject the idea, and it was a cheap way to win the President's goodwill. Ben-Gurion was hesitant, but he finally agreed.

Kennedy beamed. "Thank you, Mr. Prime Minister. Blessed be the peacemaker!"

As Ben-Gurion rose to leave, the President, now bursting with goodwill, placed his hand on the Prime Minister's shoulder, took him aside and said: "I owe my victory to the support of the American Jews. How can I repay them?"

Ben-Gurion was stunned by his candor. And delighted. The President of the United States felt obligated to the Jews. He replied diplomatically, "Do what is best for the free world."

But as he left, Ben-Gurion wondered whether he himself had done what was best for Israel. He had reluctantly agreed to take back some Arab refugees, but he must somehow renege on his promise. After the meeting he told newsmen that he had reached a "large measure of agreement with the President on the Arab refugee problem." Since he said nothing about any Israeli concessions, the Arabs soon screamed that Kennedy had sold them out, and Washington, terrified, furiously denied there was any agreement. Israeli diplomats shuddered. Their boss had barged in as an unwelcome guest and now departed leaving ashes on the rug!

But not before another president, Harry S Truman, who had pulled a rug of his own from under the State Department at Israel's birth, came to see Ben-Gurion. The Prime Minister recalled that feat and told his visitor, "I don't know what the Americans are saying about you. . . . But in the eyes of the Jewish people you will live forever!"

The tough former president had coolly ordered the dropping of atomic bombs on Japan, decisively hurled troops against the Communists in Korea, and daringly fired General MacArthur. But now he broke into tears.

No less sentimental was a meeting with Winston Churchill, whom Ben-Gurion visited in London on his way back to Israel. As he entered Churchill's secluded home, he was excited by this chance to exchange views at last with the man who, he felt, had embodied all the virtues displayed by the British people when they stood alone under a rain of bombs. But he gazed with sadness and compassion at the old warrior hunched in his chair, pathetically grandiose in striped trousers and morning coat, a man drained of energy and waiting to die. Churchill, now eighty-six, perhaps sensed Ben-Gurion's sorrow as the visitor sat down beside him. Yes, he was an old man. . . .

Old? After all, said Ben-Gurion, "Moses lived to a hundred and twenty."

And then they talked about Moses and rambled past the milestones of Jewish and British history—the Balfour Declaration, Chaim Weizmann's work, the rise of modern Israel, Churchill's devotion to Zionism.

"You are a brave leader of a great nation," said Churchill.

"And your stand against the Germans in World War II will be remembered for generations," replied his guest.

But Churchill was no longer entirely lucid, and Ben-Gurion left depressed. He had in the past tried in many ways to pattern himself after this great leader. Now, apparently frightened, he told Yitzhak Navon, who had been with him, "Look, Yitzhak, what can happen to a man when he gets old."

In Paris, Ben-Gurion dropped in again on President De Gaulle, who embraced Ben-Gurion more warmly than ever and described Israel not only as a friend but as an "ally." With good reason. Three months earlier, the Prime Minister had proved his friendship for De Gaulle by helping to save the General's life. An agent of French right-wing forces in Algeria asked an Israeli friend in Paris whether Israel would collaborate in a plot to assassinate De Gaulle and thus thwart his effort to give the Algerians independence. If the plot succeeded and the rightists came to power, they would ship to Israel all the arms it needed free of charge. But the moment Ben-Gurion heard of the conspiracy, he ordered his ambassador in Paris to warn De Gaulle urgently. The conspiracy failed and Ben-Gurion now received the General's gratitude.

The Prime Minister was so sold on personal diplomacy that one trip would follow another. Hardly a country in Europe, big or small, did not celebrate the coming of this powerful gnome-like man who, to the wonder of all, had carved out a state and built an "invincible" army. It is not clear, though, how many celebrated the coming of Paula, who left strewn in her wake battered egos, baffled gapes and bemused grins. During a visit to Norway, she was furious when the King asked to see only her husband. Unaware that it was tradition for an unmarried monarch to invite a guest without his wife, she raged to the chief of protocol, "The King of Sweden is much nicer than your king. . . . Is yours afraid of women?"

Israelis in the entourage gasped. One more vote lost in the General Assembly! But the following day an official invitation arrived from the King, and Paula was shortly sitting with him explaining that she was a "nurse by profession" and an "expert" in medicine. As she departed, the chief of protocol asked, "Are you pleased?"

"Of course! He's nice, your king! Why were you afraid to show him to me?"

With much of the West now won, Ben-Gurion turned East, where he had so far made few conquests, most notably Burma. In Asia were vast lands that would be ripe for redemption if they understood Israel's mission. But they knew almost nothing about Judaism or Zionism. At the same time, Israel had much to learn from Asia. Ben-Gurion felt that Buddhism was one of mankind's most rational, humanistic moral philosophies. He found no conflict between Judaism and Buddhism, since Buddhism was not a religion. The individual could expect *nirvana,* or "salvation," only by personal effort and good deeds, not by prayer to Buddha. Human selfishness was, according to Buddha, the basic cause of all evil acts.

"Just think of it," Ben-Gurion told a colleague about Buddha, "here is a man who could preach, five hundred years before Jesus, that hatred cannot be defeated by hatred, only by love."

Ben-Gurion would now go to Burma, whose prime minister, U Nu, he knew well. In 1955, Nu had visited Israel, and the two men had become friends, though Ben-Gurion reportedly demonstrated that he knew the teachings of Buddha better than he understood their spirit. Though humility is the heart of Buddhist philosophy, Ben-Gurion, at a banquet for Nu, did not hesitate to show his modest guest which one had a greater command of Buddhist literature. According to Moshe Sharett, who was present, Ben-Gurion "exploited his superiority mercilessly. U Nu was in distress. This was a clash between a European for whom Buddhism is only a subject for intellectual argument and an unsophisticated and faithful Buddhist for whom the teachings of Buddha are a way of life and spiritual atmosphere."

Ben-Gurion wanted Paula to go with him to Burma, but to his dismay, she declined. Without telling him, she would, in his absence, have an eye operation. The Prime Minister departed, and hardly had he landed in Burma in December 1961 when he was swept up in a flurry of receptions from Rangoon to Mandalay as dancing girls with flowers in their flowing black hair swirled in flickering lantern light to the beat of drums, cymbals, flutes and bamboo sticks. Evil spirits, supposedly frightened by the rhythm, fled, and good spirits prevailed. Ben-Gurion even donned the traditional Burmese dress—colored sarong, white shirt, collarless jacket and silk piece wound around the head over a thin framework made of cane. A prophet who looked like Aunt Jemima!

A prophet, nevertheless, and no one who visited several jungle villages with him could doubt it. The bush had receded and scientifically run cooperative farms now flourished on soil so fertile that a piece of bamboo lying on the ground would strike root and grow anew. Israeli technicians and Burmese trained in Israel had built these communities, and Ben-Gurion was elated. The light had pierced even the thickest jungle.

Now Ben-Gurion sought to understand better the light emanating from the East: Buddhism. He wanted to learn something that he could not find in books—how intelligent modern Buddhists viewed their faith. He mingled with shaven-headed, saffron-robed monks and asked endless questions, often improving on their answers. With two of the priests, he entered a small, dark temple in Prime Minister Nu's Rangoon residence and remained there for eight days meditating, fasting until noon each day, reading only Buddhist literature (though he insisted on scanning the daily Hebrew newspapers flown in from Israel). Concentrate, the monks told him, on one idea at a time, such as breathing technique or body control. And so for eight days Ben-Gurion did what he usually did anyway. When he emerged, pale but healthy, an aide asked him if he had learned anything. "Nonsense! Nonsense!" he replied. "I need them to teach *me* how to concentrate?"

Ben-Gurion did, however, "gain a deeper understanding of modern Buddhist thinking." Especially of the fundamental Buddhist concept, *anicca,* or "nonpermanence," which holds that "everything is in a constant state of change and constantly renews itself"; that "no man can step twice into the same river, for the second time it is not exactly the river it was."

The river of political life, Ben-Gurion would confirm on returning home, was no exception.

CHAPTER FOURTEEN

Because he was righteous in his own eyes

JOB 32:1

THE river flowed unevenly for Paula too after Ben-Gurion's return. While the Prime Minister was away, word was mysteriously leaked to reporters about Paula's eye operation, and they rushed to the hospital to interview her. She would talk, but they must not print a word—yet. The local newspapers were being sent to Ben-Gurion, and she didn't want him to worry. They must wait—until he was home.

If Paula hoped to impress her husband, she did. He was more tender to her than usual, and his tenderness was even greater after she suffered what was apparently a minor heart attack. Feeling faint while at the hairdresser's, she suddenly cried, "Call an ambulance! Quickly, before I lose consciousness!"

But before losing it, she phoned Teddy Kollek and gasped that she was blacking out. He must swear, however, not to tell her husband. Shortly the ambulance arrived—together with a deathly pale Ben-Gurion. Paula recovered swiftly, but the Prime Minister didn't.

Paula needed all the emotional support she could muster, for not only was Ben-Gurion busier than ever, but she suspected that he wasn't just working when he stayed late at the office. And sometimes he wasn't. Paula was especially worried when Doris May came from London to work for her husband shortly before the Sinai campaign. The Prime Minister and Doris had occasionally written to each other in the years since World War

II—affectionate but unromantic letters that reflected the largely intellectual nature of their relationship—and finally he invited her to come to Israel and join his staff. Doris had mixed feelings, arguing good-naturedly that "foreigners on a P.M.'s doorstep are seldom 'well-seen.' The last thing I would wish would be to give your opponents any excuse for accusing you of being too much tied to the British coattail." Nevertheless, she was his "to command."

But when Doris flew in and was given a job in Teddy Kollek's office, it was Paula who commanded. Almost every day she telephoned one of her husband's secretaries and insisted on knowing where Doris was and what she was doing. "Is she in Teddy's office—or in Ben-Gurion's? *Where is she?*"

After a few months, Doris, constantly hounded by Paula and unable to see much of the busy Prime Minister anyway, quit her job and returned to England.

But one "rival" Paula could not hound out of her husband's life was Rachel. And his ties with "that woman" would tighten, she feared, after the death of Rachel's husband in 1958. Ben-Gurion seemed to hint they might when he failed to send condolences to Rachel, who, though deeply hurt, was also somewhat flattered that Ben-Gurion had never quite forgiven her husband for marrying her.

In any case, they continued to see each other occasionally, most often at his home. The guards had orders to let Rachel in at any time, and Ben-Gurion would drop whatever he was doing and rush to the door to greet her before Paula could. They would sit alone in the living room and talk while Paula peeked in periodically, straining her ears, it seemed, for some hint of *mishegas* ("mischief"). But one conversation, apparently, was not overheard. Rachel asked Ben-Gurion if he could induce Polish officials to grant her cousin a visa to immigrate. Though the Prime Minister was usually reluctant to do special favors for anyone, he readily agreed. "For you, half the kingdom," he said, quoting a Hebrew proverb.

"Be careful," Rachel laughed, "when you used to say that, you had nothing to give. But now you have a kingdom."

"And half is yours," Ben-Gurion replied.

Another time, Rachel patched up a feud between Ben-Gurion and Shlomo Zemach, persuading the Prime Minister to visit his ailing boyhood chum, whom he embraced in a moving reunion. Once, Rachel asked Ben-Gurion to write a chapter for a book being published on the old *shtetl* of Plonsk. The editor was skeptical. How would the Prime Minister ever find time?

"I can assure you," she answered confidently, "that he will—for me." And he did.

Ben-Gurion also found time for his other great love—Renana. She and her husband, Shlomo, visited her parents almost every evening, and sometimes, after dinner, her father would even join them in educational games—quizzes, mathematical riddles from the *Scientific American,* or charades. Paula sat by, bristling with impatience. He had plenty of time for such foolishness with his daughter, but how much time did he have for *her?*

Though not as close to Amos as to Renana, Ben-Gurion was proud of him. Amos had become assistant inspector general of the Israeli police and displayed what his father viewed as an admirable spirit of independence, reminiscent of his own when he was a young man. One time, at the state funeral of an Israeli leader, the crowds had gotten out of hand and ministers found themselves caught in the crush, infuriating Ben-Gurion, who called over his son and demanded, "Are you the senior police officer here?"

"Yes, sir."

Apparently wanting everyone to understand that he played no favorites, the father cried, "This is a disgrace to the police and the nation!"

Amos saluted and stalked off, but later confronted his father at home. "I'm going to resign! You insulted me in public and I was not to blame for the chaos. Investigate what happened, and if you find that I am right you owe me an apology."

Ben-Gurion investigated and unabashedly apologized to his son.

Outside his immediate family, Ben-Gurion felt a special affinity to his first grandchild, Yariv, who was now a teen-ager. He was proud that the boy was tall, and constantly measured him, once standing him back to back with Ben-Zvi, who was also tall, to show that his grandson would never have to look up to other men—even the President. Ben-Gurion often exchanged political views with Yariv, who, seeking to escape the Old Man's huge shadow, deliberately disagreed with him on many matters in an angry assertion of independence. Yariv deeply loved Ben-Gurion, but he remembered how he missed the toys that other grandfathers gave their grandsons. Yes, he enjoyed the hundreds of books he had received, but could a child live on knowledge alone? Ben-Gurion had even wanted to give Yariv and his bride a book as a wedding gift—until Paula forced him to put his signature to a check.

On rare occasions Yariv was able to breach the wall enclosing his grandfather's soul. This happened once when the boy visited him with several schoolmates and everybody sat around till three in the morning bragging how they cheated on examinations, went AWOL in the army, and won the favors of girlfriends. Ben-Gurion, who hated small talk, suddenly refound his own youth and matched the stories of his young guests exploit for exploit. Yariv was stunned. Ben-Gurion had never seemed so relaxed and happy.

Sometimes Ben-Gurion's sister Zippora was also able to tap his inner feelings. Still a nurse, still full of energy and resolve, she visited him at his home—if Paula would let her in—or he would visit her in Haifa. There they would gaze at photographs on the wall from their youth and reminisce about their days in Plonsk, and sometimes they would even sing the melodies of Zion that they had sung then.

There were few other living memories of family life in Plonsk; almost everyone was gone and, it seemed, forgotten. His brother Avraham had died shortly after Israel's independence, crushed by the murder of his daughter, Sheindel, in the Holocaust. His sister Rivka had passed away in 1944, and Ben-Gurion had to be reminded by Rachel where she was buried. And he even forgot that his brother Michael's wife had died, asking about her as if she hadn't. Michael himself was alive, but Ben-Gurion hardly noticed. This family "black sheep" had the kind of job, the Prime Minister appeared to feel, that best suited him—operating a refreshment kiosk in Tel Aviv. Michael would die in 1962, and on the first anniversary of his death his daughter Chaya would plead with Ben-Gurion to visit the grave. But he would reply that he had no time, walking away in embarrassment when she started to cry.

"When he discussed politics," Chaya says bitterly of her uncle, "he remembered everything, even in his old age. But he always forgot about his family."

If, in general, Ben-Gurion was little obsessed with the fortunes of his own family, he constantly dwelled on the fate of his national family—those who did not live to come home, as well as those who did. A million children. Artists. Scientists. Perhaps even prophets. And yet Israeli youth seemed almost ignorant of the Holocaust, and the world was, too. Anti-Semitism was poisoning gentile minds again, cultivating, perhaps, the seeds of a new catastrophe.

It was, therefore, with hope, if not a little skepticism, that he heard one day in 1960 a report about Adolf Eichmann, Hitler's chief Jew-exterminator. He had been seen in Buenos Aires. "Bring him here dead or alive," Ben-Gurion ordered Isser Harel, as the intelligence chief was about to leave for Argentina. But he added, "Try to bring him alive."

Ben-Gurion wanted to capture the Nazi killer, not to take vengeance, he said—how could one avenge the murder of six million souls?—but to place the butcher on trial and remind his forgetful people, and the world, why a Jewish state was necessary and why it had to guard against any attempt by its Arab neighbors, in collaboration with fugitive Nazis, to destroy it. Could a more powerful condemnation of anti-Semitism, a more revealing light, be beamed unto the nations?

Harel flew off to Buenos Aires, and on May 13, 1960, while Eichmann was walking home from work, Israeli agents drove up to the curb and dragged him into their car. That night, in Jerusalem, an aide rushed to Ben-Gurion with a coded cable, "Monster in chains." The Prime Minister silently rejoiced. But would his agents be able to smuggle the "monster" out of Argentina? He called in Abba Eban and instructed him to fly in a special plane to Buenos Aires to attend Argentine Independence Day ceremonies. What Eban didn't know was that he would be flying back in a commercial airliner; the special plane would be carrying Eichmann.

On May 22, Harel returned to Jerusalem and burst into Ben-Gurion's office.

"I have brought you a gift," he said with a smile. "I have brought with me Adolf Eichmann."

Ben-Gurion's eyes shone, but he remained stonily calm, a sign that he was seething with emotion.

After two Holocaust survivors had seen the prisoner and confirmed that he was indeed Eichmann, Ben-Gurion strode into a cabinet meeting and reported the news; and to make sure it wouldn't be leaked prematurely, he refused to let anybody leave the room until the Knesset met a little later. Why diminish the impact on the world? Shortly he stood before the Knesset and said in a casual manner, apparently to enhance the drama, "A short while ago the Israeli Security Services captured one of the greatest Nazi criminals, Adolf Eichmann. . . . [He] is already in detention in Israel and will soon be put on trial here."

Muted for a moment, the Knesset suddenly exploded into bedlam as members swarmed to the rostrum and congratulated Ben-Gurion. "The praise should go to the security services, not to me," the Prime Minister insisted. And his modesty, as usual, magnified his heroic image. As did his bristling answer later to some juridical sticklers who advised him to let Eichmann be tried in an international court, since Israel might be too emotionally involved to give the Nazi a fair trial.

Hitler's Final Solution was a "unique crime without precedent or parallel in the annals of mankind," he cried, and "historic justice and the honor of the Jewish people demand" that the "monster" be tried "only by a Jewish court in the sovereign Jewish state." And most of the world agreed—though not Argentina, which was outraged by the violation of its sovereignty and demanded that Israel return Eichmann. But even Argentina was silent after public fury had cooled there.

And so Ben-Gurion sat day after day by the radio and, as he worked, listened to the mechanics of genocide prosaically grinding out of the Eichmann trial, which ended in the Nazi's conviction and hanging. All those millions lost to Israel. . . . Yes, an education for those who doubted or no longer dreamed. And in their trauma, Ben-Gurion's pupils loved him all the more. For had *he* ever doubted or stopped dreaming?

But the higher Ben-Gurion stood on his pedestal, the more vulnerable a political target he became. And even an apparent indiscretion by Police Inspector Amos threatened to stain the father's image. A private university group investigating government corruption suggested that Amos' friendship with a suspected criminal might have tainted a police investigation of the man, especially since Amos continued to see the man after his arrest. Amos sued his accusers for libel in 1959 and won the case, but the Supreme Court censured him for withholding evidence and ordered him to repay some of the damages the lower court had awarded him. Amos' future in the police force was thus rendered uncertain—and he would eventually resign and become a business executive.

Paula was enraged, and she tongue-lashed one Supreme Court justice when he dared show up at the Ben-Gurion home for a Bible-study class. But the Prime Minister seemed more sad than angry. How could anyone harbor the slightest doubt that his son was morally impeccable? The son of a man ordained by destiny to lead the struggle for an exemplary state!

Whether Amos' "indiscretion" hurt Ben-Gurion politically isn't clear, but he didn't need his son to help him earn political enemies. Reluctant to compromise on key issues, he constantly battled with his foes, many in his own government and party. His feud with the religious groups often boiled over into mutual frenzy, and the Prime Minister and the Sephardic chief rabbi even tried to topple each other from power. To Chief Rabbi Yitzhak Nissim, Ben-Gurion was seeking to smash some of the most sacred traditions of Judaism. The Prime Minister had dared to invite him to a prayerless memorial service for Chaim Weizmann on the *goyishe,* not the Jewish, date of his death! He had the gall to let a company that stayed open on the Sabbath print books about the Torah and the Bible! And he even permitted pigs to be raised in the *kibbutzim,* arguing that God, after all, "created the pig"! Sacrilege! Besides, Ben-Gurion was a "bad sport." He had "dragged" the chief rabbi's son Moshe out of the *yeshiva* (religious school) and thrown him into the army on grounds that he wasn't a full-time student—although other religious pupils were allowed to continue studying.

Ben-Gurion had other problems with the Orthodox as well. Two religious members of the cabinet resigned and even an old friend like Rabbi Maimon publicly condemned him in 1958 for refusing to accept the Orthodox definition of a Jew for census purposes. There had to be a distinction, Ben-Gurion declared, between Jewish nationality and Jewish religion. "Whoever is conscious of being a Jew is a Jew" and should be able to register with the government as one.

No, cried Maimon, any gentile not ritually converted by an Orthodox rabbi was not Jewish—though later the rabbinate would make an exception for Amos' children. (Since their mother had undergone only a modern, superficial conversion, they were not Jews under Orthodox law.) And adding to rabbinical fury was a bombshell Biblical theory that Ben-Gurion was propagating: Six hundred Hebrews, not six hundred thousand, had been enslaved in Egypt and had fled from there with Moses. The ultra-Orthodox demanded his resignation for this "blasphemy."

In the end, Ben-Gurion almost always backed off on religious matters, since he needed the support of the rabbis to lead a majority government. But the ferocious struggle was symptomatic of the political illness that afflicted the nation and would isolate the Prime Minister even within his own party.

Ben-Gurion felt that he had a painless cure for the illness: new blood. He remembered what happened several years earlier when he retired to Sde Boker—the chaos, the lack of leadership and, worst of all, the threat to the army's good name. Who could slip into his worn-out shoes and pursue his dream after he was gone? Obviously his protégés—Dayan, Peres, Eban and others —brilliant young men who placed state before party, pragmatism before socialism.

Prodded by Mapai's young secretary general, Giora Josephtal, who had climbed to the top almost overnight (and might one day have become prime minister if he had not died prematurely), Ben-Gurion inadvertently lit a fuse in early 1958 that would ultimately sizzle to an explosion and spiritually cripple Israel for years. He told a Mapai conference that a "new generation" must join the veterans in the leadership of the state. The veterans were shocked. Ambitious, arrogant "technocrats" like Dayan and Peres would steal their jobs and smash their dreams. The Mapai, the Histadrut, the kibbutz and other socialist institutions were not, as Ben-Gurion and his "youngsters" thought, simply tools to serve the state, asserted the old guard. The state was a tool to serve these institutions.

Dayan had resigned as chief of staff in January 1958 and enrolled as a student in Hebrew University, where he shared notes with a fellow student, his daughter Yael, and awaited the call to help save the nation from its puritanical patriarchs. On resigning, he had apparently hoped that Ben-Gurion would brush off a cabinet seat for him. But he dared not say so, for in Israel politicians who were openly ambitious were usually themselves brushed off. He wanted to be asked. Ben-Gurion sensed that he did, but was his protégé ready yet? Dayan's rigid resistance to the Sinai peace settlement that Ben-Gurion had finally accepted helped to sow doubt. Dayan would have to wait and be quiet.

And so Dayan waited, but he was not quiet. He marched into a Mapai convention in May 1958 and confronted an old enemy, Pinhas Lavon. Now secretary general of the Histadrut, Lavon had grown more powerful than he had been as defense minister. He demanded that the Histadrut be reorganized to give him almost equal power with the state leaders in economic affairs. Dayan railed against this effort to whittle down the authority of the state, only to trigger a furious barrage of charges and insults from his bitter foe. The veterans listened with barely suppressed smiles. They had distrusted Lavon long before Ben-Gurion had doubts about him, but they distrusted Dayan even more.

In a rage, Dayan called a meeting at a students' club in Tel

Aviv and, like a blind machine gunner, sent the whole country diving for cover. He tore into the kibbutzniks, the economists, the party hacks and the bureaucrats, but mostly into the Histadrut and the veterans. Bad workers must be fired. Wages must be frozen. More goods must roll out of the factories, Dayan cried. Israel needed a revolution. But "the men of the last generation have reached an age where they can no longer carry out revolutions. . . . These men look back proudly on their achievements of 1902 . . . before we were born . . . but we are interested in 1962."

Lavon and the veterans were shocked. Dayan had raised the flag of revolt. Why, he wasn't even a socialist! Or a democrat. He wanted to launch a military coup! The reaction chilled Ben-Gurion. "I did not believe my ears," he wrote in his diary after a colleague had hurled this charge. "I explained . . . the absurdity of this thought."

Dayan then announced that *he* would "explain" his over-heated remarks at a special Mapai meeting. But instead of explaining them, he merely repeated them, even shooting more arrows into sacred cowhide. Ben-Gurion rose, red-faced, and asked a wildly hostile audience to "respect" Dayan for his service to the country, even if his views were rather unorthodox. It now seemed clear to all that Ben-Gurion shared these views.

When Dayan continued to stir up audiences around the country, Ben-Gurion called him to his home and bluntly told him, "Outside the army one does not order people to do things." For his own good and the good of the party, he must stop making speeches. But the party had already been shredded by suspicion, bitterness, even hatred. And veterans who had always feared to fight their god now drew courage from the ominous threat to their careers.

Golda Meir, in particular, seethed with resentment. She had reluctantly given up her job as labor minister to take over Moshe Sharett's foreign ministry post before the Sinai Campaign because Ben-Gurion had urged her to. Although uneasy about "profiting" from Sharett's misfortune, she had been a loyal servant to the Prime Minister until now, backing all his policies, almost never contradicting him. Little wonder that Ben-Gurion, who was very fond of her anyway, viewed her as the perfect foreign minister. Unlike Sharett, she supported his tough policy toward the Arabs and wouldn't feel snubbed when he or his "youngsters" dealt with some foreign issue without consulting her. And why, Ben-Gurion wondered, should he consult her?

After all, Golda, though a fine politician, was not, in his view, a woman of great vision or intellect.

And as he expected, she gave him little trouble—until the Sinai Campaign ended. During the war, he had sent Dayan and Peres on mission after mission to France, and often Golda would be told about the meetings only when they were over. She was unhappy, but she accepted Ben-Gurion's explanation that security required direct secret talks between defense ministries. But after the war, she was less understanding. Peres began dealing with Germany without letting her know, and Ben-Gurion didn't even invite her to his meetings with Dag Hammarskjöld. He gave her a free hand only in the less important African countries. Often she would burst into his office and bitterly complain that Peres was undercutting her.

"I told Golda," Ben-Gurion wrote in his diary, "that I am worried and regret her suspicions—which are not completely groundless. . . . I said that my work will become impossible if she goes around with such a feeling."

But Golda continued to go around with "such a feeling," and kept coming back to Ben-Gurion. The Prime Minister calmed her each time and agreed to consult with her before Peres had any more foreign dealings. Ben-Gurion, however, seldom did, and Peres saw no need to remind him. Thus, a burning feud raged between Golda and Peres that would help turn Golda into one of the most inflexible foes of Ben-Gurion's plan to infuse the party leadership with new blood.

Ben-Gurion, still obsessed with pursuing destiny, only gradually realized that his party was isolating him, but he reacted quickly as the 1959 elections neared. A divided Mapai could mean a triumphant Herut. Finance Minister Levi Eshkol, a man of compromise, was almost alone among the veterans willing to bring in the "youngsters." It was thus time to win back Moshe Sharett, who remained a powerful figure in the party, as well as a disturbing one. The Prime Minister apparently still felt a certain affection for him—and a gnawing sense of guilt for having tossed him out of the government.

Ben-Gurion had offended Sharett, if inadvertently, even after he resigned as foreign minister. Wishing to justify Sharett's ouster, he declared in a speech in January 1957 that only when Golda took over as foreign minister did the "unorthodox efforts [to obtain] arms bear fruit"—since she didn't insist on "ceremony and protocol."

"Blood libel!" cried Sharett, who viewed this remark as a slight on his own ability.

Now, more than two years later, Ben-Gurion wrote him that

anyone "who reads my whole speech cannot . . . draw your destructive conclusion about a blood libel. . . . In my heart the comradeship that existed between us for decades, despite differences of opinion . . . was not destroyed." And in one of the few apologies he ever made, Ben-Gurion wrote: "Perhaps I said superfluous things, and I ask you to pardon me."

But the Prime Minister apparently had second thoughts about stooping to apology. For the next day he sent Sharett excerpts from his diary "proving" that large arms shipments started flowing from France only *after* Sharett had resigned as foreign minister!

Sharett wrote back "proving" that *he* had laid the groundwork for the deal. But what hurt him most was that Ben-Gurion had humiliated him publicly.

"Why did you behave with such cruelty and rigidity toward a comrade who was hurt to the depths of his soul? . . . These words burned the last bridge between us."

Ben-Gurion perhaps hoped to salvage the bridge, but with or without Sharett he would push ahead with plans for his disciples. They would run for the Knesset and entice the country's youth into the party, especially the Sephardim who had recently arrived from Arab lands. He was deeply concerned that Begin's Herut Party might lasso them with a noose of jingoist promises. (And, in fact, they would flock to Begin in 1977, when he eventually came to power.)

"The primitive element," Ben-Gurion prophetically penned in his diary, "is . . . subjected easily to political and social demagogy. Its hatred for the Arabs is great, and the talk about the conquest of historical borders captures their hearts."

But Ben-Gurion's strategy worked, and his "boys" helped to implant in the youth new seeds of purpose as they glamorously barnstormed the nation with the message that a young dynamic leadership would soon blossom in the Israeli sun.

On November 3, 1959, Ben-Gurion, surrounded in his home by party friends, smiled triumphantly as aides rushed to him with the returns. Mapai had won its biggest plurality since the state was born, and his own prestige had soared to a peak. He was even able to persuade his colleagues to share their cabinet power with several "youngsters." Dayan became minister of agriculture, and Eban, minister of education. Who could possibly challenge Ben-Gurion now?

Three months later, on February 4, 1960, Pinhas Lavon answered the bell to his apartment and greeted two visitors. Pinhas Sapir had come with a young retired army officer, and both looked tense as they sat down. The officer was former Lieutenant Colonel Yosef Harel, who had an "extraordinary" story to tell.

About what? asked Lavon.

About the "Affair," Sapir replied.

Lavon's face flushed, as it usually did when he heard that word. It meant the "Lavon Affair." It meant memories of humiliation, bitterness and betrayal. For six years he had lived in torment, and he had even suffered a heart attack.

What did he know? Lavon asked Harel, a former military intelligence officer (no relation to Isser Harel, director of security services).

Harel knew quite a bit. He spouted a horror story of criminal conspiracy involving Colonel Gibli, his deputy Ben-Zur and Avri Elad, who had led the Egyptian operation. Records had been forged, perjury committed, documents stolen.

"The evidence," Harel said, "evoked in me the feeling that a deliberate attempt had been made to conceal facts from the responsible civilian authority. [This] pus in the public body . . . should be purged."

Lavon was stupefied. "Why didn't you come to us with this information before?" he asked.

His superiors had warned him not to say a word, Harel replied. But his conscience bothered him, and now that he was out of the army he felt he must reveal the truth. He agreed to dictate his charges to Lavon's secretary, Ephraim Evron.

In May 1960, Lavon went to see Ben-Gurion and repeated to him the details of Yosef Harel's report. Ben-Gurion seemed upset, but he was not surprised. He had known the details for years—since shortly after he took over the defense ministry from Lavon. When Gibli had been transferred to a new post, his successor discovered these details and suggested that the Prime Minister investigate. But Dayan, who was still chief of staff, warned Ben-Gurion not to touch the "dynamite," and the Prime Minister didn't need much persuading. Who knew how many victims an explosion might claim? Above all, he had to protect the army's image. A prophet could understand the frailties of even a morally superior people, but could ordinary mortals? The light emanating from an exemplary state must not pass through, or be seen passing through, a corrupting filter.

But now Ben-Gurion could not ignore Yosef Harel's charges,

or those of Avri Elad, who had "revealed" the whole conspiracy while being secretly tried for the unrelated crime of passing military information to the Egyptians. (Elad, who was sentenced to prison for this crime, was also suspected of betraying his comrades in the "security mishap," but evidence was lacking in this case.) Lavon gave Yosef Harel's report to Ben-Gurion and later learned that the Prime Minister was forming an investigative committee. It would, however, be empowered to determine only whether Gibli and his deputy were guilty of forgery and perjury, not whether Lavon "gave the order." Lavon boiled. His foes, he knew, were now saying that he *had* ordered the 1954 operation, and that Gibli, trying to protect himself, had conspired against him simply because he could not "prove" this any other way. So, by this logic, the fact that Gibli might have committed crimes didn't necessarily exonerate Lavon.

Was Ben-Gurion seeking to block his exoneration? Lavon wondered. Was the Prime Minister afraid that people might think he had known Lavon was innocent all along and yet used the charges against him as an excuse to "usurp" his job back in 1955? Did he perhaps fear that Dayan and Peres would be suspected of having helped Gibli do Lavon in?

On October 26, 1960, Lavon rushed to see Ben-Gurion again in his Jerusalem office. The Prime Minister, he said, should clear him immediately. "I think it is your duty to make an announcement about this. . . . It is evident there was a plot."

Ben-Gurion was agitated. He was neither an investigator nor a judge, he replied. "For me, you are not guilty and you are not innocent. Neither is Gibli guilty until the verdict is given. Of course, I do not compare you."

"Many thanks!"

"I cannot [exonerate you]," Ben-Gurion said flatly.

Lavon was furious. "Fine," he snapped, "I regard myself free to do all I can in order to bring the matter to the public's attention. . . . I will inform the [Knesset's] foreign affairs and security committee on the matter."

Ben-Gurion frowned. The public so far knew nothing. What a disaster if the conspiracy came to light! He must assuage Lavon. "Don't do that. There is almost no doubt that Gibli will go, and this by itself will lead to your vindication."

Lavon would not budge. He wanted an official announcement. But Ben-Gurion also would not budge. Let Lavon spill it all to the Knesset committee. He couldn't prove anything. Besides, all discussion in that committee had always been held in secret. As Lavon rose to leave, Ben-Gurion remarked like a misunderstood spouse, "You're angry with me."

"I am past anger!" Lavon exclaimed in English, as if there were no words strong enough in the Hebrew language to express his feelings. And as he climbed into his car, he growled to a friend, "This means war!"

Within days, Lavon was blasting away with his heaviest artillery before the Knesset committee, and the echoes could not be contained. Someone leaked many of the tawdry details, and the scandal, secret until now, traumatized the nation. While newspaper headlines focused a lurid spotlight on crime in high places, dazed Israelis met on street corners demanding to know *"Mah nishmah?"* ("What's new?") and pondering who the characters in this incredible drama were—aside from Ben-Gurion and Lavon—since military identities were still withheld. The Affair would eat into Israel's political and social fabric as ravenously as Watergate would into America's.

Ben-Gurion sat restlessly reading reports of the battle, flesh sagging around his jaw, wrinkles creasing his cheeks, eyes glaring with rage. Lavon, he cried to a Mapai colleague, had "slandered army officers and the defense establishment, revealed secrets, distorted facts, and leaked to the opposition parties. . . . [Lavon is] simply a liar!"

Actually, Lavon's "truths" were even more disturbing than his "lies." The committee investigating Gibli and his deputy would soon find them guilty of forgery and perjury, and Ben-Gurion would drum them out of the army. But did Lavon have to reveal their crimes to the public? He even dared charge there was "corruption" in the defense ministry and singled out Dayan and Peres for some of his most "vicious" attacks, declaring it was "very likely" that they were "accessories to acts of forgery and perjury."

And the public, Ben-Gurion lamented, apparently believed many of Lavon's charges. Though the press still didn't know the details of the "security mishap" that, years earlier, had triggered the storm, it demanded that Lavon be exonerated, and so did most Israelis. In an open letter to Ben-Gurion published in *Davar*, one reader typically wrote:

> We have believed in you all through the years as Hassidim believe in their rabbi. . . . Can you let yourself become involved in such pettiness? . . . Do you not feel, my honored teacher, that the foundations of both

the Histadrut and the state are being threatened in this backbiting, which we do not understand and of which we are all ashamed?

Such censure only nursed Ben-Gurion's wrath. Before the committee's "disgraceful" revelations, he had felt no passionate dislike of Lavon, and there was nothing personal in his refusal to clear him. But now he was convinced that what Lavon really wanted was to take over as prime minister with the support of the Mapai veterans—though Lavon was equally convinced that the veterans would back Ben-Gurion against him! And so Ben-Gurion "passed judgment in his heart" about Lavon, and "that judgment is final for me."

Another man who passed judgment was Moshe Sharett. He had once called Lavon "diabolic." Now he agreed to defend him. What were the deeds of a devil compared to the cruelty of a god? With perhaps a touch of malicious pleasure, he told a reporter, "If I knew then what I know now, perhaps there would have been no need for this type of inquiry and, in any case, it may be assumed that the . . . conclusions would have been different."

Lavon was satisfied. He considered himself "exonerated" and was ready to drop his case. But Ben-Gurion wasn't ready to drop his. The army had already been "smeared," but now his prestige and that of his "boys" were on the line. Destiny seemed in the balance. Ben-Gurion called for a hearing before a judicial committee with the power to subpoena witnesses and documents, and "put the person who lied on trial." The veterans protested, fearing a long-drawn-out "trial" that could ruin the party. They would, however, form a simple ministerial committee without judicial powers. It would review all the evidence and decide, its hands unbound by legal strings, whether Lavon "gave the order" or not.

Ben-Gurion scoffed. Israel was a democracy, wasn't it? And in a democracy there must be a separation of powers—political and judicial. To the end of his life, Ben-Gurion would not budge from this "moral" stand, even when his closest supporters begged him to give way to avoid a party split and a deepening national trauma. A priest might compromise on principle, but a prophet could not.

How sincere was this moral plea? Even today, Israelis do not agree. Ben-Gurion preferred political oblivion to moral compromise, his disciples say. Not so, his foes reply. The moral issue was simply an excuse to pursue his "vendetta." And there is probably truth in both claims. While Ben-Gurion viewed the separation of powers as the master key to democracy and justice, he seems also to have felt that a judicial committee would, conveniently, never find enough evidence to reach a clear-cut conclusion. After all, if Lavon were cleared, the "youngsters" might lose stature and their precarious hold on power. And what was more important—the nation's future or Lavon's feelings? (Whatever Ben-Gurion's motivation, his moral appeal would ultimately bear fruit. In 1968 the Knesset would pass a law providing for independent judicial hearings in cases affecting the national interest. Judicial committees would thus be set up to investigate the circumstances leading to the nearly disastrous 1973 Yom Kippur War and the 1982 massacre in two Beirut Palestinian refugee camps.)

Fists pounded. Tables trembled. Finally, Ben-Gurion accepted a proposal by the veterans that a committee of seven ministers, dominated by them, would study the evidence and recommend "how to proceed" with the investigation. Ben-Gurion understood this to mean that such a committee could deal *only* with procedure and would not be empowered to reach conclusions. But Dayan and Peres suspected a "trick." Why had Ben-Gurion agreed? The committee might decide, they feared, to exonerate Lavon after all, casting a shadow on the two of them. The Prime Minister was old and seemed to have lost his fighting spirit, they felt. He might even abandon them. Now they came to him and were brutally frank.

Unless Ben-Gurion fought harder, said Dayan, he would become a mere "figurehead." "They want you to stay, but without power and influence. Nobody wants Lavon in your place, but if they think you will accept it, why should they struggle against him? . . . You should . . . say 'either Lavon or me!' If you do that . . . you might still have a chance to win."

But Ben-Gurion didn't do that. And on November 3, 1960, the seven ministers began plowing through a mountain of paper and rehashing all the facts, forgeries and figments of imagination that had overwhelmed other investigators. Yosef Harel, apparently persuaded by Dayan, disavowed his conspiracy report. But perhaps the most important testimony came from Dalia Carmel, Gibli's former secretary, who admitted that she had forged many documents dealing with the "security mishap." Everything seemed clear to the committee now. Lavon did not "give the order." The group's report would presumably appease the public, embarrass the "youngsters," and silence Lavon—and Mapai would be free to rebuild on the ruins of the Affair.

On December 20, 1960, the committee, with a collective sigh

of relief, issued its report: "We find that Lavon did *not* give the order cited by the 'senior officer' and that 'the mishap' was carried out without his knowledge. . . . The investigation of 'the Affair' should be considered closed."

Closed? Ben-Gurion was outraged as he read the report. No, he *didn't* consider the Affair closed. The committee, he charged, had no legal right to reach definite conclusions. Ben-Gurion was especially upset because it had taken the word of Dalia Carmel, who confessed to having forged the file copy of Gibli's controversial letter to Dayan so it would appear that Lavon had "given the order." If people believed her confession, Dayan could be suspected of having conspired with Gibli against Lavon.

Dalia reaffirmed to the author that she had indeed forged this document and others as described earlier in the book. And she produced a copy of a letter she had written Gibli in response to a plea from him that she withdraw her testimony. Dalia refused, calling Gibli a "cowardly feeble human being" and Ben-Gurion a "ludicrous figure" for fighting "indirectly for your honor" when "you haven't none (sic)."

Dalia, who was in the United States when the scandal broke— she had left Israel because she "feared what Gibli might do" to her—returned in 1966 and was immediately warned by Teddy Kollek, she says, not to speak to reporters. But, "driven by conscience," she did speak to Ben-Gurion, hoping to convince him that her charges were true. In a letter to Prime Minister Eshkol, whom she served as secretary after leaving the army (he was minister of finance then), Dalia would describe the encounter:

> The sight of the Old Man, seated at his desk, with mountains of books all around him, a desk lamp lighting a big book in front of him and with it the man's own white hair—made me feel as if I were walking straight into a stage setting of Faust. . . . He set aside his book and took his famous diary/notebook with carbon paper and [while he wrote I told him how] Lt. Col. [Motke] Ben-Zur [asked] whether I would be agreeable to change some documents. . . . I then stated that the famous letter from Gibli to Dayan in the U.S., dated July 19, 1954, . . . was changed. . . . I further stated that I had been asked to change other documents.
>
> He [Ben-Gurion] then stated—looking at me with his right eye half closed, and with the "friendliest" look in the world—"You were a great admirer of Gibli, weren't you?" [The Hebrew word for "admirer" is *maaritza*, suggesting intimacy.] I took strong exception to the question, both to its meaning and . . . his intonation and look. Also . . . Ben-Gurion referred to me and to you with another "romantic" innuendo, saying something—I was your *maaritza* or something similar. Again I took exception to his statement.

Dalia denied to the writer that she had had affairs with either Gibli or Eshkol, though Eshkol, she said, had helped her get a job with an Israeli company in the United States and proposed marriage to her (she declined) while on a visit there. Ben-Gurion, Dalia claimed, was trying to discredit her as an ambitious, vengeful woman scorned by men in high places. In any case, Ben-Gurion didn't seem to believe—or want to believe—anything she told him.

Why had the veterans exonerated Lavon? Because, in Ben-Gurion's view, they wanted to humiliate the Prime Minister, to force him to his knees. Accept their decision, Dayan now advised. It was too late to fight. But now it was Ben-Gurion who was determined to fight. He *must* discredit Lavon. And he would use his old "blackmail" trick to make the veterans cooperate. "I am not a member of your government!" he cried at a cabinet meeting, and he stormed out. The "youngsters" were horrified. What if his colleagues didn't call him back?

But, as always, they did. Ben-Gurion was noncommittal. He might come back. But something must be done about Lavon, he said. "He raised his hand against the army, and this hand must be cut off."

Eshkol, especially, felt relieved. He differed with Ben-Gurion, but Lavon, after all, *had* "managed to make himself a magnet for all the opponents of Mapai." Eshkol huddled with his colleagues. Most agreed. Yes, the Old Man must have his "pound of flesh." And on February 4, 1961, a few days after Ben-Gurion had resigned, the same politicians who had cleared Lavon now helped to boot him out of his Histadrut post in a ritual sacrifice to their bitter but still beloved god.

A blemished god. To Israelis already outraged by Ben-Gurion's rigid refusal to exonerate Lavon, this *coup de grâce* was a merciless, vindictive act performed by servile old men with a gun in their back. Not at all, claimed the Prime Minister. He would never punish Lavon without a trial. It was Eshkol's idea! Ben-Gurion returned to his post, but non-Mapai cabinet members, shaken by the jeers and the jokes, were vexed. Why share the punches? They resigned, forcing a new election, and on August 15, 1961, in an atmosphere acrid with enmity, Mapai limped to a new victory, though losing five Knesset seats. For all their disillusion, many Israelis still viewed Ben-Gurion as indispensable, feeling comfortable and protected under his paternal wing. But Ben-Gurion himself was uneasy.

"A catastrophe!" he exclaimed—demonstrating once more his gift for prophecy.

Ben-Gurion had promised in the election campaign to stop demanding that a judicial committee determine who "gave the order" in the Lavon Affair. But in his first speech to the Knesset, he reneged on this pledge. When his Mapai colleagues rebuked him for raking up the embers, Ben-Gurion agreed not to utter another word. The fire within, however, continued to rage.

Meanwhile, as the Lavon Affair faded in the dawn of a new regime, other shadows dimmed Ben-Gurion's image. One was cast by an officer named Israel Beer. Arriving from Europe in 1938, he fought with the Hagana during the Arab revolt of 1936–39, served as assistant chief of planning and military operations in the War of Independence, and wrote the official history of that war in the early 1950s. His egg-shaped face with Mongoloid features set off by a tiny mustache was a familiar sight in the ministry of defense, where he would greet old army comrades with a long-toothed smile, telling each what he had learned from others, thus wheedling from them ever more secrets as he moved through the corridors.

In March 1961, Beer, carrying a black briefcase, met with a Soviet diplomat in a small Tel Aviv café and gave him papers revealing some of these secrets. A few hours later, at midnight, they met again, and the Russian returned the papers. Two hours after that, Beer, in his pajamas, answered a knock on the door. Isser Harel's men, who had been closely watching the transaction, entered and found the briefcase with the documents.

It isn't clear how Beer might have hurt Israel by his spying, but it is clear how he hurt Ben-Gurion. When news of the arrest broke, the people were shocked. How could the man they had felt so secure with permit such an incredible breach of security?

Shortly, Ben-Gurion had trouble with Isser Harel himself. It began in July 1962, when four Egyptian ground-to-ground test missiles roared into the sky in a great burst of flame that sparked terror in Israel. While Nasser bragged to ecstatic Cairo crowds that two of the missiles could strike "any target south of Beirut" —meaning Israel—Harel learned of the danger like any layman. Embarrassed by his failure to detect it earlier, he scrambled for information and soon handed Ben-Gurion a thick dossier of ghastly detail. German scientists and technicians were building

nine hundred missiles that might be fitted out with either nuclear warheads or warheads with germs, gas or radioactive
wastes.

Get in touch with Chancellor Adenauer at once, Harel
pleaded with Ben-Gurion, and ask him to order the scientists
home before they destroy Israel!

Ben-Gurion shook his head. West Germany was a democratic
state, and Adenauer might refuse to force private citizens to
obey him. Besides, the Chancellor was supplying Israel with all
kinds of arms and other goods. Why rock the tank? But Harel
decided to act on his own. In Cairo, an exploding parcel blinded
the secretary of a scientist, and booby-trapped books killed five
Egyptian employees in a missile plant. In Munich, kidnapers
hustled a supplier of the missile project into a car, and he was
never seen again. In another German town, a bullet barely
missed an electronics expert. Finally, in Basel, two of Harel's
agents threatened the daughter of a Cairo-based scientist, demanding that she lure her father home. Both agents were arrested.

When Ben-Gurion, who had been unaware of Harel's activities, learned of the arrests, he was furious. His fury was rooted
not simply in moral outrage, but in a basic conflict with Harel
over relations with West Germany. Reflecting the national
mood, especially after the trauma of the Eichmann trial, Harel
hated the Germans passionately, whether Hitler's "old" ones or
Adenauer's "new" ones. But if emotion moved Harel, so did
ambition. He despised the architect of Israel's pragmatic German policy, Shimon Peres, who, together with Dayan, blocked
his own path to power. He would later volunteer, without success, to be Ben-Gurion's deputy, and apparently dreamed of
succeeding the Old Man. He thus quietly joined the "veterans"
in their struggle with the "youngsters," and drew close to Golda
Meir, who also despised both Peres and the Germans.

Now, in the Tiberias hotel where the Prime Minister was
vacationing, Harel tried to calm the Prime Minister. He would
hold a press conference to explain the Basel arrests to the people. He would let them know what Nasser and his Nazi scientists were concocting in their laboratories.

No, Ben-Gurion replied, apparently wary of Harel's motives.
It was vital not to force Adenauer's hand.

But Harel hurried back to Tel Aviv and called a press conference anyway. And the next morning headlines around the world
screamed comic-book catastrophe. Ex-Nazis were making
atomic, chemical, bacteriological and radiological weapons in

Egypt, including the death ray! And what was the West German government doing about it? Nothing! Panic seized Israel as the final Holocaust seemed at hand. Arguments raged; which cataclysmic end was the least agonizing—bombs, bugs, beams?

The Knesset met and foes of Ben-Gurion's German policy loosed devastating verbal missiles of their own. All the while, Ben-Gurion continued to soak himself in the mineral baths of Tiberias. In his younger days he would have plunged into the fray, but now he was old and tired. Let them fight it out. Let them say what they wanted. In the end, all of them would obey him anyway. Perhaps. But now the Knesset echoed with defiance of Ben-Gurion and his policies.

"You send our Uzi [submachine gun] to Germany," Menachem Begin addressed him, "and the Germans send microbes to our enemies!"

"The German people cannot disclaim responsibility," Golda Meir cried. The German government must stop "the evil activities of its nationals."

When Harel persisted with his dire prophecies, the Prime Minister asked his chief of staff to find out how accurate his reports were. Military intelligence checked and found them greatly exaggerated—in fact, almost pure fantasy. Ben-Gurion hurried back from Tiberias and confronted Harel. He, the Prime Minister, would inform the Knesset committee on foreign affairs and security that the Egyptian missiles were primitive and impractical and did not pose a serious threat to Israel, and Harel must back him up.

Harel was indignant. How could Ben-Gurion expect him to deny the "truth"? If Ben-Gurion went before the committee with such "misinformation," Harel said, he would "enter as prime minister and exit as a private citizen." That day, Harel resigned, infuriating Ben-Gurion. He was already under fire and now if his chief of security services quit, the Prime Minister would surely be blamed. He sent word to Harel that he must stay on a while longer. And, incidentally, would he please send him immediately his intelligence sources in Egypt. Harel responded succinctly, "Send over someone to take over the operation and the keys!"

In a rage, Ben-Gurion wanted to arrest Harel for withholding intelligence information, but finally sent over someone for the keys. He now wondered how long he would keep his own.

Lonely and depressed, Ben-Gurion felt strangely helpless. Leadership of Israel was slipping from his withered hands. With no more great fateful decisions to make, he seemed unsure of his priorities. He did little party work and had even left it to Eshkol to form a Ben-Gurion government. Nor did he always remember who had which job, or so it seemed. Once, Minister of Education Abba Eban called on him and was greeted by the question, "Why aren't you in Washington?"

Eban was shocked. "I've been your minister of education for three years," he replied.

Ben-Gurion had apparently forgotten that Eban was no longer his ambassador to Washington.

"Once he appointed me minister," explains Eban, "he didn't care what I did. I received only five personal notes from him in three years."

Still, Eban was never quite sure whether Ben-Gurion's memory was really that poor or whether he simply used his "forgetfulness" to put his ministers down and make the point that he was still boss and not, as Dayan had warned, a mere "figurehead."

In any case, Ben-Gurion hesitated to step down. "Man is not free," he would tell an interviewer. "There are forces . . . obliging him to persist."

Ben-Gurion began to show signs of paranoia. Enemies were closing in on him from all sides. A mere declaration by Egypt, Syria and Iraq in April 1963 that they would unite and demolish the "Zionist threat" threw him into near-panic. For weeks he kept his secretaries rapping out a plea to world leaders: Urge the Arab states to make peace! He tried to arrange meetings with Nasser through U Nu and a British newsman, and he sent an agent to Yugoslavia with messages for Marshal Tito, but all these moves failed.

Well, if not a peace, at least a pact. And without bothering to test the diplomatic temperature, he pressed President De Gaulle for a military alliance and President Kennedy for American-Soviet action to bring about total disarmament in Israel and the Arab states, and a joint declaration guaranteeing the "territorial integrity and security of every state in the Middle East." When both leaders sent their regrets, Ben-Gurion wrote Kennedy again: Why not a wider alliance—Israel, the United States, *and* its allies? Kennedy, who was already asking Israel for closer inspection of its nuclear reactor and the return of some Arab refugees, was, it seems, stunned by such *chutzpah*. The time, he replied, wasn't quite ripe.

In his apprehension, Ben-Gurion refused to end military restrictions on the Israeli Arabs, though advisers urged him to do so. Thus, the Arabs, unless they had a pass, remained confined to their areas of residence. They were not surprised. Many years earlier, they recalled, Ben-Gurion had led the struggle to re-place Arab fellaheen with Hebrew labor in all Jewish settle-ments, and for a long period he would not allow Arab workers to become full partners in the Histadrut. Nor would he set foot in Arab villages or homes.

Ben-Gurion expected the Arabs to be anti-Zionist and thought it was hypocrisy for Zionists to accept their hospitality. All he demanded of them was to refrain from plotting against the state. Still, no Israeli prime minister showed greater willingness to improve Arab living standards, to build schools and sewage sys-tems. One didn't have to be liked to be fair. The Israeli Arabs, Ben-Gurion thought, should be dealt with as potentially danger-ous but unavoidable political orphans who were entitled to ben-efit from Jewish accomplishments as all peoples were, not as cousins or dinner companions.

Yet, the Prime Minister was disdainful of those Arabs who cooperated with the Israeli government, for they were ob-viously "opportunists" who had no influence with the Arab masses. But the leader of an Arab state? He would go anywhere to see him, for this man would be in a position to talk peace. Trouble was, the leaders were all talking war.

If the Arabs did not destroy Israel, Ben-Gurion feared, Begin's Herut Party might. Surely if it came to power it would kill any hope of an exemplary state. To strengthen his own party he pushed for a merger of all labor parties against the common threat. And he stepped up his endless campaign for a new elec-toral law that would spawn a two-party system and spell a Mapai majority. At the same time, Ben-Gurion, his face blustery red, his eyes squinting with contempt as they focused on Begin, shouted almost hysterically to the Knesset on May 13, 1963:

"He would replace the army and police command with his thugs and rule as Hitler ruled Germany, brutally suppressing the labor movement; and he would destroy the state. . . . Begin may hate Hitler, but this does not mean he differs from him."

If not Begin, perhaps Isser Harel, whom Ben-Gurion had once so trusted, would slither into power. Like Lavon, he might try to ingratiate himself with the Mapai leaders and play the role of "hypocritical vulture. . . . And such insanity would do more than anything else to place Israel under fascist rule."

To make matters worse, most of the veterans, Ben-Gurion was sure, had joined his enemies. Golda had already threatened to resign when her ally, Harel, was forced to quit. On June 15, 1963, she came to Ben-Gurion's Tel Aviv home and, while she sat in the kitchen with her host munching on Paula's cookies, bitterly blasted Israel's ties with West Germany. That night Ben-Gurion got little sleep, and in the morning he was haggard as he staggered into his office. Casually, he told aides the news: *He* was resigning.

Was this a new ruse? Or had Ben-Gurion finally collapsed under the crushing political burden growing out of the Lavon Affair? He was deadly serious, he insisted. It seems that he wanted private status for at least a while so that he could more easily deal with the Affair, which still obsessed him. As a politician, he could no longer pursue "justice." But as a prophet, he could. He had already hired a journalist to probe all aspects of the Affair, hoping to find enough evidence to justify a new call for a judiciary committee. And, in fact, he resigned the day before his investigator was to hand him a full report, apparently so he could work on it. Although Ben-Gurion's aides and "youngsters" predictably bemoaned his latest resignation, the veterans had no difficulty suppressing *their* tears. For the first time, they did not beg him to return.

Even as a private citizen, Ben-Gurion evidently hoped to manipulate the new prime minister as he had manipulated Moshe Sharett in 1954. His first choice was archeology professor Yigael Yadin, his old army chief of staff, though Yadin had previously rejected two cabinet posts. He was young and dynamic and, unlike Dayan, would be acceptable to the veterans. But Yadin refused for a third time to be lured out of the dusty past.

Next in line was Levi Eshkol, the senior veteran in the cabinet, who wasn't told he was merely second choice. Eshkol, after all, was willing to work with the "youngsters." He was no leader, in Ben-Gurion's view, but that only ensured that he would consult his old master.

No, Eshkol would not forget who was boss.

CHAPTER FIFTEEN

The shadows of the evening are stretched out
JEREMIAH 6:4

Eshkol lived up to expectations. Like many other Israelis, great and humble, he would make the pilgrimage to Sde Boker to pay homage to the prophet, who was once more dispensing wisdom from the wild infinity of the desert. People soon forgot their antipathy to Ben-Gurion, the "vindictive" politician. Here was the old Ben-Gurion, the father of his country, living as Abraham once did; the symbol of Jewish rebirth, of Israeli pride and power. On holidays, busloads of workers came to see him and sometimes to seek favors. Would Ben-Gurion please ask the transport ministry to issue him a taxi license? someone urged. One day, hundreds crowded a sandy plateau near the kibbutz to watch him lay the cornerstone of the first building of a projected College of the Negev, which he envisioned as a "combined Oxford and M.I.T.," a key institution for dispersing light to the world.

Not every visitor departed with the treasured memory of the Old Man bestowing a benevolent smile upon him. Sometimes the memory was of Paula growling outside his cabin door, still driving people off with a piercing stare. When one young female journalist showed up dressed in a miniskirt, Paula was especially abrupt. Her husband should sit with a half-naked woman? "Ben-Gurion will not see you!" she exclaimed. But the prophet came out and agreed to be interviewed, while Paula moodily stood nearby muttering, *"Feh, feh!"*

When Ben-Gurion wasn't greeting visitors, he was usually hunched over his desk editing the voluminous reports that his journalist-investigator—as well as two lawyers—had prepared on the Lavon Affair. Let the people chide him. Was it not the prophet's mission to search for the "truth" wherever it led, as Nathan had done while traipsing the streets of Jerusalem—and, incidentally, immortalizing himself?

The truth, according to the reports, was that Ben-Gurion had been right—not surprising, since these reports were a compendium of selected facts and tortuous interpretations tailored to his need. Yes, Lavon "gave the order." And now that Ben-Gurion had confirmed the "truth," he would, in October 1964, submit the "proof" to the attorney general and the minister of justice with demands that the ministerial committee be censured and a judicial committee be set up.

Eshkol was not usually given to extreme emotion, but he was outraged when he learned of Ben-Gurion's plan. He was a modest, good-humored man with twinkling, bespectacled eyes, thin, easily smiling lips, and a broad, pleasant face, a face that aptly reflected his distaste for confrontation. Unlike Ben-Gurion, he was a compromiser by nature, constantly seeking consensus. He had thus been a highly valuable counterpoint to Ben-Gurion throughout the years, the loyal troubleshooter who would smooth out ruffles when Ben-Gurion issued his "edicts." He had even acted as a kind of referee in the tug of war between the generations. And now Eshkol, egged on by his aggressive young wife, found himself confronting the man he had always served so willingly. For the party's sake, he pleaded, don't stir up the Lavon Affair again. But Ben-Gurion was adamant: "It is a matter of conscience."

Eshkol finally rebelled. Lavon, he decided, would be "rehabilitated" and become a major force in the party again. This new reversal was necessary, the Prime Minister felt, to appease Lavon's influential comrades in Mapai, and also in the left-wing Ahdut HaAvodah Party, which had taken the name of Ben-Gurion's pre-Mapai party. Its members (like those of Mapam) had broken with Mapai in 1944, but they were now being urged by Eshkol to join with the mother party in a coalition government, and Lavon's reinstatement seemed a modest price to pay—especially since Ben-Gurion's messianic services were no longer required.

It was now Ben-Gurion who was outraged; Eshkol had "betrayed" him! But good news took the edge off his bitterness. The two cabinet officials studying his report recommended that a judicial committee examine the 1954 "security mishap." Stunned, Eshkol agonizingly agreed, only to spark a storm. Was he their leader or wasn't he? the veterans roared. Was he a *man* or wasn't he? his wife raged. Within three hours, Eshkol changed his mind. And in a masterful maneuver he resigned, declaring that he would not open a "Pandora's box." The party, he cried, must choose between him and a judicial committee, between a big Mapai win and a possible Mapai loss in a new election.

The party faithful mulled it over. Ben-Gurion was now dispensable, but was the party? Even Dayan did not favor a judicial hearing "to the point of wishing the government to resign." The party thus shelved the Lavon Affair, so infuriating Ben-Gurion that he resigned from the Mapai secretariat. Eshkol had succeeded with a stratagem right out of his old mentor's book!

Ben-Gurion now had one more chance to salvage victory—at a Mapai convention that would stagger Israel in the chilly gloom of February 1965.

Ben-Gurion listened to the deafening ovation with a strange impatience, as if too little time was left to indulge in such demonstrative nonsense. Too little time to make sure that Israel was on the right road to destiny before he faded into history. He stood rigidly behind the rostrum on the flower-adorned stage of Mann Auditorium in Tel Aviv waiting for silence, looking tired, worried, and perhaps a little guilt-ridden. . . .

Life had been hard since his humiliating defeat by Eshkol—especially for Paula. The reporters were constantly banging on the door, whether in Sde Boker or in Tel Aviv, seeking more information they could twist into "slander." Old colleagues who had voted against him knocked, too, hoping to ease their conscience with "hypocritical" explanations. When one party leader, Shraga Netzer, called, Paula glared at him and, hissing that Ben-Gurion "receives only friends," slammed the door in his face.

But she welcomed his "real" friends. "Save him from his misery," she would beg. "Speak to him. Make him give up this Lavon business. Tell him he should make up with Eshkol."

Paula kept all hate mail from her husband and even secretly spoke with Eshkol and Lavon's wife, scheming for some kind of *modus vivendi* that would give her husband peace. She herself felt helpless, Paula told a friend. She no longer even gossiped to her husband over dinner. "What shall I tell him? That Eshkol has friends and you haven't? How can I hurt him?"

Yet Paula knew that her husband was already deeply hurt, though, as a prophet, he tried not to show it. He was like a radio, she felt. He would simply "turn the knob off and go back to Spinoza." But the radio was never really turned off. It played the same music over and over again. . . .

"I don't know what the people want," Ben-Gurion cried when the ovation had ended, "but I know what it *should* want—that truth and justice shall reign in our land." And he demanded once more a judicial inquiry into the Lavon Affair.

Ben-Gurion's old comrades, baring their wounds, replied in anguish. There was Levi Eshkol, the man of compromise who could not compromise now and remain a man. He asked gently, almost pathetically: "A judicial committee? God in Heaven . . . what are we doing here trying to restore the Roman forum? . . . I say to [Ben-Gurion]: Give me a chance, give me room!"

There was Moshe Sharett, dying from cancer and speaking from a wheelchair, a poignant figure as words gushed from his seared soul: "We must free ourselves of this *dybbuk* [evil spirit]. The public is sick of it. We must ask Ben-Gurion either to forsake the issue and join the mainstream of our life or to relinquish the crown of leadership."

And there was Golda Meir, who had worshiped Ben-Gurion since the day he visited Milwaukee about fifty years earlier. She kissed Sharett on the forehead, then rained more acidic rhetoric on Ben-Gurion. He was a "hypocrite" who spoke of justice but "accuses and . . . judges from the outset!"

Ben-Gurion listened to the insults with flushed dismay as he sat on the stage at the president's table, which many party leaders had abruptly abandoned when he took his place. Golda, his dear Golda! "The ugliest thing at the convention," he would write in his diary, "was Golda's vicious speech. It was sad to hear her speak like this, spouting hate and poison. . . . If I hadn't heard it with my own ears, I wouldn't have believed she could do it."

Not since the dawn of his career in Palestine had comrades so cruelly attacked him. In those early years he had marched out of clandestine, mosquito-infested meetings and, with only the rags on his back, gone off to sulk in the wilderness and await destiny's call. Now, in the dusk of his career, he stalked out again after Golda's speech and went home. "Everything is finished," he muttered to an aide who accompanied him.

After midnight a group of supporters called, pushed past a protesting Paula, and found their leader sitting in his pajamas and talking to himself. "What does she want from me? What did I do to her? Where does that wickedness come from?" Then, seeing his visitors, he added as if seeking to protect the woman who had so wounded him: "After all, Golda had a difficult childhood."

"Ben-Gurion was very restrained and self-controlled," one of the guests would later report, "but I had never seen such an expression on his face before—and would not see it again until he was close to death."

Nu? So what happened at the convention?

Sixty percent of the delegates voted against a judicial committee, but forty percent voted for it. Not bad.

Not good, Ben-Gurion replied.

Then why didn't Ben-Gurion seek power again? his comrades asked. Not only would Eshkol be out, but Golda and the other veterans who had "betrayed" him could be ousted, too.

Golda? All his old comrades? But they had helped him to forge the state. How could he rule without them? Suddenly the full tragedy of the Lavon Affair lay shatteringly bare.

A judicial committee was no longer enough for Ben-Gurion. Eshkol must go, he demanded; but he decided not to put himself forward as the man who should succeed him, apparently fearing a new humiliating defeat. Eshkol, he charged, had "lied," "undermined all moral values in the party and in the state," and was "not fit to be prime minister!"

The veterans gasped, and Golda replied that if Eshkol "is a liar, we are all liars." The "youngsters" tried to calm their master, especially after the party ignored his protests and renominated Eshkol in June 1965. Eshkol might have the upper hand now, they argued, but Ben-Gurion's minority would eventually swell into a majority. Ben-Gurion, however, was impatient. He and his followers, he decided, would run in the next election— in November 1965—on a separate slate within the party. They would probably pile up enough votes to hold the balance of power in any government and could thus manipulate Mapai.

But the "youngsters," afraid that they would be thrown out of the party, rebelled, and Abba Eban even switched to Eshkol's side. Peres, who was still director general of the defense ministry and personally liked Eshkol, walked out of one meeting in Ben-Gurion's house and held his own to seek ways to thwart the Old Man's strategy. Ben-Gurion found out and sent Paula bursting in with the order: Everyone to Ben-Gurion's! Another time, her husband personally crashed a press conference that Peres had called and demanded that his comrades leave and come with him immediately. Later, Ben-Gurion called Peres and apologized, pleading for his support, and Peres, who owed his career to him, could not refuse. Moshe Dayan, who had earlier left Eshkol's cabinet, also felt indebted to Ben-Gurion, but was angry with him for not having pressed Eshkol to name the best man—Dayan—defense minister. Now Dayan ignored Ben-Gurion's pleas, stalling until he could determine the shortest route to power.

Meanwhile, Ben-Gurion decided to force the issue. He called a meeting at his home on June 29, 1965, and, after some heated debate, rapped for silence. "Anyone who wants to go on a new slate with me has the right to speak," he said. "Anyone who doesn't will keep quiet."

Dayan rose and tramped out, though he would reluctantly rejoin Ben-Gurion later. And Peres, turning pale, sputtered, "But Ben-Gurion—"

"I don't want to hear any more. Sit down and write an announcement to the press!"

And that night the Voice of Israel broke the news: Ben-Gurion would set up a new slate.

A Mapai "court" then convened and drummed all those who supported the separate slate out of the party that Ben-Gurion had founded, ironically, as a monument to labor unity! The founder, according to the Mapai prosecutors, was now a "coward" and a "danger to Israeli society." But some who voted for Ben-Gurion's expulsion were horrified by their own action.

"I'd rather have cut off my hand than expel [him] from the party," said one. "Can you expel your father from the family? But [if we hadn't], the whole party structure would have disintegrated."

Now Ben-Gurion's group, called Rafi (Israeli Workers' List), would fight Mapai at the polls as a separate party, though Ben-Gurion, hurt and humiliated, was confident that the divorce would be temporary. Rafi would win so many votes that Mapai would never be able to rule without its backing. And then Rafi would return to the fold—in charge!

The applause echoing through the huge amphitheater in Haifa gradually tapered off, and the outcast prophet got set to shrill his usual message into the klieg-lit night: Israel, in sum, must be an exemplary state, a light unto the nations. . . . Suddenly, there was no light at all—as if a godly hand had mockingly pulled the switch. Ben-Gurion's voice wailed in the dark like a broken flute and finally whined into silence.

Sabotage! cried his supporters. But Ben-Gurion was "less disturbed by the lights going out physically than by those going out morally." And indeed the lights "morally" flickered all over Israel as the election campaign bogged down in mud, oozing acrimony and anger. This was the "ugliest election campaign ever held in Israel," charged Ben-Gurion, who hurled his share of stinging epithets. Yet "slander" could neither tarnish the awesome image of a modern Moses nor enhance the pathetic one of a spiteful old man. The crowds left neither loving less nor hating more; they left bored. Who cared whether Lavon "gave the order" or not? Who cared about being a messianic nation? Who cared about past deeds and destiny?

Gradually, the crowds grew smaller. They had seen the prophet, perhaps touched him. Something to tell their children about. But in November 1965 they voted to give Rafi only 10 seats, and the new alignment—Mapai and Ahdut HaAvodah—45 out of a total of 120. They voted to send their prophet back to the desert, where his voice would roar harmlessly into eternity.

Many Israelis, nevertheless, missed the roar. And on Ben-Gurion's eightieth birthday in October 1966, ten thousand trekked down to the lion's den to listen and luxuriate in the glorious past. Only two minor ministers, however, bothered—or dared—to join the crowd. And even President Zalman Shazar, whom Ben-Gurion had chosen to succeed Yitzhak Ben-Zvi when Ben-Zvi died in 1963, tried to renege on a commitment to serve as honorary chairman of the anniversary committee, though mutual friends finally shamed him into keeping it. Even so, under pressure from Eshkol and Golda not to attend, Shazar went to congratulate Ben-Gurion only on a "private" visit. Eshkol at first even refused to let him fly in a government helicopter, though he finally gave in for fear of a new press scandal. The Prime Minister had not yet recovered from an earlier scandal in August. The new Knesset building had opened in Jerusalem, and celebrities from all over the world took part in the pomp, but the nation's founder was not among them. Relegated to the stands and passed over as a speaker, Ben-Gurion had declined to come.

Now, on his birthday, however, Israel had come to him. And the moonlit desert echoed with the thunder of ten thousand voices singing "Happy birthday, dear Ben-Gurion," as flags fluttered along sandy paths and long beams of light danced amid the stars. Israel's finest actors portrayed scenes from his life, and speaker after speaker thanked him for redeeming his people.

"You have put faith into our hearts with the flame of your vision," said one. "This faith has enabled us to hold our heads high, to fortify ourselves in our agony; you have been a partner to our lives."

Ben-Gurion smiled, yet rather sadly. So many people, so much love. But where were his old comrades who had struggled with him through all the crises, keeping pace with destiny? He gazed upon the floodlit multitude and felt alone.

Ben-Gurion was never more convinced that Eshkol was a menace to Israel than on May 19, 1967, when the Prime Minister partly mobilized the army and brought the nation to the brink of war. Nasser's troops had marched into the Sinai; but, to Ben-Gurion, that was no reason to wage war. He had hesitated to launch the Sinai Campaign almost a decade earlier, even with the support of France and Britain. Now, all the Western powers would condemn a preemptive Israeli strike.

He stressed the danger to Army Chief of Staff Yitzhak Rabin when the General, depressed and worried, stopped by his house for advice. "I very much doubt whether Nasser wants to go to war," he said. "You, or whoever gave you permission to mobilize so many reservists, made a mistake. We must not go to war."

Rabin was stunned. "It was painful to see him in his present state," he would say, "totally cut off from any source of information and, worse, clinging staunchly to outmoded concepts. . . . Having come to Ben-Gurion for encouragement, I left him feeling doubly despondent."

With Eshkol wallowing in indecision, many Israelis, unaware of Ben-Gurion's views, began clamoring for their slightly tarnished god to reclaim his throne and lead them to another glorious military victory. Even Menachem Begin now asked him to come back. Ben-Gurion had earlier sought to use Begin as a possible counterweight to Eshkol, finding even so "unspeakable" an enemy more palatable than a "treacherous" comrade. Reversing a policy of almost two decades, he had urged colleagues to take Begin into the government.

Now Begin reciprocated. He urged Ben-Gurion to lead a government of national unity and raise the sword against Egypt. But after paying the Old Man a visit, Begin too would leave disillusioned.

The legend of the desert lion was sullied. Ben-Gurion, it was now said, had lost his audacity and his vision. He had, in his declining years, turned docile and lived in an abstract, unrealistic world. And he had, in fact, lost some of his toughness. Even if he favored war, Ben-Gurion told a comrade, he could "no longer lead boys into battle." But he had not really changed his views. He was just voicing openly what he had said only privately while in power: War was an unacceptable risk unless Israel was mortally threatened—especially if it didn't have the support of at least one strong ally. And his old cautiously aggressive approach grew apparent when Nasser closed the Straits of Tiran. Ben-Gurion now favored an attack on Sharm el-Sheikh in order to open the waterway but would not strike elsewhere.

As Ben-Gurion's heroic image faded, Moshe Dayan's sharply emerged. Local leaders streamed into Jerusalem with identical messages: The people were demanding that Eshkol give up the defense ministry he personally headed and turn it over to Dayan. The anti-Dayan cabinet veterans preferred Yigal Allon, hero of the 1948 war, but finally bent to the wind. Dayan was offered the defense post.

Should he accept it? Rafi leaders met to decide. Ben-Gurion was wary, for Dayan favored a preemptive attack. A great soldier, a great mind, but still too impetuous. Still not ripe enough to make the big decisions, to see the full picture. At the same time, Eshkol, whom Dayan would serve, was a "coward." But Ben-Gurion's colleagues stood firm: Dayan should accept. Only *he* could raise the army's slumping morale.

Ben-Gurion back-pedaled. All right, but if Dayan was to be defense minister, why not prime minister as well? Let Eshkol take orders from *him.*

Impossible! replied the others.

"Moshe," Ben-Gurion finally said, "accept!"

Dayan smiled. "I'll accept on one condition," he said. "That I'll have your advice."

Ben-Gurion was relieved. Perhaps he could still talk Moshe into stopping a full-scale war.

"All right," he replied, "but you'll have to come to Sde Boker."

"I'm now the commander, and you'll stay in Tel Aviv! That's an order!"

Everyone laughed and drank to Moshe's success.

Ben-Gurion stayed in Tel Aviv, but Dayan did not ask for his advice. On June 4, the cabinet was to vote on war or peace—but Dayan didn't call. Finally, word came that Israel would attack the following day and Dayan would drop in for five minutes. Ben-Gurion was crushed. No, he replied, Moshe needn't bother. The following day, June 5, he lamented in his diary: "I feel certain this is a great mistake."

On the second day of the war, however, Ben-Gurion's mood changed; the Israelis were scoring stunning victories. "We must win a complete victory," he now wrote. But, as in the past, he opposed keeping the West Bank permanently: "There are about a million Arabs west of the Jordan and we don't need more Arabs in Israel."

He now tried again to meet with Dayan, but the General still avoided him. As Dayan himself would explain, "I forebore from taking counsel with him [because] I thought that he had an imperfect vision of our situation, that he was living in a world that had passed. . . . In this war I would be on my own."

Finally, when a cease-fire with Syria ended in renewed fighting, Ben-Gurion phoned and asked how it had happened. Dayan's silence was "sufficient." Israel had broken the truce. No wonder Moshe hadn't called him. He knew the Old Man would oppose such action.

"We have no need of the [Golan] Heights," Ben-Gurion would write, "because we won't remain there. . . . [And] it is wrong to show our enemies that we break our word . . . and to [risk losing] much of the world's sympathy and friendship. . . . One can't deceive the whole world."

Ben-Gurion himself had done so in the Sinai Campaign. But, of course, *then* he was a politician. A prophet had to be more careful. He couldn't afford to risk the future for an immediate gain. The immediate gain, however, was ample. After six days, total triumph. . . . East Jerusalem, the Sinai, Gaza, the West Bank, the Golan Heights. And a new era began as Israelis prayed at the liberated Western (Wailing) Wall and went skin-diving in the crystal waters of the Sinai. It was time for them to become a normal nation, to lay down the terrible messianic burden that Ben-Gurion had saddled them with, to live and die and be forgotten, their souls unlit by any burning legacy to the world.

Ben-Gurion knew, as Dayan did, that the time of the prophet was over.

Soon almost all Ben-Gurion's followers knew it. Against his wishes, most Rafi members, even Dayan and Peres, voted in December 1967 to form with Mapai and Ahdut HaAvodah a single great Labor Party. All his life Ben-Gurion had fought for labor unity, building the Histadrut and Mapai, begging his comrades to unite. But now with this new attempt at unity, he stood aloof and alone, deserted by even his closest disciples. Pathetically he joined with a handful of men, among them Isser Harel, whom he had recently condemned as a "fascist," to create another party, the State List, which would win only four Knesset seats in the 1969 elections.

The following year, the founder of the state, shorn of almost all influence, gave up his seat and retired from politics for good, an event barely noted by the press on the inside pages. How did he feel? "No comment!" he answered newsmen as he climbed into his car for the lonely drive into the Negev.

Hardly had his Rafi comrades abandoned Ben-Gurion when a new, more chilling loneliness engulfed him. Paula suffered a stroke in January 1968, and day after day Ben-Gurion stood vigil in Beersheba Hospital. Though ill for months, she had never stopped guarding him from people who would steal his time and perhaps stoke his desires. She had even journeyed with him to the United States on a fund-raising tour a few months earlier, dragging herself out of bed to be by his side.

When the doctor told Ben-Gurion that Paula would die, the Old Man paled, then said calmly, almost casually: "One day man will understand how the brain functions."

The doctor persuaded Ben-Gurion to go home, but called him soon afterward—Paula was dead. There was an agonized silence.

"Amos," Ben-Gurion said after putting down the phone, "let's find a place to bury Mother." They drove to the Sde Boker library on the sandy crest of a hill, the nucleus of Ben-Gurion's projected desert college, and explored the surrounding barrenness, cratered and crystalline, that sloped down into a plateau and rolled in amber splendor to an almost invisible horizon.

"Here!" said Ben-Gurion, pointing to a spot that overlooked a breathtaking glare of desert and sky. And when Amos proposed another place, the father protested, "Who's going to lie here, you or me?"

Yes, from here he and Paula would watch the Negev turn green and listen to the hum of factories grinding out goods for the markets of the world. And perhaps their graves would attract more pioneers to the desert, boys and girls who would make the vision come true.

Father and son drove to the hospital, where Ben-Gurion insisted that the blanket covering the corpse be lifted, even though the doctor warned that Paula's face was distorted in death. Never mind. He must see Paula once more. Guilt engulfed him. Why had he left her in her last hours? What had she said? Had she asked for him? "Paula, Paula, Paula!" he mumbled, stroking her hand.

But even at the funeral, Ben-Gurion remained the prophet.

"I've been meaning to write a reply to your article," he told a political foe.

The funeral drew many political foes, who saw an opportunity to make amends with Ben-Gurion. Even Golda Meir came, and then sat with the family at home for hours, silent and sheepish. The family, especially Renana, was furious. Didn't Golda know that after all her "ugly" charges they didn't want her around? Ben-Gurion hardly looked at her, though he could never hate her. She was, after all, a woman, a great woman. And she had suffered much in her childhood.

If Ben-Gurion didn't weep at Paula's funeral, he would when he visited her grave on the first anniversary of her death. It would take at least that long for him to fully realize that she was gone. Often as he got up from the dinner table he would say, "Come, Paula, let's go"—until it dawned on him that she was not there. He missed her more as time went on and wrote to a friend: "Paula was unique. She was a friend, a wife, a mother, a child, a sister—she was Paula."

Ben-Gurion even had a bodyguard prepare his wife's special dishes, including one that he especially disliked. Why did he eat food he disliked? his grandson Yariv asked him. "I eat it once a day," replied Ben-Gurion, "in memory of Grandma."

In all the years of their marriage, they had had little in common, little to talk about, and she had never really understood his dream. But like his mother, she had protected him and shared his suffering, and most important of all, she had accepted his neglect. Now he could no longer ease his guilt by writing passionate love letters or watching her taste the heady wine of summit society. It simply wasn't fair, he moaned, that Paula, who was younger than he (a disputable claim), should die first. And he himself began to die—"spiritually."

But at the same time, the crushing weight of decades began to lift. More than seventy years earlier, the death of his mother had triggered a gradual choking-off of emotions that could jeopardize his mission. Now the death of his wife, it seems, modified his values and to some extent liberated him emotionally. Suddenly the driven messiah, already relieved of his great political burden, mellowed into a docile old man.

"After Paula died," says her friend Esther Rubin, "Ben-Gurion was more sentimental and human. No one believed he would grieve so much. No one thought he was capable of it."

Ben-Gurion spent much time now in the company of his loved ones. Zippora had died in 1965, but his children and grandchildren came to see him often, either in Sde Boker or Tel Aviv. Perhaps the unhappiest visitor was Geula's daughter, Orit, whom he would sometimes mistake for Yariv's wife and demand that she become pregnant without delay—though she was not even married yet. Renana, who had recently given birth to a boy, had her father over for dinner every Friday night when he was in Tel Aviv. For hours they analyzed the potential of the human brain, which Ben-Gurion would come to view as the ultimate weapon in the Jewish struggle for survival. This subject especially interested him after Paula's fatal stroke—and his own memory lapses, which deeply worried him because "a man who does not remember is no longer a man." How, he wondered, would he ever complete his memoirs, which must guide future generations?

He was apparently unaware that he also began to repeat himself in his conversation and speeches, a tendency that became so serious in his last year that his aides tried to keep him from speaking in public. When Teddy Kollek sought to stop him from reciting Biblical verses at the Youth World Bible Quiz, the nation's founder appealed to Rabbi Gevaryahu, the quiz director, who reluctantly agreed to let him read two or three verses. Ben-Gurion was euphoric.

Worried about her father, Renana asked him if she and her family could move in with him for a while, and he gladly agreed. But then he wondered if they simply wanted to ease his loneliness. No, he now said, they couldn't move in. Yet he was so lonely that when a ninety-one-year-old British woman he had never met wrote to ask if she could stay with him, he invited her to come—though his dismayed aides never sent the invitation.

One day in 1970 a "miracle" happened that drew Ben-Gurion even closer to his newly discovered family. Amos called Sde Boker: He was a grandfather! Some minutes later, Geula phoned: She was a grandmother! Ben-Gurion was confused and thought at first that they were talking about the same baby. Then it dawned: He had just become a great-grandfather *twice.* Incredible! This had to be an act of God! "If only there were some way," he wailed, "that I could let Paula know!"

And Ben-Gurion related to his great-grandchildren with uncharacteristic warmth and intimacy. Grandson Yariv could barely believe his eyes when he returned home with his wife one night—their babysitter, Ben-Gurion, was rolling on the rug with his giggling great-grandchild, his face aglow.

While Ben-Gurion's family kept in frequent touch with him, he seems to have quietly despaired that his friends had abandoned him. One Independence Day, a friend visited him and found him in bed reading a book while the echoes of celebration sounded in the distance. Why were the people celebrating? "Because of what you did for them, Ben-Gurion!" It seemed ironic. The same will and vision that had created the state had made him a pariah. Ben-Gurion smiled and when their chat had ended went back to his book. His visitor left with tears in his eyes. All alone on *his* day. . . .

Apparently fearing criticism by future historians and remembering Paula's pleas for reconciliation, Ben-Gurion soon forgave almost everybody "for what he did to them," as one pundit put it, including Lavon. He even forgave Begin, and wrote him: "Paula . . . was for some reason an admirer of yours. I opposed your road . . . but personally I never harbored any grudge against you, and as I got to know you better . . . my esteem for you grew and my Paula rejoiced in it."

Sharett and Eshkol died before they could be forgiven, and Ben-Gurion did not even attend their funerals, but he now had kind words for them too. Still, Ben-Gurion perhaps never fully forgave Eshkol, for Eshkol had "betrayed" him. Politicians born and bred in Eastern Europe did not lose their instinct for devouring their heaviest debtors, especially close comrades.

Many of Ben-Gurion's former foes joyously responded to his sudden serenity at a festive Mapai luncheon held in 1971 to mark his eighty-fifth birthday. Ben-Gurion listened impassively as Golda, who had succeeded Eshkol as prime minister, espressed her "pain and sorrow for what took place between us during a certain period of time." Then, at a special session of the Knesset, friends and enemies who had worked and fought beside him throughout his life—from his early days in Petah Tikvah to the Six-Day War—jammed the hall to hear him speak once again of the "uniqueness of the Jewish people," the "vision of redemption," Spinoza, Hess and Herzl. When Ben-Gurion had entered, he could barely believe that he was being shown to the speaker's chair. "Are you sure I sit here?" he asked. But after his momentous reception, he knew, apparently with mixed feelings, that everybody had forgiven him. . . . For what? Was it a crime to insist that they live up to his dream?

Having performed their duty and salved their consciences, Ben-Gurion's old comrades ignored him once again. At the Independence Day parade in May 1973, Israel's twenty-fifth anniversary, Golda did not even invite him to sit in the same box with her and the President. And his friends seldom found time to visit him. When someone did, he would usually find it difficult leaving. There was no Paula now to shoo him out, and Ben-Gurion would often clutch the person's arm and press him to remain and reminisce about old times—though he had always deplored "small talk."

Ben-Gurion talked most often now of the distant past. One night, on a trip, he pattered barefoot in his long underwear into the adjoining hotel room of his aide, Elchanan Yishai, and cried, "Elchanan, wake up! I want to talk to you about my mother." And after extolling her virtues for an hour, he plodded back to bed, still, it seemed, the child of eleven whose world had suddenly exploded.

Ben-Gurion also reminisced sometimes about a beautiful young girl from Plonsk whom he said he had loved in his youth, though he never mentioned her name. "He spoke of her over and over," one visitor recalls. "He spoke tenderly, and his expression became soft and almost angelic. I felt embarrassed, as if he were revealing something to me that no one had a right to know."

Ben-Gurion would reveal very little even to Rachel herself, though he continued to see her occasionally. Sometimes he would send a chauffeured car to drive her and her daughters to Sde Boker, and he spent one particularly memorable day with her in her home after the filming of a documentary on his life. Rachel, now frail, gray and gaunt, was introduced in the film as a "childhood comrade," but there was not a hint of their deeper relationship. Ben-Gurion refused to leave, and a bodyguard virtually had to drag him out so he could keep an appointment. Following Paula's death, he wrote Rachel more often than he had done at any time since their youth.

In one note, he wrote: "Your letter . . . enchanted me. The friendship of youth is eternal—how good it is to know this." In another: "I presume that you know well how precious you have been to me since our youth."

Finally, in 1970, he no longer addressed her as "My dear Rachel," but as "Dear and beloved Rachel." Referring to a letter she sent him, he wrote: "The memories are yours as well as mine, from Plonsk and our journey to *Eretz Yisrael* with Shlomo Zemach and your mother, from the life we shared in Petah Tikvah and our numerous meetings since then and until today."

And then Ben-Gurion reflected on his dream: "There is hope, dear Rachel, that peace is approaching, not quickly, but slowly, slowly, and . . . it appears to me that by the end of this century the prophecy of Isaiah will be fulfilled."

Ben-Gurion had shared the euphoria that bubbled through Israel's veins after the Six-Day War. The first thing he did was to visit conquered Jerusalem and symbolically order a soldier to tear down a sign in Arabic by the Western Wall. Jerusalem was transformed. And so were his people. Never had he seen them fizz with such optimism, confidence and faith. In the heady atmosphere, immigrants from Western nations streamed in, together with their duty-free refrigerators and cars; tourists crammed new luxury hotels that scarred ancient Biblical skylines; foreign businessmen fiercely competed for investment bonanzas; merrymakers crowded bustling cafés and rock-blaring discotheques late into the night. The economy boomed, and Israel, it seemed, was on the edge of Eden.

But as Ben-Gurion peeked under the froth, his spirits gradually soured. What sort of country would he leave behind? A powerful, modern nation had sprouted in the desert, but had he failed Isaiah? Israel still wasn't an exemplary state. The people were splintered and many had become materialistic and smug; increasing numbers of thieves, racketeers and prostitutes were helping to turn the country into one like any other; and violence had become common as a means of persuasion or protest—even among religious groups, which hurled rocks at nonobservant Jews or at each other if one sect didn't conform to another's standards. Tragically lacking the vision of the pioneer, most Israelis craved the "good life," the mediocrity of "normalcy," and they refused to move to the Negev. Ben-Gurion still felt like Moses dragging his people through the wilderness, seeking to turn sinners into saviors. And now he could lure them toward the Promised Land only with the written word—his memoirs and other papers that he would leave behind.

Was Israel even governable? Ben-Gurion was not at all sure. Politically only a stable two-party system could end the chaos of multiparty coalition. But the parties, with their greed for power outweighing their concern for the state, rejected a new system. And this greed not only had crippled political life but had produced a bureaucratic crust that stifled business incentive and labor productivity, indeed, the Israeli spirit. Was this democracy? Was this moral rule?

Socially this nation was bitterly split between the Sephardim and the Ashkenazim, the largely impoverished Oriental community and the more prosperous European community. The Sephardim had once accepted life in leaky tents, but now their children, many of them angry dropouts from school, craved a bigger share of the power and wealth. Jammed into slums, eight or ten to a room, they rioted for better housing and better benefits, overturning cars, stoning police, breaking shop windows.

Did Ben-Gurion realize that he was at least partly responsible for Sephardic discontent? Though he had patronizingly repeated many times that he hoped one day to see a "Yemenite chief of staff," he did little, in fact, to groom the Sephardim for such exalted jobs—not with the entrenched Europeans jealously guarding their fiefdoms of power. He had tried to raise their educational level, but their social and economic progress was not one of his top priorities in an era of ingathering and insecurity. He had once planned to carve an Oriental Jewish province out of the Ottoman Empire, but he would create a European culture, alien and isolated in this part of the world. Had Ben-Gurion's priorities saved the nation only to jeopardize the dream?

Whatever the answer, Ben-Gurion did not stop dreaming. He hoped that five million more Jews would eventually settle in Israel—to make a total of eight million—confident that one day the expanded population would build an exemplary state. In pursuing this goal, he pleaded with mothers to bear at least four children; he told one woman who had twenty that she "set an example for all Israeli girls!"

"As long as the people of Israel remain small in number," he would say, "they will face the world alone; but when there is a big, strong nation in Israel it will dwell securely among the nations and many will seek its friendship."

Israel must first live securely among the Arab nations. Despite his initial joy after the Six-Day War, Ben-Gurion did not view that war as a victory, but simply as an escape from another Holocaust. Only real peace could mean real victory. And real peace, he felt, was likely only in about ten years—and then only with Egypt. Young Egyptian intellectuals, eager to build up their country and convinced that Israel was here to stay, would demand peace and, he prophesied, an Egyptian leader would emerge who would support their view. This leader might have been Nasser had he not died in 1970, since, Ben-Gurion was persuaded, this old foe had seriously wanted to talk peace with

him in his last days. As for Nasser's successor, Anwar Sadat, the
Prime Minister felt, ironically enough, that he would not seek
peace.

Ben-Gurion was pleased that American arms shipments
begun under President Kennedy had multiplied under President Lyndon Johnson, reflecting Israel's new tight bond with
the United States. Yet, not only had real peace eluded Israel up
to now, but many valuable friends were slipping away. President De Gaulle had warned Israel not to attack and was now
demanding that it withdraw from all conquered areas. In one
speech he called the Jews an "elite people, self-assured and
domineering."

Unfair and untrue, Ben-Gurion wrote him.

No insult intended, De Gaulle replied. He meant the description as a compliment!

But it was clear that Israel could no longer rely on France for
rescue in an emergency. And almost as troubling to Ben-Gurion
was his personal disillusion. How could so great a man as De
Gaulle utter words smelling of anti-Semitism? Nevertheless,
Ben-Gurion virtually excused the French leader. "After all," he
told the press, "we cannot judge a man only according to his
attitude toward the Jewish people."

Ben-Gurion agreed with De Gaulle that Israeli troops should
pull out of the conquered areas, though he would keep Jerusalem and the Golan Heights—and stand fast everywhere until
the ink was dry on final peace treaties. He was even ready to
relinquish the Golan Heights until the military flew him by
helicopter over the once deadly peaks so he might see how
Syrian artillery shells could rain down on Israeli settlements.
With the Arabs snubbing peace, he was willing to let a limited
number of Jews stake their claims in unoccupied sectors of the
West Bank, but would grant autonomy to the Arabs and, perhaps
later, statehood. In fact, Jews, he wrote, "can live in Hebron in
a friendly Arab state, just as they live in London." And he told
one interviewer:

> First, never forget that historically this country [Palestine] belongs to
> two races. . . . Second, remember the Arabs drastically outbreed us, and
> to insure survival a Jewish state must at all times maintain within her
> own borders an unassailable Jewish majority. Third, the logic of all this
> is that to get peace, we *must* return in principle to the pre-1967 borders.
> . . . Peace is more important than real estate.
>   Militarily defensible borders, while desirable, cannot by themselves
> guarantee our future. Some sections of our people still have not learned
> this lesson. *Real* peace with our neighbors, mutual respect and even

affection, perhaps an Arab-Israeli alliance, in any case, a settlement they will not reluctantly agree to live with, but will enthusiastically welcome from their hearts as essential for our common future—that is our only *true* security. Then together we could turn the Middle East into a second Garden of Eden and one of the great creative centers of the earth.

With final peace, Ben-Gurion even envisaged the United Nations building a shrine of the prophets in Jerusalem to serve a "federated union of all continents." Jerusalem would also be the seat of a supreme court of mankind "to settle controversies among the federated continents, as prophesied by Isaiah."

Ben-Gurion's perceptions had changed drastically since his days in Sejera, when he had fought Arab raiders with a sooty old rifle, utterly unaware that they coveted anything more than Jewish possessions and lives. He had led his people to war in 1948 so they might survive, and in 1956 so they might breathe more freely. He had opposed war in 1967 and now would pay a heavy price in territory to avert any future war. Ben-Gurion wanted his people not only to live, but to live without fear. Yes, they now did, but only because fantasy had replaced fear. They were, he felt, still dazzled by the "illusion" of victory in 1967, by a dangerous omnipotent image of themselves. He himself was far less optimistic. "Ask me," he said to a colleague, "whether my son, Amos, has a chance of dying and being buried in a Jewish state, and I would answer: fifty-fifty." Yes, what if the Arabs suddenly struck back? They might prove Isaiah wrong, for a state that no longer existed could not be exemplary. . . .

In October 1973, on Yom Kippur, the Arabs struck back.

"Happy birthday, Ben-Gurion!"

This time only a handful of relatives and close friends visited him—he was eighty-seven.

"May you live to a hundred and twenty."

Coughing hard as he lay in bed with bronchitis in his Tel Aviv home, Ben-Gurion made a motion with his hand, apparently to suggest that in fact the end was near. He was alarmed —not about his own fate but about that of the state. Would the state die with him? A few days earlier, it seemed, this might be the cruel logic of their linked destinies, for the Egyptian and Syrian armies had caught Israel by surprise. And though Israeli troops were now striking back on both fronts, the danger was still not over.

When one friend assured Ben-Gurion that Israel would win, he suddenly sat up and asked, "What makes you so confident?"

And he refused to say another word about the war. Instead, he sought solace in the Bible, mumbling a pertinent passage to Rabbi Gevaryahu, who didn't yet know that his son had been killed in battle:

"The eternal God . . . shall say, Destroy them. Israel then shall dwell in safety alone: the fountain of Jacob shall be upon a land of corn and wine; also his heavens shall drop down dew. Happy art thou, O Israel. . . ."

But even if Israel survived, would it dwell in safety and happiness? The attack had confirmed Ben-Gurion's worst fears: Israel was frighteningly vulnerable. The fantasy had burst, and the land of "corn and wine" would never be the same. What would now happen to his people? With their prophet gone, who would protect them from their enemies and themselves? Could he die without knowing that his beloved state would live?

When Geula told him some days later that her daughter had given birth to a boy, his eyes gleamed for a moment. "He will be a good soldier," he said.

Soon afterward, Ben-Gurion suffered a stroke and was rushed to the hospital. He did not know that only shortly before, Amos' son, a good soldier, had been gravely wounded in battle. But though the Old Man was partially paralyzed and no longer able to speak, his sunken eyes spoke for him. "They were full of agony," Geula would say. Was he thinking of all the good soldiers who might fall in the future—possibly obeying the orders of men who would corrupt his dream and compromise the state?

The gleam, it seems, returned when Rachel visited him. Sitting by his bed, she gently caressed his trembling hand and they silently exchanged stares. Reliving, perhaps, moments of youth and love and a voyage of destiny. As Rachel rose to leave, unable to suppress tears, Ben-Gurion's bodyguard consoled her: "I'm sure he recognized you."

On December 1, 1973, David Ben-Gurion, the father of his country, died. And Rachel followed a few months later.

The voyage had ended.

NOTES

Notes are keyed to the text by page number and identifying words at the beginning of the note. A single phrase (e.g., *If an opportunity*) is used to indicate the first words of the material covered by the note. This material either ends where the material covered by the next note begins, or, if no other note follows in the same paragraph, extends to the end of the paragraph.

Two phrases (e.g., *Tel Aviv bakes* to *Jewish people wait*) indicate the first words and the last words of the material covered by the note. This form is used to cite more than one paragraph, or a portion of one paragraph when material covered by a subsequent note in the paragraph does not immediately follow.

Full titles and names of authors (first-name initials of article writers), as well as the location of documents, are indicated in the Bibliography. Full names and identities of interviewees appear in the Acknowledgments.

If an author has more than one book listed in the Bibliography, any one cited may be identified by key words in its title.

Page numbers are cited for all books except those in the Hebrew and Yiddish languages.

"Ben-Gurion" refers to David Ben-Gurion unless another first name or an initial precedes it.

Other forms of citation are:

IDFA—Israel Defense Forces Archives
Int.—Interview
JA—Jewish Agency
JO—*Jewish Observer and Middle East Review*
JP—*Jerusalem Post*
JPS—Jewish Publication Society
LA—Labor Archives
LPA—Labor Party Archives
NJM—*National Jewish Monthly*
NYT—*New York Times*

(o.h.)—Oral History
PP—*Palestine Post*
PZ—Poalei Zion
WZO—World Zionist Organization
ZA—Zionist Archives

Prologue (pages 19–39)

19–20: *Tel Aviv bakes* to *Jewish people wait*—Kurzman *Genesis 1948* pp. 248–50; Sharef pp. 281–82; Yorman pp. 26–32; Brilliant in NJM 3/1970; JP 4/30/1968

20–21: *It wasn't easy* to *"birth certificate" had arrived*—Kurzman *Genesis 1948* pp. 248–50; Sharef pp. 281–82; Yorman pp. 39–64; Brilliant in NJM 3/1970; JP 4/30/1968; Int. Ben-Tov, Rosen, Sharef, M. Sharett

21–23: *The comically amateurish* to *powerful new nation*—Yorman pp. 39–40; Int. Ben-Gurion, Sharef, M. Sharett, Yadin

23–24: *At 4 P.M.* to *declares the meeting over*—Kurzman *Genesis 1948* pp. 250–51; Sharef pp. 282–88; Yorman pp. 39–41, 65–75; Brilliant in NJM 3/1970; JP 4/30/1968

24: *And then, as he steps down*—J. and D. Kimche *Clash.* (The reporter was Jon Kimche.)

24: *Propelled by an unbendable* to *one brick at a time*—Int. Z. Kesse, M. Sharett

25: *"People call Ben-Gurion*—Int. M. Sharett

25: *"When I'm in a rage*—Emanuel Neumann in memorial tribute to Ben-Gurion 2/20/1974

25: *"If an opportunity*—Peres *HaShalav HaBa*

25: *Ben-Gurion's pragmatism*—Int. G. Ben-Eliezer

25: *Feeding Ben-Gurion's Zionist fervor* to *ingrained inferiority complex*—Int. Yadin

26: *Most curiously of all*—Int. Feldenkrais (*"secretly ate ham"*), Gevaryahu (*"seldom wore a hat"*)

26: *"I've read much*—Int. Burg

26: *Earlier he had written*—Pearlman *Looks* p. 216

26: *"Nothing can surpass*—Ben-Gurion *Rebirth* p. 444

26: *According to Rabbi*—Int. Gevaryahu

27: *To Ben-Gurion*—Finkelstein (o.h.)

27: *When a survivor* to *language of exile*—Int. Lubetkin

27: *And after the 1967*—Int. C. Herzog

27: *"You know"*—Finkelstein (o.h.)

27: *The key to Israel's* to *among the nations"*—JP 11/10/1975

28: *Ben-Gurion once told*—Goldmann *Autobiography* p. 292

28: *Yet, the outlawing of war*—Ben-Gurion, speech at Gen. Ass., Reconstituted Jewish Agency, Jer. 6/23/1971

28: *"In the majority*—Ben-Gurion *Recollections* p. 178

28: *Nor, he claimed, is Israel*—Pearlman *Looks* p. 231; Ben-Gurion address on "Science and Ethics," Brandeis U. 3/9/1960

29: *According to Teddy*—JP 10/8/1971

29: *Once, when he was visiting* to *just a little Jew"*—St. John *Ben-Gurion* p. 107 (quotes Ruth Gruber in NY *Post*)

29: *But when someone* to *look like Lincoln"*—Int. Goldman

29: *Only once was he known*—Int. Katzman

29: *"What difference does*—King in NYT Mag. 7/19/1959

29: *Typically, at one dinner*—Int. Beer

30: *"Never mind*—Int. Weisgal

30: *Without air conditioning*—McDonald p. 246

30–31: *But whatever the weather* to *for most of these books*—Int. P. Ben-Gurion, Lif; author's observations

31: *(Sometimes he unwittingly boosted* to *in great demand*—Int. Goldman

32: *Ben-Gurion spent*—Author's observations

32: *More accurately than modestly*—Lewis in NYT Mag. 5/6/1951

32: *With straight-faced*—Elon in *Haaretz* 4/9/1971 (quotes Shlomo Lavi)

32: *And, characteristically, when*—Goldmann *Paradox*

32–33: *He was "a self-taught*—Int. Yadin

33: *He deeply respected* to *learned men"*—Int. Gevaryahu

33: *Walter Eytan*—Int. Eytan

33: *One language he never* to *Not practical!*—Int. Strumza

33: *Yitzhak Navon, an aide* to *wouldn't miss one*—Int. Navon

34: *No, it wasn't true* to *he is a gentleman"*—Int. E. Ben-Eliezer

34: *A speaker at a meeting*—Int. Katzman

35: *Elchanan Yishai, a close aide*—Int. Yishai

35: *Ben-Gurion's relations* to *own minutes at meetings*—Int. Diskin, Gil, Lif, Rosen, Siegal

35: *A caller might leave*—Int. D. Carmel

35–36: *Sometimes, if Ben-Gurion disliked*—Ratner

36: *Or he might abruptly*—Sharett *Yoman Ishi* 12/16/1956

36: *If, however, he liked to before they were realized*—Ratner

36: *"I would rack my brain*—Gurari (o.h.; quotes Yosef Serlin)

36: *Ben-Gurion never relaxed* to *stare at the wall?*—Int. Siegal

36: *"Satisfaction? What's that?*—Peres *HaShalav HaBa*

36: *And woe to the aide*—*Ibid.*

36: *"Why is your hair* to *so squinty*—Int. Diskin

37: *He didn't realize that*—Int. Weisgal

37: *When one secretary mentioned*—Int. Diskin

37: *Since Ben-Gurion wished*—Int. Lif and other secretaries

37: *And while traveling*—Surkis (o.h.)

37: *Thus, when an aide told him*—Int. Peres

37: *United States Ambassador Ogden Reid*—Int. Reid

38: *Few people were surprised*—Goldmann *Paradox* p. 101

38: *Nor did many doubt*—Int. Masler

38: *According to his daughter*—Int. R. Leshem

39: *When an associate*—Weisgal *So Far*

Chapter One (pages 43–73)

43–44: *The Polish and Jewish communities* to *as the Jews were*—*Encyclopaedia Judaica; Sefer Plonsk*

44: *The shtetl of Plonsk* to *(shadchans) and beggars*—Mark in *Jewish Digest* 10/1963

44–45: *But their dream* to *channel their hatred*—Laqueur *Zionism* pp. 58–61; Int. B. Ben-Gurion

45: *Still, most Plonsk Jews*—Habas; Lavi; Mark in *Jewish Digest* 10/1963; Int. Rosenberg

45: *One of the alleys* to *child would survive)*—Habas; Int. E. Ben-Gurion, Arye Ben-Gurion, B. Ben-Gurion

45–46: *David was born to cookies and sweets*—Habas; Int. B. Ben-Gurion, Finkelstein, Yitzhak Kvashner, Rosenberg

46: *The host, Avigdor to even to a university*—Int. Eisenberg, Rosenberg

46: *The father's affectations*—Int. Yitzhak Kvashner

46–47: *After centuries of conditioning*—Ben-Gurion *Mémoires* p. 9

47: *To the mystical Hassidim*—Laqueur *Zionism* pp. 61–62; Litvinoff pp. 25–26

47: *Avigdor Green had to of the Jewish people*—*Ibid.*

47–48: *What path to freedom to oppression and insecurity*—Habas; Ben-Gurion in JP 9/30/1966

48: *Avigdor was in a sense*—Bar-Zohar *Ben-Gurion* pp. 1–2; Ben-Gurion in JP 9/30/1966

48: *Since Avigdor dealt*—Ben-Gurion *Israel: A Personal History* pp. 10–11; Laqueur *Zionism* pp. 70–75

48: *People streamed into*—Habas; Ben-Gurion in JP 9/30/1966; Int. B. Ben-Gurion

48: *"In those days*—Tevet *Kin'at* v.1

49: *David's third year*—Int. B. Ben-Gurion, Yitzhak Kvashner

49: *Then the other wonderful*—Habas; Ben-Gurion in JP 9/30/1966

49: *Even before David*—Int. Yitzhak Kvashner

49: *One day, when David was five*—Ben-Gurion in JP 9/30/1966; Int. E. Ben-Gurion

49: *But Sheindel was more concerned*—Ben-Gurion in JP 9/30/1966

50: *When David was seven*—Ben-Gurion *Mémoires* p. 8

50: *Gradually, David grew*—Habas

50: *But withdrawn and rather*—Int. Yitzhak Kvashner

50: *Nevertheless, he often*—Ben-Gurion in JP 9/30/1966

50: *The willingness of the Jews*—*Ibid.*

50: *And sometimes on the Sabbath*—Int. Yitzhak Kvashner

50: *He seldom played*—*Ibid.*

50: *But though David was introverted*—Int. B. Ben-Gurion, Yitzhak Kvashner

51: *David did so well*—Int. Yitzhak Kvashner

51: *His classroom was part to lower strata*—Ben-Gurion *Mémoires* pp. 12–13; *Sefer Plonsk;* Ben-Gurion in JP 10/5/1966; Int. Yitzhak Kvashner, Rosenberg

51–52: *David's Beth Hamidrash to all living things*—Ben-Gurion *Mémoires* p. 13; Laqueur *Zionism* pp. 66–67; Ben-Gurion in JP 10/5/1966; Int. Yitzhak Kvashner

52: *David was delighted*—Ben-Gurion in JP 10/5/1966

52: *But this zeal*—Habas

52: *"There was a rumor"*—Ben-Gurion in JP 9/30/1966

52–53: *Theodor Herzl, a reporter to home in Palestine"*—Litvinoff pp. 31–32; Ben-Gurion in JP 9/30/1966

53: *Like other Zionists*—Ben-Gurion in JP 9/30/1966; Int. Yitzhak Kvashner

53: *It struck when*—Int. Yishai

53: *"I used to see her*—Ben-Gurion *Mémoires* p. 13; Habas

53–54: *Avigdor tried to fill to brutal uncertainties*—Int. E. Ben-Gurion

54: *Several months after*—Lavi; Int. Ruth Beit-Halachmi, Y. Beit-Halachmi, Izhar, Turel

54: *Like Avigdor Green*—Lavi

54: *David seldom attended*—*Ibid.*; Int. Ruth Beit-Halachmi

55: *The couple, however*—Ben-Gurion in JP 9/30/1966

55: *In desperation*—Lavi

55: *David defiantly met*—

Ben-Gurion in JP 9/30/1966; Int. Finkelstein

55–56: *For David, the decision* to *over a massive head?*—Int. Finkelstein, Vereté

56: *But the two*—Ben-Gurion in JP 9/30/1966; Int. Yitzhak Kvashner

56: *Lovesickness, however*—Lavi; *Sefer Plonsk*

56: *The next day, David*—Lavi; Ben-Gurion in JP 9/30/1966; Int. Yaacov Kvashner

57: *The Yiddish-speaking*—Ben-Gurion *Mémoires* pp. 9–10; Ben-Gurion in JP 9/30/1966

57: *Rabbi Isaac paid*—Ruth Beit-Halachmi

57: *But the three comrades*—Lavi; Ben-Gurion in JP 9/30/1966

57: *With remarkable daring*—Habas

57: *For Tsar Nicholas II*—Biderman p. 6; Edelman p. 26

58: *David called a meeting*—Int. Yaacov Kvashner, Yitzhak Kvashner, Rosenberg

58: *David, however, would not*—Lavi; Int. Yaacov Kvashner

58: *Although Avigdor was proud*—Int. Yitzhak Kvashner, Rosenberg

58: *Avigdor remained close*—Habas; Ben-Gurion in JP 9/30/1966

58: *"When I was twelve*—Ben-Gurion in JP 9/30/1966

58: *A barrier had come between them*—Int. E. Ben-Gurion, Yitzhak Kvashner, Rosenberg

59: *"Leader of our people*—Avigdor Green to Herzl 11/1/1901

59: *Herzl, in any event*—St. John *Ben-Gurion* pp. 15–16; Litvinoff pp. 36–38

59: *News of the split*—Ben-Gurion *Mémoires* p. 14; Ben-Gurion in JP 9/30/1966

60: *One of the three*—Habas; Int. Vereté

60: *"I was still a boy*—Ben-Gurion to Shmuel Fuchs 6/2/1904

60: *For the first time*—Ben-Gurion in JP 9/30/1966; Int. Ruth Beit-Halachmi

60: *If David was at times*—Habas; Int. Halamish

60: *In Warsaw he would groom*—Ben-Gurion in JP 9/30/1966; Int. Yitzhak Kvashner

61: *Yes, I loved* to *do not have the time*—Ben-Gurion to Fuchs 6/2/1904

61: *Shmuel Fuchs was the first*—Int. Finkelstein, Vereté

61: *Fuchs decided to leave*—Tevet *Kin'at* v.1; Int. Yitzhak Kvashner

61: *"I felt so lonely*—Ben-Gurion to Fuchs 6/2/1904

62: *At night David would sit*—Ben-Gurion to Fuchs 6/2/1904

62: *"This time,"* he would *write*—Ibid.

62: *Despite his loneliness*—Tevet *Kin'at* v.1

62: *David finally found*—Ben-Gurion *Mémoires* p. 14; Int. Yitzhak Kvashner

63: *"It was as though* to *visionaries' visions*—Ben-Gurion in JP 10/5/1966

63–64: *I am particularly influenced* to *perhaps forever?*—Ben-Gurion to Fuchs 6/2/1904

64: *"I have a strong yearning*—Ben-Gurion to Fuchs 6/28/1904

64: *"I feel in my heart*—Ibid. 11/6/1904

64: *Another tonic turned out*—Ben-Gurion in JP 10/5/1966; Int. Yitzhak Kvashner

64–65: *Three weeks later* to *returned to Plonsk*—Ben-Gurion to Fuchs 6/14/1904; Int. Vereté

65: *This account contradicted*—Ben-Gurion in JP 10/5/1966

65: *Shlomo later denied*—Int. Vereté

65–66: *A few weeks later* to *you'll have work*—Lavi

66: *David and the others*—Ben-Gurion *Mémoires* p. 15; Int. Vereté

66: *Back in Warsaw*—Bar-

Zohar *Ben-Gurion* p. 9; Tevet *Kin'at* v.1

66–67: *David scurried* to *not the Jewish people*—Tevet *Kin'at* v.1 (incl. quotes: "the revolutionary movement" and "a vacuum was created"); Ben-Gurion to Fuchs 12/18/1904

67: *David's reserve*—Kurzman *Bravest Battle* p. 19; Litvinoff p. 35

67: *And his spirits* to *youth was harmless*—Ben-Gurion *Mémoires* p. 16; Ben-Gurion in JP 10/5/1966

67–68: *After vainly trying*—Avi-hai pp. 81–82; Ben-Gurion *Israel: A Personal History* p. 685

68: *With new enthusiasm*—Litvinoff p. 41; Int. Yitzhak Kvashner

68: *The battle between*—Ben-Gurion *Mémoires* p. 16; Ben-Gurion in JP 9/30/1966; Int. Yitzhak Kvashner, Rosenberg

68–69: *Each of the speakers* to *interior of the town*—Int. Rosenberg

69: *David's membership* to *the house maids*—Sefer Plonsk; Int. Finkelstein, Rosenberg

69: *David was amazed*—Sefer Plonsk

69: *David envisaged*—Int. Finkelstein, Rosenberg

69–70: *If a labor movement* to *blacklist to hide there*—Habas; Ben-Gurion in JP 9/30/1966

70: *"My father was not too happy*—Ben-Gurion in JP 9/30/1966

70: *At the next meeting*—Int. Yaacov Kvashner

70: *And David, trained* to *into their pockets*—Ben-Gurion in JP 9/30/1966

70: *In the shadows of night*—Habas; Ben-Gurion in JP 9/30/1966

70: *David Green was an impressive*—Int. Finkelstein, Yaacov Kvashner, Rosenberg

71: *More important were the implications*—Ben-Gurion in JP 9/30/1966

71: *Despite David's militancy*—Ben-Gurion *Mémoires* pp. 16–17; Ben-Gurion in JP 10/5/1966

71: *David would leave*—Ben-Gurion in JP 9/30/1966

71: *They would be joined*—Tevet *Kin'at* v.1; Int. Finkelstein

71–72: *Shlomo had matured* to *his final goal*—Litvinoff pp. 45–46; Int. Finkelstein, Vereté

72: *A few days before*—Tevet *Kin'at* v.1; Int. Ruth Beit-Halachmi

72: *Finally an agreement*—Rachel Beit-Halachmi to Ben-Gurion 5/1948 (quoted in Habas); Int. Ruth Beit-Halachmi, Finkelstein, Rosenberg

72–73: *"I sat on that great and historic*—Rachel Beit-Halachmi to Ben-Gurion (quoted in Habas)

Chapter Two (pages 74–99)

74: *In t hazy glow*—Ben-Gurion *Mémoires* p. 20; Int. Ruth Beit-Halachmi

74: *"Silently," David would write*—Ben-Gurion *Mémoires* p. 20

74: *From the moment David*—Litvinoff pp. 47–48; Int. Ruth Beit-Halachmi

74: *David felt a sense*—Litvinoff p. 48; Ben-Gurion in JP 10/5/1966

75: *The four travelers*—Knopf (Kurzman) in *El-Alon* fall 1971

75: *As it pulled out* to *triumph over authority*—Habas

75–76: *David's spirits remained* to *invited to visit them*—Ben-Gurion *Mémoires* p. 19

76: *David spent much* to *over*

any dream?—Int. Ruth Beit-Hal-achmi, Y. Beit-Halachmi, Izhar, Turel

76: *Dozens of rowboats*—Ben-Gurion *Mémoires* p. 20; Lavi; Litvinoff pp. 50–51

76–77: *David and the others* to *jetsam and rot*—Ben-Gurion *Mémoires* p. 20; R. Ben-Zvi p. 10; Edelman p. 35; Habas; Lavi

77: *"Waves of joy*—Ben-Gur-ion *Mémoires* p. 20

77: *"Fat Arabs squatted*—Bar-Zohar *Ben-Gurion* p. 14 (quoting Ben-Gurion)

77: *And while ragged idlers*—R. Ben-Zvi p. 11; Lavi; Zemach

77: *"The air smelled*—Edel-man p. 36 (quoting letter to Avig-dor Green)

78: *While David and his friends*—Litvinoff pp. 51–52; Tevet *Kin'at* v.1; Int. Ruth Beit-Halachmi, Y. Beit-Halachmi, Izhar, Turel

78: *The two groups* to *later in a carriage*—Habas, Lavi, Tevet *Kin'at* v.1

79: *"Hurray! This morning*—Ben-Gurion *Mémoires* p. 21

79: *Dancing, singing and jok-ing* to *Gate of Hope"*—Ben-Gur-ion *Mémoires* pp. 20–21; Lavi; Int. Ruth Beit-Halachmi

80: *Petah Tikvah was no*—Ben-Gurion *Israel: A Personal History* pp. 17–20

80: *"The howling of jackals*—Ben-Gurion *Mémoires* p. 21; Ben-Gurion *Rebirth* p. 7

80–81: *The next morning* to *as the Arabs did*—Ben-Gurion *Mémoires* p. 21; Habas; Lavi

81: *The First Aliya pioneers*—Ben-Gurion *Rebirth* p. 10

81: *Ironically, they had been*—Ben-Gurion *Israel* pp. 34–37; Morton pp. 197–209

81: *David and Shlomo now knocked*—Lavi; Int. Yitzhak Kvashner

81–82: *The next morning David* to *they were men*—Bar-Zohar *Ben-Gurion* p. 15; Ben-Gur-ion *Mémoires* pp. 22–23

82: *But not all were* to *cer-tainly not himself*—Int. Ruth Beit-Halachmi, Turel

82–83: *"Yallah! to hunger,"* he wrote—Ben-Gurion *Mémoires* pp. 23–25

83: *Wishing neither to worry* to *had the fever"*—Ben-Gurion in JP 10/5/1966

83: *Both Miriam and Rachel* to *Yehezkel Beit-Halachmi*—Int. Ruth Beit-Halachmi, Y. Beit-Hal-achmi, Izhar, Turel

83–84: *The malaria attacks* to *stick to my fingers"*—Ben-Gurion *Mémoires* p. 23; Ben-Gurion *Re-birth* pp. 8–9

84: *Nevertheless, David's spirit*—Bar-Zohar *Ben-Gurion* p. 15

84: *Disturbing him more*—Tevet *Kin'at* v.1

84–85: *But David would not confess* to *fighting for his views*—Int. Cruso

85: *David now threw*—Ben-Gurion *Mémoires* p. 26

85–86: *In October 1906* to *far-ther from Marxism*—Habas; Int. Yaacov Kvashner

86: *Before long his fervent* to *the national language*—Bar-Zohar *Ben-Gurion* p. 18

86–87: *David stayed in Jaffa* to *croaking of frogs*—Freiman; Gluskin *Memoirs;* Habas; Lavi; Tevet *Kin'at* v.1 (incl. Shochat quote)

87: *About three months later* to *or none at all*—Tevet *Kin'at* v.1; Zeid

87–88: *One man who listened* to *into the villages*—Ben-Gurion *Israel; A Personal History* pp. 684–85; Zeid; JP 12/9/1952, 4/24/1963

88: *He went first to Ness-Ziona* to *was not hungry*—Ben-Gurion in JP 10/5/1966

88–89: *David drifted to Rishon* to *state of near-delirium*—

Bar-Zohar *Ben-Gurion* p. 19; Zemach

89: *One day, David met*—Tevet *Kin'at* v.1; *Yizkor Book;* Int. S. Taub

89: *David, though boiling* to *plowman's song*—Ben-Gurion *Rebirth* p. 10

89: *Shlomo was returning* to *shoulder and left*—Int. Ruth Beit-Halachmi, Y. Beit-Halachmi, Izhar, Turel

90: *Exhausted from a three-day hike*—Ben-Gurion *Rebirth* p. 12; R. Ben-Zvi p. 118

90: *"After Judea"*—Ben-Gurion *Rebirth* p. 12

90: *It was only one* to *living in the settlement*—Hadani

91: *David and Shlomo were soon* to *labor of others"*—*Ibid.*

91: *"Beautiful are the days*—*Ibid.*

91: *All of David's problems* to *Judea shall rise"*—Hadani; *Sefer Hashomer;* Sheba; *Yizkor Book*

92: *"We were afraid*—Tevet *Kin'at* v.1

92: *When Manager Krause*—Ben-Gurion *Mémoires* p. 44; Int. Arye Ben-Gurion, Yaacov Kvashner

92: *"Working is so easy*—Ben-Gurion *Mémoires* p. 37

92: *Then suddenly David's dreams* to *Her mind was made up, she said*—Int. Ruth Beit-Halachmi, Y. Beit-Halachmi, Izhar, Turel

92–93: *David returned to Sejera* to *savored in Plonsk*—Tevet *Kin'at* v.1; Int. Ruth Beit-Halachmi

93: *And he would stare*—Ben-Gurion to his father 7/24/1907

93: *"Several times I have walked alone*—Ben-Gurion to his father (quoted in Tevet *Kin'at* v.1)

93: *As if in answer* to *three hundred rubles*—Avigdor Green to Ben-Gurion 3/1908

93: *David knew he must go*—Ben-Gurion to his father 5/5/1908

93: *As he prepared*—Int. Ruth Beit-Halachmi

93: *David's homecoming*—Bar-Zohar *Ben-Gurion* pp. 22–23; Ben-Gurion in JP 10/5/1966

93: *But before leaving*—Ben-Gurion to his father (quoted in Tevet *Kin'at* v.1)

94: *With the authorities*—Tevet *Kin'at* v.1; Ben-Gurion in JP 10/5/1966

94–95: *David landed in Jaffa* to *yearn for Rachel*—Hadani; Int. Avani, Yaacov Kvashner

95: *In early 1909*—*Sefer Hashomer; Yizkor Book*

95: *The Jewish Workers* to *the driving rain*—Ben-Gurion *Mémoires* pp. 31–32, *Rebirth* pp. 16–17

95: *David and his comrades*—Ben-Gurion *Mémoires* p. 33, *Rebirth* p. 18; *Yizkor Book*

96: *On Passover* to *choose its victim*—Ben-Gurion *Mémoires* pp. 39–40, *Rebirth* pp. 22–23; R. Ben-Zvi pp. 119–21; *Yizkor Book*

96–97: *The morning after the incident* to *stormy temperament*—R. Ben-Zvi pp. 121–22

97: *The stormy-tempered young man*—Ben-Gurion *Rebirth* p. 24; R. Ben-Zvi p. 122; *Yizkor Book*

97: *A shot rang out one night* to *prepared to meet them"*—Ben-Gurion *Mémoires* pp. 40–42, *Rebirth* pp. 24–27; *Yizkor Book*

97–98: *If the killings* to *in another village*—Hadani; Tevet *Kin'at* v.1

98: *On the way a Bedouin*—Hadani

98: *In November 1909*—Tevet *Kin'at* v.1; Ben-Gurion in JP 10/5/1966

98: *An unexpected twist*—Ben-Gurion *Mémoires* pp. 43–44

98: *David left the conference*—Int. Ruth Beit-Halachmi, Y. Beit-Halachmi, Izhar, Turel

99: *When David returned* to *"practical" Zionism over*—Ben-Gurion *Mémoires* pp. 43–44

Chapter Three (pages 100–113)

100: *The old one-story*—R. Ben-Zvi p. 149; Habas

100: *The darkness and dilapidation*—Ben-Gurion *Mémoires* pp. 44–45; Habas

101: *Living and working together*—Bar-Zohar *Ben-Gurion* pp. 27–28; R. Ben-Zvi pp. 151–52

101: *"Climbing onto the Wall" to blanket at night*—R. Ben-Zvi pp. 151–52

101: *But whether hungry*—Sittner in *Jewish Digest* 12/1975

101–2: *His views were already* to *had grandiose overtones*—Bar-Zohar *Ben-Gurion* p. 28; *Poalei Zion in the Second Aliya;* Tevet *Kinat* v.1; JP 10/24/1968

102: *Rachel hadn't replied* to *"poor and unclean"*—Tevet *Kin'at* v.1

102: *The two old friends* to *little girl and come!"*—Ben-Gurion to Rachel Beit-Halachmi, winter 1910

102: *Once more drowning*—Ben-Gurion *Mémoires* p. 45; R. Ben-Zvi (o.h.)

102: *Ben-Gurion, Ben-Zvi*—Ben-Gurion *Mémoires* pp. 45–46; Habas

103: *Before leaving for Turkey*—Int. Ruth Beit-Halachmi, B. Ben-Gurion, E. Ben-Gurion

103: *On June 13, 1911* to *children to come*—Tevet *Kin'at* v.1; Int. Ruth Beit-Halachmi, Y. Beit-Halachmi, Izhar, Turel

103: *"How much I would like*—Ben-Gurion to Rachel Beit-Halachmi 6/1911

103: *Rachel replied*—Int. Ruth Beit-Halachmi, Turel

104: *Soon after his sister's*—Tevet *Kin'at* v.1

104: *In his despair*—Int. Ruth Beit-Halachmi, Turel

104: *In July, Ben-Gurion traveled*—Protocols, PZ conf. 7/1911, LA

104: *After the conference*—Int. Ruth Beit-Halachmi, Turel

104: *On October 28, 1911*—Ben-Gurion *Mémoires* p. 46; *Saloniki;* Int. Strumza

104: *The Salonikan Jews*—Int. Strumza

105: *"My teacher"*—Ben-Gurion *Mémoires* pp. 46–47

105: *Even before Ben-Gurion*—Int. Strumza

105: *"In this animated port"*—Ben-Gurion to his father, winter 1911

105: *After nearly a year*—Ben-Gurion *Mémoires* p. 49; Int. Strumza

105: *Ben-Gurion clambered ashore*—Tevet *Kin'at* v.1; Int. Strumza

106: *"You have certainly learned*—Ben-Gurion *Mémoires* p. 51

106: *When the war finally ended*—Int. Strumza

106: *In international law*—Ben-Gurion *Mémoires* pp. 55–56

106: *In his letters home*—Tevet *Kin'at* v.1; Int. Ruth Beit-Halachmi

106–7: *Ben-Gurion had a greater* to *for such interruptions*—Int. Strumza

107: *Such dedication took its toll* to *not writing out of joy"*—Ben-Gurion to his father, 1913

107: *Ben-Gurion believed that his father* to *seemed insignificant*—Ben-Gurion *Mémoires* p. 49

108: *On July 28, 1914* to *heading for Jaffa*—Ibid. p. 58

108: *"Our destiny is bound* to *hopes of a future"*—Reuveni

108–9: *Most of his comrades* to *must help it win*—Ben-Gurion *Mémoires* p. 59; R. Ben-Zvi p. 237; Reuveni

109: *But Ben-Gurion and Ben-Zvi to* No armed Jews—Ben-Gurion *Mémoires* p. 59; Reuveni; Zerubavel

109: *On October 31, 1914*—R. Ben-Zvi p. 237; Tevet *Kin'at* v.1

109: *An even worse omen*—Ben-Gurion *Mémoires* p. 59; R. Ben-Zvi p. 239; Reuveni

109–10: *Ben-Gurion and his colleagues to Ben-Gurion's colleagues agreed*—Reuveni

110: *The protest appeared*—Ben-Gurion *Mémoires* p. 59

110: *In their terror*—Ben-Gurion *Mémoires* pp. 59–60; Reuveni

110–11: *Ben-Gurion rushed to together with Ben-Gurion*—Ben-Gurion *Mémoires* p. 60; Reuveni

111: *The Bens were charged*—Ben-Gurion *Mémoires* pp. 61–62; Reuveni

111: *They were thrown to country as aliens"*—Reuveni

111: *"We believe we have*—Ben-Gurion *Mémoires* pp. 62–64

111–12: *When the Bens were finally released*—R. Ben-Zvi (o.h.)

112: *The next day, the Poalei Zion*—R. Ben-Zvi pp. 245–46; Reuveni

112: *The Bens, it was decided*—Ben-Gurion *Mémoires* p. 65; R. Ben-Zvi pp. 245–46; Reuveni

112: *"I can't forget*—R. Ben-Zvi pp. 245–46

112–13: *Ben-Gurion stared into to cheer him or Ben-Zvi*—Ben-Gurion *Mémoires* pp. 65–66

113: *"Sitting silently*—R. Ben-Zvi pp. 246–47

Chapter Four (pages 114–40)

114: *Some weeks later to with unequaled power"*—Ben-Gurion *Mémoires* pp. 71–72

114: *"I always dreamed*—*Ibid.*

114: *En route to America*—*Ibid.* pp. 68–69

115: *Happily they were soon*—*Ibid.* p. 72; Ben-Gurion diaries 7/4/1915

115: *Within the fragmented to strange new freedom*—Ben-Gurion *Mémoires* pp. 72–73; Zuckerman (o.h.)

115–16: *But he didn't to under the Turks*—Ben-Gurion *Mémoires* p. 75

116: *But the "army"*—*Ibid.*; PZ Archives 1915

116: *Ben-Gurion was glum*—Tevet *Kin'at* v.1; PZ Archives 1915

116: *Then another tour*—PZ Archives 1915

116–17: *"The comrades," he wrote*—*Ibid.*

117: *What is more*—*Ibid.* 1915–16

117: *Hurt and embittered to following day*—*Ibid.* 1916

117: *After an exhausting*—*Ibid.*

117: *Party leaders agreed*—Ben-Gurion *Mémoires* pp. 75–76; Tevet *Kin'at* v.1; *Yizkor Book*

118: *Ben-Gurion was then blessed*—Tevet *Kin'at* v.1; *Yizkor Book* (revised)

119: *Lonelier than ever*—Avrech; P. Ben-Gurion in *Ramon* 7/30/1937; Int. Cruso, Masler

119: *Ben-Gurion seems to have found to stare at her*—Avrech; Bar-Zohar *Ben-Gurion* pp. 35–36 ("You should have seen); Ben-Gurion *Mémoires* p. 77; Tevet *Kin'at* v.1; P. Ben-Gurion in *Ramon* 7/30/1937

120: *Paula also rattled off to was a child*—Avrech; P. Ben-Gurion in *Ramon;* Int. Cruso, Masler

120–21: *And ironically, his obsession to few hours off*—Avrech; Bar-Zohar *Ben-Gurion* p. 36; Ben-Gurion *Mémoires* p. 77

121: *On November 2, 1917 to pull British lapels*—Bar-Zohar *Ben-Gurion* p. 38; Ben-Gurion *Mémoires* p. 82–83; PZ Archives 1917

121–22: *Ben-Gurion was disturbed* to *full emancipation"*—Ben-Gurion *Mémoires* p. 89–90

122: *To Ben-Gurion this statement* to *his lunch hour*—Ben-Gurion *Mémoires* p. 76–77; P. Ben-Gurion in *Ramon* 7/30/37; Int. P. Ben-Gurion, Masler

122–23: *At 11 A.M., December 5, 1917* to *married to his mission*—*Ibid.*

123: *That evening, Paula*—Ben-Gurion diaries 12/5/1917

123: *Only three days*—Bar-Zohar *Ben-Gurion* p. 38; Tevet *Kin'at* v.1; PZ Archives 1917

124: *Occasionally he did*—Tevet *Kin'at* v.1

124: *But Ben-Gurion seldom* to *destiny come first?*—*Ibid.*; Bar-Zohar *Ben-Gurion* p. 38; Int. P. Ben-Gurion, Masler

124–25: *Ben-Gurion thus marched* to *speak in Chicago*—*Ibid.*

125: *Ben-Gurion was relieved*—Tevet *Kin'at* v.1; Ben-Gurion *Mémoires* p. 76; Ben-Gurion's last will and testament

125: *On May 27, 1918* to *Hebrew flag"*—Ben-Gurion diaries 5/29/1918; PZ Archives 1918

125–26: *"We sang all the way"*—Ben-Gurion to his wife 6/1/1918

126: *"Everyone came*—*Ibid.*

126: *Acceptance by his comrades*—*Ibid.* 6/1, 3/1918

126: *"My popularity*—*Ibid.* 7/2/1918

126: *Ben - Gurion sometimes even* to *in the Legion*—*Ibid.* 6/13,16/1918

126: *One comrade pointed out* to *affection of the soldiers*—Int. Lieberman

127: *"I have been making* to *higher standard"*—Ben-Gurion to his wife 6/18/1918

127: *My darling,*—Ben-Gurion to his wife 6/1/1918

127: *I didn't realize*—P. Ben-Gurion to her husband 6/5/1918

128: *It seems you don't*—Ben-Gurion to his wife 6/14–15/1918

128: *"I am so worried*—P. Ben-Gurion to her husband 6/26/1918

128: *"I will be all right*—*Ibid.* 6/29/1918

128: *"Last night was the most miserable*—Ben-Gurion to his wife

128: *One man [she wrote]*—P. Ben-Gurion to her husband 6/17/1918

128: *Liza Voran was*—*Ibid.* 6/28/1919

128: *I wish to fall*—Ben-Gurion to his wife 6/15/1918

129: *"You are my all*—P. Ben-Gurion to her husband 7/21/1918

129: *"I have never felt*—Ben-Gurion to his wife 6/21/1918

129: *After more than a month*—*Ibid.* 7/2/1918

129: *On July 10, Ben-Gurion's*—Ben-Gurion *Mémoires* p. 98

129: *The battalion arrived*—Ben-Gurion to his wife 8/6/1918

130: *Under a broiling*—Bar-Zohar *Ben-Gurion* p. 39

130: *But Ben-Gurion made the best*—Tevet *Kin'at* v.1; Int. Lieberman

130: *Ben-Gurion's mood*—Ben-Gurion to his wife 10/2/1918

130: *My dearest treasure*—*Ibid.* 9/23/1918

130–31: *Day after day I wait*—*Ibid.* 10/2/1918

131: *Dear and beloved papa*—P. Ben-Gurion to her husband 10/30/1918

131: *On his release*—Ben-Gurion to his wife 10/2/1948

131: *"When I read it*—JP 7/31/1964

131: *The writer opposed*—*Ibid.*

131: *When Ben-Gurion returned*—*Ibid.*; Int. Sharett

132: *Squatting on the sandy*—Ben-Gurion *Mémoires* p. 102

132: *"At long last*—Ben-Gurion diaries 11/4/1918

132–33: *Ben-Zvi was at his side* to *would challenge it?*— Tevet *Kin'at* v.1; PZ Archives 11/6/1918

133: *"I never dreamed*—Ben-Gurion to his wife 11/20/1918

133–34: *"Poor baby*—P. Ben-Gurion to her husband 10/30/1918

134: *And she cried too*—Ibid. 4/6/1919

134: *"In case anything*—Ibid. 4/12/1919

134: *"If anything happens*—Ibid. 4/11/1919

134: *Meanwhile, she was teaching*—Ibid.

134: *"When I read what*—Ben-Gurion to his wife 11/18/1918

134: *As for their reunion*—Ibid.

134: *"Dear Paula, I know*—Ibid. 2/14/1919

134: *Apparently noting that*—P. Ben-Gurion to her husband 4/7/1919

134–35: *Despite his alarm* to *glorious Jewish Legion?*—Ben-Gurion *Mémoires* p. 102

135: *Ben-Gurion received a coveted*—Tevet *Kin'at* v.1

135: *"I'm a private*—Ben-Gurion to his wife 7/25/1919

135–36: *On December 23* to *Lord Balfour's promise*—Habas; Tevet *Kin'at* v.1; LA 1918–19

136: *As he continued*—Ben-Gurion *Mémoires* pp. 125–26

136–37: *But as usual* to *Katzenelson and Ben-Zvi*—Ibid. pp. 102–107; Ben-Gurion diaries 2/1919

137: *"Many people, including*—Ben-Gurion to his wife 3/3/1919

137: *Although the League*—Ben-Gurion *Mémoires* pp. 112–16

137–38: *No one was more impressed*—Kurzman *Genesis 1948* p. 52; Tevet *Kin'at* v.1; Int. Husseini

138–39: *Early on the morning* to *Was it possible?*—R. Ben-Zvi (o.h.)

139: *But Ben-Gurion had little time to waste*—Ben-Gurion *Mémoires* pp. 117–18

139: *And they did* to *in the assembly*—Tevet *Kin'at* v.1; Ben-Gurion diaries 4–5/1919

140: *"Decide about your future"*—P. Ben-Gurion to her husband 4/7/1919

140: *But when Ben-Gurion promised*—Ibid. 4/25/1919

140: *She needn't worry*—Ben-Gurion to his wife 5/8/1919

140: *"I am living in*—Ibid. 7/16/1919

140: *Paula was furious*—P. Ben-Gurion to husband 6/29/1919

140: *In desperation*—Tevet *Kin'at* v.1; Ben-Gurion to his wife 5/25/1919; Ben-Gurion diaries 11/1919

Chapter Five (pages 141–71)

141: *Even in the small*—Bar-Zohar *Ben-Gurion* p. 49; Int. P. Ben-Gurion, R. Leshem

141: *Meanwhile, Ben-Gurion*—Ben-Gurion *Mémoires* p. 138

142: *Before Ben-Gurion could* to *flush toilet*—Bar-Zohar *Ben-Gurion* p. 43; Ben-Gurion *Mémoires* p. 127; Litvinoff p. 84

142: *For Ben-Gurion, London's* to *drawing room*—Edelman p. 75; Hacohen (o.h.); Int. Hacohen

142: *Ben-Gurion was thus*—St. John *Ben-Gurion* p. 51

143: *Born near Pinsk* to *honest chaps*—Crossman *Nation* p. 36 (quote); Int. Kimche, Linton

143–44: *Weizmann's grandiose style*—Ben-Gurion *Mémoires* p. 110; Int. Hacohen

144: *Weizmann and other Zi-*

onist to man apologized—Litvinoff p. 84; protocols W.Z.O. conf.
London 7/7–21/1920

144: *But Weizmann, vain to
pillars of Zionism*—Ben-Gurion
Mémoires pp. 135–36; Int. Hacohen

145: *In August 1920 to real Zionist*—Tevet *Kin'at* v.2; PZ Archives 8/1920

145: *Ben-Gurion felt drained*
—Ben-Gurion *Mémoires* pp. 126–
27 (Ben-Gurion to his father from
Jaffa)

145: *Avigdor wrote back*—
Habas

145: *"This question depends*
—Ben-Gurion to his father quoted
in Bar-Zohar *Ben-Gurion* pp. 43–
44

146: *Apparently troubled*—
Ben-Gurion *Mémoires* pp. 128–29

146: *Before Avigdor could
reply*—*Ibid.* p. 129

146: *Ben-Gurion was joyous*—
Bar-Zohar *Ben-Gurion* (Heb.)

146: *"I can't say*—Ben-Gurion *Mémoires* p. 132

146: *Avigdor had asked to my
own idea"*—*Ibid.* p. 129

146: *Certainly he had loved to
raising children means"*—*Ibid.*
pp. 129–30

146: *According to one*—Hacohen (o.h.)

146: *Meanwhile, Avigdor
wrote*—Ben-Gurion to his father
quoted in Bar-Zohar *Ben-Gurion*
p. 44; Ben-Gurion *Mémoires* pp.
129–30

147: *In March 1921*—Tevet
Kin'at v.2; Ben-Gurion to Katzenelson 3/13/1921

147: *So one day in March*—
Litvinoff p. 85; Int. P. Ben-Gurion

147: *White-haired, white-
bearded*—Ben-Gurion to his father 6/6/1921; Int. B. Ben-Gurion,
E. Taub

147–48: *Relations between
Paula*—Ben-Gurion to his father
6/6/1921; Int. Finkelstein

148: *Not only was Ben-Gurion*

to *leader, of Jerusalem*—Kurzman
Genesis 1948 pp. 51–53

148: *Ben-Gurion was now*—
LPA 5/1921

149: *Paula and Avigdor could
barely*—Ben-Gurion to his father
6/6/1921; Int. B. Ben-Gurion

149–50: *In late 1921 to domi-
nated it alone*—Bar-Zohar *Ben-
Gurion* (Heb.); Tevet *Kin'at* v.2;
Int. Hacohen

150: *At this time only*—Ben-
Gurion *Mémoires* pp. 143–46

150: *Nor would the Histadrut*
—Edelman pp. 80–82; Int. Hacohen

150: *In February 1922*—Ben-
Gurion diaries 2/2/1922

150: *So small was Ben-Gurion's*—*Ibid.* 2/2–3/1922

151: *One problem was*—*Ibid.*
3/20/1922; Int. B. Ben-Gurion

151: *When Ben-Gurion was
lonely*—Ruth Beit-Halachmi

151: *Still, Paula to air for
breathing*—Ben-Gurion to his
father 3/28/1922

151: *Ben-Gurion was hard*—
Ben-Gurion *Igrot*

151: *Paula aggravated*—*Ibid.*

151: *Please return*—*Ibid.*

151: *Reluctantly Paula complied*—*Ibid.*

151–52: *No, he responded*—
Ben-Gurion to his father 8/5/1921

152: *Once more Paula*—P.
Ben-Gurion to her husband 8/23/
1921

152: *She herself had "fainting*
—*Ibid.* 8/13/1921

152: *It grew even harder*—
Ibid. 9/10/1921

152: *She then charged to Ben-
Gurion despised her*—*Ibid.* 8/23/
1921

152: *When he heard they were*
—Ben-Gurion diaries 4/5/1922

153: *Paula was shocked*—
Ibid. 4/4–8/1922

153: *No one dared to*—Bar-
Zohar *Ben-Gurion* (Heb.); Int.
Netzer

153: *At conference after Eu-*

ropean—Ben-Gurion to Shertok 11/1924

153–54: *Maybe the Communists* to *lead the Histadrut delegation*—Ben-Gurion *Mémoires* pp. 191, 289–95; Int. Netzer

154: *"Moscow is animated*—Ben-Gurion *Mémoires* p. 174

154: *This revolution has become* to *like it or not*—Ben-Gurion diaries 9/11/1933

154: *But on the other hand*—Ben-Gurion *Mémoires* p. 197

155: *Anyway, if the Bolsheviks*—*Ibid.* p. 193

155: *The exposition hall was impressive*—Int. E. Galili

155: *Would many Soviet Jews*—Ben-Gurion *Mémoires* pp. 176–77

155: *Such savage taunts*—Int. E. Galili, Netzer

155: *especially taken by* to *"What a man!"*—Int. E. Galili

155–56: *Word spread* to *show his synagogue?*—Ben-Gurion *Mémoires* pp. 185–87

156: *As Ben-Gurion sailed back* to *remains of Russian Judaism*—Ben-Gurion *Mémoires* p. 204

156: *But on arriving*—Avigur (o.h.)

156–57: *But his hopes slowly*—Int. Ben-Aharon, Netzer

157: *Ben-Gurion spoke now*—Ben-Gurion diaries 2/27/1924

157: *The Zionist far leftists* to *but also you"*—IDFA #794

157: *Ben-Gurion interpreted this*—Tevet *Kin'at* v.2

157: *Shochat bitterly retorted*—Ben-Gurion diaries 7/31–8/31/1926; *Davar* 8/26/1926

157–58: *If Ben-Gurion attacked* to *the world agreed*—Ben-Gurion *Mémoires* pp. 226–27; Int. Ben-Aharon, Netzer

158–59: *Ben-Gurion seethed* to *strength shall remain!"*—Becker (o.h.); Int. Ben-Aharon, Netzer

159: *And he was prepared*—Becker (o.h.)

159: *"At that moment"*—Ish-Shalom (o.h.)

159: *Sometimes Ben-Gurion* to *not destroy the people"*—Histadrut protocols, Exec. Com. 1/23/1924

159: *"Should help be given*—Ben-Gurion diaries 12/31/1925

159: *Once when a jobless* to *He is hungry"*—Tevet *Kin'at* v.2

159–60: *"The middle class came*—Ben-Gurion *Mémoires* p. 226

160: *In Ben-Gurion's view* to *no argument could shake*—*Ibid.* p. 206; Elon *Israelis* p. 224

160: *"According to my moral*—Litvinoff p. 93; protocols, 14th ZC Vienna 1925

160: *Ben-Gurion sounded all*—Elon *Israelis* pp. 204, 230; protocols, 14th ZC Vienna 1925

161: *Attacked by the left*—Bar-Zohar *Ben-Gurion* p. 57

161: *Still, sometimes when* to *shall I still?"*—Ben-Gurion diaries 12/1923

161–62: *With her husband seldom* to *been in Plonsk*—P. Ben-Gurion to husband 3/1926, 4/24/1926

162: *She developed "heart trouble"*—*Ibid.* 4/24/1926

162: *Paula was livid* to *a good actor*—*Ibid.*

162: *However hyperbolical*—Int. Amos Ben-Gurion

162: *Once the iceman*—Int. Sifroni

162–63: *Paula spent much time* to *caring for Ben-Gurion*—Ben-Gurion *Igrot* v.B #211 (piano quote); Int. G. Ben-Eliezer, Amos Ben-Gurion, R. Leshem

163: *Thus, the children saw*—Int. A. Remez

163: *But, for all his neglect*—Ben-Gurion diaries 3/30/1925

163: *"Today we weaned her"*—*Ibid.* 2/8/1926

163: *Never was Ben-Gurion*

closer to *write that night—Ibid.* 9/9/1926

163: *"At noon her condition* to *she won't die!"—Ibid.* 9/10/1926

164: *But tests showed* to *the other children*—Tevet *Kin'at* v.2; Int. R. Leshem

164: *"I received your drawings"* to *within the family*—Ben-Gurion *Igrot* #523

164: *Once when Paula broke* —Int. G. Ben-Eliezer

164: *Amos was less sensitive* to *with your mission"*—Int. Amos Ben-Gurion

165: *Every time Father tried* to *Benjamin to Palestine*—Int. B. Ben-Gurion

165: *After Benjamin came*— Int. Arye Ben-Gurion, E. Ben-Gurion

165: *"My dear father*—Ben-Gurion to his father 9/1921

165: *And Zippora warmly*— Zippora to Paula

165: *But shortly after* to *feeling for the family"—Ibid.* 10/13/1923

165: *Nor would Ben-Gurion help* to *shouldn't come to Palestine!*—Ben-Gurion *Mémoires* p. 131

165–66: *Avigdor had written* to *live with relatives*—Tevet *Kin'at* v.2; Ben-Gurion to his father 7/1924

166: *One day in July 1925* to *prescribed by Ben-Gurion*—Int. Arye Ben-Gurion, B. Ben-Gurion, E. Ben-Gurion

166: *But Ben-Gurion seldom* —Int. Arkis, E. Ben-Gurion, M. Taub (niece)

167: *And Paula pursued*— Ben-Gurion to his wife 10/26, 11/23/1923; Int. B. Ben-Gurion

167: *Meanwhile, Ben-Gurion flung*—Ben-Gurion diaries 6/11, 5/26/1926

167: *Occasionally there was*— *Ibid.* 7/12/1928

167: *And aboard one ship* to *the only purpose—Ibid.* 6/7/1926

168: *In the late 1920s*—Horin (o.h.)

168: *But while Ben-Gurion* to *including his own*—Davar 6/13/1927

169: *"Let me inform you* to *than bankruptcy*—Litvinoff p. 93; protocols, 14th ZC 1925

169: *"My forecasts are coming* —Bar-Zohar *Armed* p. 41

169: *Ahdut HaAvodah, which* —Hexter (o.h.)

169: *In speeches as well*— Cruso (o.h.)

169: *As a common friend*— Avigur (o.h.)

170–71: *Now, as he described* to *smiling wanly*—Litvinoff pp. 95–97; Int. Hacohen, Netzer

171: *"Pale and moved*—Gurari (o.h.)

171: *But then his voice*—LA 1V 1/405

171: *But Mapai would not*— Ben-Gurion diaries 9/5/1929

171: *When the conference*— Gurari (o.h.)

Chapter Six (pages 172–98)

172: *At 11 A.M., August 23* to *deadly weapons*—Ben-Gurion *Mémoires* pp. 23–29

172–73: *Haj Amin's studied reply* to *stabbing Jews to death*— Ben-Gurion diaries 8/25/1929

173: *The mufti had struck*— Ben-Gurion *Mémoires* pp. 233–54

173–74: *Shortly Ben-Gurion* *boarded*—Ben-Gurion diaries 8/29/1929

174: *Ben-Gurion rallied other* to *forces and more work*—Ben-Gurion *Mémoires* p. 252

174: *Ben-Gurion believed* to *Insanity!—Ibid.* pp. 253–54; Ben-Gurion diaries 10/23/1929

174: *Then the British deliv-*

ered—Ben-Gurion *Mémoires* pp. 263–68, 296–97, 305; Pearlman *Looks* p. 71

174–75: *Ben-Gurion was aghast* to *Manya with insults*—Bar-Zohar *Ben-Gurion* (Heb.)

175: *Ben-Gurion then replied* to *will of the people!*"—Groman (o.h.)

175: *And the sweepers returned*—Ben-Gurion speech, Mapai Conf. 10/25/1930; Int. M. Sharett

176: *Thus, on September 27* to *from his perch*—Ben-Gurion *Mémoires* pp. 289–93; Ben-Gurion to his wife 10/1930

176: *Weizmann was already*—Ben-Gurion *Mémoires* pp. 319–21

176–77: *But would this letter* to *Congress two years later*—Bar-Zohar *Ben-Gurion* (Heb.)

177–78: *Jabotinsky, in any case* to *world Zionist domination*—Benari pp. 3–32; Int. Weinshal

178–80: *Hardly had the Seventeenth* to *vision to help him*—Ben-Gurion *Mémoires* pp. 322–26; Ben-Gurion diaries 7/12–15/1931; Ben-Gurion to his wife 7/20/1931; protocols, 17th ZC

180: *Ben-Gurion's next step*—Ben-Gurion diaries 1/28/1932

180: *"Sport," he told*—Ben-Gurion lecture, Nat. Hapoel Ass. 10/23/1932

180: *Who would lead*—Protocols, Histadrut Exec. Com. 1931–32

180: *More powerful than ever*—Ben-Gurion *Mémoires* pp. 342–50

180: *Everyone agreed, but*—*Ibid.* pp. 364–73; Int. Netzer

181: *Not since World War I* to *anyone who threatened him*—Ben-Gurion *Mémoires* pp. 417–24, 439; Schechtman *Fighter* p. 248; Ben-Gurion to his wife 4/25/1933

182: *He thus hardly reacted*—Tartakower (o.h.)

182: *Ben-Gurion was even*

wary to *young Jews of Germany"*—Ben-Gurion *Mémoires* p. 449

182: *"People walked four*—Ben-Gurion to his wife 5/30/1933

182: *At another meeting*—Ben-Gurion diaries 5/8, 6/10/1933

182–83: *But as the election neared* to *and I fainted"*—Ben-Gurion to his wife 6/26/1933

183–84: *On the previous evening* to *hate, anger and fear*—Derogy and Carmel pp. 31–32; JP 6/16/1978; Int. Dekel, Rosenblatt

184: *Who killed Arlosoroff?*—Dekel report; Int. Dekel, Rosenblatt

184: *And Sima Arlosoroff*—Derogy and Carmel p. 25

184: *Ben-Gurion didn't* to *the right hypothesis"*—Ben-Gurion diaries 6/18/1933

184: *But as he wrote to Paula*—Ben-Gurion to his wife 6/26/1933

184–85: *Ben-Gurion's colleagues in Tel Aviv* to *ears remained plugged*—Dekel; Derogy and Carmel pp. 34–49; Schechtman *Fighter* pp. 184–205; *Jewish Chronicle* 7/9/1933; Report High Commissioner for Palestine Ref. NCF/279134 P.R.O./C.0933/266-2573 Ser. # 59; protocols, session of Gen. Zion. Council, Prague 8/17–21/1933, Cent. ZA File 2/4/287/1

186: *"It is my impression*—*Haboker* 6/14/1955; *Herut* 6/22/1956

186: *While Palestine simmered* to *our last chance"*—Ben-Gurion *Mémoires* p. 445; Ben-Gurion to Mapai secretariat 7/9/1933

186: *In the violent climate*—Yiddish *Stimme Kaunas* #1418 (incl. quote)

187: *"Cable from America*—Ben-Gurion diaries 7/18/1933

187: *"There will be no negotiation*—Ben-Gurion to Mapai secretariat 7/9/1933

187: *But Ben-Gurion was*

afraid—Ben-Gurion to Berl Locker 8/1933

188: *Hardly had the Congress begun*—Resolutions, 18th ZC p. 17

188: *When the Revisionists* to *with the Histadrut*—Ben-Gurion to Amos and Geula 9/14/1933

188: *Finally, his colleagues*—Ben-Gurion to his wife 9/6/1933

188: *Soon aware that politics*—Dobkin (o.h.)

189: *He refused to "take*—Hexter (o.h.)

189: *Living much of the year*—Bar-Zohar *Ben-Gurion* v.2 (Heb.); Int. E. Galili

189: *Hitler's rule places*—Ben-Gurion *Arab Leaders* pp. 13–14

189–90: *With a new sense* to Then *demand a state*—Int. Shapira, M. Sharett; Baruch (o.h.)

190: *The problem was* to *internecine strife"*—Ben-Gurion to Amos and Geula 9/14/1935

190: *Perhaps he had erred*—Protocols, Mapai Council 7/20/1934

190: *In the midst*—Bar-Zohar *Ben-Gurion* v. 2 (Heb.); Litvinoff p. 105; Schechtman *Fighter* pp. 245–46

191: *Delegates of the two* to *extend my hand"*—Ben-Gurion diaries 10/10/1934

191–92: *Ben-Gurion had been sure* to *relief in his diary*—Ben-Gurion diaries 10/10–26/1934

192: *The two men continued* to *too good to be true"*—Ben-Gurion diaries 10/26/1934

192: *"I hope you will forgive*—Ben-Gurion to Jabotinsky 10/27/1934

192: *Jabotinsky immediately replied*—Jabotinsky to Ben-Gurion 10/29/1934

192–93: *On October 27, the*

day—Ben-Gurion diaries 10/27/1934

193: *The first stone* to *home at once!"*—*Ibid.* 10/28/1934

193: *I am sorry*—Ben-Gurion to Mapai Cent. Com. 10/30/1934

193: *Ben-Gurion wired Moshe Shertok*—Ben-Gurion cable to Shertok 10/29/1934

193: *Movement has been wounded*—Katzenelson cable to Ben-Gurion 11/8/1934

193–94: *Though Ben-Gurion was now* to *endorsed the agreement*—Schechtman *Fighter* pp. 251–52

194: *Ben-Gurion's turn came* to *had suddenly eroded*—Litvinoff p. 114

194: *When Ben-Gurion explained*—*Ibid.*

194: *"On receiving the news*—Jabotinsky to Ben-Gurion 3/30/1935

194: *Perhaps we will have to appear*—Ben-Gurion to Jabotinsky 4/28/1935

194–95: *But their hands seldom* to *bones of the dead"*—Ben-Gurion to Jabotinsky supporter 10/1956 (quoted in Bar-Zohar *Ben-Gurion* p. 75)

195: *While Jabotinsky skidded*—Ben-Gurion to Amos and Geula 9/14/1935

195–96: *Some colleagues even wanted* to *a suit that fit!*—*Ibid.* 9/8/1935

196: *On returning home* to *know who married him?*—Int. Ruth Beit-Halachmi, Halamish

196–97: *Never mind what he said*—Netzer (8/18/1935); Ben-Gurion speech to Labor faction, 19th ZC

197–98: *Was peace with the Arabs* to *rejected the accord*—Ben-Gurion *Arab Leaders* pp. 15–17, 25–34, 35–40, 42–62, 85; JO 2/7/1964; Int. Alami

Chapter Seven (pages 209–26)

209: *The first Arab bullets*— Ben-Gurion diaries 4/20/1936

209: *Ben-Gurion's suspicion* —*Ibid.* 4/22/1936

209–10: *Ben-Gurion was not too worried* to *highwaymen and thugs*—Ben-Gurion *Rebirth* pp. 189–90

210: *But as violence spread*— Ben-Gurion diaries 4/30/1936

210: *In the dazzling glow*— Ben-Gurion *Rebirth* pp. 91–95; Kurzman *Genesis 1948* p. 133

210: *"Terrorism benefits the Arabs*—Ben-Gurion *Rebirth* p. 95

210: *Besides, there was now*— Ben-Gurion *Rebirth* p. 94

211: *The Hagana was now emerging*—Pearlman *Looks* p. 77

211: *Actually, the* Yushiv *did not have to*—Ben-Gurion *Arab Leaders* p. 104, *Rebirth* p. 118

211: *Ben-Gurion rushed to London*—Ben-Gurion to his wife 9/1/1936

211: *The Problem was Weizmann*—Bar-Zohar *Ben-Gurion* p. 87; Dugdale p. 21

212: *Ben-Gurion threatened*— Shapira *Berl*

212: *On Amos' sixteenth*—Int. Amos Ben-Gurion

212–13: *Before the fighting ended* to *wish to dominate others* —Notes of Evidence, Palestine Royal Commission 1/7/1937 pp. 288–91

213: *Only a day after*—Sykes *Crossroads* p. 201

213: *"At first," he told them*— Ben-Gurion to Amos 7/27/1937

214: *"My nerves are tense*— Ben-Gurion to his wife 6/27/1937

214: *"We are facing a complete*—*Ibid.* 6/29/1937

214: *"When I . . . weigh*—Ben-Gurion to Amos 7/27/1937

214: *But in addressing the*

Mapai—Bar - Zohar *Ben-Gurion* p. 90

214: *The Peel report was the "beginning*—Bar-Zohar *Ben-Gurion* (Heb.)

214–15: *Sentimental considerations* to *It must come*—Ben-Gurion to Amos 10/5/1937

215: *But Ben-Gurion didn't want*—Ben-Gurion diaries 6/11/1937

215: *In late July*—Ben-Gurion to Amos 7/28/1937

215: *Still, Ben-Gurion, hoarse* —Laqueur *Zionism* pp. 518–20; protocols, 20th Zion. Cong. 8/1937

216: *Only the League of Nations*—Laqueur *Zionism* pp. 521–22

216: *"He was on the verge*— Katzenelson to Konin 8/23/1937 (quoted in Shapira *Berl*)

216: *"Life is very difficult*— Ben-Gurion to his wife 10/7/1937

216: *"Hitler's prestige will rise*—*Ibid.* 9/20/1938

217: *Palestine? "They handed* —*Ibid.* 10/7/1938

217: *Frantically, Ben-Gurion rushed* to *no Jewish state*—*Ibid.* 9/20/1937

217: *Ben-Gurion returned to his hotel*—*Ibid.*

217: *"When I returned*—*Ibid.* 10/1/1938

217: *But gradually Ben-Gurion's depression*—*Ibid.* 10/7/1938

217–18: *On the same day* to *revolt and fight"*—Ben-Gurion to Amos, Geula and Renana 10/7/1938

218: *In December 1936* to *would surely bud*—Bar-Zohar *Ben-Gurion* (Heb.)

218: *The atmosphere was electric*—Bar-Zohar *Ben-Gurion* p. 93; Ben-Gurion to Amos, Geula and Renana 10/7/1938

218: *Ben-Gurion sent agents*

—Hacohen in *Jerusalem Quarterly*, Fall 1978; JO 9/20/1963

218–19: *Wingate was a Biblical* to *return as a refugee"*—Kurzman *Genesis 1948* pp. 133–35; Ben-Gurion in JO 9/27/1963

219: *He even obliquely cooperated*—Shapira *Berl*

220: *Nor would Ben-Gurion agree* to *utter irresponsibility"*—Avriel p. 35; Avigur (o.h.)

220: *Ben-Gurion not only hesitated* to *damage we shall cause"*—Beit-Zvi; minutes, JA Exec. 6/26/1938

220–21: *With the plight* to *in Evian, failed*—Minutes, JA Exec. 11/13/1938

221: *"Concentrate on the realities*—Ben-Gurion to his wife 2/7/1939

221: *With his tight stiff collar*—*Ibid.* 2/10/1939

222: *Ben-Gurion tore off*—Bar-Zohar *Ben-Gurion* p. 95

222: *The British were shocked*—Ben-Gurion to wife 3/6/1939

222–23: *Finally, a miracle!* to *And there was none*—Ben-Gurion diaries 3/7/1939

223: *Ben-Gurion was crushed*—Dugdale p. 127

223: *In a rage* to *gangsters and racketeers"*—Ben-Gurion diaries 3/15/1939

223: *When Ben-Gurion fell ill*—*Ibid.* 3/7/1939

223: *Ben-Gurion finally calmed* to *empire on earth*—Ben-Gurion to his wife 3/6/1939

224: *But so "evil, stupid and shortsighted"*—*Ibid.*

224: *For the first time*—*Ibid.* 3/16/1939

224: *Refuse to cooperate* to *Had not circumstances changed?*—Ben-Gurion in JO 9/6, 10/18, 10/25/1963

224–25: *And besides, Berl* to *bottom of the sea*—Avigur (o.h.)

225: *The dispute came to a head*—Bar-Zohar *Ben-Gurion* p. 100; Int. Avriel

225–26: *"There are some things* to *would meet again"*—Protocols, 21st Zion. Cong. 1939; Epstein (o.h.)

226: *A few days later*—Ben-Gurion diaries 9/1/1939; Ben-Gurion in JO 10/25/1963

Chapter Eight (pages 227–57)

227: *"The die is cast*—Ben-Gurion in JO 11/1/1963

227: *Drugged with hope*—*Ibid.*

227: *But not every Jew* to *there were no war"*—*Ibid.*

228: *Hardly had Ben-Gurion issued*—Ben-Gurion in JO 11/1/1963

228: *For as Ben-Gurion himself* to *Palestine after the war*—*Ibid.* 11/22/1963

228: *On February 28, 1940* to *struggle against Hitler*—*Ibid.* 12/6/1963

228: *Perhaps. But when*—Bauer *Diplomacy* p. 75

228: *Ben-Gurion's colleagues*—Ben-Gurion in JO 12/6/1963; JA Exec. 4/8/1940

229: *"He had a very arrogant*—Int. Denman

229–30: *But not every assistant* to *jealous tantrums*—JP 1/8/1959 (*veil*); Baruch (o.h.); Int. Denman (*"Catholic rubbish"*), Eytan (*Lourie*), R. Leshem (*"deaf"*), Levenberg, Linton

230: *When the Nazis began*—Meltzer report; Int. Denman

230: *Another time*—Ben-Gurion to Dugdale 9/21/1940

230: *Years later he would recall*—Ben-Gurion *Rebirth* p. 209

230: *And his own model* to

had been no Churchill—Pearlman *Looks* p. 99

230: *Was Ben-Gurion identifying to struggle for victory"*—*Ibid.* p. 102

231: *Ben-Gurion was, paradoxically*—Int. Weisgal

231: *"It is almost as great to colleagues backed him*—Dugdale pp. 102, 174–75

231: *Ben-Gurion retreated home*—Ben-Gurion diaries 9/11/1940

231: *Ben-Gurion would urge* —Ben-Gurion in JO 12/13/1963

231: *He would forge iron*— Ben-Gurion diaries 11/20/1939; JP 10/4/1972

232: *America was another world*—Ben-Gurion in JO 2/7/1964

232: *Nevertheless, Ben-Gurion scurried to Jewish psychology* —Int. Miriam Taub (secretary)

232: *Ben-Gurion was stymied* —Ben-Gurion in JO 2/7/1964; Int. Epstein

232: *On arriving home*— Shapira *Berl;* Ben-Gurion diaries 2/1941

233: *If the British withdrew*— Int. Ben-Hur

233: *Most of the other Jews*— Ben-Ami (o.h.)

233: *And the survivors to workers and technicians*—Int. E. Galili

233: *He was in such a hurry*— Maor (o.h.)

233–34: *Lord Moyne to Jews is Palestine*—Ben-Gurion in JO 3/13/1964

234: *"I am departing*—Ben-Gurion to Weizmann 11/12/1941

234: *On November 24, 1941 to would not compromise*—Ben-Gurion in JO 4/3/1964

234: *Carefully weighing*— *Haaretz* 10/3–9/1972

234–35: *Ben-Gurion soon recovered*—Bauer *Diplomacy* pp. 235–36

235: *Ben-Gurion's scenario to*

danger to Palestine"—Weisgal *So Far* pp. 174–75

235: *Ben-Gurion, however, felt*—Protocols, JA Exec. 10/26/1943 (quoted in cable from High Commissioner to Sec. of State for Palestine 11/20/1943 F0921 X/K 6634)

235: *Weizmann had himself*— Weizmann in *Foreign Affairs* 1/1942

235–36: *But Ben-Gurion didn't believe*—Protocols, JA Exec. 10/26/1943

236: *And in fact Weizmann*— Bauer *Diplomacy* pp. 238–40

236: *Actually, by the time of to duty to Zionism?*—Beit-Zvi; Int. Elam

236–37: *On May 9, 1942 to Jews a majority*—Laqueur *Zionism* p. 546; Protocols, Extraord. Zion. Conf. 5/9–11/1942

237–38: *Ben-Gurion basked to full of love"*—Ben-Gurion to his family 5/14/1942

238: *Before the echo*—Protocols, JA Exec. 10/26/1943

238: *On June 11, Ben-Gurion* —Ben-Gurion to Weizmann 6/11/1942

238: *In an angry reply*—Weizmann to Ben-Gurion 6/15/1942

238: *He then wrote*—Weizmann to Lewis Namier 6/27/1942

238: *Meanwhile, Ben-Gurion asked Rabbi*—Bar-Zohar *Ben-Gurion* pp. 110–11; Int. Weisgal

238: *There was a moment*— Weisgal *So Far* p. 175

238–39: *Weizmann, his wrinkled to profane their god?*—Bar-Zohar *Ben-Gurion* pp. 111–12; Int. Weisgal

239: *But Ben-Gurion wasn't defeated*—Bauer *Diplomacy* p. 239

239: *Weizmann could barely* —Bar-Zohar *Ben-Gurion* p. 108 (quoting Weizmann)

239: *Why hadn't Ben-Gurion* —Bauer *Diplomacy* p. 29 (quoting Weizmann)

239: *After fourteen months—* Weizmann to Locker 8/18/1942

239–40: *He found that the mood* to *dispensing their pounds* —Eliav (o.h.)

240: *Most of them didn't know* to *Hitler is sealed"*—Beit-Zvi; Gerhard Riegner report to JA 8/ 1942

240: *Yitzhak Gruenbaum— Haboker* 12/7/1942

240: *But even after Rommel—* Protocols, JA Exec. 10/25/1942

240: *Ben-Gurion, who was— Haaretz 11/9/1942*

241: *A few days later—Ibid.* 11/15/1942

241: *His job was to illustrious national leader—*Ben-Gurion in JO 5/8/1964

241: *It was time to dispose—* Bar-Zohar *Ben-Gurion* p. 112

241: *He wasn't well enough* to *grievances introspectively—* Weizmann to Zion. Exec. 10/1942

241: *In his bitterness—*Weizmann to Zion. office, London 11/2/ 1942

242: *When Ben-Gurion learned* —Sharett *Yoman Ishi* vs.2, 7, 8

242: *Ben-Gurion was equally* to *largely accepts this"*—Ben-Gurion to his wife 10/7/1937

242–43: *Did Shertok plan* to *called me 'Moshe' again—*Sharett *Yoman Ishi* 11/23/1953; *Maariv* 5/17/1974

243: *They did not believe—* Yaacov Kurtz report (quoted in Beit-Zvi)

243: *Eliahu Dobkin—*Dobkin (o.h.)

244: *The Palestine Jews* to Hatzofe *writer asked—Hatozfe* 11/26/1942

244: *Dobkin would later—* Dobkin (o.h.)

244: *Yet Dobkin, after questioning—Ibid.*

244: *Ehud Avriel—*Int. Avriel

244: *But Ben-Gurion would*

never admit to *for a long time—* Ben-Gurion *B'Maarakhah* v.3

244: *There are German nationals—*PP 12/1/1942

245: *What have you allowed—* St. John *Ben-Gurion* pp. 85–86

245: *If it is not—Ibid.*

245: *"We do not know exactly* —Ben-Gurion *B'Maarakhah* v.3 (Extraordinary Session, Elected Assembly 11/30/1942)

245: *"We shall bring you— Ibid.*

245: *And in still another—* Ben-Gurion speech in Tel Hai 3/ 18/1943

245: *Later in the war—*Beit-Zvi

246: *Typically, Ben-Gurion said—*Ben-Gurion *B'Maarakhah* v.4

246: *He would also say—*Ducovny *Own Words* p. 185

246: *It is possible to convert—* Ben-Gurion *B'Maarakhah* v.4

246: *It appears, then* to *slow down, the horror—Davar* 11/8/ 1943

246–47: *"With his realism—* Avriel memo prepared for author

247: *I came back to a satisfied* —Eliav (o.h.)

247: *"It is quite likely—*G. H. Hall, Foreign Office, to Weizmann (quoting conversation) 6/22/1944 PSO F0371/42758 XP 0/5176 Pub. Records Off., London

247: *"Ben-Gurion, who is in many—*Cable, R. M. A. Hankey, High Commissioner's Office, to Sec. of State, Colonies 6/9/1944 PRO F0371/42758 X/P 0/5176 Pub. Records Off., London

247–48: *In June 1944* to *proposed to the Allies"*—Protocols, JA Exec. 6/11/1944

248: *A few months later—*Permanent undersec. of foreign office to Weizmann 9/1/1944; *Yediot Acharonot* 4/11/1980

248: *Ben-Gurion, however, bore—*Ben-Gurion to Benjamin Nahari 2/10/1965

248: *If Ben-Gurion did not give to feet to the shoes?*—Avriel pp. 193–97; Int. Avriel

249: *The Allies "might have rescued* —Ducovny *Own Words* p. 106

249: *Speaking of Pope Pius XII*—Ben-Gurion on Mutual Broadcasting System (quoted in JP 3/5/1964)

249: *The Pope feared*—Kurzman *Race for Rome* pp. 39–50; Int. Wolff

249: *A leader of Ben-Gurion's* —Reiss (o.h.)

249: *And another associate*—Tartakower (o.h.)

250: *"What matters in a situation*—Goldmann *Autobiography* p. 149

250: *"All of Zion is standing*—Protocols, Zion. Exec. 7/11/1943

250: *Ben-Gurion, however, would not*—Dugdale 11/14/1943 p. 207

250: *And even if Ben-Gurion came*—Ibid. 12/30/1943 pp. 208–209

250–51: *He bellowed at*—Protocols, JA Exec. 10/26/1943 (quoted in cable from High Commissioner to Sec. of State for Palestine 11/20/1943 F0921 O/K 6634)

251: *"It was like a child*—Protocols, Mapai Political Com. 11/3/1943

251: *Finally, in February 1944* —Protocols, JA Exec. 2/27/1944

251: *Soon there was more tsouris to shan't leave alone!"*—Protocols, Mapai Conf. 3/5–8/1944 LPA

251: *At a Mapai conference to coop of doves*—Hacohen (o.h.)

251: *At about midnight to Berl, you can't"*—Int. Amos Ben-Gurion, Hacohen

252: *"How dear you were*—Ben-Gurion *Rebirth* p. 177

252: *Ben-Gurion's colleagues* —JO 1/10/1964

252: *At the same time, Churchill*—Maariv 5/14/1974

252–53: *Ben-Gurion would gladly to was visiting Cairo*—Kurzman *Genesis 1948* pp. 55–56

253: *Churchill hinted as much* —Churchill speech, House of Commons 11/17/1944

253: *Furthermore, that bullet to war on the British*—Moshe Sneh report, *Hagana Book* 11/9/1944

254: *"The Jewish community* —Protocols, JA Exec. 11/7/1944

254: *Thus began the "Hunting* —Kurzman *Genesis 1948* p. 544; Int. Raanan

254: *In Palestine Rachel Ben-Zvi*—R. Ben-Zvi (o.h.)

254: *Paula was convinced to more in common?*—Ibid.

254–55: *Paula would try to Israel Bar-Shira*—Int. R. Leshem

255: *"You're not very pretty to understood his priorities*—Ibid.

255–56: *Sometimes Ben-Gurion to three more children*—Int. G. Ben-Eliezer

256–57: *Ben - Gurion hardly ever saw Amos to accept the decision*—Int. Amos Ben-Gurion

Chapter Nine (pages 258–85)

258: *Amid a blazing to the other peoples*—Ben-Gurion in JO 6/12/1964; Ben-Gurion diaries 5/8/1945

258: *Ben-Gurion had flown*—Protocols, Mapai Cent. Com. 3/15/1945

259: *Britain's response*—Ben-Gurion in JO 6/12/1965

259: *Nor could Ben-Gurion count*—Ben-Gurion in JO 6/12/1965; Ben-Gurion diaries 3/21/1945; protocols, Zion. office, London 6/13/1945

259–60: *Ben - Gurion lay "stretched* to *met many years before*—Weisgal *So Far* p. 231; Int. Weisgal

260: *On July 1, 1945* to *answer the call*—Kurzman *Genesis 1948* p. 107; Int. Sonneborn

260: *July 1945 brought other*—Bar-Zohar *Ben-Gurion* p. 127; Kurzman *Genesis 1948* p. 5

260: *But Ben-Gurion did not celebrate*—Haboker 9/25/1957

260–61: *At the conference* to *the Biltmore program*—*Ibid.;* protocols, Zion. Conf. 8/2/1945

261: *Ben-Gurion kept up*—Avriel p. 205

261–62: *Ben-Gurion would now launch* to *American pledge*—Livneh in *The American Zionist* 1/1967

262: *"The time has come!"*—Kurzman *Genesis 1948* pp. 107–108; Int. Jarcho, Sonneborn

262: *The arms collected*—Ben-Gurion in JO 7/17/1964

262–63: *On October 19, 1945* to *pioneers and soldiers*—Nadich pp. 228–32

263: *That afternoon Ben-Gurion* to *air shuttle service*—Bauer *Flight* p. 94; Nadich p. 233; Ben-Gurion in JO 7/17/1964

264: *"I saw the gas chambers*—Voice of Israel 11/28/1945

264: *"This is the last will*—*Ibid.*

264: *The Hagana, the Irgun*—Ben-Gurion in JO 8/7/1964

264: *Ben-Gurion knew even before* to *unlikely prospect*—Bar-Zohar *Ben-Gurion* p. 130; Int. Linton

264–65: *So in March 1946* to *the boiling point*—Int. Ben-Gurion, Sharett

265: *The caldron finally boiled* to *Ben-Gurion in Paris*—Avriel pp. 287–88; Int. Avriel, Weisgal

265–66: *At 6:30 A.M., shortly after* to *declare a state"*—Int. Kluger

266: *But he still seemed a bit*—Kol (o.h.)

266: *Within minutes members* to *proclamation of independence"*—Avriel pp. 288–92; Int. Avriel

266: *Ben-Gurion immediately plowed*—Kollek pp. 64–65

266–67: *Ben-Gurion returned* to *British must go!*—Gvati (o.h.)

267: *And to prod them* to *evacuate the hotel*—Gervasi pp. 178–79; Kurzman *Genesis 1948* p. 465; Int. Begin, I. Galili, Paglin

267: *Ben-Gurion was enraged*—Int. Avriel, Kluger

267: *Meanwhile, the explosion*—Haaretz 8/9/1946

267: *To mend the split*—Livneh in *The American Zionist* 1/1967

268: *In edging toward*—Weisgal *So Far* p. 238; Int. Weisgal

268: *Weizmann later plotted*—Weizmann to Marc Jarblum 1/13/1947; Weizmann to Eliezer Kaplan 3/27/1947

269: *Demonstrating his new* to *see him alone*—Kurzman *Genesis 1948* p. 7; Ben-Gurion in JO 12/25/1964

269: *"I would like to know* to *And the meeting ended*—Ben-Gurion in JO 12/25/1964

269: *On February 18, 1947*—Kurzman *Genesis 1948* p. 5; Int. Ben-Gurion

270: *"This meeting must be strictly* to *need to hold out?"*—Int. Laskov

270: *This question tormented* to *with the Arab states?*—Avidar (o.h.)

270–71: *Soon after that meeting*—Ben-Gurion diaries 6/6,26/1947; Int. Laskov

271: *"We shall stand face*—Ben-Gurion in JO 6/4/1965

271: *He now asked Laskov* to *save the Yishuv*—Int. Laskov

271: *Meanwhile, Ben-Gurion issued*—Kurzman *Genesis 1948* pp. 117–18

272:    *But useful or not to flown to Palestine*—Surkis (o.h.)

272:    *"Who is willing*—Bar-Zohar *Ben-Gurion* p. 141

272:    *Ben-Gurion kept his people*—Kurzman *Genesis 1948* pp. 11–14; Int. M. Sharett, Weisgal

274:    *It was not at all clear*—Kurzman *Genesis 1948* pp. 17–19 —Int. N. Bernstein

274–75:   *Yet, even a victory* to *character if they weren't*—Aref; Kurzman *Genesis 1948* pp. 22–24; Int. Danin, Meir

275–76:   *On the chilly starlit* to *best of our youth"*—Bar-Zohar *Ben-Gurion* p. 142; Collins and Lapierre pp. 35–36

276:    *Two hundred Bren guns* —Ben-Gurion diaries 12/11/1947

276:    *Ben-Gurion would have* to *depend* to *items we need*—Int. Avriel

276–77:   *The American Jews, Ben-Gurion felt* to *plane to the United States*—Int. Meir, M. Sharett

277:    *The urgency*—Kurzman *Genesis 1948* p. 3; Int. B. Gharbieh

277:    *In the Jewish quarter*—Int. A. Halperin

277:    *Then, on January 14, 1948*—Int. Abufara

277:    *As usual when Ben-Gurion*—Int. Kaoukji

277:    *Even when Kaoukji*—Int. M. Gharbieh, Ghouri, Lurie

278:    *Each day the thought*—Ben-Gurion diaries 3/13/1948; Ben-Gurion to his wife 9/2/1947

278:    *His agents were still his main hope*—Int. Avriel

278:    *And the Jews had the money*—Int. Meir

278:    *Agents were smuggling*—Kurzman *Genesis 1948* pp. 110–13, 488–93; Int. Sonneborn

278:    *And as British soldiers*—Kurzman *Genesis 1948* pp. 114–17; Int. Flanagan, D. and M. Rutledge

278:    *Meanwhile,   Hagana agents*—Kurzman *Genesis 1948* pp. 121–23; Int. Sereni

278:    *But there was bad news* —Int. Clifford, B. Cohen

278–79:   *Then, even worse news* to *hurting innocent people"* —Protocols, Mapai Central Com. 1/8/1948 LPA

279:    *Perhaps he had been*—Ben-Gurion diaries 12/19/1947, 1/2/1948

279:    *Plan D called on*—Ibid. 5/11/1948

279:    *"We'll grow vegetables*—Ben-Gurion diaries 12/3/1947

279:    *At a meeting of Hagana* to *exodus from Egypt*—Kurzman *Genesis 1948* p. 106; Int. Allon, Ben-Gurion, Yadin

280:    *"At 0330 we shall* to *throwing kisses*—Int. Gazit, Narkis

280:    *Ben-Gurion rejoiced* to *inhabitants had escaped*—Int. Eichler, Elnakam, Gottlieb, Kassim, Lapidot, Raanan, Radwan, Shaltiel, Zetler

280:    *When Ben-Gurion learned* —Int. Ben-Gurion

281:    *In Haifa not even*—Int. M. Carmel, Makleff, Stockwell

281:    *Ben-Gurion was startled* to *left to sabotage it*—Bar-Zohar *Ben-Gurion* v.2 (Heb.); Int. Allon, Ben-Gurion

281:    *"It is not our duty*—Ben-Gurion diaries 5/1/1948

281:    *Arab fighters desperately* —Kurzman *Genesis 1948* pp. 188–99; Int. Edelman, M. Gharbieh, Jones, Passman-Epstein, Yassky

282:    *But Ben-Gurion rejected* —Memo, Presidential Adviser Max Lowenthal to Clifford ("Clark: Please do not let anyone else read this dynamite"), Clifford papers (quoted in Kurzman *Genesis 1948* p. 213)

282:    *Neither man knew that Nahum*—Davar 5/22/1973; *Maariv* 9/5/1975

282:    *There must be an immediate* to *not come to their aid*—Kurzman *Genesis 1948* pp. 213–

14; Sharett *B'Shaar;* Int. Ben-Gurion, Goldmann, M. Sharett
282: *Shertok was crestfallen*
to *nor be dismayed!"—Ibid.*
282: *Still in doubt* to *in your
report"*—Int. Ben-Gurion
282–83: *Ben-Gurion faced the*

challenge to *there will be war"*—
Int. Danin, Meir
283–85: *On May 12, three
days* to *the deciding vote*—Kurzman *Genesis 1948* pp. 242–47; Int.
Ben-Gurion, I. Galili, M. Sharett,
Yadin

Chapter Ten (pages 286–310)

286–87: *"Are you sure?"* to
before he was killed—Int. Ben-
Gurion, Yannai
287: *"Outside stood people*—
Ben-Gurion diaries 5/15/1948
287: *"I'm sorry, but we*—Baratz; Int. Baratz
287–88: *Ben-Gurion paused*
to *few gimmicky guns?—Ibid.;*
Int. Ben-Gurion, Yadin
289: *Yet even at this desperate*
to *would last that long*—Baruch
(o.h.)
289: *It would. On May 23* to
jotted in his diary—Ben-Gurion
diaries 5/23/1948
289–90: *Jerusalem again!* to
Twenty-four hours—Kurzman
Genesis 1948 pp. 403–11; Int.
Ben-Gurion, C. Herzog, Laskov,
S. Shamir, Yadin
290: *At dawn, May 25—Ibid.;*
Int. Rousan
290: *"You must look* to *we
failed miserably"*—Int. Yadin
290: *Ben-Gurion waved away
—Ibid.;* Int. Avidan, Laskov, Prulov, Rousan
290: *Marcus now had a new
idea*—Int. Ben-Gurion, Chorev
290: *But Ben-Gurion and
Marcus*—Int. Allon, M. Cohen,
Kelman
290–91: *Ben-Gurion was
shocked* to *report to me"*—Int.
Ben-Gurion
291: *Shapira immediately* to
the fatal one)—Official investigation report on Marcus' death; Int.
Linski, Shapira
291: *Ben-Gurion would publicly* to *It was the Palmach"*—Int.
Ben-Gurion
291–92: *On June 11, 1948* to

for our efforts"—Int. Allon, Ben-
Gurion, M. Carmel
292: *Ben-Gurion's obsession
—*Kurzman *Genesis 1948* pp. 457–
84; Int. Ariel, Katz
292: *On the morning of June
12* to *fighters in Jerusalem*—Int.
Begin, I. Galili
292: *Galili telephoned*—Int. I.
Galili
293: *Ben-Gurion was con-
vinced*—Int. Paglin
293: *In any case, Ben-Gurion
ordered* to *Ben-Gurion agreed*—
Int. I. Galili
293: *The* Altalena *anchored*—
Int. Fallon, Fein, Kraushar
294: *Suddenly, a Hagana officer*—Int. Even
294: *Hardly had Galili*—Int.
I. Galili
294: *Within an hour a hail*—
Int. Fallon
294: *The* Altalena *zigzagged*—
Int. Shuman
294: *One of the Irgun*—Int.
Fallon, Fein
294: *A few hours later* to *kill
the state"*—Kurzman *Genesis
1948* p. 473; Int. Gruenbaum, M.
Sharett
294–95: *After the meeting*—
Int. Allon
295: *While Ben-Gurion addressed*—Kurzman *Genesis 1948*
p. 474
295: *On the veranda*—Int. Joseph
295: *At Palmach headquarters
—*Int. Rabin
295: *Meanwhile, army troops
—*Int. Fallon, Fein
295: *At the same time, Irgunists*—Int. Allon, Rabin

295–96: *Ben-Gurion remained icily* to *We must shell her"* —Becker (o.h.)

296: *Shortly, the* Altalena— Int. Fallon, Fein

296: *Begin, who had wanted* —Int. Fallon

296: *Pondering his losses* to *Israel's war museum"*—Kurzman *Genesis 1948* p. 484; Int. Sheib

296: *The Palmach then arrested* to *through the dragnet*— Int. Kelman

296–97: *On June 29* to *draw conclusions"*—Kurzman *Genesis 1948* pp. 497–98; Int. Ben-Gurion, Yadin

297: *Ben-Gurion thus decided* to *time to fall ill*—Int. Ben-Gurion, Gruenbaum, M. Sharett, Yadin

297: *"B.G., what in heaven* to *Shertok from the room*—Int. M. Sharett

297–98: *The cabinet was stunned* to *role without the title*— Int. I. Galili, Gruenbaum, M. Sharett, Yadin

298: *Ben-Gurion suddenly made*—Int. M. Sharett

298: *And they would certainly* to *already fled!*—Int. Rutledge

299: *"Every Jew in the world* —Ben-Gurion to Yitzhak Rosental 11/25/1948

299: *[Ben-Gurion] sat frozen* to *back to the hall*—Gurari in JP 10/15/1976

299: *Ben-Gurion had rejected this plan*—Int. Ben-Gurion

300: *"If the world listens*— Int. Sheib

300: *Sheib, a wizened* to *for the crime*—Int. Y. Shamir, Sheib, Yellin-Mor

300: *The decision was immediately*—Int. Zetler

300: *Goldfoot, lanky and elegant*—Int. Goldfoot

300: *Yehoshua Cohen*—Int. Yehoshua Cohen, Zetler

300: *On the afternoon*—Int. Goldfoot

301: *About two minutes after five* to *from a scratch*—Kurzman *Genesis 1948* pp. 562–63 (assassin's identity from sources requesting anonymity)

301: *Ben-Gurion was studying* to *committed the crime*—McDonald pp. 79–80; Int. Ben-Gurion

302: *It was time for Chaim Weizmann* to *cable arrived*—Int. Linton

302: *On the occasion*—Ben-Gurion and colleagues to Weizmann 5/15/1948, Weizmann Archives

302–3: *That day Weizmann* to *or check passports*—Kurzman *Genesis 1948* pp. 571–72

303: *But once settled* to *No one can be sure*—Int. Weisgal

303: *But the battle was just*— *Yediot Acharonot* 9/30/1970; Int. Sharef, M. Sharett

304: *"The plan has been dropped*—Ben-Gurion diaries 9/26/1948

304: *Yadin now called for*— Int. Yadin

304: *Another time, on a trip*— Avigur (o.h.)

304: *And once he even ran*— Kol (o.h.); Int. Shaltiel

304: *So worried were his commanders* to *he had a cold*—Avrech

304: *Most fretful of all* to *fear was unfounded"*—Argov diary 6/16/1949

304: *Now Ben-Gurion was touring*—Ben-Gurion diaries 10/5/1948; Int. Yadin

305: *On the way back*—Argov diary 10/5/1948

305: *"We must have just made* —Ben-Gurion diaries 10/6/1948

305: *Too grave, Ben-Gurion decided*—Bar-Zohar *Ben-Gurion* pp. 182–83; Int. Allon, Ben-Gurion, Rabin, Yaari

305: *Ben-Gurion sat down*— Argov diary

305: *Now all the Israelis needed*—Int. Allon, Avidar, Gammal, Hirzallah, Prulov, Rabin, Segall, Yadin

306: *As Ben-Gurion sat* to *Galei Kinneret Hotel there*—Int. M. Carmel

306: *"Let us push all* to *the whole Galilee"*—Int. Makleff

307: *Now, with the United Nations* to *Egyptian army*—Int. Sasson, A. Tel

307: *Ben-Gurion was aghast*—Int. Ben-Gurion, Yadin

307: *Hardly had the Prime Minister*—McDonald pp. 117–21; *Yediot Acharonot* 9/30/1970

307: *The British threat*—*Ibid.;* Ben-Gurion diaries 12/6/1948

308: *But shortly afterward*—Int. Allon

308: *By the next evening* to *pondering the question*—Int. Ben-Gurion

308: *The next morning an aide* to *evacuation immediately"*—Yeroham Cohen

308: *"Shocked by this order"* to *however harsh it may be"*—Int. Allon

309: *Meanwhile, Allon made a new plea* to *West Bank territory*—*Maariv* 3/30/1980; Int. Allon, Ben-Gurion, Yeroham Cohen

309: *"I do not know* to *mass-produce miracles*—Ben-Gurion to Geula Cohen 2/4/1962

309–10: *Biblical philosophy* to *won the whole Negev!*—Int. Allon, Bromage, Yeroham Cohen, Glubb, Peri

Chapter Eleven *(pages 329–62)*

329–30: *Ben-Gurion watched in wonder* to *modern Ingathering of the Exiles*—Kurzman *Genesis 1948* pp. 26–29; Author's observations; Int. Ben-Gurion

330–32: *But many might still* to *history, they did*—Int. Ben-Gurion, Rafael

332: *Some, like the Yemenites*—Int. Y. Kesse

332: *Even more disappointing*—Int. Epstein, Goldmann

332: *And, some people say*—Lavon report on talk with Ben-Gurion 9/26/1960; Int. Ben-Porat (Israeli agent in Iraq who denies charge)

332: *Whatever the truth*—Bilby pp. 232–33; JP 7/27/1949

333: *Like the Israelites*—Sachar *Ends* pp. 355–56; Int. Y. Kesse

333: *Now he would think*—Bilby pp. 167–68; JP 1/10–26/1949

333–34: *How, Ben-Gurion wondered* to *religious friends*—Int. Burg, Goren, Rafael

334: *Meanwhile, Ben-Gurion*

struggled—Bilby p. 169; *Hadassah* 10/1961; JP 10/6/1961; R. Halperin (o.h.); Int. Epstein, Goldmann

335: *And in August 1950* to *socialist Jewish state*—Litvinoff pp. 14–15; Int. Goldmann

335: *It was a nostalgic* to *captive of your city"*—*Ibid.* pp. 2–3; NYT 5/10/1951

335: *Actually, the city*—Kollek p. 94

335: *As crowds greeted*—JP 6/7/1951

336: *One day she went to Garfinckle's*—Friend of Paula (anonymity requested)

336: *Meanwhile, in Princeton*—Ducovny *Own Words;* Pearlman *Looks* p. 217; St. John *Ben-Gurion* pp. 221–22

337: *Though his people greeted*—Horin (o.h.)

337: *Accept blood money* to *must be practical*—Ducovny *Own Words* p. 115; Gurari (o.h.)

337: *But some were not*—Ben-Gurion diaries 4/18/1953

337: *Ben-Gurion tackled rep-*

arations—Goldmann *Paradox* pp. 124–35; Int. Goldmann

337: *Ben-Gurion was delighted* to *for Grandpa and Grandma?"*—JP 1/8/1952

338: *A few blocks away* to *life or death"*—*Ibid.*; St. John *Ben-Gurion* p. 229

338: *The crowd dispersed* to *the father roared*—Int. Amos Ben-Gurion

338–39: *Suddenly stones* to *Knesset was recessed*—JP 1/8/1952

339: *Yesterday the hand*—JP 1/9/1952

340: *His fears grew*—Ben-Gurion diaries 11/21/1948

340: *To meet this possible danger*—*Ibid.* 11/29/1948

340: *But first he had to deal* to *finest officers*—Int. Allon

340: *The results were catastrophic*—Burns p. 63; Horowitz and Luttwak pp. 106–107; Dan Horowitz *Borders* pp. 5–6

340: *Adding to the chaos*—Int. Yadin

340: *If the Prime Minister*—Int. M. Carmel, Sharon, Yadin

341: *Even before World War II*—Int. Ben-Gurion

341: *He didn't look the part*—Tevet *Dayan* (Heb.)

341: *He was also adolescent*—Tevet *Dayan* p. 199; Int. Avriel

341: *Dayan commanded almost without*—Tevet *Dayan* p. 221; Int. Avneri

341: *And he lured countless*—Avneri *Zionists* p. 130; Int. Mor

341–42: *When one husband* to *will never meet"*—Pepper in NYT Mag. 5/4/1980

342: *Dayan needed political*—Int. Ben-Gurion

342: *Like his mentor*—Tevet *Dayan* p. 177; Int. Pearlman

342: *Even more important*—Int. Ben-Gurion, Pearlman

342: *Dayan's pragmatism* to *circumstances*—Avneri p. 125; Tevet *Dayan* p. 195

342: *And often his pragmatism*—Avneri *Zionists* (quoting Yael Dayan) p. 128; Tevet *Dayan* p. 205

342: *Ben-Gurion named* to *elite at once, he cried*—Horowitz and Luttwak pp. 108–109

342: *But when Unit 101*—Int. Sharon

343: *To supply this army* to *nuclear industry?*—Int. Peres

344: *"He was afraid*—Int. Dan

344: *"When the Old Man asks*—Nehemiah Argov

344: *Argov proved his love*—*Ibid.*; Int. D. Argov, Gil, Navon, Rosen, R. Siegel

344–45: *"B.G., put on* to *put it on*—Nehemiah Argov

345: *If the Prime Minister*—Int. Avriel, Goldschmidt

345: *Still, Ben-Gurion would defy* to *behind drawn curtains?*—Int. R. Leshem

345: *Another aide who became*—*Ibid.*; Int. Avriel, Pearlman

345: *Kollek, though able and warm*—Int. Pearlman

345–46: *With his young protégés*—JP 9/2/1960, 8/7/1970; Int. Gilboa

346: *Ben-Gurion felt that Israel*—Bar-Zohar *Ben-Gurion* pp. 192–93; Int. Makleff

347: *Fearful that Mapam*—Ben-Gurion diaries 12/18/1951

347: *Ben-Gurion saw his chance* to *anti-Semitic features?"*—JP 11/26/1952

347–48: *Ideologically shaken* to *wreck the coalition*—Int. Avriel, Netzer

348: *Take Jerusalem*—Ben-Gurion diaries 2/14/1949; Bader (o.h.)

348: *An ally nevertheless*—Bar-Zohar *Ben-Gurion* pp. 192–93

348: *Ben-Gurion was more trusting* to *in case of war*—Ben-Gurion diaries 7/20/1950

348–49: *Hoping to soften* to *fish for a week*—Avrech

349: *He stole away*—Int. Avriel

349: *But sometimes he also put*—Int. Ruth Beit-Halachmi

349: *And he occasionally enjoyed*—Sources requesting anonymity

350: *Ruth Goldschmidt* to *live in Israel*—Int. Goldschmidt and sources requesting anonymity

350: *Shortly Ben-Gurion found* to *defense ministry*—Sources request anonymity

351: *"X phoned*—Argov diary

351–52: *And the pioneers and soldiers*—Litvinoff p. 248

352: *"I am ashamed*—Gvati (o.h.)

352: *So frustrated were some*—Derogy and Carmel p. 102

352: *And after the report*—Gurari (o.h.)

352: *Whatever the answer*—Litvinoff p. 248; Int. Gevaryahu, Rafael, Shragai

352: *But perhaps the greatest* to *without Ben-Gurion"*—Int. Kimche

353: *He was "the only head*—Ben-Gurion *Vision* 11/2/1949

353: *"Weizmann is liable*—Ben-Gurion diaries 9/20/1948

353: *"I am . . . standing*—Weizmann to Ben-Gurion (never sent), Weizmann Archives 87/I-1 1951

353: *But Kimche would read*—Int. Kimche

353–54: *Ben-Gurion would soon* to *official functions"*—Eban *Autobiography* pp. 166–68; Pearlman *Looks* pp. 203–204

354: *Perhaps remembering the years*—Avigur (o.h.)

354: *Yet, how precious*—Bar-Zohar *Ben-Gurion* v.3 (Heb.); Int. Avriel

354: *Stop here!* to *beginning again?*—St. John *Ben-Gurion* pp. 246–48; Int. Avriel

354: *Paula was stunned*—Int. P. Ben-Gurion, Rosenblum

355: *Ben-Gurion understood Paula's* to *let them stay?*—Ben-Gurion in JP 3/29/1954

355: *But Israel's renewal* to *might drop in*—Int. P. Ben-Gurion, Rosenblum

355: *Being the Prime Minister's*—Kollek p. 106; Int. Avriel

356: *Nor did her husband* to *"fat legs"?*—Int. Jibli

356: *Still, Paula enjoyed*—Avrech; Int. R. Leshem

356: *At first the social*—Int. Jibli, E. Rubin

356–57: *Yes, Paula had been* to *older than you, isn't she?"*—Ibid.; Avrech

356: *Paula was at least relieved*—Int. Avriel

358: *"Er geht! Schweig!"*, to *teacup still full*—Int. Rosenblum

358–59: *Actually, Ben-Gurion*, to *be so "irresponsible"?*—Sharett *Yoman Ishi* 10/10/1953; Int. Ben-Gurion, Hacohen, M. Sharett

359: *Other ministers were also hard* to *torment never stop?*—Sharett *Yoman Ishi* 10/11/1953

359: *On October 14, 1953*—Ibid. 10/14,17/1953

359–60: *Thus, on the breezy starlit night* to *his own government*—Schiff in *Haaretz* 12/10/1965; Int. Dan, Sharon

360: *Ben-Gurion hurried to Jerusalem* to *whatever its shame*—Sharett *Yoman Ishi* 10/15/1953

360: *He recalled Victor Hugo's* to *purpose, be condemned?*—Int. Navon

360: *Ben-Gurion called in Sharon to attack was "shameful."*—Int. Sharon, Makleff

361: *On November 2, 1953*—Sharett *Yoman Ishi* 11/2/1953

361: *Eshkol, however, would not*—Ibid. 11/17/1953

361: *Sharett's gratitude* to *(It doesn't matter)' "*—Ibid. 11/19/1953

362: *I have endeavored"* —JP 12/8/1953

362: *A few days later*—Int. P. Ben-Gurion

362: *When several trucks to Follow me!"*—St. John *Ben-Gurion* pp. 251–52

Chapter Twelve (pages 363–89)

363: *"I feel," he wrote*—Sharett *Yoman Ishi* 12/15/1953

363–64: *Not everything, of course to she hated the desert*—Int. Baniel, Rosenblum

364: *Ben-Gurion scanned*—Louvish in *Jewish Vanguard* 3/26/1954; Strachey in *New Statesman and Nation* 11/6/1954; Int. Baniel

364–65: *It was because to special note of him*—Int. Baniel, Hirsh

365: *But they couldn't entirely*—Sharett *Yoman Ishi* 1/29/1954; Int. Baniel

365: *Though he and Paula*—St. John *Ben-Gurion* p. 256; Int. Baniel

365: *Yes, she had dreaded*—Int. L. Rivlin

365–66: *But her unhappiness to old Second Aliya mold*—Bar-Zohar *Ben-Gurion* v.3 (Heb.); Blair in NYT Mag. 1/12/1954

366: *He would even become*—Int. Baniel

366: *He wouldn't to wanted more milk*—Int. Hirsh

366: *Was Ben-Gurion just grateful*—Int. R. Leshem

367: *A healthy tan replaced to animals depended on him*—Int. Hirsh

367: *"He still kept his hand*—Meir p. 235

367: *"I received the impression"*—Sharett *Yoman Ishi* 1/29/1954

367: *Besides, the visits*—Eliav pp. 78–79; Int. Yishai

367–68: *The Israelis, Ben-Gurion decided to Very well, I agree"*—Int. Yishai

368: *But though Ben-Gurion dragged*—Int. A. Nehamkin

368–69: *And so was born to would be good farmers*—Ibid.; Int. Yishai

369: *Ben-Gurion would, first of all to sarcasm, rudeness and arrogance*—Bar-Zohar *Ben-Gurion* p. 208; Int. Ofner

369: *Ben-Gurion had not always*—Eban *Autobiography* p. 180; Int. Z. Kesse, Meisels

370: *Sharett had never been*—Dayan *Story* p. 186; (Lau-)Lavie pp. 122–23 (quoting Sharett letter to Lavon); Sharett *Yoman Ishi* 10/2/1954, 1/15/1955

370: *Nonsense! reply Lavon's*—Int. Sternberg, Yagol

370: *Finally, when Lavon refused*—Arieli (quoting Lavon testimony before Knesset committee); Dayan p. 187; (Lau-) Lavie p. 123

371: *"We have been keeping track*—Yaari pp. 40–42 (quoting cable)

371: *"The principal reason*—Ibid. pp. 40–42

371: *Persuaded that Nasser*—Sharett *Yoman Ishi* 9/27/1955; Int. Z. Kesse

371: *One Egyptian agent*—Avneri *Zionism* p. 113

371: *And shortly, Nasser invited*—Int. Yeroham Cohen

371: *He used the Indian ambassador*—Avneri *Zionism* p. 113 (based on talk with Panikar and reported statement by Orbach)

371: *"Why," he asked a visitor*—Goldmann *Paradox* p. 99

371: *"We must straighten*—Bar-Zohar *Ben-Gurion* p. 219 (quoting Ben-Gurion interview with journalist)

372:   *But if the new Jew*—Derogy and Carmel p. 102

372:   *Then came the most frightening*—Sachar *Ends* p. 352

372:   *Could the Israelis stop them?*—Bayne report in JO 12/18/1964

372:   *Colonel Benjamin Gibli to Presumably not*—*Ibid.*

372–73:   *Gibli apparently decided to fly off to Europe*—*Ibid.*; Elad pp. 133–59; Int. Dassa

373:   *Gibli was horrified*—Arieli; Eshed; *Haaretz* 2/19/1965

373:   *Several months earlier*—Evron to Lavon 12/30/1954

373:   *Dayan too was aware*—(Lau-)Lavie p. 126

373:   *But was it a coincidence*—Avneri *Zionists* pp. 117–18

373:   *When Dayan was in Washington* to *had been given*—Arieli; Eshed; Int. Olsham

373:   *He apparently made no frantic*—*Ibid.*

374:   *"He informed me about a strange*—Ben-Gurion diaries 8/24/1954

374:   *But if Dayan had rather*—Arieli; Lavon testimony, Knesset foreign affairs and security committee 10/4/1960

374–75:   *Dayan fired it back*—Int. (Lau-)Lavie

375:   *Gibli would claim*—Arieli; Eshed; Int. Gothels

375:   *Propelled by a Watergatelike*—Int. D. Carmel

375:   *(Dayan would later tell*—Int. Ben-Aharon

375:   *Dalia was soon working*—Int. D. Carmel

375:   *When the Egyptian government*—Arieli; Elad pp. 178–83

375:   *Lavon fought back*—Minutes, Lavon-Gibli meeting 12/28/1954 (made available by source requesting anonymity)

375:   *Lavon then burst into*—Int. Sternberg

375:   *Sharett, who hadn't even*—Int. Olsham

376:   *Meanwhile, Lavon, en-*

raged to *would confide to his diary*—Sharett *Yoman Ishi* 2/12/1955

376:   *Sharett secretly summoned*—*Ibid.* 1/25/1955

376:   *"He must go!"*—Ben-Gurion diaries 2/1/1954

376:   *And shortly afterward*—Sharett *Yoman Ishi* 2/2,12/1955

376:   *Delegations now streamed* to *were in trouble*—Int. Netzer, Yishai

376–77:   *After a long talk* to *first priority"*—Ben-Gurion diaries 2/17/1955

377:   *When Golda Meir returned* to *of joint comradely work*—Sharett *Yoman Ishi* 2/21/1955

377:   *The massive public turnout*—JP 2/23/1955

378:   *The stiffening process* to *for me and for him"*—Sharett *Yoman Ishi* 2/27/1955

378: *Ariel Sharon, who had commanded*—Bar-Zohar *Ben-Gurion* p. 218; Burns p. 17; Love pp. 5–20; Int. Sharon

379: *On learning of* to *failure as prime minister"*—Sharett *Yoman Ishi* 2/28/1955

379:   *Yes, Ben-Gurion had returned* to *done without war*—*Ibid.* 3/2/1955

379:   *As Sharett had guessed*—Burns p. 18

379:   *And soon the Gaza frontier*—Sharett *Yoman Ishi* 3/25/1955

379–80:   *Ben - Gurion had taught Nasser*—*Ibid.* 5/17/1955

380:   *Pain once again "gnawed* to *Sharett was incredulous*—*Ibid.* 3/27/1955

380:   *The whole Gaza Strip?*—*Ibid.* 3/2,10,16,24/1955, 4/13/1955, 7/10/1955; Kramer in *New York* 8/9/1982

380:   *Still fuming from this*—Sharett *Yoman Ishi* 3/27/1955

380:   *And the next day* to *turned down Ben-Gurion again*—*Ibid.* 4/3/1955

380–81: *Sharett also spurned* —*Ibid.* 5/16/1955

381: *In Sharett's state*—*Ibid.* 8/21/1955

381: *Nor did the elections*— *Ibid.* 8/15/1955

381: *Sharett grew frantic*— *Ibid.* 8/12,18,19,21,24/1955

381: *Some time later*—*Ibid.* 8/30/1955

382: *The thunderous collapse* —Love pp. 96–97; Dayan *Story* p. 190; Love pp. 96; A. Thomas p. 23

382: *"If they really receive*— Sharett *Yoman Ishi* 10/3/1955

382: *Though Ben-Gurion fell ill*—Dayan *Sinai* p. 19

382: *During the next months to arms to Israel*—Peres *Sling* pp. 41–65

382: *After being told of future* —Sharett *Yoman Ishi* 12/20/1955

382: *Contingency plans?* to *military solution"*—Dayan *Story* p. 192

383: *Even so, on November 2* —Dayan *Sinai* p. 19; Sharett *Yoman Ishi* 11/2/1955

383: *Robert B. Anderson* to *with all his Migs"*—Ben-Gurion *Arab Leaders* pp. 274–325

383: *Perhaps Dayan was right*—Bar - Zohar *Ben - Gurion* v.3 (Heb.); *Yediot Acharonot* 2/25/1973

384: *An opportunity arose* to *leaving the cabinet*—Meir pp. 237–38

384: *Desperately, pathetically* —Sharett *Yoman Ishi* 2/15/1956

385: *On June 6, two Mapai officials*—Bar-Zohar *Ben-Gurion* v.3 (Heb.; quoting Sapir)

385: *The curse of my relations* —Sharett *Yoman Ishi* 2/15/1956

385: *Sharett cried to by American TV"*—Bar-Zohar *Ben-Gurion* v.3 (Heb.; quoting Sapir)

385: *Sharett sweated through* —Sharett *Yoman Ishi* 6/17/1956

385: *Ben-Gurion was working* —Bar-Zohar in JP 10/14/1966

386: *Ben-Gurion's reaction*— Dayan *Story* p. 194; Love pp. 297–327

386: *"How much time*—Peres *Sling* p. 185

386: *Rushing back to Israel*— Dayan *Story* p. 194

386: *Within weeks Ben-Gurion to noted in his diary*—Ben-Gurion diaries 7/24/1956

386: *Two days later, Nasser*— Dayan *Story* pp. 194–95

386: *French and British leaders*—*Ibid.* pp. 213–20; Peres *Sling* pp. 193–96; Int. Peres

387: *Why, Ben-Gurion wanted* —Dayan *Story* p. 224

387: *Nevertheless, Ben-Gurion accepted*—Bar-Zohar *Ben-Gurion* pp. 234–35; Dayan *Story* p. 227

387: *In a magnificent villa*— Dayan *Story* pp. 230–31

387: *Israel had to appear*— *Ibid.* p. 223

388: *He suggested a compromise*—*Ibid.* p. 238–39; Peres *Sling* pp. 201–202

388: *Lloyd was doubtful* to *during the blitz!*—Dayan *Story* pp. 233–34

388: *A French general* to *a moral end*—Bar-Zohar *Ben-Gurion* p. 240

388: *Finally, everyone*—Bar-Zohar *Ben-Gurion* v.3 (Heb.)

388–89: *What did Ben-Gurion think?* to *Peres would write*—Bar-Zohar *Ben-Gurion* p. 241

389: *"He was still grappling*— Dayan *Story* p. 240

389: *"The whole gang*—Ben-Gurion diaries 10/23/1956

389: *But members of the "gang"*—Dayan *Story* p. 240

389: *Shortly before noon* to *augured peace*—Peres *Sling* p. 202

389: *But war was on his mind* —*Ibid.* pp. 202–204; Dayan *Story* pp. 243–45

389: *"Moshe's plan is good—* Dayan *Story* p. 245
389: *On the flight to Paris—* *Ibid.* p. 227

389: *"I wonder," Ben-Gurion* *mused—Ibid.* p. 245

Chapter Thirteen (pages 390–419)

390: *One night in October* to *in our shelter"*—Int. Rosenblum
390: *Few others knew*—Ben-Gurion diaries 10/26,28/1956
390: *Ben-Gurion was so anxious*—Int. M. Carmel
391: *After the cabinet meeting* —Bader (o.h.); Int. Bader
391: *Shortly two cables arrived* —Bar-Zohar *Ben-Gurion* p. 245
391: *Could American intelligence*—Y. Herzog in JP 10/8/1941
391: *"My government will be failing*—Cable, Ben-Gurion to Eisenhower (quoted in Bar-Zohar *Ben-Gurion* p. 246)
391: *Had they jumped yet?—* Dayan *Story* pp. 250–52; Int. M. Carmel, Navon
391: *At the U.S. State Department* to *in your country"*—Eban *Autobiography* p. 211
391: *In New Delhi*—Int. Hacohen
392: *The next day, October 30* —Dayan *Story* pp. 252–53
392: *The ultimatums were announced* to *costly—unnecessary* *—battle*—Dayan *Story* p. 258
392: *Shocked by the unexpected*—Cable, Eisenhower to Ben-Gurion (quoted in Bar-Zohar *Ben-Gurion* p. 247)
392: *Ben-Gurion rejected this* —Eban *Autobiography* pp. 214–15
393: *"At first," he wrote*—Bar-Zohar *Ben-Gurion* p. 249
393: *In the Israeli Arab village*—St. John *Ben-Gurion* pp. 288, 291
393: *The government of Israel* —Nikolai Bulganin to Ben-Gurion 11/5/1956 (quoted in Eban *Autobiography* pp. 227–28)
394: *The eyes of the world—*

Avrech; Bar-Zohar *Ben-Gurion* v.3 (Heb.)
394: *"The revelation of Sinai* to *talks with the Arabs*—Eban *Autobiography* pp. 228–29
394: *The United Nations General Assembly* to *assurance to the Jewish state*—Eban *Autobiography* pp. 229–31; Int. Eban
395: *[Ambassador] Eban phoned me*—Ben-Gurion diaries 11/8/1956
395: *"I made a few mistakes—* Brecher p. 283
395: *Dayan found the Prime Minister*—Bar-Zohar *Ben-Gurion* p. 251 (quoting Dayan)
395: *Around him, sleepless aides*—Int. Navon
395: *Ministers nervously sat* to *Out of the Sinai!' "*—Bar-Zohar *Ben-Gurion* v.3 (Heb.) (B-Z int. with Sapir)
395: *As mankind seemingly hurtled*—Int. Eban, Feldenkrais
396: *He called Ambassador Eban* to *speech proposing compromise*—Eban *Autobiography* pp. 231–32
396: *The Prime Minister was relieved* to *this great operation"—* Voice of Israel 11/8/1956
396: *"You advanced to Sinai* —Bar-Zohar *Ben-Gurion* (Heb.)
397: *Israel would withdraw—* Eban *Autobiography* p. 235; Int. Eban
397: *"Write and tell him—* Bar-Zohar *Ben-Gurion* p. 254
397: *But he settled for*—Ben-Gurion to Eisenhower 2/1957
397: *"This president hardly does*—Bar-Zohar *Ben-Gurion* v.3 (Heb.)
397: *But when Washington began*—Eisenhower p. 185; Ben-Gurion diaries 2/7/1957

397:   *And French Foreign Minister Pineau*—Eban *Autobiography* pp. 248–51; Meir pp. 249–54

397:   *"Tomorrow there won't be*—Int. Makleff

398:   *"Perhaps," Golda would write*—Meir p. 255

398:   *Despite reassurances from*—Cable, Eisenhower to Ben-Gurion 3/1/1957

398–99:   *But he could drive himself to people gaping at him?*—JP 12/14/1973; Int. Feldenkrais

399:   *"Let him open a circus—Maariv* 9/19/1957

399:   *And he would never sit still*—Int. E. and G. Ben-Eliezer

399:   *Feldenkrais, Paula thought*—JP 12/14/1973; Int. Feldenkrais

399:   *Perhaps, but for his services*—Int. Feldenkrais, C. Yisraeli

399:   *Paid or not, however—Ibid.;* JP 12/14/1973

399–400:   *Unfortunately, Ben-Gurion wasn't to hospital for a while*—JP 10/30/1957

400:   *"I know that you regret*—St. John *Ben-Gurion* p. 306

400:   *Paula couldn't be kept from—Ibid.* p. 311; Avrech; Int. R. Leshem

401:   *A far more serious plot*—JP 11/3/1957; Int. Lif

401:   *"I would like to die now*—Navon in *Nehemiah Argov*

401:   *But his euphoria waned*—Int. R. Leshem, Shanz

401:   *In a farewell letter*—JP 11/14/1957

401:   *But his friends did mourn*—Int. Rosenfeld

401:   *But the day after the funeral to greatest men of all time*—JP 11/6/1957 (Kollek claims *he* informed Ben-Gurion)

401–2:   *When Ben-Gurion finished*—Int. Kollek

402:   *A feeling of guilt*—Int. Gil

402:   *"I doubt if two men*—JP 11/19/1957

402–3:   *Paula, however, seemed more to kitchen sink*—Avrech; Int. P. Ben-Gurion

403:   *The next morning* to *"former terrorist"*—JP 1/4/1959

403:   *The Secretary General left—Ibid.*

403:   *Nasser had already helped*—Int. Ben-Gurion, Hacohen

403–4:   *Now Nasser was courting to Ghana and Liberia*—Avriel report prepared for author; Int. Avriel

404:   *Ben-Gurion thus embarked*—Meir pp. 263–90; Author's observations in Ghana and Ethiopia; Int. Avriel, Gilboa, Meir

404:   *But Joshua was right*—Ben-Gurion diaries 4/18/1957, 8/15/1957

405:   *Playing upon America's* to *in any way it could*—Bar-Zohar *Ben-Gurion* pp. 259–60

405:   *Thanks for the advice*—Int. C. Herzog, Lubrani, Navon

405:   *The Turks were "taking*—Ben-Gurion diaries 7/19/1958

406:   *"Why doesn't the President—Ibid.* 7/28/1958

406:   *Finally, word from Dulles*—Int. Lubrani, Navon

406:   *Ben-Gurion wasted no time to sought before World War I—Ibid.*

406:   *A few months later*—Int. C. Herzog

406:   *And while on a trip*—Int. Lubrani (Navon cannot recall meeting with Shah)

407:   *That left Ethiopia—Ibid.*

407:   *Since the Arabs had*—Minutes, Ben-Gurion meeting with subordinates 10/30/1958

407:   *Ben-Gurion thus cabled*—Cable, Ben-Gurion to Eban 8/16/1958

407:   *The real question*—Ben-Gurion diaries 7/15/1958; Ben-Gurion to Macmillan 7/17,20/1958

407:   *Both Britain and the United States*—Cable, Eban to Ben-Gurion 8/4/1958

408: *"Eisenhower's honor—* Protocols, Mapai Foreign Affairs Committee meeting 3/4/1958

408: *Ben-Gurion now wistfully looked*—Ben-Gurion diaries 3/15/1958, 7/24/1958

408: *After a rebuff—Ibid.* 7/19,22/1958 (Britain), 7/17,18/1958 (Russia)

408: *Shimon Peres charmed—* Peres *HaShalav HaBa*

408: *But the news leaked—* Ben-Gurion diaries 12/17/1957; Int. M. Carmel

408–9: *Soon afterwards* to *Jewish machine guns*—Int. Allon, M. Carmel

409: *By early 1960* to *wasn't a correct one* Bar-Zohar *Ben-Gurion* v.3 (Heb.); Int. Kollek, Navon

410: *On the morning of March 14*—JP 4/29/1966

410: *Adenauer, he would write*—Ben-Gurion in JP 10/11/1963

410: *Shimon Peres and Defense Minister*—Int. Peres

410: *But how much money* to *'five-hundred million'*—Int. Navon

411: *Ben-Gurion laughed, but* to *as a human being"*—JP 4/24/1966

411: *After the talk* to *replied Navon*—Int. Navon

411: *En route home*—JP 3/23/1960; Int. Navon

411: *Britain, however, wasn't* to *ease his disappointment*—JP 3/20/1960

411–12: *Indeed, hardly had he flown* to *Nikita Khrushchev—Ibid.* 3/24/1960

412: *Meanwhile, he must see* —Ben-Gurion diaries 11/4/1959

412: *To Ben-Gurion, De Gaulle*—Kollek pp. 140–41; Int. Avriel

412: *Yet Ben-Gurion had hesitated*—Peres *HaShalav HaBa;* Int. Avriel, Tsur

412: *This installation, De Gaulle*—De Gaulle p. 266

412–13: *At noon, June 14—* Avrech; JP 6/15/1960

413: *"Tell me, please, who* to *That's enough!"*—Avrech; Int. Tsur

413: *"You symbolize in your person* to *State of Israel"*—JP 6/15/1960

413–14: *Over coffee in the beautiful* to *genius of the other—* De Gaulle pp. 265–66 (reference to his memoirs); Peres *Lekh im HaAnashim;* Int. Eytan, Navon, Peres, Tsur

414: *Ben-Gurion was less—* Daily Express 12/16/1960; NYT 12/10/1960; Time 12/13/1960; Washington Post 12/18/1960

414: *No!, Ben-Gurion bellowed* to *with new vigor*—Bar-Zohar *Ben-Gurion* pp. 271–72

415: *Ben-Gurion was, indeed, so eager*—Ben-Gurion diaries 3/21/1961; Int. Gazit

415: *"I can't wait* to *meeting with Khrushchev*—Int. Gazit

415: *"It is hoped"*—State Dept. memo, Myer Feldman and Armin Meyer 4/25/1961

415: *Ben-Gurion sized up—* Int. Kollek, Lubrani

415–16: *But if Ben-Gurion harbored* to *Blessed be the peacemaker!"*—Int. Gazit

416: *As Ben-Gurion rose* to *for the free world"*—Int. M. Carmel, Lubrani

416: *But as he left*—Int. Gazit

416: *After the meeting—Ibid.;* JP 6/6/1961

416: *But not before another* to *broke into tears*—Bar-Zohar *Ben-Gurion* (Heb.); script *Ben-Gurion Remembers* Heb. U., Jer.

416–17: *No less sentimental* to *when he gets old"*—JP 6/4/1961; Int. Navon

417: *In Paris, Ben-Gurion*—JP 6/7/1961

417: *With good reason*—Bar-Zohar *Spies* pp. 226–30; Int. Tsur

417–18: *It is not clear, though* to *show him to me?"*—Avrech

418:   With much of the West to only by love"—Pearlman Looks pp. 189–94

418:   In 1955, Nu had—Sharett Yoman Ishi 5/30/1955

418:   Ben-Gurion   wanted Paula to go—Avrech

418–19:   The Prime Minister departed to usually did anyway—JP 12/1–9/1961; Int. Feldenkrais, Navon

419:   When he emerged to how to concentrate?"—Int. Galli

419:   Ben-Gurion did, however, "gain—Pearlman Looks p. 190

Chapter Fourteen (pages 420–43)

420:   The river flowed to the Prime Minister didn't—Avrech

420:   Paula needed all—Int. Rosen

421:   Doris had mixed feelings —Doris May to Ben-Gurion 2/1955 (quoted in Bar-Zohar Ben-Gurion p. 280)

421:   But when Doris flew in to returned to England—Int. Gil, Rosen

421:   But one "rival" Paula—Int. E. Taub

421:   In any case, they continued—Int. Ruth Beit-Halachmi, Y. Beit-Halachmi, Izhar, Turel

421:   They would sit alone—Int. Halamish

421:   But one conversation to moving reunion—Int. Ruth Beit-Halachmi, Y. Beit-Halachmi, Izhar, Turel

421–22:   Once, Rachel asked to and he did—Int. Halamish

422:   Ben-Gurion also found time to did he have for her?—Int. R. Leshem

422:   Though not as close to Amos to apologized to his son—Int. Amos Ben-Gurion

422–23:   Outside his immediate family to so relaxed and happy —Int. Y. Ben-Eliezer

423:   Sometimes Ben-Gurion's sister—The Day (London; Yiddish) 4/5/1958

423:   His sister Rivka—Ben-Gurion to Rachel Beit-Halachmi 7/24/1963

423:   And he even forgot to forgot about his family"—Int. Arkis

423–24:   It was, therefore, with hope to beamed unto the nations?—NYT Mag. ·12/18/1960; Int. Harel

424:   Harel flew off—Ben-Gurion Israel: A Personal History p. 576; Ben-Gurion diaries 5/15/1960

424:   He called in Abba Eban —Int. Gilboa

424:   On May 22, Harel returned to was indeed Eichmann—Int. Harel, Navon

424:   After two Holocaust survivors—Int. Navon

424:   "A short while ago to Prime Minister insisted—Ben-Gurion Israel: A Personal History p. 573

425:   Hitler's Final Solution—Ben-Gurion to Goldmann (quoted in Ben-Gurion Israel: A Personal History p. 575)

425:   And most of the world—Ben-Gurion Israel: A Personal History p. 576

425:   And so Ben-Gurion sat—Int. Hausner, Navon

425:   But the higher Ben-Gurion—JP 6/19,22/1960

425:   Paula was enraged—Int. Gevaryahu

426:   To Chief Rabbi Yitzhak Nissim—Int. M. Nissim

426:   Ben-Gurion had other problems to within his own party —JP 8/7/1959; exchange of letters, Ben-Gurion and Rabbi Yehuda Maimon 7/3–4/1958

427:   Prodded by Mapai's—Int. Gilboa, Ofner, Meisels

427:   Dayan had resigned—

Ben-Gurion diaries 5/4,6/1958;
Int. Yadin
427: *And so Dayan waited*—
Tevet *Dayan* pp. 286–87
427–28: *In a rage, Dayan*—
Ibid. p. 287; (Lau-)Lavie pp. 175–
76; Int. Ofner
428: *Lavon and the veterans
to absurdity of this thought"*—
Ben-Gurion diaries 11/26/1958
428: *Dayan then announced*—
Tevet *Dayan* pp. 290–91; *Haaretz*
6/8/1958
428: *When Dayan continued
to stop making speeches*—Ben-
Gurion diaries 6/15/1958
428: *Golda Meir, in particular*
—Almogi; Int. Gazit, Harel, R.
Leshem, Meir, Yishai
429: *But after the war*—Int.
Gazit
429: *"I told Golda"*—Ben-
Gurion diaries 7/12/1957
429: *But Golda continued*—
Int. Harel, Tsur
429: *It was thus time to win
back*—Int. Hacohen
429: *Ben-Gurion had offended
Sharett*—Ben-Gurion speech,
Kibbutz Givat Haim 1/18/1957
429–30: *Now, more than two
years to pardon me"*—Ben-Gurion to M. Sharett 4/7/1959
430: *But the Prime Minister
apparently*—Ben-Gurion to M.
Sharett 4/8/1959
430: *Sharett wrote back*—M.
Sharett to Ben-Gurion 5/22/1959
430: *Ben-Gurion perhaps
hoped to captures their hearts"*—
Ben-Gurion diaries 5/21/1959
431: *Three months later to
Ephraim Evron*—Lavon notes on
meeting of 2/4/1960 (anonymity
requested by custodian); Int. L.
Lavon, Sternberg
431–32: *In May 1960, Lavon
went to helped Gibli do Lavon in?*
—Ben-Gurion *Israel: A Personal
History* pp. 605–606; protocols,
Knesset foreign affairs and security committee; Int. L. Lavon,
Sternberg

432–33: *On October 26, 1960*
to *"This means war!"*—Ben-Gurion *Israel: A Personal History* p.
606; Lavon notes on meeting of
10/26/1960 (dictated afterwards by
Lavon to Evron—anonymity requested by custodian); Int. Evron,
L. Lavon, Sternberg
433: *Within days, Lavon*—JO
1/20/1961
433: *Ben-Gurion sat restlessly*
—Ben-Gurion *Israel: A Personal
History* pp. 606–25; Ben-Gurion
to Yehoshua Manosh 2/1/1961; Int.
Gilboa, Navon, Peres
433: *Lavon, he cried to simply
a liar!"*—Netzer
433: *Actually, Lavon's "truths"
to forgery and perjury"*—Ben-
Gurion *Israel: A Personal History*
p. 614
433–34: *We have believed in
you*—Reprinted in JP 1/1/1961
434: *Such censure only nursed*
—Bar-Zohar *Ben-Gurion* p. 292;
Ben-Gurion *Israel: A Personal
History* p. 292; JP 1/13/1961
434: *And so Ben-Gurion
"passed*—Int. Almogi
434: *"If I knew then what I
know now*—JP 10/20/1960
434: *Ben-Gurion called for a
hearing to who lied on trial"*—
Ben-Gurion *Israel: A Personal
History* p. 624
434: *To the end of his life*—
Int. Gevaryahu
435: *Fists pounded*—JP 11/26/
1964
435: *He might even abandon
them*—Netzer
435: *Unless Ben-Gurion fought*
—Netzer
435: *But Ben-Gurion didn't do
that*—Ben-Gurion in JP 11/1/
1965; Int. Bar-Eli
435: *But perhaps the most important to "security mishap"*—
Int. D. Carmel, Hausner
436: *"We find that Lavon to
"given the order"*—Ben-Gurion
Israel: A Personal History pp.
631–32

436:   *And she produced a copy*
—D. Carmel to Benjamin Gibli 2/
7/1965

436:   *Dalia, who had fled*—Int.
D. Carmel

436:   *The sight of the Old Man*
—D. Carmel to Levi Eshkol 3/23/
57 (copy shown to author by D.
Carmel)

437:   *"I am not a member*—
Ben-Gurion *Israel: A Personal
History* pp. 633–34

437:   *"He raised his hand*—
Int. Y. Kesse

437:   *Eshkol, especially, felt
relieved*—Ben-Gurion *Israel: A
Personal History* p. 638

437:   *Eshkol huddled*—Arieli
(quoting Ben-Gurion aide)

437:   *A blemished god*—*Ibid.;*
Bar-Zohar *Ben-Gurion* v.3 (Heb.)

438:   *"A catastrophe!"*—Int.
Allon

438:   *Ben-Gurion had promised*—Ben-Gurion *Israel: A Personal History* p. 642

438:   *Meanwhile, as the Lavon
Affair* to *breach of security?*—
Bar-Zohar *Spies* pp. 204–10;
Derogy and Carmel pp. 145–55;
Int. Harel, Manor, Navon

438–39:   *Shortly, Ben-Gurion
had trouble* to *Both agents were
arrested*—Bar-Zohar *Ben-Gurion*
pp. 298–303; Derogy and Carmel
pp. 184–201; Int. Harel, Manor

439:   *When Ben-Gurion, who
had been*—Int. Avriel, Manor

439:   *Now, in the Tiberias
hotel* to *force Adenauer's hand*—
Int. Manor

440:   *"You send our Uzi* to *activities of its nationals"*—Minutes, Knesset 3/20/1963

440:   *When Harel persisted*—
Int. Amit

440:   *Ben-Gurion hurried back*

to *infuriating Ben-Gurion*—Int.
Harel

440:   *He sent word to Harel*—
Ben-Gurion to Harel 3/26/1963

440:   *"Send over someone*—
Ben-Gurion diaries 4/4/1963

440:   *In a rage, Ben-Gurion*—
Int. Ben-Porat

440:   *Lonely and depressed*—
Elon in *Haaretz* 4/19/1963

441:   *Nor did he always remember* to *a mere "figurehead"*—
Int. Eban

441:   *"Man is not free"*—Elon
in *Haaretz* 4/19/1963

441:   *A mere declaration*—
Bar-Zohar *Ben-Gurion* p. 304

441:   *He tried to arrange meetings*—Ben-Gurion diaries 2/27/
1963 (talks between British journalist Charles Hamilton and Nasser); 5/19/1963 (messages to Tito);
report on Nasser-Hamilton talks 5/
20/1963; Ben-Gurion to U Nu 2/1/
1962 (Nasser); Edmond de Rothschild to Ben-Gurion 2/4/1963
(Hamilton); Ben-Gurion to E. de
Rothschild 3/1/1963 (Hamilton);
Ben-Gurion to Tito 12/28/1962
(Nasser)

441:   *Well, if not a peace*—
Ben-Gurion diaries 5/19,23/1963,
6/16/1963

441–42:   *In his apprehension*
to *they were all talking war*—Int.
Alami, Jabary, Lubrani, Palmon,
Zuabi

442:   *"He would replace the
army*—Minutes, Knesset 5/13/
1963

442:   *If not Begin, perhaps*—
Ben-Gurion diaries 6/16/1963

442–43:   *On June 15, 1963*—
Bar-Zohar *Ben-Gurion* p. 305

443:   *That night, Ben-Gurion*
—Int. Lubrani

443:   *His first choice*—Int.
Yadin

Chapter Fifteen (pages 444–63)

444: *Eshkol lived up*—JP 10/11/1963

444: *Not every visitor* to *muttering, "Feh, feh!"*—Int. L. Rivlin

445: *And now Eshkol, egged on* to *matter of conscience"*—Ben-Gurion diaries 10/19/1963; Int. M. Eshkol

445: *Eshkol finally rebelled*—JP 10/7/1964, 11/29/1964; Ben-Gurion diaries 8/14/1964

445–46: *It was now Ben-Gurion* to *Eshkol changed his mind*—Yanai; *Yediot Acharonot* 12/20/1964; Ben-Gurion diaries 12/17/1964

446: *And in a masterful maneuver*—JP 12/14/1964

446: *Even Dayan did not favor*—JP 12/17/1964

446: *The party thus shelved*—JP 12/16/1964

446: *Life had been hard*—Avrech; Int. Avriel

446: *"Save him from his misery*—Surkis (o.h.)

446: *Paula kept all hate-mail*—Brenner (o.h.); Int. L. Lavon. Olshan

446–47: *"What shall I tell him?* to *back to Spinoza"*—Avrech

447: *"I don't know what* to *into the Lavon Affair*—JP 2/18/1965

447: *"A judicial committee?*—*Ibid.* 2/19/1965

447: *"We must free ourselves*—*ibid.* 2/18/1965

447: *She kissed Sharett*—Bar-Zohar *Ben-Gurion* p. 309

447: *Ben-Gurion listened to the insults*—Surkis (o.h.)

447: *"The ugliest thing*—Ben-Gurion diaries 2/19/1965

447: *"Everything is finished"*—Int. Yishai

447–48: *After midnight a group* to *close to death"*—Netzer

448: *Nu? So what happened* to *lay shatteringly bare*—Int. Yishai

448: *A judicial committee was no*—*Davar* 5/13/1965; Ben-Gurion diaries 5/13/1965, 6/18/1965

448: *The veterans gasped*—Syrkin *Golda* p. 327

448: *The "youngsters" tried to calm* to *Everyone to Ben-Gurion's!*—Int. Peres

448: *Another time, her husband*—Surkis (o.h.)

448–49: *Later, Ben Gurion called*—Yanai; Int. Bar-Eli, Peres

449: *Moshe Dayan, who had earlier*—Surkis (o.h.); Int. Bar-Eli, Kimche

449: *Meanwhile, Ben-Gurion decided* to *set up a new slate*—Ben-Porat (o.h.); Int. Bar-Eli

449: *A Mapai "court" then convened*—JP 8/20/1965; Shadmi (o.h.)

449: *"I'd rather have cut off*—Becker (o.h.)

449–50: *The applause echoing* to *acrimony and anger*—Int. Gilboa

450: *This was the "ugliest*—Bar-Zohar *Ben-Gurion* p. 311

450: *Many Israelis, nevertheless, missed*—JP 10/3/1966

450: *And even President Zalman Shazar*—Ben-Ami (o.h.)

450: *The Prime Minister had not yet*—Samuels in NYT Mag. 10/16/1966

450: *Now, on his birthday*—JP 10/3/1966

451: *"You have put faith*—Guber *Path* p. 93

451: *He stressed the danger* to *feeling doubly despondent"*—Rabin pp. 72–73; Ben-Gurion diaries 5/22/1967; Int. Rabin

451: *With Eshkol wallowing*

to *would leave disillusioned*—
Bader (o.h.)

451:    *The legend of the desert
lion*—Rimalt (o.h.)

452:    *And he had, in fact, lost
to boys into battle*"—Surkis (o.h.)

452:    *And his old cautiously
aggressive*—Rimalt (o.h.)

452:    *As Ben-Gurion's heroic
image*—Netzer; Tevet *Dayan* p.
325

452:    *Should he accept it?*—
Int. Yadin

452:    *At the same time, Eshkol*
—Surkis (o.h.)

452:    *Ben-Gurion back-pedaled
to drank to Moshe's success*—Int.
Kimche

452:    *Ben-Gurion stayed in Tel
Aviv*—Ben-Gurion diaries 6/4/
1967

453:    *The following day, June 5*
—*Ibid.* 6/5/1967

453:    *On the second day* to *still
avoided him*—*Ibid.* 6/6–7/1967

453:    *"I forebore from taking*
—Dayan *Story* p. 350

453:    *Finally, when a cease-fire*
to *deceive the whole world*"—
Ben-Gurion diaries 6/9/1967

453:    *Soon, almost all Ben-
Gurion's*—Surkis (o.h.);   Int.
Netzer

454:    *Pathetically he joined
with*—Int. Harel, Netzer

454:    *"No comment!" he answered*—JO 5/22/1970

454–55:   *Hardly had his Rafi*
to *stroking her hand*—Int. Amos
Ben-Gurion

455:    *"I've been meaning*—
Surkis (o.h.)

455:    *The funeral drew many*—
Int. Amos Ben-Gurion, R. Leshem

455:    *If Ben-Gurion didn't
weep*—Surkis (o.h.)

455:    *It would take at least* to
she was not there—Int. Beer,
Amos Ben-Gurion

455:    *"Paula was unique*—
Ben-Gurion to Mrs. Archibald Sil-
verman 3/13/1968

455:    *Ben-Gurion even had a*

bodyguard to *die*—"*spiritually*"
—Int. Y. Ben-Eliezer

456:    "*After Paula died*"—Int.
Rubin

456:    *Perhaps the unhappiest*
—Int. O. Ben-Eliezer

456:    *Renana, who had recently*—Int. R. Leshem

456:    *He was apparently unaware*—Int. Gevaryahu

456:    *Worried about her father*
—Int. R. Leshem

456:    *Yet he was so lonely*—
Int. G. Ben-Eliezer

456:    *One day in 1970 to let
Paula know!*"—*Ibid.*; Int. Y. Ben-
Eliezer, Amos Ben-Gurion

456–57:   *And Ben-Gurion related*—Int. Y. Ben-Eliezer

457:    *While Ben-Gurion's family*—Int. Yishai

457:    *Apparently fearing criticism*—*Time* 10/18/1971

457:    *Sharett and Eshkol died*
—Int. Gevaryahu, Yishai

457:    *Many of Ben-Gurion's
former*—JP 10/1/1971

457:    *Then, at a special session*
—*Ibid.* 10/26/1971

458:    *Having performed their
duty*—Int. Katzman, Yishai

458:    *Ben-Gurion talked most
often* to *had suddenly exploded*—
Int. Yishai

458:    *Ben-Gurion also reminisced* to *right to know*"—Int.
Katzman

458:    *Ben-Gurion would reveal*
—Int. Ruth Beit-Halachmi, Y.
Beit-Halachmi, Izhar, Turel

458:    "*Your letter . . . enchanted
me*—Ben-Gurion   to   Rachel
Beit-Halachmi 10/25/1964

458:    "*I presume that you
know*—*Ibid.* 12/1/1968

458–59:   *Finally, in 1970, he
no longer* to *Isaiah will be fulfilled*"—*Ibid.* 11/28/1970

459:    *Ben-Gurion had shared*
—Int. C. Herzog

459:    *But as Ben-Gurion
peeked*—JP 9/30/1968; Int. Ben-
Gurion

459: *Was Israel even governable?*—Int. Amos Ben-Gurion, Yishai

459–60: *Socially this nation*—Int. Ben-Porat

460: *Whatever the answer, Ben-Gurion*—JP 11/22/1974

460: *In pursuing this goal, he pleaded*—*Ibid.* 8/15/1968

460: *"As long as the people*—*Ibid.* 11/22/1974

460: *Israel must first live*—Int. Brenner

460–61: *And real peace, he felt* to *bond with the United States*—Int. Ben-Gurion

461: *Yet, not only had real peace* to *toward the Jewish people"*—JP 1/10/1968

461: *Ben-Gurion agreed with De Gaulle*—Int. Ben-Gurion

461: *He was even ready*—Int. Navon

461: *With the Arabs snubbing peace*—Int. Ben-Gurion

461: *In fact, Jews, he wrote*—JP 9/30/1970

461–62: *First, never forget to centers of the earth"*—John M. Roots in NYT 2/8/1975

462: *With final peace*—*Jewish Frontier* 1/1974

462: *"Ask me," he said to a colleague*—Goldmann *Paradox* p. 99

462: *"Happy birthday, Ben-Gurion!"* to *hundred and twenty"*—Int. B. Ben-Gurion

462: *Coughing hard as he lay*—*Ibid.*; Surkis (o.h.)

462–63: *When one friend assured* to *word about the war*—*Ibid.*

463: *Instead, he sought solace*—Int. Gevaryahu

463: *"The eternal god*—Deuteronomy 33:27–29

463: *But even if Israel survived*—Int. B. Ben-Gurion, Ben-Porat

463: *When Geula told him*—Int. G. Ben-Eliezer

463: *Soon afterward, Ben-Gurion*—Int. Amos Ben-Gurion

463: *But though the Old Man* to *Geula would say*—Int. G. Ben-Eliezer

463: *The gleam, it seems, returned* to *he recognized you"*—Int. Ruth Beit-Halachmi

BIBLIOGRAPHY

Research on the life of David Ben-Gurion must begin at the Ben-Gurion Research Institute and Archives in the Negev desert kibbutz of Sde Boker in Israel. Here can be found most of Ben-Gurion's papers gathered throughout his adult life, including hundreds of diaries dating back to 1915. These diaries, written dryly in Hebrew, contain almost no material of a personal nature that would throw light on Ben-Gurion's character or feelings, but comprise an invaluable detailed account of the Zionist march to statehood and the history of Israel's first quarter century. Researchers have recently been given access to the diaries, which are considered state property, and can now freely examine all those up to the last thirty years as well as some extracts from later diaries if they are not militarily or politically sensitive.

English and Hebrew transcripts of taped oral histories obtained from friends and associates of Ben-Gurion constitute another extremely important collection at Sde Boker. I was fortunate to be the first researcher to see these transcripts, though some contributors have stipulated that their reports be withheld from public scrutiny until a future time. Books in all languages dealing with Ben-Gurion and Zionism crowd the shelves of the Sde Boker library.

Nor can any researcher on Ben-Gurion afford to ignore the archives of the *Jerusalem Post* in Jerusalem, where thousands of articles about him are contained in scrapbooks available to the public.

Here are the principal books, periodicals, newspapers, and unpublished documents that I consulted in the preparation of this book:

Books:

Abd Allah Ibn Husain (King Abdullah), *My Memoirs Completed* [al-Takmilah]. Washington, D.C.: American Council of Learned Societies, 1954.

Adams, Michael, *Chaos and Rebirth*. London: BBC Publications, 1968.

Adams, Sherman, *First Hand Report*. New York: Harper, 1961.

Allon, Yigal, *The Making of Israel's Army*. London: Vallentine Mitchell, 1970.

Almogi, Yosef, *Zikhronot* [Memoirs]. Tel Aviv: Yediot Acharonot-Idanim, 1980. (Heb.)

Am Yisrael U'Medinat Yisrael, HaVeida HaOlamit HaRishona shel HaNoar HaYehudi [The Jewish People and the State of Israel, The First World Conference of Jewish Youth]. Jerusalem: Jewish Agency, 1958.

American Jewish Committee, *In Vigilant Brotherhood*. New York: American Jewish Committee, 1964.

Amina, N., ed., *B'Shaarey Aza* [At the Gates of Gaza]. Hakibbutz Hadati (Israel), 1949. (Heb.)

Amrami, Yaacov, *Toldot Milchemet HaKomemeut* [History of the War of Independence]. Tel Aviv: Shelach, 1951. (Heb.)

Antonius, George, *The Arab Awakening*. London: Hamish Hamilton, 1938.

Appel, Benjamin, *Ben-Gurion's Israel*. New York: Grosset & Dunlap, 1965.

Applebaum, Syd, *Education in the IDF*. Tel Aviv: Office of the Army Spokesman, 1960.

Aref, Aref el-, *The Tragedy of Palestine* (7 vols.). Beirut: n.d. (Arabic)

Arendt, Hannah, *Eichmann in Jerusalem*, New York: Viking, 1963.

Arian, Alan, *Ideological Change in Israel*. Cleveland: Case Western Reserve University Press, 1968.

Arieli, Yehoshua, *HaKnunia* [The Conspiracy]. Tel Aviv: Kadima, 1965. (Heb.)

Atiyah, Edward, *The Arabs*. London: Pelican, 1955.

Attlee, Earl, *As It Happened*. London: Heinemann, 1954.

Avi-hai, Avraham, *Ben-Gurion, State Builder*. Jerusalem: Israel Universities Press, 1974.

———, *David Ben-Gurion: The State Building Era*. Jerusalem, 1971.

Avneri, Uri, *Bisdot Pleshet* [Fields of Palestine]. Tel Aviv: Tversky, 1950. (Heb.)

———, *Israel Without Zionism*. New York: Crowell-Collier-Macmillan, 1968.

Avrech, Mira, *Paula*. Tel Aviv: Am Hasefer, 1965.(Heb.)

Avriel, Ehud, *Open the Gates!* New York: Atheneum, 1975.

Azcarate y Flores, Pablo de, *Mission in Palestine*. Washington, D.C.: Middle East Institute, 1966.

Azeau, Henri, *Le Piège de Suez*. Paris: Laffont, 1964.

Bader, Yochanan, *HaKnesset V'Ani* [The Knesset and I]. Jerusalem: Edanim, 1979. (Heb.)

Baratz, Joseph, *Village by the Jordan*. London: Harvill, 1954.

Barker, A. J., *Suez: The Six Day War*. London: Faber, 1964.

Bar-Zohar, Michael, *Ben-Gurion* (3 vols.). Tel Aviv: Am Oved, 1977. (Heb.)

———, *Ben-Gurion: A Biography*. New York: Delacorte, 1978.

———, *Ben-Gurion: The Armed*

Prophet. New York: Prentice-Hall, 1968.

———, *The Hunt for the German Scientists*. London: Barker, 1967.

———, *Spies in the Promised Land*. Boston: Houghton Mifflin, 1972.

———, *Suez: Ultra-Secret*. Paris: Fayard, 1965.

Bat-Yehuda, Geula, *HeRab Maimon V'Dorotav* [Rabbi Maimon and His Generations]. Jerusalem: Herzl, 1979. (Heb.)

Bauer, Yehuda, *Flight and Rescue: Brichah*. New York: Random House, 1970.

———, *From Diplomacy to Resistance*. Philadelphia: Jewish Publication Society of America, 1966.

———, *The Holocaust in Historical Perspective*. Seattle: University of Washington Press, 1978.

Becker, Yaakov, *Mishnato shel David Ben-Gurion* [The Teachings of David Ben-Gurion] (2 vols.). Tel Aviv: Yavneh, 1958. (Heb.)

Beer, Israel, *Bitechon Yisrael* [The Security of Israel]. Tel Aviv: Amikam, 1966. (Heb.)

———, *Carvot Latrun* [Battles of Latrun]. Tel Aviv: Maarachot, 1953. (Heb.)

Bein, Alex, *The Return to the Soil*. Jerusalem: Zionist Organization, 1952. (Heb.)

———, *Theodore Herzl*. New York and Philadelphia: Meridian, Jewish Publication Society, 1962.

Beit-Zvi, S. B., *HaTzionut HaPost Ugandit B'Mashber HaShoa* [Post-Ugandan Zionism in the Holocaust Crisis]. Tel Aviv: Bronfman, 1977. (Heb.)

Bemis, Samuel Flagg, *The American Secretaries of State and Their Diplomacy*. New York: Pageant, 1958.

Benari, Yehuda, *Zeev Vladimir Jabotinsky*. Tel Aviv: Jabotinsky Institute, 1977.

Ben-Gurion, David, *Anahnu U'Sheineinu* [We and Our Neighbors]. Tel Aviv: Davar, 1929. (Heb.)

———, *Beit Avi* [My Father's House]. Hakibbutz Hameuhad (Israel), 1975. (Heb.) Serialized in *Jerusalem Post*, Sept. 30, Oct. 5, 24, 1966.

———, *Biblical Reflections*, New York: Jonathan.

———, *Devarim L'Iyun* [Subjects for Study]. Jerusalem: Zionist Organization, 1958. (Heb.)

———, *Devarim Kehavayatam* [Things as They Happened]. Tel Aviv: Am Hasefer, 1965. (Heb.)

———, *HaEmet Kodemet L'Kol* [Truth Above All]. Tel Aviv: Mimeo, 1961. (Heb.)

———, *Hazon V'Derekh* [Vision and Way] (5 vols.). Tel Aviv: Mapai, 1951–57. (Heb.)

———, *B'Hilahem Yisrael* [When Israel Fought]. Tel Aviv: Mapai, 1950. (Heb.)

———, *HaHistadrut V'HaMedinat* [The Histadrut and the State]. Tel Aviv: Histadrut, 1956. (Heb.)

———, *HaPoel HaIvre V'Histadrut* [The Hebrew Worker and His Organization]. Tel Aviv: Histadrut, 1964. (Heb.)

———, *Igrot Ben-Gurion* [Letters of Ben-Gurion]. Tel Aviv: Am Oved and Tel Aviv University, 1971. (Heb.)

———, *Israel: A Personal History*. New York and Tel Aviv: Sabra, 1972.

———, *Israel: Years of Challenge*. New York: Holt, Rinehart & Winston, 1963.

———, *Jewish Labor*. London: HeChalutz, 1935.

———, *The Jews in Their Land*. Garden City, N.Y.: Doubleday, 1966.

———, *Ketavim Rishonim* [Early

Writings]. Tel Aviv: 1952. (Heb.)

———, *Letters to Paula*. London: Vallentine Mitchell, 1971.

———, *Likrat HaAtid L'She'ailat Eretz Yisrael* [To the Future of the Palestine Problem]. (Heb.)

———, *B'Maarakhah* [In the Struggle] (5 vols.). Tel Aviv: Am Oved, 1957. (Heb.)

———, *Maarekhet Sinai* [The Sinai Campaign]. Tel Aviv: Am Oved, 1964. (Heb.)

———, *Medinat Yisrael Ha-Mehudeshet* [The Restored State of Israel]. Tel Aviv: Am Oved, 1962. (Heb.)

———, *MeLev L'Lev* [From Heart to Heart (letters to bereaved parents)]. Tel Aviv: Ministry of Defense, 1976. (Heb.)

———, *MeMaamad L'Am* [From Class to Nation]. Tel Aviv: Aiyanot, 1956. (Heb.)

———, *Mémoires: Israël avant Israël*. Paris: Bernard Grasset, 1971.

———, *My Talks with Arab Leaders*. Jerusalem: Keter, 1972.

———, *Netzah Yisrael* [The Eternity of Israel]. Aiyanot, n.d. (Heb.)

———, *Rebirth and Destiny of Israel*. New York: Philosophical Library, 1954.

———, *Recollections*. Edited by Thomas H. Bernstein. Tel Aviv: Bitan, 1970.

———, *Southwards*. Tel Aviv: 1956.

———, *Tenuat HaPoalim V'Ha-Revisionistim* [The Labor Movement and the Revisionists]. League for Labor Palestine, 1933. (Heb.)

———, *Zikhronot* [Memoirs] (3 vols.). Tel Aviv: Am Oved, 1971–73. (Heb.)

Ben-Jacob, Jeremiah, *The Rise of Israel*. New York: Grosby House, 1949.

Ben-Shaul, Moshe, ed., *Generals of Israel*. Tel Aviv: Hadar, 1968.

Bentwich, Norman, *Israel Resurgent*. London: Benn, 1960.

———, *Palestine of the Jews*. London: Kegan, Paul, 1919.

Ben-Yeruham, H., *Sefer Betar* [Betar Book]. Tel Aviv. (Heb.)

Ben-Zvi, Rachel, *Coming Home*. Tel Aviv: Massada, 1963.

Ben-Zvi, Yitzhak, *Igrot Yitzhak Ben-Zvi* [Letters of Yitzhak Ben-Zvi]. Jerusalem: Yad Ben-Zvi, 1968. (Heb.)

———, *Kitvei* [Works]. Tel Aviv: Mitzpah, 1936. (Heb.)

Berding, Andrew H., *Dulles on Diplomacy*. Princeton: Van Nostrand, 1965.

Berkman, Ted, *Cast a Giant Shadow*. Garden City, N.Y.: Doubleday, 1962.

Berlin, Isaiah, *Chaim Weizmann*. London: Weidenfeld and Nicolson, 1950.

Bernadotte, Folke, *The Curtain Falls*. New York: Knopf, 1945.

———, *To Jerusalem*. London: Hodder and Stoughton, 1951.

Bernstein, Edward, *Evolutionary Socialism*. New York: Schocken, 1961.

Bernstein, Marver H., *The Politics of Israel: The First Decade of Statehood*. Princeton, N.J.: Princeton University Press, 1957.

Betchy, Mohammed al, *Our Martyrs in Palestine*. Cairo: 1949. (Arabic)

Biderman, Israel, *David Ben-Gurion: Architect of a State*. New York: Jewish National Fund, 1962.

Bilby, Kenneth W., *New Star in the Near East*. Garden City, N.Y.: Doubleday, 1950.

Bilitzky, Eliahu, *Solel Bonei 1924–1974*. Tel Aviv: Am Oved, 1974. (Heb.)

Birnbaum, Ervin, *The Politics of Compromise: State and Religion in Israel*. Rutherford,

N.J.: Fairleigh Dickinson, 1970.

Borochov, Ber, *Nationalism and the Class Struggle*. New York: Poalei Zion, 1937.

Brandeis University, *Convocation Honoring David Ben-Gurion* Brandeis University, March ninth, nineteen hundred and sixty. Waltham, Mass.: Brandeis U. Publications, 1960.

Brecher, Michael, *The Foreign Policy System of Israel*. London: Oxford, 1972.

Brodetsky, Selig, *Memoirs*. London: Weidenfeld and Nicolson, 1960.

Bromberger, Merry and Serge, *Secrets of Suez*. London: Pan, 1957.

Buber, Martin, *Israel and Palestine: The History of an Idea*. New York: Farrar, Straus and Young, 1952.

Bullard, Sir Reader, *Britain and the Middle East*. New York: Hutchinson, 1951.

Bullock, Alan, *Life and Times of Ernest Bevin*. Vol. I. London: Heinemann, 1960.

Burns, E. L. M., *Between Arab and Israeli*. London: Harrap, 1962.

Burrows, Millar, *Palestine Is Our Business*. Philadelphia: Westminster, 1949.

Calvocoress, Peter, *Suez: Ten Years After*. New York: Pantheon, 1967.

Campbell, J. C., *The Defense of the Middle East*. New York: Harper & Row, 1958.

Carmel, Moshe, *Maarachot Tzafon* [The Campaigns in the North]. Ein Harod (Israel), 1949. (Heb.)

Carmichael, Joel, *The Shaping of the Arabs*. New York: Macmillan, 1967.

Casper, Bernard M., *With the Jewish Brigade*. London: Goldstone, 1947.

Celler, Emanuel, *You Never Leave Brooklyn*. New York: Day, 1953.

Childers, Erskine, *The Road to Suez*. London: MacGibbon and Kee, 1952.

Chouraqui, André, *L'État d'Israël*. Paris: Presses Universitaires, 1955.

Churchill, Winston, *Their Finest Hour*. Boston: Houghton Mifflin, 1949.

Cohen, Israel, *A Short History of Zionism*. London: Muller, 1954.

———, *The Zionist Movement*. London: Muller, 1945.

Cohen, Yeroham, *L'Or U'Bamachshach* [By Daylight and in Darkness]. Tel Aviv: Maarachot, 1969. (Heb.)

Collins, Larry, and Lapierre, Dominique, *O Jerusalem*. New York: Simon and Schuster, 1972.

Comay, Joan Francis, *Ben-Gurion and the Birth of Israel*. New York: Random House, 1967.

HaCongress HaTziyoni HaKaf-Dalet, Din V'Heshbon Stenographi [The Twenty-fourth Zionist Congress, Stenographic Record]. Jerusalem: Zionist Executive, 1956–57. (Heb.)

HaCongress HaTziyoni HaKaf-Heh, Din V'Hesbon Stenographi [The Twenty-fifth Zionist Congress, Stenographic Record]. Jerusalem: Zionist Executive, 1961. (Heb.)

Cremeans, Charles, *The Arabs and the World*. New York: Praeger, 1963.

Crossman, Richard H., *A Nation Reborn*. London: Hamish Hamilton, 1960.

———, *Palestine Mission*. London: Hamish Hamilton, 1947.

Crum, Bartley, *Behind the Silken Curtain*. New York: Simon and Schuster, 1947.

Daniels, Jonathan, *Man of Independence*. Philadelphia: Lippincott, 1950.

Dayan, Moshe, *Diary of the Sinai Campaign 1956*. London: Weidenfeld and Nicolson, 1966.

———, *Story of My Life*. New York: Morrow, 1976.

Dayan, Ruth, and Dudman, Helga, *Or Did I Dream a Dream?* Tel Aviv: Steimatsky/Weidenfeld and Nicolson, 1973.

Dayan, Shmuel, *Pioneers in Israel*. New York and Cleveland: World, 1961.

Deacon, Richard, *The Israeli Secret Service*. London: Hamish Hamilton, 1977.

De Gaulle, Charles, *Memoirs of Hope: Renewal and Endeavor*. New York: Simon and Schuster, 1971.

Dekel, Ephraim, *B'riha*. New York: Herzl, 1973

———, *Shai*. London: Yoseloff, 1965.

Derogy, Jacques, and Carmel, Hesi, *The Untold History of Israel*. New York: Grove, 1979.

Dimont, Max, *Jews, God, and History*. New York: Simon and Schuster, 1962.

Documents on Germany, Washington, D.C.: Department of State, 1961.

Douglas-Home, Charles, *The Arabs and Israel*. London: Bodley Head, 1968.

Draper, Theodore, *Israel and World Politics*. London: Becker and Warburg, 1968.

Dubnow, Semen, *History of the Jews in Russia and Poland*. Philadelphia: Jewish Publication Society of America, 1916.

Ducovny, Amram, *David Ben-Gurion in His Own Words*. New York: Fleet Press, 1968.

Duff, D. V., *Sword for Hire*. London: J. Murray, 1934.

Dugdale, Blanche, *Baffy: The Diaries of Blanche Dugdale, 1936–1947*. London: Vallentine Mitchell, 1973.

Eban, Abba, *An Autobiography*. New York: Random House, 1977.

———, *My People: The Story of the Jews*. New York: Random House, 1968.

———, *Voice of Israel*. New York: Horizon, 1957.

Eddy, William Alfred, *F.D.R. Meets Ibn Saud*. New York: American Friends of the Middle East, 1954.

Edelman, Maurice, *Ben-Gurion: A Political Biography*. London: Hodder and Stoughton, 1964.

Eden, Anthony, *Full Circle*. London: Cassell, 1960.

Eisenberg, Dennis; Dan, Uri; and Landau, Eli, *The Mossad*. New York: New American Library, 1978.

Eisenhower, Dwight D., *Waging Peace 1956–61*. Garden City, N.Y.: Doubleday, 1965.

Eisenstadt, Samuel, *The Absorption of Immigrants*. London: Routledge and Kegan Paul, 1954.

El-Ad, Avri, *Decline of Honor*. Chicago: Regnery, 1976.

Elath, Eliahu, *Israel and Elath*. London: Weidenfeld and Nicolson, 1966.

———, *Israel and Her Neighbours*. London: James Barrie, 1956.

———, *Zionism at the U.N.* Philadelphia: Jewish Publication Society of America, 1976.

Eliav, Arie L., *No Time for History*. New York: Sabra, 1970.

Elon, Amos, *The Israelis*. London: Weidenfeld and Nicolson, 1971.

Elston, Roy, *No Alternatives*. London: Hutchinson, 1960.

Encyclopaedia Judaica. Jerusalem, 1972.

Encyclopaedia of Zionism and Is-

rael. New York: Herzl and McGraw-Hill, 1971.

Even-Shoshan (Rosenberg), Zvi, *Toldot Tenuat HaPaolim B'Eretz Yisrael* [History of the Labor Movement in the Land of Israel] (3 vols.) Tel Aviv: Am Oved, 1963–66. (Heb.)

Evron, Yosef, *B'Yom Sagrir* [On a Rainy Day]. Tel Aviv: Otpaz, 1968. (Heb.)

Eytan, Teddy, *Neguev: l'Héroïque naissance de l'état d'Israël.* Geneva: Bacconière, 1950.

Eytan, Walter, *The First Ten Years.* New York: Simon and Schuster, 1958.

Farag, Sayed, *Our Army in Palestine.* Cairo: Fawakol, 1949. (Arabic)

Fein, Leonard J., *Politics in Israel.* Boston: Little, Brown, 1967.

Feiwel, T. R., *No Ease in Zion.* London: Secker and Warburg, 1938.

Forbes-Adam, Colin, *Life of Lord Lloyd.* London: Macmillan, 1948.

Forum for the Problems of Zionism, Jewry and the State of Israel (Jerusalem Ideological Conference, August 1957). Jerusalem: World Zionist Organization, 1959.

Frank, Gerald, *The Deed.* New York: Avon, 1964.

Freiman, A. M., *Rishon LeZion Sefer Rayovel (Rishon LeZion 50th Anniversary Book).* (Heb.)

Frumkin, Gad, *Shofet B'Yerushalayim* [Judge in Jerusalem]. Tel Aviv: Dvir. (Heb.)

Gerias, Sabri, *HaAravim B'Yisrael* [The Arabs in Israel]. Haifa: Al-Teahad, 1966. (Heb.)

Gervasi, Frank, *The Life and Times of Menachem Begin.* New York: Putnam, 1979.

Glass, Zrubavel, ed., *Sefer Ha-Palmach* [Book of the Palmach] (2 vols.). Tel Aviv: Hakibbutz Hameuhad, 1953. (Heb.)

Glubb, Sir John Bagot, *Britain and the Arabs.* London: Hodder and Stoughton, 1959.

———, *A Soldier with the Arabs.* London: Hodder and Stoughton, 1956.

———, *Story of the Arab Legion.* London: Hodder and Stoughton, 1948.

———, *Syria, Lebanon, Jordan.* London: Thames and Hudson, 1967.

Gluskin, Zeev, *Zikhronot* [Memoirs]. Tel Aviv: Association of Cooperative Winegrowers, 1946. (Heb.)

Goldmann, Nahum, *The Autobiography of Nahum Goldmann.* New York: Holt, Rinehart & Winston, 1969.

———, *The Jewish Paradox.* New York: Grosset & Dunlap, 1978.

Goldsmith, S. J., *Twenty 20th Century Jews.* New York: Shengold, 1922.

Golomb, Eliahu, *Hevion Oz* [Hiding Place of Boldness] (2 vols.). Tel Aviv: Ayonot, 1954. (Heb.)

Gordon, A. D., *Kitvei A. D. Gordon* [Writings of A. D. Gordon] (5 vols.). Tel Aviv: HaPoel HaTzair, 1925–29. (Heb.)

Graves, Richard M., *Experiment in Anarchy.* London: Gollancz, 1949.

Graves, Robert, *Lawrence and the Arabs.* London: Jonathan Cape, 1927.

Great Britain, Parliamentary Papers, Cmd. 3530, *Report of Commission of the Palestine Disturbances of August 1929.* London, 1930

———, Cmd. 5354, *Palestine: Partition Commission Report.* London, 1938.

———, Cmd. 5479, *Palestine:*

Royal Commission Report, London, 1938.

———, Cmd. 6019, *Palestine: Statement of Policy.* London, 1939.

Gruen, George, *Israel, the United States and the United Nations.* New York: American Jewish Committee, 1969.

Guber, Rivka, *Only a Path.* Ramat Gan: Massada, 1972.

———, *Signal Fires of Lachish.* Tel Aviv and Jerusalem: Massada, 1964.

Gutmann, Emanuel, and Dror, Yehezkiel, *Mishtar Medinat Yisrael* [The Government of the State of Israel]. Jerusalem: Hebrew University, 1969. (Heb.)

Habas, Brakha, *Ben-Gurion V'Doro* [Ben-Gurion and His Generation]. Tel Aviv: Massada, 1952. (Heb.)

Hacohen, David, *Et Lisaper* [Time to Tell]. Tel Aviv: Am Oved, 1974. (Heb.)

Hadani, Ever, *Hityashvut B'Galil Hatahton* [Settlement in Lower Galilee]. Tel Aviv: Massada and Farmers Association in Lower Galilee, n.d. (Heb.)

Halperin, Samuel, *The Political World of American Zionism.* Detroit: Wayne University Press, 1961.

Halpern, Ben, *The Idea of the Jewish State.* Cambridge: Harvard University Press, 1961.

Harel, Isser, *Anatomia shel Begida* [Anatomy of Treason]. Tel Aviv: Yediot Acharonot-Idanim, 1980. (Heb.)

Hay, Alice Ivy, *There Was a Man of Genius.* London: Spearman, 1967.

Hecht, Ben, *Perfidy.* New York: Julian Messner, 1961.

Heller, Joseph, *The Zionist Idea.* New York: Schocken, 1949.

Henriques, Robert, *100 Hours to Suez.* London: Collins, 1957.

Hertzberg, Arthur, *The Zionist Idea.* New York and Philadelphia: Meridian, 1960.

Herut, *MeParashat Lavon L'Parashat Ben-Gurion* [From the Lavon Affair to the Ben-Gurion Affair]. Tel Aviv: Herut, 1961. (Heb.)

Hill, Christopher, *Lenin and the Russian Revolution.* Middlesex, Eng.: Penguin, 1971.

Historical Branch of General Headquarters, Israeli Army, *The Sinai Campaign.* Tel Aviv, n.d.

Horowitz, Dan, *Israel's Concept of Defensible Borders.* Jerusalem: Hebrew University, 1975.

Horowitz, Dan, and Hasin, Eliyahu, *HaParashat* [The Affair]. Tel Aviv: Am Hasefer, 1961. (Heb.)

Horowitz, Dan, and Lissak, Moshe, *MeYishuv L'Medinah* [From *Yishuv* to State]. Jerusalem: Hebrew University, 1972. (Heb.)

Horowitz, Dan, and Luttwak, Edward, *The Israeli Army.* London: Penguin, 1975.

Horowitz, David, *State in the Making.* New York: Knopf, 1953.

Hughes, Emmet John, *The Ordeal of Power: A Political Memoir of the Eisenhower Years.* New York: Atheneum, 1963.

Hurewitz, J. C., *Diplomacy in the Near and Middle East: A Documentary Record.* Princeton, N.J.: Van Nostrand, 1956.

———, *Middle East Politics: The Military Dimension.* New York: Praeger, 1969.

———, *The Struggle for Palestine.* New York: Norton, 1950.

Hutchinson, Elmo H., *Violent Truce.* New York: Devin-Adair, 1956.

Hyamson, A. M., *Palestine Under*

the Mandate. London: Methuen, 1950.

Infeld, Henrik, *Cooperative Living in Palestine*. London: Kegan Paul, 1946.

Ionides, Michael, *Divide and Lose: The Arab Revolt, 1955 to 1958*. London: Geoffrey Bles, 1960.

Israel and the United Nations. New York: Carnegie Endowment for International Peace, 1956.

Israeli, Yosef, *B'Shlihut Bithonit* [On a Security Mission]. Tel Aviv: Am Oved, 1972. (Heb.)

Jabotinsky, Eri, *Zeev Jabotinsky*. Jerusalem, 1953. (Heb.)

Jabotinsky, Vladimir, *Neumin* [Speeches] (2 vols.). Jerusalem, 1947–48. (Heb.)

Jamal, Ahmed Pasha, *Memoirs of a Turkish Statesman*. New York: Doran, 1922.

The Jewish Case Before the Anglo-American Committee of Inquiry on Palestine. Jerusalem: Jewish Agency for Palestine, 1947.

The Jewish Plan for Palestine. Jerusalem: Jewish Agency for Palestine, 1947.

Johnson, Paul, *The Suez War*. London: MacGibbon and Kee, 1957.

Joseph, Dov, *The Faithful City*. Tel Aviv: Schocken, 1950.

Kagan, Benjamin, *The Secret Battle for Israel*. New York and Cleveland: World, 1966.

Katz, Samuel, *Battleground: Fact and Fantasy in Palestine*. New York: Bantam, 1973.

———, *Days of Fire*. London: Allen, 1968.

Katzenelson, Berl, *Igrot* [Letters]. Tel Aviv: Am Oved. (Heb.)

———, *Ktavim* [Works]. Tel Aviv: Am Oved. (Heb.)

Kedourie, Elie, *England and the Middle East*. London: Bowes, 1956.

Kerr, Malcolm, *The Arab Cold War*. London: Oxford, 1964.

Khatib, Mohammed Nemr al-, *The Result of the Catastrophe*. Damascus: Matba Umomeya, 1951. (Arabic)

Khronologia shel Toldot HaYishuv B'Eretz Yisrael [Chronology of the History of the Yishuv in Palestine]. Jerusalem: Yad Ben-Zvi, 1979. (Heb.)

Kimche, Jon, *Both Sides of the Hill*. London: Secker and Warburg, 1960.

———, *Palestine or Israel*. London: Secker and Warburg, 1973.

———, *Seven Fallen Pillars*. London: Secker and Warburg, 1950.

Kimche, Jon and David, *A Clash of Destinies*. New York: Praeger, 1960.

———, *The Secret Roads*. London: Secker and Warburg, 1954.

Kirk, George, *The Middle East in the War 1939–45*. London, Oxford, 1952.

———, *A Short History of the Middle East*. New York: Praeger, 1964.

Knohl, Dov, ed., *Siege in the Hills of Hebron*. New York: Yoseloff, 1958.

Koestler, Arthur, *Promise and Fulfillment*. London: Macmillan, 1949.

Kollek, Teddy, *For Jerusalem*. London: Weidenfeld and Nicolson, 1978.

Kovetz Min HaYesod [Collection of articles by the Min HaYesod]. Tel Aviv: Amikam, 1962. (Heb.)

Kraines, Oscar, *Government and Politics in Israel*. Boston: Houghton Mifflin, 1961.

Kurzman, Dan, *The Bravest Battle: The 28 Days of the Warsaw Ghetto Uprising*. New York: Putnam, 1976.

————, *Genesis 1948: The First Arab-Israeli War*. New York: World, 1970.

————, *The Race for Rome*. Garden City, N.Y.: Doubleday, 1975.

————, *Subversion of the Innocents*. New York: Random House, 1963.

Laqueur, Walter, *Communism and Nationalism in the Middle East*. London: Routledge, 1956.

————, *A History of Zionism*. London: Weidenfeld and Nicolson, 1972.

————, *The Middle East in Transition*. London: Routledge, 1958.

————, *The Road to War*. London: Weidenfeld and Nicolson, 1968.

Landau, Jacob, *The Arabs in Israel*. London: Oxford, 1969.

Lankin, Eliahu, *Sipuru shel Mefaked Altalena* [The Story of the Commander of the Altalena]. Tel Aviv: Herut, 1954. (Heb.)

Laufer, Leopold, *Israel and the Developing Countries*. New York: Twentieth Century Fund, 1967.

(Lau-)Lavie, Naphtalie, *Moshe Dayan*. London: Vallentine Mitchell, 1968.

Lavi, Shlomo, *Aliato shel Shalom Laish* [*Aliya* of Shalom Laish]. Tel Aviv: Ayanot, 1957. (Heb.)

Lavon, Pinhas, *Derekh Ha-Histadrut B'Medinat* [The Path of the Histadrut in the State]. Tel Aviv: Histadrut, 1959. (Heb.)

————, *Hevrat HaAvodah* [A Labor Society]. Tel Aviv: Mifaley Tarbut Vehinuch, 1968. (Heb.)

Lawrence, Thomas Edward, *Seven Pillars of Wisdom*. Garden City, N.Y.: Doubleday, 1935.

Levenberg, S., *The Jews and Palestine*. London: Poalei Zion, 1945.

Lever, Walter, *Jerusalem Is Called Liberty*. Jerusalem: Massada, 1951.

Levin, Harry, *I Saw the Battle of Jerusalem*. New York: Schocken, 1950.

Lewis, Bernard, *The Emergence of Modern Turkey*. New York and London: Oxford, 1968.

————, *The Middle East and the West*. London: Weidenfeld and Nicolson, 1963.

Lie, Trygve, *In the Cause of Peace*. New York: Macmillan, 1954.

Lilienthal, Alfred M., *What Price Israel?* Chicago: Regnery, 1953.

Liron, Aaron, *Yerushalayim Ha-Atika B'Matzor V'B'Bakrav*. [Old Jerusalem: Under Siege and in Battle]. Tel Aviv: Maarachot, 1957. (Heb.)

Litvinoff, Barnett, *Ben-Gurion of Israel*. New York: Praeger, 1954.

Lloyd, Selwyn, *Suez 1956*. London: Jonathan Cape, 1978.

Lorch, Netanel, *The Edge of the Sword*. New York: Putnam, 1961.

Love, Kennett, *Suez: The Twice-Fought War*. New York: McGraw-Hill, 1969.

Lowdermilk, Walter C., *Palestine, Land of Promise*. New York and London: Harper, 1944.

————, *The Untried Approach to the Palestine Problem*. New York: American Christian Palestine Committee, 1948.

Lowenthal, Marvin, ed., *Diaries of Theodor Herzl*. London: Gollancz, 1958.

Lukan, Kadri, *After the Catastrophe*. Beirut: Dar el Elm, 1950. (Arabic)

Mansfield, Peter, *Nasser's Egypt*. London: Penguin, 1966.

Manuel, Frank E., *The Realities*

of American-Palestine Relations. Washington, D.C.: Public Affairs Press, 1949.

Mardor, Munya, *Hagana*. New York: New American Library, 1966.

Marlowe, John, *Rebellion in Palestine*. London: Cresset, 1946.

———, *The Seat of Pilate*. London: Cresset, 1959.

Mason, Alpheus Thomas, *Brandeis: A Free Man's Life*. New York: Viking, 1946.

McDonald, James G., *My Mission in Israel, 1948–1951*. New York: Simon and Schuster, 1951.

Meeker, Owen, *Israel Reborn*. New York: Scribner, 1965.

Meinertzhagen, Richard, *Middle East Diary*. London: Cresset, 1959.

Meir, Golda, *My Life*. New York: Putnam, 1975.

Miller, William, *The Ottoman Empire and Its Successors*. Cambridge, 1923.

Millis, Walter, *The Forrestal Diaries*. New York: Viking, 1951.

Monroe, Elizabeth, *Britain's Moment in the Middle East, 1914–1956*. Baltimore: Johns Hopkins, 1963.

Montgomery, Bernard Law, *Memoirs*. New York and Cleveland: World, 1958.

Morton, Frederic, *The Rothschilds*. New York: Atheneum, 1962.

Mosley, Leonard, *The Cat and the Mice*. London: A. Barker, 1958.

———, *Gideon Goes to War*. New York: Scribner, 1955.

Murphy, Robert, *Diplomat among Warriors*. Garden City, N.Y.: Doubleday, 1964.

Nadel, Baruch, *Bernadotte*. Tel Aviv: 1968. (Heb.)

Naguib, Mohammed, *Egypt's Destiny*. London: Gollancz, 1955.

Nakdimon, Shlomo, *Likrat Sha'at HaEfes* [Toward H-Hour].

Tel Aviv: Ramdor, 1968. (Heb.)

Nasser, Gamal Abdel, *Egypt's Liberation: The Philosophy of the Revolution*. Washington, D.C.: Public Affairs Press, 1955.

———, *The Truth about the Palestine War*. Cairo, n.d.

Nehemiah Argov, Tel Aviv: published by friends, 1960. (Heb.)

Netzer, Shraga, *Reshimot Me-Yomani* [Notes from My Diary]. Tel Aviv: Am Oved, 1980. (Heb.)

Nofal, Sayed, *Ben-Gurion's Version of History*. Cairo: Arab League, 1962.

Nutting, Anthony, *No End of a Lesson*. London: Constable, 1967.

O'Ballance, Edgar, *The Arab-Israeli War, 1948*. London: Faber, 1956.

———, *The Sinai Campaign*. London: Faber, 1959.

Oliphant, Laurence, *Haifa, or Life in Modern Palestine*. London: William Blackwood, 1887.

Olshan, Yitzhak, *Din Udvarim* [Controversy]. Tel Aviv: Schocken, 1978. (Heb.)

Palestine Royal (Peel) Commission, *Minutes of Evidence*. London: Colonial No. 134, H.M.S.O., 1937.

Palestine: Termination of the Mandate 15th May 1948. London: H.M.S.O., 1947.

Parkes, James, *Arabs and Jews in the Middle East*. London: Gollancz, 1967.

———, *Five Roots of Israel*. London: Vallentine Mitchell, 1954.

———, *A History of the Jewish People*. London: Penguin, 1964.

———, *A History of Palestine*. London: Gollancz, 1949.

———, *The New Face of Is-*

rael. Leeds, Eng.: University Press, 1964.

Pearlman, Moshe, The Army of Israel. New York: Philosophical Library, 1950.

———, Ben-Gurion Looks Back. London: Weidenfeld and Nicolson, 1965.

———, The Capture of Adolf Eichmann. London: Weidenfeld and Nicolson, 1961.

———, Mufti of Jerusalem. London: Gollancz, 1947.

Peres, Shimon, David's Sling. New York: Random House, 1970.

———, HaShalav HaBa [The Next Stage]. Tel Aviv: Am Hasefer, 1965. (Heb.)

———, Lekh im HaAnashim [Go with the People]. Tel Aviv: Am Hasefer, 1979. (Heb.)

Peretz, Don, Israel and the Palestine Arabs. Washington, D.C.: Middle East Institute, 1958.

Perlmutter, Amos, Military and Politics in Israel. London: Cass, 1969.

Philby, Harry St. John Bridger, Arabian Jubilee. New York: Day, 1953.

Poalei Zion B'Aliya HaShniya, [Poalei Zion in the Second Aliya]. Tel Aviv: Mapai and Poalei Zion, 1950. (Heb.)

Poliakov, Leon, Harvest of Hate. London: Elek, 1965.

The Political History of Palestine under British Administration. New York: Reprinted by British Information Services, 1947.

Polk, William R.; Stamler, David M.; and Asfour, Edmund, Backdrop to Tragedy. Boston: Beacon, 1957.

Preuss, Walter, The Labour Movement in Israel. Jerusalem: Reuben, 1965.

Prittie, Terence, Eshkol: The Man and the Nation, New York: Pitman, 1969.

———, Israel: Miracle in the Desert. New York: Praeger, 1967.

Rabin, Yitzhak, The Rabin Memoirs. Boston: Little, Brown, 1979.

Rabinowicz, Oskar K., Fifty Years of Zionism. London: Anscombe, 1952.

———, Vladimir Jabotinsky's Conception of a Nation. New York: Beechhurst, 1946.

———, ed., Winston Churchill on Jewish Problems. London: Lincolns Prager, 1956.

Rackman, Emanuel, Israel's Emerging Constitution, 1948–1951. New York: Columbia University Press, 1955.

Ramsaur, E. E., The Young Turks. Princeton, N.J.: Princeton University Press, 1957.

Ramsay, Sir William, The Revolution in Constantinople and Turkey. London: Hodder and Stoughton, 1919.

Ratner, Yohanan, Hayay V'Ani [My Life and I]. Jerusalem and Tel Aviv: Schocken, 1978. (Heb.)

Record of Israel's Peace Offers to the Arab States, 1948–1963. Jerusalem: Ministry for Foreign Affairs, 1963.

Reuveni, A., Al Yerushalayim [About Jerusalem]. Jerusalem: Rubin Mass, 1968. (Heb.)

Reynier, Jacques de, À Jérusalem un drapeau flottait sur la ligne de feu. Neuchâtel, Switzerland: La Baconnière, 1950.

Reynolds, Quentin, Leave It to the People. New York: Random House, 1949.

Ribalow, Harold, ed., Fighting Heroes of Israel. New York: New American Library, 1967.

Robertson, Terence, Crisis. London: Hutchinson, 1965.

Roosevelt, Eleanor, and De Witt, William, U.N.: Today and To-

morrow. New York: Harper, 1953.

Roosevelt, Kermit, *Arabs, Oil and History*. New York: Harper, 1949.

Rousan, Mahmoud al-, *Battles of Bab el-Wad*. Amman: n.d. (Arabic)

Rustow, Dankwart, *A World of Nations*, Washington, D.C.: Brookings Institute, 1968.

———, ed., *Philosophers and Kings*. New York: Braziller, 1970.

Sachar, Howard E., *Aliyah: The Peoples of Israel*. New York and Cleveland: World, 1961.

———, *The Course of Modern Jewish History*. London: Weidenfeld and Nicolson, 1958.

———, *From the Ends of the Earth: The Peoples of Israel*. New York and Cleveland: World, 1964.

Sacher, Harry, *Israel: The Establishment of a State*. London: Weidenfeld and Nicolson, 1952.

———, *Zionist Portraits and Other Essays*. London: Blond, 1959.

Sadat, Anwar, *Revolt on the Nile*. London: Allan Wingate, 1957.

Safran, Nadav, *From War to War*. New York: Pegasus, 1968.

———, *The United States and Israel*. Cambridge: Harvard University Press, 1963.

St. John, Robert, *Ben-Gurion*. Garden City, N.Y.: Doubleday, 1971.

———, *The Boss: The Story of Gamal Abdel Nasser*. New York: McGraw-Hill, 1960.

———, *Shalom Means Peace*. Garden City, N.Y.: Doubleday, 1949.

Samuel, Horace, *Unholy Memories of the Holy Land*. London: Hogarth, 1930.

Samuels, Gertrude, *B.G.: Fighter of Goliaths*. New York: Crowell, 1974.

Sanders, Ronald, *Israel: The View from Masada*. New York: Harper & Row, 1966.

Sayed, Nejal, *Ben-Gurion's Version of History*. Cairo: League of Arab States, 1962.

Schechtman, J. B., *The Jabotinsky Story: Fighter and Prophet*. New York: Yoseloff, 1956.

———, *The Jabotinsky Story: Rebel and Statesman*. New York: Yoseloff, 1956.

———, *The Mufti and the Fuehrer*. New York: Yoseloff, 1965.

Schoenbrun, David, *The New Israelis*. New York: Atheneum, 1973.

Schwartz, Leo Walder, *The Redeemers*. New York: Farrar, Straus and Young, 1953.

Schwarz, Walter, *The Arabs in Israel*. London: Faber, 1959.

Sefer Aliya Shnia [Second *Aliya* Book]. Tel Aviv: Am Oved, 1949. (Heb.)

Sefer Hashomer [Hashomer Book]. Tel Aviv: Ovir, 1957. (Heb.)

Sefer HaPalmach [Book of the Palmach]. Hakibbutz Hameuhad, 1953. (Heb.)

Sefer Plonsk [Plonsk Book]. Tel Aviv: Plonsk Association, 1963. (Heb.)

Sefer Saloniki—Ir Va Em B'Yisrael [Salonika Book—Mother City in Israel]. Jerusalem and Tel Aviv, 1966. (Heb.)

Seligman, Lester G., *Leadership in a New Nation: Political Development in Israel*. New York: Atherton, 1964.

Shahan, Avigdor, *Kanfer Ha-Nizachon* [The Wings of Victory]. Tel Aviv: Am Hasefer, 1966. (Heb.)

Shakti, *Ben-Gurion, Friend of India, 80 Years*. New Delhi, 1966.

Shapira, Anita, *Berl Katzenelson*. Tel Aviv: Am Oved, 1980. (Heb.)

——, *The Dream and Its Solution*. Tel Aviv: Tel Aviv University, 1967.

——, *HaMaavak HaMeakhzev* [The Disappointing Struggle]. Tel Aviv: Hakibbutz Hameuhad, 1977. (Heb.)

Sharef, Ze'ev, *Three Days*. Garden City, N.Y.: Doubleday, 1962.

Sharett, Moshe, *B'Shaar HaUmot* [At the Threshold of Statehood]. Tel Aviv: Am Oved, 1966. (Heb.)

——, *Yoman Ishi* [Personal Diary] (8 vols.) Tel Aviv: Maariv, 1978. (Heb.)

——, *Yoman Medini* [Making of Policy—Diaries]. Tel Aviv: Am Oved, 1968. (Heb.)

Shavit, Yaacov, *MeRov L'Medina* [From Majority to State]. Tel Aviv: Yariv and Hadar, 1978. (Heb.)

Sheba, Shlomo, *Shevet Ha-Amitzim* [The Tribe of the Bold]. Tel Aviv: Siforat Poalim, 1969. (Heb.)

Sheib, Israel, *Maaser Rishon* [The First Tithe]. Tel Aviv: Hamatmid, n.d. (Heb.)

Sherwood, Robert, *Roosevelt and Hopkins*. New York: Harper, 1948.

Shihor, Schmuel, *Hollow Glory*. New York: Yoseloff, 1960.

Slater, Robert, *Golda: The Uncrowned Queen of Israel*. New York: Jonathan David, 1981.

——, *Rabin of Israel*. London: Robson, 1977.

Spiro, Melford, *Kibbutz: Venture in Utopia*. New York: Schocken, 1963.

Stein, Leonard, *The Balfour Declaration*. London: Vallentine Mitchell, 1961.

Steinberg, Alfred, *The Man from Missouri*. New York: Putnam, 1962.

Stock, Ernest, *From Conflict to Understanding*. New York: Institute of Human Relations, 1968.

——, *Israel on the Road to Sinai, 1949–1956*. Ithaca, N.Y.: Cornell University Press, 1967.

Stone, Isidor, *This Is Israel*. New York: Boni, 1948.

Storrs, Sir Ronald, *Lawrence of Arabia: Zionism and Palestine*. New York and Middlesex, Eng.: Penguin, 1943.

Sykes, Christopher, *Cross Roads to Israel*. London: Collins, 1965.

——, *Orde Wingate*. London: Collins, 1959.

Syrkin, Marie, *Golda Meir: Woman with a Cause*. New York: Putnam, 1964.

——, *Nachman Syrkin*, New York: Herzl, 1960.

Syrkin, Nachman, *Essays on Socialist Zionism*. New York: Young Poalei Zion Alliance of America, 1935.

Tabenkin, Yitzhak, *Devarim* [Subjects]. Tel Aviv: Hakibbutz Hameuhad, 1967. (Heb.)

Talmai, Ephraim, *Israel B'Maareicha* [Israel in Battle]. Tel Aviv: Amihai, 1952. (Heb.)

——, *Sefer HaNegev* [Book of the Negev]. Tel Aviv: Amihai, 1953. (Heb.)

Talmai, Menahem, *Shayarot B'Esh* [Convoys under Fire]. Tel Aviv: Amihai, 1957. (Heb.)

Taylor, Alan R., *Prelude to Israel*. New York: Philosophical Library, 1959.

Tcherikowe, Elias, ed., *The Early Jewish Labor Movement in the U.S.* New York: Yivo, 1961.

Tel, Abdullah, *The Tragedy of Palestine*. Cairo: Dar al-Salam, 1959. (Arabic)

Tevet, Shabtai, *Kin'at David* [David's Zeal]. Vols. 1 and 2. Tel Aviv: Schocken, 1977, 1980. (Heb.)

————, *Moshe Dayan*. London: Weidenfeld and Nicolson, 1972.

Thayer, I. W., *Tensions in the Middle East*. London: Oxford, 1958.

Thomas, Abel, *Comment Israël fut sauvé*. Paris: Albin Michel, 1978.

Thomas, Hugh, *The Suez Affair*. London: Weidenfeld and Nicolson, 1967.

Tobias, Henry J., *The Jewish Bund in Russia*. Stanford, Calif.: Stanford University Press, 1972.

Toldot Milhemet HaKomemiut [History of the War of Liberation]. Tel Aviv: Maarakhot, 1959. (Heb.)

Trevor, Daphne, *Under the White Paper*. Jerusalem: Jerusalem Press, 1948.

Truman, Harry S, *Years of Trial and Hope*. Vol. 2 of *Memoirs*. Garden City, N.Y.: Doubleday, 1956.

Tsur, Yaacov, *Prélude à Suez*. Paris: Plon, 1968.

Vaze, Pinhas, *HaMesima: Rechesh* [Objective: To Acquire Arms]. Tel Aviv: Maarachot, 1966. (Heb.)

Vester, Bertha, *Our Jerusalem*. Garden City, N.Y.: Doubleday, 1950.

Vilnoy, Zeev, *HaMaaracha L'Shichrur Yisrael* [The Battle to Liberate Israel]. Jerusalem: Tor-Israel, 1953. (Heb.)

Weisgal, Meyer, *Meyer Weisgal . . . So Far*. New York: Random House, 1972.

Weisgal, Meyer W., and Carmichael, Joel, eds., *Chaim Weizmann: A Biography by Several Hands*. London: Weidenfeld and Nicolson, 1962.

Weissberg, Alex, *Advocate for the Dead*. London: André Deutsch, 1958.

Weitz, Raanan, *Agricultural and Rural Development in Israel*. Jerusalem: Jewish Agency, 1963.

Weizman, Ezer, *On Eagles' Wings*. New York: Macmillan, 1976.

Weizmann, Chaim, *The Jewish People and Palestine*. London: Zionist Organization, 1939.

————, *Letters and Papers of Chaim Weizmann*. Jerusalem: Israel Universities Press, 1977.

————, *Selected Speeches of Chaim Weizmann: A Tribute*. London: Zionist Organization, 1945.

————, *Trial and Error*. London: Hamilton, 1950.

Weizmann, Vera, *The Impossible Takes Longer*. New York: Harper, 1967.

Welles, Sumner, *We Need Not Fail*. Boston: Houghton Mifflin, 1948.

Wheelock, K., *Nasser's New Egypt*. New York: Stephens, 1960.

Williams, Francis, *Ernest Bevin: Portrait of a Great Englishman*. London: Hutchinson, 1952.

————, *A Prime Minister Remembers*. London: Heinemann, 1961.

Wilson, R. D., *Cordon and Search*. Aldershot, Eng.: Gale and Polden, 1949.

Winer, Gershon, *The Founding Fathers*. New York: Bloch, 1971.

Wischnitzer, Mark, *To Dwell in Safety*. Philadelphia: Jewish Publication Society of America, 1948.

Wise, Stephen, *Challenging Years*. New York: Putnam, 1949.

World Zionist Organization, American Section, Dept. of Education and Culture, *David Ben-Gurion*. New York, 1974.

Wynn, Wilton, *Nasser of Egypt: The Search for Dignity.* Cambridge, Mass.: Arlington, 1959.

Yaari, Ehud, *Egypt and the Fedayeen 1953–1956. Givat Haviva:* Center for Arabic and Afro-Asian Studies, 1975. (Heb. with Eng. summary)

Yalkut Ahdut HaAvodah [Ahdut HaAvodah Anthology] (2 vols.) Tel Aviv: Zionist-Socialist Organization of Palestine Workers, 1929–32. (Heb.)

Yanai, Natan, *Kera B'Zameret* [Split at the Top]. Tel Aviv: Levin Epstein, 1968. (Heb.)

Yavneli, Shmuel, *Haroe L'Mershok* [The Far-Sighted One]. Tel Aviv: Am Oved, 1972. (Heb.)

Yehezkel Beit-Halachmi. Tel Aviv: Brochure published by family.

Yivo Annual of Jewish Social Science. Vol. IV. History of New York's Jewish Community. New York: Yivo, 1949.

Yizkor Book. New York: Poalei Zion Palestine Committee, 1918. (Yiddish)

Yorman, Pinhas, *The First 32 Minutes.* Tel Aviv and Jerusalem: Massada, n.d.

Zasloff, Joseph Jeremiah, *Great Britain and Palestine.* Geneva: Droz, 1952.

Zeid, Alexander, *Yoman* [Diary]. Tel Aviv: Am Oved, 1940. (Heb.)

Zeine, Z. N., *The Struggle for Arab Independence.* Beirut: Khayat's, 1960.

Zemach, Shlomo, *Shana Rishona* [First Year]. Tel Aviv: Am Oved, 1965. (Heb.)

Zerubavel, Jacob, *Aley Hayim* [Leaves of Life]. Tel Aviv: Peretz, 1960. (Heb.)

Zionist Organization, Book of Documents Submitted to General Assembly of U.N. New York, 1947.

———, *The Jewish Case Before the Anglo-American Committee.* Jerusalem, 1947.

———, *The Jewish Plan for Palestine,* Jerusalem, 1947.

Zisling, A., *David Ben-Gurion: Emet V'Selef* [David Ben-Gurion: Truth and Falsehood]. Tel Aviv, 1959. (Heb.)

Zuckerman, Baruch, *Memoirs.* [Zikhroynes]. New York: Yiddischer Kempfer, 1962. (Yiddish)

Zurayk, Constantine R., *The Meaning of the Disaster.* Beirut, 1956.

Periodicals:

Alami, Musa, "The Lesson of Palestine," *Middle East Journal,* Oct. 1949. (Condensed translation of *Ibrat Falasteen,* Beirut, 1949)

"Allon Attacks Ben-Gurion," *Jewish Observer and Middle East Review,* Apr. 7, 1967.

Alpert, C., "Ben-Gurion's Blunder," *Reconstructionist,* Jan. 11, 1952.

"Army's Farewell to Ben-Gurion," *Israel Digest,* June 21, 1963.

"As Israel Views Ben-Gurion's Return," *The American Zionist,* Mar. 1955.

Avi-Hai, A., "Ben-Gurion at 84," *Hadassah Magazine,* Oct. 1970.

———, "Ben-Gurion in Retrospect," *Midstream,* May 1974.

Avriel, Ehud, "Some Minute Circumstances," *The Jerusalem Quarterly,* Winter 1980.

Bar-David, M. L., "Mrs. Paula Ben-Gurion," *Zionist Review,* Feb. 23, 1951.

Bar-Natan, M., "Ben-Gurion at 80," *Jewish Frontier*, Nov. 1966.

Bauer, Y., "When Did They Know?" *Midstream*, Apr. 1968.

Bayne, E. A., "The Lavon Affair: 1954–1964," *Jewish Observer and Middle East Review*, Dec. 18, 1964. (Based on report for American Universities Field Staff).

Begin, M., "Ben-Gurion Is Playing with Cards He Hasn't Got in His Hand," *Jewish Herald*, Dec. 30, 1955.

———, "Ben-Gurion and Sharett: Two Men Who Have Failed," *Jewish Herald*, Apr. 10, 1953.

———, "Ben-Gurion's Tragedy," *Jewish Herald*, Dec. 23, 1955.

Bendon, J., "Ben-Gurion—A Controversial Figure," *Jewish Newsletter*, May 14, 1951.

Ben-Dor, L., "Ben-Gurion," *Jewish Digest*, Feb. 1974.

———, "Israel Scene," *Congress Bi-Weekly*, Oct. 24, 1966.

Ben-Eliezer, Yaacov, "Grandpa David," *Hadassah Magazine*, Jan. 1974.

"Ben-Gurion," *Jewish Spectator*, May 1967.

"Ben-Gurion and the English," *Jewish Observer and Middle East Review*, Apr. 1, 1966.

"Ben-Gurion As Nahum Goldmann Sees Him," *National Jewish Monthly*, March 1970.

"Ben-Gurion Charges Bankruptcy of American Zionist Organization," *Christian Century*, Dec. 26, 1951.

"Ben-Gurion Compared to Joshua," *Jewish Observer and Middle East Review*, Dec. 14, 1973.

Ben-Gurion, D., "On the Road to the State," *Jewish Observer and Middle East Review*, 28 installments from Aug. 16, 1963, through Mar. 13, 1964.

"Ben-Gurion at 80," *Hadassah Magazine*, Nov. 1966.

"Ben-Gurion at 84," *Jewish Observer and Middle East Review*, Oct. 23, 1970.

"Ben-Gurion at 86," *Jewish Observer and Middle East Review*, Sept. 29, 1972.

"Ben-Gurion Envisages 'Oxford in the Negev,'" *Israel Digest*, Oct. 25, 1963.

"Ben-Gurion at Herdsman's Fields," *The American Zionist*, Dec. 5, 1953.

"Ben-Gurion of Israel, Encircled, Unafraid," *U.S. News & World Report*, Mar. 8, 1957.

"Ben-Gurion Is 85," *National Jewish Monthly*, Oct. 1971.

"Ben-Gurion Looks Down," *Jewish Observer and Middle East Review*, May 10, 1968.

"Ben-Gurion Offends American Jews," *Christian Century*, June 27, 1962.

"Ben-Gurion Outlaws the Diaspora," *Christian Century*, Jan. 18, 1961.

Ben-Gurion, P., "My Life with Ben-Gurion," *Ramon Magazine*, July 30, 1957.

"Ben-Gurion Pushes New Electoral Reform Plan," *Israel Speaks*, Oct. 11, 1954.

"Ben-Gurion Raises the White Flag," *Israel Horizons*, July-Aug. 1953.

"Ben-Gurion Remembered," *Jewish Observer and Middle East Review*, Oct. 3, 1975.

"Ben-Gurion's American Tour," *Israel Digest*, Mar. 10, 1967.

"Ben-Gurion's Attempt to Unite the Nation," *Jewish Vanguard*, Jan. 14, 1955.

"Ben-Gurion Says Farewell to America," *Jewish Observer and Middle East Review*, Mar. 24, 1967.

"Ben-Gurion's Challenge: Come to Sde Boker," *Jewish Observer and Middle East Review*, Apr. 8, 1966.

"Ben-Gurion's Credo: Extracts," *Jewish Digest*, Feb. 1975.

"Ben-Gurion's Crusade Against

Private Capital," *Jewish Herald*, Nov. 18, 1949.

"Ben-Gurion Shocks Followers," *Jewish Observer and Middle East Review*, Sept. 29, 1967.

"Ben-Gurion's Inside History," *Jewish Observer and Middle East Review*, Sept. 6, 1963.

"Ben-Gurion's Legacy," *Progressive*, Jan. 1974.

"Ben-Gurion's Room Is an Index to His Character," *Zionist Record*, Oct. 24, 1952.

"The Ben-Gurions Settle Down," *Israel Speaks*, Feb. 5, 1954.

"Ben-Gurion's Silent Retirement," *Jewish Observer and Middle East Review*, May 22, 1970.

"Ben-Gurion's Uplifting Vision," *Jewish Observer and Middle East Review*, Aug. 21, 1970.

"Ben-Gurion's Vision of Arab-Israeli Harmony," *Jewish Observer and Middle East Review*, Nov. 14, 1975.

"Ben-Gurion and the Turks," *Jewish Observer and Middle East Review*, June 17, 1966.

"Ben-Gurion Woos the Diaspora," *Christian Century*, June 16, 1965.

"Ben-Gurion and the Youth Movements," *Israel Youth Horizon*, July 1954.

Ben-Horin, E., "Not Mr. Ben-Gurion," *Reconstructionist*, June 11, 1965.

Ben-Jacob, J., "Profile of David Ben-Gurion," *National Jewish Monthly*, Dec. 1950.

Ben-Zvi, M., "The Vision of Sde Boker," *Israel*, Feb. 1974.

Ben-Zvi, S., "Shattering the Tools," *Israel Horizons*, July 1954.

Berlin, I., "We Shall Not See His Likes Again," *Jewish Observer and Middle East Review*, Dec. 21, 1973.

"Bible Brain from Brooklyn," *Jewish Observer and Middle East Review*, May 10, 1968.

"Birth of the Jewish Brigade," *Jewish Observer and Middle East Review*, Jan. 10, 1964.

Blair, W. A., "Visit with Ben-Gurion in the Desert: Sde Boker," *New York Times Magazine*, Jan. 12, 1964.

Brainin, J., "The Ben-Gurion Saga," *Opinion*, Jan. 1954.

Brilliant, M., "Ben-Gurion at 70," *New York Times Magazine*, Oct. 14, 1956.

———, "The Birth Certificate," *National Jewish Monthly*, Mar. 1970.

———, "Israel Changes the Guard," *National Jewish Monthly*, Sept. 1963.

Cale, R., "Ben-Gurion's New Home," *Israel Speaks*, Nov. 27, 1953.

———, "Settlers of the Desert," *Israel*, Feb. 1954.

"Citizen Ben-Gurion: Memoirs with a Difference," *Jewish Observer and Middle East Review*, Oct. 4, 1963.

Comay, J., and Justman, J. H., "Man Who's Israel," *Israel Speaks*, Apr. 29, 1951.

Coughlan, R., "Modern Prophet of Israel," *Life*, Nov. 18, 1957.

Currivan, G., "Ben-Gurion: Key Man of Israel," *New York Times Magazine*, June 6, 1948.

"David Ben-Gurion," *Israel Digest*, Mar. 22, 1949.

"David Ben-Gurion, Premier of Israel," *Zionist Review*, June 11, 1948.

"The Death of Ben-Gurion," *Jewish Observer and Middle East Review*, Dec. 7, 1973.

"Desert Saga," *Time*, Oct. 18, 1971.

Epstein, M., "David Ben-Gurion," *World Over*, Nov. 30, 1973.

Flapan, S., "Dispute Over the Jordan," *New Outlook*, Feb. 1960.

"Founding Father," *New Statesman and Nation*, Dec. 7, 1973.

Fraenkel, J., "Ben-Gurion and the Turks," *Jewish Observer and Middle East Review*, June 24, 1966.

Frank, M. Z., "Ben-Gurion at 80," *The American Zionist*, Oct. 1966.

———, "Ben-Gurion and His 'Boys,'" *The American Zionist*, Dec. 1965, Jan. 1966.

———, "Ben-Gurion Today: Curmudgeon or Iconoclast?," *Congress Bi-Weekly*, Mar. 6, 1967.

Fredenthal, D., "Some Agonizing Moments of Israel's Great Decision," *Life*, Mar. 18, 1957.

Freund, M. K., "A Man for History: Ben-Gurion at 85," *Hadassah Magazine*, Oct. 1971.

Gershater, C., "Inside Story of Ben-Gurion's Farewell Speech," *Zionist Record*, June 29, 1954.

Gevaryahu, C., "Reminiscences about Ben-Gurion," *Dor le Dor, The World Jewish Bible Society*, Winter 1974–75.

Gilboa, Y. A., "Ben-Gurion at 85: Still Facing the Desert," *Israel*, Nov. 1971.

"Golda Talks about Ben-Gurion," *Jewish Digest*, Aug. 1972.

Goldsmith, S. J., "Ben-Gurion at 83," *Jewish Observer and Middle East Review*, Oct. 10, 1969.

———, "Man of Destiny—Ben-Gurion's Greatness," *Jewish Observer and Middle East Review*, Oct. 8, 1971.

———, "Paula Ben-Gurion," *Jewish Observer and Middle East Review*, Feb. 2, 1968.

Goldstein, A., "Ben-Gurion Emerges from Sde Boker with a New Idea," *Jewish Herald*, Feb. 11, 1955.

———, "Ben-Gurion for Lavon," *Jewish World*, March 1955.

Goldstein, B., "Thoughts on a Visit to Sde Boker," *Pioneer Woman*, Feb. 1954.

Gordis, R., "David Ben-Gurion and the Bible," *Congress Bi-Weekly*, Jan. 18, 1974.

"The Greatest Chalutz of All Time," *Young Judean*, Dec. 1970.

"The Greatness of David Ben-Gurion," *Jewish Observer and Middle East Review*, Dec. 7, 1973.

Gruenbaum, Y., "What Ben-Gurion Really Wants," *Israel Horizons*, Feb.–Mar. 1955.

Guber, R., "Ben-Gurion: A Personal Memoir," *Jewish Frontier*, Nov. 1971.

Hacohen, D., "Smuggling Arms for the Haganah," *The Jerusalem Quarterly*, Fall 1978.

Handlen, O.; Himmelfarb, M.; Shulman, C. E., "Ben-Gurion against the Diaspora," *Commentary*, Mar. 1961.

Hauslich, A., "Ben-Gurion Blames U Thant: New Light on Sinai Diplomacy," *Jewish Observer and Middle East Review*, Nov. 8, 1968.

———, "Ben-Gurion at Four Score and Two," *Jewish Observer and Middle East Review*, Oct. 18, 1968.

———, "Birthday in the Desert: Ben-Gurion Is 77," *Jewish Observer and Middle East Review*, Oct. 4, 1963.

"Israel: Chairman Mao and Ben-Gurion," *Jewish Observer and Middle East Review*, Sept. 17, 1976.

"Israel Mourns Paula Ben-Gurion," *Israel Digest*, Feb. 9, 1968.

Jabotinsky, E., "Ben-Gurion—the 'Revisionist,'" *Jewish Herald*, Jan. 20, 1950.

Kimche, J., "Ben-Gurion's Unanswered Charges: Is the Zionist Movement Evading the Issue?," *Jewish Observer and*

Middle East Review, Mar. 26, 1954.

———, "People vs. Ben-Gurion's Government: The Present Crisis in Israel," *Commentary*, Sept. 1952.

———, "The Priest Goes—the Prophet Remains: Ben-Gurion at 80," *Jewish Observer and Middle East Review*, Sept. 30, 1966.

King, S., "New Battle for Israel's Happy Warrior," *New York Times Magazine*, July 19, 1959.

Klutznick, P. M., "Remembering Ben-Gurion—Debater, Thinker, Statesman," *National Jewish Monthly*, Jan. 1974.

Knopf (Kurzman), F., "Hey Mom, I'm a Movie Star!" (article on Ben-Gurion film), *El-Alon Magazine*, Fall 1971.

Kramer, M., "Israel's Man of War," *New York Times Magazine*, Aug. 9, 1982.

Lania, L., "A Prophet Abdicates," *World*, Feb. 1954.

Laqueur, W. Z., "Israel Back to 'Normal,' "*Commentary*, June 1957.

Lask, I. M., "Ben-Gurion and His Background," *The American Zionist*, Jan. 1965.

Lerner, M., "Ben-Gurion in the Desert," *Israel Life and Letters*, Oct. 1953.

"The Lesson of Palestine," *Middle East Journal*, Oct. 1949.

Lewis, F., "Ben-Gurion: Man on a Mountaintop," *New York Times Magazine*, May 6, 1951.

Litvin, J., "The Great Meeting," *Gates of Zion*, Jan. 1954.

———, "Prophet in the Wilderness," *New Statesman and Nation*, Dec. 10, 1955.

Livneh, E., "Ben-Gurion's Immortal Hour," *The American Zionist*, Jan. 1967.

Louvish, M., "All Eyes on Sde Boker," *Jewish Vanguard*, Jan. 1967.

———, "Ben-Gurion's Credo," *Jewish Vanguard*, Jan. 1954.

———, "Sde Boker—Ben-Gurion's Retreat," *Jewish Frontier*, Apr. 1954.

"Maker of History, Statesman and Pioneer," *Israel and Middle East*, Jan.–Mar. 1951.

"Malice in Wonderland," *Israel Horizons*, July–Aug. 1953.

Mark, Y., "The Shtetl," *The Jewish Digest*, Oct. 1963.

McClelland, D. C., "The Two Faces of Power," *Journal of International Affairs*, 1970.

Meir, G., "Tribute to Ben-Gurion," *Jewish Frontier*, Nov. 1971.

Michaelson, S. H., "An Incident in the Young Days of David Ben-Gurion," *Zionist Record*, Oct. 1951.

Morris, Y., "Ben-Gurion and the Youth Movement," *Jewish Observer and Middle East Review*, July 9, 1954.

Nets, Y., "The Secret of Sde Boker," *Jewish Herald*, Feb. 19, 1954.

Neumann, E., "Ben-Gurion—Profile, 1951," *The American Zionist*, Mar. 1967.

———, "David Ben-Gurion," *The American Zionist*, May 1974.

"An Old Man in a Hurry: Ben-Gurion's Sad Visit to France," *Jewish Observer and Middle East Review*, Oct. 31, 1969.

"On Hearing of the Passing of Itzhak Ben-Zvi," *Jewish Frontier*, June 1963.

"Our Greatest Genius," *Jewish Observer and Middle East Review*, Apr. 22, 1955.

"Paula Ben-Gurion: An Interview with the Prime Minister's Wife," *Pioneer Woman*, June 1951.

Pepper, B., "Moshe Dayan: Reflections on a Life of War and

Peace," *New York Times Magazine*, May 4, 1980.

Remba, I., "Jabotinsky and Ben-Gurion," *Jewish Herald*, July 14, 1950.

"Remembering Ben-Gurion," *Jewish Observer and Middle East Review*, June 18, 1976.

"Remembering David Ben-Gurion, Dreamer, Doer, Scholar," *National Jewish Monthly*, Jan. 1974.

Rosenberg, S. E., "Paula Ben-Gurion and the Bible," *Hadassah Magazine*, Oct. 1968.

Rosenthal, D., "David Ben-Gurion: Some Reflections," *Jewish Frontier*, Jan. 1974.

Samuels, G., "Israel at 13, Ben-Gurion at 75," *New York Times Magazine*, Sept. 24, 1961.

———, "Man of Sde Boker," *New York Times Magazine*, Oct. 16, 1966.

———, "Visit with Ben-Gurion," *New York Times Magazine*, Feb. 6, 1955.

Scalapino, R. A., "The New Role of Nationalism," *Problems of Communism*, Jan.–Apr. 1971.

Segal, M., "Ben-Gurion," *Jewish Digest*, Dec. 1972.

———, "Ben-Gurion of Israel: The First 85 Years," *Jewish Observer and Middle East Review*, Oct. 8, 1971.

Selden, H. L., "For Ben-Gurion Is an Honorable Man," *Answer*, July 2, 1948.

———, "Luck of Ben-Gurion," *Answer*, Sept. 24, 1948.

Sherman, C. B., "Ben-Gurion and Rafi," *Jewish Frontier*, Oct. 1965

Shimoni, S., "His Excellency Prime Minister Yariv," *Israel Horizons*, Mar. 1953.

———, "Yiftah 'Pacified,' British Style," *Israel Horizons*, July–Aug. 1953.

Sittner, A., "The Day They Almost Hanged Ben-Gurion," *Jewish Digest*, Dec. 1975.

Sterling, C., "Old Man and the Young Sabras," *The Reporter*, Nov. 4, 1965.

Strachey, J., "Visit to Ben-Gurion," *New Statesman and Nation*, Nov. 6, 1954.

"Suez Crisis and Ben-Gurion," *Foreign Affairs*, July 1960.

Swet, G. H., "David Ben-Gurion," *Israel Life and Letters*, May 1951.

Syrkin, M., "Ben-Gurion at 70," *Jewish Frontier*, Dec. 1956.

Teller J. L., "The Making of the Ideals That Rule Israel," *Commentary*, Jan., Feb. 1954.

"Truth about Ben-Gurion Parley," *Israel Horizons*, July–Aug. 1953.

"Two Unique Attributes Mark Ben-Gurion's Life," *Mizrachi Woman*, Oct. 1956.

Weiser, R., "Ben-Gurion's Dispute with American Zionists," *Commentary*, Aug. 1954.

Weisgal, M. W., "A Personal Portrait," *Hadassah Magazine*, Nov. 1966.

Weizmann, C., "Palestine's Role in the Solution of the Jewish Problem," *Foreign Affairs*, Jan. 1942.

Whartman, E., "Ben-Gurion at 80," *National Jewish Monthly*, Oct. 1966.

"What Made Ben-Gurion Go to London?" *Jewish Observer and Middle East Review*, Mar. 25, 1966.

"Who Is Amos Ben-Gurion?" *Here and Now*, Jan. 25, 1956.

Yaari, M., "Ben-Gurion Broke Faith," *Labour Israel*, Mar. 25, 1949.

Yaffe, R., "Ben-Gurion vs. Eban in the U.N.," *Israel Horizons*, Jan. 1953.

Newspapers and Radio-TV Stations

American: *Christian Science Monitor, New York Herald-Tribune, New York Times, Wall Street Journal, Washington Post, Washington Star, Yiddisher Kempfer.*

British: BBC, *Daily Telegraph, The Day* (Yid.), *Jewish Chronicle, Manchester Guardian, The Observer, The Times.*

Egyptian: *Akhbar el Youm, Aker Saa, Al Ahram, Rose el Yussef.*

French: *Le Figaro, Le Monde.*

Israeli: *Ahdut, Al Youm, Davar, Haboker, Jerusalem (Palestine) Post, Kol Yisrael (Voice of Israel), Maarachot, Maariv, Yediot Acharonot.*

Jordanian: *Al-Dafa, Falestin, Palestine News.*

Lebanese: *Daily Star, Hayat.*

Polish: *Hamelitz, Hatzefira.*

South African: *South African Jewish Times.*

Unpublished Documents:

The Arlosoroff Case, report by Joseph Delek—Vladimir Jabotinsky Archives, Tel Aviv.

Correspondence between David Ben-Gurion and Rachel Beit-Halachmi—Ruth Beit-Halachmi, Givatayim, Israel.

Correspondence between David and Paula Ben-Gurion—Ben-Gurion Research Institute and Archives, Sde Boker, Israel.

Correspondence between David Ben-Gurion and Shmuel Fuchs—Sde Boker.

Correspondence involving Jewish Agency and World Zionist Organization—Central Zionist Archives, Jerusalem.

David K. Niles and U.S. Policy toward Palestine, thesis by David B. Sachar, Harvard University, Cambridge, Mass.

Diaries of David Ben-Gurion (from 1915 to 1973)—Sde Boker.

Diary of Nehemiah Argov—Sde Boker.

From Legionnaire to Leader, report by Julian Meltzer—Sde Boker.

"A Jewish Combined Infrastructure," speech by Zvi Kesse, Tel Aviv.

Knesset proceedings—Knesset Archives, Jerusalem.

Material on Hagana and Israeli military history—Israel Defense Forces Archives (IDFA), Tel Aviv.

Material on the Holocaust—Central Archives for the History of the Jewish People, Hebrew University, Jerusalem.

Official Records of the United Nations General Assembly—U.N. Headquarters, New York.

Papers and correspondence of David Ben-Gurion—Sde Boker.

Papers and correspondence of Yitzhak Ben-Zvi—Yad Ben-Zvi, Jerusalem.

Papers and correspondence of Vladimir Jabotinsky—Vladimir Jabotinsky Archives, Tel Aviv.

Papers and correspondence of Chaim Weizmann—Weizmann Archives, Rehovot, Israel.

Provisional State Council Proceedings—Israeli State Archives, Jerusalem.

Protocols, Ahdut HaAvoda Executive Committee—Labor Archives, Tel Aviv.

Protocols, American Poalei Zion meetings—Israeli Labor Party Archives, Beit Berl, Kfar Saba, Israel, and Yivo Institute for Jewish Research, N.Y.

Protocols, Mapai Central Committee meetings—Israeli Labor Party Archives, Kfar Saba, Israel.

Protocols, Jewish Agency and World Zionist Organization meetings—Central Zionist Archives, Jerusalem.

Protocols, Secretariat of Histadrut

Executive Committee and Histadrut conferences—Histadrut Executive Committee Archives, Tel Aviv.

Truman Administration papers on Palestine (including speech by Clark M. Clifford to American Historical Association, Dec. 28, 1976: "Factors Influencing President Truman's Decision to Support Partition and Recognize the State of Israel")—Clark M. Clifford's private archives, Washington, D.C.

Oral Histories
(made available to author at Sde Boker)

Yosef Avidar
Shaul Avigur
Yohanan Bader
Tal Baruch
Aharon Becker
Oved Ben-Ami
Chaim Ben-Asher
Mordechai Ben-Porat
Rachel Yanait Ben-Zvi
Zvi Brenner
Pinchas Cruso
Chaim Dan
Eliahu Dobkin
Lova (Arie) Eliav
Judith Epstein
Rabbi Louis Finkelstein
Elkana Gali
Rabbi Chaim Gevaryahu
Israel Goldstein
Chief Rabbi Shlomo Goren
Jacob Groman
Moshe Gurari
Chaim Gvati

David Hacohen
Rose Halprin
Maurice Hexter
Yehuda Horin
Mordechai Ish-Shalom
Katriel Katz
Moshe Kol
Arthur Lourie
Yaacov Maimon
Rabbi Irving Miller
Eliezer Peri
Anshel Reiss
Eliezer Rimalt
Nahum Shadmi
Eliezer Shoshani
Zalman Shragai
John Slawson
Mordechai Surkis
Arie Tartakower
Zerah Wahrhaftig
Baruch Weinstein
Israel Yeshayahu

INDEX